International Directory of
COMPANY
HISTORIES

International Directory of
COMPANY HISTORIES

VOLUME 65

Editor

Jay P. Pederson

ST. JAMES PRESS

An imprint of Thomson Gale, a part of The Thomson Corporation

Detroit • New York • San Francisco • San Diego • New Haven, Conn. • Waterville, Maine • London • Munich

THOMSON

GALE

International Directory of Company Histories, Volume 65

Jay P. Pederson, Editor

Project Editor
Miranda H. Ferrara

Editorial
Virgil Burton, Donna Craft, Louise Gagné,
Peggy Geeseman, Julie Gough, Linda Hall,
Keith Jones, Lynn Pearce, Maureen Puhl,
Holly Selden, Justine Ventimiglia

Imaging and Multimedia
Randy Bassett, Lezlie Light

Manufacturing
Rhonda Williams

Product Manager
Gerald L. Sawchuk

LIBRARY OF CONGRESS CATALOG NUMBER 89-190943

ISBN: 1-55862-510-0

BRITISH LIBRARY CATALOGUING IN PUBLICATION DATA

International directory of company histories. Vol. 65
I. Jay P. Pederson
33.87409

Printed in the United States of America
10 9 8 7 6 5 4 3 2 1

CONTENTS _____

Company Histories

PREFACE

The St. James Press series *The International Directory of Company Histories (IDCH)* is intended for reference use by students, business people, librarians, historians, economists, investors, job candidates, and others who seek to learn more about the historical development of the world's most important companies. To date, *IDCH* has covered over 6,800 companies in 65 volumes.

Inclusion Criteria

Most companies chosen for inclusion in *IDCH* have achieved a minimum of US$25 million in annual sales and are leading influences in their industries or geographical locations. Companies may be publicly held, private, or nonprofit. State-owned companies that are important in their industries and that may operate much like public or private companies also are included. Wholly owned subsidiaries and divisions are profiled if they meet the requirements for inclusion. Entries on companies that have had major changes since they were last profiled may be selected for updating.

The *IDCH* series highlights 10% private and nonprofit companies, and features updated entries on approximately 50 companies per volume.

Entry Format

Each entry begins with the company's legal name, the address of its headquarters, its telephone, toll-free, and fax numbers, and its web site. A statement of public, private, state, or parent ownership follows. A company with a legal name in both English and the language of its headquarters country is listed by the English name, with the native-language name in parentheses.

The company's founding or earliest incorporation date, the number of employees, and the most recent available sales figures follow. Sales figures are given in local currencies with equivalents in U.S. dollars. For some private companies, sales figures are estimates and indicated by the abbreviation *est.* The entry lists the exchanges on which a company's stock is traded and its ticker symbol, as well as the company's NAIC codes.

Entries generally contain a *Company Perspectives* box which provides a short summary of the company's mission, goals, and ideals, a *Key Dates* box highlighting milestones in the company's history, lists of *Principal Subsidiaries, Principal Divisions, Principal Operating Units, Principal Competitors,* and articles for *Further Reading.*

American spelling is used throughout *IDCH*, and the word ''billion'' is used in its U.S. sense of one thousand million.

Sources

Entries have been compiled from publicly accessible sources both in print and on the Internet such as general and academic periodicals, books, annual reports, and material supplied by the companies themselves.

Cumulative Indexes

IDCH contains three indexes: the **Index to Companies**, which provides an alphabetical index to companies discussed in the text as well as to companies profiled, the **Index to Industries**, which allows researchers to locate companies by their principal industry, and the **Geographic Index**, which lists companies alphabetically by the country of their headquarters. The indexes are cumulative and specific instructions for using them are found immediately preceding each index.

Suggestions Welcome

Comments and suggestions from users of *IDCH* on any aspect of the product as well as suggestions for companies to be included or updated are cordially invited. Please write:

The Editor
International Directory of Company Histories
St. James Press
27500 Drake Rd.
Farmington Hills, Michigan 48331-3535

AB	Aktiebolag (Finland, Sweden)
AB Oy	Aktiebolag Osakeyhtiot (Finland)
A.E.	Anonimos Eteria (Greece)
AG	Aktiengesellschaft (Austria, Germany, Switzerland, Liechtenstein)
A.O.	Anonim Ortaklari/Ortakligi (Turkey)
ApS	Amparteselskab (Denmark)
A.Š.	Anonim Širketi (Turkey)
A/S	Aksjeselskap (Norway); Aktieselskab (Denmark, Sweden)
Ay	Avoinyhtio (Finland)
B.A.	Buttengewone Aansprakeiijkheid (The Netherlands)
Bhd.	Berhad (Malaysia, Brunei)
B.V.	Besloten Vennootschap (Belgium, The Netherlands)
C.A.	Compania Anonima (Ecuador, Venezuela)
C. de R.L.	Compania de Responsabilidad Limitada (Spain)
Co.	Company
Corp.	Corporation
CRL	Companhia a Responsabilidao Limitida (Portugal, Spain)
C.V.	Commanditaire Vennootschap (The Netherlands, Belgium)
G.I.E.	Groupement d'Interet Economique (France)
GmbH	Gesellschaft mit beschraenkter Haftung (Austria, Germany, Switzerland)
Inc.	Incorporated (United States, Canada)
I/S	Interessentselskab (Denmark); Interesentselskap (Norway)
KG/KGaA	Kommanditgesellschaft/Kommanditgesellschaft auf Aktien (Austria, Germany, Switzerland)
KK	Kabushiki Kaisha (Japan)
K/S	Kommanditselskab (Denmark); Kommandittselskap (Norway)
Lda.	Limitada (Spain)
L.L.C.	Limited Liability Company (United States)
Ltd.	Limited (Various)
Ltda.	Limitada (Brazil, Portugal)
Ltee.	Limitee (Canada, France)
mbH	mit beschraenkter Haftung (Austria, Germany)
N.V.	Naamloze Vennootschap (Belgium, The Netherlands)
OAO	Otkrytoe Aktsionernoe Obshchestve (Russia)
OOO	Obschestvo s Ogranichennoi Otvetstvennostiu (Russia)
Oy	Osakeyhtiö (Finland)
PLC	Public Limited Co. (United Kingdom, Ireland)
Pty.	Proprietary (Australia, South Africa, United Kingdom)
S.A.	Société Anonyme (Belgium, France, Greece, Luxembourg, Switzerland, Arab speaking countries); Sociedad Anónima (Latin America [except Brazil], Spain, Mexico); Sociedades Anônimas (Brazil, Portugal)
SAA	Societe Anonyme Arabienne
S.A.R.L.	Sociedade Anonima de Responsabilidade Limitada (Brazil, Portugal); Société à Responsabilité Limitée (France, Belgium, Luxembourg)
S.A.S.	Societá in Accomandita Semplice (Italy); Societe Anonyme Syrienne (Arab speaking countries)
Sdn. Bhd.	Sendirian Berhad (Malaysia)
S.p.A.	Società per Azioni (Italy)
Sp. z.o.o.	Spólka z ograniczona odpowiedzialnoscia (Poland)
S.R.L.	Società a Responsabilità Limitata (Italy); Sociedad de Responsabilidad Limitada (Spain, Mexico, Latin America [except Brazil])
S.R.O.	Spolecnost s Rucenim Omezenym (Czechoslovakia
Ste.	Societe (France, Belgium, Luxembourg, Switzerland)
VAG	Verein der Arbeitgeber (Austria, Germany)
YK	Yugen Kaisha (Japan)
ZAO	Zakrytoe Aktsionernoe Obshchestve (Russia)

$	United States dollar	ISK	Icelandic krona
£	United Kingdom pound	ITL	Italian lira
¥	Japanese yen	JMD	Jamaican dollar
AED	Emirati dirham	KPW	North Korean won
ARS	Argentine peso	KRW	South Korean won
ATS	Austrian shilling	KWD	Kuwaiti dinar
AUD	Australian dollar	LUF	Luxembourg franc
BEF	Belgian franc	MUR	Mauritian rupee
BHD	Bahraini dinar	MXN	Mexican peso
BRL	Brazilian real	MYR	Malaysian ringgit
CAD	Canadian dollar	NGN	Nigerian naira
CHF	Swiss franc	NLG	Netherlands guilder
CNY	Chinese yuan	NOK	Norwegian krone
COP	Colombian peso	NZD	New Zealand dollar
CLP	Chilean peso	OMR	Omani rial
CZK	Czech koruna	PHP	Philippine peso
DEM	German deutsche mark	PKR	Pakistani rupee
DKK	Danish krone	PLN	Polish zloty
DZD	Algerian dinar	PTE	Portuguese escudo
EEK	Estonian Kroon	RMB	Chinese renminbi
EGP	Egyptian pound	RUB	Russian ruble
ESP	Spanish peseta	SAR	Saudi riyal
EUR	euro	SEK	Swedish krona
FIM	Finnish markka	SGD	Singapore dollar
FRF	French franc	THB	Thai baht
GRD	Greek drachma	TND	Tunisian dinar
HKD	Hong Kong dollar	TRL	Turkish lira
HUF	Hungarian forint	TWD	new Taiwan dollar
IDR	Indonesian rupiah	VEB	Venezuelan bolivar
IEP	Irish pound	VND	Vietnamese dong
ILS	new Israeli shekel	ZAR	South African rand
INR	Indian rupee	ZMK	Zambian kwacha

International Directory of
COMPANY HISTORIES

ABB Ltd.

P.O. Box 8131
CH-8050 Zurich
Switzerland
Telephone: (043) 317 7111
Fax: (043) 317 7958
Web site: http://www.abb.com

Public Company
Incorporated: 1988 as ABB Asea Brown Boveri Ltd.
Employees: 116,464
Sales: $18.80 billion (2003)
Stock Exchanges: Swiss London Stockholm Frankfurt
New York
Ticker Symbol: ABB
NAIC: 334416 Electronic Coil, Transformer, and Other
Inductor Manufacturing; 334513 Instruments and
Related Products Manufacturing for Measuring,
Displaying, and Controlling Industrial Process
Variables; 334514 Totalizing Fluid Meter and
Counting Device Manufacturing; 335311 Power,
Distribution, and Specialty Transformer
Manufacturing; 335999 All Other Miscellaneous
Electrical Equipment and Component Manufacturing

Often called the General Electric of Europe, ABB Ltd. has two core business segments: power technologies and automation technologies. Serving electric, gas, and water utilities, and also industrial and commercial customers, the power technologies division offers a wide array of products, systems, and services for power transmission and distribution and power plant automation. Offerings include transformers, medium- and high-voltage products, power systems, and utility automation systems. The automation technologies division specializes in manufacturing-automation and process-automation products, services, and systems. ABB transacts 55 percent of its total sales in Europe, 19 percent in the Americas, 18 percent in Asia, and 8 in the Middle East and Africa. The Wallenberg family dynasty of Sweden holds about a 10 percent stake in the company. ABB (formerly known as ABB Asea Brown Boveri Ltd.) was formed in 1988 from the merger of Sweden's ASEA AB and Switzerland's BBC Brown Boveri Ltd.—two companies founded in the late 19th century.

Early History of ASEA

Elektriska Aktiebolaget in Stockholm was established in 1883 by Ludwig Fredholm to manufacture electrical lighting and generators based on the designs of a young engineer named Jonas Wenström. Wenström's innovative designs quickly led to financial success, and Fredholm soon wanted to expand the scope of his firm's operations. He arranged a merger with Wenströms & Granströms Elektriska Kraftbolag, a company founded by Jonas Wenström's brother Goran.

Allmänna Svenska Elektriska Aktiebolaget (whose name was later shortened to ASEA AB) was created on November 18, 1890, to provide electrical equipment for Swedish industry. Goran Wenström shared presidential responsibilities with Fredholm, who also served as chairman of the board. After Fredholm's death in 1891, Wenström become sole president and Oscar F. Wijkman was appointed chairman.

The dawning of the electrical age provided ASEA with large new markets as the industrial and residential use of electricity became commonplace in Sweden. The company quickly established itself as a pioneer in the industrial field. ASEA's installation of electricity at a rolling mill in the town of Hofors is believed to be the first of its kind in the world, and in 1893, ASEA built Sweden's first three-phase electrical transmission, between Hellsjon and Crangesberg.

ASEA's early success was short-lived. In 1896 one of Sweden's leading inventors and industrialists, Gustaf de Laval, acquired a 50 percent interest in the company and both Wenström and Wijkman were ousted in a management reorganization. But Laval's mismanagement of ASEA soon led the company into severe financial difficulties. With the help of the Stockholms Enskilda Bank, management opposed to Laval eventually extricated the company from his control. Disorganized and deeply in debt, the firm lost a significant share of the electrical equipment market in Sweden.

Stockholms Enskilda Bank played a major role in ASEA's financial recovery. In fact, it was only after the bank agreed to guarantee his salary that J. Sigfrid Edstrom, the former manager of the Gothenburg Tramways Company, agreed to become president of ASEA in 1903. Under Edstrom's direction, the com-

---

Company Perspectives:

ABB is a global leader in power and automation technologies that enable utility and industry customers to improve performance while lowering environmental impact. We are present in around 100 countries.

We leverage our technology leadership, global presence, application knowledge and local expertise to offer products and services that allow our customers to optimize their operations. Our integration platform, Industrial IT, enables our customers to manage their installations better and link up in real time with their own suppliers and customers. The result is a leap in efficiency, quality and competitiveness.

We focus on our core businesses in power and automation technologies and have simplified our organization. This ensures that our customers have quick and easy access to ABB's offerings, when and where they need us—whether they buy from us directly or through distributors, wholesalers, system integrators or other partners.

Our businesses work together with one simple and seamless set of values for customers.

---

pany began to show a substantial profit by 1907. In addition, he expanded the firm's markets in Europe: subsidiaries were established in Great Britain, Spain, Denmark, Finland, and Russia between 1910 and 1914.

Although Sweden remained neutral during World War I, the company was adversely affected by the conflict. ASEA prospered during the early years of the war because the scarcity of coal stimulated the development of electricity, including the company's first major railway electrification project. Eventually, however, the firm lost many of its European markets because of the success of German submarine warfare. In Russia, all of ASEA's operations were interrupted by the revolution beginning in 1917.

The postwar years brought a deep recession to Sweden that lasted from 1920 to 1923. Yet Edstrom's cautious spending policies enabled the company to survive. By the late 1920s, ASEA was once again on the road to profitability and growth. In 1926 the company provided the electric locomotives and converter equipment for the first electric trains on the Stockholm-Gothenburg line, and in 1932 ASEA built the world's largest naturally cooled three-phase transformer.

During the 1930s, company management decided to concentrate on expanding and improving its domestic operations. After several years of negotiations, ASEA and LM Ericsson Telephone Company signed a pact in 1933 stipulating that the two companies would not compete with each other in certain sectors of the electrical market. As part of the agreement, ASEA purchased Elektromekano from Ericsson, giving ASEA undisputed control over a large portion of the electrical equipment market in Sweden.

In addition to its production of electric locomotives and rail equipment for Sweden's national railway electrification program, the firm expanded into new markets. ASEA purchased AB Svenska Flaktfabriken, a firm specializing in air-freight handling technology, and a large electric-motor manufacturer in

Poland to augment its domestic production. In 1934 Edstrom was named chairman of the board and Arthur Linden, executive vice-president and a close Edstrom associate for many years, was named president. These two men directed the company's successful growth and expansion strategy until World War II.

Although Sweden remained neutral during World War II, once again war severely affected the country's economy. The Nazi occupation effectively curtailed ASEA's operations throughout Europe, and even to a significant extent in Sweden. A new president, Thorsten Ericson, was appointed in 1943, but this management change had little impact on the company's fortunes for the remainder of the war.

During the immediate postwar years, domestic power demands skyrocketed, forcing utility companies to expand rapidly. ASEA was unable to meet this demand for electrical equipment because of shortages of material. To make matters worse, a five-month strike by metal workers played havoc with the company's delivery schedule, leaving ASEA unable to meet the demand from the Soviet Union for electric equipment based on a 1946 trade agreement between Sweden and the U.S.S.R.

In 1947 ASEA broke into the American market by signing a licensing agreement with the Ohio Brass Company for the local production of surge arrestors. During this time, ASEA also received substantial orders for the first stage of the massive Aswan Dam project in Egypt.

In 1949 Ake T. Vrethem, formerly with the Swedish State Power Board, was named president of ASEA and Ericson became chairman of the board. Under their direction, the company continued its pioneering efforts in several areas: ASEA supplied electrical equipment and technical expertise to the world's first 400 kilovolt AC transmission, between Harspranget and Hallsberg in 1952; the company claims to have produced the world's first synthetic diamonds using high-pressure technology in 1953, two years before General Electric Company announced a similar achievement in the United States; and ASEA supplied the first permanent high-voltage, direct current (HVDC) transmission, linking the Swedish mainland with the island of Gotland in 1954.

The company continued to play a critical role in Sweden's rail transit system. ASEA's locomotives accounted for virtually all the traffic on the country's rail network. In the mid-1950s, the firm introduced its "Ra" light-class electric locomotive, which was an immediate success and gave a boost to ASEA's efforts to market competitive locomotive models internationally.

Curt Nicolin Era at ASEA: 1961–80

In 1961 Curt Nicolin was appointed president. Nicolin restructured the parent company, introduced a new divisional organization, and relocated some of ASEA's manufacturing facilities. The company formed an electronics division, signaling the start of ASEA's transition from a traditional heavy electrical equipment manufacturer to an electronics company in which high-technology played an increasingly important role.

In the mid-1960s, ASEA's American market expanded considerably and became more important to the company's overall sales strategy. After serving customers such as the Tennessee

Key Dates:

1883: Ludwig Fredholm establishes Elektriska Aktiebolaget in Stockholm as a manufacturer of electrical lighting and generators.

1890: Elektriska Aktiebolaget merges with Wenströms & Granströms Elektriska Kraftbolag to form Allmänna Svenska Elektriska Aktiebolaget (name later shortened to ASEA AB).

1891: Charles E.L. Brown and Walter Boveri establish BBC Brown Boveri in 1891 in Baden, Switzerland; initially known as Brown, Boveri & Cie, the company's early activities include manufacturing electrical components such as electrical motors for locomotives and power-generating equipment for Europe's railway systems.

1926: ASEA provides the electric locomotives and converter equipment for the first electric trains on the Stockholm-Gothenburg line.

1968: After receiving an order to build Sweden's first full-scale nuclear power station, ASEA merges its nuclear division with the state-owned Atom-Energi to form ASEA Atom.

1980: Percy Barnevik is named ASEA's managing director and initiates a major reorganization, placing greater emphasis on such areas as robotics, state-of-the-art electronics, and automation technologies.

1982: ASEA purchases full control of ASEA Atom.

1988: ASEA and Brown Boveri merge the assets of their respective companies, forming ABB Asea Brown Boveri Ltd.; the new entity, based in Zurich, is 50–50 owned by ASEA and Brown Boveri.

1989: ABB acquires the power transmission and power distribution systems business of Westinghouse Electric Corporation.

Early 1990s: Company makes concerted push into eastern European and Asian markets.

1996: ABB merges its rail transportation unit with that of Germany's Daimler-Benz AG to form ABB Daimler-Benz Transportation GmbH (ADtranz), a 50–50 joint venture; ABB's parent companies change their names, ASEA becoming ABB AB and Brown Boveri becoming ABB AG.

1998: Elsag Bailey Process Automation N.V. is acquired in a $2.1 billion deal.

1999: Half interest in ADtranz is sold to DaimlerChrysler AG; ABB merges its power generation business with that of ALSTOM to create ABB Alstom Power; parent companies ABB AB and ABB AG are merged as ABB Ltd., whose stock begins trading on the Zurich, Stockholm, London, and Frankfurt exchanges.

2000: ABB sells its nuclear power operations to BNFL Inc. and its interest in ABB Alstom Power to ALSTOM.

2001: $470 million charge for asbestos liabilities contributes to $691 million net loss for the year—the first of three straight years in the red.

2002: ABB restructures to focus on two core businesses: power technologies and automation; structured-finance unit is sold to General Electric.

2003: "Prepackaged" bankruptcy plan is offered for Combustion Engineering that would cap asbestos liabilities at $1.2 billion; ABB's capital base is strengthened by more than $4 billion.

Valley Authority, the company firmly established itself in the United States when it was chosen to supply HVDC equipment for the Pacific Internie Project on the West Coast.

ASEA also received an order to build Sweden's first full-scale nuclear power station during this period. The company then merged its nuclear division with the state-owned Atom-Energi to form ASEA Atom in 1968. ASEA acquired the remaining 50 percent state interest in Atom-Energi in 1982.

In 1963 ASEA achieved a major technological breakthrough with the introduction of an improved thyristor able to handle substantially more electrical current than existing devices. As a result, the company began manufacturing thyristor locomotives for Swedish and European rail systems. In the mid-1970s, ASEA worked with its American licensee, the electromotive division of General Motors, to secure an order for 47 thyristor locomotives for use on Amtrak lines in the Boston–New York–Washington, D.C. corridor.

Nuclear power became an increasingly controversial issue in Sweden during the late 1970s. ASEA continued to manufacture nuclear reactors and received its first foreign order, from Finland. But in a 1980 national referendum Sweden voted to phase out nuclear power programs over a period of 25 years. The company was still allowed to complete orders for foreign reactors, but ASEA Atom's future looked bleak.

Curt Nicolin was also appointed chairman of the board in 1976. During the 1970s, however, Nicolin's management style was overwhelmed by the fast pace of changing technology. A large number of utility and electrical equipment manufacturing companies, including ASEA, experienced falling profits and lackluster growth.

Percy Barnevik Era at ASEA: 1980–88

ASEA began to revive in 1980, when 39-year-old Percy Barnevik was named managing director and, eventually, CEO. Barnevik immediately began a reorganization of the company's management strategy. ASEA had previously bid on projects with low profit margins for the sake of maintaining a minimum sales level and a certain number of employees, but under Barnevik's direction the company would emphasize high profit margin projects. Barnevik's strategy began to pay off quickly.

ASEA initiated a major expansion into high-tech areas, investing heavily in robotics and other state-of-the-art electronics. The development costs of robotics at first held profits down in that sector, but Barnevik viewed robotics as a long-term, high-growth area.

Barnevik also considered ASEA's industrial controls business, with products such as large automation controls, a high-growth sector. ASEA already had a major share of the rapidly expanding market for industrial energy controls, such as those that recycle waste heat. In addition, the company positioned itself to take advantage of a growing demand for pollution controls, spurred in part by the acid-rain controversy in Europe and North America.

In 1985 the company was accused of an illegal diversion of proprietary U.S. technology to the Soviet Union. A former ASEA vice-president was charged by Swedish authorities with tax evasion and violation of foreign exchange regulations in connection with the sale of six sophisticated computers with possible military applications. Barnevik insisted that the diversions occurred without management's approval. By 1986 ASEA reported revenues of SEK 46 billion and earnings of SEK 2.6 billion, and its workforce had reached 71,000.

Early History of BBC Brown Boveri

Charles E.L. Brown and Walter Boveri established BBC Brown Boveri in 1891 in Baden, Switzerland; it was initially known as Brown, Boveri & Cie. The company's development is interesting because it was one of only a few multinational corporations to operate subsidiaries that were larger than the parent company. Because of the limitations of the Swiss domestic market, Brown Boveri established subsidiaries throughout Europe relatively early in its history, and at times had difficulty maintaining managerial control over some of its larger operating units. The merger with ASEA, a company that was praised for its strong management, was expected to help Brown Boveri reorganize and reassert control over its vast international network.

Brown Boveri's early activities included manufacturing electrical components such as electrical motors for locomotives and power-generating equipment for Europe's railway systems. In 1919 the company entered into a licensing agreement with the British manufacturing firm Vickers that gave the British firm the right to manufacture and sell Brown Boveri products throughout the British Empire and in some parts of Europe. The agreement gave Brown Boveri a significant amount of money and the promise of substantial annual revenue, and also helped the company expand into foreign markets at a time when protectionist policies inhibited international expansion.

In the early 1920s, Brown Boveri, already a geographically diversified company with successful operating subsidiaries in Italy, Germany, Norway, Austria, and the Balkans, suffered losses because of the devaluation of the French franc and the German mark. At the same time, in the Swiss domestic market, production costs increased while sales remained static, causing the company further losses. In 1924 Brown Boveri devalued its capital by 30 percent to cover the losses it had incurred. In 1927 the agreement with Vickers ran out and was not renewed.

During the same time, Brown Boveri's various subsidiaries grew rapidly. Industrialization throughout Europe created strong demand for the company's heavy electrical equipment. Italy's burgeoning railroad industry provided a particularly strong boost to Brown Boveri's Italian subsidiary, and the company's German facility actually did considerably more business than the Swiss parent. For the next few decades Brown Boveri grew as fast as technological developments in electrical engineering. Each of the company's subsidiaries tended to develop

individually, as if it were a domestic company in the country in which it operated, and broad geographic coverage helped insulate the parent from severe crises when a certain region experienced economic difficulties.

This sort of segmented development had its drawbacks, however. After World War II, the cold war presented a variety of business opportunities for defense-related electrical contractors, but Brown Boveri's subsidiaries were seen as foreign companies in many of the countries in which they operated, sometimes making it difficult for the company to win lucrative contracts involving sensitive technology and other government contracts. The company, nevertheless, excelled at power generation, including nuclear power generators, and prospered in this field. Electrification efforts in the Third World also provided Brown Boveri with substantial profits.

Reorganization of Brown Boveri in 1970

In 1970 Brown Boveri began an extensive reorganization. The company's subsidiaries were divided into five groups: German, French, Swiss, "medium-sized" (seven manufacturing bases in Europe and Latin America), and Brown Boveri International (the remaining facilities). Each of these groups was further broken down into five product divisions: power generation, electronics, power distribution, traction equipment, and industrial equipment.

Throughout the 1970s, Brown Boveri struggled to expand into the U.S. market. The company negotiated a joint venture with Rockwell International Corporation, the American manufacturer of high-tech military and aerospace applications, but the deal fell through when the two companies could not agree on financial terms. While Brown Boveri counted a handful of major U.S. customers as its clients, among them large utilities such as the Tennessee Valley Authority and American Electric, Brown Boveri's American market share was dismal considering the company's international standing (North American sales accounted for only 3.5 percent of total sales in 1974 and 1975), and the company continued to search for a means of effectively entering U.S. markets.

In 1974 Brown Boveri acquired the British controls and instrument manufacturer George Kent. The deal at first raised concern in Britain over foreign ownership of such highly sensitive technology, but Brown Boveri prevailed with the encouragement of George Kent's rank-and-file employees, who feared the alternative of being bought by Britain's General Electric Company, PLC (GEC). The newly acquired company was renamed Brown Boveri Kent and made an excellent addition to the parent company's already diverse product line.

In the mid-1970s growing demand in the Middle East for large power-generating facilities distracted the company from its push into North America. Oil-rich African nations, such as Nigeria, attempting to diversify their manufacturing capabilities, also created new markets for Brown Boveri's heavy electrical engineering expertise.

In the early 1980s Brown Boveri's sales flattened out and the company's earnings declined. In 1983 Brown Boveri's German subsidiary in Mannheim, West Germany, which accounted for nearly half of the entire parent company's sales, rebounded. In spite of an increase in orders, however, the company's cost structure kept earnings down. In 1985 the subsidiary's performance improved as a result of cost-cutting measures but price decreases in the international market and unfavorable shifts in currency exchange rates largely offset these gains. In 1986 the parent company acquired a significant block of shares in the Mannheim subsidiary, bringing its total stake to 75 percent. That year, Brown Boveri's revenues amounted to SEK 58 billion, while earnings were SEK 900 million; the company had 97,000 employees.

In the later 1980s Brown Boveri took steps to reduce duplication of research and development among its various groups. While each subsidiary continued to do some product development research for its individual market, theoretical research was unified under the parent company, making more efficient use of research funding. In 1987 the company introduced a supercharging system for diesel engines called Comprex. This system was capable of increasing an engine's horsepower by 35 percent and delivering up to 50 percent more torque at lower speeds. The Japanese automaker Mazda planned to use the new supercharger in its new diesel passenger models.

Formation of ABB in 1988

In August 1987 ASEA and Brown Boveri, who had been fierce competitors in the heavy-electrical and power-generation fields, announced their intent to merge their assets for shares in a new company, ABB Asea Brown Boveri Ltd., to be owned equally by each parent company—which maintained separate stock listings in their own countries and acted as holding companies for ABB. When the merger took effect on January 5, 1988, ASEA's Curt Nicolin and Brown Boveri's Fritz Leutwiler became joint chairmen. ASEA's CEO, Percy Barnevik, became the new operating company's CEO, while his Brown Boveri counterpart became deputy CEO. ABB's headquarters were established in Zurich.

The joint venture between the two former competitors allowed them to combine expensive research and development efforts in superconductors, high-voltage chips, and control systems used in power plants. In addition, ASEA's strength in Scandinavia and northern Europe balanced Brown Boveri's strong presence in Austria, Italy, Switzerland, and West Germany. The merger, which created Europe's largest heavy-electrical combine, was also designed to take advantage of ASEA's management strengths and Brown Boveri's technological and marketing expertise.

The integration of the giant was the new management's first task. CEO Barnevik had been applauded for his excellent job of rationalization at ASEA. When he took the helm of that company in 1980 it was struggling but by 1986 it was earning 5.5 percent of total sales, compared to Brown Boveri's 1.5 percent. The companies hoped Barnevik would have similar success with Brown Boveri's operations. For his part, Barnevik aimed for ABB to achieve an overall operating margin of 10 percent.

In 1988 and 1989, ABB reorganized its existing operations by decentralizing and ruthlessly slashing bureaucracy. The combined corporate headquarters alone went from 2,000 to 176 employees. During the same period, ABB also went on an acquisition spree in Western Europe and the United States, purchasing a total of 55 companies. Perhaps most importantly, ABB was able to gain a foothold in North America, something both halves of ABB had struggled to achieve for the previous two decades. In early 1989 ABB formed a joint venture with the American electrical firm Westinghouse Electric Corporation. ABB owned 45 percent of the new subsidiary, a manufacturer of power transmission and power distribution systems for international markets. Then, in December 1989, ABB exercised its option to buy Westinghouse out of the venture, leaving ABB the sole owner of the company. That same month, the company agreed to buy Stamford, Connecticut-based Combustion Engineering Group, an unprofitable manufacturer of power generators and related equipment, for $1.56 billion. These U.S. investments, however, were not immediately successful for ABB, and the company, over the next few years, had to reorganize the acquired businesses, divesting $700 million in assets and trimming their payroll from 40,000 to 25,000.

Expansion in Asia and Eastern Europe and Major Restructurings in the Early to Mid-1990s

With recession plaguing the markets of Western Europe and North America in the early 1990s and with the continuing maturation of those markets, ABB decided that its future lay in the emerging markets of Eastern Europe and Asia, where opportunities for growth were plentiful and where it could set up lower-cost manufacturing operations. Although the company had virtually no operations in Eastern Europe at the beginning of the decade, through a series of acquisitions and joint ventures in Eastern Germany, Poland, and Czechoslovakia, ABB had established a considerable presence in the region by 1992, employing 20,000 people in 30 companies. By the end of 1995, ABB had a network of 60 companies in Eastern Europe and the former Soviet Union, giving it the largest manufacturing operation of any Western firm in the region. Operations in Poland and the Czech Republic continued to lead the way, but significant operations had also been established in Russia (3,000 employees), Romania (2,000 employees), and the Ukraine (1,500 employees).

At the same time, ABB began to expand more cautiously in Asia, laying the groundwork for $1 billion in investments there by the mid-1990s. In 1992 an operating structure was created for the Asia-Pacific region and more than 20 new manufacturing and service operations were established in the region through acquisitions, joint ventures, and other investments. Investments in Asia continued in 1993, the year that ABB carried out another major restructuring. This one involved the reorganizing of the company's global operations into three geographic regions: Europe (including the Middle East and Africa), the Americas, and Asia; the folding of six industrial business segments into the following four: power generation, power transmission and distribution, industrial and building systems, and rail transportation; and the streamlining of the executive committee to eight members (Barnevik, the heads of the three geographic regions, and the heads of the four business segments).

In 1994, in addition to making additional investments in Asia, ABB entered into a contract to build a $1 billion combined-cycle power plant in Malaysia. On January 1, 1996, ABB merged its rail transportation unit with that of Germany's Daimler-Benz AG to form ABB Daimler-Benz Transportation

GmbH (ADtranz), a 50–50 joint venture that immediately became the largest provider of rail systems in the world. As part of the agreement, Daimler-Benz paid ABB $900 million in cash for its half share of the new venture because its rail operations were only about half the size of those of ABB.

In February 1996 the parent companies of ABB changed their names, with ASEA becoming ABB AB and Brown Boveri becoming ABB AG. At the same time, changes were made to ABB's board of directors. These changes were intended to reflect the company's increasingly global nature and to improve the relationship between the subsidiary and its parent companies. Further management changes came in October 1996 when Barnevik relinquished his position as chief executive of ABB in order to take over the chairmanship of Investor, the Wallenberg family holding company. Assuming the position of president and chief executive was Göran Lindahl, a 25-year company veteran who had been executive vice-president for power transmission and the Middle East and North Africa region. Barnevik remained ABB chairman. In June 1997 the Wallenberg group, in need of cash for a takeover, reduced its indirect voting stake in ABB from 32.7 percent to 25.5 percent.

In June 1996 ABB was awarded a contract by the government of Malaysia to play the lead role in the building of a $5 billion-plus hydroelectric power generation plant and transmission system at Bakun on the Balui River, but this project ran into problems in the following year. As a result of the Asian economic crisis, which hit Malaysia particularly hard, the Malaysian government was forced to announce an indefinite delay in the project in September 1997. Despite this setback, and the continuing uncertainty surrounding Asian economies, ABB did not pull back from its expansion in that region. In October 1997 the company announced yet another major restructuring in which it planned to shift thousands of jobs from Europe and the United States to Asia, cutting 10,000 jobs over an 18-month period. This was in addition to a 3,600-job cut announced just a few days earlier at ADtranz. ABB's executives were betting that the Asian economic crisis would be of relatively short duration and reasoned that, although they might lose business in the region in the short term, they could recoup some of these losses by taking advantage of the countries' weakened currencies, which brought manufacturing costs down even further. To cover the costs of the reorganization, ABB took a charge of $850 million in the fourth quarter of 1997.

From its first year of operation in 1988 through its ninth year in 1996, ABB Asea Brown Boveri Ltd. nearly doubled in size, increasing revenues from $17.83 billion to $34.57 billion. Although it failed to reach Barnevik's goal of a 10 percent operating margin for even a single year, the merged company was much more profitable than its predecessors, ASEA AB and BBC Brown Boveri Ltd., achieving a peak operating margin of 9.7 percent in 1995 before falling back to 8.8 percent in 1996. ABB was already much stronger, better managed, and more global in nature than its parent companies had been when operating independently.

1998–2000: Lindahl's Transforming Moves

During the late 1990s and into 2000, Lindahl left his mark on ABB through a number of significant initiatives. In August 1998 the company launched a major restructuring that did away with the group's regional reporting structure in favor of a realignment of business activities on global lines. In addition, some existing business segments were broken up into smaller, more focused categories. For example, the industrial and building systems segment was split into three new segments: automation, products and contracting, and oil, gas, and petrochemicals—the latter being the largest of the three. The power transmission and distribution segment was divided into two covering power transmission and power distribution. Remaining unchanged were the power generation and financial services segments.

Next, Lindahl spearheaded a series of moves to shift ABB's focus toward high-tech sectors, particularly industrial robots and factory control systems, and away from the traditional heavy engineering activities. In October 1998 ABB completed the largest acquisition in company history, buying Elsag Bailey Process Automation N.V., a Netherlands-based maker of industrial control systems, for $2.1 billion, including $600 million in debt. This deal made ABB's automation segment the world's leading maker of robotics and automated control systems, with annual revenues of $8.5 billion. On the divestment side, ABB in January 1999 sold its 50 percent stake in ADtranz to Daimler-Chrysler AG for $472 million. In March 1999 ABB and France-based ALSTOM merged their power generation businesses into a 50–50 joint venture called ABB Alstom Power. For transferring to the venture operations that generated some $8 billion in annual revenues, ABB received $1.5 billion in cash. Then in May 2000 ABB sold its 50 percent interest in the venture to ALSTOM for $1.2 billion. That same month, ABB completed the sale of its nuclear power business to the U.K. firm BNFL Inc. in a $485 million deal.

The final step in the integration of the ABB predecessors ASEA and Brown Boveri also occurred under Lindahl's watch. During 1999 ABB AB and ABB AG were united under a single stock, ABB Ltd., which began trading in June on the Zurich, Stockholm, London, and Frankfurt exchanges. (A listing on the New York Stock Exchange was later added, in April 2001.) With the dramatic changes that had taken place at ABB under his relatively brief tenure—changes that had by and large been received favorably—Lindahl's sudden resignation at the end of 2000 came as a surprise. It later came to light that Lindahl had been forced out in a behind-the-scenes power struggle. Jörgen Centerman, the head of ABB's automation segment, was named to replace Lindahl as chief executive. The now smaller ABB reported net income of $1.44 billion for 2000 based on revenues of $22.97 billion.

Early 2000s: A Fallen Giant Battling for Survival

Centerman quickly launched a restructuring of his own. In January 2001 ABB reorganized around four customer-focused divisions—utilities; process industries; manufacturing and consumer industries; and oil, gas, and petrochemicals—and two divisions based on product type, power technology products and automation technology products. The new organization was intended to accelerate ABB's shift away from heavy industrial products toward new technologies and services, as well as to streamline its relationship with large corporate customers. Centerman also engineered one major acquisition during 2001, the

June purchase of Entrelec Group for $284 million. Gaining Entrelec, a supplier of industrial automation and control products based in Lyon, France, strengthened ABB's position in key North American and European markets.

During the first half of 2001, operating earnings at ABB were down 21 percent and revenues were flat as the company's key markets suffered from the economic slowdown. In July ABB announced that it planned to cut 12,000 jobs, or 8 percent of its workforce, over the following 18 months, in an effort to shave $500 million off its annual expenses. Concerns about the company's performance and growing U.S. asbestos liabilities sent the company's stock sharply lower. It was in this environment that Barnevik unexpectedly announced his resignation as chairman in November 2001. Succeeding him as nonexecutive chairman was Jürgen Dormann, who was concurrently serving as chairman of the pharmaceuticals group Aventis S.A. and had been on the ABB board for three years.

In January 2002 ABB doubled its provisions for asbestos liabilities by taking a $470 million charge against fourth-quarter 2001 earnings. ABB's exposure to asbestos lawsuits stemmed from its 1990 acquisition of Combustion Engineering, which prior to the mid-1970s was a supplier of products containing asbestos. This charge coupled with asset writedowns, a change in accounting practices, and losses on certain projects led to a $691 million net loss for 2001. Soon after announcing these dismal results, ABB became embroiled in controversy through the embarrassing revelation that former top executives Barnevik and Lindahl, apparently taking advantage of a lax corporate governance environment, walked away from the company with pension and retirement benefits worth a combined $143 million. ABB pushed them to return some of the money, and in March 2002 the two agreed to give back a combined $82 million. Saddled with $4 billion in debt, ABB next had to repair its balance sheet to avoid a financial collapse. In April the company got some breathing room by restructuring a $3 billion loan. Then in September it reached a deal to sell its structured-finance unit to General Electric; this deal, which closed in November, generated much needed cash proceeds of about $2.5 billion.

Also in September 2002, Dormann, unhappy about the pace of restructuring, took over as chief executive, replacing Centerman. Within weeks he streamlined ABB's divisional structure, cutting its five divisions down to two core businesses: power technologies and automation. The building products and oil, gas, and petrochemicals units were placed into a discontinued operations category, slated for divestment. Through this latest reorganization, Dormann hoped to realize annual savings of $800 million. In December 2002 ABB sold its water and electricity metering business to Ruhrgas Industries GmbH for $223 million. That same month, liquidity was assured for 2003 and 2004 through the securing of a $1.5 billion credit facility. For 2002, ABB posted a record net loss of $783 million on revenues of $18.3 billion. Over the course of the year, the company's stock, battered by the incessant bad news, fell 70 percent. The stock closed the year at $2.87 per share, down from $33 just three years earlier.

In January 2003 ABB and its Combustion Engineering subsidiary announced plans for a "prepackaged" bankruptcy for the U.S. unit and an offer to resolve the unit's asbestos liability through a deal that would cap payments at $1.2 billion. This plan was soon approved by a U.S. district court, but an appeal filed by a group of plaintiffs was pending in mid-2004. On the divestment front, ABB in August 2003 sold its building systems business in Sweden, Norway, Denmark, Finland, Russia, and the Baltic states to Helsinki-based YIT Corporation for about $233 million. In December the company agreed to sell its Sirius reinsurance business to the Bermuda-based White Mountains for about $425 million. In January 2004 ABB reached an agreement to sell the upstream portion of its oil, gas, and petrochemicals unit to a private equity consortium led by Candover Partners, a European buyout firm, in a deal estimated to be worth at least $925 million. During 2003, ABB also further bolstered its depleted capital base through a $2.5 billion rights issue, a $750 million bond, and a $1 billion unsecured credit facility.

The various initiatives undertaken in 2003 failed to prevent ABB from posting its third straight full-year net loss. The news of the $767 million loss, however, was soon followed by a report of the company's first quarterly profit in two years, during the first quarter of 2004. It appeared by then that the worst of the crisis was over, and that ABB had firmly pulled itself back from the brink of bankruptcy. There was nevertheless a measure of uncertainty in the form of the unresolved asbestos litigation. But Dormann felt confident enough about the company's future to announce in early 2004 that he would step aside as chief executive at the end of the year. Selected to succeed him was Fred Kindle, the head of Sulzer AG, a Swiss engineering group much smaller than ABB.

Principal Subsidiaries

ABB S.A. (Argentina); ABB Australia Pty Limited; ABB AG (Austria); ABB Ltda. (Brazil); ABB Bulgaria EOOD; ABB Inc. (Canada); ABB (China) Ltd.; Asea Brown Boveri Ltda. (Colombia; 99.99%); ABB Ltd. (Croatia); ABB s.r.o. (Czech Republic); ABB A/S (Denmark); Asea Brown Boveri S.A. (Ecuador; 96.88%); Asea Brown Boveri S.A.E. (Egypt); ABB AS (Estonia); ABB Oy (Finland); ABB S.A. (France); ABB AG (Germany); ABB Automation Products GmbH (Germany); ABB Gebäudetechnik AG (Germany); ABB Process Industries GmbH (Germany); Asea Brown Boveri S.A. (Greece); ABB (Hong Kong) Ltd.; ABB Engineering Trading and Service Ltd. (Hungary); ABB Ltd. (India; 52.11%); ABB Ltd. (Ireland); ABB Technologies Ltd. (Israel; 99.99%); ABB S.p.A. (Italy); ABB Sace S.p.A. (Italy); ABB Trasmissione & Distribuzione S.p.A. (Italy); ABB Technology SA (Ivory Coast; 99%); ABB K.K. (Japan); ABB Ltd. (Korea); ABB Holdings Sdn. Bhd. (Malaysia); Asea Brown Boveri S.A. De C.V. (Mexico); ABB BV (Netherlands); ABB Holdings BV (Netherlands); Lummus Worldwide Contracting B.V. (Netherlands); ABB Limited (New Zealand); ABB Holding AS (Norway); Asea Brown Boveri S.A. (Peru; 99.99%); Asea Brown Boveri Inc. (Philippines); ABB Sp. zo.o. (Poland; 95.98%); ABB S.G.P.S., S.A. (Portugal); Asea Brown Boveri Ltd. (Russia); ABB Contracting Company Ltd. (Saudi Arabia; 65%); ABB Holdings Pte. Ltd. (Singapore); ABB Holdings (Pty) Ltd. (South Africa; 80%); Asea Brown Boveri S.A. (Spain); ABB AB (Sweden); Sirius International Försäkrings AB (publ) (Sweden); ABB Asea

Brown Boveri Ltd.; ABB Schweiz Holding AG; ABB LIM-
ITED (Thailand); ABB Holding A.S. (Turkey; 99.95%); ABB
Ltd. (Ukraine); ABB Industries (L.L.C.) (United Arab
Emirates; 49%); ABB Ltd. (U.K.); ABB Inc. (U.S.A.); Asea
Brown Boveri Inc. (U.S.A.); Asea Brown Boveri S.A. (Venezu-
ela); ABB (Private) Ltd. (Zimbabwe).

Principal Divisions

Power Technologies; Automation Technologies.

Principal Competitors

Siemens AG; General Electric Company; Hitachi, Ltd.; Schneider Electric SA; AREVA Group.

Further Reading

"The ABB of Management," *Economist,* January 6, 1996, p. 56.

"All Over?," *Economist,* October 26, 2002, p. 56.

Andrews, Edmund L., "ABB Will Cut 10,000 Jobs and Switch Focus to
Asia," *New York Times,* October 22, 1997, p. 2D.

Barham, Kevin, and Claudia Heimer, *ABB, the Dancing Giant: Creating the Globally Connected Corporation,* London: Financial Times/
Pitman, 1998, 382 p.

"Barnevik's Bounty," *Economist,* March 2, 2002, p. 58.

Bilefsky, Dan, "Chief Dormann Shakes Up ABB Corporate Culture,"
Wall Street Journal Europe, January 22, 2004, p. A6.

Bilefsky, Dan, and Anita Raghavan, "Blown Fuse: How 'Europe's GE'
and Its Star CEO Tumbled to Earth," *Wall Street Journal,* January
23, 2003, p. A1+.

Brown-Humes, Christopher, et al., "From Admired to Mired: A Powerhouse Adrift," *Financial Times,* March 11, 2002, p. 30.

Ehrenkrona, Olof, *Nicolin: En svensk historia,* Stockholm: Timbro,
1991.

Evans, Richard, "Back from the Brink," *Barron's,* October 25, 1999,
pp. 26, 28.

Fink, Ronald, "The Tortoise Doesn't Always Win," *Financial World,*
September 27, 1994, pp. 22, 24.

Fleming, Charles, "ABB Earmarks $1.5 Billion to Purchase Elsag
Bailey," *Wall Street Journal Europe,* October 15, 1998, p. 3.

——, "New Chairman of ABB Aims to Tighten Business Focus," *Wall
Street Journal Europe,* November 23, 2001, p. 5.

——, "Percy Who? ABB's Top Officer Rapidly Re-engineers Engineering Giant," *Wall Street Journal Europe,* December 15, 1999,
p. 1.

"A Great Leap, Preferably Forward," *Economist,* January 20, 2001,
p. 65.

Gumbel, Peter, "Daimler to Pay $900 Million to ABB As They Merge
Railroad Operations," *Wall Street Journal,* March 17, 1995, p. 6A.

Guyon, Janet, "ABB Fuses Units with One Set of Values: Managers
Get Global Strategies to Work Locally," *Wall Street Journal,* October 2, 1996, p. 15A.

Hall, William, and Dan Roberts, "How a Toxic Mixture of Asbestos
Liabilities and Plummeting Demand Poisoned an Industrial Powerhouse," *Financial Times,* October 23, 2002, p. 17.

Hofheinz, Paul, "Yes, You Can Win in Eastern Europe," *Fortune,* May
16, 1994, pp. 110–12.

"Is It a Bird? Is It a Manager?" *Economist,* May 3, 1997, pp. 53–54.

Kapstein, Jonathan, and Dean Foust, "An Insider Caper in Liechten-
stein," *Business Week,* December 11, 1989, pp. 58–59.

Karlgaard, Rich, "Percy Barnevik," *Forbes ASAP,* December 5, 1994,
pp. 65–68.

Kets de Vries, Manfred F.R., with Elizabeth Florent-Treacy, *The New
Global Leaders: Richard Branson, Percy Barnevik, and David Simon,* San Francisco: Jossey-Bass, 1999, 188 p.

Lang, Norbert, *Charles E.L. Brown, 1863–1924, Walter Boveri, 1865–
1924: Gründer eines Weltunternehmens,* Meilen, Switzerland:
Verein für Wirtschaftshistorische Studien Meilen, 1992, 95 p.

Michaels, Daniel, "ABB Showcases Growing Share of Poland's Market," *Wall Street Journal,* March 1, 1996, p. 5A.

Morais, Richard C., "ABB Reenergized," *Forbes,* August 23, 1999,
pp. 58, 61.

"Mr. Barnevik, Aren't You Happy Now?," *Business Week,* September
27, 1993, p. 128L.

"Neither Lender Nor Borrower Be," *Economist,* March 30, 2002, p. 54.

Rapoport, Carla, "A Tough Swede Invades the U.S.," *Fortune,* June
29, 1992, pp. 76–79.

Reed, Stanley, "The Wallenbergs' New Blood," *Business Week,* October 20, 1997, pp. 98, 102.

Reed, Stanley, and Michael Arndt, "Work Your Magic, Herr
Dormann," *Business Week,* February 10, 2003, p. 46.

Smart, Tim, and Gail Edmondon, "Slow Boil for ABB in the U.S.,"
Business Week, September 12, 1994, pp. 72–73.

Taylor, William, "The Logic of Global Business: An Interview with
ABB's Percy Barnevik," *Harvard Business Review,* March/April
1991.

Tomlinson, Richard, "Mission Impossible? Jürgen Dormann's Job: To
Save ABB from Itself," *Fortune,* November 18, 2002, pp. 147–48,
150, 152.

Wagstyl, Stefan, "Woven into the Fabric," *Financial Times,* January
10, 1996, p. 15.

Woodruff, David, and Charles Goldsmith, "Sour Sign-Off: A Final
Pension Move Soils High Standing of Top European CEO," *Wall
Street Journal,* March 8, 2002, p. A1+.

—update: David E. Salamie

Abertis Infraestructuras, S.A.

Avda del Parc Logistic 12-20
Barcelona E-08040
Spain
Telephone: +34 93 230 50 00
Fax: +34 93 230 50 01
Web site: http://www.abertis.com

Public Company
Incorporated: 2003
Employees: 4,741
Sales: EUR 1.28 billion ($1.1 billion) (2003)
Stock Exchanges: Madrid Barcelona
Ticker Symbol: ABE
NAIC: 237310 Highway, Street, and Bridge Construction;
517110 Wired Telecommunications Carriers; 541320
Landscape Architectural Services; 561730
Landscaping Services; 811198 All Other Automotive
Repair and Maintenance

Abertis Infraestructuras, S.A. has gone beyond its position as the leading operator of toll roads in Spain to become an international transportation infrastructure specialist. As such, Abertis, through its Saba subsidiary, is Spain's leading operator of parking garages, with more than 90,000 car parking spaces in more than 35 cities. Saba is also present in 25 cities in Italy, Portugal, Morocco, and Andorra. Abertis has also extended its infrastructure operations through subsidiary abertis logistica to include CIM Vallés logistics park, the Ronda del Litoral and the Cilsa port operation in Barcelona, and two new logistics centers in Alava and Sevilla, which will add some 500,000 square meters of warehouse space and 200,000 square meters of offices under the company's management. In another infrastructure extension, Abertis has acquired control of the Tradia and Retevision radio and telecommunications transmission networks, providing analog and digital transmission capabilities at more than 2,400 sites in Spain. Lastly, Abertis has entered the airport management arena, joining Codad to manage Colombia's Eldorado airport. Nonetheless, toll roads remain the company's largest operation, accounting for 84 percent of its reve-

nues of nearly EUR 1.3 billion ($1.1 billion) in 2003. In Spain the company's network, developed through the mergers of Acesa, Aurea, and Iberpistas, comprises some 68 percent of the country's toll road system, as well as stakes in the Túnel de Cadi and Autema. Spain also represents Abertis' primary market, at 94 percent of its revenues. Abertis, however, has sought to enhance its international position at the turn of the century, and includes motorway operations in Argentina and Puerto Rico, and stakes in toll road operators Autostrade, in Italy; Brisa, in Portugal; and RMB, in the United Kingdom. Together, the company directly controls 1,500 kilometers of motorways.

Building Spain's Highway System in the 1960s

Formed through the merger of Acesa and Aurea, followed by the absorption of Iberpistas in 2003, Abertis represented the combination of nearly 40 years of road-building in Spain. Acesa started out as Autopistas, Conceionaria Española SA, and was founded in 1967 in order to build Spain's first toll road, the highway linking Montgat and Mataró. Based in Barcelona, Acesa became a major regional player, constructing nearly 550 kilometers of roadway, including the Jonquera-Salou segment, the Maresme coastal road, and the link through the Ebro corridor to Zaragoza.

Acesa, which came under control of the La Caixha insurance group, also expanded through a series of mergers and acquisitions, such as the 1979 absorption of Aecasa, which extended Acesa's network to include the toll road linking Montmeló and El Papiol. In 1984, Acesa grew again, acquiring the motorway operations of Acasa. That acquisition permitted Acesa to extend its network from Zaragoza to the Mediterranean.

Elsewhere in Spain, a number of other companies were steadily completing the country's roadway grid. Construction leader Dragados had entered the road-building market in the mid-1960s, based on its experience paving runways for the country's airports. The company's first concession in Spain was awarded in 1967, for the construction of a toll road connecting Seville and Cadiz. Dragados later emerged as a major force in the Spanish and international infrastructures market, completing more than 2,500 kilometers of highways, including toll roads, as well as more than 4,000 kilometers of other roadways, among other projects. Dragados also became active in a number of other concessions markets, including the award of the management contract for Colombia's Eldorado Airport in 1995.

Dragados began shifting its strategy in the late 1990s, seeking to reduce its reliance on construction and instead focus on its other fast-growing operations, such as its Services divisions, and also to broaden its international operations. As part of this effort, Dragados spun off parts of its concessions business, including its Spanish toll road operations, into a merger with another major Spanish toll road operator, Aumar, in 2000, creating Aurea Infraestructure e Concessions.

Founded in 1971, Aumar, or Autopistas del Mare Nostrum, began construction on the first of two toll road concessions, linking Tarragona and Valencia, in 1974. Following the completion of that first section, the company completed the successive segment, joining Valencia with Alicante. By 1985, the full length of the company's concessions had been completed, bringing the toll road to the French border. In 1986, Aumar purchased another toll road operator, Bética de Autopistas. Following its merger with Dragados's toll road business, the company reincorporated as the publicly listed Aurea. Dragados remained the company's largest shareholder, with 36 percent of its stock.

The third member of the later Abertis was Iberpistas. Owned by four families, Iberpistas originated as part of Canales y Túneles SA, which was awarded the concession to build the roadway link between Villalba and Adanero. After launching construction of the 70-kilometer highway, Canales y Túneles transferred the construction, management, and maintenance concession to a new structure, Ibérica de Autopistas, which became more popularly known as Iberpistas. That company later received the concession to operate the toll road between Bilbao and Zaragoza, including more than 300-kilometers of roadway. In 2000, Iberpistas extended its total roadway concession through the acquisition of Autopista Vasco Aragonesa, or Avasa. This acquisition positioned Iberpistas as the country's fourth largest toll road operator with a 600-kilometer network under its control.

Consolidated Infrastructure Operations for the New Century

While Aumar remained the focus toll road division of the larger Dragados group, Acesa began a drive to extend beyond toll road operations in the mid-1990s. In 1994, the company drafted new strategic objectives calling for it to become a major Spanish infrastructures group. This led to the group's movement into car parks, with the acquisition of a majority stake in Saba, in

1994, with the remainder held by La Caixa. The construction and operation of logistics area, providing warehousing and related services to the truck market, became another company focus in 1997. Acesa also acquired control of Tradia, which provided infrastructure services to radio broadcasters as well as to the telecommunications market. Acesa continued to build up its stake in Tradia, acquiring full control in September 2003.

By then, Acesa had been radically transformed. The run-up to consolidation among Europe's toll road groups had begun in earnest in the late 1990s as the launch of the new single European currency approached. Many companies began to develop a series of cross-shareholdings with foreign partners. Such was the case with Acesa, which acquired a 10 percent stake in Brisa Auto-Estradas, based in Portugal, in 2002. Brisa in turn purchased a 10 percent stake in Acesa. Earlier, Acesa had also joined a shareholding group including members of the Benetton family, which acquired a 30 percent stake in Autostrade—

which acquired 4 percent of Acesa in its turn. Observers saw Acesa international partnerships as a prelude to a possible merger early in the new century.

In the meantime, Acesa had also begun to step up its position in the Spanish market as well. In 2001, the company began acquiring the motorway investments held by its main financial institution shareholders, including La Caixa. As part of this process, Acesa began building up a controlling stake in Autopistes de Catalynya, or Aucat. By 2002, the company had gained full control of Aucat, adding its 60-kilometer concession along the Garraf Pau Casals highway. Acesa also acquired an 8 percent stake in Iberpistas, as well as an agreement to purchase stakes in toll road operator Autema and the concession operating the Túnel del Cadi.

These acquisitions helped raise Acesa's profile, making it Spain's top toll road operator—and placing it in pole position for the soon-to-be privatized road concessions still held by the Spanish government. Yet that position came under threat in early 2002 when Aurea, through Dragados, announced that it had entered talks with Iberpistas to merge the two companies toll road and infrastructures operations. The deal appeared set to go through, until Acesa responded with a higher bid for Iberpista. A bidding war ensued, as Aurea launched a new counteroffer.

Yet in May 2002, the bidding war came to an abrupt end with La Caixa and Dragados—itself under pressure from the ultimately successful hostile takeover attempt by ACS—announced that they had agreed to a merger between Acesa and Aurea, creating a new publicly listed company, Abertis Infraestructuras. The new company became the outright toll road leader in the Spanish market and the third largest toll road operator in Europe. The merger also gave the company a strong international profile, with operations and holdings in Italy, Portugal, Andorra, the United Kingdom, Argentina, Chile, Puerto Rico, Colombia, and Morocco. Following the merger, completed in 2003, Abertis reached an agreement to acquire Iberpistas, a merger which was completed in June 2004.

In the meantime, Abertis continued building up its infrastructure operations. In 2003, the company acquired La Caixa's 39.9 percent stake in Saba, giving Abertis control of 99.1 percent of the Spanish parking garage leader. After withdrawing from the bidding for the privatization of the Spanish government's roadway operator, Ena, Abertis instead turned to boosting its telecommunications infrastructure wing. In September 2003, the company acquired full control of Tradia. That purchase followed on the company's June 2003 purchase of Retevisión Audiovisual, the Spanish leader in television and radio signal transmission infrastructure management, with more than 2,400 sites under its control. As it moved toward the middle of the 2000s, Abertis had positioned itself as a major player in the increasingly global infrastructures market.

Principal Subsidiaries

abertis logística; abertis telecom; Accesos Madrid; Acesa; APR; Arasur; Aucat; Aulesa; Aumar; Ausol; Autema; Autopista A-6; Autostrade; Brisa; Castellana; Central Gallega; Cilsa; Codad; Concesiones de Madrid; Coviandes; Elqui; GCO; Gesa; Henarsa; Iberpistas; Parbla; Proconex; Rabat; Retevisión; RMG; Saba; Saba Italia; Satsa; Sevisur; Spasa; Spel; Torre de Collserola; Tradia; Túnel del Cadí.

Principal Competitors

RWE AG; Consolidated Contractors Co.; Bouygues S.A.; VINCI S.A.; Hochtief AG; Royal BAM Group N.V.; Colas S.A.; Construtora OAS Ltda.; OAS Engenharia e Parcicipacoes Ltda.; Fomento de Construcciones y Contratas S.A.

Further Reading

"Abertis se fija en Europe del este," *Epoca*, April 30, 2004, p. 83.

Blitz, James, "Autostrade, Acesa Strengthen Ties," *Financial Times,* March 27, 2001, p. 30.

Gonzalez, Emilio, "Abertis, en busca de la consolidaci?" *Epoca*, July 11, 2003, p. 78.

Levitt, Joshua, "Acesa Move Opens up Battle for Iberpistas," *Financial Times*, March 21, 2002, p. 22.

Schafer, Thilo, "Spanish Roads Operator Attracts Four Bids," *Financial Times*, May 28, 2003, p. 28.

"Spanish Acesa Group Acquires 5% of Portuguese Operator Brisa," *European Report*, April 6, 2002, p. 600.

Wise, Peter, "Brisa Road Deal Points to Merger," *Financial Times,* September 17, 2002, p. 16.

—M.L. Cohen

Air Sahara Limited

3rd Floor, Dr. Gopal Das Bhawan
28, Barakhamba Road
New Delhi - 110001
India
Telephone: +91-11-23326851
Fax: + 91-11-23755510
Web site: http://www.airsahara.net

Private Company
Incorporated: 1993 as Sahara Airlines Limited
Employees: 1,600
Sales: $264.0 million (2004 est.)
NAIC: 481111 Scheduled Passenger Air Transportation;
481112 Scheduled Freight Air Transportation; 481212
Nonscheduled Chartered Freight Air Transportation;
481211 Nonscheduled Chartered Passenger Air
Transportation; 488190 Other Support Activities for
Air Transportation; 721110 Hotels (Except Casino
Hotels) and Motels

Air Sahara Limited is a leading private airline in India, owned by the diversified Sahara India Parivar group. It flies 115 flights on a network of 20 destinations, operating a dozen Boeing 737 airliners and seven regional jets. It also operates four helicopters on charter flights between Delhi and Mumbai (Bombay). The carrier was allowed to begin flying to neighboring countries in the spring of 2003.

Origins

The Indian government opened its domestic air market to private carriers in the early 1990s. One of the first to create a new airline was the diversified conglomerate Sahara India Pariwar. The Pariwar had been formed in northern India in 1978 as a small finance company with just INR 2000 in start-up capital. As noted by *Air Transport World,* the name "Sahara" means shelter or support in Hindi.

Air Sahara began operations as Sahara Airlines Limited on December 3, 1993. A single Boeing 737 airliner made up the fleet. This aircraft crashed on a training flight in February 1994.

Most of the new start-up airlines—East West, Damania, ModiLuft, and NEPC—folded within a few years. Sahara Airlines held on. It earned INR 23.37 crore ($1.2 million) on revenues of INR 424.36 crore ($78.7 million) in the 1997–98 fiscal year ("crore" is a traditional term meaning 10 million).

Sahara began a charter service with four new helicopters in 1999. The late 1990s were characterized by fare wars as Sahara struggled to lift its market share and build its fleet. In April 1999, the airline cut fares again by 10 to 20 percent.

Parvez Damania, who had founded Domania Airways and sold it to NEPC Group in 1995, became director of Sahara Airlines in February 1999. Chief Controller Uttam Kumar Bose, who had been with Sahara Airlines since it was founded, left the airline in August 2000 and joined start-up Crown Express. He was soon back with Sahara, however, in the position of chief executive officer.

Rebranded in 2000

On October 2, 2000, Sahara Airlines was rebranded as Air Sahara. A frequent flier program called "Sahara Club Crown" had been launched the previous month. At the time, the airline operated eight Boeing 737s. Earlier in the year, the company dropped a plan to introduce a feeder airline called "Sahara Connect" using a dozen turboprop aircraft. The airline had a rather large workforce for the size of its fleet, 1,600 employees. Calcutta became the airline's third hub in October 2000.

Air Sahara reported a turnover of INR 40 crore in the 2000–01 fiscal year, and was profitable. The airline faced competition from the larger Jet Airways, and more new carriers like Royal Air and Visa Air were being launched. An e-commerce unit was established in 2001 to develop links with travel sites, and in March Air Sahara began booking flights over the Internet. Travel packages, particularly to resort destinations, were becoming more important. Air Sahara sold an estimated 10,000 packages from Delhi and Mumbai (Bombay) to Goa. In the fall of 2002, Air Sahara bought the Centaur Hotel in Mumbai from Air-India.

Revamped in 2001

A major revamp of the airline was launched in July 2001, Bose told the *Financial Express.* To improve reliability, the

Key Dates:

1993: Sahara Airlines begins operations with two Boeing 737s.
1999: Helicopter charters are launched.
2001: The company name is changed to Air Sahara.
2003: Regional Jets are added to the fleet.
2004: The first international service is inaugurated.

Dutch global airline KLM was tapped for maintenance support. On-time performance was raised from 57 percent to 96 percent.

While other airlines were scaling back during the post-9/11 slowdown in international travel, Air Sahara CEO U.K. Bose told *Business Line* it was a perfect time to increase market share. The airline actually increased frequencies on certain routes. Air Sahara went into November 2001 operating 37 flights and ended the month operating 53, to 12 destinations. The company spent INR 5 crore on promotions during the month.

To attract passengers, Air Sahara offered to accept frequent flier miles earned on other airlines in its own rewards program. Users had to earn an equal number of miles on Air Sahara, however, before they could be exchanged for free travel or consumer goods. According to the company, 1,000 people signed up for the program in the first two weeks.

Air Sahara brought a live acoustic band on board certain long-haul flights during February 2002. In another marketing scheme, the company teamed with Standard Chartered Bank to offer fliers the "Instabuy" program providing interest-free credit for air travel.

Air Sahara aggressively marketed itself toward corporations. It had package deals with 500 companies. The airline was earmarking one of its newly ordered Regional Jets for corporate charters, with a special 18-passenger VIP seating configuration—a "sky limousine." In September 2002, Bose told *Financial Express* that 40 percent of the company's passengers were business travelers.

Boosting the Fleet in 2002

Air Sahara began 2002 with just five aircraft; the fleet doubled in size within a few months, and doubled again by the beginning of 2004. A new, smaller aircraft type, the 50-seat Bombardier Canadair Regional Jet, bolstered the airline's regional connections beginning in January 2003. Sahara was the first privately owned airline in India to operate regional jets.

The added capacity allowed the airline to increase flight frequency, Bose told *Business Line*. This helped appeal to the business travelers who made up 80 percent of the company's market. The company also established business lounges in major cities across India.

Sahara aggressively marketed the new flights with its "Cosmos" frequent flyer programs, "Steal-a-Seat" auctions, and discounted advance tickets, allowing the airline to compete with trains in price and to grow the domestic air market as Southwest Airlines had in certain U.S. markets. For a 20 percent premium, U.K. Bose told *Business Line*, rail users could shorten a 36-hour trip to 2.5 hours. Sahara was supporting its expansion in capacity with an upgraded web site.

New Horizons in 2003 and 2004

In the spring of 2003, Air Sahara connected 13 destinations with 63 flights per day. It operated hubs at Mumbai (Bombay), Delhi, Kolkata, and the recently added Chennai.

In 2003, only Jet Airways was larger among private airlines in India. Both it and state-owned Indian Airlines had a domestic market share of about 45 percent, while Air Sahara was claiming 12 percent of the market. There was plenty of room to grow the market; according to CEO U.K. Bose, only 0.75 percent of the population flew.

Air Sahara launched an unprecedented 24 new flights on a single day, September 7, 2003. This expanded the route network to 20 destinations. Most of the new flights originated in Chennai.

The Indian government, pursuing an open skies policy, then began allowing the country's private airlines to operate limited international flights to six neighboring countries forming the South Asian Association of Regional Co-operation (SAARC): Nepal, Bangladesh, Bhutan, Maldives, Pakistan, and Sri Lanka. These routes traditionally had been reserved for the state-owned carriers Air-India and Indian Airlines.

Air Sahara was the first of the private airlines to launch such long awaited service with a flight from Chennai (Madras) to the Sri Lankan capital of Colombo on March 22, 2004. *Business Line* reported that CEO U.K. Bose told the first passengers, "This is a flight which will be cherished and remembered by all." Rival Jet Airways was inaugurating its own Chennai-Colombo service.

Air Sahara added flights to Nepal, Bangladesh, and the Maldives in April 2004. The airline soon teamed with Cathay Pacific to offer service through Colombo to Hong Kong and Singapore. Air Sahara added two widebody jets to accommodate traffic to Colombo.

According to the *Economic Times,* Air Sahara CEO U.K. Bose expected flights to neighboring countries to account for up to 12 percent of revenues. There were plans to open up the broader ASEAN region to services from India's private carriers within a few years, increasing the possibilities for Air Sahara even more.

Principal Subsidiaries

Centaur Hotel.

Principal Operating Units

Aviation Academy; Cargo.

Principal Competitors

Air Deccan; Air-India Limited; Indian Airlines Ltd.; Jet Airways (India) Private Limited.

Further Reading

Abreu, Robin, and Priya Ramani, "Domestic Airlines: Price Warriors," *India Today,* July 12, 1999, p. 50.

"Air Sahara Charts Out Fleet Buy Plan," *Business Standard,* December 3, 2001, p. 4.

"Air Sahara Enters International Partnership," *Airclaims Airline News,* August 10, 2001.

"Air Sahara Ties Up for Onward Connections from Colombo," *Financial Express,* March 23, 2004.

Bakshi, Veeshal, "Forty Per Cent of Our Passengers Today Are Corporate Travellers," *Financial Express,* September 6, 2002.

Bhushan, Ratna, and Ashwini Phadnis, " 'Our Twin Goals Are Link, Frequency'—Mr. Uttam Kumar Bose, CEO of Air Sahara," *Business Line,* January 10, 2003.

"Bose No Longer Part of Sahara Parivar," *Economic Times* (India), August 7, 2000.

Dubey, Rajeev, "Strategy: Can Sahara Airlines Scale New Heights?," *Business Today* (India), June 7, 1999, p. 44.

Ionides, Nicholas, "India's Air Sahara Closing on Fleet Roll-Over Decision," *Air Transport Intelligence,* February 17, 2003.

"Makeover for Sahara in Growth Bid," *Airline Business,* November 30, 2000.

Malhan, Sangita P. Menon, "For Domestic Airlines, Packaging Is Buzzword," *Times of India,* March 25, 2001.

——, "Up, Up and Away," *Times of India,* May 26, 1999.

Mhatre, Kamlakar, "Sahara Girds for Growth," *Air Transport World,* May 1, 1999.

Mitra, Sidhartha, "Moving into High Gear," *Business Standard,* April 22, 2000.

Mukherjee, Rumy, "Out on a Wing," *Economic Times* (India), August 19, 1999.

Murali, Janaki, "Air Sahara Flies Higher Despite Recession," *Business Line (The Hindu),* November 11, 2001.

Phadnis, Ashwini, "Air Sahara Not to Offer Equity to Foreign Firms," *Business Line (The Hindu),* December 15, 2001.

——, "Air Sahara Soars on Web Power," *Business Line (The Hindu),* September 26, 2002.

——, "Private Airlines Fly into Open Skies, Land in Colombo to Create History," *Business Line,* March 24, 2004.

——, "Skies Open Up Over the Sub-Continent," *Business Line,* March 29, 2004.

Rao, Girish, "Air Sahara Loyalists to Gain on Foreign Flights," *Economic Times* (India), August 28, 2001.

——, "Air Sahara Sees 10–12% of Revenues from Int. Flights," *Economic Times* (India), March 17, 2004.

——, "Sahara Airlines on Expansion Spree," *Business Line (The Hindu),* November 6, 2001.

——, "Sahara All Set to Take a Jet Flight," *Economic Times* (India), December 10, 2002.

"Sahara Airlines Plans to Spread Its Wings," *Hindu,* February 2000.

"Sahara Airlines Targets Rail-Users," *Business Line (The Hindu),* October 29, 2002.

"Sahara Airlines to Sport New Name," *Economic Times* (India), September 19, 2000.

Shankar, T.S., "Air Sahara's Expansion Plans," *Hindu,* August 28, 2003, p. 1.

——, "Air Sahara's Marketing Initiatives," *Hindu,* October 29, 2002.

Sinha, Ashutosh, "Airlines: Flying into Thin Air," *Business Today* (India), November 6, 2000, p. 54.

Subramaniam, G. Ganapathy, "Air Sahara Honours Frequent-Flier Miles Earned on Rival Carriers," *Economic Times* (India), December 4, 2001.

"Uttam Bose Refutes Sahara Charges," *Business Line (The Hindu),* August 8, 2000.

Zaheer, Kamil, "Jet Airways Faces a Mini-Exodus of Pilots to Better-Paying Sahara," *Economic Times* (India), December 16, 1999.

——, "Sahara Kicks Off Yet Another Airfare War on Key Routes," *Economic Times* (India), December 17, 1999.

——, "Sahara's Plan to Induct Turboprops Hits Airpocket," *Economic Times* (India), September 7, 1999.

—Frederick C. Ingram

ALARIS Medical Systems, Inc.

10221 Wateridge Circle
San Diego, California 92121
U.S.A.
Telephone: (858) 458-7000
Toll Free: (800) 854-7128
Fax: (858) 458-7760
Web site: http://www.alarismed.com

Public Company
Incorporated: 1988
Employees: 3,000
Sales: $533.9 million (2003)
Stock Exchanges: New York
Ticker Symbol: AMI
NAIC: 339112 Surgical and Medical Instrument
    Manufacturing

ALARIS Medical Systems, Inc. (Alaris) is a world leader in intravenous (IV) drug delivery systems, infusion devices, patient vital-signs monitoring instruments, and related software, disposables, consultations, and training. The company's motto is "Medication Safety at the Point of Care." To that end, Alaris offers the Medley Medication Safety System, the Signature Edition GOLD, Gemini, ASENA, and other infusion "smart pumps," the Guardrails Safety Software Suite, SmartSite and SmartSite Plus Needle-Free Valve systems, the VITAL•CHEC Vital Signs Monitor, electronic thermometers, docking systems, alternate site infusion systems, and other IV drug administration, monitoring, and safety systems. Alaris markets its products in the United States, Canada, Latin America, Europe, the Middle East, Asia, and Australia, and maintains manufacturing facilities in San Diego, California; Creedmoor, North Carolina; Hampshire, England; and Tijuana, Mexico.

Beginnings: Merger, Rightsizing, and Renaming

Alaris was formed in November 1996 when Advanced Medical Inc. merged its wholly owned subsidiary IMED Corporation with IVAC Medical Systems. IVAC and IMED were already major players in the intravenous drug delivery market, in operation since 1968 and 1972, respectively, and their merger created an opportunity to offer a wide selection of IV devices and customer care solutions to hospitals and healthcare purchasing organizations. Products included IMED's Gemini infusion and IVAC infusion and syringe pumps, and vital signs monitors. Important new products brought to the merged company included the Signature Edition Infusion System and the SmartSite Needle-Free Valve system. The SmartSite product proved to be one of the company's most significant, establishing it as a world leader in healthcare safety and anticipating needle-stick accident legislation.

Advanced Medical financed the $400 million acquisition of IVAC through a bank credit facility, subordinated notes, and a substantial equity contribution from Advanced Medical's chairman and principal stockholder, Jeffrey M. Picower. Advanced Medical reduced the labor force in December 1996 to eliminate redundancy in the two merged workforces, the cuts most directly affecting the corporate staff and the manufacturing workers. In total the layoffs included around 240 employees. In May of the following year the newly formed company took the name Alaris Medical Systems, Inc.

1997–99: Labor Dispute, Important Early Contracts, and New Products

In January 1997 Alaris, then still IMED-IVAC, entered into a five-year agreement with Premier Inc. to supply tympanic and electronic thermometers to Premier member hospitals. In March of the same year the companies agreed to another five year deal, in which IMED-IVAC would supply IV infusion pumps and related disposable administration sets. Premier was the nation's largest healthcare alliance enterprise at the time of the deals, and the agreements allowed IMED-IVAC to provide their infusion instruments and proprietary disposables to an alliance which comprised one-third of the hospitals in the United States.

Also that year, Alaris Medical Systems faced a work dispute with its maquiladora contracting firm, Cal Pacifico, based in Newport Beach, California. Alaris's agreement with Cal Pacifico provided the medical supply company with manufacturing facilities and more than 1,200 workers in Tijuana, Mexico,

Company Perspectives:

Our Mission is to develop "smart" technology, tools and services designed to help reduce the risks and costs of medication errors, and safeguard patients and clinicians at the point of care.

where disposable intravenous administration sets proprietary to Alaris's infusion systems were produced. The Tijuana workforce had for over two years voiced a desire to be directly employed by Alaris Medical Systems, and in April of that year Alaris notified Cal Pacifico that their agreement would be terminated and the medical supply company would hire the workers on directly, which they did on June 6, 1997. The dispute caused a two-week shutdown of the plants and interruption of work. The dispute was settled with Alaris making a payment of an undisclosed amount to Cal Pacifico and taking a related $4.1 million charge that quarter.

Alaris Medical Systems held a large portion of the infusion pump market share throughout Europe, the installed base of products placing it in the number one or two position in 11 countries, and third in Italy and Germany. The company also maintained the largest installed base of infusion pumps in Canada and Australia, and increasing shares of business in Latin America and Asia. In September 1997 Alaris entered into two agreements which reflected the company's desire to increase its international business. Alaris agreed to distribute the Rhythmic ambulatory pump manufactured by Micrel Microelectronic Application Centre, a private company based in Athens, Greece. An unrelated agreement gave Alaris the rights to market and distribute StatLock securement devices in Europe, Australia, and the Middle East. These improved, tape-free IV securement devices, developed and manufactured by VENETEC International, a private company based in Mission Viejo, California, reflected a commitment to safer and better care for patients and more convenience for healthcare workers, a commitment shared by both companies. In addition to thus nicely complementing Alaris Medical's existing product line, the agreement allowed VENETEC to enjoy much greater world market penetration than they would have been able to accomplish on their own.

The next month Alaris announced another major distribution agreement for a product which combined Alaris's P6000 intravenous syringe pump with Zeneca Limited's Diprifusor Target Controlled Infusion module, providing a solution for the safe and convenient administration of Diprivan, a general anesthesia shown to have less of certain side effects and a shorter recovery time.

In December 1997 Alaris announced the release of the IVAC Vital Signs Monitor, in collaboration with Criticare Inc. This product incorporated Alaris's advanced thermometry into Criticare's full-parameter vital signs monitors. Alaris Medical held the exclusive distribution rights to the new Vital Check 4400 in the United States hospital market and the entire Canadian markets. The small and portable unit combined electronic thermometry, digital pulse oximetry, and blood pressure into a single lightweight unit. Previous to the formation of Alaris, IVAC had introduced the world's first electronic thermometer.

The following July Alaris Medical completed the acquisition of Instromedix Incorporated for a total cash consideration of $51 million, the assumption of approximately $5.1 million in debt, and an additional $1 million for transaction expenses incurred by Instromedix. The acquisition allowed Alaris to add to its existing vital signs monitoring product line Instromedix's cardiac disease diagnosis and monitoring products and technologies, including arrhythmia event recorders, pacemaker monitors and the LifeSigns System, and a hardware and software system allowing remote monitoring and data reporting of vital signs.

In November 1998 Alaris launched a major new product, the ADVANTIS DL Infusion System, a small, lightweight pole-mounted infusion device designed to appeal to more cost-conscious international customers. It was the first infusion pump Alaris ever manufactured outside of the United States, and was intended exclusively for international markets. The infusion system incorporated many of Alaris's patented technologies for patient safety, including its proprietary anti-bolus, automatic site priming and free-flow protection.

Spending about $20 million per year on research and development, Alaris continually updated technology in its existing products. In 1999 the company introduced six products which improved on existing products. These included two new ASENA syringe pumps, the Turbo Temp Thermometer, the Signature Edition Gold Infusion System, and the MedSystemIII Multi-Channel Infusion Pump.

2000–02: Medley and Guardrails Becoming Central to Healthcare Strategy

In April 2000 Alaris's Instromedix Division signed an agreement with Quality Diagnostic Services Inc. (QDS) for the purchase of Instromedix's King of Hearts Express II recorder, a cardiac event monitor which detected and recorded heart arrhythmias. QDS, the nation's largest arrhythmia monitoring service, saw the agreement as a significant opportunity for growth for both companies. Instromedix had been manufacturing quality cardiac event monitors for 20 years, and the pager-sized King of Hearts Express II was designed not only to monitor and store a patient's ECG data and transmit it to doctors via telephone, but also automatically detect any unusually high or low heart levels, potentially catching dangerous events and saving lives.

Another important distribution agreement came in August 2000, with Alaris's Instromedix Division arranging to handle the United States and Canadian distribution of advanced electrocardiographs developed and manufactured by Nihon Kohden, Japan's leading medical electronic equipment manufacturer. Instromedix signed a separate three-year distribution agreement with Biomedical Systems for their Century line of Holter Scanning Systems, both in the United States and abroad. Both moves broadened Instromedix's already strong line of heart monitoring products, making the operation attractive to a potential buyer. Hence, later in August, Alaris announced its intention to sell Instromedix to Card Guard Scientific Survival Limited, an Israeli-based company specializing in telemedicine disease management.

In November Alaris announced a major sales agreement with Novation LLC, the supply company for two major health-

Key Dates

1996: IMED Corporation and IVAC Medical merge; SmartSite Needle-Free Valve is introduced.
1997: Merged entity is renamed ALARIS Medical Systems, Inc. (Alaris).
1999: Signature Edition GOLD Infusion System is introduced; sales exceed $400 million.
2001: Medley Medication Safety System, Guardrails Safety Software are introduced.
2003: Customer contracts include safety products.

care alliances, Veterans Health Administration and University Health Care Consortium. Under the terms of the agreement Alaris and one other company would provide large volume infusion pumps and accessories to Novation's two major clients as well as other healthcare organizations. The agreement also included Alaris's award-winning SmartSite needle-free valve system. In January of the following year Alaris announced that the same SmartSite system would be added to its existing supply agreement with Premier. SmartSite provided healthcare personnel needle-free access to IV lines, greatly reducing the number of needle-stick accidents and related problems among those personnel and helping their hospitals and healthcare providers to meet needle-free workplace regulations.

Around this time Alaris received a 54-page establishment inspection report (EIR) after a two-month inspection by an FDA investigator regarding previous inspections and complaints filed. Among other issues, the EIR concentrated on malfunctions in the Alaris's MSIII models of infusion pumps, specifically regarding a report of a lithium battery rupturing in one of the pumps and three incidents of capacitors failing and pumps shutting down. These problems resulted in recalls, redesigned circuitry, and new systems of testing and verification of performance parameters.

In 2001 Alaris introduced its proprietary Guardrails Safety Software, an application designed to prevent medication administration errors, to be used with the company's Medley Medication Safety System. The important new product reflected the company's ongoing commitment to patient safety and care. At the time medical errors were the 8th leading cause of death in the United States, responsible for more than 50,000 deaths annually. Guardrails monitored the administration of IV delivered drugs, comparing the amounts and rates to preconfigured data profiles for each individual patient and warning healthcare personnel if doses were too high, given at too fast a rate, or otherwise deviated from those profiles. In the fall of 2002 Alaris announced that Guardrails would be made available to a second major line of IV infusion devices, the Signature Edition GOLD System. By making the technology available on this system Alaris realized significant new sales opportunities, as well as the potential to utilize the safety software system with an established base of 50,000 infusion instruments in service worldwide.

The Medley Medication Safety System and Guardrail Safety Software became conceptual centerpieces of Alaris's commitment to the finest healthcare and the safest administration of that care. Using the latest technology Alaris developed a system for the monitoring of patients and the delivery of their intravenous treatments that prevented error and injury at the point of the IV's delivery, prevented needle-stick injuries due to needle-free valves, monitored the actual fluids being administered, to prevent over-dosing or any treatment outside of or contrary to the patient's computer profile, and provided detailed reporting of deviations and errors. It was difficult to assess the large amount of human injury, and even death, Alaris had prevented through its commitment to safety. Alaris refined the Medley System even further. In October 2002 the company added the SpO2 module capable of accurately measuring arterial oxygen and pulse, even against significant interference or motion. This gave the Medley System unprecedented mobility and had an impact throughout the health profession. In 2003 Alaris introduced the Medley Syringe Module for the systems using syringe infusion. Alaris expanded customer contracts to include the new safety systems, including for AmeriNet, Premier, and Novation. AmeriNet and Premier extended their contracts to 2006 and 2009, respectively.

In late 2003 Alaris announced a three-year agreement to provide the Medley Medication Safety System, along with Guardrails Safety Software, to Magnet, a purchasing consortium with over 775 acute-care provider members. Safety products contributed to a 16 percent increase in sales in 2003, to $533.9 million; however, except for 2002, the company continued to operate at a loss.

2003 and The Future: Patent Rights, Recapitalization, and Overseas Business

In May 2003 Alaris settled a patent lawsuit with Filtertek relating to Alaris's needle-free products. The settlement gave Alaris the worldwide patent license for this technology and eliminated the danger of patent infringement litigation in the future. The license was fully paid up, irrevocable, and unrestricted. The weight of such ongoing legal action lifted, Alaris was free to sell its SmartSite needle-free valves. Alaris was a leader in implementation following the 2000 Needle Stick Safety and Prevention Act. Less than a month after the end of litigation Alaris was awarded the Gold Medal Design Excellence Award for the SmartSite valves at the Medical Design and Manufacturing Conference and Exposition.

In June 2003 Alaris announced its intention to sell 9.1 million shares of its common stock in a move to recapitalize. The company realized the sale on June 30, for $12.50 a share, and also sold $175 million worth of senior notes. Also, the company offered $200 million in bonds and established a bank loan in excess of $200 million and a $30 million revolving credit facility.

At this time Alaris launched its redesigned global web site, www.alarismed.com, showcasing the corporate philosophy and history, investor information, detailed product information, and much more.

In late 2003 Alaris announced a three-year agreement to provide its Medley Medication Safety System with its proprietary Guardrails Safety Software to the purchasing consortium

Magnet and its over 775 acute care provider members. Alaris also began to seek more international business, announcing its attention at the beginning of 2004 to sell its ''smart pumps'' outside of the United States. Guardrails was added to the new ASENA CC Syringe Pump for sale outside the United States in 2003 and the company planned to add the software to other products sold overseas.

Alaris already obtained a third of its business from overseas customers, even without selling the Medley and Guardrails suite, and anticipated success for its established sales force abroad.

Principal Competitors

Abbott Laboratories; Baxter International, Inc.; B. Braun Medical, Inc.; Becton, Dickinson and Company; Fresenius Medical Care AG; Graseby Medical Limited; Sherwood-Davis & Geck; Welch Allyn, Inc.

Further Reading

Acello, Richard, ''Alaris Medical Inc. Survives a Feast of Changes,'' *San Diego Business Journal*, October 27, 1997, p. 4.

Brooks, Karen, ''Improving and Extending the Quality of Human Life,'' *San Diego Business Journal*, October 2, 2000, p. 74.

''Israel: Card Guard Scientific Survival Signs New Deal (Buys Istromedix from Alaris Medical Systems Inc.),'' *IPR Strategic Business Information Database*, August 24, 2000.

Lau, Gloria, ''Alaris Medical Systems, Inc. San Diego, California; CEO Guides Medical Firm to Higher Ground,'' *Investor's Business Daily*, July 14, 2003, p. A08.

Much, Marilyn, ''Alaris MEDICAL SYSTEMS San Diego, California; Medical Device Maker Pumps Up Global Sales,'' *Investor's Business Daily*, February 12, 2004, p. A10.

''New Editions of Guardrails Safety Software,'' *Journal of Clinical Engineering*, Fall 2002, p. 267.

''Small Parts Yield Alaris 11 Recalls During Audit,'' *Inspection Monitor*, June 2001.

—Mary Tradii and Jim Mooney

Albertson's, Inc.

250 Parkcenter Boulevard
Boise, Idaho 83706-0020
U.S.A.
Telephone: (208) 395-6200
Fax: (208) 395-6349
Web site: http://www.albertsons.com

Public Company
Incorporated: 1945
Employees: 212,000
Sales: $35.44 billion (2003)
Stock Exchanges: New York Pacific Exchange
Ticker Symbol: ABS
NAIC: 445110 Supermarkets and Other Grocery (Except
   Convenience) Stores; 446110 Pharmacies and Drug
   Stores

Albertson's, Inc. (the company omits the apostrophe in its brand marketing) is the second largest operator of grocery stores in the United States, trailing only the Kroger Co.—although in overall food retailing it also trails Wal-Mart Stores, Inc., the leader in that category. Following the April 2004 $2.47 billion acquisition of the Shaw's and Star Markets chains, Albertson's operated more than 2,500 stores in 37 states, mainly in the West, Southwest, Midwest, Mid-Atlantic, and New England. The units include about 1,350 combination food-and-drug stores as well as around 420 conventional supermarkets (under the Albertsons, Acme Markets, Jewel Food Stores, Shaw's, and Star Markets names); about two dozen warehouse stores (Max Foods and Super Saver Foods); and more than 700 stand-alone drugstores (Osco Drugs and Sav-on Drugs). Among the combination stores were a number of outlets operating under dual banners: Albertsons Osco, Albertsons Sav-on, and Jewel-Osco. More than 230 of the company's stores include onsite gasoline stations. Albertson's had small-town beginnings but had evolved by the early 2000s into a suburban-oriented operation; despite its expansion into a coast-to-coast operator, it also remained a predominantly western chain, with more than half of its stores located in that U.S. region. The company's history turns on the expansion of the one-stop shopping concept upon which it was founded, which led to the growth of larger stores carrying more diverse products and eventually to the jumbo food-and-drug stores that were the key to Albertson's tremendous success.

Early Years

In 1939 Joe Albertson left his position as a district manager for Safeway Stores and—with partners L.S. Skaggs, whose family helped build Safeway, and Tom Cuthbert, Skaggs's accountant—opened his first one-stop shopping market, called Albertson's Food Center, on a Boise, Idaho corner. Albertson thought big from the start—his first newspaper ad promised customers "Idaho's largest and finest food store." Indeed, the store was huge by contemporary standards; at 10,000 square feet it was approximately eight times as large as the average grocery store of that era. The store included specialties such as an in-store bakery, one of the country's first magazine racks, and homemade "Big Joe" ice cream cones. Customers liked what they saw, and the store pulled in healthy first-year profits of $9,000 on sales of more than $170,000.

Albertson's grew slowly at first. Sales remained constant during the war years, and in 1945 Joe Albertson dissolved the partnership and Albertson's was incorporated. By 1947, the chain had six stores operating in Idaho and had established a complete poultry processing operation. In 1949 the Dutch Girl ice cream plant opened in Boise, and Albertson's adopted the Dutch Girl as its early trademark.

Albertson's expanded during the 1950s into Washington, Utah, Oregon, and Montana. In 1957 the company built its first frozen foods distribution house, which served its southern Idaho and eastern Oregon stores. Albertson's also operated a few department stores during the 1950s, but these were phased out rapidly as the company decided to focus on the sale of food and drugstore items. In 1959 Albertson's introduced its private label, Janet Lee, named after the executive vice-president's daughter. The company also went public in 1959 and with that capital began to expand its markets aggressively.

Albertson's moved into its sixth state, Wyoming, in 1961, and opened its 100th store in 1962. In 1964 the company broke into the California market by acquiring Greater All American Markets, based in Los Angeles. The same year, Albertson turned the position of chief executive over to J.L. Berlin, although Albertson continued to chair the executive board.

Under Berlin's leadership, the company strengthened its Californian position by merging with Semrau and Sons, an Oakland-based grocery store chain, in 1965. This added eight markets in northern California, which Albertson's continued to operate under the name of Pay Less. In 1967 the company purchased eight Colorado supermarkets from Fury's Inc., a Lubbock, Texas concern. Between these purchases and construction of new units, Albertson's operated more than 200 stores by the end of the decade and annual sales were substantially more than $400 million.

In the late 1960s, Albertson's set several company policies that would secure its snowballing success. One of these was the company's ongoing renovation program. In 1980 Vice-Chairman Robert D. Bolinder pointed out that "almost every failure of previously profitable supermarket companies can be attributed to stores becoming outdated." Albertson's avoided this pitfall by constantly upgrading its facilities, remodeling and enlarging older stores, and closing those that had become obsolete.

Anticipating the ever increasing competition for profitable operating sites, Albertson's also took care during the 1960s to build a sophisticated property development task force of lawyers, economic analysts, negotiators, engineers, architects, and construction supervisors that allowed the company to stay on top of industry trends. In addition, it expanded its employee training and incentive programs to encourage employees to make a lifetime career with the company.

Combination Format in the 1970s

During its first three decades Albertson's primarily sold groceries, although it did introduce drugstore departments into units where possible. In 1970, however, the company pioneered a unique and exceptionally profitable concept in supermarket design. J.L. Scott, who had become chief executive officer in 1966, announced in 1969 that Albertson's would enter into partnership with Skaggs Drug Centers, Inc., based in Salt Lake City, Utah, and headed by Albertson's former partner, to jointly finance and manage six jumbo combination food-and-drug stores

in Texas. Whereas the average contemporary supermarket was 30,000 square feet or smaller, the combination stores covered as much as 55,000 square feet. In addition, while conventional stores carried strictly grocery items, which have a slim profit margin of 1 to 2 percent, the Skaggs-Albertson's combination stores stocked not only groceries but also nonfood items such as cosmetics, perfumes, pharmacy products, camera supplies, and electrical equipment. Banking on the higher profit margin of nonfood items as well as on an aggressive five-year plan, Scott also predicted in 1969 that Albertson's sales would double within five years. His optimism was not unfounded. By 1974, sales reached $852.3 million, with net earnings of $8.9 million.

The first Skaggs-Albertson's combination stores were opened in Texas in 1970, the year after the New York Stock Exchange began to trade Albertson's shares. In the early 1970s, Albertson's and Skaggs considered merging, but ultimately decided against the move. Albertson's continued its beneficial partnership with Skaggs until 1977, opening combination drug and grocery stores throughout Texas, Florida, and Louisiana.

Along with rapid growth, Albertson's faced some minor setbacks during the early 1970s. In 1972 Albertson's had acquired Mountain States Wholesale of Idaho, a subsidiary of DiGiorgio Corporation. In 1974 the Justice Department filed a civil antitrust suit against Albertson's, asserting that at the time of the purchase Albertson's was the largest retail grocer in the southern Idaho and eastern Oregon market, while Mountain States carried 43 percent of the wholesale grocery market, and that Albertson's purchase created an illegal monopoly.

Robert D. Bolinder, CEO from 1974 through 1976, claimed that the suit was without basis and that Albertson's had in fact preserved competition in the area by acquiring Mountain States. Bolinder still claimed that the Justice Department had misunderstood Albertson's reasons for buying the wholesaler, noting that the subsidiary was not financially integral to the company but accounted for only 3.4 percent of its total sales in 1973. The settlement, in 1977, required Albertson's to divest Mountain States and barred the company from acquiring any retail or wholesale grocery businesses in southern Idaho or eastern Oregon for five years.

Also in 1974, in the Portland, Seattle, and Denver areas, the Federal Trade Commission (FTC) found fault with Albertson's advertising practices. The company complied with an FTC order requiring that advertised sale items be available to customers and that rain checks be issued when sale items were out of stock, although Bolinder maintained that Albertson's had not violated any laws and emphasized that compliance would not require any change in the company's previously established advertising policies.

In 1976, after chairing the board for 37 years, Joe Albertson became chairman of the executive committee. Warren McCain, who began his career with Albertson's as a merchandising supervisor in 1951, became chairman of the board and CEO. In the same year, Albertson's began to build superstores, which would carry an even higher ratio of nonfood items. A slightly smaller version of the combination store, the superstores ranged in size from 35,000 to 48,000 square feet and featured more fresh foods and perishables. It was during 1976 that the corporation slowly

Key Dates:

1939: Joe Albertson, with partners L.S. Skaggs and Tom Cuthbert, opens his first one-stop shopping market, called Albertson's Food Center, in Boise, Idaho.

1945: Albertson dissolves the partnership and incorporates the business as Albertson's, Inc.

1950s: Company expands into Washington, Utah, Oregon, and Montana.

1959: Company goes public.

1964: Albertson's breaks into California market by acquiring Greater All American Markets.

1969: Company enters into partnership with Skaggs Drug Centers, Inc. to open combination food-and-drug stores.

1976: Company begins building superstores and slowly starts phasing out its conventional supermarkets.

1977: Albertson's and Skaggs dissolve their partnership, evenly splitting the assets.

1979: First warehouse stores are opened.

1988: Company completes its first fully mechanized distribution center, in Portland, Oregon.

1992: Albertson's acquires 74 Jewel Osco food-and-drug stores in Texas, Oklahoma, Arkansas, and Florida from American Stores Company.

1999: In an $11.7 billion deal, Albertson's acquires Salt Lake City-based American Stores Company, operator of 288 combination stores, 514 supermarkets, and 783 stand-alone drugstores.

2004: Albertson's acquires the Shaw's and Star Markets chains in New England for about $2.5 billion.

began to phase out its conventional markets. Although a few profitable ones remained open, most were closed or converted into larger stores during the late 1970s and early 1980s. Albertson's also installed its first electric price scanner in 1976. By the late 1980s, 85 percent of Albertson's stores used scanners.

Relying principally on outside distributors, Albertson's successfully penetrated markets located throughout a broad geographic area, but the rapid expansion of its markets during the 1970s called for expansion of company-owned distribution facilities. Two of the company's four full-line distribution facilities were built during this period. The first of these went up in 1973 in Brea, California, and the other was completed in 1976 in Salt Lake City. All Albertson's distribution facilities were built, and operated, as profit centers, contributing a return on investment that equaled or exceeded that of the company's retail stores.

Continued Expansion in the Late 1970s and 1980s

In 1977 Albertson's and Skaggs dissolved their partnership amicably, splitting their assets equally. For Albertson's, the breakup resulted in the formation of Southco, the company's Southern division. Southco assumed operation of 30 of the 58 combination stores formerly run by the partnership. Albertson's continued opening combination stores, concentrating them principally in Southern states, but also opening a few in South Dakota and Nebraska. In 1978 Albertson's strengthened its

stronghold in southern California by acquiring 46 supermarkets located in the Los Angeles area from Fisher Foods, Inc.

In 1979 Albertson's took the "bigger is better" concept to the drawing boards again and introduced its first warehouse stores. As inflation drove prices up, Albertson's needed to cut overhead to preserve its profit margin. To this end, it converted, between 1979 and 1981, seven stores into full-line, mass merchandise warehouse stores run under the name Grocery Warehouse. These no-frills stores carried nonfood items but emphasized groceries, with substantial savings on meat and liquor. Although these stores continued to be successful, they did not eclipse the profitability of the more broadly appealing superstores.

The introduction of the combination store and the continuing readaptation of older stores (87 percent of the company's stores were newly built or completely remodeled during the 1970s) allowed Albertson's to prosper despite the economically hostile environment of the late 1970s and early 1980s. In 1983, just after the country's most severe recession since the Great Depression, Albertson's boasted 13 years of record sales. The combination stores, both jumbo and smaller, were in large part responsible for this success. In 1983 these units accounted for only one-third of the chain's 423 stores but were the source of 65 percent of its profits.

Because Albertson's had grown by expanding over a wide geographic region rather than increasing its dominance in a smaller area, it did not hold superior market share in many of the areas where it operated. But it was this diversification, in part, that had allowed Albertson's to weather the economic storms of the 1970s and 1980s so successfully. As it happened, the areas of Albertson's concentration were the areas of relative economic prosperity. In 1981 Albertson's was operating in 17 of the fastest-growing standard metropolitan areas, as identified by the U.S. Department of Commerce. Stores in comparatively stable areas helped balance losses in more depressed markets.

Although Albertson's did break into the Nebraska and North and South Dakota markets in 1981, during the 1980s it concentrated principally on increasing its presence in established markets. For example, in an effort to expand its market in Texas, Albertson's modified its advertising strategy. In 1984 Albertson's reentered the Dallas-Fort Worth area, a competitive market that no new firm had entered since Skaggs opened its first store there in 1972. The standard advertising strategy was to offer gimmicks such as double-value coupons and promotional games to attract customers. Albertson's had used such techniques, but chose to approach the Dallas-Fort Worth market with an "everyday low-cost" image instead. Store circulars explained, "We won't be advertising weekly specials . . . we'll pass the savings on advertising costs on to you. Tell your friends and neighbors to help us keep prices down." The campaign sparked fierce competition, but the Albertson's units continued to prosper. Although the company traditionally held an upscale profile, it began to extend the new image to other suitable markets.

As Albertson's continued to build larger concentrations of stores, its behind-the-scenes operations continued to grow. In 1982 retail management was reorganized into four operating units/regions: California, Northwest, Intermountain, and South. This subdivision allowed each regional director and management team to more effectively focus marketing and retail sales strategies as well as to more closely guide employee and real estate development. Albertson's built another distribution center in the Denver area in 1984 and completed its first fully mechanized distribution center in Portland, Oregon, in 1988. In addition, the Salt Lake City facility was expanded substantially in late 1988 and the Brea, California, center was expanded and mechanized in 1989.

Innovation and Improvements in the Early 1990s

The expansion of Albertson's distribution network, combined with new computerized inventory and checkout scanners, enabled the chain to begin to handle its own distribution in 1990. By 1993, almost two-thirds of the items purchased by Albertson's stores were distributed by its own system.

In December 1991 Albertson's announced a five-year expansion plan that called for a $2.4 billion investment in the construction of 250 new stores, the renovation of 175 older stores, and the acceleration of computerization chainwide. By the end of fiscal 1991 (January 1992), more than half of Albertson's stores had computerized time and attendance systems, all of the pharmacies had automated prescription systems, and 96 percent of the stores were equipped with checkout scanners. In 1992 the company acquired 74 Jewel Osco food-and-drug stores in Texas, Oklahoma, Arkansas, and Florida from American Stores Company, along with a nonfood distribution center in Ponca City, Oklahoma—all for a total of $442 million. Albertson's had ambitious plans at this time, especially considering that it took the company all of the 1980s to build or acquire 283 stores. Albertson's was targeting its growth for California, Texas, Florida, and Arizona, some of the United States' fastest-growing markets. CEO Warren McCain targeted growth for smaller cities and suburbs where plentiful, inexpensive land allowed Albertson's to maximize profits.

Gary Michael became chairman of the board and CEO of Albertson's on February 1, 1991, and initiated the "Service First" employee award program. The plan recognized and rewarded excellence in customer service. Michael also implemented a quarterly video news program that promoted employee understanding of Albertson's goals and objectives. The employee relations efforts resulted in a 16 percent decrease in the worker turnover rate.

Public relations in the 1990s focused on "Service First" and a new advertising theme, "It's Your Store." It was hoped that the slogan would instill in customers a sense of partnership through convenience, quality, competitive pricing, and service. The HOPE (Helping Our Planet's Ecology) line of environmentally safer paper products reinforced Albertson's commitment to the ecosystem.

By January 1992, Albertson's ran 562 grocery stores in 17 western and southern states, employing 60,000 workers. The company's 1991 sales and earnings hit record highs for the 22nd year: net income rose 10.3 percent to $258 million and sales grew 5.6 percent to $8.68 billion. Sales surpassed the $10 billion mark in 1993, the year that Joe Albertson died at age 86. Although modern business sensibility had cultivated Albertson's multibillion-dollar success, the solid, small-town philosophy of founder Albertson—giving customers quality merchandise at a reasonable price—was at its root.

Achieving Number Two Position by Decade's End

By the mid-1990s, Albertson's was the number four grocery chain in the United States, with about 800 stores in 19 states and revenues approaching $12 billion. The company continued building its distribution system, with a new, one-million-square-foot center in Plant City, Florida—a facility dedicated to reviving its struggling 74-unit Florida operation—opening in early 1994. By mid-1996, with the opening of a center in Houston, Albertson's had a total of 12 distribution centers. Meantime, in early 1996, Richard L. King, a 28-year company veteran, was named president and COO, with Michael remaining chairman and CEO. Also in 1996, Albertson's introduced Quick Fixin' Ideas. This concept included offering time-starved customers recipes and all the ingredients to make them in one convenient location, as well as offering several prepackaged entrees for heat-and-serve meals (the latter an example of the trend toward home meal replacement). Having been hurt by chains such as Safeway Inc. taking business away through their aggressive promotional programs, Albertson's began to put a greater emphasis on advertising and promotion to bolster its longstanding everyday-low-price approach, an approach that some analysts said bored customers. At the same time, Albertson's took steps to improve its customer service and speed up the checkout process.

Albertson's was the object of several class-action lawsuits filed in 1996 and 1997. The suits charged that the company systematically permitted its workers to work "off-the-clock," without paying them. Albertson's was potentially liable for about $200 million in back pay and damage awards. The management contended that the suits, sponsored by the United Food and Commercial Workers, were part of an effort by the union and its allies to unionize the company's stores, only a third of which were unionized. Eight suits were eventually merged into one consolidated suit. Late in 1999 Albertson's elected to settle the lawsuit by setting aside $22 million for potential payments to claimants meeting certain eligibility requirements.

During the late 1990s, Albertson's continued its ongoing program of store remodeling and achieved some growth through organic expansion. It was through acquisitions, however, that Albertson's vaulted to the number two position in grocery retailing by the end of the decade. At the end of the fiscal year ending in January 1998, Albertson's operated 878 stores in 20 states and had revenues of $14.69 billion. Less than two years later, the company had grown to a nearly nationwide chain of more than 2,400 units in 39 states, with revenues of approximately $33.4 billion, which trailed only Kroger's $43 billion (the latter the product of a May 1999 merger of Kroger and Fred Meyer, Inc.).

During the year ending in January 1999, Albertson's made several acquisitions that added some 80 stores to its system and brought the company into five new states: Georgia, Iowa, Missouri, North Dakota, and Tennessee. These included the purchase of Seessel Holdings, Inc., which included ten Seessel's stores in Memphis, Tennessee; Smitty's Super Markets, Inc., which included ten Smitty's stores in southwest Missouri; three Super One stores in Des Moines, Iowa; 14 Bruno's stores in the Nashville and Chattanooga, Tennessee, metro areas; and Buttrey Food and Drug Stores Company, which included 44 stores in Montana, North Dakota, and Wyoming. To gain approval from the FTC for the last of these acquisitions, Albertson's had to divest itself of nine Buttrey stores and six Albertson's units.

In June 1999 Albertson's made its biggest deal ever—valued at $11.7 billion, including $3.4 billion in debt—to acquire American Stores Company, the successor company to Skaggs Drug Centers, Albertson's former combination stores partner. At the time of the merger, Salt Lake City-based American Stores had 288 combination stores, 514 supermarkets, and 783 stand-alone drugstores. To gain FTC approval, Albertson's agreed to divest 145 stores plus four store sites (in overlapping markets in California, Nevada, and New Mexico), in what was believed to be the largest divestiture ever ordered in relation to a retail merger. As with other consolidation moves of the late 1990s, the acquisition was driven by projected cost savings from synergies created by the merged operations. Company officials estimated that $100 million would be saved in the first year, $200 million in the second, and $300 million per year thereafter. Albertson's also announced that it would take $700 million in after-tax charges over a two-year period to cover merger-related costs. Around the time of the completion of the merger, King resigned his executive positions to "pursue other opportunities," with Michael initially assuming his responsibilities; in March 2000 Peter L. Lynch, who had been a senior executive at American Stores, was named the new president and COO.

The American Stores deal provided Albertson's with four more grocery store brands—Acme (in the Mid-Atlantic region), Jewel and Jewel-Osco (Midwest), and Lucky (West Coast)—but the Lucky outlets were converted to the Albertsons banner shortly after the merger. In addition to increasing the number of units it operated to more than 2,400, the acquisition also provided Albertson's with its first freestanding drugstores (under the Osco and Sav-on names) and placed the suburban-oriented company into its first two urban markets, Chicago and Philadelphia. During the five years following the merger, Albertson's planned to spend about $11 billion on capital projects, including building 750 combination stores, 500 drugstores, and 600 fuel centers. The company had been experimenting with some success with fuel centers that had been added to its combination stores, featuring three to six gas pumps and either pay-only kiosks or small convenience stores. Albertson's also planned to remodel about 730 units. An area of possible concern was the meshing of Albertson's mostly nonunion workforce with the three-quarters unionized American Stores staff. But overall, the deal dovetailed with the company's goal of becoming a truly nationwide chain in order to better compete with the likes of behemoth Wal-Mart Stores, Inc., which was rapidly and aggressively delving into the food retailing sector.

Restructuring in the Early 2000s

In the fiscal year ending in January 2001, the first full year following the American Stores merger, Albertson's reported profits of $765 million on revenues of $36.76 billion. The resulting profit margin of 2.1 percent was well below the 3.5 percent average for Albertson's in the late 1990s. The company's travails were traced to difficulties integrating the American Stores acquisition, which had brought together two very different companies. For example, Albertson's had adopted a no-frills approach to marketing and its stores were of the cookie-cutter variety,

whereas American took a much more aggressive marketing stance and designed its stores more for the local market.

When Michael announced that he intended to retire in 2001, the Albertson's board concluded that it needed to go outside the company for a new leader to implement a much needed restructuring. In April 2001 Lawrence R. Johnston was named chairman and CEO, becoming the first outsider to lead the company. A veteran of General Electric Company (GE), Johnston most recently headed up GE's appliance manufacturing business. Possessing neither a grocery nor drugstore background, he was nonetheless a well-respected manager with much experience in integrating acquisitions. Though passed up for the top spot, Lynch stayed on as president and COO until July 2003, when he resigned as part of a flattening of management. Johnston added the title of president at that point.

Johnston wasted no time making changes at Albertson's. In July 2001 he announced that more than 1,300 corporate and administrative jobs were to be cut, four of the 19 divisional offices would be closed, and 165 underperforming stores spread across 25 states would be closed or sold. In early 2002 the company exited from the New England drugstore market by selling its 80 Osco outlets in that region to Maxi Drug Inc., operator of the Brooks Pharmacy chain, for about $240 million. Then in March 2002 Albertson's launched the second phase of its restructuring, which involved the complete exit from four underperforming markets: Memphis and Nashville, Tennessee; and Houston and San Antonio, Texas—including the closure or sale of 95 stores and two distribution centers in Houston and Tulsa, Oklahoma. The number of divisional offices was reduced further, to 11. All told, these moves were aimed at paring annual operating costs by $750 million by the end of 2004. The freed-up capital was earmarked for remodeling existing stores, opening new stores in key markets such as California and Florida, and bolstering technology in such areas as ordering, distribution, and online shopping (the existing albertsons.com online business in Seattle, San Diego, and Vancouver was expanded to include Los Angeles, San Francisco, and Portland).

Albertson's also took two pages out of the American Stores playbook. The latter company's chains had joined in the trend toward frequent-shopper programs, but Albertson's had been a holdout. Under Johnston, Albertson's reversed this policy, and the Albertsons chain began rolling out its Preferred Customer membership program in the summer of 2002. American Stores had also brought to Albertson's its dual-branded Jewel-Osco combination food-and-drug stores. Albertson's transferred this strategy to the Albertsons chain. Stores in Tucson and Phoenix, Arizona; Omaha, Nebraska; and El Paso, Texas, were converted to Albertsons Osco combo stores. At the same time, Albertsons Sav-on combo units were launched in Reno, Nevada; and later in Las Vegas, Nevada, and southern California. Another new development, launched in the fall of 2003, was a store-within-a-store initiative designed to make the company's stores more of a one-stop shopping destination. Through a partnership with toy retailer Toys "R" Us, Inc., more than 1,100 Albertsons stores began opening small Toys "R" Us "Toy Box" sections carrying about 500 products priced under $25. Similarly, in an alliance with retailer Office Depot, Inc., 18 of the company's supermarkets in Chicago, Los Angeles, and Phoenix began sporting small Office Depot departments that featured more than 700 products, principally school and office supplies. Johnston hoped to complete similar deals with other retailers.

Not all the news at Albertson's was positive. The company, along with Kroger and Safeway, endured a four-and-a-half-month strike in southern California—the longest grocery strike in U.S. history. By the time the strike ended in late February 2004, it had cost Albertson's $90 million in profits and $700 million in revenues in the fourth quarter of fiscal 2003. Overall at Albertson's, sales for 2003 remained flat, at $35.44 billion, while the profits of $556 million translated into a profit margin of just 1.6 percent. In 2004 the company launched a new divisional consolidation that would further reduce the number of divisions to seven.

As its three-year-long restructuring neared completion, Albertson's stepped back into the acquisition arena in April 2004, snapping up the Shaw's and Star Markets chains—202 stores in all—from their British parent J Sainsbury plc for $2.1 billion in cash and the assumption of about $368 million in capital leases. Albertson's thereby gained its first presence in the supermarket sector in New England with slightly higher-end stores that would be easier to differentiate from low-priced Wal-Mart outlets. Annual revenues at Albertson's were now expected to surpass $42 billion as the company neared its goal of becoming the number one operator of supermarkets in the country. Toward that end, the company was likely to pursue additional acquisitions, particularly smaller deals involving individual stores or groups of stores rather than whole chains as there were few attractive opportunities for the latter.

Principal Subsidiaries

Acme Markets, Inc.; American Drug Stores, Inc.; American Food and Drug, Inc.; American Stores Company; Jewel Companies, Inc.; Jewel Food Stores, Inc.; Jewel Osco Southwest, Inc.; Osco Drug of Massachusetts, Inc.; Osco Drug of Texas, Inc.

Principal Competitors

Wal-Mart Stores, Inc.; The Kroger Co.; Safeway Inc.; Royal Ahold N.V.

Further Reading

"Albertson's Massive Deployment," *Discount Merchandiser,* March 1991, pp. 26–27.

Alster, Norm, "One Man's Poison . . . ," *Forbes,* October 16, 1989, pp. 38–39.

Baldo, Anthony, "Fleming: Food Fight," *Financial World,* January 8, 1991, pp. 40–41.

Barrett, Amy, "Albertson's: A Shopper's Delight," *Financial World,* May 12, 1992, pp. 13+.

Barron, Kelly, "Albertson's Gets a Makeover," *Forbes,* September 6, 1999, pp. 107–08.

Beauchamp, Marc, "Food for Thought," *Forbes,* April 17, 1989, p. 73.

Berner, Robert, "Albertson's Says King Has Resigned His Executive Posts," *Wall Street Journal,* June 23, 1999, p. A11.

Bernstein, Aaron, "This Union Suit Could Really Scratch," *Business Week,* March 10, 1997, p. 37.

Blumenthal, Robin, "Grocer on a Diet: Albertson's Sheds Stores and Plumps Up Its Prospects," *Barron's,* May 6, 2002, p. 17.

Burton, Jonathan, "Bagging Profits," *Chief Executive* (U.S.), April 2002, pp. 46–51.

Byrne, Harlan S., "Albertson's: Food and Drug Retailer Boasts Top Earnings Growth, High Rate of Return," *Barron's,* April 13, 1992, pp. 55–56.

Campanella, Frank W., "The Right Combination: Albertson's Huge New Outlets Are Paying Off Handsomely," *Barron's,* June 29, 1981, pp. 39+.

Coleman, Calmetta Y., "Albertson's Leaves Industry Trends in the Checkout Line," *Wall Street Journal,* August 6, 1997, p. B4.

——, "Albertson's Plans to Buy American Stores: Largest Supermarket Firm to Be Created in Deal for $8.4 Billion of Stock," *Wall Street Journal,* August 4, 1998, p. A3.

Desjardins, Doug, "Albertsons Sees Dual-Brand Store As Key to Staying Competitive," *Drug Store News,* December 15, 2003, pp. 19–20.

Feldheim, David, "Outlook at Albertson's Brightened by Streamlining," *Barron's,* December 28, 1970, pp. 17+.

Gordon, Mitchell, "Albertson's to Ring Up Fresh Advance in Profits," *Barron's,* April 8, 1974, pp. 30+.

——, "Express Lane: Albertson's Keeps Earnings on the Rise with New Stores, Widening Margins," *Barron's,* February 18, 1985, pp. 71+.

Guidera, Jerry, and Robert Berner, "Albertson's Agrees with FTC Demand to Divest More Stores Than Expected," *Wall Street Journal,* June 22, 1999, p. A4.

Hays, Constance L., "Albertsons Buying Shaw's, New England Grocery Chain," *New York Times,* March 27, 2004, p. C1.

Hughes, Teni, editor, "Yesterday and Tomorrow, 1939–1989," *Albertson's Today,* July 1989.

Johnston, Melanie, "Supermarkets Feed Phoenix Glut," *Advertising Age,* November 13, 1989, p. 66.

Lublin, Joann S., "Albertson's Picks an Outsider—GE Veteran Johnston—for Top Posts," *Wall Street Journal,* April 24, 2001, p. B1.

Orgel, David, "Albertson's in Action: A Multidimensional Approach Is Working for the Country's Fourth-Biggest Chain," *Supermarket News,* June 24, 1996, pp. 1+.

Stavro, Barry, "In the Bag," *Forbes,* December 5, 1983, p. 118.

Tosh, Mark, "Reorganization Effort Puts Chain on the Right Track," *Drug Store News,* March 26, 2001, pp. 15–16, 122.

Urbanski, Al, "The New Albertsons," *Progressive Grocer,* October 15, 2002, pp. 18–22.

Zwiebach, Elliot, "Albertson's Advancing on Many Fronts," *Supermarket News,* August 31, 1998.

——, "Albertson's American Plan," *Supermarket News,* August 10, 1998, p. 1.

——, "Albertsons Purchasing New England Presence," *Supermarket News,* April 5, 2004, p. 1.

——, "Albertson's Stealthy Growth: Analysts Say This Quiet Chain Has a Sound Future," *Supermarket News,* July 12, 1993, pp. 1+.

——, "Albertson's Still Has Eye Out for Buys," *Supermarket News,* May 3, 1999, p. 10.

——, "Albertson's to Acquire Buttrey for $134 Million," *Supermarket News,* January 26, 1998, pp. 1+.

——, "Albertson's to Open 1,250 New Stores After Merger," *Supermarket News,* December 21, 1998, p. 1.

——, "The $33 Billion Chain: Albertson's Is Going All-American, Expanding into 14 New States and Entering Two Urban Areas As Well As the Drug-Store Business with Its Acquisition of American Stores Co.," *Supermarket News,* June 28, 1999, p. 1.

—Elaine Belsito
—updates: April Dougal, David E. Salamie

Alleanza Assicurazioni S.p.A.

Viale Luigi Sturzo, 35
20154 Milan
Italy
Telephone: +39 02 62961
Fax: +39 02 6552356
Web site: http://www.alleanzaassicurazioni.it

Public Subsidiary of Assicurazioni Generali Spa
Incorporated: 1898
Employees: 3,239
Sales: $58.64 billion (2003)
Stock Exchanges: Borsa Italiana
Ticker Symbol: AL
NAIC: 524113 Direct Life Insurance Carriers; 524114
    Direct Health and Medical Insurance Carriers; 524126
    Direct Property and Casualty Insurance Carriers

Alleanza Assicurazioni S.p.A. is Italy's leading life insurance company and the largest publicly listed company focusing almost exclusively on the domestic life insurance market. The company boasts more than two million customers, generating some EUR 4.2 billion ($5 billion) in premiums. The company is present throughout Italy with a network of more than 320 sales offices, backed by over 3,200 employees and 20,000 commission-based sales agents, as well as 1,000 specially trained and certified financial advisors. Agency sales, together with sales made through financial advisors, account for nearly half of the group's total premiums. The single-largest outlet for the group's insurance, assets management, pension, and related products comes through the bancassurance channel, and particularly through the company's 45 percent holding in the Intesa Vita joint venture set up with Intesa in 2003. Alleanza Assicurazioni typically targets the lower to middle-class consumer segment, providing door-to-door service, and boasts an especially strong penetration of Italy's rural provinces. Founded in 1898, Alleanza has long been majority-owned by Assicurazioni Generali, Italy's largest insurance company. The company is headed by Chairman Sandro Salvati and CEO Franco Viezzoli and is listed on the Borsa Italiana.

Pioneering the Italian Life Insurance Industry in the 1890s

Alleanza Assicurazioni was founded in 1898 by a group of investors led by Evan Mackenzie. Mackenzie, who was born in Florence at the middle of the century to Scottish parents, had already built a distinguished career in the insurance industry, acting as the Italian representative for a number of foreign insurance companies. Based in Genoa, Mackenzie worked for such European insurance institutions as France's Union, England's Merck Fink & Co., and the German-Austrian company Munchener Ruckversicherungs Gesellschaft, the latter giving Mackenzie experience in the reinsurance market as well.

Mackenzie set up a number of companies on his own as well, such as Iniziativa Insurance Company, which issued policies for workers' insurance, in 1891. Into the next century, Mackenzie's companies included Ausonia, a reinsurance specialist, founded in 1903, and La Consorziale, providing reinsurance and retrocession services, in 1918.

Yet Alleanza Assicurazioni became Mackenzie's most lasting success. The "insurance alliance" united backers such as the Italian Credit Bank, Berlin-based Nationalbank fur Deutschland, and Rome's Manzi & Co., with Mackenzie as the company's first director. Alleanza initially operated in the broader insurance market, issuing policies in a range of fields, such as transport, health, and accident insurance. Yet the company was also one of the first Italian insurance companies to begin issuing life insurance policies.

Until the end of the 19th century, the Italian economy remained dominated by agriculture. The move toward industrialization at the beginning of the 20th century, and the creation of a rising working class, led to a new level of demand for insurance products, and particularly life insurance policies.

Life insurance quickly became a primary focus, as the company attracted a growing number of customers. As it entered its second decade in business, Alleanza already had sold some 13,000 policies. Alleanza also distinguished itself through its progressive social policies. The company became one of the first to employ women in its administration, and also provided healthcare, medical assistance, and free medicine to its staff.

Company Perspectives:

To operate in today's market requires not just suitable products able to satisfy the diversified needs of customers, but also highly qualified human resources and state-of-the-art technologies.

With this in mind, aware of the innovations that serve to constantly enhance customer service, Alleanza devotes an ongoing commitment—together with the professional training of its Consultants—to the development of Information Technology, in keeping with the High tech-High touch business model on which the Company has based its role in the market.

Yet Alleanza faced near disaster in 1912 when the Italian government, under Giolotti, nationalized the life insurance sector, setting up the Istituto Nazionale Assicurazioni (INA) to take over all existing life insurance policies in the country. The purpose of the monopoly was to prevent foreign insurance companies from gaining undue influence in Italy's financial markets. The move spelled the end of a number of insurance companies, which withdrew from the Italian market. Alleanza, in the meantime, was forced to fall back on its non-life insurance operations.

These were not enough to shield the company from difficulties during and especially immediately after World War I. Indeed, for a time, Mackenzie, who remained at the head of the company, had even begun to consider shutting the company down as it struggled in the postwar period.

Nonetheless, Mackenzie held on, and in 1923, the INA, itself hit hard by reconstruction payments and by the growing political unrest, abandoned its life insurance monopoly. With the market once again opened to competition, Alleanza was reorganized. Now, the company exited its other insurance markets and instead focused exclusively on its life insurance products.

Life Insurance Specialist in the Mid-20th Century

Alleanza continued to grow slowly through the rest of the 1920s. At the beginning of the 1930s, as it struggled through the Great Depression, Alleanza found new financial backing with Assicurazioni Generali, which bought majority control of the life insurance specialist. Generali, founded a century earlier, had long held a position as a major European insurance group. After becoming a full-fledged Italian company in 1913, Generali built itself into Italy's predominant insurance group. The change in ownership led to Alleanza's emergence as the country's preeminent life insurance provider.

Following the sale to Generali, Alleanza appointed a new general manager, Mario Gasbarri, who was to remain at the head of the company into the late 1970s. Gasbarri restructured Alleanza, creating a decentralized organization that received much of the credit for the company's success. The company began establishing a network of sales agencies, which, while remaining under corporate control, were operated more or less autonomously. Agency heads received a basic salary, yet had the potential to double their pay upon meeting corporate sales targets.

The company also introduced a pyramid-like sales structure. Placed under the head of the agency were several salespeople, who also received a large percentage of their income based on their performance and on the performance of the sales agents in their charge. Sales agents in turn were paid entirely on commission, and often worked only part-time. In this way, Alleanza was able to maintain a lean corporate structure, and yet deploy a large, motivated, and mobile sales force. The company soon achieved a high degree of penetration, with a strong geographic balance and a particularly strong presence in the country's rural provinces.

Under Gasbarri, Alleanza also oriented itself firmly as a provider of popular life insurance policies for the country's lower to middle income classes. Gasbarri, and Alleanza as a whole, became an important proponent of the need for developing savings among the lower and working classes, and especially the need for creating retirement pension plans. The company launched a new series of policies based on fixed monthly payments that the company collected by sending its agents door to door.

Forced to shut down during World War II, Alleanza returned to business in the second half of the war. The economic boom years of the 1950s and 1960s led to a boom in the life insurance market, and Alleanza grew strongly into the 1970s. In 1971, Alleanza listed on the Borsa Italiana, although Generali remained the group's major shareholder and maintained its majority control of the company into the late 1990s.

Developing New Sales Channels: 1990s–2000s

Changes in the economic situation, brought about in part by the oil crisis in the 1970s, and the high inflation rates of the period, led Alleanza to drop its fixed-rate popular policies and instead launch a new set of index-linked policies. The company continued to roll out new products through the 1980s, such as its DR revaluable policy.

The arrival of Alfonso Desiata as the company's chairman in 1990 heralded the beginning of a new growth period for the company. Under Desiata, Alleanza saw exponential growth in its premium collections—from the equivalent of EUR 300 million in the mid-1990s, the company's premium totals topped EUR 2 billion by the end of the 1990s and passed EUR 4 billion by the beginning of 2004.

Part of the motivation behind Alleanza's growth spurt was new legislation authorizing Italy's banks to begin selling life insurance products at the beginning of the 1990s. Faced with this new competition, Alleanza responded by acquiring a 16 percent stake in Banco Ambroveneto and striking a deal with the bank that established Alleanza as its exclusive provider of life insurance products. The deal gave Alleanza access to Ambroveneto's 500-strong branch banking network (later expanded to 650 branches) and also introduced it to an important new sales channel. Indeed, while its agency sales remained an important contributor to its revenues, bancassurance sales quickly became a major outlet as well, reaching nearly half of the group's sales by the beginning of the next decade.

At the same time, Alleanza began expanding its range of products and services. The company added an assets management operation, acquiring La Venezia in 1993 from parent

Key Dates:

1898: Evan Mackenzie founds Alleanza Assicurazioni in Genoa, which begins offering insurance products, including life insurance policies.

1912: The Italian government forms the INA life insurance monopoly, which takes over Alleanza's life insurance business.

1923: INA loses its monopoly on the life insurance sector and Alleanza reincorporates, now focusing wholly on the life insurance market.

1933: Assicurazioni Generali acquires majority control of Alleanza; new head Mario Gasbarri introduces a new streamlined corporate structure and popular fixed-rate life insurance policies.

1971: Alleanza Assicurazioni goes public on the Borsa Italiana.

1980s: In response to high inflation rates, Alleanza launches index-linked policies and revaluable policies.

1993: After banks are allowed to sell life insurance, the company acquires a stake in Banco Ambroveneto and enters an agreement to provide life insurance products to the bank's customers; Alleanza acquires La Venetia from Generali and begins offering asset management services.

1995: Fondi Alleanza is created, as the company enters the mutual fund market.

1997: Banco Ambroveneto merges with Cariplo, creating Banca Intesa, and Alleanza gains control of Cariplo's Carivita life insurance subsidiary.

1998: The company establishes new sales network of Financial Advisors.

2003: Alleanza and Intesa agree to merge their bancassurance operations, creating Intesa Vita, held at 45 percent by Alleanza.

2004: Alleanza becomes the top life insurance company in Italy.

merger gave Alleanza access to Cariplo's life insurance operation, carried out as Carivita, and its network of 1,600 sales branches. As part of the merger agreement, Alleanza acquired a 50 percent direct stake in Carivita, in addition to an 8 percent stake held through its interest in Ambroveneto. For the time being, however, the company's bancassurance operations remained separate from those of Intesa.

The diversification of Alleanza's operations and product portfolio led the company to create a new class of sales agents called Financial Advisors in 1998. Recruited in large part from the company's own staff, the financial advisors were given special training and certification; the new program quickly became an important revenue stream for the company, nearly matching that of its sales agent network. Meanwhile, after Salvati left the group to become head of the Italian insurance association ANIA, the company appointed Sandro Salvati as its new CEO.

Into the new century, Alleanza's growth remained strong. Sales leapt from EUR 2.5 billion in 2000 to more than EUR 4 billion in 2004, despite the difficult economic climate. In 2003, the company at last moved to merge its bancassurance business with that of Intesa, creating a three-way venture, together with France's Crédit Agricole, called Intesa Vita. Alleanza's share in the new company stood at 45 percent. The new outlet, which boasted a branch network of 3,000 and more than 1,700 financial advisors, was expected to help Alleanza maintain its strong growth as it moved into its second century as Italy's leading life insurance group.

Principal Subsidiaries

Agricola San Giorgio; Alleanza Investments PLC (Ireland); Finagen; Fondi Alleanza; La Venezia Assicurazioni; Timavo Vita; Torcello.

Principal Competitors

Allianz Subalpina SpA; Fondiaria-SAI, S.p.A.; Riunione Adriatica di Sicurtà S.p.A.

Further Reading

"Alleanza Assicurazioni: Moving Places," *Financial Times,* June 16, 1998, p. 11.

Dickson, Bill, "Alleanza Move Stuns Investors," *Financial Times,* May 4, 2001, p. 44.

Fanfani, Tommaso, *Alleanza Assicurazioni: cento anni di storia,* Milan: Alleanza Assicurazioni S.p.A., 1998.

—M.L. Cohen

Generali. That acquisition enabled the company to begin marketing investment products through its new subsidiary's 300-strong network of financial promoters. In 1995, Alleanza launched a new product group, that of mutual funds, establishing Fondi Alleanza. That operation later built up a portfolio of nine different funds. On the life insurance side, Alleanza began developing a new range of life insurance policies targeting specific market segments—such as families with small children, or middle-aged men seeking fixed-duration policies.

New expansion for the company came in 1997 when Banco Ambroveneto merged with Cariplo, forming Banca Intesa. The

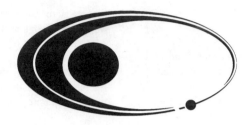

The Allied Defense Group, Inc.

8000 Towers Crescent Drive, Suite 260
Vienna, Virginia 22182
U.S.A.
Telephone: (703) 847-5268
Toll Free: (800) 847-5322
Fax: (703) 847-5334
Web site: http://www.allieddefensegroup.com

Public Company
Incorporated: 1961 as Allied Research Associates, Inc.
Employees: 577
Sales: $171.41 million (2003)
Stock Exchanges: American
Ticker Symbol: ADG
NAIC: 332992 Small Arms Ammunition Manufacturing;
    332993 Ammunition (Except Small Arms)
    Manufacturing; 332995 Other Ordnance and
    Accessories Manufacturing; 334290 Other
    Communications Equipment Manufacturing

The Allied Defense Group, Inc. (ADG) owns several defense- and security-related businesses. ADG's largest unit, MECAR S.A. of Belgium, is a leading supplier of medium- to heavy-caliber ammunition and grenades, specializing in quick turnarounds on small orders. In 2004 MECAR was setting up a U.S. subsidiary at the site of Titan Dynamics, ADG's Texas-based pyrotechnics business. ADG also owns security equipment companies in the United States and Belgium.

Origins

The Allied Defense Group, Inc.'s history can be traced to Allied Research Associates, Inc., a Delaware corporation organized on July 20, 1961. It was originally headquartered in Boston and had connections to MIT. According to the *Washington Post,* the company's first line of business was studying the effects of nuclear tests on aircraft.

Martin B. Ruffin acquired Allied Research in 1967 and eventually became chairman. A native of Tarboro, North Carolina, Ruffin had studied at the University of North Carolina and earned an engineering degree from the Naval Academy in 1941. During his career, he worked at Lear Industries and at MECAR S.A., Allied's Belgian munitions subsidiary, where he oversaw development of the first bullet-trap grenades (BTUs), which could be mounted on assault rifles. According to his obituary in the *Washington Times,* Ruffin's design team also pioneered tungsten dart ammunition, which was used in MECAR's star product, the Kinetic Energy Weapons System (KEWS), a high-velocity 90mm gun.

Allied sold most of its subsidiaries in the late 1970s after running into hard times. It acquired complete control of MECAR in 1983, reported the *Baltimore Business Journal.* The company immediately set out expanding its product line, from 15 items to more than 65. Revenues were $30.5 million in 1985, up from $25.8 million the year before. Net income slipped from $3 million to $2.5 million.

Allied itself had just two employees at the time, President and Chairman Martin Ruffin and Reinald W. Carter, then executive vice-president. MECAR was Allied's only holding at the time. Its history in Belgium dated back to 1938. Although MECAR had virtually no U.S. competitors, Allied management sought an American company to acquire to help increase Allied's marketability with the U.S. Department of Defense.

Allied acquired Barnes & Reinecke, Inc., based in Arlington Heights, Illinois, on May 26, 1987. Barnes & Reinecke was an engineering and manufacturing company specializing in technology and support related to military equipment such as the M109 self-propelled 155mm Howitzer and M55 Sheridan Light Tank. It had 300 employees and produced a $1 million profit on sales of $17 million in 1986.

Allied Research Associates became known as Allied Research Corporation effective June 1, 1988. In the same year, headquarters moved from Severna Park, Maryland, to Legg Mason Tower on Baltimore's Inner Harbor. The company moved again five years later to Vienna, Virginia, to be closer to the Pentagon. Allied ended the 1980s with about 500 employees.

A U.K. unit, Allied Research Corporation Limited, was established in 1989 to develop the business abroad. Its London office

Company Perspectives:

The Allied Defense Group (AMEX· ADG) is a diversified international defense and security firm, which provides an array of products and services as solutions to defense and security needs worldwide. The capabilities of Allied's five operating units include: development and production of conventional ammunition marketed to defense departments worldwide; the design, production and marketing of sophisticated electronic and microwave security systems principally for European and North American markets; manufacturing battlefield effects simulators and other training devices for the military; and designing and producing state-of-the-art weather and navigation software, data, and systems for commercial and military customers. Each unit has a dedication to agility, diligence, and precision, as well as a commitment to defending and securing the future for every American and our allies.

was closed five years later due to a lack of business, although the entity remained in existence, awaiting further contracts.

New Leadership in the 1990s

In early 1990, Reinald Carter, then chief financial officer, took over the positions of president and chief operating officer from Chairman Martin B. Ruffin, who passed away on November 16, 1990. Carter also was named chief executive officer in May 1990. He was tasked with restoring the company's profitability, and this was achieved quickly. Revenues reached $51.2 million in 1990. The company had managed to break even after posting a $7.4 million loss the year before and an $8.5 million loss in 1988. It had contracts with 35 free world nations. In December 1990, the company had been able to acquire the inventory of bankrupt Belgian munitions maker PRB S.A.

Engineering firm Barnes & Reinecke produced armored cars at its facility in Illinois. Founded in 1934, it was also known for developing the first pop-up toaster for Toastmaster in the late 1930s.

Grumman Corp. veteran and former Assistant Secretary of the Army Jay R. Sculley was named president and chief operating officer of Allied in April 1992. He became chief executive officer as well after Reinald Carter retired at the end of the year. Allied shares migrated from the NASDAQ (symbol: ARAI) to the American Stock Exchange (ticker: ALR) in October 1992.

Sales were up to $217.3 million in 1992, producing income of $18 million. Most of the company's revenues came from sales of Belgian-made ammunition to clients in the Middle East, an area that did not see the steep decline in defense spending that affected the United States after the Cold War. Asia was another key market.

Looking to hedge against U.S. military downsizing, Allied entered the weapons and chemical cleanup business in the early 1990s. It announced the creation of a dedicated new unit, ARC Services Inc., in January 1993. Allied also was negotiating with

Austrian arms and vehicle maker Steyr-Daimler-Puch Spezialfahrzeug AG (SSF) on possible joint ventures.

In 1991, Kusai H.M. al Azawi of Saudia Arabia, Allied's largest shareholder at the time with a 20 percent holding, had unsuccessfully attempted to take over the company. A 1993 attempt to acquire Allied by Florida investor Malcolm Glazer also collapsed after several months.

In 1993, MECAR entered the medium-caliber ammunition market, producing a 25mm round for use against light armor and support vehicles. MECAR, based in Petit-Roeulx-lez-Nivelles, Belgium, had developed a specialty in quick turn-arounds on small orders larger armament manufacturers would not touch.

Beyond Defense in the Mid-1990s

Allied took a major step toward diversifying into non-defense markets in the mid-1990s. Its MECAR subsidiary acquired companies making up Belgium's VSK Group in 1994 and 1995. These included VSK Electronics, S.A., Teletechnique Generale, S.A., and IDCS, S.A. VSK supplied security systems and components. Belgian video surveillance company Vigitec was acquired in December 1999.

In the mid-1990s MECAR accounted for more than three-quarters of Allied's total revenues. It posted a $9 million loss on annual sales of $54 million in 1994. In April 25, MECAR's plant in Belgium suffered an explosion that shut down operations for three months.

Allied entered the mid-1990s with more than 500 employees, but cut 200 jobs to recover profitability. Revenues slipped a bit to $65.8 million in 1995; the company narrowed its losses from $11 million to $2 million. By 1996, Allied was in recovery; revenues rose 30 percent to $134.5 million in 1997 as net income doubled to $8.6 million. By this time, the company had 442 employees, just five of them at its headquarters.

Allied's poor stock performance in the bull market of the late 1990s prompted a 1999 takeover battle led by New York-based Zilkha Capital Partners. Allied sold a lower-performing unit, Barnes & Reinecke, to United Defense Limited Partnership, Inc., a unit of The Carlyle Group, in March 2000. Rising gas prices in 2000 prompted Allied's Middle Eastern customers to stock up on ammo, noted the *Washington Post*.

Post-9/11 Acquisitions

The September 11, 2001 terrorist attacks on the United States brought homeland defense to the forefront. Allied soon bought a U.S. electronic security firm to complement its European business. News/Sports Microwave Rental, Inc. was acquired on the last day of 2001. NS Microwave, based in Spring Valley, California, supplied surveillance equipment for law enforcement and security applications. It also made mobile command centers. The company had been founded in 1986 by Everett Shilts and employed 53 people at the time of its acquisition by Allied.

In June 2002 Allied bought Titan Dynamics. Titan produced pyrotechnics used in combat simulation. SeaSpace Corporation

```
┌─────────────────────────────────────────┐
│              Key Dates:                  │
│                                          │
│  1961:  Allied Research Associates, Inc. │
│         (ARAI) is incorpo-               │
│         rated.                           │
│  1970:  Martin B. Ruffin acquires ARAI.  │
│  1987:  ARAI buys Illinois engineering   │
│         firm Barnes & Rei-               │
│         necke.                           │
│  1988:  ARAI is renamed Allied Research  │
│         Corporation;                     │
│         company moves to Baltimore.      │
│  1993:  Headquarters are relocated to    │
│         Vienna, Virginia.                │
│  1995:  MECAR subsidiary acquires        │
│         security system sup-             │
│         plier VSK Group.                 │
│  2000:  Barnes & Reinecke is sold to     │
│         United Defense.                  │
│  2002:  Acquisitions include NS Micro-   │
│         wave, Titan Dynam-               │
│         ics, and SeaSpace Corporation.   │
│  2003:  Allied Research is renamed The   │
│         Allied Defense                   │
│         Group, Inc.                      │
└─────────────────────────────────────────┘
```

was added at the end of July 2002. SeaSpace provided technology for satellite-based sensing equipment. It employed 40 people.

In late 2002, MECAR bought a critical supplier, Netherlands-based pyrotechnics firm Eugene Hendrickx N.V., from a division of Euro Metaal. MECAR added nine new nations to its list of clients in 2003, bringing the total to 20. In April 2003, in cooperation with L-3 Communications, MECAR won a contract to supply high-explosive 105mm rounds to the U.S. Army, and was opening a plant at the Titan Dynamics site in Marshall, Texas, in late 2004.

MECAR was looking to expand sales in South America. The company was left as the world's premier supplier of 90mm ammunition after France's GIAT Industries scaled back operations. MECAR also specialized in 105mm tank rounds.

VSK's four units (VSK Electronics N.V., Intelligent Data Capturing Systems N.V., Télé Technique Générale S.A., and VIGITEC S.A./N.V.) provided security alarm, access control, and video recognition systems. Based in Belgium, VSK made significant progress in penetrating markets in Germany, France, and the United Kingdom in 2003. It also made inroads in the Polish banking industry.

Allied Research was renamed The Allied Defense Group, Inc. (ADG) effective January 2, 2003. Its ticker symbol on the American Stock Exchange changed from ALR to ADG. Total ADG revenues rose from $130.9 million to $171.4 million in 2003. Net income slipped to $8.8 million from $10.7 million. Ordnance and Manufacturing was the largest segment, taking in $129.7 million. Electronic Security (VSK Group) accounted for $33.3 million while Environmental Safety and Security accounted for $7.1 million. A fourth segment, Software, Training and Simulation, had revenues of $1.3 million.

General (Ret.) J.H. Binford Peay, III, former head of the U.S. Central Command, became Allied's CEO in January 2001. He left in June 2003 to lead the Virginia Military Institute (VMI). He was succeeded at ADG by the company's chief operating officer, Major General (Ret.) Gil Meyer, who had formerly served as chief of army public affairs.

Principal Subsidiaries

ARC Europe, S.A. (Belgium); Allied Research Corporation Limited (U.K.); Energa Corporation; News/Sports Microwave Rental, Inc.; Titan Dynamics Systems Inc.; SeaSpace Corporation; MECAR USA, Inc.

Principal Operating Units

Ordnance & Manufacturing; Electronic Security; Software, Training & Simulation; Environmental Safety & Security.

Principal Competitors

Alliant Techsystems Inc.; Esterline Technologies Corporation; General Dynamics Corporation; General Electric Company; Honeywell Automation and Control Solutions.

Further Reading

"Allied Chairman to Retire," *Sun* (Baltimore), December 3, 1992, p. 13F.

"Allied Defense Group to Enter U.S. Ammo, Pyrotechnic Markets," *Defense Daily International*, December 5, 2003.

Baumgardner, Neil, "MECAR Looks to Build on Ammo Production Flexibility for Future Orders," *Defense Daily International*, July 11, 2003.

Biesecker, Calvin, "Allied Research to Bring in Key Supplier for Ammunition Business," *Defense Daily International*, November 8, 2002.

Chartrand, Sabra, "Allied Research Receives $76 Million Offer," *New York Times*, April 13, 1993, p. D4.

Clabaugh, Jeff, "Allied Research on Acquisition Mission," *Washington Business Journal*, November 6, 2002.

——, "Local Firm Plays Big Brother in Baltimore," *Washington Business Journal*, April 10, 2002.

——, "New Day Dawns for Allied Defense," *Washington Business Journal*, January 2, 2003.

Drickhamer, David, "Out of the Shadow; As the Complexity and Demand of Global Manufacturing Increase, So Do Demands on COOs," *Industry Week*, January 2003, p. 37.

Fisher, Eric, "Allied Reaps Benefits of Layoffs, Cost Cutting," *Washington Times*, April 1, 1997, p. B9.

——, "Allied Research Finds Life After the Cold War," *Washington Times*, November 25, 1996, p. D20.

Fromson, Brett Duval, "Companies to Watch: Allied Research Associates Inc. (Munitions Maker Aims at New Markets)," *Fortune*, July 6, 1987, p. 46.

"General (Ret.) J.H. Binford Peay, III: Allied Research Corp.," *Wall Street Transcript*, Company Interview, November 26, 2001.

"General (Ret.) J.H. Binford Peay, III: Allied Research Corporation," *Wall Street Transcript*, Company Interview, June 24, 2002.

"General (Ret.) J.H. Binford Peay, III: The Allied Defense Group, Inc.," *Wall Street Transcript*, Company Interview, May 5, 2003.

Graves, Brad, "Allied Research Buys Second Local Company," *San Diego Business Journal*, August 12, 2002, pp. 10+.

Grocer, Stephen, "Allied Defense Taps New M&A Pro," *Mergers & Acquisitions Report*, May 3, 2004.

Hamilton, Susan, "Annapolis Arms Maker Is Looking to Buy a Metal Fabricator for Up to $35 Million," *Baltimore Business Journal*, December 15, 1986, p. 1.

Hetrick, Ross, "Ex-Grumman Official Named Allied Research President," *Sun* (Baltimore), April 7, 1992, p. 3E.

Hinden, Stan, "How Much Is Allied Research Really Worth?," *Washington Post*, August 16, 1993, p. F27.

——, "The Unraveling of the Allied Research Buyout," *Washington Post,* November 1, 1993, p. F33.

Kleiner, Kurt, "Allied Battle Fizzled, CEO Packed Parachute, Anyway," *Baltimore Business Journal,* June 10, 1991, p. 8.

——, "Allied Research Continues Rebound, Profits Shoot Up," *Baltimore Business Journal,* August 23, 1991, p. 8.

——, "Allied Swallows Poison Pill As Saudi Buys Bigger Share," *Baltimore Business Journal,* June 17, 1991, p. 3.

——, "Saudi Now Seeks Control of Allied: Investor Trying to Oust Management in Surprise Proxy Battle," *Baltimore Business Journal,* May 27, 1991, pp. 1+.

Knight, Jerry, "Corporate Raiders Train Their Sights on Allied Research," *Washington Post,* May 31, 1999, p. F7.

Maier, Timothy W., "Allied Armed Against Budget Cuts," *Baltimore Business Journal,* February 26, 1990, p. 8.

"Making Money Making Soviet Ammo," *Baltimore Business Journal,* December 15, 1986.

"Martin B. Ruffin, 72, Allied Research Chairman," *Washington Times,* Obituaries, November 20, 1990, p. B4.

Page, Douglas, "Police Hit the Street in AWACS on Wheels," *Law Enforcement Technology,* March 2003, pp. 70–75.

Reddy, Anitha, "Local Firms Respond to a Changing U.S. Military; Smaller Contractors Benefit from High-Tech Emphasis," *Washington Post,* April 26, 2004, p. E3.

Royall, Roderick, "Allied Set for Govt. Bids After Takeover of Firm," *Baltimore Business Journal,* June 8, 1987, p. 8.

Schneider, Greg, "Earnings Over a Barrel; Ammunition Maker's Sales Are Up on a Cyclical Oil Market," *Washington Post,* August 21, 2000, p. F6.

Shelsby, Ted, "Allied Creates Unit to Dispose of Military Waste," *Sun* (Baltimore), January 29, 1993, p. 14C.

——, "Allied Research Mines Success; But Proxy Fight Threatens CEO's Job," *Sun* (Baltimore), May 29, 1991, p. 1C.

——, "A Major New Direction: Defense Contractor Eyes Other Markets," *Sun* (Baltimore), December 21, 1991, p. 12C.

Zuckerman, Gregory, "Allied Evaluates Takeover Bid," *Mergers & Acquisitions Report,* May 10, 1993, p. 4.

——, "Allied Research Said to Rebuff Another Offer," *Mergers & Acquisitions Report,* January 17, 1994, p. 2.

——, "Allied Research Takeover Falls Apart," *Mergers & Acquisitions Report,* November 1, 1993, p. 3.

—Frederick C. Ingram

Altiris, Inc.

588 W. 400 South
Lindon, Utah 84042-1914
U.S.A.
Telephone: (801) 805-2400
Toll Free: (888) 252-5551
Fax: (801) 226-8506
Web site: http://www.altiris.com

Public Company
Incorporated: 1998
Employees: 600
Sales: $99.3 million (2003)
Stock Exchanges: NASDAQ
Ticker Symbol: ATRS
NAIC: 334611 Software Reproducing

Based in Lindon, Utah, Altiris, Inc. offers software and related services to manage information technology (IT) systems. The company's suite of 18 modules enables IT professionals to deploy, migrate, patch, and restore software on servers, desktop PCs, notebook computers, and handhelds. Altiris is able to greatly reduce software installation times and also allow IT managers to correct problems and counteract viruses without interrupting users. Changes to an entire system can be completed in a matter of minutes and if necessary rolled back to the previous stable condition, thereby providing IT managers with a margin for error and the confidence that they can quickly recover from a mistake. In addition, Altiris software is able to keep track of a company's computer assets as well as the performance history and diagnostic metrics of both hardware and software. The products rely on a Web-based infrastructure and are multi-tiered, allowing them to be used by small businesses as well as large corporations. Altiris benefits from both good economic conditions and poor. When budgets are tight, companies turn to Altiris to help save money managing their IT assets, because the purchase price represents only 20 percent of the costs associated with a computing device. During prosperous times, companies add hardware and use Altiris software and services to help in rollout and management.

A global company, Altiris has forged alliances with such major corporations as Dell, Hewlett-Packard, and Microsoft. It is publicly traded on the NASDAQ.

Starting in 1996 As KeyLabs' Software Division

Altiris was launched by KeyLabs, which was started in Provo, Utah, in January 1996 as a full-service Internet and network-testing company for large corporations as well as hardware and software developers. KeyLabs was founded by J.D. Brisk and two partners: Jan Newman and Kevin Turpin. Brisk had worked as a test engineer and manager for Provo-based Novell Labs and became director of engineering. He designed and managed Novell's SuperLab, the largest network test facility in the world, which tested third-party software applications and hardware devices. He then decided to strike out on his own and along with Newman and Turpin started an independent network-testing company. Because KeyLabs had a large number of computers in its laboratory that needed regular software updates and had to be reconfigured before each test, company engineers created a solution to automate the process. Now a single technician at one console could redeploy KeyLabs' entire inventory of computers in a matter of minutes. It was an impressive display of power and control and when customers visited the lab this in-house software tool often upstaged the company's actual testing business. Thus KeyLabs created a software division and began selling a commercial version of its management software, primarily targeting schools and corporations that maintained large computer labs.

Both KeyLabs divisions were doing well, but in 1998 management decided to split the company to allow management and employees to better focus on their particular businesses. The separate companies would also have a clearer mission and avoid confusion in the marketplace about what they offered. Moreover, the testing business needed to maintain its neutrality, and having a software IT management product was a potential conflict of interest. In August 1998 Keylabs' 12-person software division was spun off as Altiris, Inc.

Funding had not been easy to find. The company was rejected by a number of venture capital firms before a deal was reached with a firm that shared Novell's roots, Canopy Group, a high-tech incubator and venture capital firm established in Lindon, Utah, in 1995 by legendary Ray Noorda, Novell's longtime chairman and chief executive officer. Noorda was raised in Ogden, Utah, during the Great Depression, earned an electrical engineering degree from the University of Utah, and then worked for General Electric until starting his own business career in the 1970s. He earned a reputation for building successes out of troubled companies. In 1983 he was asked to take over Novell, Inc., a PC components manufacturing company that had been struggling since its start three years earlier. Noorda transformed Novell into a network-software company and was instrumental in the growth of the local area network (LAN) concept that linked personal computers and allowed organizations to lessen their need for large and expensive mainframe computers. By the time Noorda retired in 1994, Novell had grown to become one of the largest software companies in the world. Although 70 years old, Noorda remained active, mostly through Canopy Group, funding a number of start-up companies including Altiris, which set up shop in Lindon where he could easily visit them.

Forging an Alliance with Compaq in 2000

Initially Altiris concentrated on software for deployment and imaging. The company's first migration product was leased in 1999. Revenues grew steadily, improving from $1.8 million in 1998 to $3.6 million in 1999. A major step in the growth of the company came in January 2000, when it forged an alliance with Compaq, which agreed to bundle Altiris software on its commercial desktop computers. A month later, another important development took place when Jan Newman, who had been serving as chief executive for both KeyLabs and Altiris, decided it was time to turn over the helm of Altiris in order to take the company to the next level in its growth. Greg S. Butterfield, another Novell alumnus, was tapped for the job. He had more than 15 years of experience as a sales and marketing executive in the software industry, working at WordPerfect Corporation, Vinca Corporations, and two years at Novell, where he served as regional director of sales for the Rocky Mountain region.

Under Butterfield's leadership, Altiris began to make a series of calculated acquisitions that filled out the company's business. In the fall of 2000, Altiris paid $3.8 million for Computing Edge, a Utah company that provided systems and asset management solutions for the Windows and UNIX operating systems. The addition of Computing Edge gave Altiris a complete Web-based operations management and inventory and asset management solution. In February 2001, Altiris paid $800,000 for Tekworks, acquiring products that it had previously leased from Tekworks and that were major parts of its helpdesk and problem resolution products. A month later, Altiris acquired Compaq's Carbon Copy technology for $3.6 million, adding remote control capability and further help desk and problem resolution support. Then, in September 2002,

Altiris spent $1.1 million to acquire technology assets from San Diego-based Previo Inc., filling out its data protection and recovery capabilities by adding Previo's Web-based data backup software suite. By now the company was enjoying steady growth in revenues, although it continued to lose money as the business was established. Sales totaled $10 million in 2000 and jumped to $34.5 million in 2001. Net losses, however, increased from $6.5 million in 2000 to more than $10.2 million in 2001.

In the early months of 2002, Altiris completed three rounds of private stock sales, raising $24.5 million. The company was well financed, yet management needed new capital to speed up product development and for other reasons decided that the time was right to take the company public. According to an interview Butterfield gave to the *IPO Reporter* in 2002, "We concluded that based on where we were as a company . . . based on the fact we were doing much larger transactions with larger companies who wanted to get confidence and drill down in the financial stability of the company, that it made sense at this time [to go public]." To serve as lead underwriter of the initial public offering (IPO), Altiris chose Credit Suisse First Boston, which had been cultivating a relationship with the company for the past 18 months, making their analysts and merger and acquisitions people available to provide advice as Altiris engineered its acquisitions and new product releases. The company had hoped to raise $70 million, but conditions were hardly ideal. The NASDAQ was plummeting as the tech bubble burst and the business world was still reeling from a series of corporate scandals, including Enron and WorldCom. Altiris's accountant, Arthur Andersen, was also on the verge of self-destruction. To make matters worse, Altiris was a money-losing company whose business model was all too similar to Peregrine Systems, which was in trouble and about to restate its earnings. Altiris dropped its asking price from a range of $12–$14 to $10–$12, and proceeded with the offering in May 2002. It had to settle for the low end of the range, $10 a share, and at the end of the day netted $43.8 million. Further disappointment followed as the price of the company's stock immediately fell and continued to decline for the next few weeks, eventually bottoming out at $4.50 in June.

Rebounding from Disappointing 2002 IPO

Butterfield described to *Varbusiness* the sensation of watching the company's IPO on television monitors in New York City: "There I was in what was supposed to be one of the happiest moments for a CEO, watching a nightmare unfold right before my very eyes." The disappointment over the offering and the collapse of the stock price cast a pall over the company. Butterfield called a companywide meeting to rally the employees. He turned to the movie *Hoosiers* about a troubled coach who guides a small school in overcoming great odds to become Indiana state high school basketball champions. "I remembered when Hackman had his team in the arena where the big game was to be played," Butterfield told *Varbusiness*. "He could tell his players were a little awestruck, so he takes out a tape measure and shows them that the rims were still only 10 feet tall." Butterfield told his employees that despite investors' negative take on the company's offering and prospects, their products had not changed: They were still just as good and the company had just as much potential to prosper as before the IPO.

```
┌─────────────────────────────────────────────────┐
│                  Key Dates:                      │
│                                                  │
│  1996:  KeyLabs starts a software division.      │
│  1998:  KeyLabs spins off Altiris.               │
│  2000:  Greg Butterfield is named CEO.           │
│  2002:  Altiris goes public.                     │
└─────────────────────────────────────────────────┘
```

Altiris soon benefited from a downturn in the economy and the dropoff in IT spending. First, because companies were not hiring, no disillusioned employees decided to leave Altiris, an event that might have caused a snowball effect, and possibly destroyed the company. Instead, Altiris retained all of its key people. Moreover, because IT budgets were slashed, companies were looking to maximize their resources and found that investing in Altiris products was a prudent, money-saving investment. As a result, momentum began to shift and the company renewed its march toward profitability. It also began to change the minds of investors who gradually came to recognize the company's worth and began bidding up the price of Altiris stock. A year after the IPO, Altiris stock traded at more than $20. Revenues grew to $62.9 million in 2002, an 83 percent increase over the year before, and the company's net loss was reduced to just $86,000. Efforts to expand international sales also were beginning to pay off, as revenues outside of the United States grew from $5.4 million in 2001 to $12.8 million in 2002.

In August 2003 the company made a secondary offering of stock, this time netting $66 million. Altiris completed another strategic acquisition in 2003, paying $43 million in cash and stock for Wise Solutions, a Michigan software management company. The two had worked together for the past year, and Wise Solutions had been helpful to Altiris in winning some important contracts. More important, the acquisition added a patch delivery module to Altiris's suite of software applications. Patches, used to ward off attacks from computer viruses and worms, were becoming increasingly more important to IT managers in maintaining the security of their networks. Altiris was able to incorporate the patch module into the first upgrade of its software in two years, Altiris 6, which offered the new patch delivery module as well as an improved user interface, faster performance, and an increased number of language options. The software also offered what the company called a type of "pre-flight testing," allowing IT managers more options in patch management, so that if something should go wrong, they would be able to restore their computers to their prior stable state. In March 2004 Altiris added to its application management capabilities by acquiring the file system layering technology of FRLogic Inc., purchased for $1.8 million.

In 2003 Altiris reached $99.3 million in sales and turned its first net profit, totaling more than $14 million. The company appeared well established and was known to be very aggressive in closing deals. Moreover, the functionality and ease of use of its products gave Altiris a competitive advantage. Because it took a module approach, both small or large customers could choose the options suited to their needs. But there was little margin for error. There were some 200 companies vying for business in a highly competitive field, and giants like Microsoft and Hewlett-Packard were becoming more involved in management software. While the prospects for Altiris remained bright, they were far from certain.

Principal Subsidiaries

Altiris Computing Edge, Inc.; Wise Solutions, Inc.

Principal Competitors

Computer Associates International, Inc.; IBM Software; Peregrine Systems, Inc.

Further Reading

Bonasia, J., "Tiny Altiris Attracts Big Rivals in Security-Patching Arena," *Investor's Business Daily,* March 16, 2004, p. A06.

Brammer, Rhonda, "Dancing with Giants," *Barron's,* June 16, 2003, p. 32.

Collins, Lois M., "KeyLabs Turned Altiris into a Happy Byproduct," *Deseret News,* August 21, 200, p. C03.

"Computer Testing Lab Spins Off Software Company," *Enterprise,* August 17, 1998, p. 8.

Doyle, T.C., "Altiris Is Back from IPO Disaster," *Varbusiness,* August 4, 2003.

—Ed Dinger

Ambac

Ambac Financial Group, Inc.

One State Street Place
New York, New York 10004
U.S.A.
Telephone: (212) 668-0340
Toll Free: (800) 221-1854
Fax: (212) 509-9190
Web site: http://www.ambac.com

Public Company
Founded: 1971 as American Municipal Bond Assurance
   Corporation
Employees: 400
Total Assets: $16.74 billion (2003)
Stock Exchanges: New York
Ticker Symbol: ABK
NAIC: 551112 Offices of Other Holding Companies

Ambac Financial Group, Inc.'s (Ambac) primary operating subsidiary, the AAA-rated Ambac Assurance Corporation, was the first to offer insurance on municipal bonds. The subsidiary is now the cornerstone of its increasingly diversified parent company. Ambac Financial's core business areas involve public, structured, and international finance.

In Wisconsin: 1960s–70s

Ambac's story begins in Milwaukee, Wisconsin. MGIC Investment Corp., a holding company with its primary business in home mortgage insurance, began a diversification drive in the late 1960s. The company first expanded into commercial building mortgage insurance and then picked up home building and land development concerns. Gerald L. Friedman, nephew of founder Max H. Karl, was instrumental in the establishment of an endeavor that took them further from their core business area.

American Municipal Bond Assurance Corporation (AMBAC) was created in 1971 to insure the principal and interest of municipal bonds against default. The company's first issue was a general obligation bond for construction on an Alaskan medical facility. AMBAC's first competitor came along three years

later. The Municipal Bond Insurance Association (MBIA) was formed as a consortium of major insurance companies—Aetna, Fireman's Fund, Travelers, Cigna, and Continental—according to *Business Week*.

Just as AMBAC faced its first challenger in the industry it had pioneered, MGIC's fortunes turned toward the worse. The company suffered a $1.9 million loss in 1974. Reorganization followed. Lines of business were dropped. Friedman took over operations as president, with his uncle in the post of chairman.

The difficulties of another entity actually helped AMBAC at this time. New York City's well publicized financial woes drove up the demand for bond insurance in 1975.

Back on track in the late 1970s, MGIC drew the attention of a suitor, Baldwin-United Corp. The multibillion-dollar holding company owned insurance and savings and loan operations and was identified with annuities and S&H Green Stamps.

In 1981, MGIC lost its independence and its president. In addition, AMBAC moved to the Big Apple.

New York Minutes: 1980s

"Friedman says he fought selling MGIC to Baldwin-United because he feared an alliance with a 'second-rate company with weak management and a very weak balance sheet' would undermine his plans to move AMBAC into other kinds of financial guarantees," according to *Business Week*. He left in protest of the deal.

The weight of the $1.2 billion price tag on MGIC contributed to the collapse of Baldwin-United in 1983. In addition, a for-sale sign went up on its subsidiaries. AMBAC was forced into a defensive posture just as a new competitor entered the market. Friedman established Financial Guaranty Insurance Co. (FGIC) in alliance with General Electric Credit, Merrill Lynch, Morgan, General Re, Shearson Lehman/American Express, and Kemper Group.

Coming off a record year in 1982, AMBAC's prospects for 1983 looked even better. But uncertainty surrounding its future, plus heavy-hitting competition, knocked the bond insurer off its top spot in the industry. MBIA usurped AMBAC as the leader in municipal bond insurance in 1984.

Furthermore, AMBAC had to begin paying on Washington Public Power Supply System bonds. AMBAC's liability on the default, which totaled $2.25 billion, was an estimated $75 million. Even though the claims would be paid over the life of the bond, AMBAC was required to up its reserves.

Yet, it was just this financial vulnerability of large institutions that drove the industry in which AMBAC operated. "When you step back and look at the growth of financial guarantees, it is a sad commentary on the condition of the municipal and corporate sectors," Robert Mebus, a managing director of Standard & Poor's told *Business Week*.

In 1985, Citibank (the principal subsidiary of Citicorp) acquired majority control of Ambac Inc., parent company of AMBAC. Other investors, including Xerox Corp., Ambac management, and Stephens Inc., an investment banking firm, held the remaining equity. The estimated sale price ranged from $150 million to $200 million, according to the *Wall Street Journal*.

Citibank infused the company with additional capital. At the time of purchase, AMBAC held about 40 percent of the municipal bond insurance market. Anticipating the Tax Reform Act of 1986, municipalities doubled the high watermark of any previous year and issued $207 billion of long-term debt in 1985.

AMBAC's share of the insured new municipal issue market was 26.2 percent in 1986. But the Citibank subsidiary was regaining ground, climbing to 30.6 percent in 1988.

In 1989, Citibank gained sole ownership of the municipal bond insurer, purchasing the remaining shares it had not already secured from its former partners. About that time, allegations regarding Citibank's parent company, pertaining to its business practices, were leveled by a competitor. "FGIC said it believes Citicorp is exploiting a loophole in banking regulations and that it 'double-counts' Ambac's capital for its own banking purposes. That allows Ambac to unfairly cut prices and expand its market share," according to the *Wall Street Journal*. Citicorp denied the double-counting charge.

Open to the Public: 1990s

Ambac's net premiums written exceeded $100 million in 1990. But Citicorp was trying to exit the business. When a direct deal to sell failed, Citicorp switched gears and offered slightly more than half of its ownership in the company as common stock to the public.

"By reducing its stake, Citicorp removed Ambac from its books and cut by nearly $1 billion the amount of capital it needs to meet regulators' minimum capital standards, moving the giant banking company into compliance with the minimum capital standards that become effective at the end of 1992," reported the *New York Times*. More than $86 billion in municipal bonds was insured by Ambac.

Phillip B. Lassiter, moving over from Citibank, was named Ambac Inc. chairman and CEO following the public offering. Citibank sold its remaining shares to the public in February 1992, making Ambac the first bond insurer to be 100 percent publicly held. Trading at nearly $32 per share, the stock had climbed more than 50 percent since the initial public offering in July 1991.

The complete divestiture was prompted by the strength of the stock market, difficulty in Citicorp's core businesses, and a call by the feds for Citicorp to cease double counting its capital, according to the *Bond Buyer*.

As a part of a streamlining effort, Lassiter took on the additional role of president in August 1992. Product diversification was ratcheted up. In 1993, Ambac entered the fray for guarantees on asset-backed and structured issues. Finally, in 1994, the company began making municipal interest rate swaps, the only company of its type to do so. The move put Ambac into competition with investment banks and securities dealers, among their customers for the core municipal bond insurance business. The demand for bond insurance by states, counties, cities, and towns continued to grow, and the top four insurers held the lion's share of the market.

The bankruptcy of Orange County, California, in 1994 was a double-edged sword for the industry. The potential for municipal failure was once again highlighted but so was the risk to investors in publicly held municipal bond insurers. Seeking to broaden its business outside the country, in 1995, Ambac established a joint venture with MBIA for reinsurance and marketing purposes.

In 1997, the company changed its name to reflect its expansion into new areas of business. Ambac Inc. was renamed Ambac Financial Group, Inc. The municipal insurance subsidiary was renamed Ambac Assurance. The company continued to fine-tune its product mix by buying and selling smaller operations.

The municipal bond business had experienced two decades of double-digit growth. Although growth continued to be strong, market penetration for new bond issues had reached about 50 percent by 1998. Analysts engaged in speculation over the level of success new ventures by bond insurers could achieve, relative to their core business area.

Ambac dropped to fourth place among insurers of municipal bonds during 1998, but outshined its publicly held rivals in terms of the stock market with a rise of 31 percent. Ambac's unwillingness to discount premium prices had eroded market share, but its entry into sectors with higher premiums and brighter growth prospects helped drive up its value on The Street. Ambac's nonmunicipal activities, which accounted for just 6 percent of business in 1994, reached 43 percent in 1998.

Key Dates:

1971: The company is founded as a subsidiary of MGIC Investment Corp.
1982: Baldwin-United Corp. purchases MGIC and subsidiary companies.
1985: Citibank gains majority control of Ambac.
1991: The parent company, Ambac Inc., goes public.
1997: The company's name is changed to Ambac Financial Group, Inc.
2000: Ambac joins the S&P 500.
2003: International operations produce record results.

Riskier Business: 2000–04

The new century marked Ambac's inclusion on the S&P 500. Technology stocks took a beating during the year. Financial guarantors, still producing double-digit growth, outperformed the market. In addition, Ambac outpaced the two other publicly held bond insurers, once again, with stock rising 67.6 percent on the year.

Ambac dissolved its international joint venture with MBIA in 2000 and opened offices in Tokyo and Sydney in 2001.

The events of September 11, 2001, traumatized the financial industry. Ambac employees had to evacuate their offices near the World Trade Center. Potential claim exposure lay in its credit risks attached to airports and airlines, sectors hard hit by the attacks and the post-9/11 environment.

Bond insurers recorded their best ever year in 2002, with $176.75 billion in volume. The industry benefited from investor fears in the wake of credit defaults, a lowering of interest rates by the Federal Reserve, which drove refunding, and a drop-off in municipal revenue, which forced more borrowing, according to the *Bond Buyer*. The strength of the bond market helped Ambac achieve 89th place on The Boston Group list of the world's best performing financial stocks during the period from 1998–2002.

Economic conditions helped drive up claims paid during 2003, but Ambac continued to produce strong growth and profit. The country's pressing infrastructure needs and budget shortfalls contributed to record municipal bond issuance. Activity in the United Kingdom helped yield record results in international operations. Structured finance, which included asset-backed business, faced a challenging year. Mortgages and home loans had dominated this segment, but Ambac also had added riskier auto loan and credit card receivables.

Lassiter stepped down as CEO in January 2004 but continued to serve as chairman of the board. Robert J. Genader, 18-year veteran of Ambac and president and chief operating officer, succeeded him.

Principal Subsidiaries

Ambac Assurance Corporation.

Principal Competitors

Financial Guaranty Insurance Co.; Financial Security Assurance; MBIA Insurance Corporation.

Further Reading

Birger, Jon, "Market Share? Who Cares?," *Crain's New York Business,* January 18, 1999, p. 3.

Boyle, Nicholas, "AMBAC Considering Stock Sale to Public Series: 7," *Bond Buyer,* April 8, 1991.

——, "Citibank Sells Remaining Stake in AMBAC, Oldest Bond Insurer Is 100% Publicly Owned," *Bond Buyer,* February 20, 1992, p. 28.

Carpenter-Kasprzak, Sheri, "Bond Insurers: As Tech Stocks Bombed, Ambac and MBIA Shares Soared," *Bond Buyer,* February 20, 2001, p. 40.

"Citibank Acquires 80% of Ambac from Unit of Baldwin-United," *Wall Street Journal* (Eastern Edition), July 1, 1985, p. 1.

"Citicorp's Bank Unit Buy Remaining 3% of Ambac Indemnity," *Wall Street Journal* (Eastern Edition), July 14, 1989, p. 1.

Dickson, Steven, "AMBAC to Sell $75 Million in Corporate Debentures to Beef Up Reserves," *Bond Buyer,* March 10, 1993, p. 7.

——, "Year Isn't Over and Insurers Already Break 1991 Record," *Bond Buyer,* October 15, 1992, pp. 1+.

Forde, John P., "AMBAC Calls Double-Counting Charge a Ploy," *American Banker,* June 27, 1989, p. 7.

Fredrickson, Tom, "5 NY Financial Companies Singled Out for Stock Appeal," *Crain's New York Business,* August 18, 2003, p. 14.

Homa, Lynn, "Ambac President Resigns," *American Banker,* December 14, 1988, p. 3.

"Orange County Victim," *Forbes,* January 2, 1995, p. 297.

"PFI Global Awards," *Project Finance International,* March 17, 2004.

Quint, Michael, "Citicorp Sells Majority Stake in Bond Insurer Subsidiary," *New York Times,* July 12, 1991, p. 4D.

Reynolds, Katherine M., "Ambac's Swaps Success Draws Fire Over Dual Role As Insurer, Provider," *Bond Buyer,* June 8, 1998, p. 1.

Rudnitsky, Howard, "What's in a Rating," *Forbes,* September 12, 1983, p. 4.

Sheeline, Bill, "How to Play the Muni Boom and Earn Around 35%," *Money,* March 1993, pp. 80+.

Smith, Aaron T., "Bond Insurers: AGFI Head: Diversified Insurers Prepared for Falling Volumes," *Bond Buyer,* April 29, 2003, p. 28.

"Top Bond Insurers: All of 2003," *Bond Buyer,* January 5, 2004, p. 39.

Ulick, Jude, "There's More to Life Than Insurance: Ambac Goes Beyond Traditional Role," *Bond Buyer,* June 25, 1998, p. 1.

"What's Behind the Bittersweet Boom in Financial Guarantees," *Business Week,* September 17, 1984, pp. 116–18.

—Kathleen Peippo

American Healthways, Inc.

3841 Green Hills Village Drive
Nashville, Tennessee 37215
U.S.A.
Telephone: (615) 665-1122
Toll Free: (615) 665-7697
Fax: (615) 665-7697
Web site: http://www.americanhealthways.com

Public Company
Incorporated: 1981 as American Healthcorp, Inc.
Employees: 1,511
Sales: $165.5 million (2003)
Stock Exchanges: NASDAQ
Ticker Symbol: AMHC
NAIC: 624120 Services for the Elderly and Persons with
    Disabilities

American Healthways, Inc. is a publicly traded company based in Nashville, Tennessee, offering disease management and comprehensive care enhancement programs. The company is contracted by health plans, physicians, medical management organizations, and hospitals to help patients better manage their diseases. Registered nurses maintain regular contact to provide education, encouragement, and reminders. Moreover, American Healthways studies members' medical records looking for symptoms that might lead to a particular disease, such as diabetes, contacts those patients, and gives them a chance to enroll in a proactive, preventive program. More than a million people across the country are served by American Healthways programs. The approach has been called ''professional nagging,'' but patients and nurses are known to develop close and caring relationships, and the effectiveness of the disease management programs in reducing medical costs and increasing worker productivity are positively reflected on an insurer's balance sheet. American Healthways has experienced tremendous growth since taking on its first contract in 1996. Clients now include CIGNA Healthcare, WellChoice, Oxford Health Plans of New York, Blue Cross and Blue Shield of Minnesota, Health Plus of Michigan, The Principal Financial Group, Lowe's, and US Bank.

Company's Founding in 1981

American Healthways was founded in 1981 as a hospital company called American Healthcorp, Inc. by Thomas G. Cigarran, senior vice-president of development at Hospital Affiliates International, along with four other executives from Hospital Affiliates: James A. Deal, Henry D. Herr, Robert E. Stone, and David A. Sidlowe. The new company then bought four hospitals in Tennessee and Virginia and in 1983 acquired an alcohol treatment company, Koala Centers. The following year the company branched into hospital-based diabetes programs under the name Diabetes Treatment Centers of America. Because of a consolidation trend in hospitals, American Healthcorp decided in 1984 to divest its hospital division and focus on disease management services for hospitals. Over the course of the next five years the company built up its alcohol treatment division, American Treatment Centers, but it was divested as well, in 1989. In that same year, the company paid more than $2 million to acquire MWM, Inc. and other assets of the Houston Center for Health Promotion.

American Healthcorp went public in 1991 and began trading on the NASDAQ. In November 1992 it acquired a controlling interest, 57 percent, in a newly founded Nashville company, AmSurg Corp., which would acquire, develop, and manage specialty outpatient surgery centers in partnership with physicians. The centers offered insurers and patients a less expensive alternative to surgery centers in hospitals, which were saddled with much higher overhead costs. AmSurg grew steadily over the next five years, and in March 1997 American Healthcorp elected to spin off the subsidiary in a tax-free distribution to its shareholders.

Launching a Population-Based Program in 1993

While AmSurg had pursued its niche in the healthcare field, its corporate parent concentrated on its diabetes management services. In 1993 American Healthcorp launched Diabetes Healthways, a population-based—rather than hospital-based—diabetes management program designed for health plans. Diabetes was a strong candidate for such a service because of the nature of the disease. It could not be cured, only managed, and if not properly cared for, a patient could develop a wide range of problems, including heart attacks, strokes, blindness, and nerve and kidney damage. Diabetes was also a leading cause of death in the United States. As a result, poorly treated diabetes put a strain on the entire healthcare system and drove up costs. American Healthcorp banked on health plan administrators recognizing that a diabetes management program would save money while offering patients better care.

American Healthcorp may have been the leading diabetes disease management company in the hospital market, but its management team was convinced that the future was in the managed care market and elected to invest $12 million in the development of a managed care product. The cost would grow to $20 million, the company would suffer in the short term, much to the concern of investors, but management remained committed to making the transition. In late 1995 American Healthcorp signed its first managed care diabetes contract to Principal Health Care, a part of Principal Financial Group. To service the contract, American Healthcorp centralized its call-center operations in 1996, a key step in the growth of the company. Not only was it able to house more nurses, the company gained the advantage of spreading its overhead over a number of contracts, thereby allowing it to price its service more advantageously. American Healthcorp had seen revenues for its hospital-based diabetes service peak in 1994 at $41.1 million; then sales fell to $30.5 million in 1997 as the company began to make the switch to a population-based approach. During 1997, 91 percent of the company's revenues still came from hospital contracts and just 7 percent from health plan contracts. A year later, 60 percent of revenues came from hospitals and 39 percent from health plans. The company lost $2.3 million in 1998 but revenues returned to the 1994 level and, more important, the company was now well positioned for a return to profitability and long-term growth. In 1999 health plan revenues exceeded hospital revenues for the first time, 54 percent versus 45 percent. The company also was gaining credibility. American Healthcorp was able to document the clinical as well as financial success of its approach in a large-scale, multi-site study, confirmed by third parties and subjected to peer review.

American HealthCorp began to expand beyond diabetes. It launched a comprehensive cardiac disease management program called Cardiac Healthways, and followed up with Respiratory Healthways, a program to manage respiratory diseases. To further promote ''Healthways'' as a recognizable brand, the company late in 1999 decided to change its name from American Healthcorp to American Healthways, Inc., which took effect at the start of 2000. In addition, the Diabetes Treatment Centers of America name was phased out and the company's hospital contracts were now folded into the new brand. A new product also would adopt the Healthways tag in 2000, Myhealthways, which was subsequently changed to Care Enhancement. This program moved American Healthways beyond chronic disease management to providing a positive healthcare relationship between health plans and all of its members. Another important step in 2000 was the signing of the first multiple-disease contract. Because a large number of patients suffered from more than one serious ailment, and it was unwieldy to assign a separate nurse to work with a patient on each disease, there was a clear need for a program that could provide one-call, comprehensive disease management. A further milestone for American Healthways in 2000 was the company's issuance of the first set of disease management standards in the United States. By now, annual revenues topped the $50 million mark.

In 2001 American Healthways sold a number of major contracts. Of particular importance was a ten-year contract, the first of its kind in the industry, to provide a total-population care enhancement program for Blue Cross and Blue Shield of Minnesota. The program would focus on the 15 percent to 20 percent of the members responsible for 75 percent to 80 percent of medical costs. To accomplish this task, American Healthways adopted a multiple-disease approach, with the capability of dealing with 17 chronic conditions. Later, the Care Enhancement approach would be rolled out to the plans of more than two million members, helping them to prevent disease and maintain a healthy life. To help achieve these lofty goals, American Healthways added to its capabilities by way of acquisition. That May American Healthways used stock to purchase two-year-old CareSteps Inc., a healthcare management firm that had developed a health risk appraisal tool. Shortly after the CareSteps deal, American Healthways added to its Care Enhancement program by acquiring Empower Health, a Connecticut-based compiler of market research data.

Johns Hopkins Approval in 2002

Because the healthcare industry had for the past decade offered up numerous cost-saving strategies that were also supposed to provide better care, doctors and patients alike needed reassurance that the Care Enhancement program was more than just hype. Johns Hopkins University's Outcomes Verification Program was brought in by American Healthways and Blue Cross and Blue Shield of Minnesota to study the new program, both in terms of cost savings and improved health for members. Johns Hopkins would then be free to publish its findings, favorable or not, in medical journals. In May 2002 the advisory board of Johns Hopkins's Outcomes Verification Program approved American Healthways' cardiac and diabetes care enhancement programs, the first such approvals since the university established the program in 2001. American Healthways received further commendation in June 2002, becoming the first organization to be issued accreditation under the new Disease Management Accreditation program administered by the National Committee for Quality Assurance (NCQA). American Healthways also would be certified by the other major healthcare accreditation bodies. URAC (Utilization Review Accreditation Commission) issued a full, two-year accreditation for the company's care enhancement programs, and JCAHO (Joint Commission on Accreditation of Healthcare Organizations) also accredited the program. As a result, American Healthways became the first company to be certified by all of the country's leading healthcare accreditation bodies. Moreover, in 2002 Ernst & Young LLP completed a study that confirmed savings from 20 to 29 percent in total healthcare costs for congestive heart failure patients.

Because American Healthways had proven it could deliver both good healthcare and save money, there was no wonder that

---

Key Dates:

1981: American Healthcorp is founded to run hospitals.
1984: The Hospital division is divested; a hospital-based diabetes care program is launched.
1991: The company is taken public.
1995: The first population-based diabetes management contract is signed.
1999: The company name is changed to American Healthways.
2001: CareSteps Inc. and Empower Health are acquired.

---

the company began to enjoy a robust business. In 2001 it posted net income of $3.2 million on sales of $75.1 million. Those numbers improved to $10.4 million in earnings and $122.8 million in revenues. In 2003 revenues advanced to $165.5 million and net income grew to $18.5 million. Estimated sales for 2004 were $255 million. As a result of this impressive record, American Healthways was ranked fifth by *Fortune* magazine in its 2003 list of the nation's 100 Fastest Growing Companies, and was also ranked by *Fortune* as the number one fastest growing publicly traded small business in the United States. In addition, American Healthways cracked *BusinessWeek* magazine's 2003 list of America's top 100 "Hot Growth" companies, and was added to the Standard & Poor "S&P SmallCap 600 Index." Also in 2003, American Healthways continued to grow externally. It paid $65 million to acquire Status One Health Systems, provider of health management services to high-risk health plan customers.

After more than 20 years of heading American Healthways, Cigarran stepped down as chief executive, while retaining the chairmanship. His replacement, Ben R. Leedle, although just 42, was well prepared to take over in September 2003. Leedle had played an important role in the company's transformation from a hospital-based to population-based company and steadily rose through the management ranks after that. After being named senior vice-president of operations from September 1997 to September 1999, he served as chief operating officer and added the presidency in May 2002, when he was made Cigarran's heir apparent. He was groomed for the top position over the next year and a half. Tapped to make presentations and meet with investors, Leedle also took a course at Harvard Business School to improve his knowledge of international markets. Because its methods could be applied elsewhere in the developed world, American Healthways was already beginning to look to foreign markets for foreign growth.

In the meantime, there were plenty of opportunities in North America. The disease management approach to healthcare was still very much in its infancy, but American Healthways' success was already impressive. In 2003 the company saved Blue Cross and Blue Shield of Minnesota $40 million, which allowed the health plan to reduce its cost increase by three percentage points. Wall Street estimated that disease management would soon grow into a $20 billion business, a huge increase over the $600 million in combined sales for the industry in 2002. As a consequence, of course, American Healthways would face greater competition, both from other third-party companies and internal programs launched by health plans. But start-up costs would be high, and many insurers would rather outsource the operation to a proven company like American Healthways, which was well positioned to garner a significant share of this growing market.

Principal Subsidiaries

American Healthways Services, Inc.; Arthritis and Osteoporosis Care Center, Inc.; American Healthways Management, Inc.; CareSteps.com, Inc.; Axonal Information Solutions, Inc.; StatusOne Health Systems, Inc.

Principal Competitors

Express Scripts, Inc.; Landacorp, Inc.; Matria Healthcare, Inc.

Further Reading

Alva, Marilyn, "American Healthways Inc. Nashville, Tennessee News Flash: Staying Healthy Can Save Money," *Investor's Business Daily,* January 8, 2002, p. A08.

Lau, Gloria, "American Healthways Inc./ Nashville, Tennessee Sick of HMO's? These Guys Might Have Cure," *Investor's Business Daily,* April 26, 2001, p. A08.

Reeves, Amy, "American Healthways Inc. Nashville, Tenn.; Job Should Be a Cinch for Chief in Waiting," *Investor's Business Daily,* June 13, 2003.

Russell, Keith, "Firm Finding Success Through Managed Care Market," *Nashville Business Journal,* January 12, 1999.

Stires, David, "RX for Investors," *Fortune,* May 3, 2004, p. 158.

—Ed Dinger

AMVESCAP PLC

30 Finsbury Square
London EC2A 1AG
United Kingdom
Telephone: +44 (0) 20 7638 0731
Fax: +44 (0) 20 7638 0711
Web site: http://www.amvescap.com

Public Company
Incorporated: 1997
Employees: 6,844
Total Assets: $7.33 billion (2003)
Stock Exchanges: London New York
Ticker Symbol: AVZ
NAIC: 523920 Portfolio Management; 551112 Offices of
   Other Holding Companies

AMVESCAP PLC is one of the largest independent investment managers in the world, a global player. Principal brands include AIM, INVESCO, and Atlantic Trust. Through mergers and acquisitions, AMVESCAP has developed significant footholds in the North American, European, and Asian markets and offers a sweeping range of products and services.

Southern Roots: 1970s–80s

AMVESCAP PLC's early history is tied to the ambitions of two men. After stints as an engineer, Navy officer, and stockbroker, Charles W. Brady signed on, in 1964, with the trust department of Atlanta's Citizens and Southern National Bank. When regulatory changes allowed banks to register with the Securities and Exchange Commission as investment advisers, his employer created, in 1971, Citizens and Southern Investment Counseling Co. Loan problems for the bank would open a door of opportunity for Brady later in the decade.

In 1978, Brady and eight other employees bought the investment business, renamed it INVESCO, and set out to capture the large corporate pension fund clients of major banks. As the company's assets under management grew, so did Brady's ambitions. He wanted to expand internationally. In the mid-1980s, he sold 45 percent of the company to U.K.-based, publicly held Britannia Arrow, which also owned London's Montagu Investment Management (MIM). The deal was problematic from the get-go and Brady ended up selling the rest of INVESCO to Britannia in 1988. The company, renamed INVESCO MIM, had $14 billion in managed assets at the time.

Brady stayed on to run the Atlanta-based U.S. operations and Britannia's Denver mutual fund business. The future of the company was jeopardized by a string of problems: London-based trusts performance dropped off; expansion in Europe and Asia proved costly; and investigations into sales practices and fund management were in progress in the United Kingdom. In the United States, however, sales remained strong.

As a result, in 1993, Brady was named CEO and the company was renamed INVESCO PLC. In 1995, the operation had $83 billion in assets under management and $78 million in operating profits from $300 million in revenues, according to *Institutional Investor International.*

Meanwhile, in Houston, another company had been getting under way. Charles T. Bauer left American General Insurance Co. when plans for a spinoff or sale of the $1.8 billion capital management unit he had built failed to materialize. In 1976, Bauer—a Navy pilot in World War II—and five former American General managers, including Robert H. Graham and Gary T. Crum, formed AIM Management Group, with $487,000 in capital and a $2 million line of credit. The group held 38 percent of the company and two outside investors held the rest. The firm struggled, nearly tanking in late 1980. In a last-ditch effort, an institutional money market fund with deeply discounted fees was introduced. In a year the company had $2.5 billion in assets.

Success bred success and new equity funds were launched. Then in 1986, AIM purchased the Weingarten Fund, Constellation Fund, and Charter Fund, which formed their core product line. Aggressive marketing boosted assets under management to $9.9 billion by 1987. Because its assets were primarily in money market funds at that time, AIM sustained little damage when the equity market crashed.

Company Perspectives:

AMVESCAP's mission is to Help People Worldwide Build Their Financial Security, and we do that by delivering superior investment performance and client service around the world. Our overall goal is to become one of the top players in every market we choose to compete in.

International Aspirations: 1990s

Between 1989 and 1993 AIM really took off, and assets under management grew from $12 billion to $25.3 billion. New products and strong fund performance helped drive the growth. But like his counterpart in Atlanta, Bauer wanted more and looked beyond American borders.

The death of one of the original outside backers provided the opportunity. Dutch insurance company Nationale Nederlanden became a new investor. A merger, in which the Dutch company became International Nederlander Group (ING), put a halt to its plans to exercise the right to buy a controlling interest of AIM, which had appreciated in value beyond what ING wanted to pay. In 1993 Bauer, Graham, Crum, and 60 AIM insiders gained 70 percent control of the company in a leveraged buyout backed by Boston concern TA Associates.

In 1996, INVESCO and AIM announced plans to merge. INVESCO brought its international presence and AIM its strong distribution system to the table. Brady would serve as chair, with Bauer as vice-chair.

Graham, AIM president and cofounder, headed up the North American retail fund business: AIM's $61 billion under management and INVESCO's approximately $20 billion. AIM's funds, carrying sales charges and annual fees, were sold by intermediaries such as stockbrokers and financial planners, while INVESCO's no-load funds were sold directly to investors.

The pair's stock strategy differed as well: AIM was more aggressive, buying companies whose earnings were on the rise and selling when profits fell. The more conservative INVESCO leaned toward value stocks, those that were inexpensive relative to value of the company.

AIM's strategy propelled it to a spot among the top U.S. mutual fund companies, but the booming mutual fund industry was no small factor in AIM's success. Assets under management had risen from $50 billion in 1976 to $3.3 trillion in 1996, according to the *Houston Chronicle.*

Business Week called AIM "one of the fund industry's hottest companies," about the time of the merger. The company's annualized growth had exceeded the industry during the 1990s and helped put its sale price at a premium.

"More important, performance is what sells mutual funds in the U.S., and that's where AIM has excelled: Eight of its 18 rated funds have earned either four or five stars, the highest rating from Morningstar Inc., the mutual-fund data company," wrote Gary McWilliams and Heidi Dawley for *Business Week.* Yet AIM had a vulnerable spot—its reliance on growth stocks.

The $1.6 billion merger came during a time when a number of investment management companies were consolidating to bring a broader range of products and services to customers from a single source. The INVESCO/AIM deal, completed in early 1997, was one of the largest deals to date. The new company, AMVESCAP PLC, held $200 billion in funds under management.

But the urge to merge was not satisfied. LGT Asset Management was up for grabs. The global operation had been losing assets, peaking at $65 million in early 1997. By acquiring the company, AMVESCAP would gain market share in key areas of the world where it had little or no market share. Included in the deal was GT Global Inc., an international mutual fund company strong in Asia, as well as Chancellor LGT Asset Management, a U.S. institutional money management company.

AMVESCAP was particularly interested in enhancing its position in the personal retirement account segment of the international market. A global shift from government and corporate pensions to personal retirement accounts was taking place, according to INVESCO Global unit CEO Michael Benson, in *American Banker.* The United States' own growth in the mutual fund industry had been part of that trend.

INVESCO Global handled non-U.S. retail and institutional marketing and had offices in France, Italy, The Netherlands, Japan, Hong Kong, Canada, Argentina, and Bermuda. Funds also were marketed in Eastern Europe and the Middle East. GT Global put the company into the German market for the first time and propelled it up the ladder ranking foreign-owned investment companies in important markets, including Japan.

Even with increased size, AMVESCAP faced a number of challenges in the global marketplace. Banks dominated the U.K. and continental European investment markets, according to *American Banker,* and they were reluctant to distribute independent funds. Investment firms tried to make inroads into the market by putting emphasis on fund performance.

Moreover, most fund sales in Europe, Japan, and elsewhere in Asia were made via banks, brokers, and financial planners. AMVESCAP was positioning itself for direct sales in those regions. Establishing a brand name on a worldwide level was a costly endeavor and the GT Global acquisition was expected to help. Following the acquisition the level of assets under management from investors outside the United States rose to 14 percent.

The 1998 LGT purchase, at $1.3 billion, established AMVESCAP as a truly global company. But company executives knew that mere physical presence was not enough to ensure success. "Many people go overseas and wind up with an outpost that does a little research and tries to solicit accounts, and that's what they call global business," Brady told *American Banker* in 1999. "You've got to design a product from the ground up in the country you're in. You're not going to dictate it from some other part of the world."

Mergers, the kind that helped AMVESCAP grow, had their pluses and minuses. Other financial services companies, such as Alliance Capital Management, Merrill Lynch & Co., and Fidelity Investments, had experienced integration problems.

Key Dates:

1976: AIM is founded in Houston.
1978: INVESCO is founded in Atlanta.
1997: INVESCO and AIM merge to form AMVESCAP PLC.
1998: The purchase of LGT Asset Management solidifies the company's position as a global operation.
2003: Investigation of the financial industry hits U.S. fund business.

AMVESCAP found the governing structure challenging when it brought together INVESCO and AIM, and when AMVESCAP took another quantum leap with the purchase of LGT, operating margins took a hit.

Complications in the New Century: 2000–04

In 2000, AMVESCAP positioned itself as a leading financial company in Canada with the purchase of Trimark Financial Corporation, and in the United Kingdom through a deal for Perpetual PLC. Acquisitions in the growing Australian and Taiwanese markets followed.

National Asset Management, a U.S. concern, was added in 2001, and enhanced institutional product offerings. That same year, AMVESCAP moved to secure the assets in the rapidly growing segment of wealthy individual investors with the establishment of Atlantic Trust Private Wealth Management. The company commenced gathering firms serving high-net-worth individuals: Pell Rudman in Boston, Whitehall Asset Management in New York, and Stein Roe Investment Counsel.

Despite the growth by acquisition, AMVESCAP had been feeling the strain of the steep market drop-off that had begun in 2000. Heavy into growth stocks, the company had been hit harder than most. INVESCO Funds Group, for example, had used the rise of technology stocks to grow from $16 billion in managed assets in 1998 to $55 billion in 2002.

Aldo Svaldi reported for the *Denver Post,* "At one point, the group received nearly $1 out of every $20 going into a mutual fund, not an easy feat considering its smaller size." The Denver-based operation confidently entered into costly endeavors of acquiring naming rights for the Broncos' new stadium and erecting a new headquarters. Furthermore, when the company shifted to load stocks in 1998, it established its own distribution network instead of dovetailing with AIM.

About mid-year 2003, AMVESCAP started to merge some funds into AIM to try to stem the negative flow of assets. Yet bad news continued. Late in the year, New York Attorney General Eliot Spitzer, the Colorado attorney general, and the SEC brought trading abuse charges against INVESCO Funds and its former CEO. Although the unit was a relatively small part of INVESCO, the brand name was tarnished. AMVESCAP took a fourth quarter charge to cover anticipated costs related to the investigations.

Principal Subsidiaries

AIM Management Group Inc.; INVESCO PLC.

Principal Competitors

FMR Corp.; Merrill Lynch & Co., Inc.; Schroders plc.

Further Reading

De Aenlle, Conrad, "Growth-Fund Giant Tries to Cope," *New York Times,* July 7, 2002, p. 22.

"Doing M&A the AMVESCAP Way," *Global Investor,* February 2001, p. 39.

Garmhausen, Stephen, "AMVESCAP Plans to Be Among First Global Asset Managers," *American Banker,* April 9, 1999, p. 8.

Hoffman, David, "INVESCO Name Lives On, But for How Long?," *Investment News,* May 17, 2003, p. 28.

Lappen, Alyssa A., "Think Global, Act Local," *Institutional Investor International,* May 1999.

Lipin, Steven, and Charles Gasparino, "AMVESCAP to Pay Up to $900 Million to Purchase LGT Asset Management," January 30, 1998, p. 1.

McWilliams, Gary, and Heidi Dawley, "We've Brought Both Companies into the Future," *Business Week* (Int'l Edition), November 18, 1996.

Milstead, David, "$41 Million Legal Bill: Parent Sets Aside Money to Cover Costs of Fund Scandal," *Rocky Mountain News* (Denver), February 4, 2004.

Mintz, Bill, "AIM to Unite with INVESCO to Form Giant," *Houston Chronicle,* November 4, 1996.

Pizzani, Lori, "AMVESCAP Fires Andersen," *Mutual Fund Market News,* April 1, 2002.

Stoneman, Bill, "AMVESCAP Sees Big Shift in Pension Savings," *American Banker,* May 14, 1998.

Svaldi, Aldo, "INVESCO's Decline Result of Risk-Taking, Bear Market, Management, Analysts Say," *Denver Post,* June 22, 2003.

——, "INVESCO Gets New Denver Manager; Marketing Chief to Assume Post," *Denver Post,* May 5, 2004, p. C1.

—Kathleen Peippo

Antofagasta plc

5 Princes Gate
London SW7 1QJ
United Kingdom
Telephone: +44 20 7808 0988
Fax: +44 20 7808 0986
Web site: http://www.antofagasta.co.uk

Public Company
Incorporated: 1888 as The Antofagasta (Chile) and
    Bolivia Railway Company Plc
Employees: 2,458
Sales: £659.4 million ($1.1 billion) (2003)
Stock Exchanges: London New York
Ticker Symbols: ANTO.L; ANFGY
NAIC: 482111 Line-Haul Railroads; 212221 Gold Ore
    Mining; 212234 Copper Ore and Nickel Ore Mining;
    221310 Water Supply and Irrigation Systems; 237210
    Land Subdivision; 334290 Other Communication
    Equipment Manufacturing; 522293 International Trade
    Financing

Antofagasta plc is one of the world's leading producers of copper, with total production levels nearing 472,000 tons in 2003. The focus of the company's operations is its Los Pelambres mine site, which began production in 2001 and has extended its life expectancy to some 50 years. The Los Pelambres site represents nearly three-quarters of the group's mining revenues. The shift of its mining focus to the Los Pelambres site has also enabled Antofagasta to claim a position as one of the global copper market's lowest cost producers, at just 36.4 cents to the pound. Antofagasta also holds controlling stakes in two other mines, El Tesoro, which adds 16 percent to the group's revenues; and Michilla, which represents 9.5 percent of Antofagasta's total mining revenues. Since the late 1990s, Antofagasta has restructured itself as one of the industry's most focused mining groups—more than 93 percent of the company's revenue comes from its mining operations. Nonetheless, the company continues to participate in two other important and related areas. The company's Transportation division oversees its monopoly control of the FCAB railroad linking Antofagasta in Chile to the Bolivian border, a 650-kilometer stretch of railroad crossing the Andes, which also represents the company's historic core operation. The company also operates the Bolivia-based Andino rail network, and a road-based door-to-door transportation subsidiary, Train Ltda., servicing the northern Chile region. Antofagasta's Water and Forestry division oversees its water pipeline and treatment operations, originally an offshoot of its railroad business, as well as the company's 32,000-hectare forest holdings. The company has moved to expand its water operations, and in 2004 was awarded a 30-year concession for the water distribution and treatment rights in the Antofagasta region. Yet mining remains the focus of the group's efforts, with an active exploration program in place, including a stake in Chile's Esperanza Project, and exploration partnerships in Peru. Listed on the London and New York stock exchanges, Antofagasta is controlled at more than 60 percent by Chile's powerful Luksic family.

Railroad Origins in the 19th Century

Toward the mid-1800s, British interests joined with the Bolivian government to construct a railroad crossing the Andes mountain and linking Huanchaca to the port of Antofagasta, along the Pacific coast. Founded in 1867 as a small fishing village, Antofagasta, which means "hiding place for copper" in Quechua, soon after became an important port town with the discovery of significant nitrate and other mineral deposits, including copper, in the Atacama desert.

The construction of the initial interior portion of the railroad, starting from Antofagasta, was originally completed under Compañía de Salitres de Antofagasta. Construction continued into the 1870s, and the resulting railroad represented one of the era's significant feats of engineering—as it neared the Bolivian border on its Collahausi branch (later shut down) the line topped an altitude of 4,827 meters, becoming the world's highest railroad.

Antofagasta and the Atacama region originally belonged to Bolivia and represented that country's link to the Pacific ocean. Nonetheless, Chilean interests were active in the region's early mining operations, including the production of nitrates, used for fertilizers and explosives, and copper. The importance of the nitrate trade in particular led the Bolivian government to attempt to increase its control over the region, and in 1879, the government imposed new, stiffer taxes on the Chilean-owned nitrate mines. When the mine owners balked at paying the higher tax, the government attempted to confiscate their holdings, then instituted an embargo on all Chilean goods entering Bolivian territory. This move precipitated in the five-year War of the Pacific, in which Chile emerged victorious over Bolivia and its ally Peru. As a result of the Treaty of 1884, Antofagasta and the Atacama region, as well as a significant portion of the Peruvian coast, fell under Chilean control.

With hostilities ended, construction of the Antofagasta railroad was renewed. Companhia Huanchaca de Bolivia became the controlling force behind the railroad, which featured a proposed 650-kilometer length of the line. By the late 1880s, the Huanchaca company had succeeded in building some 440 kilometers of rail from Antofagasta to the Andes.

In 1888, the Huanchaca company began negotiations to cede its concession on the railroad to a group of British entrepreneurs, which launched the Antofagasta (Chile) and Bolivia Railway Company Plc in 1888. The company listed its stock on the London Stock Exchange that same year, and used the proceeds of the public offering to back completion of the railway. The Huanchaca company remained responsible for the actual construction operations, which were scheduled for completion by 1890, at a price of £300,000. The new London-based company became known alternatively as FCAB, or, for its British investors, "Fags." In addition to its railroad concession, Fags also gained the concession for developing the water treatment and distribution network for the region.

Based on the booming nitrate trade, Antofagasta quickly developed into Chile's fourth largest city, and Fags found itself in control of the country's largest and most lucrative independently operated railway. Throughout its history, Fags maintained a monopoly on the railroad serving northern region's mining communities. The importance of the nitrate trade through the turn of the century and into the early decades of the 20th century stimulated the growth of a string of towns and villages along the railroad.

By the 1930s, however, the development of chemically derived nitrates spelled the end of the nitrate mining sector. Steady decreases in production led a significant loss in importance of the Fags-owned railroad. As nitrate mines shut down, the villages along the line were abandoned. Fags remained in business through the 1970s, yet lack of investment had resulted in a decrepit railroad and unreliable service, and had led the company to the edge of bankruptcy.

Transporting Copper Mining Success in the 1980s

Fags might have faded out entirely if not for the rapid development of a new mining sector in the northern Chilean region, that of copper, and particularly the efforts of Andrónico Luksic. Luksic was the son of Policapro Luksic, a former native of Croatia under the Austro-Hungarian empire. In 1910, the elder Luksic immigrated to Chile at the age of 17, and came to Antofagasta, where he married into a prominent local family. Son Andrónico went on to study law in Santiago, then, following World War II, went to Paris to study at the Sorbonne.

In Paris, Luksic worked in the monetary exchange market, raising enough capital to purchase a 10 percent stake in the Ford automobile concession in Antofagasta. Soon after, Luksic returned to Chile and joined a law firm. Luksic then went to work at the Ford automobile business, and later acquired full control of the concession.

Luksic had long held an interest in geology and mining, and was especially attracted to the opportunities presented by the Atacama desert region. In the early 1950s, Luksic was approached by one member of a three-way partnership of Frenchmen that had been developing a nearby copper mine. Disagreements had led to a falling out among the partners, and Luksic agreed to buy out the initial one-third share. Unable to pay outright, Luksic negotiated an agreement to pay back the stake over a 25-year period.

Shortly after, Luksic acquired the remaining shares in the mine by 1952. Then, in 1954, Luksic had a stroke of luck. Lacking the resources to develop the copper mine, Luksic instead sought a buyer for the holding. As the legend had it, Luksic approached Nippon Steel, offering to sell the mine for CLP 500,000, worth about $45,000 at the time. Yet the Japanese were said to have misunderstood Luksic, and agreed to pay him $500,000 instead.

Luksic founded the Luksic Group that same year. Over the next two decades, Luksic developed widely diversified business interests, becoming a major force in the country's fishing industry through his purchase of the local Star-Kist operation in the 1950s, as well as redeveloping the Ford dealership as an equipment rental company for the fast-growing mining industry in the region. At the same time, Luksic remained a force within the mining industry itself, conducting exploration and production operations, and buying stakes in a number of mining operations through the 1960s. In addition to interests in copper mining, Luksic controlled the Carbonifera Lota Schwager coal mining group, while his holding company, Madeco, in addition to being the country's leading producer of copper wire and tubing, emerged as one of the country's top conglomerates.

Luksic's fortunes met with a setback in 1970 when Salvador Allende was elected president of Chile. Allende's government quickly nationalized much of the mining and other industries. Luksic was granted some compensation for the expropriation of Madeco and other holdings, and his Ford equipment rental business remained a primary supplier to the northern mining industry now controlled by the Chilean government.

The company was forced to turn to the international market for continued investment in the 1970s. Luksic's string of business successes continued outside of Chile, and included control of Salta, Argentina's largest brewery, farming interests, canneries in Colombia, and an extension of his Ford dealership concession into Argentina and Brazil.

The overthrow of the Allende government by a U.S.-backed military dictatorship in 1974 led to a new reversal of fortune for Luksic. The new government began privatizing the businesses appropriated by the Allende government during the decade, yet Luksic found himself barred from acquiring the newly privatized companies—because of the compensation he had received from the Allende government and his continued trade with the government-controlled mining industry. Instead, Luksic concentrated his Chilean activities on redeveloping his copper exploration and mining interests in the northern region.

The blacklisting turned out to be a blessing in disguise. Unlike competing Chilean groups, which took on high levels of debt in order to acquire the privatized companies, Luksic remained financially solvent. With the collapse of the Chilean economy amid the Latin American debt crisis of the early 1980s, Luksic found himself in position to acquire a significant number of the bankrupted companies, establishing himself as the company's most powerful businessman.

At the same time, Luksic had spotted a new opportunity. Exasperated by the poor and unreliable service of the Antofagasta (Chile) and Bolivia Railway Company at the end of the 1970s, Luksic decided to gain control of the company. In 1979, Luksic acquired a majority stake in Fags, a move that largely went unnoticed by the investment community at the time. By the early 1980s, Luksic had succeeded in restoring Fags' operation, transforming it into a highly profitable enterprise. These profits in turn fueled Luksic's investments in other industries, such as his buyback of Madeco, and his partnership in the acquisition of CCU, another of Chile's largest and most profitable conglomerates.

Fags rapidly grew into the holding company for much of Luksic's industrial and mining operations, as well as its railroad and water concessions. By the end of the 1990s, the Luksic empire had expanded to include such significant operations as Indelqui SA, a leading copper products company in Argentina that had been expanding into the telecommunications sector, acquired in 1990. In 1992, the company joined Argentina's Perez Companc at the head of a consortium providing electric power generation and distribution to Buenos Aires.

Focused Copper Group for the New Century

During this same period, Fags had been building up new copper mining businesses. In 1983, the company acquired the concession for the Michilla copper mine. By the mid-1990s, that mine was producing more than 50,000 tons of copper per year. Fags also controlled another important mine, El Chacay, an underground operation. Then, in 1992, Fags joined a consortium to buy a controlling stake in the El Mince copper mine, together with Outokumpu Oy of Finland.

By then, Fags had already become the lead partner in developing a new and highly important mining concession. Fags had originally purchased the Los Pelambres concession in 1986, paying ARCO $6.2 million to acquire porphyry copper reserves estimated at more than 1.4 billion tons. The original life expectancy of the mine was placed at 30 years. Work began on developing the site in the early 1990s. Instead of constructing an underground mine, Fags opted for an open-mine model, allowing the Los Pelambres site to become one of the world's lowest-cost copper mines. Similar development began at a second, smaller site, El Tosoro, which featured total reserves of 178 million tons.

As the launch of production at the Los Pelambres site drew nearer, Luksic, by then joined by sons Andronico, Jr., Guillermo and Jean-Paul, began taking steps to streamline the operation. In 1996, the Luksics created a new holding company, Quinenco, which took over most of the family's industrial and financial holdings. The Luksic group held a 65 percent stake in Quinenco, with the remainder owned by Fags.

Fags now concentrated its efforts on developing the low-cost Los Pelambros and El Tosoro sites. In 1997, the company announced its decision to shut down the El Chacay underground site. By 1999, the company, which adopted the name Antofagasta plc that year, had launched production at Los Pelambros, ramping up to full production by 2001. At the same time, construction began on the El Tosoro site, which launched production in 2002.

By the end of 2003, Antofagasta had emerged as one of the world's largest focused copper mining groups, with a total production that topped 427,000 tons. At the same time, the company was riding the crest of the copper pricing cycle—driven in part by the surge in demand from China and other Asian markets—which boosted its total revenues from just $185 million in 1998 to more than $1 billion in 2003. In that year, Antofagasta sold its stake in Quinenco to the Luksic Group.

Antofagasta successfully boosted the life expectancy of the Los Pelambros site to 50 years in early 2004. The company had also launched a series of exploration operations in Chile and Peru in order to develop future copper reserves. Meanwhile, the company expanded its water concession in the region, paying

$194 million to acquire the water rights and distribution and treatment concession for the Antofagasta region in December 2003. Soon after, in March 2004, the company's rise in revenues earned it a spot on the prestigious FTSE 100 index of the London Stock Exchange. With more than 100 years in Chile's northern region, Antofagasta had repositioned itself as a major player in the global copper market.

Principal Subsidiaries

Aguas de Antofagasta S.A. (Chile); Antofagasta Minerals S.A. (Chile); Antofagasta Railway Company plc (UK); Chilean Northern Mines Limited (UK); Empresa Ferroviaria Andina S.A. (Bolivia; 50%); Forestal S.A. (Chile); Minera Anaconda Perú S.A.; Minera El Tesoro (Chile; 61%); Minera Los Pelambres (Chile; 60%); Minera Michilla S.A. (Chile; 74.2%); Servicios de Transportes Integrados Limitada (Chile); Train Ltda.

Principal Competitors

Samancor Ltd.; CESBRA; Corporacion Nacional Del Cobre De Chile, Codelco; Gordo y Cia Eulogio; Empresa Nacional de Mineria; Cia Minera El Indio; American Pacific Honduras Incorporated S.A.; Cia Minera Huaron S.A.; Empresa Minera de Mantos Blancos S.A.

Further Reading

Blakemore, Harry, *From the Pacific to La Paz,* London: Lester Crook Academic Publishing, 1989.

Bream, Rebecca, "Gains in Copper Turn Investors on to Antofagasta," *Financial Times,* February 19, 2004, p. 21.

Cave, Freiderike Tiesenhausen, "Downbeat Reaction to Antofagasta Data," *Financial Times,* July 28, 2004, p. 20.

Conway, Edmund, "The Andean Ascent to the FTSE," *Daily Telegraph,* February 21, 2004.

——, "Antofagasta Makes Its Debut in the Top Flight," *Daily Telegraph,* March 10, 2004.

John, Peter, and Kevin Morrison, "Antofagasta Benefits from China Sales," *The Financial Times,* March 10, 2004, p. 22.

Millman, Joel, "Follow the Philosophy of the Ant," *Forbes,* October 12, 1992, p. 132.

Spence, Bruce, "Luksic Open to Selling Part of Mining Interests—Chile," *Business News Americas,* March 15, 2004.

Yafie, Roberta C., "Antofagasta Stays Upstream," *American Metal Market,* September 6, 2000, p. 1.

—M.L. Cohen

Ask Jeeves, Inc.

5858 Horton Street, Suite 350
Emeryville, California 94608
U.S.A.
Telephone: (510) 985-7400
Fax: (510) 985-7412
Web site: http://www.ask.com

Public Company
Incorporated: 1996
Employees: 306
Sales: $107.29 million (2003)
Stock Exchanges: NASDAQ
Ticker Symbol: ASKJ
NAIC: 541990 All Other Professional, Scientific and
   Technical Services; 518111 Internet Service
   Providers; 541512 Computer Systems Design Services

Ask Jeeves, Inc. owns a number of information retrieval web properties, or search engines, that allow users to pose questions in plain language rather than by using keywords. The company's web properties include Ask.com, AJKids.com, Ask.co.uk, Excite .com, IWon.com, Maxonline.com, MySearch.com, MyWay.com, MyWebSearch.com, and Teoma.com. Ask Jeeves generates revenue by directing users to advertiser-supported web sites and by syndicating its search technology to third-party web sites.

Origins

Ask Jeeves was incorporated in June 1996, nearly a year before the company established itself as a pioneer on the Internet. Its founders, software developer David Warthen and venture capitalist Garrett Gruener, were intent on creating a product innovative in large part due to its simplicity of use. The pair began developing a new type of search engine, one that would respond to queries phrased in complete sentences rather than posed by keywords. In April 1997, Warthen and Gruener launched the first natural language search engine on their web site Ask.com, offering a service that the entrepreneurs hoped would attract users, which, in turn, would attract paying advertisers.

Ask Jeeves's novel and simple search engine proved popular shortly after its introduction. The company, like the operators of other search engines, wanted to create the most practical and relevant tool to help users navigate the Web. Search engines served as gateways to other sites offering information, products, and services—the conduit through which many Internet searchers passed to get where they wanted to go. By creating a popular destination that handled a high volume of traffic, Warthen and Gruener could command fees from the corporate web sites their search engine revealed to customers. Ask Jeeves, emerging as the first search engine capable of responding to natural language questions, found a receptive audience among Internet users, giving Warthen and Gruener the leverage to court advertising dollars. In October 1998, Ask Jeeves reached 300,000 searches per day, a figure that extended to one million by May 1999 and two million by October 1999. The company's cartoon mascot, a portly butler based on the English valet in P.G. Wodehouse novels, was a ubiquitous fixture on the Internet by the end of the 1990s.

Ask Jeeves took advantage of its recognition by completing an initial public offering (IPO) of stock, exposing the company to the public spotlight. The IPO, completed in July 1999, was a spectacular success, ranking at the time as the third most successful first day performance in business history. The company by this point was led by Robert W. Wrubel, who was appointed president in May 1998 and chief executive officer in November 1999. Wrubel, who held various executive positions at an educational software company, Knowledge Adventure, Inc., before joining Ask Jeeves, ushered the company through its public debut and presided over one of the greatest success stories of Internet-related business in the late 1990s. The company's stock value soared, rising as high as $190 per share in 1999, the same year Ask Jeeves launched its first national advertising campaign. The campaign, intended to create a national brand, was far-reaching, exemplifying "the excesses of the dot-com era," as *Forbes* noted in its February 3, 2003 issue. The company's branding campaign included sticking Ask Jeeves logos on apples and bananas. It entailed sending a troupe of individuals dressed as butlers to business districts, where resemblances of the company's icon were seen at popular lunch locations.

The heady mood pervading Ask Jeeves headquarters during the late 1990s was typified in areas other than the company's wide-ranging advertising campaign. The company leased expansive new office space, adding tens of thousands of square feet to its existing property holdings. Ask Jeeves also expanded internationally, launching Ask Jeeves UK as a joint venture with two British media companies in December 1999. The company completed several acquisitions as well, purchasing Net Effect Systems, Inc. in November 1999. Net Effect provided live help service to corporate web sites, enabling companies to communicate with their customers with real-time text messaging. In February 2000, Ask Jeeves acquired Direct Hit Technologies, Inc., a company whose technology aggregated and organized online content.

Collapse Beginning in 1999

As Ask Jeeves expanded and its natural language online services grew increasingly popular, the company's revenues increased exponentially. Ask Jeeves generated $23,000 in sales in 1997, $800,000 in 1998, $22 million in 1999, and $58 million in 2000. Profits, however, failed to materialize amid the energetic revenue growth. The company sustained annual net losses that reached $675 million by 2001. Perhaps more disheartening to Wrubel and his executive team, investors were losing faith in the company, causing Ask Jeeves's stock value to plummet severely. From a high of $190 per share in 1999, the company's stock began spiraling downward, falling to just $.86 per share by 2002. The company was in trouble, but before its share price reached its nadir, sweeping changes were made to arrest its spectacular fall. Ask Jeeves's efforts to effect a turnaround began in earnest in December 2000, an occasion marked by the arrival of a new chief executive officer.

A. George "Skip" Battle, an Ask Jeeves board member since 1998, was named chief executive officer at a critical juncture in the company's development. "The product offering wasn't developed very well," he explained in a February 3, 2003 interview with *Forbes,* commenting on his impression of Ask Jeeves when he took the helm. "We were very badly organized," he added. In the years before his appointment as chief executive officer, Battle was in semi-retirement, having left Anderson Consulting in 1995 after working for the company for 27 years. He faced a considerable challenge at Ask Jeeves, charged with reviving what had once been one of the great success stories of the late 1990s. When Battle arrived, the company began streamlining its operations in an effort to increase revenues, reduce costs, and realign the company for a more stable future. Battle replaced most of the company's senior management and reduced the company's payroll by over 50 percent in a three-year period following his arrival. Perhaps the most important accomplishment of Battle's tenure occurred in September 2001, when the company addressed the technological flaws in its search engine.

During the early years of the new decade, the novelty of a natural language search engine had faded. Ask Jeeves had pioneered the concept, but by the time the company's stock value began to shrink, it was joined by a number of competitors with natural language search engines, most notably Google Inc. Of critical importance to a search engine's popularity was its effectiveness, its ability to produce relevant results to the query posed by the user. The technology employed at the company's web sites, which included Ask.com, Ajkids.com, and DirectHit .com, produced results that were at times irrelevant, compounding the company's organizational problems and its over-zealous marketing efforts. Battle knew the company's technology needed to be revamped, and in September 2001 he attempted to correct the problem with an acquisition. Ask Jeeves purchased a Piscataway, New Jersey-based company named Teoma Technologies, Inc., an acquisition that was credited with injecting new life into Ask Jeeves.

Teoma possessed the search technology that helped Ask Jeeves launch a comeback. Teoma was a small company founded by nine professors from Rutgers University who focused on creating a mathematically based solution that could produce the most relevant search results. The technology they developed centered on a ranking system that listed web sites according to how many other pages linked to the same subject, a system that represented an improvement over Ask Jeeves's existing technology. At the time the acquisition was completed, Ask Jeeves ranked as the 17th most visited web property, receiving more than 14 million unique visitors a month. With the addition of Teoma's technology, which was integrated into Ask.com in December 2001, the company hoped to expand its reach on the Web.

Posting Its First Profit in 2002

Few other Internet-related companies who collapsed at the dawn of the 21st century were able to mount a comeback, but Ask Jeeves responded to failure with a demonstration of strength. With its operations realigned and with the incorporation of Teoma's search technology, the company gradually emerged as a profitable, growing enterprise. In 2001, as the company focused on staging a turnaround, its revenues dropped 45 percent, falling to $32 million. In 2002, buoyed by the integration of Teoma's technology and the addition of a sponsored links service with Google, the company's revenues swelled to $74 million. The increase in sales was encouraging, but the most impressive achievement of the year was the company's first profit. In the final fiscal quarter of 2002, Ask Jeeves posted $2 million in net income.

The first signs of a turnaround in 2002 were confirmed in 2003, as Ask Jeeves again stood as one of the most impressive performers on Wall Street. Internet marketing represented an estimated $3 billion business during the early years of the decade, and Ask Jeeves attracted the attention of investors who were intent on sharing in the riches. In 2003, the company was the 51st best-performing stock on NASDAQ, ranking ahead of 3,178 other companies traded on the exchange. The company's stock value rose from the depths of $.86 per share, increasing in value more than 500 percent during 2003. As Ask Jeeves recovered its balance and began to stride forward, Battle stepped aside as chief executive officer and accepted the post of chairman of the board. Steve Berkowitz, who joined Ask Jeeves in May 2001, was selected to take over day-to-day manage-

---

Key Dates:

1996: Ask Jeeves is founded.
1997: The Ask.com web site is launched.
1999: Ask Jeeves completes its initial public offering of stock.
2000: Direct Hit Technologies, Inc. is acquired.
2001: Teoma Technologies, Inc. is acquired.
2004: Interactive Search Holding is acquired.

---

ment, his challenge being to maintain the company's startling resurgence.

The beginning of Berkowitz's tenure was highlighted by an acquisition that rivaled the purchase of Teoma Technologies. By the spring of 2004, Ask Jeeves was ranked, according to Forrester Research, as the fastest growing search property on the Internet. The company, after recording $26 million in net income in 2003, had established its first genuinely stable business foundation and Berkowitz and Battle were committed to building on that base. In May 2004, after a 1,600 percent increase in the company's stock during the previous two years, the pair engineered a signal acquisition, one that promised to double the company's market share. The company was Interactive Search Holding, an Irvington, New York-based enterprise that owned a portfolio of web sites, including Iwon.com, MySearch.com, and Excite.com.

The acquisition of Interactive Search Holding provided a tremendous boost to Ask Jeeves's business, fueling confidence that it faced a promising future. The deal was valued at an estimated $343 million, bringing together two companies of roughly the same size. During the fourth quarter of 2003, Ask Jeeves performed 680 million searches, while Interactive Search Holding performed 700 million searches. Combined, the companies controlled 7 percent of the Internet search market, doubling Ask Jeeves's share of the market. As the company prepared for its future, it hoped to narrow the large lead its competitors held. The two largest companies, Google and Yahoo, controlled 35 percent and 27 percent of the Internet search market, respectively. Microsoft's MSN Network and Time Warner's America Online (AOL) followed, with Ask Jeeves occupying the fifth position.

Principal Subsidiaries

Ask Jeeves Internet Limited; Ask Jeeves International, Inc.; Ask Jeeves (Jersey) Limited; The Ask Jeeves U.K. Partnership.

Principal Competitors

America Online, Inc.; Google Inc.; Yahoo! Inc.

Further Reading

"Ask Jeeves Is Acquiring Interactive Search Holding, Which Counts Excite Among Its Brands, for Around $343 Million," *Internet Magazine,* June 2004, p. 10.

"Ask Jeeves Makes Its First Buy," *San Francisco Business Times,* November 19, 1999, p. 11.

Carrel, Lawrence, "Ask Jeeves, and Ye Shall Receive," *SmartMoney .com,* March 4, 2004, p. 34.

Dolan, Kerry A., "Ask Jeeves Still Answering Questions," *Forbes,* February 3, 2003, p. 45.

Karpinski, Richard, "Search Tool Uses English," *InternetWeek,* March 29, 1999, p. 19.

Mathewson, James, "What Makes a Good Search Engine?," *Computer User,* April 2003, p. 32.

Rynecki, David, "Seeking Answers on Ask Jeeves," *Fortune,* May 17, 2004, p. 180.

—Jeffrey L. Covell

Autoliv, Inc.

World Trade Center
Klarabergsviadukten 70
Section E, Box 70381
Stockholm
Sweden
Telephone: +46-8-587-206-00
Fax: +46-8-411-70-25
Web site: http://www.autoliv.com

Public Company
Incorporated: 1996
Employees: 38,900
Sales: SEK 38.14 billion ($5.3 billion) (2003)
Stock Exchanges: New York Chicago Stockholm
Ticker Symbol: ALV
NAIC: 334519 Other Measuring and Controlling Device
    Manufacturing; 336399 All Other Motor Vehicle Parts
    Manufacturing; 421120 Motor Vehicle Supplies and
    New Parts Wholesalers

Autoliv, Inc. is the largest producer of automotive safety equipment in the world. Its product lineup, manufactured at facilities in nearly 30 countries, includes air bags, seatbelts, child seats, and electronics. The company estimates these products save 20,000 lives a year. The company was formed by the 1997 merger of Sweden's Autoliv AB with U.S. air bag pioneer Morton ASP.

Origins

Autoliv, Inc. is a spinoff of the Swedish company Autoliv AB, an early pioneer of seatbelts for automobiles in the 1950s. The company developed retractor belts and air bag inflators in the late 1960s.

About the same time, another company, ASP, was pioneering air bag technology in the United States. (Autoliv would merge with ASP in 1997.) Autoliv began testing air bags in the United States in the late 1970s.

Gränges Weda AB, a manufacturer of seatbelt retractors, bought Autoliv AB in 1974. Electrolux acquired Gränges in 1980, and renamed it Electrolux Autoliv four years later.

Over the next decade and a half, Autoliv acquired related businesses in Sweden (Klippan Italia S.p.A.), Great Britain (Britax Overseas Ltd.; it also had operations in Germany and Australia), Germany (Autoflug Sicherheitstechnik GmbH), and India (IFB Industries). It also formed joint ventures with partners in Japan (Fuji Kiko, NSK), South Korea (Suskan Life Ind), and France (SNPE).

The company developed an automatic seatbelt in the late 1980s to satisfy a U.S. mandate for passive restraint systems.

Expanding Air Bag Technology in the 1990s

Autoliv began producing its own air bag inflators in bulk in 1991. It introduced the first non-azide inflator the next year and also began producing its own air bag electronics. A number of developments in side airbags were rolled out during the 1990s.

Autoliv produced nearly 30 million seatbelt units and more than one million air bag systems in 1993. By this time, Autoliv had manufacturing operations in ten countries concentrated in Europe, which accounted for 91 percent of sales. It also was involved in more than a dozen joint ventures. The company had 4,400 employees. Seatbelt products accounted for three-quarters of revenues, which rose 51 percent in 1993 to SEK 5.3 billion. Autoliv was Europe's largest manufacturer of auto safety equipment.

Toward the end of 1994, Autoliv opened a new plant in Sweden to produce hybrid gas generators for air bags. They were less expensive to manufacture and were safer, since they deployed in two stages, the first of which corrected the occupant's sitting position.

Autoliv continued to create global partnerships, forming a seatbelt joint venture in the Philippines with Qualibrand, a local company, and Autobelt of Malaysia in 1995. At about the same time, Autoliv launched a joint venture with Nanjing Honguang Airborne Equipment to produce steel safety belt parts in China. Also in 1995, the company acquired 49 percent of Isodelta SA of France, Europe's fourth leading steering wheels producer. A pair of Dutch auto parts suppliers, Hammarverken of Vaxjo and Hassleholms Automotive, were acquired from United Parts Group NV in 1996.

1997 Morton ASP Merger

The company went public on the Stockholm stock market on June 9, 1994, as Autoliv AB. It was one of the country's most successful flotations of the year. Three years later Autoliv AB merged with U.S. air bag pioneer Morton ASP to form Autoliv, Inc. Morton International, based in Chicago, was selling its auto safety division to concentrate on its salt and chemicals business.

The new company was the world's largest air bag producer, with sales of SEK 20 billion ($3 billion) and 15,000 employees. Although incorporated in the United States, the company's headquarters were located in Sweden. Former Autoliv AB President and CEO Gunnar Bark was the new company's first chairman, and ASP President Fred Musone was named chief executive officer.

Europe still accounted for more than half of sales. Autoliv had acquired a leading European steering wheel manufacturer, France's Isodelta, in 1995. This opened a new market to Autoliv and allowed it to begin producing steering wheels with integrated air bags.

In the late 1990s, Autoliv was working on ways to adjust the deployment pattern of air bags to reduce the potential for them causing passenger injury.

Globalization for the New Millennium

In 1999, Autoliv acquired a 50 percent interest in Norma AS, an Estonian factory that had been making seatbelts since 1971. Before then, it had produced toys, noted London's *Financial Times*. Norma had revenues of EEK 482.7 million ($31.6 million) in 1998; nearly 90 percent of its production went to Russian and Eastern European car manufacturers. Autoliv

moved some of its steering wheel operations to Tunisia in 1999 and also opened a $10 million plant in Turkey.

Autoliv bought the seatbelt operations of Japanese auto parts supplier NSK in 2000, paying an initial $72 million plus a later performance-based bonus. The unit had sales of about $300 million a year and operations in the United States, Mexico, and Thailand as well as Japan, where Autoliv had until then not made its presence felt. Autoliv announced a joint venture with Korean parts supplier Mando Corporation in November 2000. Autoliv also had operations in the growing Chinese auto market. It formed a new joint venture in northern China in 2002. The next year, the company bought out Japanese steering wheel manufacturer Nippon Steering Industries, which had been created as a joint venture between its own subsidiary Autoliv-Isumi and Japanese parts maker KIW. In 2003, Autoliv expanded its Malaysian plant to 14,500 square feet.

Autoliv made an important U.S. acquisition in 2000, buying OEA of Arapahoe County, Colorado, for $306 million (including $100 million in assumed debt). OEA produced propellant-actuated devices used to deploy air bags. It had been founded in 1957 as Ordnance Engineering Associates Inc. by Turkish immigrant Ahmed Kafadar. At the time of the acquisition, OEA had sales of about $250 million a year and 1,700 employees around the world; its shares were traded on the New York Stock Exchange. Autoliv had been one of OEA's largest customers.

Autoliv's revenues were $4.1 billion in 2000 with net income of $170 million. The company began shrinking its workforce in the United States and Europe as it shifted production to lower-cost areas. An air bag cushion plant in Utah, where the company employed 5,000 people, was relocated to Mexico in 2001. After losing 10 percent of its Utah workforce, Autoliv was still the state's largest manufacturer, according to the *Salt Lake Tribune*. The OEA plant in Colorado closed in 2003. Autoliv also began to reduce the number of countries in which it had operations, more than 30 at the time.

Visteon Corporation, a spinoff of Ford Motor Company, sold Autoliv its Restraint Electronics air bag sensor business for $25 million in 2002. The unit employed 1,000 workers in Ontario and 200 engineers in Michigan. The next year, Autoliv acquired Nippon Steering Industries and the remainder of shares in European air bag inflator supplier Livbag.

Autoliv's Utah operations received a boost when a group of ten automakers committed to install head-curtain air bags in half of their models by the model year 2008. These air bags, designed to reduce head injuries in side-impact collisions, were already available as an option; Autoliv sold less than ten million units in 2001.

Revenues were $5.3 billion (SEK 38.1 billion) in 2003. Analysts were impressed that the company managed 19 percent revenue growth even as U.S. vehicle production fell 2 percent. Air bags and related products accounted for nearly 70 percent of sales, with seatbelts and associated items making up the remainder.

Autoliv ASP announced an expansion of its Whitley County, Indiana facilities in July 2004. The project was expected to more than triple employment there, adding 678 jobs by

<table>
<tr><td colspan="2">Key Dates:</td></tr>
<tr><td>1956:</td><td>Autoliv AB introduces an automotive seatbelt.</td></tr>
<tr><td>1968:</td><td>ASP pioneers air bag technology.</td></tr>
<tr><td>1974:</td><td>Gränges Weda AB acquires Autoliv AB.</td></tr>
<tr><td>1980:</td><td>Electrolux acquires Gränges.</td></tr>
<tr><td>1984:</td><td>Gränges Weda is renamed Electrolux Autoliv.</td></tr>
<tr><td>1994:</td><td>The company goes public as Autoliv AB; Electrolux sells shares.</td></tr>
<tr><td>1997:</td><td>Autoliv AB merges with Morton ASP to form Autoliv, Inc.</td></tr>
<tr><td>2000:</td><td>NSK's seatbelt business is acquired.</td></tr>
<tr><td>2002:</td><td>Ford spinoff Visteon Restraint Electronics is acquired.</td></tr>
<tr><td>2003:</td><td>Nippon Steering Industries is acquired.</td></tr>
</table>

2009. The new capacity was earmarked for producing inflatable curtains, or side-impact air bags.

Night vision had been one project in development since 2000. It was expected to hit the market in 2006. The company also was working on an automatic accident notification system, as well as air bag systems for the hood and windscreen areas of cars to protect pedestrians in the event of an accident.

Principal Subsidiaries

Autoliv AB; Autoliv ASP, Inc.

Principal Competitors

Delphi Corporation; Honeywell International; Key Safety Systems, Inc.; Takata Corporation; TRW Automotive Holdings Corporation.

Further Reading

Accola, John, "OEA to Be Bought by Swedish Firm; Manufacturer of Air-Bag Triggers Bought by One of Its Biggest Customers," *Denver Rocky Mountain News,* March 14, 2000, p. 8B.

Arellano, Kristi, "Autoliv Factory to Close," *Denver Post,* November 24, 2002, p. K3.

"Autoliv and Korean Auto Parts Supplier Form JV," *Nordic Business Report,* November 8, 2000.

"Autoliv Buys Seat-Belt Ops for Initial 72 Mln USD from Japan's NSK," *AFX Europe,* February 25, 2000.

"Autoliv: Components Industry Glamour Stock," *Automotive Components Analyst,* June 1, 1994.

"Autoliv Develops New Airbag Technology," *Dagens Industri,* December 7, 1994, p. 7.

"Autoliv Inc. Acquires Steering Wheel Operations in Japan," *Nordic Business Report,* May 16, 2003.

"Autoliv Jettisons OEA," *National Post* (Canada), December 30, 2000, p. D2.

"Autoliv of Sweden Becomes Sole Owner of Airbags International," *Dagens Industri,* August 2, 1994, p. 18.

"Autoliv Opens Turkish Plant; Will Make Seatbelts, Airbags, Steering Wheels," *AFX Europe,* December 1, 1999.

"Autoliv Sets Up Chinese Joint Venture with Maw Hung Industrial Corp.," *AFX European Focus,* September 11, 2002.

Brown-Humes, Christopher, "Electrolux Plans Global Share Offering in Autoliv," *Financial Times* (London), May 11, 1984, p. 31.

"Electrolux Autoliv of Sweden and Fuji Kiko of Japan Have Formed a Jointly-Owned Subsidiary Called Fuji-Autoliv," *Dagens Industri,* May 15, 1987, p. 7.

"Electrolux Autoliv of Sweden Is Launching an Automatic Car Safety Belt with a Two-Point Suspension System and It Sees the USA As Its Main Market," *Veckans Affarer,* May 6, 1986, p. 6.

Hinds, Gary, "Swedish Auto Safety Device Maker to Reduce U.S. Staff," *Standard Examiner* (Ogden, Utah), January 18, 2001.

Isaac, David, "Autoliv Inc., Stockholm, Sweden; Demand for Car Safety Gear Has It in the Financial Fast Lane," *Investor's Business Daily,* March 9, 2004, p. A9.

Leib, Jeffrey, "Air-Bag Giant Wants OEA; Autoliv Offers $306 Million," *Denver Post,* March 14, 2000, p. C1.

Mateja, Jim, "Myth of Smart Air Bag May Soon Become a Reality," *Chicago Tribune,* Bus. Sec., May 12, 1997, p. 6.

"Merger to Create Biggest Maker of Air Bags," *New York Times,* October 1, 1996, p. D4.

Mitchell, Lesley, "Air-Bag Plan a Big Boost for Utah's Autoliv," *Salt Lake Tribune,* December 5, 2003.

——, "Ogden, Utah-Based Air Bag Maker Pins Hopes on New Product," *Salt Lake Tribune,* June 14, 2003.

——, "Swedish Air Bag Manufacturer to Move Plant from Ogden, Utah to Mexico," *Salt Lake Tribune,* August 17, 2001.

"New Airbags Will Protect Pedestrians," *Waikato Times* (Hamilton, New Zealand), Motoring Sec., November 2, 2001, p. MT18.

Rimlinger, Craig, "680 Jobs in Whitley Expansion; State Pledging $11.6 Million to Autoliv Plan," *Journal-Gazette* (Ft. Wayne, Ind.), July 28, 2004, p. 1A.

"A Secured Future," *Financial Times* (London), February 24, 1998, p. 7.

"Sweden's Autoliv to Acquire 49% Stake in Steering Wheel Maker," *Dagens Industri,* August 3, 1995, p. 7.

"Swedish Autoliv to Take Stake in Seat Belt Maker Norma," *Estonian News Agency,* July 6, 1999.

"Visteon to Sell Air Bag Sensor Unit to Autoliv," *New York Times,* February 5, 2002, p. C12.

Yunus, Kamarul, "Autoliv Houses Malaysian Operations in New, Bigger Plant," *Business Times* (Malaysia), September 22, 2003, p. 1.

—Frederick C. Ingram

Avocent Corporation

4991 Corporate Drive
Huntsville, Alabama 35805
U.S.A.
Telephone: (256) 430-4000
Toll Free: (866) 286-2368
Fax: (256) 430-4030
Web site: http://www.avocent.com

Public Company
Incorporated: 2000
Employees: 719
Sales: $304.2 million (2003)
Stock Exchanges: NASDAQ
Ticker Symbol: AVCT
NAIC: 334119 Other Computer Peripheral Equipment
  Manufacturing

Avocent Corporation, based in Huntsville, Alabama, is the world's largest KVM (keyboard, video, and mouse) switch manufacturer. The switches, both analog and digital, are used to manage multiple computer servers. Rather than connecting a monitor, keyboard, and mouse to each server, system administrators can use a KVM switch to monitor a large number of computers, local and remote, from a single console, thus saving space, time, and money while providing better system management. Although most of the switches require a wired connection, Avocent also offers a wireless product that provides switching and A/V broadcasting capabilities between monitors, keyboards, mice, and audio devices up to 100 feet indoors. Avocent's switches and services are sold around the world. Major customers include Dell, Gateway, Hewlett-Packard, Intel, and Microsoft. Avocent is a public company trading on the NASDAQ.

Roots of the Company Dating to 1981

Avocent was formed in 2000 through the merger of Cybex Computer Products Corporation and Apex Inc., the two largest KVM switch companies in the world. The older of the two was Cybex, which was cofounded in Huntsville in 1981 by Remigius

G. Shatas. After earning a degree in mathematics from the University of Alabama in Huntsville in 1973, Shatas went to work in the space industry in Huntsville as a computer operator and later as a programmer at SCI Systems, Inc. Due to cutbacks in the space program he lost his position and had to take a programming job at a grommet factory 50 miles away, where he often had to work overnight in order not to interfere with daytime production runs, providing him with plenty of time on the road to think about striking out on his own. Finally, at age 29 he and some other programmers formed a consulting business. He developed his first product as a way to meet his own needs. Shatas was contracted to install computers at the Marshall Space Flight Center but the units were too big for the desk. Despite being told by engineers that it was impossible to locate the computer anywhere but on the desk, he came in one Saturday morning determined to find a way to hook up a computer to a monitor and keyboard 150 feet away. From that idea, several years later, would emerge the company's first product, the Extender.

Shatas's company was incorporated as Cybex Computer Products Corp. in 1981, but it was far from an immediate success. Two of the founders quit, but in 1982 a key employee, Robert Asprey, joined the company. He earned an engineering degree from New Mexico State University and served as manager of Management Information Systems at Teledyne Brown Engineering. Asprey formed a solid partnership with Shatas, possessing the engineering talent to make Shatas's ideas work. Shatas also was acting as the company's chief executive officer, but realized that administration was not his strong suit. In 1984 he recruited a friend, Steve Thornton, to serve on the Cybex board. Thornton was the best manager Shatas had known at his previous employer, had risen to the rank of vice-president, and was now looking to move on. When asked to join the board, Thornton suggested that Shatas hire him to run the company.

When Thornton took over as CEO Cybex was attempting to become involved in the development of specialized software, but by 1986 the field was overcrowded and Cybex began to focus on hardware accessories. In that year the company introduced the Extender, which Asprey then improved upon, extending its range to 600 feet and adding peripheral support features. A major turning point for Cybex occurred when a nuclear power

Company Perspectives:

Avocent's field proven KVM switching and connectivity solutions provide smarter access and simpler manageability for "real world" IT environments.

plant contacted the company, asking if it could find a way for one operator with a single keyboard and monitor to switch between two computers separated by 25 feet. The result was the company's first switching product, named the Commander. In 1989 Shatas and Asprey teamed up to invent the AutoBoot Commander, the first KVM switch that could boot up all the attached servers following a power outage.

In KVM switches Cybex had found a niche in the computer field and devoted all of its resources to exploiting it. Cybex enjoyed steady growth in the 1990s. Revenues improved from $8.5 million in 1993 to more than $12.8 million in 1994, while net income grew from $925,000 to $1.4 million. In 1995 Cybex went public, netting $32.6 million in an initial offering of stock. With some of this money the company was able to establish a European subsidiary, located in Ireland. Revenues topped the $25 million mark in 1996 and reached $82.2 million in 1999; net income grew to $12.4 million in 1999. Although a number of competitors had emerged in the KVM switch field, Cybex's greatest rival was Apex Inc.

Launching Apex in 1992

The man behind the foundation of Apex was Kevin J. Hafer. After high school he learned electronics in the U.S. Navy, and upon his discharge used this experience to become a computer technician. He became a manager at Harris Corp., a major electronics company, then in 1990 was named general manager at Apex Computer, a Seattle-area computer services company. One of his jobs at Apex was to maintain servers at Microsoft Corporation. Each server was connected to a separate monitor and keyboard, requiring employees to move from server to server to administer Microsoft's internal network. Like many others, Hafer realized that a more logical approach would have all of the servers available to a single keyboard, mouse, and monitor. In 1992 he convinced Apex's owner, Sterling Crum, to start a dedicated division to serve the network-management field. With a handful of engineers Hafer developed software that allowed one KVM console to monitor a multitude of servers. Because the switches freed servers from monitors and keyboards, they could now be stacked, leading to the development of integrated server cabinets with built-in KVM switches.

With Microsoft as its primary customer, Apex was spun off as Apex PC Solutions Inc. in early 1993. In May 1994 it added Compaq as a customer and subsequently discontinued its computer maintenance service business to focus on KVM switches and server cabinets. Revenues grew from $7.3 million in 1994 to $33.6 million in 1996; income during this period improved from $1 million to $3.6 million. In February 1997 Apex went public, netting $28.4 million in an initial offering of stock, and later in the year the company netted $30.3 million in a secondary offering. Sales continued to grow at a strong clip, totaling

$55.4 million in 1997 and $75.6 million in 1998, while income reached $10.5 million in 1997 and $15.7 million in 1998. With strong sales to original equipment manufacturers, Apex at this stage controlled a large share of the KVM switch market and had not yet begun to tap into the market of servers already installed in the field. Because its name caused some confusion in the marketplace about its products and services, the company in July 1999 shortened its name from Apex PC Solutions to Apex Inc. For the year, Apex would experience even stronger growth, with sales totaling $107.3 million and net income $21.2 million.

Cybex and Apex were the only two publicly traded companies in the KVM switch business and took turns as the leader in market share. Sometimes they even took customers from one another, such as Cybex winning Hewlett-Packard's business late in 1999. But each had particular strengths, Apex with original equipment makers such as Dell and Gateway, and Cybex with its overseas business, which accounted for 30 percent of revenues. In 2000 the rivals decided they would be better off joining forces, creating a larger company able to pursue opportunities that neither would be able to exploit on their own. In March 2000 a merger was announced. Under terms of the deal, which was accounted for as a purchase by Apex, Apex shareholders received a 55 percent stake in the combined company, to be named Avocent Corporation. But the new company would be located in Huntsville and Thornton would become president, chief executive officer, and chairman. Hafer, on the other hand, would walk away once the merger was consummated. The six-person board would be equally divided between Apex and Cybex appointments.

Avocent's expectation was that it would be able to offer broader network management solutions and target new and emerging fields, such as management systems used by application service providers and operators of "server farms." In general, Avocent was well positioned to benefit from a growing movement toward server-based computing. A major advance for the company took place in November 2000 with the introduction of the first digital switches, regarded as a significant advance over analog switches, which sometimes experienced distortion problems and were slower than the new devices. Moreover, digital switches were cheaper to manufacture, while at the same time fetched higher prices.

Avocent quickly took steps to strengthen its position in the marketplace through acquisitions. In November 2000 it agreed to buy Sunrise, Florida-based Equinox Systems for $57 million in cash. The addition of Equinox expanded Avocent's digital console management products to the Unix platform. Equinox also was strong in products and software that supported serial device connectivity, serving ISPs (Internet service providers) and ASPs (application service providers), two of the fastest growing markets for server management solutions.

Naming John R. Cooper CEO in 2002

After closing on the acquisition of Equinox in January 2001, Avocent would suffer through a difficult year, as a downturn in the economy caused many companies to postpone technology purchases. Conditions improved in 2002 and Avocent began to enjoy some strong sales for its digital switches. In March 2002

Key Dates:

1981: Cybex Computer Products Corp. is founded.
1992: Apex Inc. is launched as a division of Apex Computer.
1995: Cybex goes public.
1997: Apex goes public
2000: Cybex and Apex merge, forming Avocent.
2004: OSA Technologies is acquired.

Thornton stepped down as Avocent's president and CEO, turning over the posts to John R. Cooper, although he remained chairman of the board. Cooper had been on Avocent's board from the beginning and before that had served on the Cybex board of directors. Previously he had served as chief financial officer of ADTRAN, Inc., maker of telecommunications products. Also of note in 2002, Avocent acquired 2C Computing Inc. for $22.8 million in cash. 2C was founded by Shatas and Asprey in 1999 to develop switching technology for desktop PCs. In 2002 Avocent recorded revenues of $260.6 million and net income of $10.7 million.

In 2003 Avocent paid $7 million to acquire Soronti Inc., a Draper, Utah-based company that made an adapter that allowed IT managers to access older analog KVM switches remotely. Later in the year, Avocent agreed to acquire Crystal Link Technologies for $1.3 million in cash and stock. Based in Escondido, California, Crystal Link was a wireless technology firm, the addition of which was expected to help Avocent make its systems wireless, thus potentially eliminating a multitude of cabling needed to connect KVM switches to servers. Avocent completed its largest acquisition in April 2004, another deal intended to add to its technology, with the $100 million cash and stock purchase of OSA Technologies, which developed embedded management firmware and software for Intelligent Platform Management Interface (IPMI) products. OSA was less than four years old, founded by former Intel employees, but it was well advanced in creating products for IPMI—a specification created by heavyweights Intel, Hewlett-Packard, NEC, and Dell—which held out the promise of replacing cards that cost

$500 to $700 with silicon chips as cheap as $5 to provide remote server management. Dell was already committed to incorporating OSA's technology into its next generation of servers, a key factor in Avocent's desire to acquire the young San Jose, California-based company.

Avocent was committed to acquiring technology and expertise that would allow it to maintain a leadership position in its field. As the market for server management products increased, there was a strong likelihood that stronger competition would crop up. As technology spending began to increase at *Fortune* 1000 companies, Avocent saw its revenues jump to $304.2 million in 2003 and net income surpass $38.6 million. When the global economy improved, technology spending would increase even further, leading to more spending on servers and an increased need for Avocent's products and services. Clearly Avocent was determined to position itself for strong long-term growth while choking off competition before it could threaten its dominant position.

Principal Subsidiaries

OSA Technologies.

Principal Competitors

Belkin Corporation; Raritan Computer Inc.; Rose Electronics, Inc.

Further Reading

Baker, M. Sharon, "Fast-Growing Apex PC Solutions Files for IPO," *Puget Sound Business Journal,* December 20, 1996, p. 3.

Brooks, Rick, "Cybex Computer, Apex Agree to Merge in Stock Deal Valued at $1.08 Billion," *Wall Street Journal,* March 9, 2000, p. B10.

Browder, Seanna, "Apex PC Solutions: Serving the Servers," *Business Week,* June 1, 1998, p. 86.

Gondo, Nancy, "Huntsville, Alabama Tech Firm's Digital Strategy Keeps It Growing," *Investor's Business Daily,* February 25, 2003, p. A08.

Shinkle, Kirk, "Switch Maker Profits by Cutting the Clutter," *Investor's Business Daily,* December 4, 2003, p. A06.

—Ed Dinger

AVTOVAZ Joint Stock Company

36 Yuzhnoe Shosse
445633 Togliatti
Samara Region
Russia
Telephone: +7 (8482) 73-71-71
Fax: +7 (8482) 73-82-43
Web site: http://www.vaz.ru

Public Company
Incorporated: 1993
Employees: 118,000
Sales: RUB 107 billion (2003 est.)
Stock Exchanges: RTS (Moscow) Frankfurt Berlin London
NAIC: 336111 Automobile Manufacturing; 333319 Other Commercial and Service Industry Machinery Manufacturing; 336399 All Other Motor Vehicle Parts Manufacturing; 423110 Automobile and Other Motor Vehicle Merchant Wholesalers

AVTOVAZ Joint Stock Company, or OAO AVTOVAZ (Avtovaz), manufactures nearly three-quarters of the light automobiles sold in Russia, producing around 700,000 cars a year. State economic planners founded the company in the late 1960s in order to provide an affordable car for the Soviet citizen, and the so-called "Zhigulis" soon became a familiar icon of life in the U.S.S.R. They were exported to European countries under the brand name "Lada." Even after the fall of the communist system, Avtovaz's cars have retained their market leadership due to their affordability, familiarity, and simplicity of design. The company's best-selling models are the new Lada 110 line and the updated version of the classic Zhiguli. Avtovaz also offers the Samara sedan and the rugged all-wheel drive Niva truck. Since privatization in 1993, Avtovaz has been struggling to improve production efficiency, develop newer models, and gain control of distribution. The company employs about one-sixth of the city of Togliatti. Recently, Avtovaz entered an alliance with General Motors to produce an updated version of the Niva truck at a new facility in Togliatti.

A Car for the Soviet People: 1966–85

The Five-Year Plan for economic development in the U.S.S.R. during 1966–70 called for the construction of a new automobile factory. This factory would provide for the first large-scale production of light cars in the U.S.S.R., producing an accessible consumer vehicle for the Soviet people and their neighbors in the Communist bloc. In July 1966 the Central Committee of the Communist Party passed a resolution calling for a plant at a site on the Volga River about 800 kilometers east of Moscow. A completely new settlement was to be built here, replacing an older village that had been flooded by a recently constructed dam. The new city was named Togliatti after Palmiro Togliatti, a longtime secretary of the Italian Communist Party. The car factory would be known as the Volga Automotive Plant, or AvtoVAZ. Viktor Nikolaevich Polyakov, the deputy minister of the automobile industry in the USSR, was appointed general director of the concern.

Avtovaz signed an agreement to work with Fiat, the Italian carmaker, on design of the car and the factory. In early 1967 ground was broken at the site, even as Fiat engineers were still working on final plans for the plant. Among the first buildings to be finished were a cafeteria and a housing development for workers. The Avtovaz project was promoted as a dynamic feat of collective socialist effort, and it brought together youth work brigades and technical specialists from a wide area. The first assembly line in the factory became operable in 1970. On April 19 of that year, the first car rolled off the production line in Togliatti. It was a four-door compact vehicle closely modeled after the Fiat 124. Officially, it was known as the VAZ-2101, but the automotive magazine Za rulyem sponsored a "Name the Car" contest for the vehicle. The winning name was "Zhiguli," after a nearby mountain range.

In 1972 Avtovaz began production of two additional models: the VAZ-2102, a hatchback, and the VAZ-2103, a speedier, more powerful version of the Zhiguli. That year the factory and its supporting enterprises already employed 43,000 people, and the number surpassed 100,000 a few years later. By the end of 1973 all three production lines were up to capacity, turning out 660,000 cars a year. As the only significant employer in Togliatti, Avtovaz also accepted much of the responsi-

Company Perspectives:
Our mission is to consolidate AVTOVAZ's position as market leader in the Russian automotive industry for the long term, providing quality vehicles to Russian people at prices they can afford.

bility for making sure that general living amenities would be available to its workers, such as medical facilities, a school, a movie theater, and a cultural center.

Avtovaz sold its first car in Great Britain in 1973 and soon thereafter began making models with right-side steering wheels for the European market. Exported cars were sold under the name "Lada." The cars sold reasonably well abroad because of their low price. Foreign markets included Germany, France, Belgium, Hungary, and Turkey. Domestically, the car sold well because it faced practically no competition. But the Zhiguli developed a reputation for mechanical unreliability. According to the *Economist,* Russians joked that a new Zhiguli would run just fine once you took it apart and replaced any missing parts. The condition of the car depended on the whim of the workers on the assembly line. Nevertheless, the cars were easy to repair and spare parts were abundant.

In 1975 General Director Polyakov departed to be the minister of the automobile industry and was replaced by A.A. Zhitkov. Zhitkov oversaw the production of several new models in the late 1970s. The VAZ-2106, referred to as the "Six," was introduced in 1976 as a modernized version of the luxury 2103 Zhiguli. In 1977 the VAZ-2121, called the "Niva," began full-scale production in a newly built facility. This was the first car fully developed by Avtovaz engineers. The Niva was a four-wheel drive vehicle with off-road capabilities. It developed a far-flung following due to its proven ability to stand up in conditions ranging from the Arctic to the desert. Decades later, an Australian fan club was still organizing periodical Niva races through the Outback. In 1979 the classic Zhiguli was updated with the introduction of the VAZ-2105 model, followed by the VAZ-2107 rear-wheel drive sedan in 1982 and the VAZ-2104, an updated version of the hatchback model, in 1984.

Avtovaz also introduced its first front-wheel drive vehicle in 1984, the VAZ-2108 three-door hatchback. This was the first member of the "Samara" family of Western-style sedans. In 1987 the Samara line was enhanced with a five-door version, the VAZ-2109. A new complex was constructed for the Samara line, but the classic Zhiguli still accounted for most sales of Avtovaz vehicles.

Economic Experimentation in the Late 1980s

By the mid-1980s seven production divisions had been established to provide for all stages of automobile production, including foundry, sub-assembly, small press, final assembly, machine building, and precision tooling. Avtovaz was a very profitable enterprise, since the Zhiguli was practically the only car available to the average Soviet citizen. But Avtovaz's production lines were now 15 years out of date and its vehicle models had not changed much since the first Zhiguli in 1970. As

the reformist doctrines of perestroika and glasnost were being formulated, Avtovaz became the site for experimentation in a more flexible form of socialist enterprise. Starting with the 12th Five-Year Plan of 1986–90, Avtovaz was to be run according to the "three pillars" of independence, paying its own way, and economic accountability. The paper stream of dictation from above was to be reduced, giving onsite managers more decision-making authority. Percentage deductions from profits were also set several years ahead of time, allowing for more stability in planning. Workers could receive bonuses for exceptional work. In return, Avtovaz would introduce new models on a regular schedule, pay for all development from its own profits, and begin replacing its production lines in order to improve efficiency and export competitiveness.

But it was difficult to reform one piece of the economy without restructuring the whole system. Avtovaz had the money to pay for development, but it could not secure the supplies it needed because its subcontractors still operated the old way, waiting for government approval before moving ahead with anything. For the first time ever, Avtovaz had to take cars off the production lines in early 1986 because of a lack of required components. The company was as entangled as ever with government regulators, trying to get the bureaucrats to approve needed projects at Avtovaz subcontractors. In April 1986 A. Yasinsky, Avtovaz's director of economics and planning, wrote in *Pravda* that "ministries and departments are still burdened by past rules and procedures that are hampering the experiment's effectiveness."

Turbulent Transition to a Market Economy: 1991–98

In the early 1990s the economic experiments of the late 1980s were subsumed by the complete collapse of the Soviet system. Avtovaz was better prepared than some enterprises to compete in a free market since it was experienced in carrying on an export business in consumer goods. But its production lines were as inefficient as ever, its workforce was bloated, and its vehicles were outdated compared to the competition. It took about 450 man-hours to make a Lada, compared to 15 hours for a Toyota. A typical capitalist firm would lay off many employees, but for Avtovaz to do so would cause unacceptable devastation and unrest in Togliatti since the firm employed about one-quarter of the workforce. Avtovaz's costs were particularly high because the company was a major provider of social services in Togliatti, such as housing, medical care, and retirement pensions.

Substantial capital investment would be needed to ensure Avtovaz's long-term survival. For this reason, Avtovaz management promoted the idea of finding a foreign investor during discussions on how to privatize the company. Shortly before Communism collapsed in 1991, the company had hired the U.S. firms Bear Stearns and Deloitte Touche to value the company and produce accounts that a Westerner could understand. Meanwhile, Avtovaz was negotiating with Fiat to buy a 30 percent stake in the company. But this initial attempt to produce Westernized accounts was never completed.

Avtovaz employees voted to turn the company into a joint stock company effective January 1, 1993. The enterprises of the Volga Automotive Plant Association became known as AO "AVTOVAZ," or AVTOVAZ Joint Stock Company (later

Key Dates:

1966: A government decree calls for the creation of an automobile factory.
1970: The first "Zhiguli" sedan is produced at the Avtovaz plant.
1977: The "Niva" truck is introduced.
1986: A new form of socialist enterprise is tried to give Avtovaz managers more flexibility.
1993: Avtovaz is transformed into a joint stock company.
1998: The devaluation of the ruble and a crackdown on criminal activity improve sales at Avtovaz.
2001: Avtovaz signs a joint venture agreement with General Motors.

changed to OAO "AVTOVAZ"). Under the original privatization plan, employees would get 51 percent of the capital—one-quarter would be auctioned off to Russian citizens and most of the remainder would go to corporate investors. Yet by the mid-1990s, after the confused whirlwind of Soviet privatization, most of the company seemed to be held by entities controlled by Avtovaz management and by the government, although the exact ownership was unclear. Vladimir V. Kadannikov, the head of Avtovaz since 1988, became general director and chairman of the board of directors of the new company. He had several decades of experience at Avtovaz, having started out as a shop floor apprentice in his youth.

Kadannikov had been abroad for training in the automotive industry, but he asserted that his foreign experience was of little use in the chaotic Russian economy of the early 1990s. "If an executive who has worked under market conditions all his life were brought to our factory, he would commit hara-kiri on the third day," he told the *Moscow News* in 1992. Many Russian firms were stuck in the habits of the Soviet era. They were used to shipping goods according to government plan, without regard for payment, which led to a complex network of mutual debt. Some firms started demanding prepayment for goods, which caused cash flow problems at Avtovaz since it could not demand prepayment on automobile sales. Occasionally, parts for the production line had to be flown in by helicopter at the last minute. Kadannikov summed up the advantages and disadvantages of the new situation for the *Moscow News:* "The old Kadannikov had to waste time and rack his brains in order to make central authorities believe he was following their instructions exactly. In actual fact, they were followed only insofar as was necessary to avoid harm to the factory. At the same time I always knew Avtovaz would get everything: funds, equipment, supplies. Now in order to get components from our former suppliers, we have to give away 190,000 cars a year for barter."

Avtovaz continued the search for a foreign investor and in 1993 hired PricewaterhouseCoopers to prepare financial accounts to international standards. It was estimated that there were only 76 cars for every 1,000 Russians, which meant that Avtovaz had a lot of room to grow and provide returns on investment. But Fiat soon announced that it had lost interest in buying a stake in the Russian company. As a result, Russian automobile moguls set up the All-Russian Automobile Alliance (AVVA) in 1993 as

a consortium with ambitious plans to collect funds and build a new factory in Togliatti. Boris Berezovsky, one of the most notorious "oligarchs" of early Russian capitalism, was a leader of the alliance. The alliance collected funds from many small investors but never raised enough to fund a factory; instead it invested in development of new vehicles. AVVA became both a subsidiary of and a major shareholder in Avtovaz. Berezovsky, meanwhile, founded LogoVAZ to distribute Avtovaz vehicles in the Moscow area and made a fortune in the mid-1990s with a string of dealerships.

Early in 1994 Avtovaz had to stop production and send more than 100,000 workers on leave due to a shortage of raw materials. Eventually it used revenue from exports to supply the needed goods. But cash flow was in very short supply; like many Russian firms, Avtovaz fell months behind in paying its workers. This led to a strike in the fall of 1994. Because of these difficulties, production fell to a low of about 500,000 vehicles in 1994 and 1995. Imports of used foreign cars also were challenging Avtovaz. High import tariffs protected Zhiguli sales to some degree. Imports were also officially capped but many vehicles were being imported illegally. In early 1996 Kadannikov was named first deputy prime minister in charge of economics under President Boris Yeltsin. He was at the position for less than a year, but the connections he developed in the Kremlin were advantageous to Avtovaz. During his tenure, for example, the tax on cars was reduced from 25 to 5 percent.

Avtovaz was teetering on insolvency by the second half of the 1990s. The company supposedly owed more than $500 million in tax arrears. When the International Monetary Fund suspended payments to Russia in 1996 because of the government's poor record in tax collection, the Kremlin pressured Avtovaz to either get serious about finding a foreign investor or transfer a block of shares to the state. In 1997 the firm reached an agreement to transfer a majority stake to the government as collateral on a plan to pay off tax debt over the next ten years. The stake was apparently given back to Avtovaz in 2001 even though the debt had not been eliminated. Another serious problem, according to reports in the *Economist* and the *Moscow Times,* was that the mafia controlled most of the distribution of Avtovaz vehicles. After the Soviet distribution network collapsed, organized crime fostered connections with some senior managers at Avtovaz. The mafia was reportedly able to receive some vehicles without even paying for them, so that it profited while Avtovaz suffered.

Improved Stability After the 1998 Crisis

Ironically, the fiscal crisis that shook Russia in August 1998 breathed new life into Avtovaz. Because the ruble was sharply devalued, Avtovaz paid less for production inputs. Its ruble-denominated cars now cost about one-quarter of what an import cost. In addition, the firm had introduced some new models just before the crisis hit. The VAZ-2110, or "Lada 110," was a modernized four-door sedan introduced in 1996. The "Lada-211," a larger five-door hatchback, was introduced in 1998. Avtovaz also cracked down on criminal distribution activities in late 1998. In the September "Cyclone" operation, state police forcibly occupied the factory in order to stop mafia agents from absconding with cars. Anti-mafia members of the Avtovaz management were constantly attended by bodyguards. After 1999 the

Russian government began a general offensive against the "oligarchs": Berezovsky had already fled the country in the face of criminal charges, and charges also were filed against some Avtovaz managers alleging embezzlement and tax evasion.

In 1999 Avtovaz had improved control of distribution and replaced the barter system with cash payment for all inputs. The days of trading cars for raw steel were over. Pricewaterhouse-Coopers was finishing up the preparation of accounts and Avtovaz was talking to General Motors, with whom it had signed an initial memorandum of understanding back in 1994 that later fizzled. In February 2001 a deal with the foreign investor was finally clinched. In a joint venture worth $332 million, General Motors would make an updated version of the Niva sports utility vehicle at a new plant to be constructed next to the existing Avtovaz facility. The vehicle would be known as the Chevrolet-Niva. The first model rolled off the assembly line in September 2002.

As the Russian economy grew during the postcrisis period, Avtovaz posted gradually increasing profits after 1999. Still, operations were far from settled. A glut of unsold vehicles in 2002 and 2003, due in part to the increased availability of secondhand imports, led the company to operate on reduced shifts for short periods. Cash flow was still a problem and the company had trouble securing capital from domestic banks. In 2003 Avtovaz had a dispute with shareholders when it tried to pass a new charter that removed the requirement for a 10 percent payout to preferred shareholders. But production was back to normal levels above 700,000 vehicles annually and Ladas still accounted for about three-quarters of car sales. In 2004 Avtovaz was discussing the construction of a $1 billion engine factory with General Motors and was introducing the "Kalina" line of its most up-to-date models. The firm had survived the chaos of the 1990s and was still the dominant car manufacturer in Russia.

Principal Subsidiaries

OAO DAAZ; OAO SAAZ; OAO AvtoVAZtrans; OAO TEVIS; OAO SeAZ; OAO Elektroset; OAO AvtoVAZstroi; Lada International Ltd. (Cyprus); OAO AVVA (85%); Oy Konela Ab (Finland; 70%); ZAO CB AFC (58.5%); ZAO IFC (51%); OOO Eleks-Polyus (51%).

Principal Competitors

GAZ Joint Stock Co.; Toyota Motor Corporation; Kia Motors Corporation.

Further Reading

Aliabyev, Boris, "AvtoVAZ Spared from Bankruptcy," *Moscow Times,* October 17, 1997.

Boulton, Leyla, "Gremlin in the Gearbox: Uncertainty for Russia's Largest Carmaker," *Financial Times,* February 15, 1994, p. 16.

——, "Lada Car Becomes Victim of Success," *Financial Times,* November 25, 1993, p. 2.

"Deals on Wheels," *Economist,* November 30, 1996, p. 74.

"First Chevy-Niva Rolls Out of Tolyatti," *Moscow Times,* September 24, 2002.

Freeland, Chrystia, "Winds of Market Buffet Old Soviet Dream," *Financial Times,* February 28, 1995, p. 7.

Katsura, P., "Volga Auto Plant to Finance Own Progress," *Current Digest of the Soviet Press,* August 21, 1985, p. 1.

"Modernising the Mastodon: Russia's Car Industry," *Economist,* June 10, 1995, p. 60.

Montgomery, Dave, "Russians Have 'Lada' Love for Domestic Automobile," *Knight Ridder/Tribune News Service,* February 10, 2002.

Ostrovsky, Simon, "Lawsuit, Probe Hang Over AvtoVAZ," *Moscow Times,* June 4, 2003.

——, "Stalling Car Giant Shifts into Low Gear," *Moscow Times,* November 26, 2002.

Radzievsky, Victor, "AvtoVAZ: Heavy Burden of Reforms," *Moscow News,* August 16, 1992, p. 33.

"Sweetly Flows the Volga," *Economist,* June 5, 1999, p. 62.

Thornhill, John, "Avtovaz Comes Under Investigation," *Financial Times,* February 20, 1999, p. 2.

——, "Car Tsar Takes Wheel of Economy," *Financial Times,* January 26, 1996, p. 2.

——, "Ruble's Crash Helps to Restock the Lada," *Financial Times,* June 5, 1999, p. 19.

Yasinsky, A., "Volga Automotive Plant's Renovation," *Current Digest of the Soviet Press,* April 9, 1986, p. 22.

Zhigulsky, Anton, "Crime Sinks the Lada As Car Market Grows," *Moscow Times,* March 5, 1996.

—Sarah Ruth Lorenz

БАЛТИКА

Baltika Brewery Joint Stock Company

3 6th Verkhny per.
Saint Petersburg
194292
Russia
Telephone: +7 (812) 329-91-00
Fax: +7 (812) 329-91-487
Web site: http://www.baltika.ru

Public Company
Incorporated: 1992
Employees: 8,700
Sales: $805.24 million (2003)
Stock Exchanges: RTS (Moscow)
Ticker Symbol: PKBA
NAIC: 312120 Breweries; 312111 Soft Drink
Manufacturing; 424810 Beer and Ale Merchant
Wholesalers

Baltika Brewery Joint Stock Company is the largest beer brewer in Russia, with about 20 percent of the domestic market. Aside from the main brewery in St. Petersburg, the company has breweries in four other cities that support the company's reach into the farthest regions of the country. The company's best-selling brand is the Baltika label, which is sold in ten varieties referred to by number, ranging from the nonalcoholic Baltika No. 0 to the extra-strong Baltika No. 9. Other brands include Arsenalnoye, a lower-priced beer, the premium beer Parnassus, and several localized labels with followings in regional markets. In addition, Baltika produces mineral water and citrus soft drinks. The company's majority shareholder is the Danish/English consortium Baltic Beverages Holding AB (BBH). After the fall of the Soviet Union, BBH's investment helped transform an aging state-owned brewery into the producer of a quality beer on par with other major European labels. Baltika's sales grew rapidly as Russians rediscovered beer, and the company's production is only just starting to level off after a decade in business.

A New Brand for the Post-Soviet Era

Baltika beer was first introduced to a market that was used to the unappealing brews of the Soviet era. Although beer had been a popular beverage under the tsars, the brewing industry suffered under the managed economy and anti-alcohol campaigns of the communist period. Very little barley was produced in the U.S.S.R., so the state-owned breweries of the Soviet era relied either on inexpensive low-quality imports or they used alternative ingredients such as rice. The resulting product was described by reporter Ben Aris as an ''acidic, pale yellow liquid tasting vaguely of yeast.'' Almost all beer was sold under the label ''Zhigulovskoye.'' Bottles came with little calendars on the label that told the buyer when the beer would start going bad, usually within a few weeks of being bottled. As a result, beer consumption was very low; vodka reigned supreme among alcoholic drinks.

The brewery that was eventually transformed into the Baltika company was one of six breweries in the Leningrad Production Association of Brewing and Non-Alcoholic Industry, also known as Lenpivo. The plan for the brewery was developed by the Institute ''Design for Food Industry-2'' in the 1970s because the other breweries in the production association had been operating for up to 200 years and were in need of major renovations. Construction began in 1978, but finishing the plant was a low priority during the 1980s because President Mikhail Gorbachev was running an anti-alcohol campaign. The plant was finally completed in 1990 and the state enterprise ''Baltika Brewery'' was established. The enterprise sent its first batch of beer to the market in November of that year. This product was still the Soviet-style beer and was sold under the brand names ''Zhigulovskoye,'' ''Rizhskoye,'' ''Admiralteyskoye,'' and ''Prazdnichnoye.'' About 27 million liters of beer were produced in the enterprise's first full year of operation.

Privatization of the brewery started in 1992 after the fall of the communist regime when the state enterprise was transformed into the Baltika Brewery Joint Stock Company. A key factor in Baltika's eventual prosperity was the early involvement of foreign investors. Personal relationships between brewery management and government officials helped Baltika make connections with potential investors. Specifically, the eventual

---

Company Perspectives:

We work to be the best Russian brewery in every aspect: in satisfying the customer—to make consumers feel they are buying the best beer; in influencing society—to convince society of benefits the Company's activities provide; in business—to ensure the growth of the Company's profits and capitalization and increase its shareholders' income; in satisfying personnel—to motivate each employee and make them feel that they are important to and appreciated by the Company.

---

general director of Baltika, Taimuraz Bolloyev, was close friends with Vladimir Putin, the future president of Russia, who at the time was deputy mayor of St. Petersburg and head of the foreign economic relations committee. Putin helped convince a Scandinavian consortium known as Baltic Beverages Holding AB (BBH) to invest in Baltika. At the time, BBH consisted of the Swedish company Pripps, the Norwegian brewer Ringes, and the Hartwall Group of Finland. BBH emerged with a 50.6 percent stake in Baltika after privatization. The remaining shares were held by corporations, private individuals, and holding companies tied to Baltika management.

The Russian plant managers, with the help of advisers from BBH, immediately began planning for the renovation of the brewery and the creation of a new brand name. The Baltika brand first appeared in June 1992. The earliest varieties were Baltika No. 1, a light golden beer; Baltika No. 3, also known as "Baltika Classic"; and Baltika No. 4, a dark beer referred to as "Baltika Original." Meanwhile, a reconstruction and development plan was drafted, which laid out an investment scheme scheduled to start in the spring of 1993 and be completed in 1998. As the plan began to be executed, brewery production grew from 60 million liters in 1993 to 113 million liters in 1995. In 1994 Baltika No. 4 "Exportnoye" was introduced in honor of the Goodwill Games in St. Petersburg; a dark porter variety, Baltika No. 6, also was available by this time.

In November 1996 the reconstruction and development plan was completed two years ahead of schedule. Renovations included the installation of new equipment at all stages of production, the installation of water purifiers, the replacement of iron pipelines with stainless steel, the computerization of production, and the utilization of beer filtering machines. Equipment had been imported from Germany, France, Denmark, and Sweden for a cost of around $44 million. The renovation made Baltika the largest brewery in Russia and the first to install equipment in line with contemporary European practices. Management's original goal had been to reach an output of 150 million liters by 1998, but in 1996 production already totaled 170 million liters.

Rapid Growth in the Late 1990s

Baltika had established a solid foundation by the mid-1990s, and the pace of the company's growth only increased in the second half of the decade. Baltika's share of the Russian beer market grew from 4.7 percent in 1995 to 20.1 percent in 2000.

At the same time, overall beer consumption in Russia was exploding now that flavorful Russian-made beers were available. The younger generation in particular was more likely to prefer beer to vodka, although vodka retained its cultural dominance and continued to be consumed in very high quantities. In 1995 both beer and vodka were consumed at an annual rate of about 16 liters per person. Five years later, Russians were drinking 36 liters of beer per person per year. Beer was seen as a relatively harmless beverage and was unregulated. Rising beer sales cut into soft drink sales rather than vodka sales, since beer was itself classified as a soft drink under Russian law. At times during the currency fluctuations of the 1990s, a bottle of domestic beer cost less than a Pepsi or a Coke, so it was a popular choice for young people. Some Russians also considered beer to have healthful properties.

In the late 1990s Baltika continued developing in order to capture as much as possible of this expanding market. After the original reconstruction plan was completed, BBH invested another $40 million to $50 million in new equipment to add production capacity. During this period Baltika also transformed itself from a single large brewery to a holding company with multiple locations. In 1997 the company purchased a controlling share of the plant "Donskoye Pivo" in the southern city Rostov-on-the-Don and began implementing a plan to update the brewery. The following year the "Don" brand was created and tailored to consumer preferences in the southern region. Don beer was described as a light, refreshing, quality brew at inexpensive prices. Four varieties were eventually created. Also in 1997, Baltika began producing mineral water under the "Khrustalnaya" ("Crystal") label on an experimental basis in St. Petersburg only. The water was marketed as a product for everyday use under the slogan "Pure water for the protection of your family."

In 1998 Russia experienced an economic crisis in which the government defaulted on its debts and the value of the ruble plummeted. The crisis had mixed consequences for Baltika. On the one hand, imported beers now cost about four times as much as they did before the devaluation, which helped domestic sales, and production costs were low by international standards, which opened the door for export sales. On the other hand, Baltika had just signed a $100 million dollar-denominated contract to expand the plant with imported equipment; the company had to refinance and take out a loan in order to meet this obligation. Baltika also switched to domestic suppliers for bottles and labels to reduce costs. Some brewing ingredients, however, were difficult to find domestically at an acceptable quality, so the company began considering the construction of a malt factory.

Meanwhile, Baltika moved ahead with its development. The company's distribution network was disorganized, loosely overseen, and allegedly involved criminal elements. Consequently, in 1998 Baltika began investing heavily in the creation of a sales network in the larger cities of Russia's regions. Baltika No. 9 also was introduced that year. Known as "Krepkoye" ("Strong"), this was a light-tasting beer with an alcohol content of at least 8 percent. Total output in 1998 reached 488 million liters.

In 1999 Baltika completed a warehouse at its St. Petersburg location. The new facility was highly automated and allowed for efficient loading onto rail or automotive transport. The company also developed a specialty beer under the Medovoye ("Honey") label in 1999, capitalizing on the traditional Russian fondness for honey. Medovoye beer was available in light and strong versions, both containing natural honey. In addition, Baltika started exporting about 2 percent of its production to Russian émigré communities, mostly in Britain, Germany, and Israel.

The year 2000 was a year of major growth and development for Baltika. Two new brands were introduced. The "Arsenalnoye" brand was developed as a popular affordably priced beer. It was available in light, dark, classic, strong, and traditional varieties and was promoted as "A Beer with a Masculine Character." A line of citrus soft drinks under the "Serebryanaya Ladoga" ("Silver Ladoga") label also was introduced. The drinks were available in lemonade, citron, and citrus mix varieties. Baltika added two new major facilities to its group as well. The plant Tulskoye Pivo in the city of Tula south of Moscow was acquired in October 2000. The plant had been established in 1974 and since 1997 had been under the control of Baltika's parent company BBH, who had carried out some modernizations. The new malt factory also was completed in October. It had been built in partnership with the French firm Groupe Soufflet and was known as the Malting Plant "Soufflet-St. Petersburg." Baltika held a 30 percent share in the plant. Now Baltika would have quality rye malt available without having to pay high prices for imports. Overall production in 2000 was up 60 percent and reached 1.06 billion liters. Revenues were up 67 percent from 1999, reaching $333 million, and net profit also rose to $79.3 million.

Slower Growth During a Maturing Market: 2001–04

In the early years of the new millennium Baltika continued expanding, although production growth slowed somewhat as the Russian beer industry matured. In early 2001 the company embarked on an ill-fated joint venture in Belarus. Baltika agreed to upgrade the Krinitsa brewery in return for a controlling interest in the plant. Baltika began installing new equipment there at the end of the year, but the Belorussian government was slow to transfer shares to Baltika and tried to reduce the agreed

upon stake in the Krinitsa brewery. Baltika halted the upgrade activities and sued to get back the $10 million it had already invested. The money did not start coming back to Baltika until the summer of 2003, after the company pushed for the seizure of a resort in southern Russia that belonged to Belarus.

Other ventures were more successful. Baltika launched a new production line for canned beer in April 2001. The line would produce half-liter cans of No. 7 "Exportnoye" and No. 9 "Krepkoye." Cans were easier to distribute than bottles, but the company had to overcome a perception among Russians that canned beer was of a lower quality. Some of the canned production was earmarked for export; Baltika announced plans to bring exports up to 10 percent of production by exporting cans of No. 7 and No. 9 to countries including Britain, Germany, Greece, Israel, China, and Mongolia. In other developments, Baltika introduced a nonalcoholic beer in 2001 known as Baltika No. 0 and a wheat beer known as Baltika No. 8. The company also introduced a new premium brand aimed at high-income consumers under the name "Parnassus." The beer was marketed under the slogan "A Beer for Goal-Oriented People."

In 2002 Baltika restructured in preparation for the addition of new breweries to its group. The Donskoye and Tulskoye breweries were merged into the Baltika Brewery and became branches of the company with its headquarters in St. Petersburg. Sales offices in 31 cities in Russia and representative offices in neighboring former Soviet countries also were integrated. Decision-making was to be centralized in order to implement more uniform policies. A recently established distributor in Germany, Baltika Deutschland GmbH, remained an independent subsidiary. There were also changes at Baltika's parent company: due to sales and mergers, the British company Scottish & Newcastle plc and the Danish company Carlsberg A/S had 50–50 control of BBH. The company continued to leave day-to-day operations in the hands of Russian managers.

Baltika introduced Baltika "Gold" No. 5 in 2002, as well as Baltika No. 2, a line of "party mix" beers in flavors such as orange, lemon, cherry, and coffee. The company also signed an agreement to begin producing Carlsberg beer under license at the Rostov brewery in May 2002; the beer had previously been imported.

In early 2003 construction was completed on two new breweries. Each was launched with the introduction of a new regional brand of beer. The plant in the city of Samara started production of Samara brand beer in classic and light varieties in January. A few months later the second plant opened in the city of Khabarovsk near the Chinese border, giving Baltika a strong presence in the Far East. Residents of Khabarovsk chose the brand name "DV" in a contest to name the region's new beer. Several other brands also were introduced in specific cities in 2003: "Leningradskoye," "Stavropolskoye," "Krasnodarskoye," "Krasnoyarskoye," "Sverdlovskoye," "Tyumenskoye," "Permskoye," and "Novosibirskoye." Each was named after its home city and was targeted at people with lower than average incomes. By the end of the year, however, production of all city brands except Leningradskoye was discontinued. Instead, in an attempt to appeal to Soviet nostalgia, in December Baltika introduced the "Zhigulovskoye" label, its own version of the low-priced familiar Soviet brand. In other efforts to broaden its product line, Baltika expanded production of bottled water nationwide. Water production in St. Petersburg was discontinued and moved to the Tula and Khabarovsk plants.

Baltika celebrated the new year in 2004 with the debut of Baltika No. 12, a dark winter-style beer. The company's annual production was now around 1.6 billion liters. Yet beer consumption in Russia was leveling off after growing at a rate of 20 percent over the past half decade and Baltika's market share was being challenged by the appearance of many popular regional brands. The company's production increased less than 1 percent in 2003 even though the overall beer market grew by 7 percent. The *Sunday Times* of London referred to beer as Russia's "liquid gold" in 2004. The boom years of the 1990s were over, however, and Baltika would have to remain vigilant and adaptable in order to retain its dominant position in the market.

Principal Subsidiaries

OOO Baltika Moskva; OOO Lizing Optimum; OOO Universalopttorg; Baltika Deutschland GmbH (Germany); ZAO Malt Factory Soufflet-Saint Petersburg (30%).

Principal Divisions

Baltika Saint Petersburg; Baltika Rostov; Baltika Tula; Baltika Samara; Baltika Khabarovsk.

Principal Competitors

Sun Interbrew Ltd.; Heineken N.V.; Ochakovo Beer and Soft Drinks Joint Stock Company; Krasny Vostok.

Further Reading

Aris, Ben, "Russian Beer Producer to Increase Exports to Western Europe," *Knight Ridder/Tribune Business News,* February 18, 2001.

"Baltika Brewery Gets Over with a Retooling Scheme a Year Earlier Than Planned," *RusData DiaLine-BizEkon News,* December 16, 1996.

"Baltika Brewery Received a Chance to Improve Its Financial Parameters," *Russian Business Monitor,* December 29, 2003.

"Baltika Brewery Released Some Results of 2003," *Russian Business Monitor,* January 26, 2004.

"Baltika to Branch Out with Own Water Label," *Moscow Times,* July 8, 2003.

Ostrovsky, Simon, "Baltika Posts 2000 Profit of $79.3M," *Moscow Times,* April 10, 2001.

Varoli, John, "Baltika Plans to Boost Output 250%," *Moscow Times,* April 22, 1999.

"Vodka Chasers," *Economist,* June 26, 1999, p. 72.

Wagstyl, Stefan, "Russia: Expanding Market Offers Heady Brew," *Financial Times,* May 10, 2000, p. 8.

Waples, John, "Russians Swap Vodka for Beer," *Sunday Times (London),* May 16, 2004, p. B1.

Yablokova, Oksana, "Baltika Hopes Canned Beer Pops Open Foreign Markets," *Moscow Times,* February 12, 2001.

Zbarovsky, Konstantin, "Baltika: Five-Year Plan of Quality Fulfilled in a Year," *RusData DiaLine-BizEkon News,* March 29, 1995.

—Sarah Ruth Lorenz

⋒ Banca Intesa

Banca Intesa SpA

Piazza Paolo Ferrari, 10
20121 Milan
Italy
Telephone: +39 02 88441
Fax: +39 02 8844 3638
Web site: http://www.bancaintesa.it

Public Company
Incorporated: 2001
Employees: 60,000
Total Assets: EUR 260.21 billion ($320 billion) (2003)
Stock Exchanges: Borsa Italiana
Ticker Symbol: BIN
NAIC: 522293 International Trade Financing

Banca Intesa SpA has merged its way into the position of Italy's top commercial bank, with total assets topping EUR 260 billion ($320 billion), and a network of more than 3,700 branches throughout the country. Intesa is also one of Italy's most international banks, operating nearly 650 branch offices in some 40 countries worldwide. Nonetheless, into the mid-2000s, Intesa has been refocusing its operations onto the domestic market, and has exited a number of foreign markets, including most of its South American holdings. The company also is exiting France, Germany, and Canada, and is considering an exit from the Eastern European market as well. Intesa was formed from a two-phase merger in the late 1990s—the first phase involved Banco Ambrosiano Veneto and CARIPLO, the world's largest savings bank. Renamed Banca Intesa, the bank next merged with Banca Commerciale Italiana (BCI), a process completed in 2001. In addition to a full range of commercial and consumer banking services, Intesa also operates brokerage services through subsidiary Caboto, as well as assets management and other financial products including mutual funds, mortgage, and leasing, and, through subsidiary Caravita, bancassurance products. Leading Intesa's ''cleanup'' is CEO Corrado Passera, who joined the company after revitalizing Italy's notoriously ailing postal system. Banca Intesa is listed on the Borsa Italiana.

Forming a National Contender in the 1990s

Banca Intesa was formed in the late 1990s from the merger between two mid-sized banks, Banco Ambrosiano Veneto and CARIPLO, which was then the world's largest savings bank, creating Banca Intesa, which then merged with another mid-sized player, Banca Commerciale Italiana to form IntesaBCI. The resulting group instantly claimed the number one position in the Italian banking sector, and became one of the top banking groups in Europe, with operations in more than 40 countries and total assets of more than EUR 250 billion ($300 billion).

The oldest part of the later Banca Intesa was the savings bank CARIPLO. Like many of Italy's banks, CARIPLO originated as part of a charitable association, with the founding of the Central Charity Commission (CCC) in Italy's Lombardy region in 1816. That association acted in two capacities, on the one hand raising funds through charitable donations, and on the other by providing financial assistance and other funding initiatives. The CCC quickly amassed a large assets base, and in 1823 used those as the foundation for the establishment of its own savings bank, patterned after the banking model pioneered by the Wien Sparkasse in Vienna. The new savings bank was named Cassa di Risparmio di Milano. The bank gradually expanded throughout the region, and later changed its name to Cassa di Risparmio delle Province Lombarde, or CARIPLO.

CARIPLO added mortgage services in 1864, which operated independently of the main bank until the beginning of the 1990s. In the 1920s, CARIPLO began lending to farmers, establishing another independent unit, the Agricultural Credit Section. Following World War II, CARIPLO played a major role in Italy's reconstruction effort. At this time, the savings bank began providing medium-term loans, primarily to small to mid-sized businesses, through a new subsidiary, Mediocredito Lombardo. The bank also provided financing for the public works and construction sector, adding a separate business unit for this operation as well.

By the end of the 1980s, CARIPLO had grown into a full-fledged commercial bank with operations throughout Italy. An important part of the group's transition to a nationally and internationally operating bank came with its acquisition of Istituto

Bancario Italiano, or IBI, in 1982. In 1991, CARIPLO—which remained a public sector bank owned by local and regional governments—converted to joint-stock status, and IBI and its other business units were then merged into a single entity, CARIPLO SpA. This move set the stage for CARIPLO to join the massive consolidation of the Italian banking sector during that decade.

Other parts of the later Banca Intesa stemmed from the end of the 19th century. The Banco Ambrosiano was created in Milan as a joint-stock bank in 1896 by a group of Lombardi Catholics. The bank grew into a mid-sized, regional player by the 1920s. In the postwar period, Ambrosiano began a long period of expansion, enabling it to emerge as one of Italy's—and even the world's—top banks. Driving the group's growth was Roberto Calvi, who joined the bank at the age of 27 in 1947 and worked his way up to become its director general. After building the bank through organic growth into the 1970s, Calvi launched Ambrosiano on an acquisition effort, acquiring Banco di Imperia in Imperia and Banca Mobiliare Piemontese in Turin in 1977.

Calvi steered Ambrosiano into a close relationship with the Vatican—indeed, Calvi himself earned the nickname as "The Banker of God." Yet Calvi's complex dealings were to lead him and Ambrosiano to ruin. In 1981, Ambrosiano suddenly found itself bankrupt, with debts as high as $1.5 billion. Calvi himself was convicted of currency trading violations in 1981. Calvi, a member of the secretive P2 masonic lodge, was later suspected of having funneled off Ambrosiano's funds through the Vatican's own bank, Istituto per le Opere Religiose (IOR), for various illegal schemes. Before he could be jailed, however, Calvi fled from Italy, and ultimately reached London. In 1982, Calvi's body was discovered hanging under the Blackfriar's bridge—a prominent landmark in freemasonry—with his pockets filled with bricks and stones. Despite the evidence to the contrary, Calvi's death was ruled a suicide, a ruling that was overturned only in 2002, with three suspects held on murder charges.

Giovanni Bazoli was appointed by the Bank of Italy to take over the failed Ambrosiano. Bazoli initiated a dramatic restructuring plan, which included a name change—to Nuovo Banco Ambrosiano—to emphasize its commitment to emerging from the Vatican scandal. Under Bazoli, Ambrosiano grew strongly through the 1980s. The successful rebuilding of Ambrosiano led Bazoli to begin planning for the next phase in the bank's development. With hundreds of small, undercapitalized banks, the Italian banking industry seemed ill-prepared for the lowering of trade barriers among European Community members in the 1990s. Bazoli recognized the need to force the consolidation of the Italian banking sector, and foster the emergence of a smaller number of larger banks capable of competing on a European and even global level. As a first step, Bazoli led Ambrosiano into its first major merger—with Banca Cattolica del Veneto.

That bank had originated as Banca Cattolica Vicentina as a cooperative bank serving the Catholic community in 1892. Vincentina reincorporated as a joint-stock company in 1916, then grew into a prominent regional bank. Vincentina came to the rescue of a number of smaller banks in its region during the Italian banking crisis of the 1930s—which led the Italian government to take over the country's top 24 banks—and then changed its name to Banca Cattolica del Veneto. Following World War II, Banca Cattolica del Veneto came under the control of the Vatican's IOR and began a steady expansion, backed by the region's own strong economic growth. At the time of its merger with Ambrosiano, the Veneto bank was considered a fast-growing, well-managed, and profitable bank.

The newly merged bank adopted the name of Banco Ambrosiano Veneto, and, under Bazoli's stewardship, began a series of mergers and acquisitions through the 1990s. Among these were the Banca Vallone, based in Galatina, in 1991, followed by the 1992 purchase of Citibank Italia, based in Naples, which formed the basis of the group's Banco Ambroveneto Sud branch. Ambrosiano Veneto continued to look for growth opportunities, and particularly national expansion. In 1994, the group acquired Società di Banche Siciliane, followed by Banca di Trento e Bolzano, and, in 1995, Banca Massicana di Sessa Aurunca. The company also had added brokerage operations through its acquisition of Caboto in 1992.

Ambrosiano Veneto's rapid growth was matched by sound financial health. As it entered the second half of the 1990s, the bank was recognized as Italy's most profitable private-sector bank. The bank remained nonetheless a relatively minor player in the European market, and even at home as well. By the middle of the decade, Ambrosiano Veneto had itself become the object of a number of takeover attempts, including from Mediobanca and Banco Commerciale Italiano. Although it had defeated the attempts, the bank remained vulnerable. To remedy this, Ambrosiano Veneto prepared the next phase of its development into Banca Intesa.

Italian Banking Powerhouse in the New Century

In 1997, Ambrosiano Veneto announced that it had entered merger talks with CARIPLO, outpacing BCI's own attempts to form a merger with Italy's largest savings bank. CARIPLO and Ambrosiano Veneto quickly reached an agreement to merge, forming Banca Intesa in 1998. The new bank now became Italy's largest private-sector bank, with more than 1,800 branches and over $150 billion in assets.

Soon after the merger, Intesa turned the tables on BCI, acquiring a stake in the recently privatized bank. By 1999, Intesa raised its stake in BCI to 70 percent, in what was described at the time as a friendly merger—although that had been strongly "encouraged" by the Bank of Italy. The bank then changed its name, briefly, to IntesaBCI, and began work converting BCI into its investment and corporate banking division. Originally BCI was to remain an independently operating part of the large Intesa, but by 2000, Intesa acquired full control of BCI, which was then absorbed into the group's overall operations.

Yet the mergers that had built Banca Intesa appeared to be mergers only in name—by as late as 2002, the bank appeared

Key Dates:

1816: Central Charity Committee (CCC) is founded.

1823: CCC uses assets from charity to launch a savings bank, Cassa di Risparmio di Milano, which evolves into Cassa di Risparmio delle Provincie Lombarde, or CARIPLO.

1892: Banca Cattolica del Veneto, which develops into a major regional bank during the banking crisis of the 1930s, is founded.

1894: Banca Commerciale Italiana (BCI) is founded.

1896: Banco Ambrosiano in Veneto is founded.

1947: The Vatican Bank acquires control of Banca Cattolica del Veneto.

1978: Ambrosiano acquires Banco di Imperia in Imperia and Banca Mobiliare Piemontese in Turin.

1982: Ambrosiano goes bankrupt and is reformed as Banco Nuovo Ambrosiano.

1989: Ambrosiano and Cattolica del Veneto merge, forming Banco Ambrosiano Veneto (BAV).

1991: BAV acquires Banca Vallone, based in Galatina.

1992: BAV acquires Caboto, then Citibank Italia, based in Naples.

1994: BAV acquires Società di Banche Siciliane and Banca di Trento e Bolzano.

1995: BAV acquires Banca Massicana di Sessa Aurunca.

1998: BAV and CARIPLO merge, forming Banca Intesa.

1999: Banca Intesa acquires 70 percent stake in BCI.

2000: Banca Intesa acquires full control of BCI, and becomes IntesaBCI.

2002: IntesaBCI is renamed Banca Intesa and begins a restructuring effort, shedding 5,000 jobs and its subsidiaries in Latin America, France, Germany, and Switzerland.

2003: Banca Intesa sells 50 percent of the Intesa Vita insurance subsidiary to Generali.

2004: Banca Intesa sells its Canadian operations to HSBC Canada; a controlling stake in Turkey's Garanti Bank is acquired.

unable to integrate its various pieces, which remained jealously controlled by their former heads, in a co-CEO setup, leading to what the *Financial Times* described as "vicious infighting among the senior ranks." In March of that year, however, the bank moved to simplify its management structure, naming Corrada Passera as its sole CEO.

Passera had already earned a reputation as a "cleanup man" by leading the resurrection of Italy's decrepit postal system. Passera set to work streamlining and revitalizing the bank, which re-adopted the name Banca Intesa in mid-2002. Under Passera, the bank shed some 5,000 employees, including 200 senior managers, in part in an effort to develop a single, unified corporate culture.

Passera next targeted the bank's widespread, and widely unprofitable, geographical focus. In 2003, the bank began exiting a number of its foreign markets, selling off its Latin American operations. The company continued its pruning effort,

selling its subsidiaries in France and Germany as well as other European holdings. In 2004, Intesa approached the end of its cleanup drive, announcing its agreement to sell its Canadian operations to HSBC Bank Canada, and its subsidiary in Uruguay to Banco ACAC Crédit Agricole. In a related move, Intesa agreed to sell 50 percent of its Intesa Vita insurance subsidiary to Generali in December 2003.

By 2004, Intesa's efforts had started to take hold, as the company's revenues rebounded and began to show steady growth. With rising sales and profits, Intesa once again began eyeing external expansion. Part of the group's future strategy involved the strengthening of its partnership with France's Crédit Agricole, which, with a 15 percent stake, remained Intesa's largest shareholder. The partnership called for the provision of combined services through Intesa's network in Italy and through Crédit Agricole's strong international network. Meanwhile, Intesa began looking for its own growth opportunities. In March 2004, the group took a new step into international markets when it acquired controlling interest in Turkey's Garanti Bank. Banca Intesa had successfully negotiated the Italian banking industry consolidation, and its own merger process, to claim a position among the world's top banks.

Principal Subsidiaries

Banca Cis S.p.A.; Banca Di Trento E Bolzano S.p.A.; Banca Intesa France S.A.; Banca Popolare Friuladria S.p.A.; Banco Comercial E De Investimento Sudameris S.A.; Banco Sudameris Argentina S.A.; Banco Sudameris Colombia S.A.; Banco Sudameris De Investimento S.A. (Brazil); Bankhaus Löbbecke & Co. Kg (Germany); Banque Sudameris S.A. (France); Caboto Sim S.p.A.; Caridata S.p.A.; Cassa Di Risparmio Della Provincia Di Viterbo S.p.A.; Cassa Di Risparmio Di Ascoli Piceno S.p.A. (Carisap); Cassa Di Risparmio Di Biella E Vercelli S.p.A. (Biverbanca); Cassa Di Risparmio Di Citta' Di Castello S.p.A.; Cassa Di Risparmio Di Foligno S.p.A.; Cassa Di Risparmio Di Parma E Piacenza S.p.A.; Cassa Di Risparmio Di Rieti S.p.A.; Cassa Di Risparmio Di Spoleto S.p.A.; Central-European International Bank Ltd. (Hungary); Comit Investment (Ireland) Ltd.; E.Tr. - Esazione Tributi S.p.A.; Esatri Esazione Tributi S.p.A.; Fundsworld Financial Services Ltd.; Intesa Bank Ireland Plc; Intesa Bank Overseas Ltd.; Intesa E.Lab S.p.A.; Intesa Fiduciaria Sim S.p.A.; Intesa Gestione Crediti SpA; Intesa Holding Centro S.p.A.; Intesa Holding International S.A.; Intesa Immobiliare S.p.A.; Intesa Leasing S.p.A.; Intesa Mediocredito SpA; Intesa Preferred Capital Company L.L.C. USA; Intesa Renting S.p.A.; Intesa Riscossione Tributi S.p.A.; Intesa Sec. Npl SpA; Intesa Sec. Npl SpA; Intesa Sistemi E Servizi S.p.A.; Intesabank Canada; Intesatrade Sim S.p.A.; La Centrale Consulenza S.p.A.; Magazzini Generali Cariplo S.p.A.; Mediofactoring S.p.A.; Nextra Alternative Investments Sgr S.p.A.; Nextra Investment Management Sgr S.p.A.; Phönix Kg (Germany); Privredna Banka Zagreb D.D. (Croatia); S.Es.I.T. Puglia - Servizio Esazione Imposte E Tributi S.p.A.; Setefi S.p.A.; Societa' Italiana Di Revisione E Fiduciaria S.I.R.E.F. S.p.A.; Vseobcna Uverova Banka (Vub) (Slovak Republic).

Principal Competitors

Sanpaolo IMI S.p.A.; Banca d'Italia; Banca Monte Parma S.p.A.; Banca Monte Dei Paschi di Siena S.p.A.; Banca

Nazionale del Lavoro S.p.A.; Banca di Roma S.p.A.; Banco Popolare di Verona e Novara.

Further Reading

''Banca Intesa,'' *Euroweek,* March 12, 2004, p. 12.

Betts, Paul, ''Intesa to Buy Rest of BCI,'' *Financial Times,* October 11, 2000, p. 34.

''Generali and Banca Intesa Cleared to Buy Italian Life Insurance Firm,'' *European Report,* December 17, 2003, p. 308.

Kapner, Fred, ''Banca Intesa Says Turnaround on Track,'' *Financial Times,* September 9, 2003, p. 29.

Kapner, Fred, and Charles Pretzlik, ''Passera Adds to His Credit,'' *Financial Times,* July 28, 2003, p. 10.

Lane, David, ''No Slowing Down,'' *Banker,* December 2001, p. 29.

Miesel, Sandra, ''The P-2 Lodge,'' *The Best of Crisis: Politics, Culture & the Church,* Vol. 1, 2003, p. 61.

——, ''The Vatican Bank Scandal,'' *The Best of Crisis: Politics, Culture & the Church,* Vol. 1, 2003, p. 63.

''On the Strength of Novelty and Tradition,'' *Euromoney,* June 2000, p. 11.

Pino, Francesca, and Monica Pavesi, ''Cooperation While Preserving Historical Specificity: The Experience of IntesaBci,'' presented at Corporate Archives During and After Mergers' EABH Workshop, Stockholm, May 29, 2002.

Sherwood, Sonja, ''Italy's Banking Duo,'' *Chief Executive,* July 2002, p. 14.

—M.L. Cohen

Banca Monte dei Paschi di Siena SpA

Piazza Salimbene, 3
53100 Siena
Italy
Telephone: +39 0577 294-111
Fax: +39 0577 294-313
Web site: http://www.mps.it

Public Company
Incorporated: 1472
Employees: 26,881
Total Assets: EUR 122.94 billion (2003)
Stock Exchanges: Borsa Italiana
Ticker Symbol: BMPS
NAIC: 522110 Commercial Banking

Banca Monte dei Paschi di Siena SpA (BMPS) claims the title as the world's oldest bank, operating without break since 1472. BMPS, the holding company for the MPS Group of banks, is also one of Italy's top five banks and ranks among the top 50 throughout Europe. The MPS banking group operates from more than 1,800 branches in Italy, with total assets of more than EUR 120 billion. Based on the original Banca Monte dei Paschi in Siena, BMPS has built up a fully integrated operation since the 1990s. The MPS Group also includes commercial banks Banca 121, Banca Agricola Mantovana, Banca Toscana, and CariPrato. More specialized operations include MPS Merchant, which provides loans, active in the medium and long-term loan market; private banker Banca Steinhaulin; and agricultural lender MPS Banca Verde. BMPS also offers assets management services and products through Monte Paschi Vita, Grow Life, and Monte Paschi Asset Management. Although primarily focused on the Italian market, BMPS operates subsidiaries in France, Belgium, and Switzerland, and branch offices in Germany, the United Kingdom, Spain, the United States, Hong Kong, and Singapore. BMPS also operates representative offices in another ten countries. Formerly wholly owned by the city of Siena, BMPS is listed on the Borsa Italiana.

Founding a Renaissance Pawnshop

Italy represented the heart of the banking world in the Renaissance era, as the city-states of Milan, Genoa, Venice, Florence, and Siena dominated world trade. Much of the merchant and exploration activities of the time, as well as many wars of the period, were financed by the great family-owned banking houses, the so-called "banchi grossi" represented especially by the Medici family. These banks, however, tended to act as financiers only for the country's wealthy noble, religious, and political elite, and often served only a limited number of clients—a situation that left them highly vulnerable to political and financial reversals.

Filling the gap for "lesser" clients were the "banchi in mercato," who served as moneychangers, but also provided certain services that developed into the modern banking system, such as holding deposits, transferring funds from one person to another, and debt-paying services. These "merchant bankers," generally a single person set up at a table with a coin purse and a ledger book, became an essential part of international commerce during the Renaissance period.

The merchant bankers, however, did not provide one essential service to Italy's poor farmers, artisans, and traders—loans. Yet lending was an area heavily constrained by canon law on usury. As a result, the lower classes were forced to turn to unregulated and often unscrupulous moneylenders, who charged interest rates as high as 40 percent.

In the mid-15th century, the Franciscan Friars petitioned the Vatican for permission to establish a different kind of loan bank that would offer loans at rates high enough only to cover their costs. These nonprofit banks became known as the "monti di pieta," because they took "pity" on the poor. The first began operating in 1467, in Perugia, offering small loans in exchange for interest rates as low as 5 percent. Customers provided collateral for the loans, usually by leaving jewelry or clothing. These banks now became known as "banchi di pegni" or pawnbrokers.

Banchi di pegni soon began appearing throughout Italy—and later inspired similar banks throughout Europe—and were

---

Company Perspectives:

Affirming a role of leadership through the MPS Group, BMPS aims to be a reference model within the ever-changing Italian banking industry.

BMPS will promote unity within the MPS Group, while simultaneously acknowledging the value of cultural differences and maintaining strong local roots in the areas where the Group companies operate.

The mission of Banca Monte dei Paschi di Siena (BMPS) is to create value for its shareholders, both in the short term and in the long term, thereby placing the priority on the satisfaction of the customers, the professional development of people and the interests of all stakeholders.

---

for the most part set up by Franciscans. The city-state of Siena, however, took a different approach, and instead founded its own Monte di Pieta in 1472. The bank was backed by a 5,000-florin loan from the city, raised through levying taxes. Members of the city's most prominent family were then granted seats on the board. Unlike at other banks, which were usually dominated by a single family, leadership at the Siena bank rotated among the families. In this way, the bank was guided only by the best members of each generation.

A large proportion of the Siena bank's clientele were farmers in the surrounding area. The rich agricultural climate of the region also gave Siena a remarkable degree of stability, since lending to farmers held far lower risk than backing other trade and commercial activities. Initially the bank accepted clothing and jewelry as collateral, but gradually began taking land as collateral as well. In this way, the bank developed into a powerful landholder, acquiring lands when customers defaulted on their loans. Among notable properties that entered the bank's real estate portfolio was the famed Fontanafredda estate and its Barolo wines, which became the bank's property in 1931.

After Siena became part of the Grand Duchy of Tuscany in 1624, the bank changed its name to Monte dei Paschi di Siena (BMPS). The addition of the word "paschi" (pasture) reflected the scale of the bank's land portfolio by then. With the unification of Italy in the late 19th century, the bank began extending beyond Siena, although remaining close to its home region. In the 1900s, however, BMPS began to expand into the wider national market. In 1929, the bank engineered the merger of Credito Toscano and Banca di Firenze, and then acquired a major stake in the resulting entity, Banca Toscana SpA. Later known as Mediocredito Toscana, then MPS Merchant, that bank became a specialist in mid-term loans to the industrial sector. BMPS added a stake in another bank, Istituto Nazionale per il Credito Agrario, later renamed MPS Banca Verde, which became the group's agricultural loans specialist.

Modern Italian Banking Leader

While Italy's banking sector collapsed amid the economic chaos of the early 1930s, BMPS remained financially solid. A major reason for its stability came from the bank's longstanding policy of reserving as much as half—and often much more—of

a year's profits in its treasury. The remaining funds were then spent on public works projects benefiting Siena and the surrounding area. The bank also was credited with maintaining a prudent, and generally risk-averse, loan portfolio—a policy adopted in part because of the bank's losses from participating in the funding of Christopher Columbus's expedition in 1492.

Five hundred years of conservative fiscal policies enabled BMPS to approach the end of the 20th century in an enviable condition. Indeed, in the late 1980s, BMPS was considered Italy's most profitable bank. The passage of the Amato law in 1988, meant to stimulate the consolidation of Italy's heavily fragmented banking sector, marked a new phase in BMPS's history. The new legislation encouraged Italy's banks, most of which, like Siena, were owned by local, regional, or national government foundations, to convert their status to joint-stock companies.

With the dropping of trade barriers among European Community members looming in the early 1990s, Italy's banking sector underwent a dramatic change. One of the most visible signs of this change was the rapid development of new national banking networks, as the number of branch offices grew steadily into the next decade. At the start of the 1990s, BMPS—which otherwise was said to drag its heels on its own privatization—joined in on the consolidation of the industry, using its deep reserves to engage in a period of acquisition and expansion.

Among the bank's first moves was its purchase of controlling stakes in Mediocredito Toscano and Credito Agrario. These purchases were followed in 1992 with the acquisition of Casa di Risparmio di Prato, which strengthened BMPS's Tuscany region presence. These acquisitions, however, were merely the largest of a long string of smaller banks, with acquisitions focusing especially in the Sicily and Lombardy regions. At the same time, BMPS began a diversification effort, launching the life insurance joint venture Monte Paschi Vita with partner Crédit Agricole. After taking on a new partner, SAI, Monte Paschi Vita developed into Italy's largest provider of bancassurance products. Another diversification move came in 1994, when BMPS launched an assets management subsidiary, Ducato Gestioni. The bank also began acquiring stakes in Banca Agricola Montavana, taking full control in 1999.

By the mid-1990s, BMPS had swelled into a major Italian banking group, with more than 22,000 employees. Yet BMPS's rapid expansion had quickly drained its reserves, while integrating operations cut deeply into its profits. Faced with a need to restructure operations in order to regain momentum, the bank—and especially its owner, the city of Siena—was forced to convert to a joint-stock company in 1995. The changeover placed the joint-stock company BMPS under control of a private foundation, which continued to control the group's charitable and philanthropic operations. The change of structure paved the way to a public offering.

Going Public, Growing Internationally: 1999–2004

The company nonetheless put off its public offering for as long as possible. Finally, BMPS launched its initial public offering (IPO) in 1999—an IPO qualified as a great success. Yet

Key Dates:

1467: The first monte di pieta (nonprofit bank), designed to end usury by providing low interest loans, is created.

1472: The city-state of Siena establishes its own Monte di Pieta.

1624: After Siena becomes part of the Grand Duchy of Tuscany, the bank changes its name to Banca Monte dei Paschi di Siena (BMPS).

1900s: The unification of Italy encourages BMPS to expand into the region around Siena.

1929: BMPS first steps into the national market by acquiring control of Banca Toscano.

1990: Company begins new expansion period, acquiring a number of small banks in Sicily and Lombardy, and taking controlling interest in Mediocredito Toscano and Istituto Nazionale per il Credito Agrario.

1992: Cassa di Risparmio di Prato is acquired; the joint venture Monte Paschi Vita is formed with Crédit Agricole.

1994: Company establishes an assets management business, Ducato Gestioni.

1995: BMPS converts its status to that of a joint-stock company.

1999: BMPS goes public on the Borsa Italiana; full control of Banca Mantovana is acquired.

2000: Company acquires Banca del Salenta.

2002: BMPS abandons merger talks with Banca Nazionale del Lavoro.

2004: BMPS is Italy's fifth largest bank with 1,800 branches and assets of more than EUR 120 billion.

the bank's owner foundation retained control of BMPS with more than 76 percent of shares.

Flush with the success of its public offering, BMPS began looking at fresh merger and acquisition candidates. In 2000, BMPS purchased majority control of Banca del Salento, an integrated, multichannel banking group, which added its own branch office network to BMPS, as well as its Banca 121 automated banking service. The addition of Salento helped push BMPS's branch office network past 1,800, and solidified its place among Italy's top five banks.

BMPS appeared to have found another, still larger merger partner in Banca Nazionale del Lavoro (BNL), then Italy's sixth largest bank. The two sides began talks in 2001, with BMPS acquiring an initial minority stake in BNL. Yet, as BNL's share price dwindled in the face of its heavy exposure to the crippled South American market, the two sides found themselves unable to arrange a "marriage of equals." Merger talks were called off in 2002.

Thwarted in its attempt to build position in the domestic market, BMPS nonetheless could comfort itself with its own sound financial position and strong share price. The company's conservative lending policy had enabled it to steer clear of the worst economic trouble spots, and to continue to integrate national operations. The group also began building its international operations, which already consisted of nearly 40 branch and representative offices in nearly 20 countries. In 2003, the bank received permission to open a representative office in Algeria, the first step ahead of a possible wider entry into the North African market in the new century. As the world's oldest bank with nearly 500 years of history behind it, BMPS appeared to have found the secret of eternal youth.

Principal Subsidiaries

Banca 121; Banca Agricola Mantovana; Banca Monte Paschi (Suisse); Banca Monte Paschi Belgio; Banca Steinhauslin; Banca Toscana CariPrato; Grow Life; Monte Paschi Asset Management; Monte Paschi Banque (France); Monte Paschi Vita; MPS Bancaverde; MPS Finance; MPS Leasing and Factoring; MPS Merchant.

Principal Competitors

Banca Intesa SpA; Sanpaolo IMI S.p.A.; Banca d'Italia; Banca Monte Parma S.p.A.; Banca Nazionale del Lavoro S.p.A.; Banca di Roma S.p.A.; Banca Popolare di Verona e Novara; Capitalia S.p.A.

Further Reading

"Arrivederci, bancantiquata," *Economist,* September 24, 1988, p. 99.

Betts, Paul, "Italian Bank Wins Go-Ahead," *Financial Times,* May 28, 1999, p. 28.

Green, Timothy, "From a Pawnshop to Patron of the Arts in Five Centuries," *Smithsonian,* July 1991, p. 58.

Kapner, Fred, "MPS Mulls Plan for BNL Merger," *Financial Times,* November 20, 2001, p. 29.

"MPS Determined to Take on the Might of Italian Borrowers," *MTNWeek,* January 28, 2000, p. 1.

"Rock of Ages," *Economist,* September 24, 1994, p. 83.

"Siena Bond Augurs Well As Investors Flock to First MBS," *Euroweek,* January 16, 2004, p. 73.

"Siena Holds on to MPS," *Banker,* March 2000, p. 36.

"A Thoroughbred Issuer," *Structured Finance International,* January–February 2003, p. 13, p. 4.

—M.L. Cohen

BEI TECHNOLOGIES, INC.

BEI Technologies, Inc.

1 Post Street, Suite 2500
San Francisco, California 94104
U.S.A.
Telephone: (415) 956-4477
Fax: (415) 956-5564
Web site: http://www.bei-tech.com

Public Company
Incorporated: 1997
Employees: 1,018
Sales: $213.7 million (2003)
Stock Exchanges: NASDAQ
Ticker Symbol: BEIQ
NAIC: 334513 Instruments and Related Products
    Manufacturing for Measuring, Displaying, and
    Controlling Industrial Process Variables

BEI Technologies, Inc. manufactures sensors, motors, actuators, and subsystems used by the aerospace, automotive, heavy equipment, industrial, medical, and military markets. The company is publicly traded on the NASDAQ and is based in San Francisco. BEI's actuators provide high-performance motion control for machinery. The company also makes brushless DC motors, ideal for sterile environments. Through the Duncan Electronics Division, BEI supplies position sensors to the automotive industry for greater comfort in seating as well as improved control through steering sensors. These devices also are used in agricultural equipment, drilling rigs, and medical equipment. BEI's inertial sensors use the company's GyroChip technology to provide stabilization, flight control, and guidance for the automotive, medical, aerospace, defense, and communications markets. The company's extensive line of rotary optical encoders uses a glass codewheel to measure motion, and the information then is translated into an electronic signal. BEI encoders are used in a broad range of industrial, office automation, instrumentation, military, and space applications. Displacement sensors use a fiber-optic probe to reflect light from a target surface to accurately measure displacements. BEI offers subsystems, combining controllers, and amplifiers to create a one-stop approach in providing motion-control systems used in highly automated robotic and pick-and-place applications. Finally, BEI manufactures miniscule silicon micro-electromechanical systems (MEMS), using micro-machining techniques. MEMS devices, both electrical and mechanical, are used in products such as pressure sensors, automotive anti-skid sensors, and air bag deployment sensors.

BEI's Lineage Dating to 1800s Piano Maker

Despite the high-tech nature of BEI's business, its history began with Dwight Hamilton Baldwin, a minister and school singing teacher who decided to open a music store in Cincinnati, Ohio, in 1862. As D.H. Baldwin & Co., the company became well known as a keyboard instrument dealer, then in 1889 the company began to make reed organs through its Hamilton Organ Company. A year later, Baldwin decided to make "the best piano that could be built," and a year later introduced its first piano, an upright model. Baldwin's first grand piano was introduced in 1895. Following Baldwin's death in 1899, the company achieved great fame with its concert grand pianos, which received numerous prestigious awards. It also gained valuable publicity due to the large number of artists who chose to use the Baldwin grand for their performances.

Baldwin grew into an international business, soon exporting pianos to more than 30 countries around the world. In addition to grands and uprights, Baldwin manufactured player pianos, which accounted for more than half of the company's sales by the early 1920s. But the rise of new media—movies, phonographs, and radio—soon resulted in dramatic cuts in this segment, and the situation only worsened with the advent of the Great Depression. Because it was well led and had an abundance of cash in reserve, Baldwin was able to carry on despite difficult conditions. During World War II the company was forced to cease making pianos, and to help in the war effort it used its woodworking expertise to manufacture wings and other aircraft parts.

Post-World War II Application
of Electronics to Music

When the war was over Baldwin first became involved in the application of electronics to musical instruments. The goal was to create an organ that would reproduce the sounds of pipe organs found in European cathedrals. Baldwin engineers developed a way to use optically encoded glass discs to reproduce the organ tones. The codewheel transcribed the original organ tones into etched-in opaque and transparent segments, so that when the codewheel rotated it created an alternating pattern of light and dark. Photodiodes then translated this into an electronic signal, which in turn could be processed and amplified to create the tones and harmonics needed to reproduce the source sound. In the late 1940s Baldwin introduced the electronic organ to the church and home market.

Baldwin began to venture beyond musical instruments in 1951 when the U.S. Army Signal Corp., recognizing that the company's technology could help in the pointing and tracking of radar antennas, contracted Baldwin to develop optical encoders using rotary code patterns. In 1953 Baldwin developed the first 16-bit divided circle machine, and in 1955 produced the first experimental optical encoders. With a new electronics market to service, Baldwin acquired American Radio and Television in Little Rock, Arkansas, which became the company's manufacturing center. By 1960 all coded disk manufacturing and personnel were transferred to Little Rock. In 1962 Baldwin's research resulted in an 18-bit optical encoder that was used in American Space flights. A year later the company produced the first optical encoder for space with LED light source. Also in 1963, the electronics division was incorporated as Baldwin Electronics, Inc., often referred to by its initials, BEI.

BEI's parent company appeared to take a radical change in direction in 1968 when it formed Baldwin-Central to acquire Denver-based Central Bank & Trust Co., but in truth Baldwin had been involved in financial services since the end of the 19th century. The company was a pioneer in the use of installment plan contracts and by the mid-1930s had gained a reputation as the banker of the piano industry. Some 20 years later, 65 percent of Baldwin's assets were tied to financial services. In 1969 Baldwin added a second Denver bank, Empire Savings & Loan, which two years later became involved in multifamily construction lending. Later, Baldwin acquired a third Denver bank, Jefferson Savings & Loan, and a Kansas City, Kansas, bank, Anchor Savings Association, as well as insurance interests. Baldwin's business was so heavily weighted toward financial assets that in 1973 the Federal Reserve ordered the company to divest certain assets not related to financial services or musical instruments. Thus in 1974 Baldwin's electronics subsidiary was spun off to 33 employees backed by Charles Crocker, a San Francisco venture capitalist. The company was renamed BEI Electronics Inc.

As an independent company, BEI Electronics expanded on a number of fronts. In 1975 it developed a 21-bit optical encoder used in weather satellites. BEI Industrial Encoder was formed in 1977. In 1979 the company developed the Star Selector Servo Subsystem used in the Hubble Space Telescope. During the 1980s BEI Electronics developed a linear gap displacement

transducer and the radiation-hardened optical encoders for the Galileo Space Probe. By now the company had emerged as a clear leader in encoder technology. Its space system experience was second to none, with its encoders having been used on the Gemini and Apollo missions, Galileo, the Hubble Telescope, and weather satellites. BEI encoders would later be employed on the Mars Observer missions, Spacelab, and the International Space Station. The devices were used to rotate satellite antennas, solar panels, control line-of-sight stabilization, attitude control, robotics, and shuttle arms. Also in the 1980s BEI Electronics developed a dual-ended quartz tuning fork that was employed in a gyro for use in missile guidance systems. Defense contracts soon became a major part of the company's business, in particular through the sale of the Hydra-70 rocket, which was relatively cheap, priced at $1,000 or less per rocket, making it an attractive training mission ammunition.

BEI Electronics quickly became overly dependent on its military business, so that when the company made an initial public offering of stock in 1989 it was greeted with little enthusiasm by investors, who worried that the company was too exposed to defense spending at a time when cutbacks were expected in military spending in the aftermath of the Soviet Union's collapse. The Gulf War resulted in a resurgence in rocket sales, but it was clear the BEI Electronics needed to find more commercial applications for its sensor products.

In the early 1990s BEI Electronics began an effort to diversify, initially through acquisitions, picking up Litton Encoder and Itek Encoder in 1990, which in the process eliminated its major U.S. competition. Also in that year, BEI Electronics acquired four of six divisions of Systron Donner Corp., adding the Duncan division, involved in position sensor technology; the Inertial division, makers of inertial reference and guidance components using new quartz sensor technology; the Edcliff division, which made pressure transducers; and the Sylmar division, producer of fluid controls and advanced cryogenic cooling systems for imaging sensors. Perhaps the most important acquisition in the Systron Donner purchase was the quartz technology from the Inertial division, which had the potential to transform measurement products in a way similar to what quartz had done to timekeeping. Quartz sensor technology would find a wide range of applications in miniaturized sensors. In late 1991, in a further attempt to move away from the defense industry, BEI Electronics also formed a new healthcare division, BEI Medical Systems, to take further advantage of the company's medical business. For some time its components for positioning and motors had been used in medical applications by other companies. Now BEI Electronics hoped to use these technologies to develop its own products.

To help facilitate the shift away from the defense business, Crocker took over as president and CEO of BEI Technology in October 1995 following the retirement of Peter G. Paraskos. At this stage, the company was composed of three operating units: Defenses Systems, which produced the Hydra-70 rocket and associated avionics; Sensors and Systems, which produced sensors and engineered subsystems for commercial, aerospace, and military applications; and Medical Systems, which offered proprietary instruments and supplies for medical diagnostic and some surgical procedures. While the latter two divisions were on the ascendancy, it was clear that the company's defense business was becoming increasingly less attractive and Crocker

---

Key Dates:

1948: Baldwin Piano and Organ Company uses an optically encoded disk to make an electronic organ.

1951: The U.S. Army Signal Corp. contracts Baldwin to develop optical encoders.

1962: Baldwin encoders are first used in the U.S. space program.

1974: Baldwin spins off BEI Electronics, Inc.

1997: BEI Electronics spins off BEI Technologies.

1998: BEI expands internationally through its acquisition of Ideacod, a French manufacturer of electronic sensors used in factory automation.

2000: OpticNet, Inc., a subsidiary dedicated to the development of fiber optic components for the telecommunications market, is formed.

---

began taking steps to exit the Hydra-70 rocket business in 1996. In the meantime Medical Systems continued to expand by acquisitions, buying OvaMed Corporation, which included subsidiaries Saratoga Medical and Fibertonics, involved in products for minimally invasive infertility and endoscopic procedures. Sensors and Systems succeeded in transferring its missile guidance technology, which employed quartz tuning forks in a gyro. The company's GyroChips were first used by Cadillac in 1996 to detect fishtailing and prevent the loss of traction, and a large number of carmakers soon followed suit.

Spinoff in 1997

Unable to find a buyer for the rocket business, Crocker simply shut it down and then took steps to split the remaining two divisions as a way to enhance the value of each. In June 1997 BEI Technologies, Inc. was formed to take over the Sensors & Systems division, the shares of which were distributed to BEI Electronics. BEI Electronics then changed its name to BEI Medical Systems Company. Shares of both companies now traded on the NASDAQ.

BEI Technologies was especially aggressive in selling the GyroChip to automakers. Sales of the sensors in 1998 totaled $20.2 million and grew to $54.4 million in 1999. BEI also was looking for further opportunities to take advantage of its other technologies. It expanded internationally in 1998 by acquiring Ideacod, a French company that manufactured electronic sensors used in factory automation. In 2000 it formed a new subsidiary, OpticNet, Inc., dedicated to the development of fiber optic components for the telecommunications market, using

BEI's MEMS process capability. In the previous two years, BEI had made significant investments in the development of MEMS for a number of applications. In 2001 BEI acquired from Boeing Co. the Digital Quartz Measurement Unit and the MIGITS (Miniature Integrated GPS/INS Tactical Systems) product lines, which had been co-developed by BEI's Systron Donner division. Systron Donner in 2002 would split into two units, devoted to automotive and inertial products.

The demand for BEI's GyroChip sensor in the automotive industry was the most important factor in the company's steady growth in sales. Revenues improved from $159.4 million in 1999 to $219.2 million in 2000. More than $53 million of that increase came from GyroChip sensors sold to automakers. In 2001 revenues increased 9 percent to $239 million. The sale of GyroChip sensors grew by more than $31 million, making up for a drop in sales to industrial customers, in particular the semiconductor capital equipment industry. A soft economy hurt BEI in 2002, leading to a 22.3 percent decrease in sales to $185.6 million. The company rebounded in 2003, with revenues totaling $213.7 million. Once again the sale of BEI GyroChip sensors to domestic and foreign automakers was the key factor, growing from $94.7 million in 2002 to $199.2 million in 2003. Ironically, BEI also was finding a use for GyroChip sensors in military aircraft, for which the technology was originally developed. In the foreseeable future, the company's fortunes were very much tied to the success of this one technology.

Principal Subsidiaries

BEI Sensors & Systems Company, Inc.; SiTek, Inc; BEI Ideacod, S.A.S.

Principal Competitors

CTS Corporation; Robert Bosch GbmH; Rockwell Automation, Inc.

Further Reading

"D.H. Baldwin Tuned Up for Fifth Straight Gain," *Barron's National Business and Financial Weekly,* April 17, 1972, p. 36.

Ginsberg, Steve, "BEI Spins Off Medical Care from Missiles," *San Francisco Business Times,* July 11, 1997, p. 1.

Henry, John, "From Music to Motion Control, Company Now Masters Space," *Arkansas Business,* April 23, 2001, p. 1.

Moore, Brenda L., "BEI Could Rally If Rollover Rating Buoys Sales of Car-Stability Sensors," *Wall Street Journal,* May 24 2000, CA2.

Savitz, Eric J., "Rocket and Roll," *Barron's,* September 11, 1989, p. 15.

—Ed Dinger

Bradford & Bingley

Bradford & Bingley PLC

21-27 Lambs Conduit Street
London WC1N 3BD
United Kingdom
Telephone: 44 20 7067 5500
Fax: 44 20 7067 5654
Web site: http://www.bbg.co.uk

Public Company
Incorporated: 1964 as Bradford & Bingley Building
    Society
Employees: 6,682
Total Assets: £32.2 billion ($56.64 billion) (2003)
Stock Exchanges: London
Ticker Symbol: BBG
NAIC: 522292 Real Estate Credit; 522120 Savings
    Institutions

Once Britain's second largest building society, Bradford & Bingley PLC has transformed itself into the country's tenth largest bank, with total assets of £32.2 billion ($54 billion) in 2003. Bradford & Bingley has done more than convert its status from mutual building society to a publicly listed bank; it has also shifted away from its traditional mortgage lending base. While Bradford & Bingley continues to operate its national network of Mortgage Express mortgage lending businesses, it has also built England's largest network of Independent Financial Advisors (IFAs), under primary brands The Marketplace and Charcol. Much of the company's growth in these areas has come through acquisitions, including the 2000 purchase of John Charcol and continuing through the end of 2003 with the acquisitions of IFA networks Holden Meehan and Aitchinson & Colegrave. The bank also operates the United Kingdom's fourth largest estate agency network, with more than 300 branches operating under various brand names, including Slater Hogg & Howison and Gascoigne Pees. Yet Bradford & Bingley's transformation appears not to have generated significant profit growth. In May 2004, the bank announced its intention to perform an about-face, abandoning the IFA model for the "multitie" financial products model made possible under the "de-

polarisation" reform in Britain's banking system in the early 2000s. As part of that process, Bradford & Bingley intends to sell off its newly noncore IFA networks, including the Charcol, Holden Meehan, and Aitchinson & Colgrave businesses. Leading the company's newest transformation is Steven Crawshaw, who was appointed CEO in March 2004. Bradford & Bingley PLC is listed on the London Stock Exchange.

Joining the Building Society Movement in the 1850s

The industrialization of Britain brought a demand for housing among the country's rising urban populations. The first mutual aid societies appeared in the late 18th century and, typically, featured the grouping of a number of artisans who pooled resources to build housing for themselves. Newly built houses were attributed to members of the pool by means of a ballot; when all the members had been provided housing, the pool was disbanded. For this reason, the early groups were known as "terminating societies."

As industrialization progressed in England, the population of the urban working class grew steadily. Toward the mid-19th century, the mutual aid society adapted to meet the needs of this new population. The lower wealth of individual members was compensated by their far larger number, who paid into the common pool. Instead of directly providing funding for housing, the building societies provided loans to members, who then paid back into the society. The new building societies were not meant to be disbanded, but instead were considered permanent, and indeed, many of the new type of building society incorporated the word "Permanent" into their names.

Over time, the building societies began to offer a wider range of banking services to their customers, adding savings products to their lending business. The building society movement was further solidified by the passage of a Building Societies Act in 1874, which also restricted building society operations to a limited number of financial products, such as mortgages and savings. The rise of worker's movements and the unionization of the British workforce also contributed to the rise of the building society sector, and by the late 19th century the movement had spread throughout the country. At its peak, the United Kingdom boasted some 2,700 building societies.

Company Perspectives:

Our Strategy: Our focus continues to be on growing our selective lending and retail businesses, whilst maintaining cost control. We aim to build and develop our retail business by investing in: A growing adviser base; improving the network; building new IT sales and support infrastructure. Increase margin in the selective lending business whilst offering market leading products via the Mortgage Express brand. Improve level of cross-sell from estate agency and savings customers.

The earliest building societies tended to be rather small, serving only their own local communities and outlying areas. In Yorkshire, near Leeds, two building societies were formed in the neighboring towns of Bradford and Bingley in 1851. The first was the Bradford Second Equitable Benefit Building Society, founded in August of that year. The second was founded in Bingley, and grouped two neighboring villages as Bingley, Morton and Shipley Permanent Benefit Building Society.

Following the passage of the Building Societies Act of 1874, the Bradford group reincorporated as the Bradford Second Equitable Building Society in 1882. The society grew strongly with the strong growth of Bradford's population base, and by the outbreak of World War I had topped assets of £1 million. In the meantime, more stringent legislation, put in place in the 1890s, had contributed to a sharp decline in the number of building societies in operation, and by World War I there were only 1,700 building societies. Despite their impact on British society, the building society movement remained financially modest—by 1914, the total assets of the country's building societies amounted to just £76 million. The Bradford society's strong asset base placed it among the country's top building societies.

Merger of Equals in the 1960s

Bradford continued to build its stature into the 1930s. In 1921, the society expanded by acquiring the Leeds Equitable Building Society. Then, in 1930, Bradford opened its first branch office, on London's High Holborn Street. Bradford was not alone in this geographic diversification. By 1934, the Bingley society, which had changed its name to Bingley Building Society in 1929, had opened its own London branch. Bradford later simplified its name, too, becoming the Bradford Equitable Building Society in 1946. Both societies continued building up their branch networks. By the early 1960s, Bradford's network included 22 branches stretching from Glasgow to London. Bingley, which boasted more than 30 branches, had concentrated its own growth on its northern region base. At the same time, the two societies—located within five miles of each other—began cooperating in an effort to stem the growing competition from such nearby and large-scale competitors as Leeds Permanent, the Provincial, Halifax, and local rival, the Bradford Permanent.

By then, both societies had been hit by legislation that forced building societies to raise their mortgage rates, starting in 1939. This change, and rising competition from the nation's banking sector for members' savings accounts, forced the beginning of a shakeup in the U.K. building society market, which entered a long period of consolidation. The consolidation of the sector took on greater movement in the 1960s, after the passage of a new Building Societies Act in 1960, which placed limits on the size of loans, particularly corporate loans, made by building societies. The British government encouraged the further consolidation of the sector with the passage of an additional Building Society Act in 1962, which incorporated all previous legislation governing the sector. The result was a stream of mergers and acquisitions that continued into the 1990s. By then, just 100 or so building societies remained.

The Bradford and Bingley societies proved to be survivors of the industry consolidation in large part by joining together. Bingley had started off on its own, acquiring the Kendal Model Building Society in 1963. In that year, however, Bradford and Bingley began their own merger negotiations, and soon after announced their intention to merge their operations, forming the single Bradford & Bingley Building Society. The merger of equals, completed in 1964, one of the largest to date, created the nation's eighth largest building society with total assets of more than £100 million, and a national branch network of more than 50 branches—the level of cooperation between the two societies had helped them avoid too much overlap, and the larger group possessed duplicate branches in just a small number of larger markets.

Bradford & Bingley promptly adopted a well-known logo, featuring two men—known as Mr. Bradford and Mr. Bingley—sporting bowler hats. At first operated by a joint team of managers from Bradford and Bingley, in 1966, the former Bingley head, Robert Gardner, was appointed as the sole general manager of the entire group.

Gaining Scale in the 1980s

In 1969, Bradford & Bingley began innovating, launching a new and successful savings product, known as the Save As You Earn scheme. The society also became an early adopter of computer technology, installing its first IBM computer in 1968. The company continued marketing aggressively into the 1970s, and expanded by opening a number of new branches, including 13 new branches in 1973 alone. By the end of the decade, the societies' assets had topped £1 billion for the first time.

As the consolidation of the building society sector gathered steam in the 1980s, Bradford & Bingley emerged as one of the trend's primary drivers. In 1980, Bradford & Bingley added Spread Eagle Building Society, followed by Hyde Building Society in 1981. In 1982, the society acquired Heart of Oak and Enfield Building Society, adding its 28 branches. That acquisition particularly strengthened Bradford & Bingley's presence in the southeast of England. In that year, also, the society picked up new additions in Saddleworth and Swansea Park, as well as the Target Building Society.

Into the mid-1980s, Bradford & Bingley continued its stream of acquisitions and takeovers, adding Horsham, Housing and General, Stockport, and Padiham in 1983; United Provinces, Clapham Permanent, Dover & Folkestone, and Glamorgan in 1984; and Forresters, Hibernian, and Merseyside in 1985.

Key Dates:

1851: The Bradford Second Equitable Benefit Building Society and the Bingley, Morton and Shipley Permanent Benefit Building Society are created.

1921: Bradford acquires the Leeds Equitable Building Society.

1930: Bradford opens its first branch office in London.

1934: Bingley opens a branch office in London.

1963: Bingley acquires the Kendal Model Building Society.

1964: Bradford and Bingley complete a merger, forming the eighth largest building society in the United Kingdom.

1973: Bradford & Bingley opens 13 new branches.

1978: Total assets top £1 billion.

1980: Bradford & Bingley launches an acquisition drive, taking over Spread Eagle Building Society, the first of more than 20 over the next decade.

1991: Total assets top £22 billion.

1997: The company begins expanding into the retail segment with the acquisition of Mortgage Express from Lloyds TSB.

1998: Black Rock Estate Agents is acquired from Lloyds TSB.

2000: The company acquires the John Charcol network of IFAs; ''de-mutualizes'' and lists on the London Stock Exchange as Bradford & Bingley PLC.

2001: The MarketPlace IFA network is launched within the existing branch network.

2002: The company pays £650 million to acquire the General Motors Acceptance Corporation's U.K. mortgage business.

2003: The company acquires the Holden Meehan and Aitchinson & Colgrave IFA networks.

2004: The company announces plans to sell off its IFA operations and refocus as a multi-tie operator.

The society next entered merger talks with another of the country's leading building societies, Yorkshire Building Society, in 1986. When those talks collapsed, Bradford & Bingley instead returned to the acquisition trail, acquiring Stanley Building Society in 1986 and Chilterns Building Society in 1987. After a brief pause, the society returned to expansion, adding building societies in Sheffield, Louth Mablethorpe & Sutton, and Leamington in 1990 and Hampshire and Hendon in 1991. By then, Bradford & Bingley's total assets had soared past £22 billion.

Multi-tie Transformation for the New Century

The building society consolidation had been completed in large part by the mid-1990s, and by the turn of the century, just 60 building societies remained, most of which were relatively modest in size. The fading out of the building society movement was spurred in large part by new legislation passed in the 1980s. On the one hand, banks and other financial institutions were allowed to extend their reach into mortgages, the building societies' traditional territory. On the other hand, the building societies, in a new act passed in 1986, were allowed to extend

their own operations into other financial areas. At the same time, the building societies were given the right to opt to abandon their mutual status in favor of a public offering or acquisition by a bank. Many of the country's largest building societies, such as Abbey National, took advantage of the new rules, and promptly secured their places among the country's largest financial institutions.

Bradford & Bingley remained a notable exception, sticking to its mutual status into the late 1990s and, with assets of £24 million by the end of the decade, claiming the number two spot among the country's building societies. Yet the society took advantage of the new freedom of operations and began adding new operations in the middle of the decade. One of the society's first moves was to purchase the Mortgage Express chain from Lloyds TSB in 1997. Mortgage Express was present in the specialized mortgage segment, with a focus on the self-employed market. In 1998, Bradford & Bingley branched out from mortgages for the first time, returning to Lloyds TSB in order to acquire its Black Horse Estate Agents operation, one of the country's leading estate agents with a national network of 370 offices.

This move was part of Bradford & Bingley's shifting focus from lending to retail operations. In 1999, the company solidified that transition with the purchase of John Charcol, the country's leading Independent Financial Advisor (IFA), with some 700 branches throughout the United Kingdom.

Yet Bradford & Bingley's mutual status was challenged in that year by a member revolt—under building society rules, members were allowed to petition to convert a society's status to public limited company. Management at first opposed conversion. Yet, after an early poll of membership indicated that a majority favored conversion, the management gave in, and instead backed the conversion. When the matter came to a vote in 2000, fully 80 percent of the society's membership favored conversion. Bradford & Bingley then completed its public offering in December 2000, taking on the new name as Bradford & Bingley PLC.

Bradford & Bingley now emphasized its growing retail arm, which accounted for the major part of its revenues and especially its profits. As part of its refocus, the company formed a joint venture with Alltel Corporation, based in the United States, in order to outsource its lending support operations. In 2001, the company launched a new chain of independent mortgage broking agents, called The MarketPlace at Bradford & Bingley, which provided IFA services within the former society's national network of more than 600 branches.

Under the legislation governing conversions, Bradford & Bingley was protected from hostile takeover attempts for a five-year period. Yet the company was rumored to have entered talks with the larger Barclays PLC. Those talks reportedly broke off after the two sides were unable to agree about a purchase price. Instead, Bradford & Bingley renewed its interest in the mortgage market in 2002. In that year, it ended the Alltel joint venture. At the same time, its mortgage business gained new scale with the announcement of its acquisition of General Motors Acceptance Corporation's U.K. mortgage business for £650 million.

Through 2003, Bradford & Bingley continued building up its IFA network. In June of that year, the company acquired

Holden Meehan, a leading IFA group, which was then placed under the Charcol brand name. The acquisition helped place Bradford & Bingley in the top ranks of U.K. IFA groups. Another result of the acquisition was that it caused Bradford & Bingley to lose its takeover protection.

Bradford & Bingley continued adding on to its IFA network through the end of 2003, acquiring Aitchinson & Colgrave, the Scottish leader with 20 branches. That purchase not only extended the company's geographic reach, it also extended its business into the higher-end bracket.

Yet Bradford & Bingley's IFA growth had not yielded significant improvement in profits, and the group's share price lagged behind its competitors. In March 2004, after CEO Christopher Rodriguez stepped down, the company named Steven Crawshaw in his place. Crawshaw promptly announced that Bradford & Bingley intended to change its strategy, restructuring its operation to focus on a "multi-tie" financial products model made possible by the new de-polarization of the financial products market. As part of that effort, the company announced its intention to sell off its IFA operations in May 2004. After more than 150 years Bradford & Bingley remained a prominent figure on the United Kingdom's financial landscape.

Principal Subsidiaries

Bradford & Bingley International; Charcol; Charcol Holden Meehan; The Marketplace.

Principal Competitors

Abbey National PLC; Barclays Bank; Cheltenham and Gloucester PLC; Alliance and Leicester PLC; Northern Rock PLC; Bank of Ireland; Britannia Building Society.

Further Reading

"B&B IFA Profits Plummet," *Money Marketing,* February 19, 2004, p. 7.

Bone, Alison, "Crawshaw Says Growth Is Priority at B&B," *Money Marketing,* March 11, 2004, p. 17.

Brown-Humes, Christopher, "We're Not Banks! Vote for Us!," *New Statesman,* March 19, 1999, p. XII.

Duncan, Chris, "Crawshaw Takes B&B into Multi-tie Arena," *Money Marketing,* May 27, 2004, p. 20

Griffiths, Katherine, "Landslide Vote for Conversion at Bradford & Bingley," *Independent,* July 18, 2000, p. 16.

Henshall, Angela, "IFA 'Jewels' Are Up for Sell-Off," *Money Marketing,* May 27, 2004, p. 20.

Lloyd, Tammy, "Bradford & Bingley Tops the Tree," *Financial Advisor,* October 9, 2002.

Love, Bruce, "B&B Goes North with Aitchison & Colegrave Buy," *Money Marketing,* September 25, 2003, p. 80.

Marshall, Andrew, "How Mr. Bradford and Mr. Bingley Lost Their Hats (But Not Their Heads)," *Independent,* April 18, 2001, p. 3.

Merrell, Caroline, "Has the B&B Taken Too Much on Board?," *Times,* February 9, 2004, p. 22.

"Mutually Assured Destruction?," *Economist,* May 1, 1999, p. 67.

—M.L. Cohen

C.R. Bard, Inc.

730 Central Avenue
Murray Hill, New Jersey 07974-1139
U.S.A.
Telephone: (908) 277-8000
Toll Free: (800) 367-2273
Fax: (908) 277-8240
Web site: http://www.crbard.com

Public Company
Incorporated: 1923
Employees: 8,300
Sales: $1.43 billion (2003)
Stock Exchanges: New York
Ticker Symbol: BCR
NAIC: 339112 Surgical and Medical Instrument
Manufacturing; 339113 Surgical Appliance and
Supplies Manufacturing; 334510 Electromedical and
Electrotherapeutic Apparatus Manufacturing

C.R. Bard, Inc. is a developer and manufacturer of surgical, medical, diagnostic, and patient-care instruments, concentrating on four main areas: vascular, urology, oncology, and surgical specialty products. Bard markets these products worldwide to hospitals, extended care facilities, and individual healthcare professionals. More than 70 percent of company revenues originate in the United States, 18 percent in Europe, 5 percent in Japan, and the remainder elsewhere. A pioneer in the healthcare industry, Bard developed presterilized instruments and the concept of complete sterilized disposable surgical trays. The company has grown in more recent years by acquiring companies and product lines, entering into licensing agreements and joint ventures, and making investments in companies developing new healthcare technologies.

Early History

C.R. Bard, Inc. was founded by Charles Russell Bard, an American importer of French silks as well as the exclusive distributor of a 19th-century European medicine purported to relieve urinary discomfort. In 1907 Bard began distributing a recently invented urethral catheter for a French firm, J. Eynard, his European connections enabling him to market the catheter in the United States. Bard's involvement with medical products expanded in 1915 when he became partners with Morgan Parker, who had invented a new scalpel. Parker provided the patents, Bard provided office space and $500, and Bard-Parker Co. Inc. was begun.

During World War I, imported scalpels became scarce, and demand for the Bard-Parker scalpel soared. After the war, however, Bard and Parker disagreed over manufacture of the scalpel. While Parker wanted the company to manufacture the instrument, Bard wanted to continue to subcontract for manufacture with a company in Ohio. The two partners could not resolve their differences, and in 1923 Parker bought out Bard's interest in the partnership for $23,000. Bard-Parker later became a division of Becton, Dickinson and Company, a medical instruments manufacturer.

Bard formally incorporated as C.R. Bard, Inc. in 1923, continuing to distribute Eynard catheters and other urological devices. His health failing, however, Bard hired John Frederick Willits as his sales manager. Willits, a former sales manager for a medical book publisher, understood that Bard would eventually turn over the business to him.

Bard kept his word and sold the business to Willits and accountant Edson L. Outwin in 1926 for $18,000. Willits, the older of the two men, became president of the company, and Outwin became vice-president and treasurer. Although Willits and Outwin borrowed the money to buy C.R. Bard, within a year, they were able to repay the loan with profits from the company. Bard became a company consultant until his retirement in 1932. He died in 1934.

Outwin, Willits, and James Vassar, the company's first full-time salesperson, hired by Bard in 1923, visited their sales regions twice a year and were on the road for 12 to 14 weeks at a time. Willits covered the West Coast, Outwin the Southeast and Mid-Atlantic states, and Vassar the rest of the United States and part of Canada. In 1929 the company added another sales representative, Willits's son Harris, to cover the upper Midwest,

Company Perspectives:

Over our 95-year history, Bard has responded to the needs of clinicians, health care professionals, and patients with strong, market-leading product franchises under a structure based on product expertise and technology.

To continue to help customers meet tomorrow's health-care challenges, Bard is refocusing its efforts and will now provide more specialized support for its products and services. The Bard focus is on specific Disease State Management needs, both diagnostic and interventional, in three key areas: Vascular, Urology and Oncology. In addition, Bard continues to invest in and support its complete line of advanced Surgical Specialty products and services in hernia repair, powered irrigation, and hemostasis.

With an emphasis on Disease State Management, Bard focuses its products and services across the spectrum of care—from wellness and disease prevention to early diagnosis and treatment to post-care management. By utilizing a Disease State Management strategy, Bard continues to advance the delivery of health care with technological developments that embody quality, integrity, and service.

New York, and Canada. During this time, the four men sold the company's line of urological instruments directly to practicing urologists.

In 1934 Dr. Hobart Belknap, an Oregon doctor and Bard customer, published an article in the *Urological Cutaneous Review* presenting his idea for a balloon-type instrument to control secondary bleeding in cases in which no suprapubic opening existed. Davol Rubber Co. of Providence, Rhode Island, developed a device based on Belknap's idea. During this time, American Anode, a division of B.F. Goodrich of Akron, Ohio, also developed devices based on Belknap's idea for Dr. Frederick E.B. Foley of St. Paul, Minnesota. Extensive litigation ensued for the patent for the device, until Davol and Goodrich agreed to cross-license each other's product. The generic name for the instrument became the Foley catheter. Because Bard was already the exclusive distributor of Davol's other catheters, it also began distributing the Foley catheters. Sales of Foley catheters took off when Harris Willits discovered that a surgeon in Flint, Michigan, was using the Foley on a routine basis as a retention catheter for postoperative patients.

In 1940 Germany's invasion of France halted all shipments of Eynard instruments from France to C.R. Bard in the United States. Bard added American-made catheters to its line when Norman Jeckel founded the United States Catheter and Instrument Corporation (USCI) to manufacture the first American woven catheter which he had developed. However, when the United States entered World War II in 1941, the U.S. military had first priority for purchase of the USCI catheters, limiting supplies and Bard's ability to meet the demand of civilian customers.

Soaring Postwar Sales

In 1945 Outwin and John Willits switched positions at the company, with Outwin becoming company president and

Willits, vice-president. Harris Willits became a member of the board of directors. Furthermore, a 150 percent increase in the company's net sales since 1935 led to the addition of two more sales positions. Net sales increased between 1945 and 1947 as a result of new urological procedures and the increase in the population of urologists and patients.

The soaring sales also necessitated a move to bigger headquarters. Bard commissioned a 5,400-square-foot building to be constructed in Summit, New Jersey, and in March 1948, the company moved there from its Madison Avenue offices. That fiscal year, net sales rose to above the $1 million mark, and 18 employees were added. Bard quickly outgrew its new facility, and, as more space was needed for on-the-premises packaging, Bard purchased the property next door to its facility.

During the 1950s, net sales grew more than 400 percent, and the number of employees increased to 200. Whereas in 1940 more than 85 percent of its products had been imported, by the 1950s the company's products were all made in the United States. During this time, Willits resigned as chairperson, and Outwin took his place. Harris Willits then became Bard's president.

In 1957 Bard introduced its products in presterilized packages. Initially the company sent its packaged goods to an outside laboratory for sterilization. However, packaging was soon sterilized in Bard's own laboratories. The introduction of presterilized products cut down on costs for hospitals and reduced the risk of contamination. The introduction of ready-to-use disposable products led to a contract with Resiflex Laboratory, Inc. to market Resiflex's disposable drainage tubes with the tradename Bardic. Bard also contracted with Deseret Pharmaceutical Company, Inc. to distribute its new intravenous tube tradenamed Bardic-Deseret Intracath. This soft, plastic tube could be placed in the patient's vein for intravenous feeding, eliminating the need to retain a steel needle for feeding.

The decade of the 1960s brought remarkable growth. Net sales increased by $42 million, reaching $51 million in 1969. The number of employees increased from 200 to 2,200. In 1961 the company moved its headquarters to a 50,000-square-foot building in Murray Hill, New Jersey. The company expanded its product line by marketing cardiological, radiological, and anesthesiological products, in addition to urological devices. By 1969, Bard owned 14 plants and was manufacturing 75 percent of the 6,000 products it sold.

Bard became a public company in 1963 when the Outwin family sold their stock on the over-the-counter market. Chairperson Edson Outwin, however, retained his own personal shares, representing a 2.5 percent interest in the company. Outwin remained chairperson until 1966, when he resigned due to ill health. Harris Willits then became chairperson, and Outwin was named chairman emeritus. In 1968 Bard stock began trading on the New York Stock Exchange for the first time.

Bard's thriving international mail-order business led to the formation of two new corporations in 1963. Bard-Davol Inc., located in England and owned equally by C.R. Bard, Inc. and Davol Rubber Inc., began producing surgical and hospital supplies for the United Kingdom. Bard-Davol International, headquartered in Bard's Murray Hill, New Jersey, offices, was re-

Key Dates:

1907: Charles Russell Bard begins U.S. distribution of a urethral catheter developed in Europe.

1923: Bard formally incorporates his business as C.R. Bard, Inc.

1926: Bard sells his company to John Frederick Willits and Edson L. Outwin for $18,000.

1934: Company begins distributing Foley catheters.

1948: Headquarters are moved from New York City to Summit, New Jersey; sales surpass the $1 million mark.

1957: C.R. Bard begins marketing its products in presterilized packages.

1961: Headquarters are shifted to Murray Hill, New Jersey.

1963: Company goes public with a listing on the over-the-counter market.

1964: First in-house manufacturing by Bard.

1966: Company acquires United States Catheter and Instrument.

1968: Bard's stock begins trading on the New York Stock Exchange; 172,000-square-foot plant opens in Murray Hill.

1979: Company gains the sole rights to manufacture and sell the Gruntzig angioplasty catheter.

1980: Davol Inc. is acquired.

1993: C.R. Bard pleads guilty to 391 criminal charges and agrees to pay $61 million in fines in connection with a scandal involving faulty catheters; three former executives are later found guilty of criminal charges connected to the same scandal.

1998: Company sells its coronary catheter laboratory business, including its angioplasty operations.

2001: C.R. Bard agrees to be acquired by Tyco International Ltd. for $3.1 billion.

2002: Drop in Tyco shares leads to a cancellation of the sale to Tyco.

sponsible for all other export trade. A year later, Bard formed C.R. Bard Limited, headquartered in Toronto, specifically to handle distribution in Canada.

Entering Manufacturing in the Mid-1960s

Bard's first in-house manufacturing began in 1964 with the molding and assembling of medical plastic tubing. Bard began making its own intravenous tubes and disposable surgical masks when Bard's and Deseret's association ended on friendly terms.

Bard bought USCI in 1966 after a 25-year association with this leading producer of urological instruments and cardiovascular products. USCI was a well-respected and innovative company, whose founder, Norman Jeckel, had collaborated with Nobel Prize winner Andre Cournand to develop the first intravenous heart catheter. USCI scientists had also collaborated on the development of artificial arteries and Dacron grafts.

In 1968 the MacBick Company of New England and Lowndes Products Inc. of Easley, South Carolina, also became part of the Bard corporation. MacBick designed and manufactured hospital supplies and equipment, including mobile carts, workstations, and disposable presterilized patient-care items. Lowndes produced underpads, diapers, mattress covers, surgeons' caps and masks, and other products for the medical market.

Once again, Bard found itself in need of more space because of its expanded packaging and in-house sterilization operations. As a result, the company doubled the size of its headquarters and built a 172,000-square-foot manufacturing plant, also in Murray Hill. With the completion of the new plant, the company consolidated all of its New Jersey manufacturing and product assembly operations.

Bard also began manufacturing its own extruded tubing at this plant. By 1982, it was producing 14,000 miles of extruded tubing rather than purchasing it from outside vendors. Bard also expanded by building a 100,000-square-foot plant in Covington, Georgia, to produce Foley drainage trays and clean catch kits.

Pursuing Acquisitions in the 1970s and 1980s

During the 1970s, Bard made several acquisitions as its business rapidly grew. The company acquired Homer Higgs Associates, Inc. of Fairfield, New Jersey, a distributor of convalescent and home-care products, and Burnett Instruments Co., Inc. of Lawrence, Kansas, a manufacturer of disposable instruments, orthopedic and physiotherapy products, and electronic heat and related products for hot compress therapy. LeMoyne & Grant Inc., of Montreal, Canada, which produced mobile stretchers, also became part of Bard during this time. Furthermore, Med-Econ Plastics of California, a maker of disposable plastic respiratory products, was acquired in 1972, as well as Sani-Pac Corp. of New York, manufacturers of bed pads and adult diapers. Two years later, Bard acquired a company that made suction collection instruments, Deaton Medical Co. of Oklahoma.

Acquisitions continued throughout the decade, including American Membrane Corp. of California—which held a license from the federal government to develop a membrane for kidney dialysis—and William Harvey Research Corp. of California, the developer of the disposable bubble oxygenator and cardiotomy used in open-heart surgery. Bard also acquired Medical Device Laboratory, Aerway Laboratories Inc., and MI Systems, Inc. By 1976, Bard was distributing 13,000 products.

In 1979 Bard obtained the sole rights to manufacture and sell the Gruntzig angioplasty catheter. This device, with a small balloon at the tip, could be used to open up artery walls by pressing fatty deposits against the walls. This device and procedure, called angioplasty, became a well-accepted alternative to the more costly and riskier heart bypass surgery. In using the Gruntzig catheter, the surgeon inserted a long wire through the femoral artery near the groin and up through the patient's arteries to the clogged arteries of the heart. A tiny balloon at the end of the wire was then inflated, compressing the fat against the walls of the artery and opening the passage to allow more blood to flow to the heart.

The 1970s brought growth in Bard's international operations as well. Bard entered into joint ventures with companies in

Japan and Denmark, and it acquired Brazilian company Rossifil Industria Produtos Plasticos Ltda., a producer of intravenous administration, blood collection, and transfusion sets.

In the late 1970s, Robert H. McCaffrey was elected CEO and George T. Maloney was elected president and chief operating officer. Harris Willits retired from his honorary chair in 1979. He died in 1992.

Bard's growth prompted the company to decentralize in 1980, forming divisions based on product lines, including urological, cardiopulmonary, implants, cardiology and radiology, medsystems, electro/medical, home health divisions, and international divisions. Divisions designed and carried out their own product development, working with medical specialists.

The 1980s brought another healthy growth spurt for Bard. In 1980 Bard continued to expand by purchasing Davol Inc. and Davol International from International Paper Company. This acquisition was significant as Davol manufactured Foley catheters, still Bard's single largest selling product. Bard also acquired Shield Healthcare Management Inc., Catheter Technology Corp. and the assets of Radi Medical Systems AB, all in the early 1980s.

Some acquisitions sent the company in new directions. The purchase of Automated Screening Devices Inc., which produced a blood pressure monitoring system, moved Bard toward more technologically advanced products. Bard also entered the orthopedic implants arena by becoming the sole distributor in the United States and Canada of the orthopedic line of German firm Waldemar Link GmbH & Co.

By the late 1980s, the company operated domestic plants in 12 states and Puerto Rico and plants or offices in several foreign countries, including Canada, Mexico, Australia, Japan, Hong Kong, India, Singapore, as well as most countries in Europe and Great Britain. In 1990 McCaffrey retired, and Maloney became president and CEO. Shortly after that, William H. Longfield was named company president.

Catheter Scandal in the Early 1990s

During this time, Bard faced some challenges regarding its coronary balloon angioplasty catheters. In 1990 the company had to temporarily withdraw its catheters from the market, pending approval from the Federal Drug Administration (FDA), after modifications were made to the devices. While catheter sales for that year were virtually nonexistent, Bard reentered the angioplasty market in April 1991.

In the early 1990s, Bard began to focus more carefully on its major markets, selling those divisions incidental to their main focus of development of single-patient-use products for diagnosis and treatment for the urological, cardiovascular, and surgical markets. In 1990 the company sold its Shield Healthcare Centers subsidiary to a subsidiary of Kobayashi Pharmaceutical Co. of Japan and also sold its MedSystems infusion pump division to Baxter International Inc.

In 1992 Bard had net sales of more than $990 million, a 13 percent increase over 1991 sales of $876 million. The company attributed the sales increase in part to its reentrance into the balloon angioplasty market following FDA approval of several of Bard's designs. Furthermore, the company looked forward to a healthy sales increase from the marketing of an implant from Collagen Corp. that would combat urinary incontinence. The product was available in several foreign countries, and FDA approval was pending in the United States in 1992.

Late in 1993 litigation connected with the defective catheters the company had sold from 1987 to 1990 began to play itself out. C.R. Bard pleaded guilty to 391 criminal charges of lying to regulators and illegally altering and marketing catheters, essentially, according to prosecutors, turning patients into human "guinea pigs." Use of the flawed catheters had resulted in scores of emergency surgeries and was linked to two deaths. Prosecutors called the company's actions "a truly egregious example of corporate criminal conduct," and said that Bard had engaged in the illegalities in order to get the catheters to market quickly "to maintain market share and reap huge profits." The company agreed to pay $61 million in fines—the largest such fine ever imposed in an FDA investigation. In October 1993 Maloney and five former Bard executives were indicted for their alleged involvement in the scandal, the charges centering on conspiracy, mail fraud, making false statements, and shipment of adulterated devices. Maloney immediately resigned to concentrate on his defense. He and two other defendants were eventually acquitted, but the other three were found guilty in August 1995, and one year later each was sentenced to 18 months in jail.

Eventually succeeding Maloney in the top position was Longfield, who was named president and CEO in June 1995. Longfield became chairman as well in September 1995. Throughout the mid-1990s, C.R. Bard continued to add to its product lines through acquisitions. Late in 1993 the company acquired Redmond, Washington-based Bainbridge Sciences Inc., developer of diagnostic tests for early detection of prostate, bladder, cervical, and lung cancer. During 1994, when revenues exceeded $1 billion for the first time, Bard bought Angiomed AG, a German maker of specialty healthcare products, such as self-expanding vascular stents (tiny tubular devices used to maintain the opening of veins and arteries). Through a stock swap valued at about $100 million, the company acquired MedChem Products, Inc., of Woburn, Massachusetts, in mid-1995. MedChem specialized in catheters, catheter kits for neonatal and adult intravenous therapy, and other surgical products. In its largest deal yet, Bard paid about $143 million for Impra, Inc. late in 1996. Headquartered in Tempe, Arizona, Impra produced vascular grafts used for blood-vessel replacement surgery.

In 1998 Bard restructured globally along disease-state management lines and also made some divestments. The most significant latter move was the sale of the coronary catheter laboratory business, which included the company's angioplasty operations. This had once been Bard's star performer, but the business never recovered from the early 1990s scandal. Bard sold the business to Arterial Vascular Engineering Inc. for $550 million. The company also sold its diagnostic sciences unit and its intra-aortic balloon-catheter and pump business in 1998 and its cardiopulmonary division the following year. C.R. Bard ended the decade by reporting 1999 profits of $118.1 million on revenues of $1.04 billion.

Early 2000s: Remaining Independent in Wake of Failed Buyout by Tyco

During 2001 Bard acquired Surgical Sense, Inc., maker of the Kugel patch, which was used in the surgical repair of hernias. The biggest news that year, however, came in May when the company agreed to be acquired by Tyco International Ltd. for $3.1 billion in stock. As a midsize player in a consolidating industry, Bard had felt increasing pressure to sell out to a larger rival, and officials believed they needed a larger research-and-development budget to stay competitive. After the deal was delayed later in the year because of Federal Trade Commission concerns about the combined company having too large a piece of the market for urology products, it was killed altogether in February 2002 because of a drop in Tyco shares that coincided with rising concerns about possible accounting irregularities and other potentially scandalous activities at the once-mighty conglomerate.

In the immediate aftermath of the failed Tyco deal, Bard moved ahead with a consolidation of business units that aimed to yield savings of $25 million in annual operating costs. This money would then be plowed back into new product research. In August 2003 Longfield retired, though he remained on the board of directors. Succeeding him as chairman and CEO was Timothy M. Ring, who had been president of the vascular products group. Ring stayed the course, continuing to seek out acquisitions to strengthen existing product lines. For example, in July 2004 the company acquired Onux Medical, Inc., producer of a system used to fixate prosthetic patches in place during hernia surgeries. The acquired system perfectly complemented Bard's market-leading line of hernia surgery patch products. In August 2004 C.R. Bard announced an agreement to sell its line of disposable endoscopes used to diagnose lung and digestive-tract conditions to Conmed Corporation for $80 million.

Principal Subsidiaries

B.C.P. Puerto Rico, Inc.; BCR, Inc.; Bard Access Systems, Inc.; Bard ASDI, Inc.; Bard Canada Inc.; Bard Cardiopulmonary, Inc.; Bard Devices, Inc.; Bard Healthcare, Inc.; Bard Holdings Limited (U.K.); Bard Implants, Inc.; Bard International, Inc.; Bard Shannon Limited (Ireland); Dymax Corporation; EndoMatrix; IMPRA, Inc.; MedChem Products, Inc.; Navarre Biomedical, Ltd.; Productos Bard de Mexico S.A. de C.V.; Productos Para el Cuidada de la Salud, S.A. de C.V. (Mexico); ProSeed, Inc.; Roberts Laboratories, Inc.; Shield Healthcare Centers, Inc.

Principal Competitors

Baxter International Inc.; Becton, Dickinson and Company; Johnson & Johnson; Abbott Laboratories; United States Surgical Corporation; Guidant Corporation; St. Jude Medical, Inc.

Further Reading

Bailey, Maureen, ''Poetry in Catheters?,'' *Barron's,* April 21, 1980, p. 54.

Bard World, Volume 2, Number 4, 75th Anniversary Edition, Murray Hill, N.J.: C.R. Bard, Inc., 1982.

Bulkeley, William M., ''Former Executives of Bard Receive 18 Months in Jail,'' *Wall Street Journal,* August 9, 1996, p. B2.

Carton, Barbara, ''Bard Ex-Officials Are Found Guilty in Catheter Case,'' *Wall Street Journal,* August 25, 1995, p. B2.

Cochran, Thomas N., ''Redoubtable Bard: It Has Its Own Special Rx for Success,'' *Barron's,* December 7, 1987, pp. 15+.

Diller, Wendy, ''More FDA Woe for Bard: Angioplasty Catheter Is Taken Off Market,'' *Northern New Jersey Record,* February 21, 1990, p. E1.

Dodge, Catherine, ''Bard Calls Off Deal After Drop in Tyco Shares,'' *Bergen County (N.J.) Record,* February 7, 2002, p. B1.

Kennedy, John H., and Matthew Brelis, ''Firm Admits Guilt in Flawed Catheters,'' *Boston Globe,* October 16, 1993.

Kindel, Stephen, ''A Deadly Probe,'' *Financial World,* December 11, 1990, pp. 52–4.

Maremont, Mark, and Nikhil Deogun, ''Tyco Is Near Deal to Acquire C.R. Bard, Medical-Products Maker, for $3.1 Billion,'' *Wall Street Journal,* May 30, 2001, p. A3.

McCoy, Frank, ''Can a 'Microprobe' Get Bard's Blood Pumping?,'' *Business Week,* February 15, 1988, pp. 98F+.

Silverman, Ed, and David Schwab, ''Tyco Buying C.R. Bard for $3.2B,'' *Newark (N.J.) Star-Ledger,* May 31, 2001, p. 55.

Tanouye, Elyse, and George Anders, ''C.R. Bard Chairman and Five Others Are Indicted in Heart-Catheter Scandal,'' *Wall Street Journal,* October 18, 1993, p. A3.

Todd, Susan, ''Bard Marches On,'' *Newark (N.J.) Star-Ledger,* April 25, 2002, p. 31.

——, ''C.R. Bard Appoints Chief Executive Officer,'' *Newark (N.J.) Star-Ledger,* February 14, 2003, p. 48.

Twitchell, Evelyn Ellison, ''Sweet New Song: A Broken Engagement Leaves Bard Strong,'' *Barron's,* February 18, 2002, p. T8.

Weiss, Gary, ''Despite a Tough Blow, Bard Is Up and Swinging,'' *Business Week,* November 19, 1990, p. 128.

Wyatt, Edward A., ''You Gotta Have Heart: Bard Strives to Bounce Back from a Rough Patch,'' *Barron's,* February 12, 1990, p. 22.

—Wendy J. Stein
—update: David E. Salamie

Capitalia S.p.A.

Viale Tupini 180
Roma I-00144
Italy
Telephone: +39 06 5445139
Fax: 39 06 54452351
Web site: http://www.capitalia.it

Public Company
Incorporated: 1992 as Banca di Roma
Employees: 28,000
Total Assets: EUR 128.38 billion ($159 billion) (2003)
Stock Exchanges: Borsa Italiana Frankfurt
Ticker Symbol: CAP
NAIC: 551111 Offices of Bank Holding Companies

Capitalia S.p.A. is a holding company created in 2002 as Italy's fourth largest bank, with total assets of EUR 128.38 billion ($159 billion)—ranking the company among the world's top 50 banks in 2003. The largest of Capitalia's assets is the Banca di Roma. Other banking assets include the southern region's Banco di Sicilia and northern region banking group Bibop-Carire. Together, the banks allow Capitalia to operate a national network of banking branches offering the full range of traditional commercial banking services and products. In addition to its banking operations, Capitalia also owns a 44.7 percent stake in Fineco, which offers such consumer-oriented banking services as bancassurance, asset management, credit and leasing products, and the like. MCC, the new name for Medio Credito Centrale, targets the corporate and investment banking markets and is held at 75.4 percent by Capitalia. The company also has a significant stake in Mediobanca, Italy's powerful investment fund, and controls its own empire of mostly financial and Internet-related investments. Since 2002, Capitalia also has operated an insurance joint venture with Fiat's Toro insurance subsidiary. Although Capitalia has inherited Banca di Roma's long notoriety as one of Europe's worst banks—with a nonperforming loan portfolio more than double the European banking industry average—the company, under new leader Matteo Arpe, has launched an ambitious restructur-

ing effort expected to be completed by the end of 2005. Nonetheless, Capitalia's past has come back to haunt it, notably through its involvement in a series of financial scandals, including the collapse of dairy giant Parmalat in 2004.

Gathering Italian Banking History in the 1990s

Capitalia S.p.A. emerged as one of Italy's top four banks as a result of a series of major events in the 1990s. The first involved the creation of Banca di Roma from the merger of Banca di Roma with Cassa di Risparmio di Roma and Banco di Santo Spirito in 1992. The three-way merger placed the majority control of the bank under the foundation behind Cassa di Risparmio, although the government maintained a significant stake of more than 36 percent. Banca di Roma was privatized in a controversial public offering in 1997, at which time Cassa di Risparmio reduced its share in the bank to 10 percent. At the time, Banca di Roma enjoyed the status of Italy's second largest event. But the massive consolidation of the Italian banking industry soon overtook the bank, and Banca di Roma itself became a subject of a takeover attempt, by Sanpaolo IMI. The Bank of Italy quashed that deal, however, in part in an effort to maintain at least one of the country's top banks outside of the rich northern region.

Instead, Banca di Roma itself joined in the consolidation effort, acquiring Banco di Sicilia in 1999 and the north's Bipop-Carire in 2002. Following the latter merger, Banca di Roma created a new holding company for itself and its other assets, called Capitalia S.p.A. That bank, with total assets of more than EUR 128 billion ($159 billion), ranked fourth among Italy's largest banks, behind Intesa BCI, Sanpaolo IMI, and Unicredito Italiano.

Despite its recent formation, Capitalia remained firmly rooted in Italy's banking history. In addition to the Banca di Roma, originally known as the Banca di Roma and created in 1880, Capitalia regrouped the histories of several notable Rome-based financial houses. The oldest of these was the Monte di Pietà di Roma, founded by a papal bull in 1539. Two other Italian banks participated in the development of what became Capitalia: the Banco di Santo Spirito, created in 1605; and the Cassa di Risparmio di Roma, founded in 1836.

Franciscan Charity in the 14th Century

Monte di Pietà di Roma was founded in the aftermath of the sack of Rome in 1527 and the famine of 1538. The rebuilding effort drained the city of credit capital and encouraged the development of usurious interest rates. In response, Pope Paul III issued a bull establishing the Monte di Pietà di Roma. The new institution, which was placed under the protection of the Franciscan Order, was established with the express and exclusive purpose of providing credit at low interest rates for the city's poor.

Successive changes to Monte di Pietà di Roma's charter enabled it to develop from an essentially charitable institution into a more traditional banking institution. This process was accomplished especially in 1617, when Monte di Pietà's charter separated its loan operations from its deposit taking operations. The bank was also obliged to record all transactions in its ledgers. Monte di Pietà also played a role in creating and circulating currency in Rome. By the end of the 18th century, Monte di Pietà's "cedole," or certificates of deposit, were accepted as legal tender in Rome.

Monte di Pietà was forced to suspend its operations for a time during the French Revolution. Following France's invasion of Italy in the early 1800s, Monte di Pietà lost its independence, and in 1814 was placed under the direction of the Vatican's Treasurer General of the Apostolic Camera. After Rome was annexed to the Kingdom of Italy in the mid-19th century, Monte di Pietà came under control of the Italian government. The bank began expanding beyond its single site in the early 20th century, adding a number of branches in Rome starting in 1908. At last, in 1937, during the banking crisis that led to the nationalization of Italy's banking industry, Monte di Pietà was placed under the control of the Cassa di Risparmio di Roma.

Roman Banking Leader in the 19th Century

Cassa di Risparmio di Roma had been established just 100 years earlier, backed by the famed Borghese and other of Rome's important noble and merchant families. Created in 1836, the Cassa di Risparmio di Roma's charter established the savings bank with the specific purpose of serving the lower classes, imparting to the city's poor such values as thrift and economy. In this respect, the new institution followed a prevailing trend of the time, which sought to replace traditional charitable activities with means of encouraging the poor to accept responsibility for their own financial situation. Cassa di Risparmio itself was set up as a nonprofit institution.

Initially situated in the Palazzo Borghese, Cassa di Risparmio grew strongly into the mid-19th century, becoming the city's leading savings bank in total deposits. By 1862, the bank had outgrown its original quarters and in that year acquired the Piazza Sciarra. Work began on remodeling the Piazza soon after, but Cassa di Risparmio only moved to its new headquarters in 1874.

By then, the bank had become an important part of the Italian economy—the annexation of Rome, and its subsequent emergence as the capital city of the newly unified Italy placed Cassa di Risparmio at the top of the Italian banking industry, second only to Cassa di Risparmio di Provincie Lombarde (also known as Cariplo). In 1891, in accordance with new legislation governing the country's savings and thrift organizations, Cassa di Risparmio di Roma reorganized and adopted new statutes. By then, the bank had emerged as a significant institutional lender and investor, stimulating industrial activity in the region around Rome.

The economic and political turmoil of the post-World War I years proved a boon for the savings bank, which attracted large amounts of deposits due to its reputation as something of a safe haven. The banking policies enacted by the Fascist government also stimulated Cassa di Risparmio di Roma's growth, and in 1934, it began expanding its branch network in Rome. The collapse of Italy's banking system in the 1930s led to a drastic reorganization of the country's banks, with much of the sector nationalized and placed under government control through the newly created Istituto per la Ricostruzione Industriale (IRI). As part of that restructuring, Cassa di Risparmio di Roma took over Monte di Pietà in 1937. Two years later, the savings bank paid ITL 10 million for a share of Istituto Federale di Credito Agrario per l'Italia. That purchase enabled Cassa di Risparmio di Roma to expand into the agricultural credit market, starting with the provinces of Rome and Frosinone, and later extended to Littoria province as well.

In the 1950s, Cassa di Risparmio continued to expand, adding branches in Rome and Lazio, then extending its geographic reach into Centocelle and Colleferro in 1951. The bank received permission to begin offering mortgage and other loans to the real estate and building sector in 1957. Then, in 1960, the bank began offering loans to the public works sector as well.

Through the 1980s, Cassa di Risparmio di Roma expanded its branch network throughout Italy, and established its first overseas offices in Germany and the United Kingdom. The bank also began a series of acquisitions of smaller banks, notably the Banca Generale di Credito in Milan, the Cassa di Risparmio Molisana-Monte Orsini, located in Molise and Campanio, and France's Banque Generale du Commerce. Cassa di Risparmio's acquisition drive culminated with the purchase of majority control of Banco di Santo Spirito in 1989.

Creating an Italian Banking Leader in the 21st Century

Banco di Santo Spirito was founded as Rome's first public deposit bank in 1605 under the auspices of Pope Paul V, a member of the Borghese family. Banco di Santo Spirito was founded in order to raise funding for charitable operation of the Arch-hospital Santo Spirito, which itself dated from 1201. The hospital-owned bank became a major lender to public works projects, such as the Trajan aqueduct project begun in 1608.

In the early 19th century, Banco di Santo Spirito faced competition from a new generation of banks that began offering

---

Key Dates:

1539: Monte di Pietà di Roma is founded.
1605: Banco di Santo Spirito is founded.
1836: Cassa di Risparmio di Roma is founded.
1880: Banca di Roma is founded.
1937: Cassa di Risparmio di Roma acquires Monte di Pietà di Roma; Banca di Roma becomes the bank of national interest under Istituto per la Ricostruzione Industriale (IRI).
1946: Banca di Roma participates in the founding of Mediobanca.
1989: Cassa di Risparmio di Roma acquires Banco di Santo Spirito.
1992: The merger of Banco di Santo Spirito and Banca di Roma forms Banca di Roma.
1997: Banca di Roma is privatized in a public offering.
1999: Banca di Sicilia is acquired.
2002: The company acquires Bipop-Carire and changes its name to Capitalia.
2003: A joint venture is formed with Archon Group to collect on EUR 6 billion in nonperforming loans.

---

interest on savings deposits. Banco di Santo Spirito's charter barred it from paying interest, however. Instead, the bank entered a new area of operation, that of real estate lending, founding the Credito Fondiario in 1873. The bank rode Rome's building boom into the 1890s. Yet when that market slumped, Credito Fondiario was separated from Banco di Santo Spirito, and entered liquidation procedures, completed in 1932. By then, Banco di Santo Spirito had itself undergone a liquidation process before being restructured as a joint-stock company in 1924. The new bank then began building its own branch network in Rome, focusing on the surrounding areas, and also in Lazio, Orvieto, and Assisi.

After its acquisition by Cassa di Risparmio di Roma, Banco di Santo Spirito became the group's primary banking vehicle, taking over the banking operations of its parent, which then changed its status to that of a foundation, Ente Cassa di Risparmio di Roma, in 1991. The new foundation controlled Banco di Santo Spirito at 87 percent, with the remainder held by the Italian government through IRI. The following year, Banco di Santo Spirito took over another IRI holding, Banca di Roma.

That bank had been founded in 1880 as a deposit bank for the Vatican and other religious groups, wealthy and middle class Romans, members of the city's aristocracy and others who had formally held their savings at the French bank Union Générale. Banca di Roma quickly emerged as a major industrial investor, and enjoyed particular success through investments in Rome's fast-growing real estate market. At the dawn of the 20th century, after listing its stock on the Paris and Alexandrian stock exchanges, Banca di Roma began expanding throughout Italy, with branches in the Piedmont, Liguria, Tuscany, and other regions. The Italian government also encouraged Banca di Roma to expand internationally, including an initial branch in Alexandria. In 1907, the bank opened branches in Tripoli and Bengasi, which were followed by

offices in Cairo, Barcelona, and other cities in 1909, and a branch in Constantinople in 1911.

During World War I, Banca di Roma expanded through the acquisition of shares in Italy's industrial groups. The bank also played a role in the peaceful expansion of the Fascist empire. In Italy, the bank's branch network grew to more than 150 by 1920. These were complemented by foreign branches in Turkey, Palestine, and Syria, among other countries, reaching a total of 43 overseas branches in 1920.

Over the next decade, Banca di Roma suffered through a series of crises, both within the Italian banking sector and throughout the world. By the mid-1930s, the collapse of the Italian banking industry brought it under government control, with the establishment of the IRI. Banca di Roma was then reformed as one of the country's three "banks of national interest," alongside Banca Commercial Italiana and Credito Italiano.

Following World War II, Banca di Roma contributed to the 1946 formation of Mediobanca, which grew into Italy's major investment fund. Banca di Roma also entered the financing market for the agricultural and building sectors in the 1950s, and began a steady international expansion throughout the 1960s and 1970s. Yet by the end of the 1980s, Banca di Roma, like Banco di Santo Spirito, had long been struggling with a heavy nonperforming loan portfolio, in large part because of government interference.

The merger between Banca di Roma and Banco di Santo Spirito in 1992, which created Banca di Roma, also created the country's second largest bank in terms of total assets, and its largest bank in terms of its branch network. Yet Banca di Roma remained highly unprofitable throughout much of the decade. In an effort to shore up its losses, the bank began selling off a number of its industrial investments at the middle of the decade. Then, in 1997, the bank underwent a privatization effort. The public offering sparked a great deal of controversy, however, in part because the bank targeted the country's small shareholders—and was accused of failing to reveal important information regarding its finances in its prospectus.

Nonetheless, the public offering went through in 1997. Two years later, the bank, which continued to enjoy the protection of the Bank of Italy to help it ward off potential takeover attempts, joined the consolidation of the Italian banking industry. In 1999, Banca di Roma acquired Sicily's Banco di Sicilia. That acquisition was followed in 2002 by the merger with northern bank Bipop-Carire. Yet the acquisitions of these two struggling banks were criticized as Banca di Roma itself attempted to restructure its way to health.

That effort was led by new CEO Matteo Arpe, then just 39 years old, who joined the bank in 2001. Arpe launched the bank on the formulation of a new business plan, expected to be completed in 2005. Part of the bank's new strategy called for a drastic reduction in its nonperforming loan portfolio. In 2003, the bank took a strong step in that direction when it transferred some EUR 6 billion in bad loans to a joint venture with Archon Group, set up as a collection agency of sorts. Banca di Roma, now Italy's fourth largest bank, hoped that the 2000s would represent a new beginning to the nearly 500-year-old institution.

Principal Subsidiaries

Bafico S.A. (France); Banca di Roma International S.A.; Banca di Roma S.p.A.; Banco di Sicilia S.p.A; Banque Bipop S.A. (France); Bipop-Carire S.p.A.; Bipop Espana Holding S.A. (Spain); Bipop Finance Limited (Ireland); Corit - Concessionaria Riscossione Tributi S.p.A.; Entasi S.R.L.; Entrium Direct Bankers AG (Germany); Eurofinance 2000 S.R.L.; European Trust Società Fiduciaria Per Azioni; Figeroma - Fiduciaria E Di Gestione Roma - Sim S.p.A.; Fineco Asset S.R.L.; Romafides - Fiduciaria E Servizi S.p.A.; Serit S.p.A.; Società Amministrazione Immobili S.A.Im. S.p.A.; Spaget S.p.A.; Trevi Finance S.p.A.

Principal Competitors

Banca Intesa S.p.A.; Sanpaolo IMI S.p.A.; Unicreditor Italiano S.p.A.; Banca d'Italia; Banca Monte Parma S.p.A.; Banca Nazionale del Lavoro S.p.A.; Banca di Roma S.p.A.; Banco Popolare di Verona e Novara.

Further Reading

"Banca di Roma Commits Itself to Privatisation," *European Banker,* May 9, 1997.

Buerkle, Tom, "Arpe diem," *Institutional Investor,* January 2003, p. 60.

"Capitalia Sticks to the Plan," *European Banker,* May 2003, p. 5.

"Fire Sale As Capitalia Tries to Avoid Disaster," *Retail Banker International,* October 9, 2002, p. 3.

Galbraith, Robert, "New Bank of the Regions," *European Banker,* March 2002, p. 4.

——, "Tricky Rescue Mission on the Cards," *European Banker,* January 2002, p. 4.

——, "Wanted: Leader with Own Strategy," *European Banker,* July 2001, p. 5.

Israely, Jeff, "The Italian Exception," *Time,* April 25, 2004.

Kapner, Fred, "Matteo Arpe, Capitalia," *Financial Times,* April 20, 2004, p. 14.

Semler, Peter, "Roma's New Empire," *Euromoney,* September 1992, p. 261.

—M.L. Cohen

cascade corporation

Cascade Corporation

2201 NE 201st Avenue
Fairview, Oregon 97024-9718
U.S.A.
Telephone: (503) 669-6300
Toll Free: (800) 227-2233
Fax: (503) 669-6716
Web site: http://www.cascorp.com

Public Company
Incorporated: 1943 as Cascade Manufacturing Company
Employees: 1,700
Sales: $297.75 million (2004)
Stock Exchanges: New York
Ticker Symbol: CAE
NAIC: 333924 Industrial Truck, Tractor, Trailer, and Stacker Machinery Manufacturing

Cascade Corporation is a publicly traded company based in Fairview, Oregon, that manufactures forklift attachments, forks, hydraulic cylinders, and replacement parts under two brand names: Cascade and Cascade-Kenhar. In addition to its primary market, the lift truck industry, Cascade also manufactures materials handling products for construction and agricultural vehicles. The company sells worldwide to industries such as pulp and paper, grocery products, textiles, recycling, and general consumer goods, through lift truck dealers and original equipment manufacturers. Cascade's CEO, Robert C. Warren, Jr., is the son of the company's founder.

Founding the Company in 1943

Cascade was founded by Robert C. Warren, Sr., in 1943. He was born in Portland, Oregon, in 1918. After graduating from Stanford University in 1940 he went to work for Henry Kaiser as the chief expediter at the Kaiser Shipyards, where he became interested in manufacturing. In 1943 he was recruited by several Esco Corp. executives to run a machine shop in Portland. The business was called Cascade Manufacturing Company, funded by $7,500 in seed money. Warren started out modestly, possess-

ing nothing more than a single employee, an old lathe, and a drill press. In the first year he added three more employees to machine and assemble stainless steel valves, pipe fittings, and other components. After recording first year sales of $60,000, Cascade grew steadily, so that by the end of five years the company employed 40 people and revenues totaled $330,000. In the 1940s Cascade designed and manufactured its first hydraulic cylinder, which proved to be a turning point in the company's history. During the 1950s Cascade expanded into designing and making hydraulic attachments for forklifts. By the time the business was 15 years old, sales had improved to $2.3 million, and the workforce had grown to 180. Cascade was now ready to open a second manufacturing plant, located in Springfield, Ohio.

Cascade experienced a number of changes during the 1960s. At the start of the decade, the company began looking to international markets, and acquired interests in companies in Australia, the United Kingdom, and The Netherlands. Ultimately the company would operate three manufacturing plants in The Netherlands and another in the United Kingdom. The company changed its name to Cascade Corporation in 1964 and a year later became a public company, making an initial offer of 200,000 shares of stock. Cascade also grew through acquisition. In 1967 it acquired C.M. Scott Fluid Power, Ltd., and in 1968 used stock to acquire Ramey Hydraulic Loaders, Inc., a Roseburg, Oregon, company.

Founder's Son Joining the Company in 1972

Warren was joined by his son, Robert C. Warren, Jr., in 1972. The decade also was marked by the acquisition of Diamond Corp. and the start of a relationship with the People's Republic of China. The younger Warren met with a Chinese government engineer while attending a technical conference in Bulgaria. He became convinced that China was determined to grow industrially and eager to find Western partners. Warren realized that more business in China meant more forklifts to move goods, which in turn meant the need for the kind of forklift attachments and parts that Cascade manufactured. Finally in 1995 a joint venture was forged with the Ministry of Machine Building, an agency with strong connections to

China's 15 forklift manufacturers. A plant was built in Xiamen, located south of Shanghai, to manufacture forklift parts and carry on sales and service activities. Cascade provided the funding, while the Ministry supplied the customers and a well-connected general manager who was able to guide the venture through a maze of local regulations and taxes.

Although it grew to be the largest company in its field, Cascade after 40 years in existence was barely known to the investment community. Part of the problem was the company's limited number of shares of stock. For many years there were only 750,000 shares, of which few were traded. In 1986 Cascade engineered a four-for-one split, raising the number of shares to three million, and a year later looked to increase that number to ten million. The maneuvers proved successful, as evidenced by a money manager in the late 1980s telling *Barron's* that Cascade was his favorite stock. Not only did the company make more of its stock available to the public, it also took significant steps in the 1980s to fend off foreign competition, such as the Japanese, Taiwanese, and Koreans, all of which had an edge on labor costs. Cascade met the challenge by increasing productivity, and the labor force worked in concert with management to initiate changes that were needed. Rigid job descriptions were replaced with flexible work assignments. Everyone was put on salary, and a cash incentive program based on productivity was implemented. Employees eventually decided to do without their traditional union.

Cascade also grew through the introduction of innovative products. The company introduced a forklift clamp attachment that did away with the usual forks that slipped under a pallet to lift a load. The new product pinched a load from all sides, eliminating the need for pallets, which were expensive, cumbersome, and took up valuable space. Cascade also brought out another product, a forklift mast, or vertical lift mechanism at the front of a forklift. Called the "World Mast" because it could be used on any forklift manufactured by any company, the product was built in a new 110,000-square-foot plant built in Westminster, South Carolina, Cascade's fifth and largest domestic operation. The primary market for the mast was the U.S. operations of Japanese forklift manufacturers, which by law were required to increase the domestic content of their products or pay large penalties.

Cascade's revenues approached $170 million in 1991, with net income of $9.8 million, but a recession soon began to take its toll. Sales slumped, bottoming out at $141.3 million in 1993, and did not begin to improve until 1994. In the meantime, in August 1993, Robert Warren, Sr., retired as chairman of the company. He was replaced as chair by longtime Cascade executive Joseph J. Barclay, who had been president of the company since 1972 and chief executive officer since 1983. Barclay retained the CEO position, while Robert Warren was promoted

to president and chief operating officer, after serving as vice-president of marketing since 1990. Prior to that appointment he had been named vice-president of administration in 1986. In 1996 he would become chief executive officer of the company his father founded. A year later, his father would die from heart failure in his home in Palm Springs, California, at the age of 78.

Cascade's revenues grew to $234 million in 1995, but dipped the next year to $218.5 million. Net income decreased from $18.3 million to $17.4 million. To increase its product offering and spur growth, the company completed a flurry of acquisitions. In January 1997 it completed the $23.7 million purchase of Industrial Tires Limited, a Canadian company that was a global manufacturer of solid rubber tires for forklift trucks, ground support, and construction equipment. Next, Cascade acquired Australia-based Hyco-Cascade Pty. Ltd., paying $12.6 million in cash and stock. For three years Hyco had been Cascade's exclusive distributor in Australia and New Zealand and also designed and manufactured container handling products. In March 1997, Cascade completed the acquisition of Kenhar Corporation at a cost of nearly $72 million.

As a result of the acquisitions, as well as strong economic conditions, Cascade saw its revenues jump to $369.9 million in 1998 and $407.9 million in 1999. Net income during this period totaled $21 million in 1998 and $21.4 million in 1999. But with the acquisitions also came some disappointing quarters, which began to adversely impact the price of Cascade's stock. To help rectify the situation management made a pair of divestitures in 1999. It sold the World Mast product line, which had not performed to the level the company had envisioned, to a Cascade executive who led a buyout effort. Cascade also sold Industrial Tires to Maine Rubber Company for $381 million, electing to focus resources on its core attachment and fork business. As a result of these divestitures, revenue in 2000 fell to $324.8 million and net income dipped below $5 million, declines that caused further concern in the investment community.

Failed Sale of Company in 2002

Cascade was a profitable company but the price of its stock, in the opinion of management, was much too low, overshadowed at the time by the high-tech sector. Shares that traded at more than $18 in late 1997 barely fetched $8 by early 2000. Because there was little reason now to remain public and to placate disgruntled shareholders, Warren and his management team indicated they were interested in pursuing a leveraged buyout and taking the company private. The board of directors led by Chairman Jim Osterman, on the other hand, decided in May 2000 to retain Gleacher & Co. as a financial advisor to pursue all options in increasing shareholder value, including fielding other offers for the business. By July, the management team was working with Chicago-based investment firm Code Hennessy & Simmons L.L.C. to fashion an offer, while the board had winnowed the number of outside suitors to six. The process continued into early 2001 when the privately held Lift Group finally emerged as the board's choice to buy Cascade at a cost of $320 million. The deal was delayed because of pending environmental litigation that involved a $19 million damage claim made by the City of Portland. A second delay was the result of Wall Street's negative reaction to the terms of the deal, with investors making it clear that they believed Lift was paying

Key Dates:

1943: The company is founded as Cascade Manufacturing Company by Robert C. Warren, Sr.
1959: A second manufacturing plant is opened in Springfield, Ohio.
1964: The name is changed to Cascade Corporation.
1965: The company is taken public.
1996: Robert C. Warren, Jr., is named CEO.
1997: The company founder dies.
2001: An attempt to take the company private fails.

too much for the company by causing the price of Cascade stock to tumble below $10. Lift Group attempted to lower its per share offer price to $15.75 from $17.25, prompting the Cascade board to decide in April 2001 to simply scuttle the acquisition. In the short term the company needed to deal with more pressing matters, focusing on the business and settling the environmental litigation. Perhaps later the board could revisit the idea of taking the company private. The decision did little to placate some of Cascade's unhappy shareholders.

Cascade's environmental problems dated back to the 1980s when the Department of Environmental Quality determined that ground water had been contaminated from industrial cleaning solutions at Boeing, which was situated close to a Cascade facility. Two years later, in 1988, the ground water under Cascade also was found to be polluted. Boeing and Cascade took immediate steps to prevent contaminants from leaking into the downstream well field that supplied backup water to Portland's water system, agreeing to split the costs until the courts could decide levels of responsibility. During a drought in 1992 Portland was still unable to access its backup water, which led the City to sue Boeing and Cascade. The matter would linger for the next ten years before a lawsuit was filed in 1999 and the matter finally reached a courtroom in 2002. On the first day of the trial, the city asked for $20.5 million in damages, and the companies countered with a $1 million offer. In the end, the sides agreed to a $6.2 million settlement to finally end the matter.

Due to poor economic conditions, revenues fell to $252.7 million in 2002 before beginning to rebound. To better focus on its core business, Cascade decided in 2002 to sell off its hydraulic cylinder division, then in 2003 it acquired FEMA Forks GmbH, a German manufacturer of forks and lifting tines that supplied European lift truck manufacturers. Later in 2003 Cascade acquired Roncari S.r.L., a supplier of materials handling equipment to the Italian lift truck market. Cascade's revenues reached $297.8 million in 2004 and net income improved to $18.5 million. During the ensuing quarter, the company enjoyed even stronger growth, the result of strong sales, a weak dollar, and recent acquisitions. As the economy continued to improve there was every reason to expect that Cascade would continue to enjoy renewed growth. Whether its mundane business would ever win over Wall Street, or the company would eventually go private, remained open questions.

Principal Subsidiaries

Cascade Xiamen Forklift Truck Attachment; Cascade Kenhar, Inc.; Hyco-Cascade Pty. Ltd.; Roncari S.r.l.

Principal Competitors

CLARK Material Handling Company; Crown Equipment Corporation; NACCO Industries, Inc.

Further Reading

Cochran, Thomas N., "Cascade Corp.: It Fills a Secure Slot in the Fork-Lift Market," *Barron's National Business and Financial Weekly,* January 9, 1989, p. 35.

"Entrepreneur Robert Carlton Warren Sr. Dies," *Portland Oregonian,* February 22, 1997, p. B05.

Stepankowsky, Paula L., "Cascade Corp. Sees Growth in Sales, Cites Demand for Forklift-Truck Gear," *Wall Street Journal,* June 15, 1998, p. 1.

Strom, Shelly, "Cascade Calls Off Plans to Take Company Private," *Business Journal, Portland,* June 22, 2001, p. 1.

—Ed Dinger

Cascade General, Inc.

Portland Shipyard
5555 North Channel Avenue, Building 71
Portland, Oregon 97217
U.S.A.
Telephone: (503) 285-1111
Fax: (503) 285-0361
Web site: http://www.casgen.com

Wholly Owned Subsidiary of Shipyard America
Incorporated: 1987
Employees: 425
Sales: $113.7 million (2003 est.)
NAIC: 336611 Ship Building and Repairing; 332710
    Machine Shops

Cascade General, Inc. owns and operates Portland Shipyard, a 57-acre, integrated facility that is connected to the Pacific Ocean by the 40-foot, Columbia/Willamette shipping channel. Assets include two dry docks, 17 Whirley cranes, and 550,000 square feet of covered craft shops and state-of-the-art ship repair equipment. Regular customers include the cruise ship industry, North Pacific factory trawlers, VLCCs engaged in the Alaska oil run, ferries from the Alaska Marine Highway Department, tugs and barges, cable-laying ships, and Corps of Engineers dredges. Cascade General also provides emergency topside repairs at any location on the West Coast and operates two permanent voyage repair stations at Port Angeles, Washington, and in Astoria, Oregon.

1987–95: The Early Years in the Portland Shipyard

In 1987, Cascade General, Inc., a small operation based in Vancouver, Washington, moved to the Portland Shipyard, along with West State Inc., to begin operations there as one of several ship repair contractors to lease space from the Port of Portland. At the time, business in the yard was booming, and the yard's more than 3,000 employees handled about 40 percent of all West Coast commercial ship repair.

The Portland Shipyard was the largest publicly run commercial yard in the country and had been in business since installing its first dry dock in 1903. Located in the Swan Island section of Portland, it had been purchased and developed by businessman Henry Kaiser in 1940. During World War II, it was the site for the construction of Liberty ships. In 1953, the Port of Portland repurchased the then dormant Kaiser yard and installed two dry docks at the facility. Three contractors opened up shop in the Portland shipyard: Dillingham Ship Repair, Willamette Iron and Steel Corp., and Northwest Marine Iron Inc.

Throughout the 1960s and 1970s, the yard expanded aggressively. In 1963, the Port built Dry Dock 3, then the largest floating dry dock in the Americas. In 1976, tri-county voters opted to build another dry dock capable of handling Alaskan oil tankers and liquefied natural gas carriers. Dry Dock 4, the new largest floating dock in the Western Hemisphere, was financed with an $84 million bond offering. Construction on Dry Dock 4 began in 1976 along with an array of support facilities, including piers and outfitting berths, heavy-lift cranes, and a water treatment plant. By 1979, the new dry dock and other improvements were complete.

However, throughout the 1980s, the shipyard consistently lost money. An oil crisis led to a worldwide slump in shipbuilding and repair, and military spending cutbacks created an oversupply of ship repair companies. The market for liquefied gas never developed, while Far East shipbuilders increased competition in the domestic market. Dillingham was bought out by Cascade; Willamette moved to San Diego. Bankrupt Northwest Marine was bought out by Southwest Marine.

Another slump in the world ship repair market depressed the Portland shipyard's business still further in the early 1990s. American shipyards had to cope with the effects of the Asian economic crisis. Currency exchange rates led more businesses than usual to take their repairs to foreign shipyards. Falling oil prices put a damper on Alaskan oil tanker repairs and the Navy initiated further cutbacks. In 1993, Southwest Marine left the yard, and the Port initiated another unsuccessful search for a financially sound operator to move in and bolster business. In 1994, West State went bankrupt, leaving Cascade General as the sole contractor in the Portland Shipyard.

In 1994, an investment company headed by Tore Steen, former chief executive of defunct West State, purchased Cascade General. The next year, Frank Foti and Andrew Rowe purchased Cascade General from Steen. Rowe had a background in international business, exporting American goods and services to the offshore industry, as well as experience in the sphere of robotics. Foti, a native of Seattle, was the former president of Global Marine Services and a former Cleveland construction executive.

Mid- to Late 1990s: Acquisition of Portland Shipyard by Cascade General

At the time of the purchase, the port commissioners, concerned about the shipyard's dwindling business and failed ship repair companies, had voted to go to a single operator system and were soliciting bids from companies interested in managing the yard. Cascade General had no ship repair contracts, and there was no assurance that it would continue its operations at Portland Shipyard. However, Foti and Rowe's first move together was to enter the public bidding process to win the contract to run the Portland Shipyard. They put together a detailed proposal and won the contract in the face of competition from National Steel and Shipbuilding and Todd Pacific. Cascade General gained charge of the yard for an initial five years at $5.8 million per year with a further 25 years covered by options. Before turning over stewardship of the yard, the port built a river water system allowing use of river water, rather than potable water, for washing ships and a water containment system for the dry docks.

Under Foti and Rowe, the company pursued new kinds of business and worked to improve its productivity. The Portland Shipyard had the largest dry dock in the Americas, but was in direct and tough competition with several other shipyards on the West Coast. Foti and Rowe set their sights on the market for foreign ships, which was twice the size of the home market. They also targeted the commercial as opposed to government market in ship repair. "I want to redefine the way we work with the owner. We wish to develop strategic partnerships with owners to bring us work," said Rowe in a 1995 *Lloyd's List* article. Although the yard still had shortfalls in 1995, by May the company was working on six ships—three fishing vessels, a Navy fuel oil tanker, a privately owned crude oil tanker, and a passenger cruise ship. In May, it picked up another contract to repair two crude oil tankers owned by SeaRiver Maritime, Inc., a company for which it had worked since 1993. More contracts followed and by June, according to Foti, the company had a backlog of about $18 million in pending business and was employing 1,200 workers a day.

Immediately following the transfer of the shipyard to Cascade General in 1996, the company enjoyed a string of suc-

cesses. Throughout 1996 and 1997, Cascade General made strides to establish its international reputation as a shipyard on the comeback. The yard upgraded its electrical systems to handle larger cruise ships and purchased new automated welding equipment for work on large-size bulkhead and deck structure projects. It successfully built its presence in the floating production, storage, and offloading and drillship conversion sectors. By 1997, a year of record turnover of more than $130 million for the company, about 45 percent of the yard's business involved the maintenance of tankers operating in the Alaskan trade. Cascade General was also part of a consortium of shipyards that had a ten-year contract with VSE-Corporation of Washington, D.C., to carry out reactivation work aboard naval ships destined for sale to friendly countries under the military sales program.

In 1997, Cascade General had sales of $132 million and employed 1,200 workers. Its bread and butter business involved the repair of super oil tankers. But in 1998, those numbers dropped to $80 million and 650 workers. Foti and Rowe made a proposal to buy the Portland Shipyard from the Port of Portland in an effort to keep the yard competitive.

In 1998, after a year of negotiations, the Port of Portland's commissioners voted to sell the Portland Shipyard to Cascade General; however, the company did not assume ownership of the yard until 2001.

In 1998, the company generated revenues of slightly more then $80 million as it performed repair and conversion work on 135 vessels. Of these 117 were commercial vessels with 24 from the international market. Unfortunately, the ship repair market of the late 1990s went soft as depressed freight rates and competition in the containership and bulk carrier markets headed it for a prolonged downturn. Lower oil prices in 1999 began to have a negative effect on Cascade General as oil companies deferred their regularly scheduled maintenance programs and the tanker trade along the West Coast weakened. Only the Alaska cruiseship market seemed destined for good times. However, the growth in the Asian ship repair market meant increased competition for the industry internationally. In 1999, Cascade General's sales increased only slightly to around $90 million.

As a result, Cascade General reemphasized diversification and long-term partnerships, in keeping with the trend towards link-ups between shipowners and repairers. At the end of 1999, it entered into an agreement with the Alaska Tanker Company of Beaverton, Oregon, the largest operator of American-flagged ships, to repair its ships. Also in 1999, it made a bid to dismantle nearly 200 decommissioned naval ships in an attempt to offset the slump in its main business of ship repair. The Port ordered Cascade General to conduct public outreach to inform its neighbors and other interested parties about ways in which it would protect the Willamette River and the health of its workers should it win the bid.

The ship dismantling business was typically one in which workers were maimed and the environment contaminated. Cascade General proposed that, rather than hacking ships down to the waterline with cutting torches and hauling them ashore, it would float them into dry dock and then remove all hazardous

Key Dates:

1987: Cascade General begins operations in the Portland Shipyard.
1994: Cascade General becomes the sole contractor in the Portland Shipyard; Tore Steen purchases Cascade General.
1995: Frank Foti and Andrew Rowe purchase Cascade General.
1999: The company enters into an agreement with Alaska Tanker Company.
2001: Portland Shipyard LLC and Cammell Laird Holdings purchase the Portland Shipyard.

materials before dismantling them. This would ensure that no asbestos, lead-based paint, or other toxic material would find its way into the environment. Cascade General's proposal won the support of an important environmental group, and the Navy awarded the company its contract.

The company's system of environmental precautions proved successful. In 2000, less than a week after arriving for dismantling and salvaging, a fishing vessel in the shipyard caught fire and burned for more than 24 hours. Significantly, there were no releases into the Willamette River from the runoff, although Cascade General lost thousands of dollars in dismantling equipment and $200,000 in furnishings and fixtures that would have been salvaged from the ship.

Portland Shipyard LLC, an affiliate of Cascade General, officially took control of 57 acres of the Portland Shipyard for $30.8 million in 2001 along with Cammell Laird Holdings, Britain's largest ship repair and conversion company, which had become a partner in the investment in 2000. The arrangement included all of the port-owned cranes, related ship repair equipment, and Dry Dock 4. Dry Dock 1 remained the property of the U.S. government, although Cascade General managed the facility. The whole property had to remain a shipyard for at least five years, after which time, if Cascade General opted to get out of the ship repair business, it had to offer the Port of Portland the chance to repurchase the yard before selling it to another buyer. The Port of Portland assumed the responsibility for $2.5 million in environmental cleanup costs at the time of the purchase.

Even as Foti and Rowe set about implementing plans for expanding the company into specialty shipbuilding markets and Navy ship dismantling, another hardship hit Cascade General in 2001. Cammell Laird went bankrupt as lenders began to seek repayments from Cascade General. "If we don't find a way to

do that, the lenders could take over our entire business." To ease its cash crisis, the company decided to sell Dry Dock 4. Amid local concern that this move would lead to the loss of jobs, Foti announced in an April 2001 *Oregonian* article, "The jobs that are primarily associated with that large dock left when two-thirds of the tanker companies that carry oil out of Alaska decided it was much more economically viable to do their business in Asia." He also commented that "[t]he lenders have a right to demand that we pay back all of the money we owe them" in a written statement printed in the *Oregonian*. Dry Dock 4, which was large enough to hold three football fields, was bought for $25 million by a Bahamian company which planned to use it to repair cruise ships.

Still experiencing hard times in 2003, Cascade General decided to turn the shipyard's underutilized space into a leasing opportunity, marketing its unused manufacturing, warehouse, office, and yard space to manufacturing, industrial, and other potential commercial users. Dubbed the Shipyard Commerce Center, the rental areas had truck, rail, and barge access and offered crane power and compressed air capacity as well as an in-house environmental consulting team and first aid staff. The Center would do both short- and long-term leases. By April 2003, Cascade General had several prospective tenants and was optimistic about the future of its newest endeavor.

Principal Competitors

Todd Pacific; The Greenbrier Companies.

Further Reading

Curl, Aimee, "Cascade General Making Room for New Tenants," *Daily Journal of Commerce*, April 24, 2003.
DiBenedetto, William, "Portland, Oregon Leases Shipyard to Cascade General," *Journal of Commerce*, August 14, 1995, p. 6B.
Hill, Gail Kinsey, "Portland, Oregon Port Approves Sale of Shipyard to Cascade General," *Oregonian*, December 17, 1998, p. B1.
——, "When—and If—Port of Portland Officials Sign the Final Papers for the $38.8 Million Sale of the Portland Ship Yard, They'll Do More Than Transfer Ownership to Cascade General, Inc.," *Oregonian*, February 28, 1999, p. B1.
"Portland, Oregon Shipyard Owner to Sell Dry Dock to Ease Cash Crisis," *Oregonian*, April 13, 2001, p. A1.
Prescott, John, "Portrait: Challenge of Taking Over Ailing Yard," *Lloyd's List*, November 25, 1995, p. 5.
Rivera, Dylan, "Port of Portland, Oregon Won't Block Sale of Dry Dock," *Oregonian*, April 19, 2001, p. B10.
Rose, Michael, "Breaking Up (Ships) Is Hard to Do—Safely," *Portland Business Journal*, April 16, 1999, p. 1.
Strom, Shelly, "Cascade's First Attempt at New Work Hits Snag," *Portland Business Journal*, November 24, 2000, p. 8.

—Carrie Rothburd

Cavco Industries, Inc.

1001 North Central Avenue Suite 800
Phoenix, Arizona 85004
U.S.A.
Telephone: (602) 256-6263
Fax: (602) 256-6189
Web site: http://www.cavco.com

Public Company
Incorporated: 1968
Employees: 1,105
Sales: $128.9 million (2004)
Stock Exchanges: NASDAQ
Ticker Symbol: CVCO
NAIC: 321991 Manufactured Home (Mobile Home)
   Manufacturing

Cavco Industries, Inc. produces and markets manufactured homes, selling them wholesale through independent dealer outlets and through company-owned retail stores. Manufactured home products include park model homes under 400 square feet and single-wide and multi-section homes from 500 square feet to 2,700 square feet. Homes feature up to five bedrooms and three bathrooms, and floor plans can be custom designed. Basic I-Beam construction styles are offered under the Sun Villa Homes, Winrock Homes, Westcourt Homes, and Villager Litchfield brands. Luxury styles with cathedral ceilings are offered under the Profile Series, Vantage Series, Sun Built Homes, and Cavco Homes. The Santa Fe Series provides manufactured homes in the Southwest style, with a flat roof and stucco exterior. Cavco Cabins are designed in a rustic style to blend with natural surroundings. Like site-built homes, manufactured homes are equipped with appliances, light fixtures, custom wood cabinets, carpet, and other basic features. Optional amenities include skylights, custom fireplaces, bay window treatments, built-in entertainment centers, as well as many practical features, such as vinyl dual glaze windows and climate zone insulation. Cavco manufactures commercial structures used for offices, showrooms, and classrooms.

Success and Turmoil in Mobile Home Industry

Cavco Industries originated as a truck camper and travel trailer manufacturer, operating as an unincorporated association named Roadrunner Manufacturing Company. Founded in 1965, the company took the name Cavalier Manufacturing the following year. Cavalier began custom mobile home production in 1969, selling its products wholesale through dealerships in Arizona. Mobile home production became the sole focus of the company in 1973, when the original product lines were discontinued. Cavalier Manufacturing changed its name to Cavco Industries in 1974. That year Aldo Ghelfi retired as president and his son, Alfred Ghelfi, was promoted from simultaneous multiple positions of vice-president, secretary, and treasurer to the position of president.

Cavco grew with the mobile home industry during the late 1970s. The company opened a second plant in Phoenix in 1977 to meet the backlog of orders for double-wide mobile homes. In 1979 Cavco formed the Modular Housing Division, using the brand name Sun Built Homes to provide larger, multi-section homes for permanent residential site location. Cavco sales rose from $4.2 million in 1975 (fiscal year December 31) to $20.4 million in 1979 (fiscal year September 30).

Market conditions changed in the early 1980s, however, as high interest rates, a difficult financing environment, a weak real estate market, and general economic recession hindered sales of prefabricated homes. Cavco's revenues hovered at $13 million to $15 million annually between 1980 and 1982, but the company earned modest profits through the implementation of cost-saving measures. To offset a problematic market, Cavco introduced a lower-priced model under the Progressive Homes label and increased its advertising to gain a greater share of the Arizona market. The company experimented with site development as a means to increase sales and Sun Built Homes completed a 12-unit condominium development in early 1983.

While lower mortgage rates benefited site-built housing construction, the manufactured home industry continued to struggle. Cavco halted plans to enter the Texas market in 1985 and decided to diversify its businesses and product offerings. In 1986 the company began to manufacture relocatable commer-

Company Perspectives:

Quality is built into every Cavco home. Beginning with the high quality materials used in construction to the complete system tests before shipment and every step in between, emphasis is on durability and lasting value. Beauty is more than skin deep in a Cavco home. Consistent quality is monitored by the ongoing structural and cosmetic audits performed by qualified factory people.

cial modular structures, primarily used by construction companies as work-site offices. A subsidiary, CVC Leasing, handled leasing and sales. CVC expanded quickly, opening sales and marketing offices in six Western states by 1989, in Arizona, Nevada, New Mexico, Colorado, Utah, and southern California. That year CVC Leasing reported revenues of $3.4 million from a fleet of 418 units.

Cavco was offered an opportunity in healthcare utilization review and cost management and in 1987 founded Action Health Care, Inc. At Action Health Care registered nurses consulted with physicians to evaluate proposed treatment in contrast to national norms as described on a computer database. Through reviews of length of hospital stay, outpatient care, and other issues, health insurance providers sought to maximize care while minimizing costs. Within three years Action Health Care served more than 40 clients and opened an office in southern California.

Creative Marketing in the 1990s

While Cavco succeeded in finding new sources of revenue, the market for manufactured housing in the United States remained stagnant, prompting Cavco to introduce a new product and to enter new markets. Cavco succeeded selling "park models," mobile homes of less than 400 square feet, but with all the amenities of a travel trailer. Retirees liked the park models as an affordable second home for recreation, and Cavco quickly became the largest manufacturer of park model homes in the United States.

Cavco expanded its dealer network to markets outside Arizona for the first time, including New Mexico, Colorado, and California, and found new opportunities overseas. Through Operation Independence, a nonprofit organization promoting trade with Israel, Cavco obtained a $4 million contract to manufacture 420 mobile homes to be used to house Jewish immigrants from the former Soviet Union. Each 480-square-foot unit met specific requirements of the Israeli government, including proper electrical wiring and outlets. Cavco delivered the homes to an intermediary in Houston in January 1991, which resold the units to the government of Israel. The contract option added another 770 units, for $5.6 million, pushing Cavco sales to $42.5 million in 1991. This foray into international markets prompted Cavco to seek other opportunities abroad, resulting in an exclusive dealer relationship with Auto Borg Enterprises in Japan.

As the manufactured home industry showed signs of improvement in the United States, Cavco founded Sun Built Homes, Inc. in 1991 to develop manufactured housing subdivi-

sions, as well as to sell the homes directly to potential residents of manufactured housing subdivisions. Cavco initiated the Canyon View and Lynx Creek subdivisions in Green Valley and Dewey, Arizona, respectively.

As the market for manufactured homes thrived again during the early 1990s, Cavco opened a third manufacturing facility in Goodyear, Arizona, in May 1993. Products sold from that facility increased revenues 17 percent, while manufactured home sales increased 30 percent overall, to $53.4 million. A larger dealer network supported the revenue increase, with Cavco products sold through 75 dealers in Arizona, 11 in New Mexico, seven each in Colorado and California, five each in Nevada and Texas, two in Oregon, and four each in Utah, Washington, and Idaho, six in British Columbia, Canada, and two in Japan. Also, Cavco succeeded in enlarging its share of the Arizona market, from 23 percent in 1987 to 35 percent in 1993, becoming the largest producer of manufactured homes in Arizona. The average retail price was $22,000 for a park model home and $37,500 for residential homes; prices ranged from $12,000 to $99,000.

In 1994 Cavco signed a two-year agreement with Auto Borg Enterprises, the exclusive dealer of Cavco homes in Japan, to market park model homes under the name Cavco Homes-Japan. Cavco built the manufactured homes to meet Japanese preferences, for instance, a shoebox at the front door to accommodate the custom of removing shoes before entering a residence. Auto Borg purchased 12 home models for its showroom.

CVC Leasing began to lease security storage containers in 1993, leading Cavco to sell the relocatable commercial structures leasing operation in 1994. Cavco applied $20.2 million from the sale of CVC Leasing to pay debt on assets sold and costs of the sale; a net gain of $3.7 million funded a new subdivision development and expansion of the container fleet. Cavco formed National Security Containers (NSC) to operate the security storage container business and added trailer van leasing as well. NSC refurbished containers at a facility in Texas, and then leased them through offices in San Antonio, Houston, Dallas, El Paso, and Phoenix. Cavco opened offices in Colorado and Louisiana in late 1995.

While manufactured housing and lease containers generated positive cash flow, Action Health Care operated unprofitably with fluctuating sales despite the company's efforts to increase business. Cavco decided to exit the business, selling assets at a loss in August 1996.

The manufactured housing industry flourished with the housing industry as a whole during the 1990s, especially as quality improvements in manufactured homes made them indistinguishable from site-built homes. In September 1996 Cavco announced plans to build its fourth manufacturing plant, on a 23-acre site near Albuquerque. After its completion in the spring of 1997, Cavco manufactured ten houses per day at maximum capacity at the 143,000-square-foot facility, producing single-wide and double-wide manufactured homes for the Colorado and New Mexico markets.

Through a joint project with the Arizona Public Service Remote Solar Option, Cavco improved the design of window and exterior wall construction and electrical appliances and light fixtures on its manufactured homes to accommodate a solar energy system. Through the program Arizona's utility company provided customers in remote locations an alternative to power line extension or use of an electrical generator. Cavco became the first manufactured home builder to be approved for participation in the project. Cavco debuted the energy-efficient homes at the Arizona Manufactured Home Show in January 1997, and then placed model homes at two shopping centers, one each in Tucson and Mesa.

1996 Merger with Centex Providing Capital for Vertical Integration

In December 1996 Cavco merged with the Centex Corporation, through Centex's acquisition of 80 percent of Cavco's outstanding stock. At $26.75 per share, the $75 million transaction paid shareholders above market rates. Centex, a large homebuilder and mortgage provider, acquired Cavco as a low-cost complement to its existing home-building operations. While Cavco provided a ready market for Centex's financial services, Cavco would benefit from Centex's expertise in subdivision development and capital for expansion. The merger combined companies of vastly different size, however. In 1996 Cavco generated $130.1 million and net income of $6.2 million from 4,893 homes delivered, while Centex generated $3.1 billion in revenues and $53.4 million net income from more than 12,000 site-built homes. Centex maintained existing executive management at Cavco, including Brent Ghelfi, who replaced his father as president and chief executive officer earlier in 1996.

Under changed ownership, Cavco sought to increase revenue and to retain profits through the integration of manufacturing, retail sales, and financing. With the formation of Centex Finance Company in late 1997, retail dealers of Cavco products gained a financing option from a company with strong leverage capabilities. Centex Finance offered loans to all Arizona manufactured home dealers through its main office in Phoenix, while marketing representatives in Denver, Salt Lake City, and Albuquerque expanded the company's geographic reach. Cavco entered the retail market with the February 1998 acquisition of

AAA Homes, Inc., the largest retailer of manufactured homes in Arizona, with revenues of $40 million in 1997. AAA Homes operated sales centers in Tucson, Sierra Vista, Casa Grande, Yuma, Mesa, and Apache Junction, Arizona, and sales offices in Fort Collins, Colorado, and Albuquerque.

Cavco entered the Texas market in 1998 with a complete plan for manufacturing, retailing, and financing. Centex Finance opened an in office in Dallas, and Cavco began construction on a facility at acquired land in Sequin, near San Antonio, for the manufacture of multi-section homes. The acquisition of Boerne Homes, Inc., also near San Antonio, provided Cavco with a retail outlet, as well as a management base for further retail expansion; founder Doug Bunnell became Regional Manager of Cavco's retail division.

As production began at the Sequin facility in January 1999, Centex sold National Security Containers, receiving $8 million in redeemable preferred stock and $17.5 million in cash, providing funds for expansion of Cavco's retail network. The Cavco Retail Group opened stores in New Mexico, south central Texas, Colorado, and Arizona, for a total of 23 retail outlets in operation by the end of March 31, 2000.

While a slowing economy and higher interest rates negatively impacted the housing market as a whole, a new federal law hampered manufactured home financing in particular. Personal loans, referred to as chattel loans, had been the primary form of financing used by manufactured home buyers, but the new law required a real estate mortgage, with the home attached permanently to specific land. Though mortgage financing offered lower interest rates, the costs for private mortgage insurance and requirements for foundation preparations more than offset the savings. The poor financing practices of one manufactured home company led to creation of the law, but impacted the entire industry as about 75 percent of chattel loans were effected. The financing issue, along with declining market conditions, led to an excess inventory in the manufactured housing industry.

At Cavco the combination of industry oversupply and new retail outlets shifted its base of revenues. In fiscal 2000, retail sales increased 53 percent, but overall sales rose only 3 percent, to $183.5 million. Cavco responded by closing the Belen plant in August 2000 and the Seguin plant in March 2001. Centex formed Factory Liquidators as a new sales outlet, with 75 percent of inventory being acquired from failed dealerships. Retail and wholesale sales declined about 30 percent each in 2001, however; net homes delivered declined from 5,950 in 2000 to 4,242 in 2001. Revenues declined to $123 million and resulted in an operating loss of $6.9 million. Cost controls and improvements to production efficiency temporarily stalled losses in 2002, but continuing poor sales in a slow economy led to an operating loss of $11.4 million for 2003, prompting Cavco to close several retail dealerships.

Cavco Independent Again in 2003

After an evaluation of Cavco's performance and the minor place Cavco operations had in Centex's overall business, in April 2003 Centex decided to spin off Cavco as an independent company. The share distribution, noted as a tax-free dividend, was completed June 30, with Joseph Stegmayer as chief executive officer. While sales increased slightly in late 2003, Stegmayer planned to proceed cautiously.

Principal Subsidiaries

Cavco Retail Group, Inc.; Sun Built Homes, Inc.

Principal Competitors

Champion Enterprises, Inc.; Fleetwood Enterprises, Inc.; Palm Harbor Homes, Inc.; Reorganized Sale OKWD, Inc.; Skyline Corporation.

Further Reading

"Belen Plant Closing Temporarily," *Associated Press State & Local Wire,* June 29, 2000.

"CAVCO Homes Signs Exclusive Agreement with Japanese Company," *Business Wire,* November 13, 1995.

"Cavco Industries Inc. and Arizona Public Service Company Join Forces to Provide Solar Powered Manufactured Housing," *Business Wire,* December 18, 1996.

"Cavco Industries, Inc. Announces It Has Completed the Sale of CVC Leasing," *Business Wire,* August 1, 1994.

"Centex, Cavco Complete Merger Joining Conventional and Manufactured Home Builders, *PR Newswire,* March 27, 1997.

"Centex, Cavco Merger Will Join Conventional and Manufactured Home Builders," *Business Wire,* December 5, 1996.

"Centex Corporation—Re Subsids New Operations," *Regulatory News Service,* December 29, 1997.

"Centex's Cavco Industries Adds Manufactured Home Retailer in Texas," *PR Newswire,* July 1, 1998.

"Centex's Cavco Industries Entering Texas Market," *PR Newswire,* May 19, 1998.

"Centex Names Head of Manufactured Housing Group," *PR Newswire,* September 18, 2000.

"Centex Unit Acquires Arizona's Largest Manufactured Housing Retailer," *PR Newswire,* February 5, 1998.

Fischer, Howard, "Cavco Supplies Mobile Homes to Israel to House Immigrants," *Business Journal-Serving Phoenix & the Valley of the Sun,* January 21, 1991, p. 5.

Jarman, Max, "As World Seeks Better Housing, State May Gain," *Arizona Business Gazette,* February 7, 1992, p. 1.

Luebke, Cathy, "Cavco Industries, Inc.," *Business Journal-Serving Phoenix & the Valley of the Sun,* June 25, 1993, p. 19B.

"Mobile Mini, Inc. to Acquire National Security Containers," *Business Wire,* April 5, 1999.

Much, Marilyn, "Centex Corp. Dallas, Texas; Planned Spinoff Lets Builder Narrow Focus," *Investor's Business Daily,* May 9, 2003, p. A08.

Pesquera, Adolfo, "Phoenix-Based Manufactured-Home Builder Cavco Bucks Industry Slump," *San Antonio Express-News,* March 15, 2002.

Reagor, Catherine, "Dallas' Centex Buying Big Stake in Arizona, Manufactured-Home Builder," *Knight Ridder/Tribune Business News,* December 6, 1996.

"Will Create 300 Jobs for Area: CAVCO Industries to Build Plant in New Mexico; Will Help Company Meet Growing Product Demands of Region," *Business Wire,* September 5, 1996.

—Mary Tradii

Ceradyne, Inc.

3169 Red Hill Avenue
Costa Mesa, California 92626
U.S.A.
Telephone: (714) 549-0421
Fax: (714) 549-5787
Web site: http://www.ceradyne.com

Public Company
Incorporated: 1967
Employees: 500
Sales: $101.47 million (2003)
Stock Exchanges: NASDAQ
Ticker Symbol: CRDN
NAIC: 327112 Vitreous China, Fine Earthenware and
    Other Pottery Product Manufacturing; Porcelain
    Electrical Supply Manufacturing; 334411 Electron
    Tube Manufacturing; 334419 Other Electronic
    Component Manufacturing

Ceradyne, Inc. develops and manufactures advanced ceramic products and components for defense, industrial, automotive, and commercial applications. The company's ceramic products possess a number of attractive characteristics, including the ability to withstand extremely high temperatures, resistance to corrosion and wear, and hardness coupled with light weight. Ceradyne relies heavily on defense spending, producing ceramic armor for military personnel and attack helicopters. The company also manufactures ceramic diesel engine components, and aesthetic ceramic orthodontic brackets through a partnership with 3M. Ceradyne operates five manufacturing facilities in California, Kentucky, and Georgia.

Origins

Joel Moskowitz was 28 years old when he started his entrepreneurial career, a venture that began at his kitchen table in 1967. In the years leading up to the formation of Ceradyne, Moskowitz gained the experience he needed to launch his own company. After earning a degree in ceramics engineering from Alfred University in 1961, he spent five years at Interpace working in ceramics research. At night, he worked toward an M.B.A. degree at the University of Southern California; he received his degree in 1966. Moskowitz's faith in the potential of ceramics drove him to start his own company, a conviction that shaped Ceradyne's strategic focus and positioned it on the leading edge of technology related to technical ceramics. "I have always felt that advanced technical ceramics would be the pacing material that would allow other technologies to advance," he recalled in a June 2002 interview with *Ceramic Industry.* "I believed, even early on," he added, "that Ceradyne should focus in the area of non-oxide structural ceramics where, even as a small company, its technology focus would allow it to excel."

Moskowitz teamed with another Interpace ceramics researcher to start Ceradyne, an enterprise founded with $5,000 of Moskowitz's wife's savings. At the kitchen table, Moskowitz and his colleague discussed the intricacies of their idea: to create a single crystal of potassium tantalate niobate for use as an electro-optic modulator—a device that modified light passing through material. The initial project was a success, eventually giving Ceradyne its first federal government contract and spawning the development of proprietary technology. With its own technology, Ceradyne could focus on developing more advanced technical ceramics, which enabled the company to focus on defense applications, a market of extreme importance to Ceradyne's growth.

Moskowitz was able to leverage Ceradyne's initial success into physical expansion. During the early 1970s, he moved the company to a larger facility in Costa Mesa, California, and installed hot presses for the production of hot pressed boron carbide, a material used to produce Kevlar systems for U.S. and allied military attack helicopters. Ceradyne's ability to produce hot pressed boron carbide anchored the company to a vast, lucrative market, positioning it as a leading supplier of ceramic armor. In the years to come, ceramic armor would be incorporated into a variety of defense applications, including its use for personnel protection and military ground-based vehicles.

For Moskowitz, the start was positive, but Ceradyne's business volume was not sufficient to sustain a capital-intensive operation. The company was barely surviving on small research projects. Advanced ceramics was a forward-looking business, one that required continual and extensive research and development efforts to produce products for anticipated needs. Ceradyne, in relation to other massive defense contractors, was small, dwarfed by the likes of Martin Marietta and McDonnell Douglas. Moskowitz, trying to compete against industry behemoths, was struggling. He was forced to take another job to help keep Ceradyne in business. "We were going after markets that didn't exist," he recalled in a July 14, 1986 interview with *Forbes,* "and developing technology that had no products."

Strategic Alliances: 1970s–80s

What Moskowitz needed was a financial partner, a company able to give Ceradyne the resources to compete in a capital-intensive business. During the mid-1970s, Moskowitz's salvation arrived. TRE Corporation, a $70 million-in-sales construction supplies conglomerate, approached Moskowitz, offering to buy his company. TRE executives gave Moskowitz the opportunity he wanted, promising to provide Ceradyne with the capital that would enable the company to move into higher-profit-margin manufacturing. Further, TRE officials promised to let Moskowitz manage Ceradyne without interference. Moskowitz agreed to the proposal, leading to the merger between TRE and Ceradyne in 1974.

Moskowitz's hopes for salvation were dashed not long after he agreed to TRE's proposal. TRE's construction supplies business faltered soon after the merger, causing the company's earnings to plunge. TRE reorganized its business and the company was forced to divest some of its assets to raise cash. Ceradyne was put up for sale in the wake of TRE's financial debacle, fueling Moskowitz's apprehension about his future and about the future of Ceradyne. A corporate suitor, Kyoto Ceramics, a company based in Japan, inquired about Ceradyne, expressing an interest in purchasing the small company. Moskowitz's position was precarious, but he was able to negotiate a deal with the Japanese buyers that calmed his fears. Kyoto executives agreed that Ceradyne would maintain its own facilities and keep its management after the deal was completed, which renewed Moskowitz's hope that salvation had arrived in the guise of another partnership. The transaction was completed in 1978, when Ceradyne generated $1.5 million in sales. The company was allowed to establish its own performance goals and its identity as a Kyoto subsidiary was shrouded.

Not long after the acquisition of Ceradyne by Kyoto, the prospects for the use of advanced ceramics in defense applications brightened considerably. The use of ceramics in military applications had supported Ceradyne for years before its corporate marriage to Kyoto, but during the early 1980s the Pentagon's attraction to ceramics intensified, its interest piqued by the material's light weight, strength, and high melting point. When the immense financial resources at the Pentagon's disposal were focused on advanced ceramics, a slew of federal contracts followed, invigorating Ceradyne's business significantly. There was a problem, however. The Pentagon disliked foreign companies having any equity interest in defense contractors, a posture that worked against the Kyoto-owned Ceradyne. In response to the federal government's stance, the Japanese company was forced to sell Ceradyne to American interests, leading to the leveraged buyout of Ceradyne by Moskowitz and his business associates for $2.3 million in cash and an agreement for a 3 percent royalty on sales.

After a couple of failed partnerships, Moskowitz found himself in charge of his company in the purest sense for the first time in a decade. Pentagon-sponsored contracts flowed after he severed ties with Kyoto, but the debt incurred from the leveraged buyout weighed on Ceradyne's ability to function effectively. Moskowitz led his company through an initial public offering (IPO) of stock in July 1984, but the capital raised from the offering was not enough to vanquish Ceradyne's weakness as an under-capitalized company competing in a research-and-development-intensive industry. As before, Moskowitz needed a partner. "We're small," he said in his July 14, 1986 interview with *Forbes.* "We can't spend 15 years researching something before we market it."

Moskowitz's need for a partner was answered not long after he completed Ceradyne's IPO. In mid-1985, he was approached by Ford Motor Company, a company whose involvement in ceramics research began in the early 1970s, when the automobile manufacturer sponsored an extensive exploration into advanced uses for ceramics. Ford was interested in forging a joint venture partnership with Ceradyne, a proposal that Moskowitz accepted. In March 1986, the two companies consummated the deal, forming a joint product development program with the long-term objective of developing ceramic components for automobiles. Under the terms of the agreement, Ford invested $10 million in Ceradyne, which eventually gave the automobile manufacturer a 16 percent stake in Moskowitz's company. Ford also gave Ceradyne technology it had developed, which included roughly 80 ceramic patents. The partnership with Ford promised great things, giving Ceradyne much needed financial support and the opportunity to diversify. In the year before its partnership with Ford, Ceradyne generated $16.8 million in sales, 90 percent of which was derived from defense-related work. Although ceramic automobile engine parts were not commercially viable in the mid-1980s, the prospect of a new, nonmilitary source of revenue boded well for Ceradyne's future.

The partnership with Ford occurred at roughly the same time Moskowitz completed another important move toward diversifying his product line. In 1986, Ceradyne forged a relationship with 3M's Unitek Division. The two companies joined forces to develop and manufacture ceramic orthodontic brackets. The brackets, marketed under the brand name Clarity, became an important part of Ceradyne's business, eventually accounting for nearly one-fifth of the company's annual sales. Moskowitz also completed two acquisitions in 1986, purchasing Lexington,

Key Dates:
1967: Joel Moskowitz cofounds Ceradyne.
1974: TRE Corp. acquires Ceradyne.
1978: Kyoto Ceramics acquires Ceradyne.
1984: Ceradyne completes its initial public offering of stock.
1986: Ceradyne begins developing ceramic orthodontic brackets and forms a joint venture with Ford Motor Co.
1995: After losing more than $20 million during a seven-year period, Ceradyne posts a profit of $2 million.
2001: The use of Ceradyne's ceramic body armor by U.S. military forces in Afghanistan fuels the company's growth.
2003: Ceradyne's sales reach $100 million for the first time.

Kentucky-based Semicon Associates and Scottdale, Georgia-based Thermo Materials. Semicon manufactured cathodes that were used in satellite communications and microwave applications. Thermo Materials produced fused silica ceramic products used by the glass and metal fabrication industries.

The additions to Ceradyne's operations in 1986 caused the company's revenue to soar. After posting $16.8 million in sales in 1985, the company recorded $25.6 million in sales in 1987. The surge in sales was fleeting, however. The total recorded in 1987 would not be eclipsed for nine years. The company's sales volume steadily shrank during the late 1980s and early 1990s, reaching a low point of $15.9 million in 1993. The cause for the extended decline stemmed from the company's reliance on defense spending, which had been reduced somewhat after the diversification of 1986 but not enough to compensate for the end of the ''Cold War.'' The collapse of the Soviet Union left the Pentagon without its greatest perceived threat, leading to a decline in defense spending. Ceradyne lost one of its principal defense contracts and suffered cutbacks in several other defense contracts. Sales of Ceradyne's translucent ceramic orthodontic brackets also declined, dropping from a peak of $6.2 million in 1988 to $400,000 in 1994, a consequence of excess inventory levels accumulated by Unitek and technical problems experienced by orthodontists. As revenues sagged, the company's profitability suffered, resulting in annual net losses that dragged on into the mid-1990s.

Ceradyne suffered through years of disappointing financial results before prosperous times returned. The company posted a loss every year between 1987 and 1994, racking up more than $20 million in losses. Ceradyne returned to profitability in 1995, when the company recorded $2 million in net income. The company remained profitable for the remainder of the decade, but it demonstrated only modest revenue growth. The $23.4 million generated in 1995—a total less than the amount recorded in 1987—increased to only $30.3 million by the end of the decade. The company was helped somewhat during this period by an improved ceramic orthodontic bracket it developed and by the market introduction of ceramic diesel engine parts, but the lack of escalating defense spending held its growth in check.

Rapid Growth in the 21st Century

The early years of the 21st century were years of dynamic growth for Ceradyne. Military spending increased dramatically, as the United States launched attacks against Afghanistan and Iraq, creating a wealth of business for defense contractors. Ceradyne's defense-related business thrived, particularly the company's bullet-resistant vests, which accounted for one-quarter of sales in 2001. In the fall of 2001, the U.S. military distributed Ceradyne's vests to special forces in Afghanistan, where the performance of the ceramic garments convinced the U.S. Defense Department to seek bids for a lighter vest to be worn by infantry troops. The military also used Ceradyne's ceramic pads for other uses, including providing a defensive layer on helicopter seat bottoms. Ceradyne's business flourished as the military campaigns intensified. In 2001, the company's sales reached $45 million and its net income swelled to $4 million, more than three times the total registered two years earlier.

The invasion of Iraq in 2003 helped Ceradyne record the most impressive financial year in its history. Driven by the demand for ceramic body armor, the company's sales soared, eclipsing $100 million for the first time. The company's net income reached $11.2 million in 2003, more than quadruple the total recorded in 2002. Flush with cash, the company was able to complete an acquisition in May 2004, when it purchased San Diego, California-based Quest Technology LP, a privately held company that molded ceramic shapes for medical applications. The acquisition of Quest represented an important step toward diversifying away from defense-related business, but as the company prepared for its future much of its financial vitality depended on a robust defense budget and its ability to bid competitively for military work.

Principal Divisions

Ceradyne Advanced Ceramic Operations; Ceradyne Thermo Materials; Semicon Associates.

Principal Competitors

Cookson Group PLC; CoorsTek, Inc.; Kyocera Corporation.

Further Reading

''Ceradyne Gets Its Acquisition,'' *Performance Materials,* May 24, 2004, p. 2.

''Ceradyne Reaches New Record,'' *Performance Materials,* May 10, 2004, p. 6.

''Ceradyne Revenues Soar, Profits Sag,'' *Performance Materials,* March 17, 2003, p. 3.

''Ceradyne Sees Rising Sales, Buys Factory,'' *Performance Materials,* October 27, 2003, p. 3.

Chafee, John H., ''The Hug of the Bear,'' *Forbes,* July 14, 1986, p. 56.

Cole, Benjamin Mark, ''Small-Cap Ceradyne Finds Niche in Equipping Troops,'' *Los Angeles Business Journal,* October 29, 2001, p. 52.

''Military Buildup May Boost Ceradyne Fortunes,'' *Performance Materials,* November 12, 2001, p. 3.

Payne, Susan, ''Advancing Technical Ceramics,'' *Ceramic Industry,* June 2002, p. 12.

—Jeffrey L. Covell

China Life Insurance Company Limited

16 Chaowai Avenue
Chaoyang District
Beijing 100020
China
Telephone: +86 10 8565 9999
Fax: +86 10 8525 2232
Web site: http://www.chinalife.com.cn

Public Company
Incorporated: 1996
Employees: 66,886
Sales: $9.53 billion (2003)
Stock Exchanges: New York Hong Kong
Ticker Symbol: LFC
NAIC: 524113 Direct Life Insurance Carriers; 524114
Direct Health and Medical Insurance Carriers

China Life Insurance Company Limited is the largest life insurer in the People's Republic of China. The company offers individual life insurance, group life, accident insurance, and health insurance policies. China Life commands 45 percent of that market, and holds the number one position in 29 of the country's 31 major markets—only Shanghai and Beijing, where the company nonetheless is number two, escape its dominance. Formed from the breakup of former government-owned monopoly People's Insurance Company of China, China Life is the only life insurance company in China with a national operating license, which has permitted it to develop a network of more than 8,000 field offices, 4,800 branch offices, 3,000 customer service offices, and 87,000 sales outlets in such locations as banks, post offices, hotels, airports, travel agents, and the like. The company's nearly 67,000 employees are complemented by a network of 650,000 exclusive independent sales agents. The company also operates a ''one-stop'' 24-hour telephone sales and service hotline. Together, China Life serves more than 100 million long-term policy holders and more than 150 million short-term policy holders, generating nearly CNY 51 billion ($6.2 billion) in net premiums and policy fees in 2003. The group's total sales topped $9.5 billion that year.

China Life listed on the Hong Kong Stock Exchange and the New York Stock Exchange at the end of 2003, raising $3.5 billion in that year's largest initial public offering (IPO). China has indicated its intention to expand into other financial areas, such as asset management, brokering, and banking.

Inheriting China's Pre-Revolution Insurance Industry

The opening of China to the West in the early years of the 20th century led to a variety of new business opportunities. By the end of World War I, China, and especially Shanghai, had become a major center for international trade, although dominated by foreign interests. The lively commercial market in that city offered entrepreneurs seemingly unlimited potential; among these was the young C.V. Starr, an American, who founded an insurance agent's office in Shanghai in 1919. At first, Starr's company, American Asiatic Underwriters (AAU), served as a local representative for foreign insurers.

AAU originally dealt in fire and marine insurance policies. In the early 1920s, however, Starr recognized the vast potential for life insurance among the country's Chinese population. Starr set up a new company, Asia Life Insurance Company, which became the first to market life insurance products to the Chinese. The company's head start allowed it to build quickly into a leading insurance provider not only across the Chinese mainland, but throughout much of the Asian region. Starr's company eventually evolved into U.S. leader American Insurance Group.

In the meantime, Asia Life's success inspired a raft of competitors. Most of these were local representatives of large foreign companies. A number of local groups appeared, however, and played an important role in developing the life insurance market among the indigenous population.

One of the earliest and most important of these companies was the Tai Ping Insurance Company, which was incorporated in Shanghai in 1929. Founded by H.C. Tung and H.N. Ting, the new company received start-up investments from a number of Chinese banks and began issuing general insurance policies. The following year, Tai Ping added a life insurance component, Tai Ping Life Insurance Company. Tai Ping developed strongly

---

Company Perspectives:

Our Mission: Work for the well-being of the people and revitalize national life insurance industry.

---

through the 1930s, adding nearly 20 branches in major cities in China as well as elsewhere in southeast Asia. The company also opened some 400 secondary offices across the Chinese mainland, before adding representative offices in Europe and in the Americas.

By the mid-1930s, Tai Ping had grown sufficiently large to become a member of the Shanghai Insurance Association, the only Chinese-owned company to be included in what had previously been an exclusive club for foreign insurers. Tai Ping's fortunes began to dwindle after the start of the Sino-Japanese War in 1937, and especially with the Mao-led Communist revolution in 1949.

Tai Ping in the meantime had been joined by a growing number of other Chinese-owned insurance companies. Among these were China Insurance Company, founded in 1931 in Shanghai, which opened a life insurance subsidiary, China Life Insurance Company in 1933. Later insurance market entries included Ming An Insurance Company, established in Hong Kong in 1949. By then, China boasted more than 240 insurance companies—some 180 of which were Chinese owned.

Following the revolution, the Mao government set up the People's Insurance Company of China (PICC), which took over all insurance interests on the mainland. Tai Ping's leadership fled to Taiwan in 1950, reestablishing the company's operations there. Other companies, especially those that had set up foreign branches in Hong Kong, Singapore, Taiwan, and elsewhere, withdrew from the mainland to rebuild their businesses around their foreign holdings. Foreign insurance companies were simply expelled outright, and their holdings regrouped under PICC as well.

At first the PICC monopoly continued to operate its various insurance services, integrating the assets of the former independent insurance sector. By 1952, PICC represented a national network of 1,300 branches and 3,000 agency outlets. Yet the Chinese government, in its effort to develop its regime, determined that insurance was superfluous in a state where the government was meant to provide for all social welfare for its citizens. In 1959, therefore, all domestic insurance business was ended. PICC's role was reduced to providing insurance covering the country's foreign policy needs, such as for the marine and aviation sectors. Following the reform, PICC was converted into a department of the government's central bank.

Reforming in the 1980s

Economic reforms launched under Deng Xiaoping in 1978 paved the way to a rebirth in China's insurance sector. In 1979, the People's Insurance Company of China was separated from the central bank and reestablished as an independently operating, although state-controlled, company. In that year, PICC began offering general (i.e., non-life) insurance policies. In 1980, as the first initiatives to bring foreign investment capital in the country emerged, PICC formed a joint venture with American Insurance Group—allowing the American company to test the waters before making a broader return to the mainland insurance market in the 1990s.

PICC began offering life insurance policies again in 1982, targeting the small but growing numbers of middle-class and wealthy Chinese, as well as government officials. Nonetheless, the Chinese life insurance market remained tiny—as late as 2004, per capita spending on life insurance amounted to the equivalent of just $28, compared with average per capita spending of as much $2,800 or more in Japan, offering tantalizing prospects for future growth.

PICC officially retained its monopoly on the Chinese insurance market into the late 1980s. In 1988, however, the company's monopoly was abolished. Licenses were granted to the company's first competitors, including Ping An, which established that year, grew into the country's second largest life insurer, with a dominance in the important Beijing market. Other early domestic competitors included China Pacific, based in Shanghai, which also started business in 1988, and American Insurance Group, which, in 1992, became the first foreign company to be granted a license to operate a self-standing business on the mainland (i.e., not as part of a joint venture with a local partner). Nonetheless, PICC remained the clear insurance champion on the mainland, with a strong national presence. The company also began opening offices overseas, adding locations in Singapore, Hong Kong, Tokyo, and London.

Public Company for the New Century

The Chinese government began a wider opening of the country's insurance market in the early 1990s. By the end of the decade, the government had granted licenses to a total of 16 companies—including such returning groups as Tai Ping Insurance Company and China Insurance Company.

The increasingly competitive environment led to a need to change PICC's structure. In 1996, the company reorganized as a holding company, called PICC Group. Its operations were then broken up into three subsidiaries, PICC Life, PICC Property, and PICC Reinsurance. PICC Group initially operated under the control of the People's Bank of China.

Despite the restructuring, PICC Group was somewhat hampered in its growth. The arrival of AIG had introduced a new tied-agency system into the market, encouraging the development of branch networks. Yet PICC Group, as a state-owned enterprise, was initially barred from developing its own network of branch offices and tied agents. As a result, the company was forced to cede the leadership spot in two of the country's most important markets, Beijing, captured by Ping An, and Shanghai, taken by China Pacific.

In 1998, the Chinese government transferred oversight of the country's growing insurance market to a new body, the China Insurance Regulatory Commission (CIRC). Under new rules, insurance companies were prohibited from operating in both the non-life and life insurance markets. As a result, PICC Group was broken up into its four primary components: PICC, which took over the company's general insurance business; China Re, for its reinsurance operations; China Insurance, which handled the group's international activities; and China Life. All four companies remained controlled by the Chinese state.

Yet the former members of PICC Group began moving toward an opening of its share capital at the beginning of the 2000s. In 2000, China Life announced its intention to diversify its own shareholding in advance of a future public offering. In the meantime, the company continued to build up its business across China, solidifying its dominant position in 29 of the country's 30 major markets. China Life also was helped by the government's rule for foreign corporations operating in China, which stipulated that all employees in these companies must be covered by unified insurance policies. In response, China Life concentrated its unified insurance operations at its Guangdong Branch, close to the rapidly expanding free-trade zone, in which the majority of foreign enterprises had set up their Chinese operations. By 2001, China Life had captured 80 percent of the unified insurance business for the top 500 foreign firms operating in China.

China Life then began petitioning the CIRC for authorization to go public, which was granted in June 2003. As part of the run up to the company's IPO, China Life restructured its operations, splitting into three entities: China Life Insurance Company and China Life Asset Management Company, both of which were placed under a new holding company, China Life Insurance Corporation.

In order to make its IPO more attractive, the parent holding transferred only long- and medium-term policies issued on or after June 10, 1999, to China Life. This move was made in order to avoid launching China Life with the burden of a large number of loss-making policies issued at return rates as high as 6.5 percent. The June 10, 1999 date corresponded to an emergency ruling by the CIRC, which lowered return rates to just 2.5 percent.

To attract as wide a pool of investors as possible, China Life launched its IPO on both the Hong Kong Stock Exchange and the New York Stock Exchange in December 2003. The IPO was a huge success, raising $3.5 billion and becoming the world's largest for that year. The retail offer had been oversubscribed by 172 times, and the total order had reached $80 billion.

The success of its IPO encouraged China Life to begin eyeing expansion into new markets in 2004. China Life's unlisted parent company announced its intention to diversify its insurance business to include property insurance and develop an insurance intermediary agent business as well as add other financial services. China Life itself announced its intention to diversify into new services, such as asset management, brokerage services, and banking in the near future. In the meantime, China Life had emerged as the dominant player in what many expected to become the world's fastest-growing and largest life insurance market.

Principal Competitors

Ping An Insurance Company Ltd.; China Pacific Insurance Company Ltd.; AIG; AIU Insurance Co.; Allianz Dazhong Life Insurance Company Ltd.; Chubb Group of Insurance Cos.; Cigna Corporation; Manulife-Sinochem Life Insurance Company Ltd.

Further Reading

Bei, Hu, "China Life's a Beach for Top-Selling Agents," *South China Morning Post*, May 13, 2004.

——, "Moody's Queries China Life's Distance from Poor Policies," *South China Morning Post,* June 30, 2004.

Chan, Christine, "New China Life Step Nearer Listing," *South China Morning Post,* June 18, 2003.

"China Life Insurance Earns $713m in 2003," *China Daily,* April 25, 2004.

"China Life Probed on IPO Share Allocation," *South China Morning Post,* May 3, 2004.

"China's Largest State-Owned Life Insurer to Embrace Diversified Ownership," *Xinhua News Agency,* July 25, 2000.

Hamlin, Kevin, "The China Life Premium," *Institutional Investor International Edition,* January 2004, p. 60.

Howard, Lisa S., "China Plans to Split State Insurer into Three Parts," *National Underwriter Life & Health Financial Services Edition,* August 24, 1998, p. 29.

"Insurer Plans Expansion," *New York Times,* May 20, 2004, p. W1.

"Investors Welcome China Life IPO," *Reactions,* January 2004, p. 8.

"Off with a Bang," *Economist,* December 20, 2003, p. 105.

Oshins, Alice H., "Changes in the Chinese Insurance Industry," *Risk Management,* December 1992, p. 52.

Sanchanta, Mariko, and Dave Shellock, "China Life Struggles with Growing Pains," *Financial Times,* February 6, 2004, p. 28.

—M.L. Cohen

ChoicePoint Inc.

1000 Alderman Drive
Alpharetta, Georgia 30005
U.S.A.
Telephone: (770) 752-6000
Toll Free: (800) 342-5339
Fax: (770) 752-6005
Web site: http://www.choicepoint.com

Public Company
Incorporated: 1997
Employees: 4,500
Sales: $750.4 million (2003)
Stock Exchanges: New York
Ticker Symbol: CPS
NAIC: 511140 Database and Directory Publishers;
    524298 All Other Insurance Related Activities

Spun off from Equifax Inc. in 1997, ChoicePoint Inc. serves the insurance industry, government, and businesses through a variety of information services it provides. After numerous acquisitions during its short history, the company has streamlined itself around the core areas of data collection and information brokering. Background checks, motor vehicle reports, property inspections, and drug screening are just a few of the services ChoicePoint provides to many of the nation's leading businesses.

In the Beginning: Early and Middle 1990s to 1997

The ChoicePoint story begins with credit report giant Equifax Inc., based in Atlanta, Georgia. The publicly traded billion-dollar company compiled and maintained credit information on more than 350 million credit cardholders around the globe by the late 1990s. Originally founded at the end of the 19th century by brothers Cator and Guy Woolford to gather information for their *Merchants Guide,* the firm officially became Equifax in 1976. Equifax, which stood for "equitability in the gathering and presentation of facts," grew exponentially in the remaining years of the 1970s and into the 1980s. By the late 1980s Equifax ruled the information-compilation industry, but was not without its detractors.

While gathering information had always riled privacy rights proponents, Equifax did make some questionable moves in its stellar climb to the top of the information industry. Its Insurance Information Services group, which assisted health, life, property, and casualty insurers in the investigation of potential clients, was losing its way, and Derek V. Smith, who had been with the company since 1981, took over the ailing division in 1993. In Smith's capable hands, the division returned to profitability and by 1996 Equifax was prepared to spin the insurance group (which had sales of around $365 million for the year and represented about 30 percent of Equifax's revenues) off on its own.

By this time in its corporate life, Equifax was no stranger to controversy and had decided to divest itself of any noncore or nonfinancial assets. It had already negotiated to sell its healthcare and direct marketing units, skirmished with California lottery officials, faced multiple lawsuits over privacy rights, and run into trouble with a new acquisition called CDB Infotek Inc. Once the decision was made to spin off the insurance group, Equifax approached New York-based Kroll Associates in early 1997 to become part of the spinoff and merge into the new ChoicePoint.

The privately held Kroll was the nation's largest private detecting and risk assessment firm, had sales of $70 million by 1996, and had let it be known that it was looking for growth opportunities. Unfortunately for both parties, executives could not agree on several salient points. Merger talks fell through with Kroll but Equifax bought Advanced HR Solutions Inc. in June and spun off ChoicePoint on July 31, 1997. ChoicePoint began trading on the New York Stock Exchange on August 8, 1997; Kroll went on to merge with Ohio-based armored car manufacturer O'Gara-Hess & Eisenhardt to become Kroll-O'Gara.

Growth and Acquisitions: 1997–2000

Newly minted ChoicePoint, headed by Smith as president and CEO, hit the ground running by acquiring Medical Information Network, LLC in October and Drug Free, Inc. in November 1997. ChoicePoint had also inherited the Equifax/CDB Infotek imbroglio. CDB had been accused of violating privacy protection rights in early 1997 for allegedly selling voter registration lists to bill collectors (it is illegal to sell voter registration information commercially). The lawsuit was filed by Aristotle Publishing Inc., a voter registration collection firm with whom CDB had done business. CDB countersued and Equifax washed its hands of it all by spinning CDB off with ChoicePoint. In early 1998 ChoicePoint bought the remaining 30 percent interest of CDB and announced that it would "review" CDB's information selling practices.

Not long after buying the remainder of CDB, ChoicePoint merged Attest National Drug Testing Inc. into its medical services unit and also bought Application Profiles Inc., Informus Corp., Customer Development Corp., Tyler-McLennon Inc., EquiSearch Services Inc., and DATEQ Information Network Inc. Year-end operating revenues for 1998 had fallen short of the previous year's $417.3 million (still part of Equifax for half the year) at $406.5 million, but operating income in 1998 rose to $61.4 million, a significant climb from 1997's $46.1 million.

ChoicePoint continued its flurry of acquisitions in 1999, buying six companies and landing several lucrative contracts as well. Through its Business & Government Services division, which had become the largest provider of background and screening services for employers in the United States, as well as the leading provider of online research gathering, ChoicePoint handled work for the U.S. Federal Marshals, Federal Bureau of Investigation, Drug Enforcement Administration, Internal Revenue Service, Department of Justice, and corporate clients including First Union and GTE. ChoicePoint's other division, the Insurance Services group, topped competitors as the leading underwriter and information products provider to property and casualty companies nationwide, with the second largest insurance testing facility in the industry. The Insurance unit also had won lucrative contracts with Progressive Insurance, Kemper, and CNA. Revenues for 1999 surpassed $430 million with operating income increasing from the previous year's $61.4 million to more than $78 million.

In 2000 ChoicePoint celebrated the new year by initiating another buying spree. Within the next several months ChoicePoint bought seven companies and then merged with Florida-based competitor DBT (Database Technologies) Online Inc. DBT specialized in court-related documents and the two companies merged operations (under the ChoicePoint banner) for a stock swap said to be worth $440 million. Yet, as with the CDB purchase, ChoicePoint was once again embroiled in controversy. This one stemmed from DBT's $4 million contract with the state of Florida. Hired in 1998 to clean up Florida's voter registration lists after a fraudulent 1997 mayoral election,

DBT was supposed to "purge" the lists of deceased citizens, duplicates, and convicted felons. DBT ended up purging more than 170,000 of the state's 8.6 million voters in error, and ChoicePoint was caught in the crossfire as DBT's owner.

Emerging Victorious in 2001 and Beyond

The new century brought a myriad of new opportunities for ChoicePoint and further friction. By the spring of 2001, the furor over Florida's now infamous voter registration flaws had reached a fever pitch since thousands of citizens had been told they were ineligible to vote. The improbably close race between presidential nominees George W. Bush and Al Gore only added fuel to the fire. In its defense, DBT told investigators they had been given very broad information to input into the firm's computer system, which in turn led to mistakes over similarly spelled names, those with the same middle initials, and a host of smaller errors causing thousands to be "scrubbed" from voter registration lists. Although DBT maintained that it had told Florida officials the list of those removed from the voter lists needed to be verified, Florida pointed the finger at DBT and registration officials, and several lawsuits were filed over the fiasco. Many ultimately held DBT responsible for the voting debacles, including the NAACP (National Association for the Advancement of Colored People), which filed a lawsuit over African Americans who were denied votes in the presidential election of 2000.

For every complaint or negative view, however, ChoicePoint had a multitude of satisfied customers. The firm's expertise in background checks and screening services continued to evolve, with new programs and even lower costs. One such advance was ScreenNow, a prospective employee screening program for smaller companies. Whereas large corporations could easily afford ChoicePoint's premium services, smaller businesses needed the same services but could not afford the price. ScreenNow provided much of the same data, was web-based, and even the smallest employers with workforces of less than 50 could afford to use it.

After the terrorist attacks of September 11, 2001, ChoicePoint gained new business as companies of all sizes were more concerned about security and exactly who might be working for them. One such commission was from the Transportation Safety Administration (TSA) to screen job applicants for the thousands of airport baggage screeners needed to beef up airport security in the wake of 9/11. ChoicePoint was hired for $19 million to do background and criminal records checks on more than 55,000 applicants. ChoicePoint devised a system of flagging applicants with colors. Prospective workers were assigned a color based on suitability for the job: green for go (meaning a clean record or no infractions found); red for those who had committed what was deemed a "serious" crime or a felony; and yellow for those whose records either could not be verified for one reason or another, or who had committed a "less serious" crime or misdemeanor.

Again ChoicePoint and its methods were criticized when it was learned that numerous airport baggage screeners had criminal records. It was with the TSA, however, where most of the blame rested since agency members admitted to hiring applicants from ChoicePoint's "red" and "yellow" lists because they had been under tremendous pressure to hire such a huge number of screeners to comply with the government's demands.

Key Dates:

1976: Equifax is incorporated (company originally founded in 1899).
1992: Equifax restructures its operations.
1993: Derek V. Smith heads up Equifax's insurance services business.
1996: Equifax withdraws from healthcare information services.
1997: Equifax decides to spin off its insurance services unit and launches ChoicePoint Inc.
1998: ChoicePoint begins an acquisition spree that includes the merger of Attest National Drug Testing Inc. into the firm.
1999: ChoicePoint acquires six additional companies.
2000: ChoicePoint acquires seven more companies and merges with DBT Online.
2001: ChoicePoint buys seven more firms, including the famed Pinkerton Services Group.
2002: Another six companies are purchased; the company changes from two divisions to three.
2003: ChoicePoint divests its home inspection services and acquires two more data-driven firms.

Both ChoicePoint and the TSA further explained to Homeland Security investigators that many applicants did change "colors," simply because information was either verified or had been erroneously attributed to their records.

Amidst the finger pointing, ChoicePoint had carried on business as usual, which for the last several years had meant buying an increasing number of like-minded companies. In 2001 ChoicePoint acquired seven more firms, including the well-known Pinkerton's Inc. Pinkerton's was widely regarded as the country's first investigative agency, founded in 1849 by Allan Pinkerton to chase counterfeiters. It seemed a bit ironic for Pinkerton's—a forebear of Equifax, ChoicePoint, and the entire data collection and sleuthing industry—to come into the ChoicePoint fold. Yet however one chose to look at this and its many other acquisitions, ChoicePoint was becoming a powerhouse in the information industry with 2001 revenues of $693.4 million, up from 2000's $631 million and operating income of slightly less than $120 million, a hefty leap from the previous year's $90.1 million.

In 2002 ChoicePoint continued to augment its business units with more acquisitions (six), Smith added the title of chairman while passing COO Doug C. Curling the duties of president, and the company shifted from two divisions to three: Business & Government Services, Insurance Services, and Marketing Services (marketing previously had been part of the business group). Its numbers—in all facets—were impressive: ChoicePoint clients amounted to about 40 percent of the country's top 1,000 firms according to its estimates, and the company had furnished or worked with virtually "all major U.S. law enforcement and homeland security agencies" since its spinoff from Equifax (which, incidentally, it outperformed on a regular basis). Year-end numbers backed up the rhetoric, with revenue hitting $792 million for 2002 and operating income reaching $193.2 million.

Early in 2003 ChoicePoint bought two more companies, which brought the total of acquisitions since its incorporation as an independent company to 38. The firm then sold off CP Commercial Specialists, a property inspection service, to focus on its core businesses of data collection and informational services. In six years the company had transformed itself from an Equifax subsidiary to one of the most powerful and increasingly successful information brokers in the world. In CEO and Chairman Smith's words in the company's 2002 annual report, "ChoicePoint strives to create a safer and more secure society through the responsible use of information." While some civil libertarians argued with this assessment and likened ChoicePoint's methods to Big Brotherish tactics, its information services not only saved corporations, governmental agencies, and law enforcement officials time and money, but more important, undoubtedly saved many lives.

Principal Subsidiaries

ChoicePoint Asset Co.; ChoicePoint Public Records Inc.; ChoicePoint Services Inc.

Principal Divisions

Business & Government Services; Insurance Services; Marketing Services.

Principal Competitors

Insurance Services Office, Inc.; Kroll Inc.; Reed Elsevier Group; Trans Union LLC.

Further Reading

Campbell, Ronald, "California's CDB Infotek, Rival in Court Fight on Alleged Voter Sales," *Orange County Register,* March 22, 1997.
"ChoicePoint Inc.: Accord Is Reached to Buy the Rest of CDB Infotek," *Wall Street Journal,* February 26, 1998, p. 1.
"ChoicePoint Says It Has Called Off Acquisition of Kroll," *New York Times,* August 8, 1997, p. D3.
Clark, Kim, "The Detectives," *Fortune,* April 14, 1997, p. 122.
Flickenscher, Lisa, "Equifax Plans Another Spinoff—This Time Insurance Info Unit," *American Banker,* December 13, 1996, p. 9.
Getter, Sarah, "Florida Anti-Voter Fraud Program Mismanaged," *Chicago Tribune,* May 21, 2001, p. 12.
Goo, Sara Kehaulani, "TSA's Hiring Practices to Be Probed," *Washington Post,* May 28, 2003, p. E02.
Kuczynski, Alex, "Companies Dig Deeper into Executives' Past," *New York Times,* August 19, 2002, p. A1.
Moore, Michael, "Equifax Rival Demands Privacy Probe," *American Banker,* June 2, 1997, p. 20.
Morse, Dan, "ChoicePoint Agrees to Buy Rival DBT for $444 Million," *Wall Street Journal,* February 15, 2000, p. 1.
Palast, Gregory, "The Wrong Way to Fix the Vote," *Washington Post,* June 10, 2001, p. B1.
Pulliam, Liz, "Equifax Buys 70 Percent Stake in Santa Ana, Calif., Database Firm," *Orange County Register,* September 5, 1996, p. 9.
Silverman, Rachel Emma, "Workplace Security," *Wall Street Journal,* March 11, 2002, p. R15.
Simpson, Glenn R., "Big Brother-in-Law: If the FBI Hopes to Get the Goods on You, It May Ask ChoicePoint," *Wall Street Journal,* April 13, 2001, p. A1.

—Nelson Rhodes

CIRCUIT CITY.

Circuit City Stores, Inc.

9950 Mayland Drive
Richmond, Virginia 23233-1464
U.S.A.
Telephone: (804) 527-4000
Fax: (804) 527-4164
Web site: http://www.circuitcity.com

Public Company
Incorporated: 1949 as Wards Company
Employees: 42,258
Sales: $9.75 billion (2004)
Stock Exchanges: New York
Ticker Symbol: CC
NAIC: 443112 Radio, Television, and Other Electronics
    Stores; 443120 Computer and Software Stores;
    443130 Camera and Photographic Supplies Stores;
    451220 Prerecorded Tape, Compact Disc, and Record
    Stores; 454110 Electronic Shopping and Mail-Order
    Houses

Circuit City Stores, Inc., is the nation's second largest retailer of consumer electronics, personal computers, and entertainment software, with more than 600 stores located throughout the United States. The company trails only Best Buy Co., Inc. in consumer electronics sales. Aside from its signature U.S. superstores, Circuit City, through its subsidiary InterTAN, Inc., operates about 1,000 retail stores and dealer outlets in Canada under the RadioShack, Rogers Plus, and Battery Plus names. Circuit City also sells its products online. The company, based in Virginia, pioneered the concept of the electronics superstore, providing a broad variety of products in a cavernous setting. In perfecting this formula, the company became the dominant marketer in many of the areas into which it expanded.

Ushering in the Television Era

Circuit City was founded by Samuel S. Wurtzel, an importer-exporter who owned a business in New York. Wurtzel had sold his business and was vacationing in Richmond, Vir-

ginia, in 1949 when he went to get a haircut and, while chatting with the barber, learned that the first commercial television station in the South would shortly go on the air in Richmond. Learning this, Wurtzel got the idea that it would be a good business proposition to open a store to sell television sets, reasoning that sales in the area would increase because of consumer interest in the new station's local broadcasts.

Wurtzel moved his family to Richmond and opened a store named "Wards," an acronym of its founder's family's names: "W" for Wurtzel, "A" for his son Alan, "R" for his wife Ruth, "D" for his son David, and "S" for his own name, Samuel. In addition, Wurtzel took a partner, Abraham L. Hecht. From its base in retailing televisions, Wurtzel soon branched out his business, initially called Wards Company, to include other home appliances. Within ten years, the business had expanded to encompass a chain of four stores, all of which were located in Richmond. Combined sales volume was about $1 million a year.

In 1960 Wards started to expand in another direction, as it began to operate licensed television departments within larger discount mass merchandisers in different areas of the country. The company ran television and other audio equipment sales operations in G.E.M., G.E.S., and G.E.X. stores. In the following year, Wards offered stock to the public for the first time, selling 110,000 shares in the company for $5.375 through a Baltimore stockbroker.

In 1962 Wards increased its commitment to customer service by implementing a new service plan that included a free loan of a television set if a customer's television could not be repaired in the home. Two years later, the company opened its fifth television and appliance store, in Richmond's Southside Plaza Shopping Center. This, along with the company's earlier stock offering, signaled a period of quick expansion for the company.

In 1965 Wards made its first moves to grow through acquisition. The company purchased the Richmond Carousel Corporation, a discount department store in Richmond, from the T.G. Stores company. By taking over this company, Wards moved into the sale of automotive supplies, gasoline, household supplies, clothing, and children's toys, as well as appliances. In addition, in September 1965 Wards purchased Murmic, Inc., a

Company Perspectives:

In 1949, when Samuel Wurtzel opened Ward's—Richmond, Virginia's first retail television store—his goal was to provide the community with a new technology that would change the face of consumer electronics forever. More than 50 years, over 600 stores and several name changes later, the technology continues to change, but Circuit City's commitment to our customers remains strong.

The technologies and solutions we provide can make your life easier and more enjoyable. And it's our goal to ensure just that. So, whether you're browsing through one of our stores or surfing our website, we're with you.

Delaware company that operated hardware and housewares sales areas in department stores located in the Southeast.

The following year, Wards opened its sixth Virginia store, this one located in the Walnut Mall Shopping Center in Petersburg. Each of the company's stores featured 5,000 to 8,000 square feet of space in which to display and sell televisions, audio equipment, and other household appliances. With the additional revenue from this facility, company sales reached $23 million. Also in 1966, one of Samuel Wurtzel's sons, Alan, a lawyer, returned to Richmond to take a role in the family business, in preparation for eventually taking over the reins from his father.

Geographic Expansion in the 1970s

In 1968 Wards offered additional stock to the public, selling 1,700 shares on the American Stock Exchange. With the revenue generated by this offering, in May 1969 the company purchased Custom Electronics, Inc., an outfit that sold audio and hi-fi equipment. The company owned four stores in the Washington, D.C. area, as well as a mail-order audio supplies operation called Dixie Hi-Fi; it also ran nine stereo departments in department stores located in an area stretching from Mobile, Alabama, to Albany, New York. Five months later, Wards continued its rapid expansion in the Mid-Atlantic states by buying the Certified TV and Appliance Company of Virginia Beach, Virginia, which operated three stores in the Tidewater area. The company also opened an additional Carousel store in the Richmond area.

One month later, Wards branched out from its familiar geographical area and its core business of appliance retailing when it purchased The Mart, located in Indianapolis, Indiana. This company had as one of its major components the tire retailing operations of the Rose Tire Company and its affiliates, but it also sold televisions, appliances, and furniture. In its furthest geographical leap, Wards also signed a contract to operate licensed television departments in Zody's Department Stores in Los Angeles.

The company's rapid expansion continued in 1970. Wards bought Woodville Appliances, Inc., which ran five television and appliance stores in Toledo, Ohio. Also in the Midwest, it acquired the operations of the Frank Dry Goods Company, which ran a television, appliance, and furniture store in Fort Wayne, Indiana.

By this time, Wards' rapid growth had brought it to a new era, and this was symbolized in 1970 by the transfer of power from the founders of the company to a younger generation. Samuel Wurtzel, its founder, stepped down as president, although he remained chairman of the board, and Abraham Hecht, his partner, retired. In their stead, Alan Wurtzel was named president of the company.

Among the first moves made by the new president was the opening of two specialty stores in Richmond, called Sight 'N Sound, that sold only audio equipment. These outlets were designed to take advantage of the boom in demand for high-tech stereo equipment.

In 1972 Alan Wurtzel, still president, assumed the responsibilities of chief executive officer of Wards. In an effort to eliminate weaker areas of the company, he closed the Franks of Fort Wayne store that Wards had purchased two years earlier and shut down three stores formerly run by Certified in Virginia. Following this consolidation, the company began to expand in the next year. Five audio stores were opened: three in the east, in Washington, D.C.; Richmond, Virginia; and Charlottesville, Virginia; and two in California. In the following year, Wards began to suffer the adverse effects of its rapid expansion and diversification into areas not related to its core business of television and appliance retailing. In 1974 the company lost $3 million on overall sales of $69 million. In an effort to stem the red ink, Wurtzel withdrew Wards from areas in which it was not turning a profit, such as tire sales. In addition, Wards was losing a large amount of money on its licensed appliance departments in three discount department store chains that were doing very badly. To cut its losses, the company began to move out of its leased audio and television operations in department stores, retaining only its involvement in the California Zody's stores.

Birth of the Superstore in the Mid-1970s

In a shift in direction also occurring in 1974, Wards closed two of its original stores in Richmond, opting instead to risk half the company's net worth opening a $2 million electronics superstore. With this move, Wards began to shift its focus from appliances in general to the growing market in consumer electronics. The company called its pioneering venture "The Wards Loading Dock." With 40,000 square feet, the warehouse store displayed and sold a very large selection of video and audio equipment and major appliances. This enormous facility, with its exceptionally broad offerings of more than 2,000 products, enabled Wards to take a strong lead against its competitors. In addition, the superstore's high volume of sales meant that the company could afford to offer lower prices than its smaller competitors, as well as such amenities as home delivery and in-store repairs. In this way, by locating its stores in medium-sized markets otherwise served only by smaller, mom-and-pop operations, Wards was able to exploit growing consumer interest in new electronics products. The successful superstore concept became the innovation upon which Wards built its future growth.

Also in 1974, Wards expanded its Dixie Hi-Fi line of discount audio stores, adding nine new properties. In the next year, as its Richmond superstore showed promising returns, Wards began to streamline its operations. The company sold its four Woodville television and appliance stores in Toledo, Ohio, and also shuttered four of its five Mart stores in Indianapolis. In addition, the company shed its two Carousel stores in Richmond.

Two years later, in 1977, anticipating that the boom in stereo sales would eventually slow, Wards began to broaden the offerings of its Dixie Hi-Fi and Custom Hi-Fi discount audio equipment stores, transforming them into full-service electronics specialty markets. With this new concept, Wards changed the name of the stores to ''Circuit City,'' opening six of the new facilities in the Washington, D.C. area. With 6,000 to 7,000 square feet of space, the new stores featured video and audio equipment made by well-known brand names, as well as in-store service capabilities and a pick-up area for people to load purchases into their cars.

To shift its operations toward the Circuit City concept, Wards continued to streamline in 1978. The company left the mail-order electronics business, which it ran under the name ''Dixie,'' and also closed its four Richmond Sight 'N Sound stores. In the following year, the company continued its progress toward large retail outlets, opening a second Wards Load-

ing Dock in Richmond. The company ended 1979 with $120 million in sales.

In 1981 Wards made its first incursion into a significant and challenging new market when it merged with the Lafayette Radio Electronics Corporation, which ran eight consumer electronics stores in the New York City metropolitan area. The company paid $6.6 million for the bankrupt retailer, earning $36.5 million in tax credits as a result of the acquisition, a benefit that observers predicted would drive up its own earnings. Lafayette's reputation within the highly competitive New York market was that of a small specialty seller that provided obscure, high-priced brand-name goods to hi-fi hobbyists. Wards faced an uphill battle in its struggle to broaden the chain's appeal and return it to profitability, especially since other New York electronics retailers routinely discounted items 50 percent or permitted haggling over the price of their products.

At the same time that Wards moved into the New York market, the company began to expand its Loading Dock superstore concept in the geographical areas where it already had a presence. Capitalizing on its other name, the company christened its new outlets Circuit City Superstores. The first four stores under this name opened in Raleigh, Greensboro, Durham, and Winston-Salem, North Carolina. In the following year, Wards simplified the naming of its outlets by changing the names of its Richmond Wards Loading Dock stores to Circuit City Superstores.

By 1982 Wards was operating four retail chains, including Circuit City stores, larger Circuit City Superstores, its Lafayette properties in New York, and its operations in Zody discount stores in California. Altogether, the company ran 100 outlets, twice the number it had owned just seven years earlier. A total of 80 percent of Wards' revenue was derived from sales of consumer electronics, and the company reaped solid profits from its marketing of Sony Betamax videocassette recorders (VCRs) and Pioneer stereo equipment. In Washington, D.C., Wards' Circuit City stores held the largest market share, garnering 11 percent of the sales of consumer electronics. By the end of 1983, Wards' pattern of consistent growth through emphasis on large retail outlets had led to sales of $246 million for the fiscal year.

Boosting Circuit City in the 1980s

As a sign of its shifting identity, Wards changed its corporate name to Circuit City Stores, Inc., in 1984. Also in this year, its stock was listed on the New York Stock Exchange for the first time. Although the leadership of the company changed hands—Alan Wurtzel stepped up to the post of chairman of the board, to be succeeded by Richard Sharp—its basic direction did not. Sharp's background was in computers, not retailing, and he had first come into contact with Circuit City when he installed a computer system to control sales and inventory in some of its stores. Under Sharp, the company continued to consolidate its operations in very large stores, replacing regular Circuit City stores with Circuit City Superstores. This process began in Knoxville, Tennessee; Charleston, South Carolina; and Hampton, Virginia.

These stores, some of which contained nearly an acre of floor space, used their grand scope to bring a theatrical flair to retailing consumer electronics. The stores featured solid walls of television sets, all tuned to the same channel. Customers entered by walking past the service department, a visible symbol that the company serviced what it sold. The stores were laid out like baseball diamonds, and customers were led around the displays by a red tile walkway. Particularly popular items were located at the back of the store, to encourage impulse purchasing on the way. By 1984 Circuit City was operating 113 stores, which made it the leading specialty retailer of brand-name consumer electronics. The company's growth continued briskly, fed by innovative new electronics products such as cordless telephones, microwave ovens, and VCRs, for which initial demand was high. Its superstores contributed the largest part of its earnings, while the company's New York operations continued to lose money. To fuel continued growth, Circuit City further expanded its operations. In 1984 the company planned a large expansion around Atlanta and opened 15 new stores in Florida. In locating stores, Circuit City adhered to a policy of clustering them together in the same geographic area, which allowed for economies of scale in advertising and promotion.

In 1986 Circuit City took the final step in consolidating its operations. The company closed down its 15 unprofitable stores in the New York area, run under the Lafayette name, after a five-year, $20 million struggle to crack this tough market. In addition, Circuit City withdrew from its arrangement with the 50-store Zody's discount department store chain in California. This low-rent retailer, which had long been suffering financial troubles, provided an inhospitable home to Circuit City's operations and contributed no earnings to its bottom line. Instead, the company decided to put the resources previously used to run these operations into further Circuit City Superstores, concentrating expansion in the Southeast and in California, where it planned to open its own freestanding stores. In moving into a new area, Circuit City methodically set out to win the lion's share of sales in that market. The company typically opened a large number of very large stores all at once, advertised heavily, and distributed products efficiently.

These efforts bore fruit in February 1987, when Circuit City's annual sales hit the $1 billion mark for the first time, driven in large part by the demand for VCRs, which also pushed up demand for new televisions and other audio equipment. The company faced a challenging future, however, as demand for this core product cooled and competition from other electronics superstores heated up. Despite these adverse circumstances, by 1988 the company owned 105 stores, 32 of which were located in California.

Armed with the nation's largest market share, Circuit City planned to add 20 new outlets. Among these new outlets were several that featured a new format. Called Impulse, these stores were tested by the company in Baltimore, Maryland; Richmond, Virginia; and McLean, Virginia. These stores, designed for malls, sold small electronic products for personal use or to be given as gifts. Three years later, the company announced that its test of this concept had been successful, and that it planned to open 50 more such outlets.

By 1989 Circuit City's profits had tripled in just three years to reach $69.5 million, despite a general recession in the consumer electronics retailing industry. Observers attributed the company's success to strong management and a merchandising formula that had been honed and refined for many years. That formula was adjusted further in 1989 when Circuit City began opening mini-Superstores in markets too small for a full-fledged massive outlet. Claiming that the mini-store offered the same service and selection as a larger outlet, the company opened a test site in Asheville, North Carolina. By the following year, sales overall had hit $2 billion, and earnings were up as well. In the meantime, the company's superstores expanded their product array, offering personal computers for the first time in 1989 and recorded music in 1992.

Competition and New Ideas for the 1990s

Circuit City surged ahead in the early 1990s, with strong sales growth and steady expansion into new markets. By 1994 it had close to 300 stores and had plans to open almost 200 more. But growing competition, particularly with the similar electronics superstore chain Best Buy, caused the company to fight harder for market share and to search for new ways to make money. In late 1993, Circuit City announced it would cut prices in markets it shared with Best Buy, sparking a grueling price war. The firm differed from Best Buy in offering a high-service, hard-sell sales environment, with salespeople working for commission. Best Buy was more of a help-yourself retailer. Circuit City publicly defended its more aggressive style, broadcasting the results of a survey in 1994 that claimed that consumers preferred its level of service. By 1995, half its stores were in markets shared by Best Buy, and 70 percent of its markets were classified by analysts as highly competitive. Despite the competition, Circuit City had sales of about $7 billion by 1995, and sales and earnings were rising by 20 percent annually.

The company went in a new direction in 1993, opening the first of what became a chain of used-car lots. Two years later, Circuit City was trumpeting its new chain, CarMax. Circuit City's CEO Sharp moved the company into used cars because he saw that the existing market was lucrative, fragmented, and not well run. Customers hated the haggling and distrusted salespeople, as a rule, in the traditional used-car lot. CarMax offered a huge, clean lot of cars marked with bar codes so that customers could easily locate the vehicles in which they were interested from a central computer listing. Prices were fixed, so the dreadful bargaining was out. CarMax lots held 500 to 1,000 cars, all no more than five years old, and with less than 70,000 miles on them. Each car went through a 110-point inspection, and CarMax offered a 30-day warranty. The aim was to bring Circuit City's retailing experience into this new industry and make the buying process easier on the customer. Though Circuit City was cautious about releasing sales figures for its first CarMax stores, one analyst estimated that its Richmond, Virginia, lot was bringing in about $55 million after being open one year. By 1996 there were five CarMax outlets, and one year later Circuit City sold a 25 percent stake in CarMax through an IPO that raised nearly $415 million and created a CarMax tracking stock. Circuit City retained 75 percent of the used-car retailer.

Used cars seemed like an odd leap for an electronics retailer, yet it was clear Circuit City needed something to keep it going, as the electronics market became saturated. Best Buy passed up Circuit City during fiscal 1996 and won the title of number one electronics retailer, and competition between the rivals did not let up. In 1998 Circuit City trotted out a new product, a digital movie disk called Divx, hoping to get in on a ground floor technology. Divx was pitched to Circuit City by a Los Angeles legal firm, and Circuit City threw money at it. Divx originally stood for digital video express, but it soon became known just by the acronym. It was a disk digitally encoded with a movie, and consumers could purchase it for between $4 and $5, watch the movie within 48 hours, and then throw it away. Divx players were hooked by phone line to a central computer, which registered when the movie was watched, and billed the customer an additional three dollars if the disk was used after the initial two-day period. It competed directly with another digital movie format called DVD, which were disks offered for rent, like traditional videocassette movies. Both these technologies were struggling for consumers' attention, with each format offering only a few hundred titles as they rolled out in the fall of 1998. The large video rental chains refused to sell Divx disks, fearing they would undermine their business, and only Circuit City and another chain called Good Guys initially sold Divx.

By fiscal 1999 Circuit City was enjoying strong sales in its core electronics business—helping push revenues past the $10 billion mark—but its used car and Divx ventures were not doing well. CarMax lost $23.5 million in 1998, on sales of $1.5 billion. The chain had grown to more than 30 locations, but Circuit City CEO Sharp halted further expansion in 1999, as sales declined. Competition with a copycat chain, AutoNation, had left CarMax struggling. Some new stores were way too big, and advertising costs were heavy. By 1999 Divx, too, seemed to have lost out to the competition. An estimated 10,000 retailers were selling DVD disks, the reusable digital movies that could either be rented like movies on video or purchased for about $20. Only about 740 of these 10,000 retailers also dealt with Divx, and most of these retailers were actually Circuit City stores. Both Sony's film studios and Warner Brothers declared they would not make their movies available on Divx, and the technology seemed to be getting squeezed out. In June 1999 Circuit City surrendered, pulling the plug on the venture after having invested $233 million to develop and promote the new product. It also took a $114 million after-tax charge for the first quarter of fiscal 2000. In July 1999, meantime, Circuit City launched its e-commerce web site, which allowed customers to order products online for both delivery and store pickup; customers could also return online-purchased items at the nearest store.

Remodeling and Restructuring in the Early 2000s

In June 2000 W. Alan McCollough was promoted from president and COO of Circuit City to president and CEO. Sharp remained chairman for two more years, whereupon McCollough took on that post as well. The first years of the McCollough era brought a host of changes to the company. Just one month after he was named CEO, Circuit City announced it would stop selling appliances in favor of a pure focus on consumer electronics. The company's stores had generated 14 percent of their overall sales from appliances, but the appliance sector became less appealing after Home Depot, Inc. and Lowe's Companies, Inc. aggressively entered the category and proceeded to engage in pricing battles. In connection with this category exit, Circuit City closed six distribution centers and

eliminated 1,000 jobs. At the same time, the company began a three-year, $1.2 billion overhaul of its more than 570 stores. In addition to eliminating the appliances and boosting the selection of hot-sellers such as DVD movies, video games, and digital cameras, the remodeled stores were more self-service and consumer-friendly—taking a page from the Best Buy formula for success. The new format cut back on the amount of space taken up by the store's warehouse section, where most of the products had previously been stored, inaccessible to customers without the intervention of a salesperson. Circuit City outlets now had more floor space, with more products available for customers to pick up themselves and take to a checkout for purchase. The stores had a more open format, with wider aisles, as well as shopping carts and baskets for customers to use. Although salespeople remained on commission—a practice abandoned by Best Buy in 1989—they took a less aggressive approach than before.

As this revamp was rolled out chainwide, Circuit City was hurt by a weak retail environment and strong competition, particularly by the ever expanding Best Buy. While Circuit City's core business struggled, CarMax had turned solidly profitable. The company took this opportunity to once again focus solely on consumer electronics, spinning off the used-car retailer in October 2002 as a separately traded, independent entity called CarMax, Inc.

McCollough continued his efforts at revitalizing the chain in 2003. The key initiative that year was the elimination of commissions at its stores as Circuit City adopted a single hourly pay structure chainwide. It dismissed 3,900 commissioned salespeople and replaced them with 2,100 hourly employees. In addition to reducing annual operating costs by as much as $130 million, eliminating commissions furthered the move toward a more self-service approach in the stores. Circuit City's continued weak position was highlighted that year when the owner of CompUSA, Inc., operator of computer superstores, made a bid to acquire the company for about $1.5 billion. The Circuit City board of directors rejected the proposal in June 2003.

Continuing to shed noncore operations, Circuit City sold its bank-card finance operation to FleetBoston Financial Corporation in November 2003 for $1.3 billion. Connected with this sale was an after-tax loss of $90 million. The company also closed 19 underperforming superstore locations in early 2004, taking an additional after-tax charge of $35 million. For the fiscal year ending in February 2004, overall sales fell 2 percent, to $9.75 billion. With the company's more than 600 stores barely profitable, and the $125 million in charges, Circuit City posted a net loss for the year of $89.3 million.

In 2004 Circuit City worked to open 65 to 70 new stores—its most aggressive plan of expansion in a decade. About half of these would be relocations: The company was trying to eliminate outlets that were sited in less than ideal locations and some of the older stores with huge warehouse space that made remodeling too expensive. During the spring of 2004 Circuit City completed two acquisitions: MusicNow, Inc., an online digital music store; and InterTAN, Inc. Circuit City spent about $300 million for InterTAN, a firm based in Barrie, Ontario, that operated more than 980 retail stores and dealer outlets in Canada under the RadioShack, Rogers Plus, and Battery Plus names. In addition to gaining a retailing foothold in Canada, and setting the stage for the possible expansion of the Circuit City chain north of the border, this deal was also designed to help Circuit City expand its offerings of private-label products at its U.S. stores. Plans were made to begin rolling out InterTAN private-label products into Circuit City Superstores in the fall of 2004. Fort Worth, Texas-based RadioShack Corporation had spun off InterTAN in 1987. Not done with its wheeling and dealing, Circuit City sold its private-label credit card operation to Bank One Corporation in May 2004 for approximately $400 million. Despite all these moves, the prime challenge confronting Circuit City remained the same: returning its core U.S. superstore operation to robust profitability while operating within one of the most ruthlessly competitive sectors of the retail market.

Principal Subsidiaries

CC Distribution Company of Virginia, Inc.; Circuit City Properties, Inc.; Circuit City Stores West Coast, Inc.; InterTAN, Inc. (Canada); MusicNow, Inc.; Northern National Insurance Ltd. (Bermuda); Patapsco Designs, Inc.; Tyler International Funding, Inc.

Principal Competitors

Best Buy Co., Inc.; CompUSA Inc.; Wal-Mart Stores, Inc.; CDW Corporation; RadioShack Corporation; Staples, Inc.; Office Depot, Inc.; Amazon.com, Inc.; Boise Office Solutions; Sears, Roebuck and Co.

Further Reading

Andrews, Edmund L., "Struggling for Profits in Electronics," *New York Times*, September 10, 1989.

Bautz, Mark, "How a Straight-Arrow Company Makes Out Like a Bandit," *Money*, October 1995, p. 68.

Brinkley, Joel, "DVD Leads Race for TV Disks, But It Is Looking Over Its Shoulder," *New York Times*, July 6, 1998, pp. D1, D4.

Brown, Paul R., "Some People Don't Like to Haggle," *Forbes*, August 27, 1984.

Carpenter, Kimberly, "Circuit City Lays an Egg and Hatches a Strategy," *Business Week*, April 21, 1986.

"Circuit City Expansion," *Television Digest*, April 17, 1995, p. 17.

"Circuit City Fires Back at Critics," *Discount Store News*, September 19, 1994, p. 5.

Cochran, Thomas N., "Circuit City Stores, Inc.," *Barron's*, January 2, 1989.

Foust, Dean, "Circuit City's Wires Are Sizzling," *Business Week*, April 27, 1992.

Gilligan, Gregory J., "Circuit City Buys Two Firms," *Richmond Times-Dispatch*, April 1, 2004, p. C1.

——, "Circuit City's Past Still Haunts It," *Richmond Times-Dispatch*, January 18, 2004, p. D1.

——, "Will Gawkers = Buyers? Circuit City Hopes to Boost Profits with a Line of Private Label Gadgets," *Richmond Times-Dispatch*, June 20, 2004, p. D1.

Heller, Laura, "At Circuit City, Consistency Is Key," *Discount Store News*, January 3, 2000, p. 24.

Johnson, Jay L., "Circuit City Recharged," *Retail Merchandiser*, January 2001, pp. 43+.

King, Sharon R., "Circuit City Is Learning the High Price of New Video Technology," *New York Times*, April 6, 1999, p. C9.

Lavin, Douglas, "Cars Are Sold Like Stereos by Circuit City," *Wall Street Journal*, June 8, 1994, pp. B1, B6.

Merwin, John, "Execution," *Forbes*, April 18, 1988.

Ramstad, Evan, "Circuit City Pulls the Plug on Its Divx Videodisk Venture," *Wall Street Journal*, June 17, 1999, p. B10.

——, "Circuit City's CEO Gambles to Galvanize the Chain," *Wall Street Journal*, September 18, 2000, p. B4.

——, "Circuit City Will Stop Selling Appliances," *Wall Street Journal*, July 26, 2000, p. B8.

Rudnitsky, Howard, "Would You Buy a Used Car from This Man?," *Forbes*, October 23, 1995, pp. 52–54.

Spiegel, Peter, "Car Crash," *Forbes*, May 17, 1999, pp. 130–32.

—Elizabeth Rourke
—updates: A. Woodward, David E. Salamie

Colonial Properties Trust

2101 6th Avenue North, Suite 750
Birmingham, Alabama 35203
U.S.A.
Telephone: (205) 250-8700
Toll Free: (800) 645-3917
Fax: (205) 250-8890
Web site: http://www.colonialprop.com

Public Company
Incorporated: 1970 as Colonial Properties Inc.
Employees: 950
Sales: $334.24 million (2003)
Stock Exchanges: New York
Ticker Symbol: CLP
NAIC: 525930 Real Estate Investment Trust

Colonial Properties Trust is a Birmingham, Alabama-based real estate investment trust (REIT) that takes a balanced approach in a field that has become highly focused on the accumulation of a single type of property. To provide a hedge against the cyclical nature of the real estate industry, Colonial invests in three different sectors: multifamily, office, and retail properties. The REIT targets midsized Sun Belt cities located in Alabama, Florida, Georgia, Mississippi, North Carolina, South Carolina, Tennessee, Texas, and Virginia. At the close of 2003, Colonial's portfolio consisted of 42 multifamily apartment communities containing 15,224 apartment units, 25 office properties offering 5.5 million square feet of space, and 45 retail properties with 15.3 million square feet of retail space. Colonial also owns land close to some of these properties for future development. Management services are provided by subsidiary Colonial Properties Services Limited Partnership, while Colonial Properties Services, Inc. offers development, construction, and management services for properties owned by third parties. With a total market capitalization of $2.8 billion, Colonial is listed on the New York Stock Exchange.

REIT Growing Out of 1950s Real Estate Business

Colonial grew out of the real estate business founded in 1956 by Edward L. Lowder, the father of the REIT's president, chief executive officer, and chairman, Thomas H. Lowder. Ed Lowder was a legendary Alabama businessman who grew up on a small farm. He went on to college, earning a degree in agriculture in 1934 from Auburn University, which was then known as Alabama Polytechnic Institute. Upon graduation he became a county agent for the Alabama Cooperative Extension Service, a post he held until 1942 when he went into the military. After serving in Italy as an artillery officer, Lowder resumed his work with the Extension Service, but in 1946 he was presented with an opportunity to tap into some latent entrepreneurial talent. He was asked by the Alabama Farm Bureau to launch an insurance company to provide affordable fire insurance to rural Alabama residents.

The first county farm bureau had been established in 1911 by the Binghamton, New York, Chamber of Commerce to sponsor an extension agent from the U.S. Department of Agriculture. The tag "bureau" was soon applied to other state farming organizations. By 1919, 500 members representing state farm bureaus (or representing states that were in the process of organizing) gathered in Chicago to form a national organization that would become the American Farm Bureau Federation (AFBF). More commonly the organization became known as the Farm Bureau. Alabama formed a chapter in 1921. One of the earliest commercial ventures pursued by individual state farm bureaus was auto insurance, as a "service to member" operation. The pioneer in this field was the founder of State Farm Insurance, George Mecherle of Bloomington, Illinois. He created a mutual insurance company for rural and small town drivers who in the early 1920s were paying higher premiums even though they had fewer accidents than drivers in urban areas. By linking insurance rates to risk levels, Mecherle was able to offer significantly lower premiums than his competitors. He also signed agreements with state farm bureaus, which received a fee for each of their members who purchased policies. Some state farm bureaus took Mecherle's lead and formed their own mutual insurance companies.

Lowder launched Alabama Farm Bureau Insurance Company because Alabama farmers and rural residents were having extreme difficulty in securing fire insurance. With just $10,000 and a secretary, he established a company that would become known as ALFA Insurance and add property, life, and automobile insurance products. With a foundation as an insurance executive, Lowder was able to branch out into a number of areas, including mortgage banking, broadcasting, and real estate, all of which would be folded into a holding company called Lowder Companies. The collection ultimately took on the name of The Colonial Companies.

Thomas Lowder As Head of Colonial Properties in 1976

Lowder's start in the real estate business came in 1956 when he launched Lowder Construction Company to build single-family homes in Montgomery, Alabama. From this venture emerged a full-service real estate company. In 1970 Lowder formed Colonial Properties Inc. for his real estate holdings. By now his three sons were starting to take over some of his enterprises. In 1966, the eldest, Robert E. Lowder, became the head of the Colonial Mortgage Company. James K. Lowder became president of Lowder Construction Company in 1974. James's twin brother, Thomas H. Lowder, took charge of Colonial Properties in 1976.

Thomas Lowder learned about business from his father, who sometimes compared it with football. According to a *Birmingham Business Journal* profile, Lowder said of his father, "He'd tell me that touchdowns are your long-term goal, but then, you have first downs to work toward in between, which are your short-term goals." This advice would lead Lowder to become very much focused on strategic planning, completing both short-term and long-term plans. His father also took him along on visits to Birmingham banks: "He told me not to make the mistake of only going to see your banker when you need something." Maintaining strong relationships with his lenders also would become a hallmark of Lowder's running of Colonial Properties. While growing up he also learned about salesmanship. Lowder told the *Wall Street Journal* about "tagging along summers with an apartment agent who always carried two things in his pocket when showing units to a prospective tenant: a piece of chalk, to cover up any scratches in the paint, and a can of aerosol spray to freshen the air."

Edward Lowder died in 1987. In 1993 his wife, three sons, and shareholders decided to package the real estate holdings they owned through Colonial Properties into a REIT. The primary purpose was to give the owners and shareholders a greater degree of liquidity, as well as to pay down some debt and provide increased possibilities for growth.

REITs had been created by Congress in 1960 as a way for small investors to become involved in real estate in a manner similar to mutual funds. They could be taken public and their shares traded just like stock, and were subject to regulation by the Securities and Exchange Commission. Unlike other stocks, however, REITs were required by law to pay out at least 95

percent of their taxable income to shareholders each year, a provision that severely limited the ability of REITs to retain internally generated funds. During the first 25 years of existence, REITs were allowed only to own real estate, a situation that hindered their growth. Third parties had to be contracted to manage the properties. Not until the Tax Reform Act of 1986 changed the nature of real estate investment did REITs begin to be truly viable. Limited partnership tax shelter schemes that had competed for potential investments were shut down by the Act: Interest and depreciation deductions were greatly reduced so that taxpayers could not generate paper losses in order to lower their tax liabilities. Separately, the Act also permitted REITs to provide customary services for property, in effect allowing the trusts to operate and manage the properties they owned. Despite these major changes in law, the REIT was still not a fully utilized structure. In the latter half of the 1980s the banks, insurance companies, pension funds, and foreign investors (in particular, the Japanese) provided the lion's share of real estate investment funds. The resulting glutted marketplace led to a shakeout that hampered many real estate firms. With real estate available at distressed prices in the early 1990s, REITs finally became an attractive mainstream investment option and many real estate firms went public starting in 1993.

Going Public As a REIT in 1993

Because Alabama did not have a REIT law and Alabama case law on business trusts was not settled, leaving uncertainty about a trust's liability, Colonial Properties Trusts was organized in Maryland in July 1993 with its corporate headquarters located in Orlando, Florida, where Colonial already had a strong office. (Two years later, Alabama would enact a REIT law, allowing Colonial to reorganize in the state and move its headquarters back to Birmingham.) The REIT's initial public offering (IPO) of shares was held in September 1993, underwritten by a group of underwriters headed by Lehman Brothers and that included Bear, Stearns & Co., Inc., Merrill Lynch & Co., and The Robinson-Humphrey Co., Inc. Colonial's portfolio was concentrated in Alabama, Florida, and Georgia, starting out with 16 multifamily properties containing more than 3,500 garden-style apartments, ten office properties with one million square feet, and ten retail properties with 2.8 million square feet.

Colonial wasted little time in launching a steady acquisition program, which continued a strategy of diversification. One benefit of this approach was that Colonial could buy when one of its three sectors was in a down cycle and prices were less expensive. As Thomas Lowder explained to the *Wall Street Journal,* "We try to buy our straw hats in winter time." The REIT's initial emphasis was on building up its multifamily holdings. In November 1993 management announced plans to expand on two current apartment complexes located in Orlando and Montgomery. In early 1994 Colonial acquired apartment properties in Tampa, Florida; Huntsville, Alabama; and Sarasota, Florida. In August it acquired four more multifamily properties, located in Gainesville, Jacksonville, and Orlando, Florida. At the close of 1994 Colonial completed a major deal, paying $190.8 million to acquire ten multifamily properties located in Birmingham, Alabama, and Stockbridge, Georgia. Also during 1994, Colonial added to its slate of retail properties by acquiring the 110,000-square-foot Britt David Shopping

<table>
<tr><td colspan="2">Key Dates:</td></tr>
<tr><td>1970:</td><td>Colonial Properties Inc. is founded by Edward Lowder.</td></tr>
<tr><td>1976:</td><td>Thomas Lowder is named president.</td></tr>
<tr><td>1987:</td><td>Edward Lowder dies.</td></tr>
<tr><td>1993:</td><td>Colonial Properties is formed as a REIT and is taken public.</td></tr>
<tr><td>1995:</td><td>Headquarters are moved to Birmingham, Alabama.</td></tr>
<tr><td>1997:</td><td>The first office property is acquired since the public offering.</td></tr>
<tr><td>2000:</td><td>Colonial initiates its first mixed-use development, Colonial Town Park in Orlando, Florida.</td></tr>
</table>

Center in Columbus, Georgia. For the year, Colonial increased revenues to more than $64 million and net income to $11.3 million.

Colonial's focus in 1995 was on the retail sector. The company acquired three shopping centers in the Orlando market, a regional mall in Decatur, Alabama, and a shopping center in Ocala, Florida. In addition, Colonial began work on the major expansion of a mall in Macon, Georgia, which would grow into a "super regional mall" and become the company's flagship retail property. As a result of its expansion efforts, revenues more than doubled in 1995, and net income now approached $15 million. Colonial continued to add to its retail and multifamily holdings in 1996, acquiring three retail shopping centers in central Florida and a South Carolina regional mall, and five multifamily properties in Alabama and two multifamily properties in Georgia. Colonial also pursued internal growth, beginning work on an expansion to a Montgomery, Alabama, community shopping center and building 873 new apartment units. For the year 1996, revenues totaled $134.9 million while net income showed significant improvement, topping $27.5 million.

Surprisingly, Colonial had not added to its office property portfolio since the 1993 offering. That neglect would come to an end early in 1997 with the $20.8 million purchase of Birmingham's Riverchase Center, an eight-building office park. During the course of 1997, Colonial added two more office properties in Alabama and another in Georgia. But the REIT was active on other fronts as well, completing a number of deals that expanded its presence to new Sunbelt states. It acquired nine shopping centers: one each in Alabama, Florida, Virginia, and Tennessee, two in Georgia, and three in North Carolina. Colonial acquired multifamily properties in Alabama, Florida, Georgia, Mississippi, and South Carolina, and also constructed nearly 1,200 new apartment units in seven of its properties.

In 1998 Colonial entered into a pair of joint ventures to acquire a community shopping center and an enclosed mall. It also added five more office properties containing 827,000 square feet of space, three of the properties located in Alabama,

plus one in Georgia and one in Florida. Furthermore, Colonial acquired four multifamily properties—located in Florida, Georgia, Texas, and South Carolina—and constructed another 596 apartment units. The REIT took a step back in 1999 to adjust its asset mix. It added just one office property and one enclosed mall, while disposing of seven multifamily properties. Colonial disposed of five more multifamily properties in 2000, representing 1,132 apartment units. But at the same time, it built nearly 1,000 apartment units in six of its multifamily communities. Colonial also added to three of its community shopping centers and completed the development of two office properties. In addition, it picked up another 575,000 square feet of retail space through the acquisition of an enclosed mall in Temple, Texas. Moreover, Colonial became involved in its first mixed-use development, the building of Colonial Town Park in Orlando, Florida, a project that would combine office, retail, and residential space and allow the REIT to take advantage of the expertise it possessed in all three areas. By now, annual revenues reached $294 million, with net income in 2000 totaling $38.7 million.

Colonial concentrated on internal growth in 2001, adding 440 apartment units, more than 318,000 square feet of office space, and completing the redevelopment of two retail properties. Colonial made a handful of acquisitions in 2002, buying three office properties and a Birmingham village-style retail center. In 2003 the REIT acquired two multifamily properties in Florida and Austin, Texas, and an office property located in Huntsville. Colonial also disposed of a multifamily property containing 176 units, an office property with 29,000 square feet, and a retail property with 152,667 square feet. For 2003 revenues grew to $334.24 million and net income totaled $32.5 million, a significant drop from the $57.8 million Colonial posted in 2002 and the $42.2 million in 2001. Nevertheless, Colonial remained a healthy, diversified regional REIT with every expectation of continuing to enjoy sure and steady growth.

Principal Subsidiaries

Colonial Realty Limited Partnership; Colonial Properties Services Limited Partnership; Colonial Properties Services, Inc.

Principal Competitors

Highwoods Properties, Inc.; Sizeler Property Investors, Inc.

Further Reading

Carrns, Ann, "Colonial Sets a Full Table," *Wall Street Journal,* February 7, 1997, p. B12.

Finkelstein, Alex, "Colonial Goes Public for REIT Reasons," *Orlando Business Journal,* February 4, 1994, p. 22.

Lowder, Thomas H., "Colonial Properties: Where You Live, Work & Shop," Exton, Pa.: Newcomen Society, 2003.

Milazzo, Don, "Colonial's Lowder Heeds His Late Father's Advice on Goals," *Birmingham Business Journal,* June 8, 2001, p. 6.

—Ed Dinger

Companhia Energética de Minas Gerais S.A. CEMIG

Av. Barbacena 1200
Belo Horizonte 30123-970
Brazil
Telephone: +55 31 3299 4900
Fax: +55 31 3299 3934
Web site: http://www.cemig.com.br

Public Company
Incorporated: 1952
Employees: 11,648
Sales: BRL 5.62 billion (2003)
Stock Exchanges: Sao Paulo
Ticker Symbol: CEMIG
NAIC: 221122 Electric Power Distribution

Companhia Energética de Minas Gerais S.A. CEMIG (Cemig) is one of Brazil's largest electric power public utility companies, and the largest power producer and distributor in its home base of Minas Gerais, the second largest state in the country in terms of gross domestic product. Cemig operates 48 hydroelectric power plants, three thermoelectric power plants, and one aeolic power plant, for a total production capacity of more than 5,700 megawatts. The company has also begun construction on four more power plants, with the first expected to be completed in 2004. Cemig serves a region of more than 562,000 square kilometers—equivalent to the size of France— and a total population of 16 million customers, including a number of Brazil's largest industrial corporations. Cemig's 330,000-kilometer distribution network is the longest in South America and the fourth longest in the world. The company also operates a natural gas transmission and distribution subsidiary, GASMIG, and has been building its own telecommunications network through subsidiary Empresa de Infovias. Through Infovias, the company also holds a 66.41 percent stake in Belo Horizonte cable television and Internet services provider Way TV Belo Horizonte. Publicly listed Cemig nonetheless remains controlled at 51 percent by the Minas Gerais government. New federal regulations relating to the energy sector have forced Cemig to split up into individual companies for its power

generation, transmission, and distribution operations, although Cemig as a holding company will retain control over these businesses. The company moved closer to launching this restructuring in 2004. In 2003, Cemig's net revenues topped BRL 5.6 billion, for a net income of BRL 1.2 billion. The company is one of only three Brazilian companies to be listed on the Dow Jones Sustainability and the DJSI World indexes.

Powering Brazilian Industrialization in the 1950s

Minas Gerais, with its rich mineral deposits, became a center of the Brazilian mining industry by the 19th century. The development of the first electrical power generation technologies offered the promise of increased production, and Minas Gerais became the first in Brazil to build an electrical power plant. That plant, serving the Diamantina mining operation, launched production in 1883. Several more power plants were built in Minas Gerais over the next decade; like the initial power plant, the new plants were hydroelectric plants, taking advantage of the abundant water resources in the state. Encouraged by new government legislation passed in 1891, Brazil saw a dramatic increase in the growth of its electric plants. Most of these new plants were small, meant to serve only a local area, and were often privately held, or owned by municipal governments. Although the earliest plants in Minas Gerais had been hydroelectrical plants, newer thermoelectric designs became prevalent throughout Brazil.

Power generation and other utilities and resources came under closer federal and state government control starting in the 1920s. By the end of World War II, the government moved to take full control of the utility sectors, establishing new state-owned companies. Until then, Brazil had remained relatively un-industrialized, in part because of the electricity sector's reliance on low-capacity plants. Much of the sector, including in Minas Gerais, depended on wood-burning plants for their electricity generation needs.

The Minas Gerais state government launched a new industrialization policy following World War II. In 1945, the government began studying the state's power generation capacity and its potential, and called for the establishment of a new government-controlled entity that would put into place its electricity generation and distribution policies. Although the gov-

Company Perspectives:

Mission: To play a major role in the energy sector with a mindset geared towards profitability, quality and social responsibility. Vision: Cemig shall be the best energy utility in Brazil.

ernment's policies were not immediately carried out, it outlined a transformation of the region's electrical generation capacity from a reliance on wood-burning plants to the development of a new generation of hydroelectric plants.

In 1952, under Governor Juscelino Kubitscheck, the state built the first of these new hydroelectric plants in Cafanhoto, which directly provided power to Minas Gerais's new Contagem Industrial District. The new plant was placed under the direction of a new company, state-owned Companhia Energética de Minas Gerais or Cemig. This first plant was quickly followed by the construction of plants in Salto Grande, Cajuru, Itutings and Piau, and, finally, Três Marias, one of the state's landmark engineering projects.

The company's initial power generation focus went toward serving the region's mining industry. In the 1960s, however, the company began targeting the industrial sector as well. In 1968, Cemig took a more active role in encouraging the growth of the region's industrial activities, forming the Institute of Industrial Development in Minas Gerais with the Bank of the Development of the States of Minas Gerais. In part due to Cemig's ability to ensure a strong power supply, the region succeeded in attracting such industrial heavyweights as Fiat, Mercedes Benz, Alcan, Alcoa, Açominas, and Usiminas. By the end of the century, Minas Gerais would emerge as Brazil's second wealthiest state.

Cemig also worked with the UN Development Program and the World Bank in order to identify new potential sites along the region's many river basins for additional hydroelectric plants. New plants were then built in Jaguara, Volta Grande, Sao Simao, Nova Ponte, and Emborcaçao. During this period, also, Cemig began acquiring many of the state's smaller electrical generation utilities, taking over their transmission and distribution facilities as well. By the end of the 1970s, Minas Gerais had emerged as the state's dominant electricity company, a position it was to maintain into the next century. Just 3 percent of the electrical power production in Minas Gerais remained in private hands or directly controlled by municipalities.

International Interests for the New Century

Cemig redrafted its bylaws in 1984, redefining itself as a power company—rather than an electricity company—in order to pursue an expansion into other power generation sectors. In 1986, the company took its first step in that direction, founding Gasmig. This utility then began building a natural gas distribution network.

During the period, the economic chaos in Brazil during the 1980s had led to a severe drop in the country's power generation investments, leaving many states, including Minas Gerais, with aging and increasingly decrepit distribution networks. At the same time, many of the country's government-owned utilities, which had enjoyed a long period of low-interest, government-backed loans, had developed into inefficient, money-losing operations.

The Brazilian government took steps to reverse the sector's difficulties in the early 1990s, passing new legislation in 1994 as a first step in the privatization and deregulation of the electricity generation sector. The new legislation installed stricter financing requirements, and led the way, in 1995, to the government announcement of its intention not only to privatize the industry, but also to break up the utilities' vertically integrated structure. Under this initiative, companies were expected to split up their operations into separate generation, transmission, and distribution components. As part of this development, the government also created a wholesale electricity market.

As Brazil's largest and one of the country's most efficient electricity companies, Cemig stood to benefit from the changes in the market. The company began preparations for the deregulation of the sector—which was also to permit it to extend beyond Minas Gerais itself. In the mid-1990s, the company launched an ambitious expansion program, which called for the company to spend some $3 billion in order to boost its generation capacity as well as expand its transmission and distribution network. The company's investment effort included the construction of two new hydroelectric plants, a 510 megawatt site in Nova Ponte and a 390 megawatt site at Miranda. The company also joined into a private sector consortium to build a third plant, the 210 megawatt Igarapava dam, with Cemig providing its technological expertise and its partners providing the funding for the project, marking one of the first times a Brazilian utility formed such a partnership with the private sector. As another part of its effort to make itself more competitive in the coming deregulated market, Cemig began trimming its payroll, shedding nearly 3,000 jobs by the middle of the decade.

Cemig was partially privatized in 1997, with its shares listed on the Sao Paulo exchange. Most of the shares sold off by the Minas Gerais government were placed with a consortium of companies, including Southern Energy Inc. and AES Corp. of the United States and Brazil's Opportunity Bank, which paid $1.1 billion for 33 percent of Cemig's shares. The Minas Gerais government nonetheless retained control of 51 percent of Cemig's stock.

The prospect of the deregulation of the energy market paved the way for the Minas Gerais government to pass new legislation in 1997 permitting Cemig to diversify into areas not related to its power operations. Nonetheless, Cemig stuck close to its expertise in transmission networks. In 1999, the company formed a joint venture with AES Forca e Empreendimentos Ltda, creating Infovias, a telecommunications, cable television, and Internet joint venture, which included the cable television and Internet services provider Way TV Belo Horizonte. In 2002, Cemig bought out AES's stake in Infovias, raising its own shareholding past 99 percent.

Telecommunications remained a minor part of Cemig's operations, however. Meanwhile, in the early 2000s, the company continued to expand its number of hydroelectric plants, invest-

Key Dates:

1883: Brazil's first hydroelectric plant, in Minas Gerais, is constructed.

1952: Companhia Energética De Minas Gerais S.A. CEMIG (Cemig) is created in order to take over electricity power sector in Minas Gerais.

1986: Cemig launches Gasmig, entering the natural gas transmission and distribution market.

1997: Cemig goes public, with a listing on the Bolsa de Valores de Sao Paulo.

1999: Company forms Infovias joint venture with AES Corp.

2002: Cemig buys out AES stake in Infovias.

2003: Cemig announces plan to split up its generation, transmission, and distribution operations into three separate companies.

2004: Cemig plans to spend up to $1.75 billion before 2010 in order to expand generating capacity and to acquire power companies beyond Minas Gerais.

ing some BRL 2.8 billion ($798 million) between 1999 and 2002. During that period, the company built two hydroelectric plants at Funil and Porto Estrela, and began construction on four others in Queimado, Aimores, Irape, and Pai Joaquim. In February 2003, the company began construction on two additional power plants in Capim. Cemig also expanded its thermoelectric plant capacity—used primarily to supplement its hydroelectric generating capacity during drought periods, building a thermoelectric plant in Barreiro, and buying two more in Carvalkho and Ipatinga in 2002. In 2003, the company announced its plans to invest in expanding its Gasmig subsidiary transmission capacity, earmarking BRL 86 million ($29 million) to extend its network by 157 kilometers in the cities of Belo Horizonte and Vale do Aco.

New rules governing the Brazilian power sector led to Cemig's announcement at the end of 2003 that it would break itself up into separate generation, transmission, and distribution companies, which were nonetheless to remain part of Cemig's holdings. Cemig, eager to begin sales of its surplus power beyond the Minas Gerais region, quickly drafted its breakup plan, which was accepted by the Minas Gerais government in July 2004. At the same time, Cemig announced its intention to spend BRL 5 billion ($1.75 billion) through the end of the decade in order to expand its power generation capacity by more than 10 percent, as well as to enable the company to make acquisitions beyond Minas Gerais. With more than 50 years of experience as a leading electricity company, Cemig appeared a sure bet to become a national powerhouse in the new century.

Principal Subsidiaries

Cemig Capim Branco Energia S.A.; Cemig PCH S.A.; Cemig Trading S.A.; Central Hidrelétrica Pai Joaquim S.A. (49%); Central Termelétrica de Cogeraçao S.A. (49%); Companhia de Gás de Minas Gerais - GASMIG (95.17%); Efficientia S.A.; Empresa de Infovias S.A. (99.92%); Horizontes Energia S.A.; Sá Carvalho S.A.; USIMINAS; Usina Te rmelétrica Barreiro S.A.; Usina Térmica Ipatinga S.A.

Principal Competitors

Centrais Eletricas Brasileiras S.A.; Centrais Eletricas De Santa Catarina S.A.; ELETROBRAS; Eletricidade E Servicos S.A.; Eletropaulo Metropolitana Eletricidade de Sao Paulo S.A.; Companhia Forca E Luz Cataguazes Leopoldina; CPFL Geracao de Energia S.A.; Itaipu Binacional; LIGHT Servicos de Eletricidade S.A.

Further Reading

Brass, Larisa, "Cemig to be split into three," *Business News Americas*, December 15, 2003.

"Cemig in the race for Aneel transmission line," *Gazeta Mercantil*, July 26, 2004.

"Cemig looks beyond home borders," *Business News Americas*, May 14, 2004.

Clarkin, Greg, Fred Katayama, and Stephanie Elam, "Cemig announces plan to raise resources," *Gazeta Mercantil*, April 5, 2004.

Kangas, Paul, and Susie Gharib, "Ccmig to invest $1.73bn in expansion through 2010," *Business News Americas*, April 1, 2004.

King, Larry, "Minas Gerais green lights Cemig restructuring," *Business News America*, July 8, 2004.

Romans, Christine, "Cemig to expand gas pipeline network," *Business News Americas*, September 29, 2993.

Turner, Rik, "Cemig: meeting rising electricity demand," *Institutional Investor*, July 1995, p. M8.

—M.L. Cohen

 Cousins

Cousins Properties Incorporated

2500 Windy Ridge Parkway, Suite 1600
Atlanta, Georgia 30339-5683
U.S.A.
Telephone: (770) 955-2200
Fax: (770) 857-2360
Web site: http://www.cousinsproperties.com

Public Company
Incorporated: 1961
Employees: 421
Sales: $314.8 million (2003)
Stock Exchanges: New York
Ticker Symbol: CUZ
NAIC: 525930 Real Estate Investment Trusts

Cousins Properties Incorporated is a real estate investment trust (REIT) based in Atlanta, Georgia, involved in the development of commercial office, medical office, and retail properties. Although very much focused on the Atlanta area, Cousins also has projects in Alabama, California, Florida, North Carolina, Virginia, and Texas. Cousins' office portfolio of 37 commercial office properties contains more than 13 million square feet. It owns an additional seven medical office buildings with 990,000 square feet. Cousins' retail portfolio includes 12 properties with close to 1.6 million square feet of space. In addition, Cousins owns more than 280 acres of valuable Atlanta property earmarked for future commercial development. The REIT is traded on the New York Stock Exchange.

Founder Launching a Real Estate Business in 1958

Cousins' chairman, Thomas G. Cousins, founded the real estate company that would evolve into the present-day REIT in 1958. He was born in Atlanta in 1933, the son of auto dealer I.W. Cousins. He studied pre-medicine for three years at the University of Georgia and then shifted gears, graduating in 1952 with a degree in finance. His business career, however, would be delayed because of a two-year stint in the military. After serving with the Strategic Air Command in Japan and Korea, he returned home to become a salesman for Knox Homes Corp., a manufacturer of prefabricated housing. In 1958

he struck out on his own, forming Cousins Properties to build single-family homes. The first man he hired was his father.

Cousins Properties grew at a fast clip. After recording $11,000 in sales in 1958, the company reached the $1.6 million mark in 1960 and topped $5 million in 1962, a year after the business was formally incorporated. It was during these early years in business that Cousins developed a three-part philosophy that would serve him well over the ensuing decades. First, avoid debt. Instead of building several houses and then putting them up for sale, Cousins built a model house to attract buyers and minimize his cash outlay. Second, keep control. In 1962 he took the company public, successfully raising $500,000 but in the process giving up more control than he was comfortable with. He would make sure he did not make that mistake later in his career. Finally, find reliable partners. Cousins used joint ventures as a way to expand beyond single-family homes and become involved in larger projects. He provided the land and development expertise while the investor provided the money and bore most of the risks. Ownership and profits were split. It was an arrangement he used to great effect later in his career with such partners as Coca-Cola, the Ford Foundation, and IBM.

Cousins was well positioned in the 1960s to enjoy the benefits of an economic boom that was taking place in Atlanta. In 1965 Cousins diversified beyond single-family homes, becoming involved in Atlanta-area industrial parks and downtown office buildings, as well as retail and recreational development. In essence, the company developed raw land into "communities," and independent builders bought lots and produced the homes. This approach also freed up construction money and allowed Cousins to begin building large apartment complexes and launch a mortgage company. Tom Cousins admitted later that the real estate business was so strong in Atlanta at the time that he thought it was impossible to lose money. But even as he was prospering he was sowing the seeds for problems that would emerge in the 1970s and almost lead to his ruin.

Problems in the 1970s

In October 1966 Tom Cousins was approached by attorney Bob Troutman, who owned the air rights over the Western and Atlantic Railroad yard in downtown Atlanta. But he had to

---

Company Perspectives:

The company's mission is to maximize shareholder value— while providing our customers with superior service—through the development, operation, acquisition, and management of high-quality commercial real estate properties.

commit to a $5 million commercial property by the end of the year in order to gain an inexpensive 80-year lease on those rights. Cousins agreed to build a parking deck on the sight, in reality a truss that could actually support a 40-story office building in the future. Yet few people would actually park there and Cousins soon found himself in the position of throwing good money after bad. To make use of the parking deck he decided to build an arena, but to get support from Atlanta's mayor on the project, he had to have a professional basketball team to play in it—and not just a vague commitment to move to the city in the future. As a result, Cousins bought the St. Louis Hawks in 1968 and moved them to Atlanta, where they played at the Georgia Tech fieldhouse. The facility was too small to allow Cousins to turn a profit on the team, but he was able to secure the financing to build his downtown arena, known as the Omni. Unfortunately, the Hawks did not draw enough fans to make the parking decks viable. In 1972 he bought a franchise from the National Hockey League, creating the Atlanta Flames, which added more need for parking at the Omni. Finally, in conjunction with out-of-town developer Maurice Alpert, Cousins erected what he thought would be the final piece in making his parking deck a paying concern: the construction of the Omni International, a multi-use office, hotel, and recreation complex, which opened in 1975.

Even as the Omni project was consuming a great deal of his time, Tom Cousins was active on other fronts. Cousins Properties was involved in a number of successful projects throughout the South. Moreover, in 1970 he formed a REIT called Cousins Mortgage-Equity Investments, which went public, raising $42.5 million. REITs had been created by Congress in 1960 as a way for small investors to own real estate in a manner similar to mutual funds. REITs could be taken public and their shares traded just like stock, and were subject to regulation by the Securities and Exchange Commission. Unlike other stocks, however, REITs were required by law to pay out at least 95 percent of their taxable income to shareholders each year, a provision that severely limited the ability of REITs to retain internally generated funds. In addition, limited partnership tax shelter schemes that were legal at the time proved more attractive to investors than REITs. According to a 1990 *Georgia Trend* profile, "The REIT represented a radical departure for Cousins in every way. He was using his company's own money, he didn't have control of the projects, and, in order to grow, he was aligning himself with an array of developers who would later cause him immense problems." To make matters worse, a recession was taking hold in the United States and the Atlanta real estate market, overbuilt during the boom times, now crashed.

Cousins Properties lost $33 million from 1974 to 1976, when the Depression bottomed out. Although his original business did reasonably well, the REIT's performance was so poor that it

nearly ruined Tom Cousins. Its only value was the tax credits it created because of its deep losses. He sold off the REIT in 1979 to focus his attention on his core business. Two years earlier he had sold his interest in the Atlanta Hawks and in 1981 would sell the Atlanta Flames. His most nettlesome problem during the 1970s was Omni International. He was successful in convincing the state General Assembly to build a convention center, the Georgia World Congress Center, close to the Omni. It opened in 1977 but it did little to salvage the project. Another ten years would pass before Cousins was able to sell his 25 percent interest to Ted Turner, who moved in some of his Cable News Network operations and renamed the facility the CNN Center. Only then did the project finally turn the corner and became profitable. In the words of *Georgia Trend*, "During his long involvement with the Omni Cousins lost more than $20 million as well as his reputation as the golden boy of Atlanta real estate."

Tom Cousins was able to survive only by convincing his creditors to work with him. He was able to avoid bankruptcy while holding onto Atlanta property that he was convinced would be valuable once the market bounced back, including 400 acres of what would become known as the "Golden Corridor" of north Fulton County. From 1978 to 1982 he tried building and managing some shopping centers but exited the business after concluding that the only way to make a go of such projects was to own the anchor stores. He now returned his focus to commercial development. His breakthrough project, launched in 1982, was Wildwood Office Park, built on some of the land that he had refused to part with. Wildwood also represented a return to an earlier practice of finding strong partners, with IBM in this case supplying the cash and Cousins the land. Throughout the 1980s he did not build any projections on spec, turning to other deep-pocketed partners, such as Coca-Cola, Nations-Bank, and the Dutch Institutional Holding Company.

The REIT form of real estate ownership became more attractive following the Tax Reform Act of 1986. Limited partnership tax shelter investments were shut down: Interest and depreciation deductions were greatly reduced preventing taxpayers from generating paper losses in order to lower their tax liabilities. Separately, the Act also permitted REITs to provide customary services for property, in effect allowing the trusts to operate and manage the properties they owned. To convert to REIT ownership, Cousins spun off into separate companies its management and leasing units, Cousins Management Inc. and Cousins Real Estate Corp. A separate brokerage company called Cousins Realty also was formed. Thus in 1987 Cousins Properties became a REIT and made a public offering of shares, which then began trading on the NASDAQ. Tom Cousins remained the controlling shareholder. In 1992 the REIT would gain a listing on the New York Stock Exchange and complete the largest stock offering in company history, netting $58 million.

By now the disastrous Omni period of Tom Cousin's career was well in the past. While many competitors were caught in a real estate recession in the early 1990s, his conservative approach during the previous decade now put him in an advantageous position. Cousins properties had just $1 million in debt and was awash in cash. It was now ready to return to the retail sector, which he had abandoned ten years earlier. In 1992 the REIT acquired New Market Development Company, a retail development company that pioneered the concept of "power

---

Key Dates:

1958: Thomas G. Cousins launches a real estate company.
1961: The company is incorporated.
1962: The company is taken public.
1987: Cousins becomes a REIT.
1992: New Market Companies, Inc. is acquired.
2002: Thomas Cousins steps down as CEO.

---

center'' shopping centers that were anchored by specialty giants such as Home Depot or Circuit City. When the office building sector showed signs of recovery, Cousins in 1995 returned to that business as well. In 1998 the company acquired its first medical office property and began developing other projects in the sector. There even had been talk earlier in the 1990s of pursuing development deals in Europe, but nothing ever came of the idea and the company remained focused on Atlanta.

Succession Issues in the 1990s

With Tom Cousins well into his 60s, the question of succession took on increasing significance starting in the mid-1990s. In April 1995, Vipin Patel, a longtime Cousins executive, was named president and chief operating officer and, unofficially, Tom Cousins' heir apparent. Filling Patel's position as senior executive vice-president was Daniel DuPree, who came over in the New Market acquisition. DuPree held that position for the next five years, during which time Cousins began to move aggressively into new territories. In 1996 it acquired an office building in Charlotte, North Carolina, to enter that market. A year later Cousins made further inroads in Charlotte while also moving into Birmingham, Washington, D.C., and California. In 1999 Cousins entered the Texas market by acquiring a half-interest in Faison-Stone, a Dallas-based full-service real estate company that concentrated on leasing and managing class ''A'' office properties. The unit was renamed Cousins Stone and was headed by founder R. Dary Stone.

In 2001, DuPree resigned as Cousins' president, maintaining that he needed a break after working ''nonstop for 20 years'' in real estate. During the five years he held the post, the company realized a 21 percent annualized total return for shareholders. He was replaced by Dary Stone on what proved to be a temporary basis. In January 2002 Stone stepped down and returned to

Texas to run the REIT's operations in that state. He was replaced three weeks later by Thomas D. Bell, who also took over the CEO position from the 70-year-old Tom Cousins, who stayed on as chairman and remained very much involved in running the business. Although the 52-year-old Bell had been a member of Cousins' board since the fall of 2000, he had little previous experience in real estate. Rather, he had made his mark in advertising as the chief executive and chairman of Young & Rubicam. After the agency merged with WPP Group PLC, London, in 2000, he left and joined Cousins' board. He soon became vice-chairman of the board and chairman of Cousins' executive committee. Despite a lack of expertise in real estate, Bell was tapped as Cousins' successor because he was familiar with running a large organization and was familiar with the public markets.

With the question of succession at Cousins apparently settled, the REIT carried on much the same as before. It considered starting an industrial development division and made a greater commitment to the Texas market, especially central Texas, but it remained very much focused on Atlanta, and on office buildings and retail power centers there.

Principal Subsidiaries

Cousins, Inc.; Cousins Real Estate Corporation; Cousins MarketCenters, Inc.; Cousins Development, Inc.; Cousins Texas GP Inc.

Principal Competitors

Chelsea Property Group, Inc.; CRT Properties, Inc.; Duke Realty Corporation.

Further Reading

Barry, Tom, ''Georgia's Most Respected CEO of 1995: Thomas G. Cousins,'' *Georgia Trend,* June 1995, p. 22.

Foster, David C., ''Thomas G. Cousins: A Modern Master of the Land,'' *Business Atlanta,* April 1, 1987, p. 40.

Kelly, Lindsey, ''Tom Cousins Beating the Recession,'' *Georgia Trend,* February 1993, p. 24.

Thiel, Paul, ''With a Little Help from His Friends,'' *Georgia Trend,* March 1990, p. 34.

Vinocur, Barry, ''The Ground Floor: Cousins at a Crossroads,'' *Barron's,* March 19, 2001, p. 44.

—Ed Dinger

CSM N.V.

Nienoord 13
1112 XE Diemen
P.O. Box 349
1000 AH Amsterdam
Netherlands
Telephone: +31 (0)20 590 69 11
Fax: +31 (0)20 695 19 42
Web site: http://www.csm.nl

Public Company
Incorporated: 1919
Employees: 13,800
Sales: EUR 3.48 billion ($4.13 billion) (2003)
Stock Exchanges: Euronext Amsterdam
Ticker Symbol: CSMN
NAIC: 311423 Dried and Dehydrated Food Manufacturing; 311211 Flour Milling; 311212 Rice Milling; 311312 Cane Sugar Refining; 311313 Beet Sugar Manufacturing; 311330 Confectionery Manufacturing from Purchased Chocolate; 311421 Fruit and Vegetable Canning; 311422 Specialty Canning; 311930 Flavoring Syrup and Concentrate Manufacturing

CSM N.V. is a leading food ingredients company with operations focused in four core areas: Bakery Supplies; Sugar Confectionery; Biochemicals; and Sugar. Although CSM's beet-sugar based refining division represents the company's historical core, it produced just 7 percent of the group's annual sales of nearly EUR 3.5 billion ($4.1 billion) in 2003. Since the late 1990s and early 2000s, CSM has instead transformed itself into a major bakery supplies company—the company's Bakery Supplies Europe and Bakery Supplies North America divisions combine to generate 63 percent of CSM's sales and hold the number one position in Europe and the number two position in North America. The company's baking supplies division operates under such subsidiary and brand names as Bakemark, American Ingredients, Henry & Henry, and Carpro, including Caravan Products and HC Brill Company, acquired in 2003. CSM also produces sugar confectionery, and rivals Germany's

Haribo for the top position in the European candy market—the company is already the number one candy producer in the Benelux and Scandinavian markets. Most of CSM's candy brands are regional names, including Venco, Red Band, Sportlife, and XyliFresh in The Netherlands; Jenkki and Tupla in Finland; Lutti in France; Dietorelle and Sperlari in Italy; Hops in Poland; Malaco, Bilar, and Läkerol in Scandinavia; and Chewits in the United Kingdom. CSM also controls the Leaf brand in the Benelux, Scandinavian, U.K., Italian, Asian, and other markets. The company's last division is its CSM Biochemicals division, which produced 7.8 percent of the group's sales in 2003 and operates under the Purac name. Purac is the world's leading producer of lactic acid, lactates, and gluconates, which are produced through the fermentation of sugar. CSM is listed on the Euronext Amsterdam Stock Exchange. Europe remains the group's largest market, accounting for nearly 65 percent of sales, more than 15 percent of which was generated in The Netherlands. North America adds 33.5 percent to the group's sales, with the rest of the world adding the remainder.

Merging Beet Sugar Producers in the 1920s

CSM's history begins in the late 19th century with the growth of the beet sugar industry in The Netherlands. Among the earliest and largest sugar producers in the country was Van Loon & Co., founded in 1871. Despite ups and downs in the market, notably in 1888 when the beet sugar market in Europe all but collapsed amid a wider financial crisis, Van Loon and a growing number of competitors prospered. Part of the sugar producers' success came from the rapid growth in demand for sugar and sugar products, which in turn stimulated the development of the sugar refining industry in the country.

By the end of the 19th century, The Netherlands boasted more than 30 beet sugar producers, and many more sugar refiners, including Wester Suikerraffinaderij, founded in Amsterdam in 1882, and NV Beetwortelsuikerfabrik De Mark, founded by Joannes Petrus van Rossum and two partners in 1890. Many of the country's sugar producers went on to join together in the formation of cooperatives, which later evolved into the Suiker Unie. Wester and de Mark, on the other hand, remained privately controlled companies.

Company Perspectives:

CSM aims to create value for its shareholders and the other stakeholders in the group.

CSM strives to attain, retain and further develop strong market positions in food ingredients and sugar confectionery in order to create a healthy basis for realizing growth in earnings per share. Both autonomous and acquisition-led growth play a part in this process. Growth must be realized whilst maintaining a healthy financial position.

Autonomous growth takes top priority at CSM, alongside efficiency and cost-effectiveness. Successful R&D programs are essential in this context.

CSM positions itself as an internationally operating company engaged in the development, production, sale and distribution of food ingredients and sugar confectionery.

Government subsidies for the sugar producers and refiners had encouraged the development of the sugar industry in The Netherlands. Refiners began adding to their production capacity, building new factories around the country. As a result, production capacity came to outstrip supply of raw sugar. At the same time, the government abolished the subsidies that had supported pricing on refined sugar. The situation forced a number of mergers among refiners, including De Mark, which merged into NV Algemeene Suiker-Maatschappij, or Asmij, in 1908. Van Rossum emerged as a director of Asmij, and ultimately its head.

Asmij became one of the first to turn to the United Kingdom for beet sugar imports, encouraging farmers there to begin sowing the crop. Asmij then opened its own refinery in England, in Cantley. Yet this facility, hampered in part by a reluctance to allow a foreign competitor to enter Britain's sugar market, was doomed to failure. By 1915, Asmij had been forced to shut the Cantley plant, and Asmij itself, further hit by the difficult market during World War I, was acquired by Wester Suikerraffinaderij.

Van Rossum became a prominent part of Wester's direction, and in 1918 was named the company's commercial director. Van Rossum then played a driving role in the consolidation of the Dutch beet sugar industry, focusing especially on the country's privately held producers. In 1919, Van Rossum's efforts paid off, when Wester agreed to merge with Hollandsche Fabriek van Melkproducten en Voedingsmiddelen, a producer of condensed milk and sugar products and other food ingredients, founded, like Wester, in 1882. Joining these companies in the merger was Van Loon & Co., as well as a number of other privately held and cooperative sugar refiners.

The new company became known as Centrale Suiker Maatschappij, or CSM. Following the September 1919 merger, the new sugar giant—countered only by the cooperative sugar movement in The Netherlands—restructured its holdings, shutting down four of its factories and streamlining distribution for the entire group under a single operation.

Van Rossum and J.A. van Loon were nominally simply members of the company's board of directors but soon emerged as the true leaders of the larger company. Together they led CSM into an internationalization effort. After adding a plant in Lillo, in Flemish-speaking Belgium in 1920, CSM turned to the United Kingdom, where the British government had begun offering subsidiaries in order to stimulate its beet sugar industry. Using the cash and equipment from its shuttered factories, CSM began building plants in Ely and Ipswich in 1924. The company then bought a sugar refiner, Sankey Sugar Company, based in Liverpool, and opened a third sugar plant, in King's Lynn, in 1927.

In the meantime, CSM had begun expanding elsewhere in Europe. Starting in the early 1920s, the company began buying plants in Poland, spending some 12 million guilders and acquiring seven factories in that country before the end of the decade. Van Rossum also sought to expand CSM into France and Germany, with plans to establish new companies, which would then acquire equipment unused by CSM itself.

Yet the economic crisis of the early 1930s, and the collapse of the sugar market, cut short CSM's expansion. The company was forced to restructure its operations. By 1934, the company had sold off its British holdings, then disposed of its Polish plants the following year. In that year, also, CSM completed its reorganization, and Van Rossum, who died at the age of 83 in 1943, was forced to take a more minor role in the company. CSM by then was reduced to just six sugar plants—in 1941, in a deal negotiated by Van Rossum, the company sold much of its unused equipment to the Nazis, who hoped to establish a beet sugar industry in the fertile Ukraine region.

Diversification in the 1970s

The smaller CSM made a first attempt at diversification in the late 1930s, when it acquired Taminiau te Elst, a family-owned company, in 1937. That purchase gave CSM operations in the production of jam and other conserves. During World War II and the Nazi occupation of The Netherlands, CSM was hit by the lack of resources, raw materials, and replacement parts for its machines, and the difficulties of transporting its goods and maintaining its workforce. Then, immediately following the war, much of the country's beet crop was needed as food for the population and for livestock.

CSM made a fresh attempt at diversification at the end of the war, launching a research and development wing in order to develop new sugar-based products. In 1950 the company established a test factory that was used to produce the vitamins B and B12. The project ended without success, however. Then, in 1958, CSM abandoned its conserves operation as well. Nonetheless, CSM continued developing sugar-derived products in a small biochemicals division.

By the 1960s, production of sugar in The Netherlands had reached a strong level, and threatened to outpace demand. At the same time, the company faced little prospect of selling its sugar products on an equally saturated export market. In 1964, therefore, the company shut down its Wester factory in Amsterdam. In that year, also, the company was approached by a number of sugar cooperatives in The Netherlands with an offer of a merger. When CSM refused, the cooperatives went on to form the Suiker Unie in 1966.

Key Dates:

1871: Van Loon & Sons sugar producer and refinery is funded.

1882: Wester Suikerraffinaderik in Amsterdam and Hollandsche Fabriek van Melkproducten en Voedingsmiddelen (Hollandia) are founded.

1890: NV Beetwortelsuikerfabrik De Mark is founded by Joannes Petrus van Rossum.

1908: De Mark merges into NV Algemeene Suiker-Maatschappij (Asmij).

1915: Wester acquires Asmij and Van Rossum is named the commercial director.

1919: Wester leads a three-way merger with Van Loon and Hollandia to create CSM.

1920: The company acquires a refinery in Belgium and begins buying refineries in Poland.

1924: CSM builds two factories in England and acquires a sugar refinery in Liverpool.

1927: CSM adds a third factory in England.

1935: The company undergoes restructuring, including the sale of all foreign operations.

1937: The company acquires the Dutch-based jam and conserves company, Taminiau te Elst.

1946: A research facility is established for developing sugar-based chemicals and products.

1958: Taminiau te Elst is sold.

1968: The biochemicals division is merged with Schiedamse Melkzuurfabriek, which forms the basis of the later Purac division.

1978: The company acquires Koninklijke Scholten Honig (KSH) as part of its diversification into food ingredients.

1979: The company begins a restructuring of its sugar refinery operations, shutting down its smaller refineries.

1986: The company begins a new diversification into confectionery, starting with the purchase of Red Band Venco.

1990: Droste chocolates is acquired.

1993: The company begins to acquire bakery supplies companies.

1997: The company restructures confectionery to focus on sugar-based confectionery and sells Droste; Scandinavia's Malaca is acquired.

1999: Leaf Europe is acquired.

2000: Continental Sweets is acquired; Unilever's European Bakery Supplies Division is acquired.

2003: The company acquires Unilever's Hungarian Bakery business, parts of Friesland Coberco's bakery division, and Carpro (Caravan Products and HC Brill).

2004: The company announces plans to refocus its European confectionery brands in order to create a smaller number of international brands.

The Netherlands adopted European Community regulations in 1968, further limiting the growth prospects of the sugar industry in the country, and CSM's prospects of expanding into the export markets. While sugar remained a profitable activity for CSM, its hopes increasingly turned toward diversification.

A first step toward expanding the group's business base came in 1968, when the company merged its biochemicals division with Schiedamse Melkzuurfabriek, a key maker of lactic acid and other products derived from sugar fermentation. The new operation was renamed Chemie Combinatie Amsterdam, or CCA, but later took on the name of Purac after CSM bought up full control of the company. That division then grew into the world's leading producer of lactic acid and related products.

During the 1970s, CSM sought new diversified outlets for growth. After rejecting another merger proposal from the Suiker Unie, the company decided to move into the larger food ingredients market in the late 1970s. The company's first step in this direction came in 1978, when it acquired Koninklijke Scholten Honig (KSH), which owned the Honig brand name. A steady stream of acquisitions followed through the 1980s and into the 1990s, with the company principally targeting a number of smaller Netherlands-based companies, such as Koninklijke De Ruiter, Venz BV, and HAK BV.

Yet the move into food ingredients brought CSM into direct competition with such global giants as Kraft and Nestlé, forcing a rethinking of the group's strategy. In the mid-1980s, the company's next expansion move came closer to its sugar base,

as it began acquiring noted confectionery brands, such as Red Band Venco, a maker of chewing gum and licorice based in The Netherlands, acquired in 1986. The company remained in The Netherlands for its next acquisitions, which included Droste chocolates and Tonnema peppermints in 1990.

Meanwhile, CSM had been completing an overhaul of its sugar refinery operation, shutting down its smaller refineries between 1979 and 1991, and concentrating its production at two modern automated facilities in Breda and Vierverlaten.

Adding Bakery Supplies for the New Century

CSM began phasing out its food ingredients unit toward the end of the 1990s, and at the same time refocused its confectionery division to concentrate on the European sugar confectionery market in the late 1990s. As part of that effort, CSM sold off the Droste chocolate operation in 1997. Instead, it picked up Malaca, a leader in Scandinavia, in 1997, followed by Leaf's European operations, one of the largest in the market in 1999. The following year, the company acquired Belgian-French group Continental Sweets, active in France, Belgium, The Netherlands, and the United Kingdom, for EUR 110 million.

In 2001, the company acquired Socalbe, based in Italy, giving it several strong brands in that country, including Dietorelle and Sperlari. As the company approached the mid-2000s, its confectionery wing had grown into one of Europe's top two candy makers, running neck and neck with Germany's Haribo. The company was the clear leader in a number of markets, including the Benelux countries and Scandinavia.

Yet by then, CSM had transformed itself into a world player in the bakery supplies market, with operations spanning North America as well as Europe. By 2004, CSM had gained the number one spot in this market in Europe and the number two place in the United States, a process accomplished by a long stream of acquisitions through the 1990s. These included Arizona Bakery Sales in the United States in 1994; Kirkland & Rose and Lafave & Sons, both of Canada, in 1995; Belgium's ReNa and Kwatta in 1996; Credit Valley Foods in the United States in 1998; and St. Louis Bakery, also in the United States, in 1999.

A major step in CSM's bakery supplies strategy came in 2000 when it agreed to pay EUR 700 million to buy Unilever's European Bakery Supplies Business. Following that acquisition, CSM restructured its operations, creating two new divisions, Bakery Supplies Europe and Bakery Supplies North America, which together came to account for more than 60 percent of the group's total sales. The company continued to add to its Bakery Supplies operations, buying Unilever's Hungarian bakery business and part of Friesland Coberco's bakery operations in The Netherlands, as well as the United Kingdom's Readi-Bake Ltd., part of Country Home Bakers in the United States, in 2003. Meanwhile, the company solidified its position in the United States with the purchase of Carpro, Inc., which added HC Brill Company and Caravan Products Company for $302 million.

In 2004, CSM announced its intention to continue expanding its operations through acquisitions. But the company expected to complete only smaller, bolt-on acquisitions in the near future. At the same time, the company announced its plan to snare the number one position from Haribo by restructuring its range of predominantly regional confectionery brands to develop a smaller number of international brands. CSM seemed to have a sweet tooth for growth into the new century.

Principal Subsidiaries

American Ingredients Company (U.S.A.); Arkady Craigmillar; BakeMark Danmark; BakeMark Deutschland; BakeMark Fin-land; BakeMark Hellas; BakeMark Ingredients (Canada); BakeMark Ingredients (East); BakeMark Ingrédients (France); BakeMark Ingredients (West); BakeMark International; BakeMark Italia; BakeMark Magyarország; BakeMark Polska; BakeMark Portugal; BakeMark Sverige; Baker&Baker; Bender-Iglauer Backmittel; Besser Service; Braims Italia; Carels Goes; Continental Sweets; CSM Suiker; Délices de la Tour; Dreidoppel; Express Croex; Lachaise; Lamy Lutti Belgium; Lamy Lutti France; Leaf Finland; Leaf Italia; Leaf Poland; Leaf United Kingdom; MalacoLeaf; Margo-BakeMark Schweiz; PGLA-I (50%); PURAC America; PURAC Asia Pacific; PURAC Biochem; PURAC Bioquímica; PURAC China; PURAC Deutschland; PURAC France; PURAC Glucochem; PURAC Hungary; PURAC Japan; PURAC Korea; PURAC Polska; PURAC Production USA; PURAC Russia; PURAC Sínteses; PURAC UK; RBV Leaf; Unipro Benelux.

Principal Competitors

Nestlé Suisse S.A.; Coca-Cola Co.; Orkla ASA; Pepsi-Cola Co.; MacAndrews and Forbes Holdings Inc.; Hershey Foods Corporation; American Ingredients Co.; Monsanto Co.; McCormick and Company Inc.; Cerestar.

Further Reading

"CSM Completes Carpro Purchase," *Food Ingredient News,* April 2003.

"CSM: de stille groeier," *Financieel Economische Tijd,* June 7, 2003.

"CSM Looks to Acquire U.S. Baking Ingredients Company," *Candy Industry,* January 2003, p. 11.

"CSM NV, the Dutch Food Ingredients and Sugar Confectionery Firm, Has Announced That It Will Buy Unilever's Bakery Ingredients Business in Hungary," *Oils & Fats International,* July 2003, p. 3.

"CSM wil 5% tot 10% wpa-groei," *De Telegraaf,* February 20, 2004.

Hallema, I.A., *Van biet tot suiker. J.P. van Rossum als suikerindustrieel-koopman en organisator,* Baarn: A.W.J. de Jonge, 1948.

Homer, Eric, "CSM Nourishes Buyside with $400 Million Via Royal Bank of Scotland," *Private Placement Letter,* February 17, 2003.

"Rossum, Joannes Petrus, van (1860–1943)," *Biografisch Woordenboek van Nederland 5* (Den Haag 2002).

—M.L. Cohen

Dex Media, Inc.

198 Inverness Drive West
Englewood, Colorado 80112
U.S.A.
Telephone: (303) 784-2900
Fax: (303) 784-1398
Web site: http://www.dexmedia.com

Public Company
Incorporated: 2002
Employees: 3,000
Sales: $1.63 billion (2003, includes West Predecessor
   revenue)
Stock Exchanges: New York
Ticker Symbol: DEX
NAIC: 511140 Directory and Mailing List Publishers

Dex Media, Inc. is the official publisher of telephone directory white pages and yellow pages for Qwest Communications. Dex distributes the directories in 14 states: Arizona, Colorado, Idaho, Iowa, Minnesota, Montana, Nebraska, New Mexico, North Dakota, Oregon, South Dakota, Utah, Washington, and Wyoming. Although the directories are distributed for free, income is derived from more than 400,000 local businesses and 4,000 national advertising accounts. Independent directories, in markets not served by Qwest, are published and distributed in El Paso, Texas, and Lincoln, Nebraska. In addition to the standard directories, Dex publishes an On-the-Go directory, a nine-inch by six-inch directory designed to be kept in automobiles. Available in major metropolitan cities, On-the-Go directories feature maps, shopping and entertainment guides, as well as telephone and address information for central city businesses. Dex publishes bilingual, English-Spanish directories for more than 20 markets. Dex publishes CD-ROM directories and its Internet Yellow Pages directory is available at dexonline.com. In addition to providing search capacity for the content of business advertisements, dexonline.com accesses more than 15 million basic business listings and 200 million residential listings nationwide.

Forming the Company in 2002 to Acquire Former AT&T Directory Publisher

Dex Media, Inc. originated as a regional publisher of the Yellow Pages, with operations beginning in Cheyenne, Wyoming, in 1881. A century later, as part of AT&T, the company became Mountain Bell Yellow Pages when the U.S. Justice Department divided AT&T into seven Regional Bell Operating Companies in 1984. When Mountain Bell took the name US West, Mountain Bell Yellow Pages became US West Direct. In 1996, US West launched a new brand, US West Dex, using a man with a magnifying glass as the identifying Dex character. When US West and Qwest Communications International merged in 2000, the directory business was renamed once again, to Qwest Dex. Qwest Communications decided to sell its directory businesses to offset rising debt and losses. Qwest Dex generated approximately $1.6 billion in revenue in 2001 and Qwest expected to gain up to $10 billion from the sale. Qwest received several bids from equity investment groups, but questions about Qwest's accounting practices dissuaded several of the interested parties.

In August 2002, Qwest accepted the $7.05 billion bid from Dex Media, though the purchase price was considered low, at only 7.8 times EBITDA, compared with similar transactions in the directories industry. The Carlyle Group, a global private equity company with more than $13.5 billion under management, and Welsh, Carson, Anderson & Stowe, a private equity firm with more than $12 billion under management, owned Dex Media, established for the purpose of acquiring Qwest Dex. Each company planned to invest $750 million of equity toward the acquisition and to fund the balance through bank debt and the sale of high-yield (junk) bonds.

The leveraged buyout occurred in two transactions. Qwest formed Dex Media East LLC and Dex Media West LLC to divide the directory operations according to states that demanded approval of the sale. Advertising income from the Yellow Pages offset lower utility rates for telephone customers, and the sale of the directories raised issues of potential rate increases. In November 2002 Dex Media acquired Dex Media East, the directory business for the states of Colorado, Iowa, Minnesota, Nebraska, New Mexico (including El Paso, Texas), North Dakota, and South Dakota. Dex Media acquired 155 directories in these seven

Company Perspectives:

Thanks to our scale and incumbent position, we have a substantial competitive advantage over independent directory advertising providers. During 2003, we printed and distributed approximately 43 million directories and had more than 400,000 local advertising accounts consisting primarily of small and medium-sized businesses and more than 4,000 national advertising accounts. As the incumbent directory publisher in the Dex States, Dex directories benefit from strong brand recognition as the official Yellow Pages.

states for $2.75 billion. Dex sold $975 million in junk bonds to leverage the acquisition, $450 million in senior notes at 9.875 percent interest, due in 2009, and $525 million subordinated notes at 12.125 percent interest due 2012. Term loans and a revolving credit facility supplied an additional $1.4 million in funds. The Carlyle Group and Welsh, Carson provided $655 million in equity, about 20 percent of the purchase price.

The $4.3 billion acquisition of Dex Media West, comprising 122 directories in Arizona, Idaho, Montana, Oregon, Utah, Washington, and Wyoming, was completed in September 2003, after approval by state utility commissions. Financing for the acquisition involved the sale of $385 million in senior notes at 8.5 percent interest due in 2010 and $780 million in senior subordinated notes at 9.875 percent interest due in 2013. Term loans and a revolving credit facility provided an additional $2.3 million, and the equity partners contributed $982 million, about 20 percent of purchase price.

Dex Media became the largest privately owned incumbent directory publisher in the world. The acquisitions involved a 50-year exclusive publishing agreement with Qwest Corporation, to publish all Qwest directories until 2052, and a 40-year non-compete agreement with Qwest Communications International. In addition, Dex Media agreed to retain management, with George Burnett becoming president and chief executive officer.

With an aggregate debt of $5.8 billion, only one other leveraged buyout exceeded the value of the Qwest Dex acquisition, that of RJR Nabisco in 1989. In late 2003 Dex restructured and repriced its Dex Media East debt for lower interest rates. Additional funding obtained from aggregate sales of its senior notes and senior subordinated notes at Dex West provided $1.25 billion in funds, which Dex Media transferred to Dex Holdings to pay a $1 billion dividend to The Carlyle Group and Welsh, Carson.

Competitive Environment in 2003

The Carlyle Group and Welsh, Carson entered the directory business as it became more competitive. Independent directories, those not published by or for telecommunications companies, proliferated during the 1990s and continued to expand in the early 2000s. For instance, Verizon Information Services entered 15 markets with competitive directories in 2002, and competitive directories were introduced into six of Dex's top ten markets in 2003. First Qwest Dex, then Dex Media responded by introducing directories in markets not served by Qwest Communications. In 2001 Qwest launched the company's first independent direc-

tory in El Paso, Texas, a smaller version of the local incumbent directory. Dex Media continued that strategy by introducing a competitive directory in Lincoln, Nebraska, in early 2003, where incumbent directory publisher Alltel dominated the market and independent publisher Yellow Book USA had already established a presence. Dex did not place much emphasis on independent directories, as independent publishers quickly launched directories in potential markets and Internet and bilingual directories held greater potential for return on investment.

Spanish-language directories or advertising sections provided new revenue sources in a market where demand was strong, but competitors sought revenue from this market as well. Whereas directories had previously included only a Spanish-English index to the yellow pages, Dex's bilingual directory added a complete Spanish-language section after the English yellow pages. In early 2003 Dex launched its first bilingual directories in Albuquerque, Denver, Phoenix, and El Paso. Additional bilingual directories followed in Pueblo, Colorado; Tucson and Nogales, Arizona; Las Cruces and Santa Fe, New Mexico; Salt Lake City, Utah; and the Kenniwick, Richland, and Pasco Tri-Cities area in Washington. The company launched a total of 20 bilingual directories in 2003; Dex faced a competitive market for bilingual advertising, however, as Verizon already published bilingual directories in more than 50 markets. In Greeley, Colorado, Dex faced strong competition from Hispanic Publications' Spanish-only directory, so the company decided to wait before issuing a directory there.

Another area where Dex encountered new competition, but held greater competitive strength, involved its Internet directory. As consumers used print directories less often and online directories more often, Dex faced competition from Switchboard.com and Version SuperPages.com, the latter launched in March 2004, as well as from popular search engines that catered to consumer searches for local, everyday requirements. For instance, Google began to seek new sources of revenue by selling access to results pages to local businesses in its Local Search, a test program for directory assistance online. Dex leveraged its competitive advantage in Yellow Pages publishing with an enhanced Internet search system, using state-of-the-art technology to extend search capability to the content of the more than 240,000 display advertisements from Yellow Pages in the company's directories in 14 states. The new information delivery system provided multiple search options in a single search box, allowing consumers to search by product and brands, hours of operation, payment options, and locations. For instance, a simple search for plumbers in Minneapolis returned a list of 1,200 plumbers, but a search for ''plumbers Sunday MasterCard'' returned a list of 20 businesses. Dex supported its in-depth search capacity by increasing system speed tenfold for rapid information delivery. An industry first, the enhanced online directory provided Yellow Pages advertisers with greater value than that available from other online business directories.

Dex extended an introductory offer on the print/Internet bundle to local businesses during 2003 in preparation for a 2004 launch of dexonline.com. Along with sales of other new products, revenue increased approximately 3 percent at Dex Media East, to $668.8 million, slightly more after the effects of the purchase method of accounting for acquisition. At Dex Media West, revenue declined about 6 percent overall, but showed an increase of approximately 2 percent when excluding the effects of purchase accounting. Combined with the West Predecessor company, Dex Media West reported $844.2 million in revenue. Dex Media East operated at a loss of $40.1 million due to debt service, financing fees related to the Dex West acquisition, and the costs of transition to a stand-alone company. The West Successor (Dex West from acquisition September 10, 2003) recorded a loss of $10 million on $199.4 million in revenue. Strong cash flow allowed Dex to pay debt early, however, for a total of $405 million in debt paid in 2003.

The company launched its enhanced Internet portal at dexonline.com in January 2004, renamed from qwestdex.com. The name change occurred in conjunction with a change in the print publications from the name Qwest Dex to simply Dex. A new logo design accompanied the name change, but the yellow and blue colors were retained for public familiarity. To maintain the company's identity as the incumbent publisher for Qwest, the descriptor "Official Directory of Qwest" followed the Dex name. To attract attention to the change, Dex customized covers of print directories to local communities, using photos of identifiable landmarks. An advertising campaign in 13 cities, involving television, radio, and outdoor advertising, used the tagline "Dex Knows" to affirm the company's lead in directory information assistance.

In March 2004 the Yellow Pages Integrated Media Association recognized Dex Media with four Industry Excellence Awards. These included two Gold Awards, one in the Advertising and Promotion category, for its Surprise and Delight Reward and Recognition Program, designed to build strong customer relationships in direct marketing. In the Process Innovation category, Dex was recognized for its Local to National Transfer Process, intended to support certified marketing professionals attending to national accounts. A Silver Award for Market Innovation acknowledged Dex's ValAd Program for underdeveloped business headings in the Yellow Pages. Dex Recycling/Competitive Response Initiative to benefit local charities and improve directory recycling rates earned a Bronze Award in the Distribution category.

Initial Public Offering of Stock in 2004

In June 2004 Dex Media announced its intention to offer 53 million shares of stock to the public, including 15.3 million primary shares from the company and 37.8 million shares from The Carlyle Group and Welsh, Carson; the stock offering involved approximately 35 percent of the ownership interest. The company intended to offer shares at $23 to $26 each, but slow

market trading prompted the company to lower the price to $19 per share immediately before the initial public offering (IPO), completed on July 24. Dex actually sold 19.7 million primary shares and applied net proceeds of the IPO, at $352.5 million, to pay debt and to redeem $127.7 million in preferred stock from its equity partners, leaving the company with only one class of stock.

Dex continued to pursue its primary areas of growth, bilingual publications and online access to dexonline.com. A distribution agreement, effective August 1st, with InfoSpace, Inc., provided access to dexonline to six million users of Switchboard.com. Infospace's success in generating traffic to the Switchboard site prompted Dex to make the agreement. In the Denver area Dex introduced two community directories with a Spanish-language yellow pages section, for the Northglenn-Thornton-Commerce City area and the Central-Downtown Denver area. Mango-colored pages differentiated the Spanish-language section, while the tab, "En Espanol," marked its beginning. The section included a 24-page directory providing emergency contacts and information on government agencies, educational institutions, and business assistance organizations.

Principal Subsidiaries

Dex Media East Inc.; Dex Media East Finance Co.; Dex Media East LLC; Dex Media Service, LLC; Dex Media West, Inc.; Dex Media West Finance Co.; Dex Media West LLC.

Principal Competitors

Google, Inc.; Hispanic Publications, Inc.; TransWestern Publishing Company LLC; Verizon Information Services; Yahoo!, Inc.; Yellow Book USA.

Further Reading

"Arizona to Consider Qwest Requests for Directory Sale, Long-Distance Service," *Knight Ridder/Tribune Business News*, August 30, 2003.

"Dex Adds Competitive Book in Lincoln, Launches Bilingual Books," *Yellow Pages & Directory Report*, February 28, 2003.

"Dex Expands Plans for Bilingual Books," *Yellow Pages & Directory Report*, April 11, 2003.

"Dex Introduces Spanish-Language Section in Denver," *Yellow Pages & Directory Report*, July 30, 2004.

"Dex Launches Ad Campaign to Combat Yellow Book in Twin Cities," *Yellow Pages & Directory Report*, May 14, 2004.

"Dex Media East Restructures, Reprices," *Bank Loan Report*, October 27, 2003.

"Dex Media Makes Debut," *Daily Deal*, July 23, 2004.

"Dex Media West LBO Deal Hits Ground Running," *Loan Market Week*, August 18, 2003, p. 1.

"Dex Prices $975M of Junk," *Daily Deal*, October 31, 2002.

"One Bid Rejected for Dex, Qwest Seeks $1B Upfront," *Yellow Pages & Directory Report*, May 24, 2002.

"SBC, Dex Expanding Spanish-Language Directory Products," *Yellow Pages & Directory Report*, May 14, 2004.

Smith, Jeff, "Dex Media's Ad Campaign Throws Book at Competitor," *Rocky Mountain News*, June 18, 2004, p. 6B.

——, "Turning a Page; Dex Media Chief Says IPO Will Help Company Reduce Its Debt," *Rocky Mountain News*, July 24, 2004, p. 7C.

"An Unusual Pair," *Yellow Pages & Directory Report*, August 30, 2002.

—Mary Tradii

✪ DÜRKOPP ADLER AG

Dürkopp Adler AG

Potsdamer Strasse 190
33719 Bielefeld
Germany
Telephone: +49 (0521) 925-01
Fax: +49 (0521) 925-2645
Web site: http://www.duerkopp-adler.com

Public Company
Incorporated: 1867
Employees: 2,000
Sales: EUR 111.5 million (2003)
Stock Exchanges: Frankfurt Berlin
Ticker Symbol: DKAG
NAIC: 333292 Textile Machinery Manufacturing; 333921 Elevator and Moving Stairway Manufacturing; 333922 Conveyor and Conveying Equipment Manufacturing; 333923 Overhead Traveling Crane, Hoist and Monorail System Manufacturing

---

Dürkopp Adler AG makes industrial sewing machines, including specialized automated machines for specific applications such as shoemaking, upholstery, and garment manufacturing. The company also produces overhead conveyor systems used to transport garments at distribution centers, dry cleaners, and commercial laundries. Dürkopp was founded in Bielefeld, Germany, in 1867 just as the Industrial Revolution was beginning to make its mark on the city's textile industry. The firm grew along with Bielefeld and was a major producer of automobiles, bicycles and ball bearings before limiting its activities to the textile field shortly after World War II. In 1990 Dürkopp merged with Kochs Adler, the other major sewing machine manufacturer in Bielefeld, to form Dürkopp Adler. The firm distributes its products worldwide through subsidiaries in Europe, the Far East and the Americas. Manufacturing is done in Bielefeld and, more recently, at facilities in the Czech Republic and Romania.

Sewing Machines and Bicycles: the 19th Century

The first 50 years of Dürkopp's operations were shaped by the mechanical passion of the company's founder, Nikolaus Dürkopp. Dürkopp was apprenticed to a metalworker in the village of Detmold, Germany, at the age of 14. In his free time, he strove to expand his mechanical knowledge through independent study and experimentation. After completing the apprenticeship, Dürkopp gathered further experience at larger shops in Berlin, Hamburg, and Bremen. He started working for a Bielefeld clockmaker named Böckelmann in 1860. Böckelmann had recently begun performing repairs on sewing machines, which were appearing for the first time in Bielefeld's linen industry. At the time, most sewing machines were being imported from the United States. Dürkopp studied these machines and learned enough to build one on his own in 1861. The next several years of his life, however, were taken up with military service.

In October 1867, at the age of 25, Dürkopp teamed up with a colleague, Carl Schmidt, to found the Dürkopp & Schmidt sewing machine factory. At first they operated out of the back room of the clockmaker Böckelmann on the Marktstrasse, making machines for both household and industrial use. After a year of operations they hired four workers and moved to new quarters at a varnisher's shop on the Marktstrasse. Their machines acquired a favorable reputation among local tradespeople, and soon the firm had hired about 20 workers and was once again cramped for space. In 1870 Dürkopp and Schmidt built their own factory a few blocks away on the Marktstrasse. Now they would have room to install steam-driven machinery and cut down on the work done by hand. But the firm's development was temporarily stalled when Dürkopp was called away to fight in the Franco-Prussian War.

After the war, the German economy prospered and Dürkopp expanded. The firm began producing more specialized machines for tradespeople such as shoemakers, tailors, and saddle makers. Dürkopp also began selling its machines in the farther regions of Germany. The company outgrew its existing space before long, but it lacked the capital to fund an expansion. In 1876 the firm convinced a Bielefeld councilmember by the name of Kaselowsky that the sewing machine venture was worthy of support. Kaselowsky's son Richard joined Dürkopp as a partner and financial backer and stayed at the company for two decades. Schmidt, meanwhile, had departed the firm, so its name was

Company Perspectives:

Today, Dürkopp Adler AG offers solutions in the field of sewing and conveyor equipment. The group operates with a worldwide service and distribution network of 11 subsidiaries and more than 80 authorised dealers. The objective of the company is to perfect the automation of production procedures, guaranteeing at the same time a maximum degree of flexible applications.

Complete consultation and reliable service round off a product pallet that takes a top place in major segments of the world market. The pioneering spirit and creative drive of the founding fathers is an integral part of a company philosophy, and will be used by the creative potential of the staff to meet the challenges of the next millennium.

changed in 1876 to Dürkopp & Co. Dürkopp now had about 250 employees. In 1877 the factory was destroyed by a fire that started in the paint shop. The company rescued a few machines and set them up in a shed until a new building was ready.

By the 1880s several other Bielefeld firms were competing with Dürkopp. In addition, an economic depression hit the city in the first years of the decade. Dürkopp cut back working hours in order to survive. The situation was better by 1884, but Dürkopp realized that diversification would help protect its bottom line. Bicycles seemed like a good match for Dürkopp's capabilities, and the company began producing them in 1885. Dürkopp was able to make top quality ball bearings, so its bicycles became known for their smooth ride. The bicycle division took off quickly. Soon Dürkopp was exporting its bearings to bicycle factories in England and selling its bicycles across Europe. The sewing machine branch was also developing new products such as specialized buttonhole and zigzag machines. In 1889 Dürkopp went public in order to raise more capital for expansion, including the construction of a foundry so that more metal parts could be fabricated in-house. In 1892 Dürkopp celebrated its 25th anniversary with a grand torchlight parade to Nikolaus Dürkopp's home, followed by celebratory speeches, a great banquet, congratulatory telegrams, and visits from town dignitaries. The firm now had about 1,650 employees.

Experiments in Automobile Production in the Early 20th Century

Near the end of the 19th century, Nikolaus Dürkopp turned his mechanical creativity to the field of automobiles. At first he was unable to persuade shareholders to invest in this area, so he built his first automobiles around 1894 with a few million marks of his personal funds. Dürkopp was able to apply the experience he had gathered over the past few years making gas motors for his factory to the manufacture of automobiles. In 1897, the firm was convinced to move into automobile production as a replacement for bicycle sales, which were falling drastically due to less expensive American imports. Dürkopp wanted to design the firm's car from scratch, but under the pressure of time the company became partners with a French manufacturer and used their blueprints instead. In 1899, however, Dürkopp presented its first original design, a small ''sports car,'' at an automobile exposition

in Berlin. The French partnership ended a few years later. Early automobile production at Dürkopp also focused on motorcycles, particularly three-wheeled models, since many people in the industry thought it would not work to put a motor on a two-wheeled vehicle. By the beginning of the new century, Dürkopp made two-wheeled motorcycles as well, then discontinued motorcycle production around 1905 in favor of standard automobiles. Meanwhile, Mercedes had come out with a groundbreaking automobile design that erased the lingering similarities between automobiles and horse-drawn carriages. Dürkopp, along with most other German manufacturers, scrapped current design experiments and began producing on the Mercedes model.

It took more than a decade before the automobile division became profitable, although Nikolaus Dürkopp was winning auto races with the special racing cars he built for fun. The company was reluctant to move into mass production, so it became known as a high-quality luxury producer. Many cars were built as special orders to meet the customer's specific requests for body design and luxury details. In the area of bicycle production, on the other hand, Dürkopp adopted more efficient standardized production, which helped the German bicycle industry rebound. Bicycle and sewing machine sales supported continued investments in automobile production. Dürkopp bought an automobile body factory, Wiemann & Co. of Magdeburg, in 1904. Cars were exported to England under the name Watsonia.

Technical details of bicycle mechanics influenced the design of automobiles. In particular, Dürkopp became known for a chainless drive train referred to as ''Kardan.'' The first Kardan bicycles were produced around 1898. Although they never captured a large market share overall, they became a specialty of Dürkopp's. The company produced some improved Kardan models in the 1920s and was known for its Kardan bicycles through the 1940s. This same technology was applied to Dürkopp's automobiles in the early 1900s. In most subsequent models, chain-driven wheels were replaced with a series of gears that directly transferred the engine's power to the wheels.

Dürkopp's first real automobile success was a model known as the ''Knipperdolling,'' first produced in 1906. This was a smaller car that moved away from the six-cylinder vehicles Dürkopp had been experimenting with in favor of a four-cylinder engine. Dürkopp began working with the Berlin manufacturer Oryx-Motorenwerken to further develop this model. Profits from the automobile division were now able to support experiments in other areas. Nikolaus Dürkopp even tried to build an airplane, but it never got off the ground. The company also made centrifuges, cash registers, motorboats, buses, and tractors over the years. Dürkopp was expanding, adding workshops in new areas in order to become more vertically integrated. In 1911 Dürkopp bought the Oryx company as well as some land in Bielefeld. A fire that year burnt down the older wood buildings, making room for larger facilities. In 1913 the company issued DEM 4.5 million in share capital to fund growth and changed its name to Dürkoppwerke AG.

Surviving the World Wars

During World War I Dürkoppwerke restructured its production to make cars and bicycles for the military, as well as trucks,

Key Dates:

1860: Koch & Co. sewing machine factory is founded in Bielefeld.

1867: Dürkopp & Schmidt sewing machine factory is formed.

1885: Dürkopp starts producing bicycles; Koch soon does the same.

1897: Dürkopp begins production of automobiles.

1920: The newly named Kochs Adler discontinues bicycle production.

1929: Dürkopp's automobile operations are sold.

1942: Bielefeld firms begin using forced labor from the east.

1944: A bombing raid leaves most of Bielefeld in rubble.

1961: Dürkopp discontinues production of bicycles to focus on industrial sewing machines.

1990: Dürkoppwerke and Kochs Adler merge to form Dürkopp Adler AG.

2001: Reduced demand leads to a period of net losses at the firm.

artillery transports, and other machinery. The company simplified its production method and discontinued all automobile models with the exception of the Knipperling. During the war, taxes and laws discouraged personal use of bicycles and automobiles. After the war, returning military vehicles overran the transportation market. Dürkoppwerke also lost its longtime leader: although Nikolaus Dürkopp was alive for the firm's 50th anniversary in 1917, he died a year later. He was said to have been familiar with all details of production and able to operate every machine in the factory. Dürkopp's personality had been a defining feature of the company. He was so committed to the firm's product development that he always drove prototypes rather than finished cars so that he could offer suggestions for design improvements. After his death, Dürkoppwerke became driven more by practical concerns than by mechanical experimentation, particularly during the crisis-ridden economy of the postwar Weimar Republic. Dürkopp's son Paul had made a career in the military, so an industrial businessman named Gustav Möllenberg was found to take over the firm.

Dürkoppwerke's debt grew as the German economy as a whole nearly collapsed. Banks gained control of most of the firm. The company was still stuck in a labor-intensive model of automobile production. Since this segment was performing more poorly than the bicycle and sewing machine operations, the banks sold Dürkoppwerke's automobile divisions to Mercedes-Benz around 1929. Many workers were laid off in the other segments and the factory halls were largely empty. Dürkopp tried making photo copiers for a few years, but they failed to catch on. The most successful developments of the Weimar Period were the founding of a subsidiary in Paris in 1927 and, around 1932, the development of the first overhead conveyor machines for the clothing industry.

In 1933 the National Socialist party came to power in Germany and implemented policies to promote industry and military development, such as providing free machinery to manufacturers for weapons production. Several members of Dürkoppwerke's leadership joined the Nazi party. When World War II started, Dürkoppwerke jumped into the war effort with patriotic enthusiasm, although not all workers supported the Nazis. The war brought ample work to the company. Dürkoppwerke implemented rotating shifts and bought a weapons factory in Künsebeck bei Halle. In 1941 the firm was proud to be recognized as a "Model Firm of National Socialism," the highest state honor for a German business. Georg Barthel was in charge of Dürkoppwerke now. His father Hermann, a successful manufacturer of bearings from Schweinfurt, had bought the company in 1940 but died a year later, leaving his son to take over. Dürkoppwerke was the leading manufacturer of cylindrical bearings for tanks during the war.

In 1942 Dürkoppwerke began using forced labor from the East. The firm built a camp known as "Bethlehem" to house 850 Ukrainian women; other workers were housed at camps around Bielefeld. Sanitary conditions at the camps were poor and the food was bad, but the official view was that the "guest workers" were getting a taste of life far superior to conditions under Communism. Some German employees of Dürkoppwerke brought food to the factory for the forced laborers and even invited them to dinner, although this was strictly forbidden. Dürkoppwerke marked its 75th anniversary in 1942 by issuing a solemn historical overview and newsletter noting employees who had fallen at the front and stating that it was no time for celebration. Meanwhile, the Allies intensified bombing towards the end of the war. A raid in September 1944 left Bielefeld in rubble.

Postwar Expansion and Merger

After the war Dürkoppwerke rebuilt and went back to producing sewing machines and bicycles. But by the early 1960s, the firm reduced its production to industrial sewing machines and overhead conveyer systems. The last bicycles and household sewing machines were made in 1961. In 1962 FAG Kugelfischer, a bearings manufacturer in Schweinfurt, acquired majority control of Dürkoppwerke. Dürkoppwerke's bearings operations were spun off to Kugelfischer in the 1970s. Dürkoppwerke celebrated its 100th anniversary in 1967 and converted from Dürkoppwerke AG to Dürkoppwerke GmbH. During this period, the company was making technical advances in sewing machine design and expanding its distribution worldwide. Subsidiaries were founded in Austria in 1965, Great Britain in 1983, Hong Kong in 1984, and the United States (Atlanta) in 1985. The first sewing machine steered by splints was introduced in 1964 and the first electronically steered machine in 1971.

In 1986 the decision was made to merge with Kochs Adler AG, the other major sewing machine manufacturer in Bielefeld. A mechanic named Koch had founded the first sewing machine factory in Bielefeld around 1860, and Nikolaus Dürkopp worked for him briefly before striking out on his own. The firm was known as Koch & Co. Koch went into bicycle production shortly after Dürkopp did, but the firm became focused mainly on industrial sewing systems under the brand name Adler. It discontinued bicycle production after 1920 and changed its name to Kochs Adler Nähmaschinenwerke ("sewing machine factory") AG. After World War II, Kochs Adler moved into production of typewriters, packing machinery and other new fields, but these ventures, as well as production of household sewing machines, were soon abandoned. FAG Kugelfischer, already Dürkoppwerke's parent company, acquired a 76 percent share in Kochs Adler in the early 1980s. A merger of the two companies was the logical next step. In 1986, Kochs Adler had annual sales of DEM 127.5 million and Dürkoppwerke of DEM 200.5 million.

However, the merger was held up for three years due to a legal dispute. Although a substantial majority of Kochs Adler shareholders approved the merger, three small shareholders opposed it. They criticized the proposed share exchange ratio and claimed that the official merger announcement did not sufficiently explain the reasons for the terms of the merger. However, they implied they would be willing to accept a financial settlement of the disagreement. Kochs Adler claimed that this was blackmail. After a lower court rejected the shareholders' complaint, a higher court accepted it, which meant that the merger papers could not be filed and the two companies lost money over the next three years due to the need to keep their administrations and annual reports separate. The parties finally came to a settlement in 1990 when the shareholders were offered an improved share ratio. After the merger the firm became known as Dürkopp Adler AG. The merged company had about 3,000 employees and annual sales of DEM 500 million.

Mixed Results After 1990

The 1990s were a mixed decade for Dürkopp Adler. The late 1980s had been a profitable period for the industry, but the firm hit rough times in the few years after the merger. After three consecutive years of losses, Dürkopp Adler posted a profit of DEM 16.1 million on sales of DEM 301.1 million in 1994. The firm had reduced bank debt and cut its workforce by several hundred employees the previous year. Also, Dürkopp Adler's overhead conveyer division was converted into a separate subsidiary, Dürkopp Fördertechnik GmbH, in order to improve material flow and distribution. Increased clothing production in Eastern Europe and Central and South America kept Dürkopp Adler on a profitable course into 1998, and the firm rehired some workers. That year the firm also began producing sewing machine parts in Romania; sewing machine production was being transferred to Boskovice in the Czech Republic as well. In late 1998 Dürkopp Adler bought Beisler GmbH of Hösbach bei Aschaffenburg, a manufacturer of automated sewing machines for producers of menswear.

Operations took a turn for the worse again in 1999, when Dürkopp Adler posted a net loss of EUR 6.2 million. In response, the company cut a few hundred more jobs and transferred more production to the Czech Republic. Mainly the more complex automated sewing machines were still being produced in Bielefeld. This restructuring pushed the company into the black for 2000, when net profit was EUR 5.4 million on sales of EUR 198.3 million. But the economic downturn that started in late 2001 hurt the company badly and led to three years of net losses, culminating in a EUR 10.1 million loss in 2003. Cloth-

ing manufacturers were reluctant to invest in new machinery during a time of low consumer demand. The strong euro also hurt Dürkopp Adler, since over three quarters of the company's business came from exports. In 2003 Dürkopp Adler founded a subsidiary in Shanghai, since more and more sewing was being done in east Asia. In 2004, with demand still low, the Chinese sewing machine producer Shanggong Co. Ltd. was considering purchasing Dürkopp Adler from FAG Kugelfischer. In the larger view, however, the company's current troubles looked like just another transient period in a nearly 140-year history of ups and downs.

Principal Subsidiaries

Dürkopp Fördertechnik GmbH; Beisler GmbH; Dürkopp Adler America, Inc. (U.S.A.); Dürkopp Adler Mexico S.A. de C.V.; Dürkopp Adler Far East Ltd. (Hong Kong); Dürkopp Adler International Trading (Shanghai) Co., Ltd. (China); Dürkopp Adler Italia S.r.l. (Italy); Dürkopp Adler France S.A.S.; Dürkopp Adler Austria Gesellschaft mbH; Dürkopp Adler Polska Sp. z o.o. (Poland); Dürkopp Adler Ukraine Ltd.; S.C. Dürkopp Adler masini de cusut S.R.L. (Romania); Minerva Boskovice, a.s. (Czech Republic; 84%).

Principal Divisions

Sewing Technology; Conveyor Technology.

Principal Competitors

Juki Corp.; Shanghai Industrial Sewing Machine Company Ltd.; Brother Industries, Ltd.; Singer N.V.

Further Reading

"Aufschwung bei Dürkopp Adler," *Frankfurter Allgemeine Zeitung*, April 27, 1998, p. 29.

Cohnen, Robert, "Autos aus Bielefeld: Die Entwicklung der Firma Dürkopp 1897–1930," *86th Jahresbericht des Historisches Vereins Grafschaft Ravensberg*, 2000, pp. 49–72.

"Dürkopp Adler baut in Bielefeld Personal ab," *Frankfurter Allgemeine Zeitung*, September 10, 1999, p. 18.

"Dürkopp Adler erwirbt Nähanlagenhersteller," *Bšrsen-Zeitung*, November 25, 1998, p. 25.

"Dürkopp Adler kehrt mit neuen Produkten in Erfolgsspur zurück," *DPA-AFX*, June 21, 2001.

Kühne, Hans-Jörg, *Kriegsbeute Arbeit: Der "Fremdarbeitereinsatz" in der Bielefelder Wirtschaft 1939–1945*, Bielefeld: Verlag für Regionalgeschichte, 2002.

"Fusion Dürkopp/Adler weiter in der Schwebe," *Neue Westfšlische*, May 26, 1988.

"75 Jahre Dürkopp," *Dürkopp Feldpost*, October 22, 1942.

"Shanggong Issues More Shares for German Deal," *Financial Times*, October 28, 2003, p. 30.

"Vorstand hält Dürkopp Adler für saniert," *Frankfurter Allgemeine Zeitung*, May 15, 1995, p. 20.

"Weg frei für Fusion von Dürkopp und Adler," *Neue Westfšlische*, March 7, 1990.

—Sarah Ruth Lorenz

Europe Through the Back Door Inc.

130 4th Avenue North
P.O. Box 2009
Edmonds, Washington 98020
U.S.A.
Telephone: (425) 771-8303
Fax: (425) 771-0833
Web site: http://www.ricksteves.com

Private Company
Incorporated: 1976
Employees: 60
Sales: $20 million (2003 est.)
NAIC: 561520 Tour Operators; 624190 Travel Aid
    Centers

Europe Through the Back Door Inc. (ETBD) is a $20 million enterprise that offers assistance to independent travelers and leads more than 150 tours throughout the European continent annually. ETBD was founded in 1976 by Rick Steves, who is known to many through the public television travel series that he created. ETBD is located in Edmonds, Washington, where Steves grew up, and is committed to helping travelers through its diverse operations. The company's 60 employees teach travel seminars, research and write European guidebooks, produce a public television video series, and offer travel consulting and numerous bus tours. The company maintains a well-frequented web site where ETBD sells travel merchandise including European rail tickets and a host of travel accessories.

European Exposure: 1960s–70s

As a young teen in the late 1960s, Rick Steves reluctantly took his first journey to Europe with his parents. Steves' father and mother owned a small piano importing business and were traveling abroad to select pianos from the continent. Steves was apprehensive at first of travel abroad. The thought of encountering people who did not speak his language and exploring cultural differences were not a teenager's dream summer vacation. The trip went well, however, and opened Steves' eyes to a whole new world, one that eventually became his life's work.

Steves credits his time spent observing backpackers in Copenhagen, Denmark, with changing his mind about travel abroad. He explained his change of heart in a February 1996 interview in the *Seattle Times,* "I saw other kids with backpacks in the Copenhagen train station, as free as birds. I vowed to go back to Europe. And now I've gone every year since I was 18."

It was not long before Rick Steves began earning his own money and taking trips throughout Europe with his friends. In the 1970s college students were backpacking their way around the world and Steves and his friends counted themselves among them. A friend who accompanied Steves on his first trip without his parents recalled the trip as less of a back door and more of a gutter, but Steves' journeys improved over the years as he learned from his mistakes.

As a student and shortly after his graduation from university, Steves financed his way by teaching piano at a studio in his hometown of Edmonds. He headed to Europe on an annual basis, exploring and gathering information and travel skills that became known as his "back door travel philosophy." It was not long before he realized that his experience qualified him to teach others his offbeat travel tips. He fervently believed that it was information that others would be eager to buy.

Steves taught his first class in 1975 at the University of Washington's experimental college. The class was entitled Travel Europe: Cheap! It was well attended and confirmed for him that he was suited to teaching travel seminars, and that perhaps the travel industry had a niche that he could carve out.

In 1976, Steves founded his company and named it Europe Through the Back Door, in keeping with his particular way of seeing the world. The company began with Steves and a seasonal staff. The "Back Door" approach espoused by Steves was about seeing the authentic Europe and not a tourist's view of things. "Back Door" travel was characterized by visiting towns off the traditional beaten paths and staying at simple yet comfortable family inns and hostels, what the company web site calls "safe, smart, inexpensive travel—low on stress and high on fun."

The company continued to offer low-cost tours each season and opened a small storefront on a main street in Edmonds. For

Company Perspectives:

Our mission at Europe Through the Back Door is to equip travelers with the confidence and skills necessary to travel through Europe independently, economically, and in a way that is culturally broadening. We value travel as a powerful way to better understand and contribute to the world in which we live. We strive to keep our travel style, our world outlook, and our business practices consistent with these values.

What we do—We teach do-it-yourself travel seminars—often for free; we research and write European guidebooks and produce a public television series; we sell European rail passes; we provide travel consulting and trip planning services; we organize and lead energetic tours throughout Europe; we sell travel bags, guidebooks, maps, videos and other traveler's supplies; we sponsor our Europe Through the Back Door Travel Center and web site; and we travel a lot.

someone who loved the independence of travel Steves remained rooted to his town and his first office and home stood across the street from his parents' piano business.

In 1980 Steves self-published his first travel guidebook, *Europe Through the Back Door,* and led his first tour. The guidebook continued in print and at the time of this writing was in its 22nd edition. His book credits included *Europe 101: History & Art for the Traveler, Mona Winks: Self-Guided Tours of Europe's Top Museums,* eight Country Guides covering all of Western Europe, City Guides for European top city destinations, phrase books, and *Postcards from Europe,* a travel biography of sorts.

Steves met his wife and travel partner Anne in 1983 while giving a lecture at the University of Washington. Anne, a nurse and politically active Catholic, brought an added dimension of social and political awareness to the couple's lives. The two had two children who were very well traveled and appeared in cameos on the video series.

Rick and Anne Steves routinely took an active role throughout their marriage to live out their commitment to social justice. The company web site featured links to nonprofit partners including Bread for the World, Mercy Corps, Green Peace, NORML, and Jubilee 2000. In addition, the company gave back to the community in numerous ways.

Getting Established Through Public Television in the 1990s

Steves made his mark in the travel industry by writing and producing a series of video documentaries in 1991 entitled *Rick Steves' Travels in Europe.* The videos were sent free to public television and helped to launch the company. Produced by Small World Productions and written by Steves himself, the films helped sell books and videos as well as market ETBD's tours and other services. The interest in the series and play time throughout the country's public television network was astounding. Steves got significant coverage from public television and in turn remained one of its most faithful fund raisers, making appearances around the nation during its semi-annual membership drives.

In 1991 the company relaunched its web site, ricksteves .com, and began to market travel-related items. Its suitcases and European rail passes continued to be big sellers through the internet site.

In 1992 ETBD released a series of five videotapes that were made from Steves' original series, *Travels in Europe.* The tapes were 55–80 minutes long, compared with the original 30-minute segments, and included suggested travel destinations. The videos were *London, Paris, and Amsterdam; Germany; Switzerland; Venice and Rome;* and *Northern Italy.*

The video travel guides were not only revered by PBS viewers, who had become a loyal following, but earned recognition for their content as well. The film series segment on Bavaria won the 1992 CINE Golden Eagle Award for Outstanding Nontheatrical Film.

In 1994 Steves wrote and released a travel video entitled, "How to Get the Most out of Your Eurorailpass." ETBD quickly became one of the most successful retail outlets for Eurorail passes in the United States. The video was given free to customers who purchased their Eurorailpass through ETBD.

Steves released *Travels in Europe* in 1995. The tapes focused on areas in Europe that had never been spotlighted by ETBD before. Steves spent more air time focusing on the cultural nuances of particular areas, particularly those of Eastern Europe from Prague to Turkey. Budapest, Vienna, Salzburg, and the French coastline or Riviera also were featured in the series. All of the travel films were hosted and written by Steves and produced by Seattle-based Small World Productions.

By 1996 ETBD led nearly 70 tours of Europe each year. Its newsletter was sent to more than 50,000 subscribers worldwide. The tour business at ETBD was highly regarded. The business offered more than 16 different tours annually. According to the tour description on the company web site, the tour itineraries differed greatly: "Some routes wander through several countries, weaving together Europe's best cities and cozy back door villages. Others dive deep into a specific country or region, with local people as a priority. Tour members can sleep in an isolated Swiss Alpine village, learn drinking songs from fishermen in a rustic island pub, or chat with an imam in a Turkish village." The company had many repeat customers who ascribed to the type of travel Steves promoted. Many returned to the company to tour its other destinations.

Europe Through the Back Door offered a series of travel seminars on countless subjects geared to the European adventurer. The company offered seven travel skills classes that included subjects such as packing light 101, art for travelers, hurdling the language barrier, European rail skills, women traveling solo, writing the inner journey, and getting the most out of your travel agent. In a 1996 *Seattle Times* interview, Steves related just what it was that made him believe he could be successful at teaching others about European travel. "I realized I could package my mistakes into a class," said Steves. "Each trip I made got so much easier. I was learning from what I did wrong. And so could other people." His hunch that others would be interested in what he could teach them brought ETBD hundreds of thousands of book sales, tour revenues, and merchandise sales each year.

Key Dates:

1969: Rick Steves takes his first trip to Europe with his parents.

1973: Steves takes his first solo trip to Europe.

1975: Steves teaches his first travel class called "European Travel—Cheap!"

1976: Europe Through the Back Door (ETBD) is founded.

1978: Steves graduates with degrees in European history and business and opens a piano studio.

1980: Steves leads his first tour and self-publishes his first travel book.

1991: ETBD produces *Travels in Europe, Series I*; rick steves.com is relaunched.

1992: The company starts selling suitcases and other travel merchandise.

1996: ETBD's mailing list exceeds 50,000 for its newsletter.

2000: ETBD expands its Travel Center, and leads 130 tours annually; *Rick Steves' Europe* premieres.

2001: *Rick Steves' Europe, Series I* with 16 episodes is produced.

2002: Tour group numbers peak at 5,000 on 25 tours.

2003: The 14-episode *Rick Steves' Europe, Series II* is produced; the company leads 150 tours.

The travel store at ETBD offered a vast array of accessories and apparel. The store did a good deal of its business through online orders and sold reversible travel skirts, money belts, packing cubes, and clotheslines. Its suitcases, day bags, and totes were among the company's top sellers as were its European guidebooks, videos, and DVDs. Helpful maps and atlases also rounded out the company inventory.

Expanding at the Beginning of the 21st Century

In 2000, ETBD augmented its Travel Center in Edmonds, adding a large new building. The travel center, built with a nod to European architecture, stood complete with stone gargoyles. The building housed the corporate offices, an extensive travel library, company store, Internet stations, and staff consultants.

The travel center grand opening led to a semi-annual European Travel Festival that drew large numbers of wayfarers to the site each year. Steves and his staff taught free travel seminars and hosted a variety of travel-related experiences for guests of all ages. Continuing free Saturday travel classes were offered as part of the weekly schedule.

In 2001 *Rick Steves' Europe, Series I* was produced. The video series included 16 episodes filmed throughout Western Europe in classic Rick Steves style.

September 11, 2001 had an incredible impact on world travel and ETBD tours were not immune from the wake of the terrorist attacks. The company had more than $1 million in tour cancellations after the U.S. disaster. In the following year, travel began to rebound and tours actually stood at an all-time high. ETBD hosted more than 5,000 people on 25 tours, a record high

for the company, and sales figures for ETBD's services and products were recorded at $20 million.

In 2003 *Travels in Europe, Series II* made its debut. The series included 14 episodes with Steves touring destinations throughout Western and Eastern Europe. Once again the videos were written and hosted by Steves but the content grew over time to include more interaction with the culture and traditions of the countries featured.

The ETBD Speakers Bureau offered presentations on many topics. There were eight separate offerings on Italy, four on destinations in France, several on the British Isles, and the remainder focusing on Eastern Europe, Amsterdam, Scandinavia, and Greece.

In 2004 *Rick Steves' Best of Eastern Europe 2004* was published by Avalon Travel Publishing. The interest in Eastern Europe had grown after the fall of communism and Steves was there to promote it and give aid to the interested traveler. Such cities as Prague, Czechoslovakia, and Budapest, Hungary, were Baroque landmarks to which Americans would flock in the late 1990s and 2000s.

Rick and Anne Steves made a significant charitable contribution in March 2004. They pledged $1 million to establish a housing complex in Snohomish County, Washington. The housing units, named Trinity Way, were managed by the YWCA and housed women and their families.

Europe Through the Back Door continued its service to travelers from its unique perspective with great success. The response to the company's travel guides and videos continued to grow. The relationship Steves built with public television was to their mutual benefit. PBS gave great exposure to ETBD and Steves became one of PBS's top promoters.

Despite a lagging dollar-to-Euro ratio Americans continued to travel to the continent in record numbers. ETBD, with its recognizable and helpful Rick Steves, appeared poised for future growth. The company had an appeal that seemed to suit the aging baby boomers who once traveled Europe with backpacks in the college years but were more likely to join the ETBD tour groups as they matured. Many such boomers could be seen throughout Europe carrying their Rick Steves bags, travel guides in hand, at all ETBD's favorite destinations.

Principal Competitors

Fodors; Frommers.

Further Reading

Beauregard, Sue-Ellen, "Rick Steves' Europe: London and Paris," *Booklist,* September 15, 2001, p. 240.

Brannon, Jody, "Notes and News," *Seattle Times,* May 5, 1991, p. L10.

Clinger, Will, "A Tour of Italy in Rick Steves Ultra-Popular Footsteps," *Chicago Sun Times,* August 16, 1998, p. 2.

Jackson, Kristin, "Back Door Savant: Europe Has Become Center of His World," *Seattle Times,* February 11, 1996.

Meyers, Susan Laccetti, "Special Europe Section: Eleven Hot Spots: See the Continent Through Expert Rick Steves," *Atlanta Constitution,* March 26, 2000, p. 11K.

Molnar, Jim, "Clipped Wings, 1990s Problems—Faltering Economy, Weak Dollar, and Threat of War—Will Shape 1991's Travel Outlook," *Seattle Times,* p. B5.

——, "The Voices of Travelers Who Are Going," *Seattle Times,* February 24, 1991, p. J2.

Rhodes, Elizabeth, "Local Travel Businesses Go Beyond Package Tours," *Seattle Times,* January 27, 1991, p. J1.

"Rick Steves' Europe Through the Back Door," *Whole Earth,* Winter 2000, p. 26.

Spano, Susan, "The Right Guidebook Earns Its Ticket," *New York Times,* April 28, 1996, p. 6.

Tarzan Ament, Deloris, "A Home-Grown Video Talent: Rick Steves," *Seattle Times,* August 23, 1992, p. J5.

——, "More Video Travels in Europe from Local Guru Rick Steves," *Seattle Times,* June 25, 1995, p. K4.

—Susan B. Culligan

Excel Technology, Inc.

41 Research Way
East Setauket, New York 11733
U.S.A.
Telephone: (631) 784-6175
Fax: (631) 784-6195
Web site: http://www.exceltechinc.com

Public Company
Incorporated: 1985
Employees: 619
Sales: $122.68 million (2003)
Stock Exchanges: NASDAQ
Ticker Symbol: XLTC
NAIC: 335999 All Other Miscellaneous Electrical
    Equipment and Component Manufacturing; 333314
    Optical Instrument and Lens Manufacturing

Excel Technology, Inc. is the parent company for several independently operated manufacturers of lasers and related equipment. The company's subsidiaries are active in design, development, manufacturing, and marketing of lasers used mainly in scientific and industrial applications—from researching subatomic particles to cutting material for automotive air bags. Through its subsidiaries, Excel has become one of the most successful companies to profit from the widening commercialization of lasers. Excel was founded in 1985 by a scientist eager to develop an advanced medical laser. In 1992 the tiny company acquired Quantronix, Inc., a much larger manufacturer of lasers for the scientific and industrial sectors. The purchase brought Excel an established product line, sales team, and manufacturing facility. Excel revived the struggling Quantronix and proceeded to buy a string of other small laser manufacturers over the next decade, bringing in companies with expertise in many different laser technologies and applications.

Excel now has about nine main subsidiaries engaged in laser-related manufacturing and design. Baublys-Control Laser manufactures lasers for marking and engraving, Continuum makes high-energy pulsed lasers for research purposes, and Synrad produces low-cost carbon dioxide lasers for cutting softer materials. Quantronix focuses on powerful solid-state lasers used for scientific applications as well as semiconductor, aerospace, and automotive manufacturing. Other subsidiaries produce subsystems related to laser applications. Cambridge Technology builds scanning components used to steer lasers, while Control Systemation makes systems for automation and parts handling. The Optical Corporation and Photo Research make precise optical products that can be used to measure light and color. Excel's manufacturing facilities are on the East and West Coast and in Germany and it has sales offices in the United States, Europe, and Asia. More than half the company's sales are to non-U.S. customers.

Rama Rao's Tunable Laser: 1980s

The story of Excel Technology starts with Rama Rao, a physicist who came to Chicago from his native India in 1979 to take a position as a teaching assistant at the Laser Laboratory of the University of Illinois. The son of a bookkeeper at a steel company in India, Rao got his bachelor's and master's degrees in physics in his home country. He arrived in Chicago the day before he was to report at his new job and took a room at the YMCA after having to pay most of his cash to an unscrupulous taxi driver who drove the newcomer all over the city. Nevertheless, Rao settled in and soon was able to take advantage of the opportunities available in the United States. He earned a doctorate in physics at Illinois, where he also met his future wife, Triveni Srinivasan. Srinivasan shared Rao's background in physics in both India and Illinois. By the mid-1980s Rao was on the faculty at the City College of New York, while his wife was a senior scientist at the Brookhaven National Laboratory on Long Island. She agreed to support the family when Rao took time off to explore the possibility of founding a company to develop advanced cancer-treating lasers. Rao's idea was that a light-sensitive drug could be injected into a cancer tumor and then activated by a laser, causing the tumor to disintegrate.

Rao established Excel Technology in 1985 as a Delaware corporation and drew up a business plan with a three-year design and development schedule. He visited nearly every venture capital firm in New York looking for funding, but the only support he received was about $1 million from the federal government's Small Business Innovation Research program. Rao used the money to outfit a laser development facility with a 220-volt power line in his garage. In 1989, he introduced the result of his efforts: "The world's first and currently only all solid state tunable Ti:Sapphire laser." Like all lasers, it produced a concentrated beam of light by stimulating a medium to emit light waves that are in phase and have the exact same frequency and direction of motion. The special feature of Rao's laser was that it was tunable, which meant that the frequency of the beam could be adjusted to cut different kinds of tissue. For about $100,000, customers could get one laser to perform several tasks, rather than purchasing a special system for each application. Excel sent the laser to the Massachusetts Institute of Technology, Hughes Medical, and other laboratories for testing. In May 1991 the company raised $3.6 million with an initial public offering on the NASDAQ. Sales in 1991 were about $250,000.

Purchase of Quantronix: 1992–94

Excel shifted its focus away from medical applications in October 1992 when it bought the laser manufacturer Quantronix Corporation, with headquarters on Long Island. The company was acquired in an exchange of stock worth about $9 million. While Excel had only a dozen employees at the time, Quantronix had about 200. The acquisition more than quadrupled Excel's annual sales and gave the once tiny company an established product line, substantial manufacturing facilities, and a marketing structure including a subsidiary in Darmstadt, Germany—which became known as Excel Technology Europe GmbH. Quantronix had been founded in 1967 and pioneered the first commercial CW-pumped Nd:YAG laser. It went on to install thousands of laser systems for industrial applications. In the 1970s, Quantronix began making laser systems designed to repair the photomasks, which are used to print computer circuit images on semiconductors. This became one of the company's primary markets. By the early 1990s, Quantronix had around $30 million in annual sales and an established presence in the industrial and semiconductor laser fields. The company was losing money, however, and needed the cash and new products offered by Excel.

The acquisition of Quantronix by Excel included two subsidiaries: Control Laser and The Optical Corporation. Control Laser, founded in 1970 and acquired by Quantronix in 1987, made lasers for marking and engraving applications in the automotive and aerospace industries. It had a manufacturing facility in Orlando, Florida. The Optical Corporation, located in Oxnard, California, made precisely polished optical compo-

nents used for measurement applications. The company had been founded as John Ransom Laboratories in 1932 to make precision optics for industrial customers.

Excel moved its offices to the Quantronix headquarters and appointed J. Donald Hill as head of the company. Hill was successful in improving the company's performance. In 1993, the first full year with Quantronix, Excel made a profit of $2.88 million on sales of $29.03 million. Meanwhile, the company was seeking approval for its new dental laser, which had the potential for less painful, noninvasive treatment of soft tissue. By late 1993 the laser was approved for sale in the United States and Germany. In the summer of 1994, Excel/Quantronix introduced a laser welding system that could be used for the repair of dental crowns and bridges. The dental products, however, never caught on for Excel. They accounted for 7 percent of sales in 1996 but were not a significant part of the company's operations by the end of the decade.

Continuing Acquisitions: 1995–98

Excel made more acquisitions in 1995. In February it paid $4.75 million in cash and stock for Cambridge Technology, Inc. of Massachusetts. Cambridge made components known as laser scanners, which are used to move a laser beam with a precise speed and direction. The company had been founded in 1978 to make instruments for biomedical research. Eventually it focused solely on "closed loop galvanometer technology," working to improve the accuracy and speed of optical scanners.

In October 1995 Excel paid $3.5 million for the Photo Research Division of Kollmorgen, which was rolled into the newly created subsidiary Photo Research Inc. This firm, located in Chatsworth, California, made photometric and spectroradiometer instruments—devices used to measure light and color. Photo Research had been founded in 1941 by cinematographer Karl Freund. He won Academy Awards in technical achievement for the development of the Spectra Color Temperature Meter, used to improve the quality of pictures in movies. Photo Research subsequently expanded the technology for use in the design and testing of other light-emitting products, such as instrument panels in cars. The company won four more Academy Awards in the 1970s for its products. In the 1990s, the photometers were miniaturized to allow for convenient portable measurements. By the time of Excel's acquisition, Photo Research's products were widely used for computer-related applications such as measuring the performance of cathode ray tube monitors or the flying height of disc-drive heads. Also in 1995, Excel settled litigation with the government relating to alleged misuse of some of the grants it received in the 1980s. Excel paid $2.7 million without admitting wrongdoing.

At the start of 1996, Rama Rao stepped down as CEO. Both he and his wife Triveni resigned their board positions to pursue other interests. Subsequently, J. Donald Hill advanced from his position as head of Quantronix to be CEO and chairman of the board. Hill worked closely with Antoine Dominic, who had joined Excel as chief financial officer in 1995 and became chief operating officer and president a few years later. Under their direction, sales of industrial and scientific lasers increased. With five separate subsidiaries now, Excel's sales were $66 million in 1997. Quantronix was the most profitable subsidiary. By 1998 it

Key Dates:

1985: Excel Technology is incorporated.
1989: Rama Rao introduces a tunable laser.
1991: Excel makes its initial public offering on the NASDAQ.
1992: Excel acquires Quantronix, including Control Laser and The Optical Corporation.
1995: Cambridge Technology and Photo Research are acquired.
1996: Rao departs Excel; J. Donald Hill becomes CEO.
1998: Synrad is acquired.
2000: Baublys is acquired.
2001: Control Systemation, Inc. is created.
2002: Continuum is acquired.
2003: D Green (Electronics) Limited is acquired.

had moved from its old facility in Hauppauge to a new 34,000-square-foot design and manufacturing facility at the Stony Brook Technology Center on Long Island.

Excel branched out to yet another area of laser technology with the purchase of Synrad, Inc. in August 1998. Synrad, based in Washington State, was a leading manufacturer of sealed carbon dioxide lasers, which were generally the lowest cost lasers available. While not as powerful as other lasers, CO_2 lasers could be used for less intense cutting applications: engraving trophies, slicing air bag material, cutting paper for computer-generated architectural models, and even giving blue jeans a worn look. Synrad had been founded in 1984 as a research company in southern California. At that time, most CO_2 lasers required a constant flow of carbon dioxide, which made them expensive to operate. Company founder Peter Laakmann developed a cheaper, less powerful sealed-tube version and set up a manufacturing plant in Washington. This new product made lasers accessible to a much wider range of clients, and Synrad grew quickly as it captured most of the market for CO_2 lasers. Eventually, competing firms developed similar products, but Synrad still had a strong market share when Excel bought it in 1998 for $22 million. Most of Synrad's lasers were sold to original equipment manufacturers who incorporated them into larger assemblies for specific applications. The acquisition of Synrad brought Excel's annual sales up to $88.9 million in 1999.

Expanding Its Reach: 1999–2004

Excel's acquisition spree continued well into the new millennium. Excel Technology Asia Sdn. Bhd., based in Malaysia, was created in 1999 as a marketing and distribution subsidiary for Control Laser and Quantronix Products in southeast Asia. European operations expanded as well. First, Excel Europe opened offices in Munich and Milan. Then, in July 2000, the European subsidiary acquired Baublys GmbH of Ludwigsberg, Germany, for $4.5 million in cash. Baublys designed and manufactured laser marking and engraving machines. Its facilities would allow Excel to offer European clients more customized products. Because Baublys had products similar to Excel's Orlando-based subsidiary Control Laser, the two companies

consolidated their activities at the start of 2002, although they remained legally separate. In the fall of 2000, Antoine Dominic was promoted to CEO of Excel and J. Donald Hill stayed on as full-time chairman of the board.

Early in 2001 Excel created a new subsidiary, Control Systemation, Inc. (CSI). CSI was originally a division of Control Laser that focused on automation and parts handling applications for laser machining systems. Now it became an independent company and moved into a new 80,000-square-foot facility in Orlando. The creation of a separate subsidiary for automation was expected to strengthen Excel's offerings for the industrial market. A global recession in 2001 reduced demand for Excel's engraving, scanning, and CO_2 laser products, pushing sales down 18 percent to $88.5 million after reaching a record $107.7 million in 2000.

Excel Technology Japan Holding Co., Ltd. was established in August 2002 to acquire OptoFocus Corporation, the company that distributed Excel's product line in Japan. In October of that year Excel used $13 million in on-hand cash to buy the scientific division of Continuum from Hoya Photonics. Continuum had offices in Santa Clara, California, France, and Japan. The company was producer of pulsed lasers, a new technology for Excel. Continuum had been founded in 1975 as Quantel International by Georges Bret, a laser technology professor at the University of Orsay in France. The company developed expertise in the production of pulsed solid state Nd:YAG lasers and changed its name to Continuum in 1990. In 1991 Hoya Corporation, a Japanese optical glass manufacturer, bought the company. By this time, Continuum had developed a laser device for tattoo removal, which proved to be very successful. Under Hoya, the expansion of the medical division held back the development of the company's scientific and commercial divisions, so these were sold to Excel, where they would have room to grow. After the sale, Continuum combined its sales team with Quantronix.

In April 2003 Excel created another Asian sales office, the Excel SouthAsia JV based in Mumbai, India. Excel had 50 percent ownership in the venture, which would focus on product sales in south Asia. In December of that year Excel bought D Green (Electronics) Limited (DGE). Based in the United Kingdom, DGE developed and manufactured power supplies for laser systems. Sales in 2003 grew to $122.68 million and net income was $11.32 million, in large part due to revenues from Continuum and the new Japanese sales office. In 2004 increased sales in marking systems, scanners, and CO_2 lasers were putting Excel on a path to exceed the previous year's sales. In addition, the company had zero debt since most of its subsidiaries had been bought with existing cash reserves. As always, all of Excel's subsidiaries were pushing ahead with new product development. Excel's diverse array of laser products and the wide range of applications for its systems made it likely that the company would continue to post profits.

Principal Subsidiaries

Baublys-Control Laser Corporation; Cambridge Technology, Inc.; Continuum Electro-Optics, Inc.; Control Systemation, Inc.; Photo Research, Inc.; Quantronix Corporation; Synrad, Inc.; The Optical Corporation; Excel Technology Europe

GmbH (Germany); D Green (Electronics) Limited (U.K.); Excel Technology South-Asia Pvt. Ltd. JV (India); Excel Technology Asia Sdn. Bhd. (Malaysia); Excel Technology Japan K.K.

Principal Competitors

Spectra-Physics, Inc.; Thales Laser; Coherent, Inc.; New Wave Research Incorporated; Spectron Lasers USA Inc.; Hans Laser; ROFIN-SINAR Technologies Inc.; Fotona; Trumpf-Haas; NEC Corporation; Seiko; Alltec; Cheval Frere.

Further Reading

Bennet, Ann Becker, ''Dr. Rama Rao: A Practical Dreamer,'' *Long Island Business News,* September 14, 1992, p. 17.

Bernstein, James, ''Companies Focus Efforts to Market Laser Device,'' *Newsday* (Long Island, N.Y.), January 14, 1992, p. 37.

Darby, Edwin, ''Entrepreneur Aims New Laser Device at Cancer,'' *Chicago Sun-Times,* July 7, 1991, p. 51.

Fetters, Eric, ''The Laser's Edge,'' *Herald* (Everett, Wash.), June 10, 2002, p. C1.

Gabriele, Michael C., ''Quantronix in Deal to Buy Control Laser As Industry Shrinks,'' *Metalworking News,* May 9, 1988, p. 1.

Kincade, Kathy, ''Excel Buys Continuum Pulsed-Laser Group,'' *Opto-electronics Report,* November 1, 2002, p. 1.

Krause, Reinhardt, ''Laser Firm's Strategic Focus: Acquisitions,'' *Investor's Business Daily* (Los Angeles), April 25, 1996.

Martorana, Jamie, ''Quantronix to Expand Tech Site,'' *Long Island Business News,* September 7, 1998, p. 1A.

Noble, Moshe, ''Laser Company Continuum Expands Products, Boosts Profits,'' *Business Journal,* June 27, 1994, p. 6.

Wilhelm, Steve, ''Synrad's Laser Focus Fuels Growth,'' *Puget Sound Business Journal,* March 8, 1996, p. 12.

—Sarah Ruth Lorenz

EXX Inc.

1350 E. Flamingo Road, Suite 689
Las Vegas, Nevada 89119-5263
U.S.A.
Telephone: (702) 598-3223
Web site: http://www.newcor.com

Public Company
Incorporated: 1899 as Fitchburg Machine Works
Employees: 1,000
Sales: $135.5 million (2003)
Stock Exchanges: American
Ticker Symbol: EXXA
NAIC: 336299 All Other Motor Vehicle Parts
   Manufacturing; 339932 Game, Toy, and Children's
   Vehicle Manufacturing

EXX Inc. is a Las Vegas-based holding company with independent subsidiaries grouped into two business segments: Mechanical Equipment and Plastics and Rubber. The Mechanical Equipment segment is composed of seven companies. Deco Engineering, Inc. manufactures heavy-duty truck engines and powertrain components and assemblies. Blackhawk Engineering, Inc. produces large gray iron, nodular iron, and steel foundry castings used by companies serving the agricultural market. Rochester Gear, Inc. and Machine Tool and Gear, Inc. manufacture automobile shafts, axles, transmission parts, differential pins and gears, rear axle shafts, and other machined components. The Bay City division of subsidiary Newcor, Inc. designs and makes machines and systems used by automotive, appliance, and consumer goods customers in their welding, assembly, forming, heat treating, and testing processes. The Howell Electric Motors Division of SFM Corp. produces specialty motors used in such applications as blowers for air conditioning systems, floor scrubbing and polishing motors, and motor pump assemblies used in food machinery products. The final unit in the Mechanical Equipment Segment is TX Technology, which provides the telecommunications industry with cable pressurization and monitoring systems to prevent signal reduction while keeping tabs via telephone lines. EXX's Plas-

tics and Rubber Segment consists of five subsidiaries. Boramco, Inc. and Plastronics Plus, Inc. manufacture a variety of automotive parts, including transmission shift boots, steering column and gearshift lever seals, air conditioning ducts, body and dash panel grommets, fuel filler seals, hose and wire brackets, speaker seals, and vacuum control systems. Henry Gordy International, Inc. produces a line of impulse toys, generally sold at the point of purchase at toy stores, department stores, drugstores, and supermarkets. Handi-Pac, Inc. makes a variety of pre-school toys. Finally, Hi-Flier, Inc. is a major manufacturer of kites. Chairman and CEO David A. Segal owns a controlling interest in the publicly traded company.

Company Roots Dating to the 1800s

The corporate lineage of EXX traces back to the Civil War when Sylvester C. Wright started the Fitchburg Machine Works in Massachusetts, which was incorporated in 1899. The company acquired the plant and assets of Seneca Falls Manufacturing Company, Inc., based in Seneca Falls, New York, in 1924 and adopted the name Seneca Falls Machine Co. The company operated in Seneca Falls for the next four decades, producing automatic lathes and special machinery, such as a machine to automatically manufacture automobile camshafts. In 1968 the company moved to New Jersey, where it was reorganized and renamed SFM Corporation. In 1970 SFM acquired one of the subsidiaries that would become part of EXX, paying $2.5 million for Howell Electric Motors of Plainfield, New Jersey, where SFM maintained its headquarters.

In 1984 EXX's chairman and CEO, David A. Segal, was a director of SFM, owning 10 percent of the company's stock, when he decided to seek control of the business. With the board's blessing he took control and became SFM's chief executive. At this stage the company manufactured machine tools and electric motors, but in 1987 Segal took SFM far afield in acquiring Henry Gordy Inc., a Yonkers, New York-based manufacturer, importer, and marketer of toys. These assets were then transferred to a newly formed subsidiary, Henry Gordy International, Inc. The modification of SFM's business mix continued over the next few years. In 1991 the Seneca Falls machine tool operation was sold for $2 million and in 1993, Waterbury Headers, Inc., which had been acquired a dozen years earlier, also was divested. A year later SFM moved into the telecommunications business, forming two subsidiaries, TX Systems Inc. and TX Technology Corp., which then bought the operating assets of TX Technologies Inc. and TX Software Inc. at a bankruptcy sale. The new units made air drying systems, sensors, and monitoring systems for a number of major telephone companies. Also in 1994 SFM supplemented its toy business by acquiring Colorado-based Hi-Flier Manufacturing Co., one of the leading makers of kites and model airplanes in the United States. These assets were folded into a new subsidiary named Hi-Flier Inc.

Sudden Celebrity in 1994

SFM was a little known company in the early 1990s, generating about $18 million in annual revenues, with sales having dropped for four consecutive years. Nevertheless it was profitable, paying a dividend of 75 cents per share in 1992 and 90 cents in 1993. But the company was thinly traded on the American Stock Exchange, with a float of only 363,000 shares because Segal owned nearly half of the company's stock. On most days that the American Stock Exchange was opened, in fact, not a single SFM share changed hands. Then, in August 1994 SFM experienced sudden celebrity and became one of the hottest stocks in the country. On August 10 the company announced its second quarter numbers, which showed that sales had increased to $11.6 million from $4.7 million, and per share profits rose from 19 cents to 60 cents during the same period the year before. Most of this improvement was due to Henry Gordy adding watches to the mix and the licensing of cartoon characters, such as a line of Mighty Morphin Power Ranger toys, but also of importance was the Hi-Flier acquisition. Because kites were a seasonal item, sales were strong in one quarter and virtually nonexistent in another. SFM booked sales when they shipped to wholesalers and stores, which fell in the second quarter, and not when the kites were actually sold to consumers. Whatever the reasons for the strong numbers, SFM caught the wave of investor enthusiasm over the sudden jump in sales, and combined with the limited number of shares available the price of SFM shares skyrocketed. In one day the price jumped from $5.5 to $14.875, with more than 50,000 shares trading hands, a number that was eight times the volume for the previous month. Over the next 11 sessions another 550,000 shares traded and the price topped $34. In fact, in a single week more shares were traded than in any previous year. Segal, although pleased, was somewhat puzzled by the run-up. He told the *Sunday Gazette-Mail* that he received calls from brokers who had just bought several thousand shares of SFM stock for their clients and wanted to know what business the company was in. The price approached $42 before receding to $26.25 early in September, only to go on another run that would bring the price of SFM stock to a new high of $46.25 before the hysteria finally began to subside.

In late July SFM had already taken steps to increase the float through the issuance of two new classes of shares and a four-for-one stock split. For each unit of current SFM stock, shareholders received three shares of Class A stock and one share of Class B stock. The class A stock elected one-third of the SFM board, while the Class B stock elected two-thirds. As explained by *Barron's*, ''Because of the different voting rights, Segal can easily maintain near-majority control of the company by keeping his B shares, while greatly diluting current holders by selling his A shares.''

The stock split took place in October 1994. As part of the issuance of two classes of stock, the company also decided to reorganize as a holding company with each of its businesses operating as separate units. Thus, in October 1994, shareholders approved the merger of SFM Corp. with a new holding company named EXX Inc. The new name was adopted in November 1994. Subsequently the company's headquarters was moved from Plainfield, New Jersey, to Las Vegas. For 1994 the company recorded sales of nearly $45.5 million, a significant increase over the $18 million generated a year earlier. Net income improved from $611,000 or 23 cents per share to $2.7 million, or 99 cents per share. Almost all of the improvement came in the toy segment, which experienced an increase in sales from $10.7 million to $37.2 million.

Business fell off in 1995, due primarily to decreasing popularity of the Mighty Morphin Power Rangers. Sales declined to $30.5 million, but net income remained strong, totaling $2.3 million or 86 cents per share. Sales of the Mighty Morphin Power Rangers continued to slide in 1996 and the company failed to sign any successful new licenses to fill the gap. As a result toy sales dropped from $21.4 million to $9.5 million, and although the Mechanical Equipment Group showed some improvement, EXX as a whole posted sales of $19.8 million, leading to a net loss on the year of $1.6 million.

EXX looked to bolster its toy business in 1997 through acquisitions. In February of that year, through a newly formed subsidiary, Steven Toy Inc., it paid $400,000 for Handi Pac, Inc., manufacturer of preschool, ride-on, classic, educational, and other toys. Later in 1997, EXX acquired the assets of Northbrook, Illinois-based Novelty Design International, LLC, which made candy-filled toy products. These additions to the company's toy lines helped the toy segment to increase sales by $2.7 million over the previous year, but a softening in the telecommunications equipment market resulted in declining sales from the Mechanical Equipment Group. As a consequence EXX lost $223,000 in 1997 on sales of $22.3 million.

Buying Newcor Shares in 2000

Over the next two years the Mechanical Equipment Group posted modest gains, the result of an improvement in the telecommunications area, but the toy segment continued to deteriorate, a condition all too common in the toy industry at the time. EXX was unable to secure any new licenses, and suffered from increased product costs and stagnant consumer demand. Revenues in the toy segment fell to $9.6 million in 1998 and $7.3 million in 1999. Although overall sales fell to $20.9 million in 1998, EXX returned to profitability, earning $761,000 or 6 cents per share. In 1999 revenues improved to $21.2 million and net

Key Dates:

1899: Fitchburg Machine Works is incorporated.
1924: Fitchburg Machine is renamed Seneca Falls Machine Co.
1933: National Electric Welding Machines Company is incorporated.
1968: Seneca Falls Machine is renamed SFM Corp.
1969: National Electric Welding is renamed Newcor, Inc.
1994: SFM is renamed EXX, Inc.
2003: EXX acquires Newcor.

income grew to $2.5 million, or 19 cents per share. While the Mechanical Equipment Group was able to benefit to some extent from the Y2K phenomenon in 1999, sales for the year decreased, and the toy segment continued to flounder.

It was clear by now that EXX needed to make an adjustment to its business mix to sustain any kind of significant growth. In 2000 EXX attempted to acquire Detroit-based Newcor, Inc., which Segal believed would fit well with the company's Mechanical Equipment Group. Newcor made precision machined products, rubber and plastic parts, and special machines for the automotive, medium and heavy-duty truck, agricultural vehicle, and appliance industries.

Newcor was founded in 1933 as National Electric Welding Machines Company, and adopted the Newcor name in February 1969. The company expanded rapidly in the 1980s and 1990s, completing a number of acquisitions, including several of the subsidiaries that would be key components of EXX. Rochester Gear was added in 1985, Blackhawk Engineering in 1994, Boramco in 1996, Plastronics Plus in 1997, and Machine Tool & Gear in 1997. The company made other acquisitions during the late 1990s, but overall it grew too quickly and had difficulty turning a profit. As a result, its stock price slipped, and in the final months of 1999 Segal began acquiring Newcor stock for both EXX and himself. By early 2000 EXX had a 13.24 percent stake in the company and Segal made it clear that he might make a hostile takeover attempt. The Newcor board adopted a

shareholder's rights plan to check his attempt. In April, when Newcor stock was trading from $1.80 to $2.75, Segal's offer of $4 a share to buy the company was rejected. Segal bided his time and continued to buy Newcor stock on the open market while the company's business continued to slip. In 2001 he controlled a large enough stake to gain a seat on the Newcor board and by the summer EXX-backed executives began to take over. In February 2002 Newcor filed for Chapter 11 bankruptcy and would not emerge for another year, at which time EXX bought the business for $5.9 million. Later in 2003 EXX also acquired a Newcor subsidiary, Midwest Rubber and Plastic Inc.

The addition of Newcor, a much larger company, transformed EXX, as it shifted away from the toy industry. In 2003 the company posted sales of $135.5 million, compared with $16.2 million the year before. Net income grew from $836,000 to $6.2 million. EXX was beginning a new chapter in its history. How it would fare as a company heavily dependent on the automotive industry remained to be determined.

Principal Subsidiaries

Newcor, Inc.; SFM Corp.; Henry Gordy International, Inc.; Hi-Flier Inc;.; TX Systems, Inc.; TX Technology.

Principal Competitors

A.O. Smith Corporation; Baldor Electric Company; Franklin Electric Co., Inc.

Further Reading

Lacter, Mark, "Toymaker Stocks Play Well on Wall St.," *Los Angeles Daily News,* October 12, 1994, p. B1.
Miel, Rhoda, "Newcor's Suitor Helping It Through Chapter 11," *Crain's Detroit Business,* March 4, 2002, p. 6.
"SFM Corp. Holder Says He Might Seek Control of Company," *Wall Street Journal,* October 18, 1984, p. 1.
"Speculators Send Toy Company Stock on Roller-Coaster Ride," *Sunday Gazette-Mail,* September 4, 1994, p. 10B.
Wyatte, Edward A., "High As a Kite," *Barron's,* August 29, 1994, p. MW4.

—Ed Dinger

First Industrial Realty Trust, Inc.

311 S. Wacker Drive, Suite 4000
Chicago, Illinois 60606
U.S.A.
Telephone: (312) 344-4300
Fax: (312) 922-6320
Web site: http://www.firstindustrial.com

Public Company
Incorporated: 1993
Employees: 329
Sales: $359.9 million (2003)
Stock Exchanges: New York
Ticker Symbol: FR
NAIC: 525930 Real Estate Investment Trust

First Industrial Realty Trust, Inc. (FIRT) is a real estate investment trust (REIT) based in Chicago, Illinois, focusing on the acquisition, development, and management of industrial properties in the top 25 industrial markets in the United States. At the close of 2003, FIRT's portfolio included 423 light industrial properties, 163 research and development or flex properties, 123 bulk warehouse properties, 92 regional warehouse properties, and 33 manufacturing properties. All told, FIRT controlled 57.9 million square feet of gross leasable area located in 22 states. The REIT's shares are traded on the New York Stock Exchange.

Forming the REIT in 1993

FIRT was established as a REIT in 1993, growing out of the real estate holdings of Jay H. Shidler, FIRT's chairman of the board. After earning a degree from the University of Hawaii, Shidler launched a real estate business in 1970, opening an office in Honolulu. He expanded his interests to the mainland and through his company, The Shidler Group, acquired property in 39 other states and Canada. In 1986 he hired Michael T. Tomasz, who would serve as FIRT's first chief executive officer, as the managing partner of his Chicago office. Tomasz, who grew up in Illinois, had spent a decade working as an industrial real estate broker before going to work for Shidler. He proved to

be aggressive, quickly snapping up $100 million worth of Chicago buildings. But then the stock market crashed, followed by a savings and loan scandal and a recession, all of which combined to dry up the capital that Shidler, Tomasz, and others needed to continue building their real estate portfolios. In the early 1990s property buyers rediscovered the REIT structure as a way to raise funds from the public markets, as well as to gain the use of shares as a currency in making acquisitions.

REITs had been created by Congress in 1960 as a way for small investors to become involved in real estate in a manner similar to mutual funds. REITs could be taken public and their shares traded just like stock, and they also were subject to regulation by the Securities and Exchange Commission. Unlike traditional stocks, however, REITs were required by law to pay out at least 95 percent of their taxable income to shareholders each year, a provision that severely limited the ability of REITs to retain internally generated funds for expansion. During the first 25 years of existence, REITs were allowed only to own real estate, a situation which hindered their growth. Third parties had to be contracted to manage the properties. Not until the Tax Reform Act of 1986 changed the nature of real estate investment did REITs begin to become truly viable. Limited partnership tax shelter schemes that had competed for potential investments were shut down by the Act. Separately, the Act also permitted REITs to provide customary services for property, in effect allowing the trusts to operate and manage the properties they owned. Despite these major changes in law, the REIT was still not a fully utilized structure. In the latter half of the 1980s the banks, insurance companies, pension funds, and foreign investors (in particular, the Japanese) provided the lion's share of real estate investment funds. The resulting glutted marketplace led to a shakeout that hampered many real estate firms. With real estate available at distressed prices in the early 1990s, REITs finally became an attractive mainstream investment option and many real estate firms went public starting in 1993.

Shidler split his real estate holdings, creating two REITs. In 1993 he took the first public, San Francisco-based TriNet Corporate Realty Trust, Inc., which focused on specialty commercial properties and would make its mark in corporate leaseback arrangements. The second would be FIRT, headed by Tomasz, which packaged Shidler's midwestern industrial holdings as well as the holdings of three other developers, whose properties were either recently purchased or would be purchased through the proceeds of the initial public offering (IPO). The other components of the REIT were the industrial properties of Troy, Michigan-based Damone/Andrew Associates Inc., Minnesota-based developer Steven Hoyt, and Pennsylvania-based developer Anthony Muscatello. Management of the three developers would stay on to run the properties. When FIRT completed its IPO in June 1994 it owned 226 industrial properties containing 17.4 million square feet of gross leasable area located in nine cities.

Growing Pains in the Mid-1990s

Envisioned as a national REIT focusing on predictable manufacturing, distribution, and warehouse properties, FIRT expanded quickly, but in the drive to achieve scale it bought some second-tier properties—older buildings with less-creditworthy tenants, located in less desirable markets. During good times, these assets were not a problem, but later in the 1990s they came back to trouble FIRT. The REIT also quickly accumulated a lot of secured debt, which prevented it from selling properties and adjusting its asset mix. That situation was rectified in 1996 when FIRT took steps to shift its capital structure to unsecured debt. According to *National Real Estate Investor*, "The company deleveraged itself by lowering its debt-to-market cap, and it did two equity offerings ... which together raised $250 million of common equity. Once this was completed, First Industrial went to the rating agencies and received a BBB rating from all. . . . This enabled the company to pay off the secured debt and replace it with long-term, fixed-rate debt, which in return freed up the company's assets." As a result, FIRT was able to sell assets as needed, and with the increased flexibility it could follow an even more aggressive acquisition strategy.

FIRT preferred to acquire entire portfolios using stock in a process known as the UPREIT transaction. The company used its size to its advantage by convincing acquisition targets to sell out for stock. In essence, sellers traded their stock for a higher market cap company, the stock of which traded more freely and was safer and more likely to increase in value. Moreover, these were "entity deals," which left management teams in place. Not only was the retention of management an important selling point, it also served FIRT's effort to build up its management depth. Because the real estate industry had been devastated from the late 1980s to the early 1990s, there had been little opportunity to train new real estate talent. Entity deals provided a significant way for FIRT to recruit the people it needed to grow the business.

In the first three years, FIRT shied away from speculative development, but in 1996 it formed a Development Services Group, geared toward serving existing tenants who might be looking to move or expand. Although most of the construction

projects would be build-to-suit projects, they still required the establishment of a dedicated unit to serve that function. For the time being, however, growth resulted solely from acquisitions. In 1996 FIRT expanded its portfolio by 45 percent and entered five new markets through five UPREIT transactions: Indianapolis, Cincinnati, Columbus, Dayton, and Cleveland. Revenues improved from $106.5 million in 1995 to more than $140 million in 1996. Net income grew from $12.3 million to $35.7 million.

FIRT grew at an even faster clip in 1997. It paid $862.3 million in eight UPREIT transactions, acquiring 389 properties, containing 22.9 million square feet. During the course of the year, it entered nine new markets. The company also added 1.7 million square feet through ten developments that were placed in service during the year, at a cost of $50.3 million. Another 12 projects were in progress. Revenues increased to $210.4 million in 1997, with net income approaching $52 million. FIRT was now the third largest REIT in the country.

REITs had enjoyed a strong run, but in 1998 the bubble burst and the price of REIT stocks plummeted. FIRT was hit harder than most, its shares losing 30 percent of their value from January to November, as some of the early, less desirable acquisitions now came back to hurt the company. The *Wall Street Journal* described the predicament that FIRT and other REITs experienced during this period: "With shares plunging, the dealmakers couldn't make acquisitions with stock. They didn't have much cash for deals because strict regulations require REITs to pass on most of their cash flow to investors. And forget about debt, one of the favorite tools of the private real-estate industry." Tomasz and other REIT executives were "stuck in dealmaking limbo—even as the property market itself, fueled by the long economic expansion sizzled."

Making Changes and Targeting the Top 25 Industrial Markets in the Late 1990s and Early 2000s

As the price of its stock fell, Tomasz saw deal after deal fall through. One FIRT executive told the *Wall Street Journal* that the period between May and September 1998 was "like the Bataan death march." Tomasz was forced to conduct constant road shows in order to convince analysts, rating agencies, and shareholders that FIRT had a bright future. But the REIT's problems began to take their toll on Tomasz, leading to high blood pressure and chest pains. Unable to make deals, FIRT had become little more than a property management company, which was not his strong suit. He was blamed when expenses got out of line and profits were not maximized on some properties. In November, Tomasz resigned in what was described by all parties as a mutual decision. He was replaced by his protégé, chief operating officer Michael W. Brennan, in November 1998. Brennan had started working with Tomasz in 1986, serving as an acquisition executive for The Shidler Group in the Chicago office.

Brennan believed that most of FIRT's problems were more perception than reality. Nevertheless, he recognized that the REIT had to prove it could act as a sound real estate manager. He also looked to sell $150 million in properties, initiate cost-cutting measures, and develop other revenue streams, such as renting rooftops for telecommunication antennas, pursuing commissions on vending machines, payphones, and billboards, and selling insurance and recycling services to tenants. FIRT

Key Dates:
1993: The REIT is formed.
1994: An initial public offering is completed.
1996: The Development Services Group division is started.
1998: The CEO is replaced.
2000: The top 25 industrial markets are targeted.

also developed a novel plan to, in effect, sell tax deferrals. Individuals who had just sold property and had a period of time to reinvest the money to avoid capital gains taxes could buy a FIRT property and lease it back to the REIT for less than the property's value. FIRT pocketed the difference and the individual could later sell the property back to FIRT. In this way, the investor deferred taxes and FIRT earned a fee.

In 1999 FIRT began adopting a strategy of concentrating on the top 25 industrial real estate markets in the United States in an effort to take advantage of the rising demand of the e-commerce and supply chain management industries. The goal was to become the "stockroom for e-commerce." After a year-long process completed in early 2000, FIRT researched and identified what it considered to be the top 25 markets for industrial real estate. The REIT was already involved in 21 of those markets and launched plans to enter the other four: Miami, San Diego, San Francisco, and Seattle. In addition, FIRT decided to exit eight markets: Cleveland, Columbus, Dayton, Des Moines, Grand Rapids, Hartford, Long Island, and New Orleans/Baton Rouge. FIRT began divesting properties to follow this plan, but with the collapse of many Internet start-ups, the demand for industrial properties by e-commerce companies failed to meet expectations and began to actually shrink. Because dot-coms never added much space, their loss had little impact on FIRT. Of more importance to the REIT was the supply-chain revolution, a move by companies to reorganize their facilities to improve the costs of labor, freight, and materials handling. As the economy began to falter, making such changes became even more important to companies, and FIRT became the beneficiary.

In 2002 FIRT began to rearrange its portfolio, exiting such second-tier markets as New Orleans, Des Moines, and Columbus, Ohio. At the same time, the REIT looked to increase its

presence in Los Angeles, New Jersey, and at home in Chicago. FIRT also looked for new sources of income. In 2002 it established an Institutional Fund with the Kuwait Financial House, a global investor with more than $8 billion in assets, to acquire industrial properties in the United States. In 2003 FIRT expanded its relationship with the Kuwait Financial House, creating a $25 million fund to target the acquisition of net lease industrial properties in the United States. For the most part, however, during the early years of the new century, FIRT became more of a seller than a buyer. Analysts, according to press reports, grew concerned that the REIT was propping up its dividend through property sales, implying that FIRT was not as strong as it appeared. As a result, despite being the largest diversified industrial REIT in the country, FIRT saw its stock trading at a discount to its rivals. There was also concern about the company's large number of leases, some 60 percent, that would soon expire. FIRT's management downplayed these questions, and carried on with attempts to grow during difficult economic conditions in the real estate market. In the early months of 2004, the REIT entered the San Diego market and opened a regional office in Milwaukee.

Principal Subsidiaries

First Industrial Finance Corporation; FI Development Services Corporation; FR Brokerage Services, Inc.; FR Management Services, Inc.

Principal Competitors

CenterPoint Properties Trust; EastGroup Properties, Inc.; Highwoods Properties, Inc.

Further Reading

Andreoli, Tom, "Will This REIT Fly," *Crain's Chicago Business,* May 30, 1994, p. 4.

Avidon, Eric, "First Industrial to Focus on Top 25 Markets," *National Mortgage News,* February 7, 2000, p. 19.

Corfman, Thomas A., "Market's Message to Unsettled REIT: It's the Properties, Stupid," *Crain's Chicago Business,* November 23, 1998, p. 3.

Heath, Tracy, "First Industrial Continues Growing Talent Pool," *National Real Estate Investor,* August 1997, p. 34.

Martinez, Barbara, "Mike T Is Back!," *Wall Street Journal,* September 2, 1999, p. A1.

—Ed Dinger

FLANDERS
PRECISIONAIRE®
FOREMOST IN AIR FILTRATION

Flanders Corporation

2399 26th Avenue North
St. Petersburg, Florida 33734
U.S.A.
Telephone: (727)822-4411
Toll Free: (800) 800-2210
Fax: (727) 823-5510
Web site: http://www.flanderscorp.com

Public Company
Incorporated: 1950 as Flanders Filters, Inc.
Employees: 2,166
Sales: $182.78 million (2003)
Stock Exchanges: NASDAQ
Ticker Symbol: FLDR
NAIC: 333412 Industrial and Commercial Fan and
    Blower Manufacturing; 551112 Offices of Other
    Holding Companies

Flanders Corporation designs and manufactures air filters that are used in residences, commercial office buildings, and by a broad range of industries with a need for maintaining specialized manufacturing environments. Aside from its residential and commercial heating, ventilation, and air-conditioning systems, Flanders supplies high-performance air filtration systems to industries associated with semiconductor manufacturing, pharmaceutical production, and nuclear power and materials processing. The company also designs and manufactures most of its own production equipment, as well as the glass-based air filter media for most of its products. Flanders' customers include Wal-Mart Stores, Abbott Laboratories, Motorola, Merck, Upjohn, and Home Depot.

Origins

Flanders was founded as Flanders Filters, Inc. in 1950. The company was started by A.R. Allan, Jr., who formed the enterprise in Riverhead, New York, the home of Flanders for the first two decades of its existence. Allan created the company to manufacture technologically advanced filters that were used for specific industrial applications. Flanders' first filters were sold to operators of atomic power reactors and nuclear fuel manufacturing facilities. In the ventilating systems of such plants, Flanders' filters served as safety devices that played a critical role in radioactive containment, removing small irradiated particles that otherwise would be released into the atmosphere. From its founding to the late 1950s, Flanders relied almost exclusively on supplying filters to atomic power reactors and nuclear fuel manufacturing plants, establishing itself as one of the first companies to compete in the market for highly specialized filters.

Given the limited demand for the type of filters Flanders made during its first decade, the company's growth potential was restricted. The design and production of filters for nuclear power facilities, however, did position the company on the vanguard of technological advancements in filter development. As new demands for sophisticated filters emerged, the potential for Flanders' growth increased. Such was the case during the 1960s, when researchers discovered that the manufacturing process used by film developers could be made significantly more efficient by incorporating high efficiency particulate air (HEPA) filters and lower-efficiency filters into production facilities. Flanders responded to the discovery by expanding its filtration product line to cater to the new demand, marking a turning point in the company's development.

The diversification into designing and manufacturing HEPA and lower-efficiency filters added significantly to Flanders' growth potential. The lower-efficiency filters, which eventually became known as ASHRAE-grade filters, increased efficiency standards for manufacturers involved in numerous other industries, giving Flanders its first exposure to widespread market demand. The company's production output increased substantially, driving its revenues upward and stretching its manufacturing capacity to the limit. The growth sparked by the foray into HEPA and ASHRAE-grade filters also led to an important decision made by the company's management; the decision to vertically integrate the company's operations as it grew. As part of the production process for its filtration products, Flanders used paper media consisting of a nonwoven matrix of glass microfibers. By the mid-1960s, the company was producing its own media, giving it a level of self-sufficiency that distinguished it from nearly all its competitors.

Company Perspectives:

Flanders Corporation, headquartered in St. Petersburg, Florida, designs, manufactures and markets precision high-performance filtration products. Flanders is a vertically integrated company, with nine filter assembly plants, two metal working facilities, and a paper mill among its thirteen operating sites. The Company's air filtration products are critical to many high-technology industries, including semiconductors, ultra-pure material handling, biotechnology, pharmaceutical production, synthetics manufacturing, and the containment of airborne radioactive particulates in nuclear facilities.

Flanders experienced its first sense of mass-market appeal for its products during the 1960s. The discovery of the benefits of using high-performance filters in the film developing industry led participants in other industries to consider incorporating sophisticated ventilating systems in their facilities. Flanders, using its skills in developing filtration products designed for radiation containment to diversify into answering the needs of film developers, was poised to reap the benefits of the widespread interest in high-performance filters. The company's business grew encouragingly, creating a bustle of activity at the Riverhead manufacturing plant. Before the end of the decade, the company was pressed to meet supply with demand, forcing management to consider the expansion of the Riverhead facility or the erection of a new, larger facility. Management, which by this point included Thomas T. Allan, who joined Flanders in 1964, decided to build a new facility, a decision that also led to the company's abandonment of Riverhead as its headquarters. Beginning in 1968, Flanders began to move its entire operation from Riverhead to Washington, North Carolina. The move took almost two years, ending in 1969 when the company settled into its new, 65-acre site in Washington.

By the time the move to Washington was completed, Flanders had its second generation of management in place. Thomas Allan, who would steward the company for the next two decades, built upon the foundation established during the 1960s. By the mid-1970s, the growth of Flanders' filter business required Allan and his team to confront the company's need for additional manufacturing capacity. The Washington plant was expanded in 1978, its tenth year in operation, and expanded again in 1984, further testifying to the increasing strength of the company's business. The efforts to vertically integrate Flanders' operations recorded progress as well, resulting in the establishment of a second paper mill abutted by additional warehouse space and a new sheet metal work area.

Flanders in the 1990s

Flanders' success during its first four decades of business established its reputation as a respected manufacturer of high-performance filters. The company's manufacturing activities were almost exclusively restricted to HEPA and ASHRAE-grade filters, however, confining the company within a niche of the filter industry. By the beginning of the 1990s, the company had yet to record more than $20 million in annual sales. Flanders' stature, both physically and financially, did not begin to increase substantially until the company broke free from its niche and diversified into other areas of the filter industry. This turning point in the company's history occurred 45 years after its inception, ushering in a new era of accelerated growth.

One of the principal architects of Flanders' strategic diversification program was Robert R. Amerson. Amerson joined Flanders in 1987 as the company's chief financial officer. The following year, he was appointed chief executive officer and president of the company. The decision to substantially expand Flanders' product line was made in the mid-1990s, long after Amerson had established himself in his leadership position. The move toward diversification was triggered in December 1995, when Flanders was acquired by a company named Elite Acquisitions, Inc. At the time of the acquisition, Elite, which was formed in 1986, operated as a publicly traded corporate shell without any significant assets. In January 1996, Elite formed a new subsidiary named Flanders Corporation (Flanders Filters, Inc. became an Elite subsidiary one month earlier) and merged with the subsidiary, leaving Flanders Corporation as the parent company for Flanders Filters, Inc.

The corporate maneuverings signaled the beginning of Amerson's campaign to diversify, a campaign to be conducted primarily by acquiring other companies involved in the filter industry. In May 1996, Flanders completed its first major acquisition, purchasing a Bath, North Carolina-based company named CSC, which operated as a charcoal filter manufacturer. CSC's activated charcoal filters were used in the containment of potentially dangerous biologically engineered microorganisms. One month after acquiring CSC for $4.5 million, Flanders spent $2.2 million for a Stafford, Texas-based company named AirSeal that produced mid-range custom filter housings for heating, ventilation, and air-conditioning (HVAC) systems. In September 1996, Flanders completed the largest acquisition in its history, paying $25.2 million for Precisionaire. A manufacturer of filter products for commercial and residential HVAC systems, Precisionaire operated manufacturing facilities in Bartow, Florida; Terrell, Texas; and Auburn, Pennsylvania.

The acquisitions completed in 1996 broadened Flanders' market exposure, driving its sales upward. Annual revenues during the early 1990s hovered around $20 million, rising to $38 million in 1995, the year before Flanders embarked on its acquisition spree. In 1996, the company's sales soared to $73 million. Flanders' net income for the year totaled $3.5 million, or more than ten times the amount posted four years earlier. Physically, the company had recorded robust growth as well, with the acquisitions of 1996 giving Flanders five separate manufacturing plants. By the end of the year, the company operated seven production facilities ranging in size from 40,000 square feet to more than 200,000 square feet.

Flanders' acquisition campaign continued after 1996, as the company sought to increase its product line and to strengthen its existing businesses. At the end of 1997, after completing several small acquisitions during the year, the company secured a $30 million credit line with SunTrust Banks to finance further acquisitions. The money was to be used to purchase as many as five companies in 1998. One of the biggest acquisitions completed in 1998 was the purchase of San Diego-based Eco-Air

Key Dates:

1950: Flanders Filters, Inc. is founded in Riverhead, New York.
1968: Flanders moves to larger manufacturing facilities in Washington, North Carolina.
1995: Flanders is acquired by Elite Acquisitions, Inc., triggering accelerated expansion; Elite merges with Flanders the following year.
1996: Flanders' acquisition spree begins with the purchase of three filter companies.
1998: Flanders acquires Eco-Air Products, Inc.

Products, Inc., an air filter manufacturer, in June. The transaction, valued at nearly $20 million, was hailed by Amerson. "Eco-Air is a regional powerhouse on the West Coast, our weakest domestic sales territory," he explained in a June 30, 1998 interview with *Business Wire.* "In addition, their four additional manufacturing facilities, including a large plant in Mexico, give us complete coverage of the United States."

Growth Slowing in the Early 21st Century

As Flanders entered the 21st century, the effect of the company's mission to diversify through acquisitions was apparent in its stature, both physically and financially. The less than $40-million-in-sales company that existed before the decision to diversify was made in late 1995 grew to a company with nearly $200 million in sales by 2000. Physically, the commitment to acquire had created a company of genuine national scope, with ten separate manufacturing facilities in operation, stretching from Bartow, Florida, to San Diego, California.

During the first years of the new decade, Flanders focused its development efforts on creating air filtration systems designed to maintain clean air in residential and commercial settings. The growth of this market niche, which after the terrorist attacks of September 11, 2001, was fueled by concerns about anthrax and other microbes, was expected to accelerate the expansion of the global air filter market. According to the McIlvaine Company, a leading industry analyst, the worldwide market for air filters

was expected to grow from $3.5 billion in 2000 to $5 billion by 2005. Flanders' executives also were looking for growth from other segments of the air filter market, including the increasing use of higher-performance filters in commercial and residential spaces.

Against the backdrop of expected industrywide growth, Flanders recorded static sales during the early years of the 21st century. After generating $194 million in sales in 2000, the company's sales volume decreased for three successive years, slipping from $189 million in 2001 to $184 million in 2002 and $182 million in 2003. The anemic sales growth stood in sharp contrast to the robust gains recorded during the late 1990s, giving Amerson and his team some cause for concern. As the company prepared for the future, it hoped to reverse the trend of waning sales growth and return to the dynamic progress achieved during the late 1990s.

Principal Subsidiaries

Flanders Filters, Inc.; Flanders Precisionaire Inc.

Principal Competitors

American Air Filter International; Farr Company; HEPA Corporation; Purolator Air Filtration Company; Donaldson Company, Inc.; Clark Corporation.

Further Reading

"Flanders Announces 1997 Earnings of $5.8 Million, or $0.32 Per Share," *Business Wire,* March 26, 1998.
"Flanders Corp. Acquires New Carbon Filtration Technology," *Business Wire,* April 7, 1997.
"Flanders Corp. Announces Two Expansions," *Business Wire,* April 8, 1997.
"Flanders Corporation Completes Acquisition of Eco-Air Products, Inc.," *Business Wire,* June 30, 1998.
Roberts, Ricado, "Deal Flow Alert: Flanders Airs Its Alternatives," *Mergers & Acquisitions Report,* April 3, 2000.
Stuart, Scott, "In Flanders Field, Acquisitions Will Come," *Mergers & Acquisitions,* December 15, 1997, p. 43.

—Jeffrey L. Covell

Genting Bhd.

24th Fl., Wisma Genting, Jalan S
Kuala Lumpur 50250
Malaysia
Telephone: +60 3 2161 2288
Fax: +60 3 2161 5304
Web site: http://www.genting.com.my

Public Company
Incorporated: 1965 as Genting Highlands Sdn Behad
Sales: MYR 4.23 billion ($1.11 billion) (2003)
Stock Exchanges: Kuala Lumpur
NAIC: 551112 Offices of Other Holding Companies;
113210 Forest Nurseries and Gathering of Forest
Products; 213112 Support Activities for Oil and Gas
Field Exploration; 221122 Electric Power
Distribution; 237210 Land Subdivision; 311225 Fats
and Oils Refining and Blending; 322130 Paperboard
Mills; 423430 Computer and Computer Peripheral
Equipment and Software Merchant Wholesalers;
522291 Consumer Lending; 522298 All Other Non-
Depository Credit Intermediation; 531110 Lessors of
Residential Buildings and Dwellings; 531120 Lessors
of Nonresidential Buildings (Except Miniwarehouses);
541511 Custom Computer Programming Services;
541512 Computer Systems Design Services; 541611
Administrative Management and General Management
Consulting Services; 561110 Office Administrative
Services; 561520 Tour Operators; 713120 Amusement
Arcades; 713990 All Other Amusement and
Recreation Industries; 721110 Hotels (Except Casino
Hotels) and Motels

Genting Bhd. is one of Malaysia's most powerful corporate conglomerates and serves as a holding company for a variety of domestic and international businesses developed by Chinese-born tycoon Lim Goh Tong. Genting's most well-known holding is its majority control of publicly traded Resorts World Bhd, Tong's vehicle for the huge Genting Highlands Resort complex not far from Kuala Lumpur. That complex also features the world's largest hotel, First World Hotel, which will top 6,300 rooms upon completion and bring the total number of rooms in the resort, including staff accommodations, to more than 15,000. Genting's Hospitality and Leisure division is also its largest, and includes the Awana resorts hotel chain and a controlling stake in Star Cruises Ltd., the world's leading cruise ship operator. In addition to its Malaysia holdings, Genting has expanded its hospitality interests internationally through casino development and management agreements in Australia, the Philippines, and the Bahamas, as well as stakes in Canada's Pacific Lottery Corporation and the United Kingdom's London Clubs International. Related Genting holdings include its Plantation division's control of more than 63,000 hectares of oil palm and other plantation property. The company's Property division meanwhile owns a 6,800-acre plot of land in Kulai, which Genting has been developing through another publicly listed subsidiary, Asiatic Indahpura. Since the early 1990s, Genting has diversified its operations somewhat, including a move into Paper & Packaging through its majority ownership of the Genting Sanyen Paper Mill complex in Kuala Langat, one of Malaysia's largest paper producers. The company has also entered the power generation market through its control of Genting Sanyen Power Sdn Bhd, which operates the power plant at the group's Kuala Langat paper complex. Genting Sanyen Power also controls the Lanco Kondapalli gas-fired power plant in India. Genting's final division is its Oil & Gas division, with oil and gas exploration and recovery operations and interests in China and Indonesia. Lim Goh Tong, Malaysia's wealthiest businessman, retired as head of the company in early 2004 at the age of 86, and has been succeeded by son Lim Kok Thay. Genting's shares are listed on the Kuala Lumpur stock exchange. In 2003, the company posted sales revenues of MYR 4.2 billion ($1.1 billion).

Rags to Riches in the 1960s

A native of China's Fujian province, Lim Goh Tong, the fifth of seven children, was forced to leave school at the age of 16 after his father's death. Then, in 1937, Lim immigrated to Malaysia, taking with him a suitcase and the equivalent of just $175. Lim's initial journey to Malaysia ended soon after, however, when the Japanese occupation of the country—and a beating—sent him back to China. Yet, when Japan later occupied the Fujian province, Lim returned to Malaysia.

Steeled by these experiences, Lim set out to build a business empire in his new homeland. Marriage, to Lee Kim Hua, whose grandfather founded the Bangkok Bank, helped Lim establish strong connections with the region's expatriate Chinese community, and by the early 1950s, Lim had already built up a thriving business as an engineering contractor, as well as a plantation owner. Among Lim's most successful projects was the Kemumu Irrigation Scheme in Ketalan.

Lim's destiny was to change in the mid-1960s, however. In 1964, while working as a subcontractor for the Cameron hydroelectric plant, Lim visited the Cameron Highlands resort, which had long attracted British colonists seeking to escape the tropical heat of the Malaysian lowlands. Located far from Kuala Lumpur, the journey to Cameron was arduous and long. Yet the resort provided Lim with an inspiration: that of building a retirement retreat for himself and other Malaysians nearer to Kuala Lumpur.

Lim began scouting for a location for his project, settling on the mountain range between Genting Sempah and Gunung Ulu Kali, just 58 kilometers from Kuala Lumpur. Yet, arriving at the top of the mountain, some 1,800 meters above sea level, Lim quickly expanded his proposed project from a simple retirement retreat to a full-scale resort catering to the Malaysian tourist trade, and especially to the large Chinese community in the country.

Lim then learned that the young Malaysian government, led by Tunku Abdul Rahman, had been formulating its own plans to develop the Gunung Ulu Kali location, but lacked the financial and political stability to do so. Lim approached Rahman with his own idea, and received the go-ahead to proceed, on the condition that Lim himself build a road leading from Kuala Lumpur to the mountain top. Lim, backed both politically and financially by Haji Mohd Noah, as well as members of the increasingly wealthy Chinese community, established a new company, Genting Highlands Sdn Behad, in 1965.

Lim himself invested much of his savings, which he augmented by the sale of his 810-acre rubber plantation, in Segamat. With capital of MYR 2.5 million, Lim began petitioning the governments of Pahang and Selangor for the more than 6,000-hectare site spanning the two Malaysian provinces. Genting's acquisition of the freehold for the entire site was only completed in 1970.

In the meantime, Lim personally led the work on the construction of the 20-kilometer road leading to the site, originally slated to be completed over a six-year period. Lim also offered to install a telecommunications tower on the site that the government had planned to build lower down on the mountain. The government agreed, and promised a subsidy of MYR 900,000 if Lim built the road in three years instead of six.

Genting met that deadline, and by 1969 was ready to begin construction on the resort itself, starting with the Highlands Hotel. The company received a surprise boost from Prime Minister Rahman, who, during the cornerstone ceremony for the hotel, suggested that the government would be willing to grant Lim a license to open a casino at the resort. Lim soon after filed the petition for the license—the only casino license to be granted in the majority Muslim country. Lim also expanded the original 38-room hotel design to 200 rooms.

The Highlands Hotel opened in 1971 and proved an immediate success, attracting the Chinese community in Malaysia, but also—as the only casino in the region—from neighboring countries. Lim quickly expanded his concept for the resort, and received a five-year tax break from the government in order to invest in the resort's expansion. The development of the resort from a casino-focused hotel operation to a full-scale resort featuring tourist attractions and other family-oriented amenities also opened the site to Malaysia's Muslim population, who were barred from the resort's casino. In addition to the tax-break from the Malaysian government, Genting raised fresh investment capital through a listing on the Kuala Lumpur stock exchange in 1971.

Expanding Holdings in the 1980s

Lim's direct involvement in the construction and expansion of the Genting Highlands resort did not prevent him from extending Genting's business interests into other areas. One of the company's first expansion moves was the creation, in 1977, of a Plantation Division to oversee Genting's growing palm oil and other holdings. The Plantation Division was placed under a new company, Asiatic Development, which was listed on the Kuala Lumpur exchange in 1982. By 2000, Genting's plantation holdings would top 63,000 hectares.

Genting also developed other property and resort interests. The company later launched its own chain of resorts in Malaysia, starting with the Awana Genting highlands Golf & Country Resort, located at the original Genting site. The Awana brand was then extended to include the Awana Kijal Golf, Beach & Spa Resort, a beachfront site in Terengganu; and Awana Porto Malai on Langkawi Island.

Genting's expanding hospitality interests led the company to restructure in 1989. Genting itself was reestablished as a holding company, while its hospitality and leisure businesses, including the Genting Highlands resort, were transferred to a new company, Resorts World Bhd. The new subsidiary was then listed on the Kuala Lumpur exchange.

Resorts World immediately launched a new and ambitious five-year development program that helped transform the Genting Highlands site into one of the world's largest and most popular tourist destinations. Into the mid-1990s, the company spent more than MYR 2 billion adding three new hotels, as well as new attractions, including two new theme parks—one of

Key Dates:

1937: Fujian province, China, native Lim Goh Tong immigrates to Malaysia and later establishes successful engineering contracting business.

1965: Lim Goh Tong decides to build a tourist resort, called Genting Highlands, and begins constructing a roadway to the top of the Genting Sempah and Gunung Ulu Kali, near Kuala Lumpur; forms Genting Highlands Bhd.

1969: Company begins construction of first hotel and receives first and only casino license in Malaysia.

1971: Highlands Hotel opens for business; Genting Highlands Bhd goes public with listing on Kuala Lumpur exchange.

1977: Company launches Plantation division.

1982: Plantation division goes public as Asiatic Development Bhd.

1989: Company restructures as Genting Holdings, placing hospitality and leisure operations into new subsidiary, Resort World Bhd, which goes public that year.

1990: Five-year development plan is implemented, adding three new hotels as well as theme parks and other amenities to Genting Highlands resort site.

1993: Company launches Star Cruises, which becomes Asia-Pacific's leading casino cruise operator.

1994: Company diversifies with purchase of Sanyen Paper Mill complex, which also includes a 720 MW power plant, placed under Genting Sanyen Power Sdn Bhd.

1996: Genting enters oil and gas exploration market with purchase of 45 percent stake in British Gas' Muturi PSC in Irian Jaya, Indonesia.

1998: Paper mill moves into packaging with launch of corrugated packaging plant.

2000: Construction begins on new 6,300-room First World Hotel, at Genting Highlands, the world's largest hotel.

2001: Stake in Muturi PSC is sold to British Petroleum.

2003: Genting acquires equity interest in power plant in India as part of continued industrial and geographic diversification.

2004: Lim Goh Tong retires at the age of 86.

which was built indoors. By the end of the decade, the resort already featured seven hotels with some 4,000 rooms. The company also began development of a new 17-kilometer roadway providing easier access from the northern side of the mountain, and built the Asian region's longest—and the world's fastest—Skyway monorail connecting Gohtong Jaya at the base of the mountain to the resort, at a total cost of MYR 128 million. In the early 2000s, Resorts World also became responsible for widening the original ten-kilometer road into a four-lane highway.

This latter project was completed in large part to ease the expected increase in traffic to come with Genting's most ambitious development project—that of the construction of the 6,300-room First World Hotel. Upon completion, the hotel, which featured its own indoor theme-park, was slated to become the world's largest hotel. The company began adding 4,000 new rooms for its staff accommodations, raising the projected total number of rooms on the resort site to 15,000.

Diversification for the New Century

Much of Genting's success was due to its monopoly position as the sole casino owner in Malaysia. The increasingly conservative mood of the Muslim population in the country made it unlikely that new challengers would appear in the domestic market. However, that same shift in religious sentiment raised the possibility that Genting's own license might one day be withdrawn. At the same time, Genting faced new competition elsewhere in the region, as a number of neighboring countries began authorizing the construction of casinos.

Genting took a multifaceted approach to confronting this situation. On the one hand, the company continued redeveloping the resort site itself away from its earlier emphasis on its casino operation to expand more broadly into the tourist and family entertainment market. Yet the company also began expanding its hospitality and leisure operations beyond its sole focus on the Genting Highlands resort.

One of the company's earliest diversification moves was the establishment of the Star Cruise line in 1993. The company began operating casino cruises in southeast Asia, building up a fleet of 18 ships with more than 23,000 beds. By the end of the decade, Star Cruise was already the Asia Pacific region's largest cruise operator. The acquisition of NCL Holdings and its Miami, Florida-based Norwegian Cruise Lines in 2000, helped position the company as one of the world's top three cruise line operators.

Genting also began expanding its hospitality operations into other markets, acquiring casino management and development contracts in such markets as Australia, the Bahamas, and the Philippines. The company also launched a new Property division, conducted through subsidiary Asiatic Indahpura, which began developing a 6,800-acre landsite in Kulai, Johor.

Genting increasingly sought to expand its international holdings, while at the same time seeking to buttress its reliance on the more volatile tourism market with an extension into other industries. This effort was led in large part by Lim's son, Lim Kok Thay. In 1994, the company launched a new Paper & Packaging division through the creation of Genting International Paper holdings Ltd. and the acquisition of the Sanyen paper mill in Kuala Langat, the country's largest brown grade paper manufacturer. In 1998, the company expanded that operation downstream, launching production of corrugated packaging. The new subsidiary was then renamed the Genting Sanyen Group.

As part of the Sanyen acquisition, the company also extended into the power generation market, taking over the paper site's 720 MW gas-fired power plant. This operation took on the name of Genting Sanyen Power, and in 1994 became Malaysia's first Independent Power Producer, launching production in 1996. Genting later turned to the international power generation market, acquiring an equity stake in the Lanco Kondapalli gas-fired plant in India in 2003.

In the meantime, Genting had ventured into the oil and gas exploration market. In 1996, the company bought a 45 percent stake in British Gas's Muturi exploration operations in Indonesia (sold to British Petroleum in 2001). Genting continued developing its oil and gas interests, however, which included the launch of the Enhanced Oil Recovery Project in China's Gulf of Bohai in 2000. In June 2004, another Genting subsidiary, Sanyen Oil and Gas Ltd., acquired the production sharing contract for the Anambas Block in West Natuna, Indonesia.

By then, Lim Goh Tong, who had been honored with the title Tan Sri in 1979, had already announced his decision to retire at the age of 86. At the beginning of 2004, leadership of Genting was passed to Lim Kok Thay. Inheriting the multibillion-dollar empire established by his father just 40 years before, the younger Lim promised to remain true to the values that had enabled Lim Goh Tong to build up one of Malaysia's—and the Asian region's—largest fortunes.

Discussing future plans with *The Star*, Lim Kok Thay stated: "My father's advice to me is to hold the group steady as she goes, rather than to rush headlong into any wild expansion programme. That's my intention too as we need to digest what we have already done." The younger Lim nonetheless pointed to a further internationalization of the group's operations in the future. Yet the company's hospitality and leisure component, including its iconic Genting Highlands resort complex, appeared certain to remain its largest and most emblematic division into the new century.

Principal Subsidiaries

Asiatic Development Berhad (54.9%); E-Genting Holdings Sdn Bhd; Genting Highlands Tours and Promotion Sdn Bhd; Genting Hotel & Resorts Management Sdn Bhd; Genting (Labuan) Limited; Genting Management and Consultancy Services Sdn Bhd; Genting Overseas Holdings Limited (Isle of Man); Resorts World Bhd (56.8%).

Principal Competitors

Sime Darby Berhad; PPB Group Berhad.

Further Reading

Burton, John, "Genting Bets on the Benefits of Extending Its Global Reach," *Financial Times*, January 7, 2004, p. 29.

"Gambling on a Dream," *Malaysian Business*, October 16, 2002.

"Getting up High Where It Belongs," *New Straits Times*, March 21, 2004.

Knipe, Michael, "Profits and Family Values," *Times*, March 31, 2004, p. 21.

Ng, Pauline S.C., and Elaine Ang, "A Tribute to Tan Sri Lim Goh Tong," *Star*, January 1, 2004.

Tan Sri Lim Goh Tong, *My Dream*, Kuala Lumpur: Genting Bhd., 2003.

—M.L. Cohen

Great Plains Energy Incorporated

1201 Walnut St.
Kansas City, Missouri 64141-9679
U.S.A.
Telephone: (816) 556-2200
Fax: (816) 556-2418
Web site: http://www.greatplainsenergy.com

Public Company
Incorporated: 1922 as Kansas City Power & Light
    Company
Employees: 2,475
Sales: $2.14 billion (2003)
Stock Exchanges: New York
Ticker Symbol: GXP
NAIC: 221112 Fossil Fuel Electric Power Generation;
    221113 Nuclear Electric Power Generation; 221121
    Electric Bulk Power Transmission and Control;
    221122 Electric Power Distribution

Great Plains Energy Incorporated is the holding company for Kansas City Power & Light Company (KCPL), which serves both residential and commercial customers in 24 counties in western Missouri and eastern Kansas, an area that covers some 4,600 square miles. Nearly a half million residents use the electricity provided by KCPL. Great Plains Energy's other principal subsidiary is Strategic Energy, which the company plans to use to expand into new territories.

Arrival of Electricity in Kansas: Late 1800s

KCPL and Great Plains Energy exist today because a young man named Edwin Ruthven Weeks witnessed an electric arc light demonstration at a Philadelphia exposition in 1876. Weeks, who eventually became the company's first superintendent, was so impressed that he immediately returned home and persuaded three men—Joseph S. Chick, L.R. Moore, and Judge William Holmes—to consider investing in the new technology. Holmes became the first president of the new company. In 1881 the men purchased an exclusive contract for $4,000 to provide power to two counties; in 1882 they incorporated the Kawsmouth Electric Light Company.

Originally serving 13 commercial customers, the plant became one of the first to use dynamos with automatic regulators. The system utilized Professor Elihu Thomson's Thomson-Houston regulator, an invention that balanced electric output to make service possible to multiple customers. Downtown Kansas City was the first section of town to be lighted; by the end of 1882, 48 merchants utilized the system.

The company reincorporated as the Kansas City Electric Light Company in 1885—the earliest of many corporate changes. As former company President Robert A. Olson explained in *Kansas City Power & Light Company: The First Ninety Years,* ''A popular reason for the change of name was that 'Kawsmouth' suggested some hungry monster. Today we might say it did not project the right image.'' That same year, the company's chief competitor, Kansas City Gas Works, was demolished in an explosion. Former customers turned to the electric company for lighting. The system was at capacity by 1887.

Because the early Thomson-Houston arc lighting system was bulky and required frequent adjustments, residential customers began demanding incandescent lights. Weeks developed the Edison Electric Light & Power Company to meet this need and tied its operations closely to the Kansas City Electric Light Company.

New Management Bringing New Struggles and Successes: Early 1900s

Over the course of the next decade, increased competition, rate wars, and the 1893 financial panic created difficult times for the utility industry. Rather than invest the significant amount of capital needed for expansion, Kansas City Electric Light Company's directors looked around for a purchaser. J. Ogden Armour, one of the owners of the Metropolitan Street Railway Company of Kansas City and heir to the famous meat-packing company, became interested in the floundering firm. He and several associates purchased the Kansas City Electric Company in early 1900. Meanwhile, the company's pioneer, Edwin Weeks, became friends with Thomas Edison and eventually founded the National Electric Light Association, later known as the Edison Electric Institute.

Infused with new capital, the company was able to buy up competing electric suppliers and eliminate costly duplication of power distribution lines. Eventually the Kansas City Electric Light Company was the city's only source for electrical power, warranting a new power plant. The new plant, built in 1903, near the Kaw River on Central Avenue, was nearly destroyed by a flood that poured 20 feet of water and mud into the plant shortly after its completion; but after three months of cleanup, service was resumed. One year later a larger plant was constructed at Second and Grand River. Kansas City Electric Light Company also began supplying steam heat to the downtown area.

Armour and his partners managed two major businesses, the lighting system and the street railway. Because they expected the streetcar industry to grow more rapidly than the electric industry, any planning for expansion of power-production facilities was geared toward the railway system. Increasing power demands of the railway system took precedence over the needs of electrical customers. Eventually this dual operation took a toll on Kansas City Electric Light Company.

When Armour took steps to refinance his corporate debt around 1911, investors had become wary of dealing with a company combining railway and electrical interests. The company suffered from this new tide of opposition and, in 1911, went into receivership. After five difficult years, the U.S. District Court approved a reorganization plan. The street railway was separated from the electric company, although the streetcar interests retained control of several major power plants. The new electric corporation formed at this time was named Kansas City Light & Power Company. John H. Lucas, the former attorney for both railway and electric companies, was appointed president.

Armour was still the company's principal stockholder, but he and Lucas wanted an experienced manager leading the company. They hired 55-year-old Joseph F. Porter. The well-known electrical equipment installer and troubleshooter took over in the fall of 1917. He found the weakened company's most urgent needs were for more energy and more efficient plants. Porter ordered work begun on the Northeast Power station, the company's first modern generating complex. Savings from this new plant helped the company's net income increase from $8,550 in 1919 to $562,000 in 1920, and reach $2.6 million five years later. All the while rates to customers decreased.

Increased construction costs forced the company to refinance, prompting a second reincorporation, as Kansas City Power and Light Company in 1919. Three years later, another reorganization occurred when the company acquired the Carroll County Electric Company. At this time, the company underwent its final name change, becoming the Kansas City Power & Light Company. In 1923, Armour's interest was sold; one year later, the Continental Gas & Electric Corporation purchased the controlling interest. Under the umbrella of the United Light and Power holding company system, the corporation maintained this position until 1950.

Under Porter's 21-year watch the company prospered. He enlarged KCPL's service territory through acquisition of other utilities in western Missouri and eastern Kansas, and he increased generating capacity from 60 to 260 megawatts. Assured of a strong financial base, he was able to order construction of the 32-story Power & Light office building. This structure became the tallest building west of the Mississippi River at the time of its construction and has remained a prominent feature on the downtown Kansas City skyline ever since. Capitalization rose from $7 million to $82.5 million under his leadership. In 1938 Porter resigned his position as president, though he remained chairman of the board until his death in 1942. Olson offered this statement, written by Porter in 1934, to demonstrate Porter's philosophy of change: "We were a struggling utility, held in low esteem by the community . . . but we became a corporation recognized by all alike as a fair-dealing organization which had adequately, effectively served and developed the territory."

Growth and Rising Demand for Power: Mid-1900s

World War II slowed any domestic industrial expansion, including activity at KCPL. Instead the utility concentrated on providing service to 129 defense industries. The end of the war created new demands for service though. Harry B. Munsell, a quick decision-maker who was committed to customer relations, became KCPL's president and soon instituted several changes. In 1947 KCPL interconnected utilities in Missouri, Kansas, and Iowa for the first time, enabling the various companies involved to share reserve capacity. The Hawthorn Station, situated on the Missouri River, was started in 1948, and the first of two units were completed in 1951. Two other units followed and were fully operational by 1955. The total power output from this plant nearly doubled the company's capacity prior to its construction. The units burned coal or natural gas or a combination of both. In 1950 the holding company dissolved and KCPL again became independent.

In 1952 KCPL acquired assets of Eastern Kansas Utilities, but still found that additional power was required. Work began in 1954 on the Montrose Station in Henry County, Missouri. This site was selected on the basis of close proximity to west central Missouri's surface coal mines and was made possible by the development of high-voltage transmission lines to carry electrical current over longer distances.

In the early 1950s the advent of air conditioning caused such a strain on the power system—one window unit could more than double a customer's energy usage—that KCPL managers realized a drastic change was needed to meet demands. In 1954 KCPL adopted a new concept called load center system design. Large capacity distribution substations, each serving up to 15 square miles, were constructed to ease the handling of large electric loads. The company sold several assets in the late 1950s and early 1960s to raise capital and concentrate operations around Kansas City.

In 1960 Harry Munsell retired as president; he died one year later. Recalling Munsell's impact during 13 years at the helm of KCPL, Olson stated, "His years were marked by significant efforts to expand, modernize, and decentralize, and his leadership prepared the company for the decade of opportunity that was ahead."

The demand for power in and around Kansas City was not leveling off. Analyses indicated the company's customer load was doubling every ten years. Because the need for additional power was so great, five utilities in western Missouri and Kansas entered into a 33-year cooperative agreement called the Mokan Pool in 1962. This enabled the participants to share reserve capacity and coordinate planning of expensive new generating facilities.

Diversification and Continued Growth: 1960s to Early 1990s

In 1969 KCPL built its first large-scale service center, a 500-megawatt addition to the Hawthorn Station. The five units at the station were constructed to burn either coal or natural gas. The first phase of the 1,370-megawatt, two-unit La Cygne station began operating in 1973, burning high-sulfur coal. This facility became the largest single investment ever made in Kansas upon completion in 1977, at a cost of $190 million. Due to inflation, this was more than twice the cost of the Hawthorn Station.

Customers' conservation measures taken after the 1973 Arab oil embargo affected operations. Growth slowed within the company as demand decreased. Concern for the environment grew nationwide during these years, resulting in expensive pollution-control requirements. KCPL adopted several cost-

cutting measures in response to these events. In 1975 KCPL sold distribution properties in Wyandotte County, Kansas, to Kansas City's Board of Public Utilities. KCPL sold other distribution facilities and the city's traffic signal system in 1977.

That same year construction began on a 1,150-megawatt nuclear facility called Wolf Creek near Burlington, Kansas, about 90 miles southwest of Kansas City. The plant was erected to supplement KCPL's coal-fired systems. In 1980 the coal-burning Iatan station, located about 40 miles northwest of Kansas City, began operating, while Wolf Creek opened in the fall of 1985. Since construction, the Wolf Creek nuclear plant, which represented almost 16 percent of KCPL's generating capacity, had been closed five times for refueling. The $3.05 billion facility attracted some negative publicity for KCPL over subsequent rate increases.

In the early 1980s, KCPL celebrated a centennial of operation. At this time the utility underwent an extensive reorganization, streamlining financial operations and emphasizing personnel training and development. The company also adopted KCPLAN, a formal corporate strategy for the future. In developing this plan, KCPL consulted with an advisory panel representing various community interests. KCPLAN detailed strategies for energy conservation, pricing policies, and production facility rehabilitation.

In 1990 KCPL sold its steam system to Trigen Energy Corporation with the provision that the steam not be used to generate competing electricity. During the same year, KCPL attempted a hostile takeover of Kansas Gas and Electric Company—the first attempt of this kind by a utility company in more than 50 years. Kansas Gas and Electric held half interest in KCPL's La Cygne and Wolf Creek generating facilities and some insiders noted that the two companies disagreed on expansion plans. KCPL management felt that the company would benefit from Kansas Gas and Electric's excess capacity and tendered an offer of $27 per share directly to stockholders. After Kansas Gas and Electric took measures to fight the takeover and considered merging with other companies, KCPL dropped the pursuit at the end of the year.

Compliance with federal pollution regulations became a major challenge facing KCPL and other utilities, especially after the Clean Air Act of 1990. The measure was designed to decrease acid rain by reducing sulfur dioxide emitted into the atmosphere by ten million tons between 1980 and 2000. The government began using an emission credit system in 1990, so that electric companies using coal-burning plants would receive credits allowing a limited amount of sulfur dioxide emissions and then could purchase more credits if their emissions were above target levels. KCPL anticipated these regulations as early as 1983 and began using low-sulfur coal from mines in Wyoming. The company expected to have extra credits available to sell to other utilities because of this early compliance.

In 1991 KCPL transferred headquarters from the landmark Power & Light Building, which had been occupied by the utility for more than 60 years, to new offices at 1201 Walnut. This was part of a $23 million upgrade of corporate facilities, which also included construction of two service centers to handle an increased customer base. Company representatives indicated that moving into state-of-the-art, all-electric offices would help KCPL test new technology, thereby speeding availability to customers.

That same year KCPL initiated several programs to increase responsiveness to the concerns of employees, customers, and the community. After realizing that some employees were failing tests for promotions because they were unable to read, the company started a confidential literacy program for plant employees and their families. In addition, in response to public concerns about utilities' adverse impact on the environment, KCPL opened the Environmental and Research Services Division to oversee regulatory compliance and design community programs. Some of the environmental issues with which this division was involved included planting native prairie grass near power plants, reinstating the peregrine falcon to the area by attaching nests to downtown Kansas City buildings, and restoring wetlands. KCPL executives hoped that community involvement would increase employee morale, improve the company's public image, and facilitate expansion by demonstrating environmentally safe practices.

Uncertainty and Reorganization: Mid-1990s to 2000s

In the mid-1990s KCPL became embroiled in discussions of mergers and hostile takeovers that lasted for several years. In 1994 KCPL entered merger talks with Western Resources, Inc., a Topeka-based energy provider. KCPL rejected Western's advances, however, and two years later, in January 1996, KCPL agreed to merge with UtiliCorp United Inc. The deal, worth an estimated $1.3 billion, would result in the 12th biggest energy provider in the nation, serving some 2.2 million customers and having $6.4 billion in assets. UtiliCorp, which also was based in Kansas City, had grown significantly in the mid-1990s through acquisitions, including pipelines in Kansas and Missouri. It provided electricity and gas to areas in the United States as well as to Canada, Britain, New Zealand, Australia, and Jamaica.

Shortly after KCPL and UtiliCorp announced the merger plans, Western tried to intervene by tendering a hostile bid to purchase KCPL for about $1.7 billion. Western, which had about 600,000 electricity customers in eastern Kansas and some 650,000 gas customers in Kansas and Oklahoma, acquired Kansas City Gas in 1992 and was looking to expand further. Western claimed its deal would benefit ratepayers more than a UtiliCorp merger would. KCPL responded by rejecting Western's offer. KCPL Chairman Drue Jennings voiced his displeasure regarding Western's unfriendly takeover bid by stating, "It's a brazen, 11th-hour, desperation attempt to derail a very formidable new competitor." UtiliCorp increased its offer from $1.35 billion to $1.7 billion in the hope that KCPL shareholders would back the UtiliCorp merger, and in June 1996 Western upped its bid to $1.9 billion. In the summer of 1996 shareholders of UtiliCorp and KCPL voted on the proposed merger. While UtiliCorp shareholders supported it, KCPL voted it down.

In 1997, a year after Western's hostile takeover attempt was initiated, KCPL agreed to sell the company to Western in a friendly, $2 billion deal. Yet another year later, the companies continued to negotiate. In March 1998 KCPL and Western agreed to combine KCPL with KPL and KGE, Western's two electricity subsidiaries, to form a new company—Westar En-

ergy. The plan was to put $800 million of KCPL's debt into Westar and the remaining $350 million into Western. Western would own 80.1 percent of the new company, with the remaining 19.9 percent going to KCPL shareholders. Westar would be dedicated entirely to electricity and would have an estimated annual revenue of $2.1 billion.

In spite of the company's preoccupation with talks of mergers and takeovers, business continued, as did diversification. In early 1997 KCPL announced that it had acquired a major stake in Digital Teleport Inc., a St. Louis-based telecommunications firm building a fiber optics system in Missouri, through its subsidiary KLT Telecom Inc. Digital Teleport planned to provide local telephone service to Kansas City residents in the summer of 1997 and to expand throughout the Midwest. The company would divest its telecom interests in the early 2000s.

In early 1999 an explosion at KCPL's Hawthorne electric power generating plant resulted in the near-total destruction of a boiler building. The plant produced some 15 percent of KCPL's electricity, but it was undergoing routine maintenance and was not operational at the time of the explosion. Although KCPL's net costs in 1999 were expected to go up an additional $6.5 million as a result of the blast, the company said they did not anticipate a rise in customers' bills. KCPL moved ahead with plans for reconstruction and hoped to have the new boiler plant operational by the summer of 2001.

Nearly four years after hints of a merger between Western and KCPL began, the deal died. On January 3, 2000, KCPL withdrew from the agreement, blaming Western's falling stock price. Western's stock traded at $16.125 per share at the time of KCPL's withdrawal. In March 1998, when the two companies came to a revised merger agreement, Western's stock traded at $43.125 per share. In the stock purchase deal made between Western and KCPL, the lower stock price meant the deal was worth less than $1.3 billion in early 2000, a significant drop compared with the original amount of $2 billion.

No longer bound to another company, KCPL announced its desire to form a holding company, Great Plains Energy Incorporated, with three units: a competitive power generation company that would include the company's power plants (Great Plains Power), a regulated utility company (KCPL), and an unregulated subsidiary (KLT). The new structure was intended to make KCPL more competitive in a deregulated energy market. KCPL received the green light from the Missouri Public Service Commission for the restructuring in August 2001, and on October 1, 2001, Great Plains Energy was established.

Great Plains Energy restructured again in 2002 into three units: KCPL; Strategic Energy, LLC, which delivered wholesale power in competitive marketplaces; and KLT Gas, which specialized in the development and exploration of natural gas properties, specifically coalbed methane. For 2003 KCPL reported sales of $2.1 billion, a 15 percent increase compared with 2002. Net income was $144.9 million, which also represented a 15 percent increase over the previous year. After again rethinking its position in the competitive power generation market, Great Plains Energy decided in February 2004 to exit the natural gas production business and to remain focused on its original mainstay, electricity.

Principal Subsidiaries

Kansas City Power & Light Company; Strategic Energy LLC.

Principal Competitors

Ameren Corporation; The Empire District Electric Company; Westar Energy, Inc.

Further Reading

Everly, Steve, "Kansas City, Mo.-Based Utilities Firm Begins Formal Reorganization Process," *Missouri,* May 18, 2000.

——, "Missouri Regulators Approve Kansas City Power & Light's Restructuring Plan," *Missouri,* August 1, 2001.

Field, David, "Two Mergers Give Jolt to Electric, Gas Utilities," *Washington Times,* April 16, 1996, p. B7.

"Great Plains Outlines Strategy, Updates Coal Information," *Platt's Coal Outlook,* September 2, 2002, p. 8.

Groene, Lee Ann, and Brian Kaberline, "Industry Observers Foresee Battle in KCP&L's Bid to Purchase KG&E," *Wichita Business Journal,* July 30, 1990.

Holden, Benjamin A., "KCPL Agrees to Western Bid for $2 Billion," *Wall Street Journal,* February 10, 1997, p. B8.

——, "UtiliCorp and Kansas City P&L Agree to Combine in a $1.35 Billion Merger," *Wall Street Journal,* January 23, 1996, p. A3.

Jeffrey, Balfour S., *Kansas City Power & Light: Through Fifty Years to the Electric Company,* New York: Newcomen Society, 1975.

Kaberline, Brian, "Falcons Soar Over Concrete Cliffs, Prairies Surround Power Plants," *Kansas City Business Journal,* May 15, 1992.

"Kansas City Power & Light Rejects Unsolicited Western Resources Offer," *Star-Tribune Newspaper,* April 23, 1996, p. D3.

Kranhold, Kathryn, "Western Resources, Kansas City P&L Revise Plans to Combine," *Wall Street Journal,* March 19, 1998, p. A4.

Lipin, Steven, "Deals & Deal Makers: How Western Resources' Merger Failed," *Wall Street Journal,* January 4, 2000, p. C22.

——, "Utilicorp Merger Could Be on the Rocks—Bid by Western Resources for Kansas City Power Is Gaining Supporters," *Wall Street Journal,* May 20, 1996, p. A3.

——, "Western Resources Makes Bid for Kansas City Power," *Wall Street Journal,* April 15, 1996, p. A3.

Olson, Robert A., *Kansas City Power & Light Company: The First Ninety Years,* New York: Newcomen Society, 1972.

Pepper, Miriam, "In Kansas and Missouri, a Saga of Power Plants and Power Plays," *Washington Post,* October 14, 1990.

Smith, Rebecca, "Kansas City Power Scraps Merger Plan," *Wall Street Journal,* January 4, 2000, p. A3.

Washington, Barbara A., "KC Utilities Could Clean Up on Pollution Credit Boon," *Kansas City Business Journal,* June 28, 1991.

Wolcott, Steven, and Brian Kaberline, "KCP&L Will Leave Historic Building for 1201 Walnut," *Kansas City Business Journal,* March 22, 1991.

—Carol Hopkins
—update: Mariko Fujinaka

Greenberg Traurig, LLP

1221 Brickell Avenue
Miami, Florida 33131
U.S.A.
Telephone: (305) 579-0500
Fax: (305) 579-0717
Web site: http://www.gtlaw.com

Private Company
Incorporated: 1967
Employees: 1,100
Sales: $572.5 million (2003)
NAIC: 541110 Offices of Lawyers

Miami-based Greenberg Traurig, LLP is an international law firm with approximately 1,100 lawyers in 24 offices located in such major U.S. cities as Atlanta, Boston, Chicago, Dallas, Denver, New York, and Washington, D.C. The firm in recent years has also expanded into Europe, opening offices in Amsterdam and Zurich. The Miami office handles the firm's Latin American business. According to the *National Law Journal*, Greenberg Traurig ranked as the 12th largest law firm in the United States in 2003. It was also listed by *Fortune* magazine as one of the top 25 most influential lobbying firms in Washington, D.C. During the 2000 Presidential election controversy in Florida, Greenberg Traurig represented George W. Bush.

Founding of Firm: 1967

Greenberg Traurig was founded in Miami in 1967 by three area lawyers: Melvin Greenberg, Robert Traurig, and Larry Hoffman. According to a 1991 *Miami Review* profile of the firm, "partners Greenberg and Traurig say one of the reasons the trio established the firm 24 years ago was that, as Jews, they didn't feel they'd fit in Miami's white-shoe corporate practices. So they opened their own firm, modeled after New York' smaller transactional practices that also are largely Jewish in population, Greenberg says." Greenberg became the chief executive officer, and Hoffman, in the words of the *Miami Review,* assumed the role of "a behind-the-scenes hatchet man and numbers cruncher." Traurig, a 1950 University of Miami

School of law graduate, became something of a rainmaker for the firm in the real estate field of Miami-Dade County, much of which he attributed to fortunate timing. He told the *Miami Herald* in 2003, "As the population increased and the need for new residential communities became more obvious, I was in the right place at the right time. There were few people at that point who were representing builders and land developers at public hearings and I was the beneficiary of good luck." Perhaps of more importance was Traurig's ability to make important political connections in Miami-Dade. When major developers decided to become involved in the market, they quickly learned that the zoning lawyer who had the most pull and could deliver was Robert Traurig. He was instrumental in westward development to the Everglades, which some critics charged was detrimental to the long-range health of the area's environment. According to the *Miami Review,* "Traurig asserts that his work and the westward growth serve the county's long-range needs, specifically accommodating population growth. Damage to the environment, Traurig says, is minimized by environmental regulations and county reviews. Still, when he talks about the issue, Traurig admits he's 'defensive.' "

Greenberg's management style was conservative, and the firm was slow to expand beyond south Florida. A move into Palm Beach failed to take hold, primarily because Greenberg Traurig brought in Miami lawyers rather than hire locally connected attorneys. The business eventually petered away. The firm would not make the same mistake when it opened a Broward office in August 1985, and during its rapid expansion in the 1990s Greenberg Traurig became notorious for cherry-picking local talent to establish a beachhead in a new city on which to build—rather than to rely on growth through acquisitions. In the meantime, the firm carried on as a Miami firm that was mostly known for its real estate work. According to the *Miami Review,* Greenberg Traurig targeted "small and mid-sized companies," hiring "Jewish and Hispanic attorneys to attract similar clients." Greenberg intended to move into such practices as admiralty, labor, and immigration practices but, in his own words, "never got around to it."

In 1987, after being in business for 20 years, Greenberg Traurig took formal steps to transfer leadership from the name

Company Perspectives:

For more than three decades, our firm has challenged traditional approaches and worked to provide practical business-focused solutions for emerging companies and Fortune 500 Corporations.

partners to a select group of 14 younger partners. It was a long-range plan that also included the turnover of the chief executive position to a second generation lawyer, which the older partners expected would emerge from a group of candidates. An ex-firm attorney told the *Miami Review* these candidates were ''all Mel and Larry's favorites,'' and went on to state that the senior partners ''cultivate people as their favorites. In exchange, those people provide them with information. They become their extra eyes and ears.''

Hoffman Succeeds Greenberg in 1991 As CEO

With the onset of a recession, Greenberg Traurig's business suffered in 1990. It was a difficult year on another front as well. In the fall Greenberg underwent brain surgery, and although the operation appeared to be successful, in January 1991 he suddenly quit as chief executive, but only—according to the *Miami Review*—''after firing a number of lawyers and cutting partners' pay. Then, instead of passing the mantle to the next generation of lawyers the firm had been nurturing for the past several years, the top management job went to Larry Hoffman.'' There was even some speculation that the firm might break up.

To the surprise of many, Hoffman proved to be an extremely aggressive leader. He immediately announced that the firm would become involved in new practice areas such as admiralty, trade, immigration, labor, and domestic relations, and would open new Florida offices. After opening an office in Fort Lauderdale, in January 1992, the firm acquired the north Florida law firm of Roberts, Baggett, LaFace & Richard, adding 13 lawyers and giving Greenberg Traurig a major presence in Tallahassee and Jacksonville. Hoffman's vision proved to be even more expansive. In little more than a year, Greenberg Traurig not only opened offices in three Florida markets it set up shop in New York City, and a Washington, D.C. office soon followed. Then, in 1995, Hoffmann opened a central Florida operation headed by former U.S. Congressman Jim Bacchus, who had a previous association with Greenberg Traurig in the early 1980s before serving two terms in the U.S. House of Representatives.

The firm's second generation of lawyers would now continue the expansion set in motion by Hoffman. When he stepped down as CEO in 1997—although he remained chairman of the board—the firm had grown to 325 lawyers. His replacement as chief executive was Cesar L. Alvarez, who became the first Hispanic head of a major law firm, a fact that held little value to him. ''I view it as a statistical anomaly,'' he told the *National Law Journal* in a 1999 interview. ''I don't think anybody ought to be anything because they're Latin or black or Jewish or anything else. I would feel very badly and I would not have taken the job if they gave it to me because I'm Latin.'' Alvarez was born in Cuba in 1947 and fled the country in 1960 with his family. He was educated at the University of Florida, earning an

economics degree in 1969, an M.B.A. in 1970, and a law degree in 1973. He was recruited by Mel Greenberg at a time when only a handful of Cuban-Americans worked at the major Miami law firms. He became lawyer number 13 at Greenberg Traurig, practicing securities, corporate, and international law. From 1981 to 1982 he served as executive vice-president at Air Florida, then resumed his career at Greenberg Traurig. Fifteen years later he was the unanimous choice of the board to lead the firm into the future.

Alvarez's plan was to make Greenberg Traurig an international law firm, as well as continue domestic growth. His first step was to open an office in Sao Paulo, Brazil, where he hoped to take advantage of corporate finance opportunities and build on relationships with lawyers in other Latin American countries to beef up the firm's referral network. The Brazil office, however, would eventually be abandoned, and the firm's Latin American business was folded into the Miami office. Alvarez was also keen on opening a London office, but instead of entering Europe through London, Alvarez for the next five years focused on extending the firm's U.S. reach.

In 1997 Greenberg Traurig added another Florida office, located in Boca Raton, Florida. In May of that year the firm also opened an office in Philadelphia, which started out with just three attorneys. Greenberg Traurig entered the Atlanta market in 1998 by merging with Atlanta-based Katz, Smith & Cohen, a major entertainment law firm whose clients included B.B. King, Willie Nelson, George Strait, and Jimmy Buffett. As a result, Greenberg Traurig gained an office in Atlanta and bolstered its presence in entertainment law, supplementing the New York office's involvement in corporate entertainment and litigation entertainment practices, and the Miami office's Latin America-based entertainment practice. A year later the Atlanta office, with 12 lawyers, would be significantly enlarged, again by way of acquisition. The unit merged with Minkin & Snyder, a deal that added 26 lawyers and the addition of nine new practice groups. Also in 1998, Greenberg Traurig opened an office in Tysons Corner, Virginia, with nine established attorneys hired from area law firms. This office targeted northern Virginia's slate of high tech companies, to serve start-ups as well as emerging and mature companies in the sector.

New Office Openings: 1999

Greenberg Traurig was especially active in 1999. It hired 36 new lawyers to support its Florida offices in Miami, Fort Lauderdale, Boca Raton, and West Palm Beach, and opened four new offices outside the state. In January the firm opened its first Midwest office, in Chicago, hiring several area lawyers to initially focus on business bankruptcy and commercial litigation. Later in 1999 Greenberg Traurig entered the Boston market by hiring three high-profile, well-connected lawyers from the Boston office of Eckert, Seamans, Cherin & Mellott LLC. Next, Greenberg Traurig opened its first office in Phoenix. Rather than cherry-pick on this one, it hired 30 lawyers that had been employed by the 40-year-old firm of O'Connor Cavanaugh, the area's third largest law firm which had broken up several weeks earlier. The new unit specialized in corporate securities, commercial litigation, employment law, financial services, and technology and intellectual property. In September 1999, Greenberg Traurig established a Wilmington, Delaware, office in order to

Key Dates:

1967: Firm is founded in Miami, Florida.
1985: Broward County office is opened.
1991: Larry Hoffman succeeds Melvin Greenberg as CEO.
1997: Cesar Alvarez succeeds Hoffman as CEO.
1999: Firm enters Chicago, Boston, Delaware, and Los Angeles.
2002: Offices are opened in Amsterdam and Zurich.

serve clients who appeared in Delaware's important bankruptcy and business courts. Finally, late in 1999 Greenberg Traurig opened an office in Los Angeles by acquiring a pair of small firms: the solo practice of Carol Perrin, who became managing partner, and the ten attorneys of Goldberg, Scott, Belfield, Steinberg & Cohen. It was a move that would lead to much unwanted publicity.

According to *American Lawyer,* "Greenberg Traurig bungled its entrance onto the Los Angeles stage. For a year, its new office was home to a bitter partnership feud. It was one part human drama and one part farce." The magazine quoted a former shareholder from another Greenberg Traurig office, who maintained that the firm entered "markets too quickly and they don't thoroughly check the quality of the lawyers they're hiring. . . . When you do that enough times, it's inevitable that things will go wrong." According to the *Miami Herald,* "Almost immediately, lawyers and staffers complained to management in Miami that Perrin was abusive and dishonest. . . . The most serious accusation was that Perrin delegated work to subordinates, then billed clients at her much higher rate." When Perrin was cleared of these charges by Greenberg Traurig, Los Angeles partner Steven Goldberg quit and then filed suit, alleging that the firm breached its employment contract with him by allowing Perrin to engage in dishonest, unprofessional, and unethical conduct. Perrin maintained that Goldberg, her chief antagonist, was pursuing a vendetta against her because she had spurned his efforts at courting her. (Both lawyers were divorced, lived close to one another, and their children were friends.) After more than a year of turmoil, Greenberg Traurig put the matter behind it by settling Goldberg's suit. Perrin stayed on, although she no longer served as managing partner.

Greenberg Traurig nearly doubled the size of its New York office in 2000. First it picked up 50 attorneys from the office of Graham & James, and a month later, in August 2000, it added 40 more attorneys from the defunct Manhattan firm of Camhy Karlinsky & Stein. As a result, Greenberg Traurig's New York office now housed 220 lawyers, making it one of the 30 largest law firms in the city. In New York size clearly mattered, and picking off lawyers one or two at a time was not a viable strategy in a market undergoing a wave of consolidation among law firms. In particular, the added slate of lawyers helped

Greenberg Traurig to beef up its underwriting, mergers and acquisitions, real estate, and telecommunications practices.

At a time when other firms were forced by difficult economic conditions to cut back, Greenberg Traurig responded by launching another growth spurt in 2002. The Arizona office added high-tech legal expertise by acquiring the law practice of Weinberg Cummerford Legal Group. The firm also opened a new office in Morristown, New Jersey, following its longtime model of cherry-picking local talent. In this case it was Phillip R. Sellinger, a former assistant U.S. Attorney and former chairman of the litigation department at Sills, Cummis, Radis, Tischman, Epstein & Gross. Sellinger became the managing partner, and only attorney, of the new office, but he took with him from Sills Cummis such major clients as Hitachi Data Systems and Toshiba. Also in 2002, Alvarez realized a longheld goal of moving into the European market. Rather than London, which was saturated with corporate law firms, he selected Amsterdam as an entry point. A second office on the continent was opened in Zurich, where the firm hired five attorneys who represented European-based film and television production companies and already had relationships with Greenberg Traurig attorneys in the Los Angeles Office.

Further expansion followed in 2003 and 2004. The firm opened its first office in Dallas in 2003, luring away the 15-attorney unit of St. Paul, Minnesota-based Larson King, which had launched its Dallas effort a year earlier. In 2004 Greenberg Traurig opened two new offices in California, in Irvine and Palo Alto, to become involved in legal work in Silicon Valley. Alvarez considered the time to be right to enter the market. An earlier move, during the superheated days of the tech sector in the late 1990s, would have been too costly. Moreover, rather than open an office right after the tech bubble burst, Alvarez opted to wait until there were signs that the sector was beginning to pick up. It was an important step for Greenberg Traurig, filling in one of the gaps in its aggressive quest to become one of the United States' leading international law firms.

Principal Competitors

Holland & Knight LLP; Paul, Weiss, Rifkind, Wharton & Garrison LLP; Stroock & Stroock & Lavan LLP.

Further Reading

Braverman, Paul, "Firm Anxiety," *American Lawyer,* July 2001, p. 98.
Bronstad, Amanda, "She Said, He Said, They Said," *Los Angeles Business Journal,* November 26, 2001, p. 1.
Fakler, John T., "Greenberg Traurig Remains Big Dog of So. Fla. Law Firms," *South Florida Business Journal,* January 14, 2000, p. 47.
Goodman, Cindy Krischer, "Miami-Based Law Firm to Expand into Europe," *Miami Herald,* November 15, 2002.
——, "New Chief at Miami's Largest Law Firm Has International Ambitions," *Miami Herald,* April 17, 1997.
Itkoff, Valerie Greenberg, "Greenberg's New Stripes," *Miami Review,* June 21 1991, p. 11A.

—Ed Dinger

GREGGS
—plc—

Greggs PLC

Fernwood House, Clayton Road, Jesmond
Newcastle upon Tyne NE2 1TL
United Kingdom
Telephone: (44) 191 281 7721
Fax: (44) 191 281 3033
Web site: http://www.greggs.co.uk

Public Company
Incorporated: 1984
Employees: 17,900
Sales: £456.97 million (2003)
Stock Exchanges: London
Ticker Symbol: GRG
NAIC: 311812 Commercial Bakeries; 311811 Retail
    Bakeries

Greggs PLC is the operator of the largest bakery chain in the United Kingdom, specializing in sandwiches, savories, and other bakery-related products. Greggs' stores operate under two names, Greggs, which focus on takeaway sales, and Bakers Oven, which offer in-store dining. The company's Bakers Oven units feature in-store bakeries. The Greggs units rely on large regional bakeries that serve clusters of retail outlets. The company's stores are located throughout the United Kingdom. Greggs also operates two stores in Belgium, units that represent the beginning of the company's expansion campaign into mainland Europe.

Origins

For the first three decades of its existence, Greggs was a small, local business, never displaying any sign that it later would become the largest chain of its kind in the United Kingdom. The business was founded by John Gregg during the 1930s, when he opened a small bakery in the Tyne suburb of Newcastle, England. There the business stood, mostly unchanged for the next 30 years, as John Gregg served nearby residents his selection of breads, rolls, cakes, and related items. Greggs did not begin to assume the stature of an industry giant until John Gregg died unexpectedly in 1964. His son, Ian Gregg, who had planned a career in law, was forced to shelve his professional aspirations and take over the family business. Ironically, it was its founder's death that gave Greggs new life.

Ian Gregg, who served as Greggs' chairman into the 21st century, took to his new career with relish. Instead of serving as a mere caretaker of the small bakery and its shop, Ian Gregg perceived the modest business as the beginning of a much larger corporation. He began expanding his father's company in the region surrounding Newcastle, establishing the company's model of expansion not long after his father's death. Although the property he inherited consisted of a shop with a bakery in the rear, Ian Gregg decided to separate the two functions, making production and retail sales geographically distinct operations. He established additional stores in clusters whose breads, rolls, and other items were supplied by a single, central bakery. The mode of expansion gave Greggs the divisional structure that later defined the company, with each wave of expansion adding another regional division to the company's operations. More important at the time of its creation, Ian Gregg's methodology also enabled the company to achieve production, managerial, and financial efficiencies, efficiencies that would increase as the size of Greggs increased.

By the beginning of the 1970s, Ian Gregg was ready to expand Greggs beyond northeastern England. He expanded outside the northeast by acquiring established, regional bakery chains, first moving to the north before expanding to the south. Greggs established a presence in Glasgow, Scotland, in 1972 and acquired properties in Leeds in 1974 and in Manchester two years later. The addition of these territories gave Greggs four regional divisions, the structure of the company when it took its next evolutionary leap in 1984.

In 1984, Greggs hired a new managing director, Mike Darrington, who presided over the company's day-to-day operation into the 21st century. He took the helm of a chain composed of 261 shops, the result of Ian Gregg's work during the previous two decades. With Darrington in charge, the company prepared for its next major surge in growth, an expansion to be funded by its debut on the London Stock Exchange. In 1984, the £37-million-in-sales Greggs completed its initial public offering (IPO) of stock, finding a wealth of investors willing to pay 135 pence per share for a stake in the company's future.

With the proceeds raised from its IPO, Greggs pressed ahead with its expansion plans, growing by internal means and by acquiring other bakery outlets. The company established several new regional operations in the years immediately following its IPO, forming a division in Birmingham in 1984, in South Wales in 1985, and in north London in 1986.

Acquiring Bakers Oven in 1994

A decade after its IPO, Greggs stood as a towering chain, with the creation of new divisions spawning clusters of new shops. By 1994—a significant year in the company's history—Greggs consisted of more than 500 stores operating in seven regional divisions. The stature of the company at this point was about to increase substantially, providing a fitting tribute to the company's tenth year as a publicly traded concern. In mid-1994, Greggs acquired the retail baking interests belonging to Allied Bakeries Limited. The transaction nearly doubled the size of the company, adding 424 shops and a new brand to the company's portfolio, Bakers Oven.

The acquisition of Allied Bakeries added a new dimension to Greggs' business strategy, one that contrasted and complemented the company's operations. Unlike the shops operating under the Greggs banner, the Bakers Oven shops featured in-store bakeries. Rather than assimilate the acquired units into the company's network of large central bakeries that served a cluster of retail shops, Darrington and his management team decided to develop Bakers Oven as a separate brand, a decision that opened new markets for the company's expansion. Through Bakers Oven shops and their in-store bakeries, the company was able to establish a presence in markets with lower population densities than the Greggs units demanded. For the Greggs model of a central bakery serving satellite shops to make financial sense, numerous retail outlets needed to be in close proximity to the bakery, which, in turn, required a population big enough to support numerous shops. The Bakers Oven units, in contrast, were self-sufficient thanks to their in-store bakeries and able to survive in sparsely populated regions, markets that Greggs was forced to avoid. Accordingly, once the Bakers Oven chain was added to Greggs' operations, the company began pursuing a two-pronged expansion strategy: building clusters of Greggs shops in large markets and establishing Bakers Oven units in smaller markets.

In the wake of the Allied Bakeries acquisition, Greggs became a chain with two complementary vehicles for growth and two distinct formats. The traditional Greggs shops concentrated on takeaway sales, while the Bakers Oven shops offered seating to its customers, functioning more like restaurants. Not all of the units acquired from Allied Bakeries conformed to Greggs' needs, including more than 90 outlets in south and west London, which were used to form the company's eighth division, Greggs of Twickenham. A ninth division was added when the company completed its next major acquisition, the December 1996 purchase of J.R. Birkett & Sons Ltd., a family-owned baking company. The Birkett division eventually was disbanded when the stores were converted to Greggs units.

By the end of the 1990s, Greggs' revenues eclipsed the £300 million mark for the first time, 15 years after the company generated £37 million in sales. The company's long-range plans included two ambitious goals. By 2010, the Greggs management team hoped to reach £1 billion in sales and at least 1,700 stores. To attain these objectives, much needed to be achieved in the decade ahead. By the end of 1999, the company operated more than 1,000 shops throughout the United Kingdom, realizing the majority of its sales from the 825 Greggs stores in operation.

Greggs in the 21st Century

As the company entered the 21st century, the Greggs units were driving its growth, both in physical and financial terms. The catering market, in which the company's Bakers Oven units operated, was proving to be less vibrant than the takeaway sector. Accordingly, the company focused on improving the performance of its existing Bakers Oven stores rather than expanding the chain. In 2001, Greggs' capital expenditure amounted to £27.4 million, which was used in large part to open additional stores and refurbish existing units. During the year, the company opened 67 new shops and closed 28 shops, giving it 905 Greggs units and 239 Bakers Oven shops. The year-end totals, when compared with the figures for 2000, reflected the company's reliance on the Greggs format to drive its growth. In 2001, the company increased the number of stores operating under the Greggs banner by 47, while the 239 Bakers Oven units in operation at the end of the year represented a loss of eight stores.

The beginning of the new decade marked the end of an era at Greggs, as the company, for the first time in its history, plotted its future course without a Gregg at the helm. After more than 30 years of presiding over the company's fortunes, Ian Gregg announced that he was retiring as chairman of the board. The announcement, made in 2001, led to the appointment of Derek Netherton as chairman designate in March 2002.

With Netherton and Darrington in charge, Greggs pressed ahead with its expansion. During the first half of 2002, the company opened 24 new stores and began to convert 50 Birketts shops in Cumbria, Lancashire, and southern Scotland to Greggs stores. The company also was exploring opportunities to expand into mainland Europe by mid-2002, with Belgium selected as the first target market. "We're hoping to have one store open this year and a couple early next year," Darrington explained in an August 3, 2002 interview with the *Express*. "We will start driving it about 12 months after that."

Key Dates:

1964: After his father's death, Ian Gregg takes control of his family's small bakery, named Greggs.
1972: Greggs expands outside northeastern England for the first time, establishing a regional division in Glasgow, Scotland.
1984: Greggs begins trading on the London Stock Exchange.
1994: Greggs acquires the retail baking interests of Allied Bakeries Limited, giving the company 424 Bakers Oven shops.
2003: Greggs opens two stores in Belgium, its first stores outside the United Kingdom.

Greggs entered mainland Europe in early 2003, when the company opened two stores, one in Antwerp and another in Leuven. After experiencing slow sales at first, the two Belgian stores began to perform well by mid-2003, when the company announced that it intended to open two more Belgian stores within the ensuing six months. By this point, the company also was developing new retail formats designed for nontraditional locations. In July 2003, the first such store opened when an outlet debuted at a gas station near Edinburgh, Scotland. Greggs' property director, in an August 2003 interview with *UK Retail Briefing,* disclosed other nontraditional settings for company stores, listing "office area, industrial estates, transport hubs, and roadside," as among possible sites for future expansion.

At the beginning of 2004, Darrington celebrated his 20th year as managing director of Greggs. During his tenure, the company store count increased from 261 to more than 1,200, a period that saw annual revenues swell from £37 million to more than £450 million and annual profits increase from £1.7 million to £40.5 million. The company stock, valued at 135 pence per share when Darrington joined the company, was trading at £31.40 at the end of 2003. The growth was impressive, but if the company was going to reach its goal of £1 billion in revenues by 2010, a more remarkable rate of growth needed to be recorded in the years ahead. The foray into mainland Europe and the development of stores in nontraditional locations offered two new avenues of growth. In the future, much would depend on the company's success with these two experimental programs, as Greggs endeavored to become a more diversified retailer and assert its national dominance in new directions.

Principal Subsidiaries

Charles Bragg (Bakers) Limited; Greggs (Leasing) Limited; Thurston Parfitt Limited; Greggs Properties Limited; Olivers (UK) Development Limited.

Principal Competitors

Tesco PLC; Burger King Corporation; Pret A Manger (Europe) Limited.

Further Reading

Cole, Robert, "Greggs; Tempus," *Times,* March 4, 2000, p. 28.
"Greggs," *Retail Business,* December 1995, p. 96.
"Greggs," *U.K. Retail Briefing,* August 2003, p. 114.
"Greggs . . . and Keeps Expanding," *U.K. Retail Briefing,* April 2004, p. 7.
"Greggs Emphasises Heritage As Bakery in Two New TV Spots," *Campaign,* April 16, 2004, p. 6.
"Greggs Expansion Goes On," *Grocer,* July 13, 2002, p. 109.
"Greggs: International Expansion," *U.K. Retail Briefing,* April 2004, p. 7.
"Greggs Is Slow to Roll," *Express,* August 3, 2002, p. 93.
"Specialist Food Retailers," *U.K. Retail Briefing,* July-August 2002, p. 115.
White, Jeremy, "Bakery Chain Holds Pitch for £3 Million," *Campaign,* January 11, 2002, p. 5.

—Jeffrey L. Covell

Haier Group Corporation

1 Haier Road, Hi-Tech Zone
Qingdao 266101
China
Telephone: +86-532-893-9999
Fax: +86-532-893-8666
Web site: http://www.haier.com

Government-Owned Company
Incorporated: 1984 as Qingdao Refrigerator Co., Ltd.
Employees: 30,000
Sales: $4 billion (2003 est.)
NAIC: 333415 Air Conditioning and Warm Air Heating
   Equipment and Commercial and Industrial
   Refrigeration Equipment Manufacturing; 334111
   Electronic Computer Manufacturing; 335221
   Household Cooking Appliance Manufacturing

Haier Group Corporation is one of the world's top-selling makers of white goods and other home appliances. The Qingdao, China-based company has grown rapidly to capture the number two spot worldwide in its core refrigerators segment, trailing only the United States' Whirlpool. At home, however, Haier has captured the lead in that segment, accounting for more than one-third of all refrigerators sold each year, and is also the leader in a number of other appliance categories, such as air conditioners and dishwashers. Since the late 1990s Haier has dramatically expanded its range of products in a diversification move that has brought the company into such markets as mobile telephones and personal computers. At the same time, Haier has pursued an aggressive globalization effort, building a sales network in more than 160 countries, with a presence in more than 38,000 retail outlets worldwide. The company's sales and distribution are backed by a vast network of subsidiaries with production facilities throughout China and 12 manufacturing plants outside of China. The company's foreign facilities include operations in Pakistan, Jordan, Indonesia, the Philippines, Malaysia, Iran—and Camden, South Carolina, in the United States. The latter plant, opened in 2000 and supported by a U.S. sales and marketing head office in New York City, is part of Haier's plans to take a 10

percent share of the U.S. refrigerator market by as early as 2005. Credit for Haier's success goes to CEO Zhang Ruimin, who transformed the small, ailing, state-owned company into a global powerhouse at the dawn of the 21st century. The company remains controlled by the Chinese government, but operates independently. Subsidiary Qingdao Haier Refrigerator Co., Ltd. is listed on the Shanghai Stock Exchange. The company is also seeking a backdoor listing on the Hong Kong Stock Exchange through its 2004 purchase of a controlling stake in the Haier-CCT Holdings joint venture. Haier Group's sales are estimated at more than $4 billion per year.

Rebuilding a Refrigerator Plant in the 1980s

The 1920s saw the construction of a factory to build refrigerators in China's coastal Qingdao (then spelled as Tsingtao, which later lent its name to the famous beer as well). Following the Communist revolution in 1949, the factory was taken over by the government. Under socialist control, however, the factory went into a long decline. By the early 1980s, its production had slowed to a trickle. Burdened by a heavy debt, the company, then known as Qingdao Refrigerator Company, had been losing money and, unable to pay its 600 workers, was close to bankruptcy. As Haier itself later admitted, the company, where production struggled to top 80 refrigerators a month, consisted of little more than "a row of shabby buildings containing several lathes."

Yet the early 1980s also marked the first opening of mainland Chinese economy to the international market. A large number of foreign companies traveled to China seeking investment opportunities. One of these was Germany's Liebherr Haushaltgerate, a leading appliance maker in that country. Liebherr proposed a partnership with the Qingdao refrigerator plant, including the sale of Liebherr's refrigerator technology to the Chinese company. Its owner—that is, the city of Qingdao—agreed to the partnership.

Technology alone was not enough to rescue the company, however. Instead, the Qingdao company's rebirth relied on the arrival of a new managing director, Zhang Ruimin, in 1984. Zhang, the son of a Qingdao textile worker, had joined the municipal government in the 1960s, when the Cultural Revolution had shut down the country's school system. Zhang, an avid

Company Perspectives:

Haier Is the Sea

Haier should be like the sea. Because the sea can accept all the rivers on earth, big and small, far and near, coming all the way to empty into it.

Once in the bosom of the sea, every drop will function as a whole and rush together pertinaciously and dauntlessly, under the command of the sea, to a common goal. They will rather be smashed to pieces than retreat as deserters, hence the overwhelming force of the sea.

The sea offers all of itself to mankind and never demands anything in return. Only through this bounty and unselfishness can the sea become an everlasting existence providing for all living beings.

Haier should be like the sea—accepting all talented people from around the world for an ambitious goal. Every Haier employee should be capable rather than mediocre and redundant, for they are the backbone and guarantee of Haier's future development.

Concerted efforts will generate power of the sea. This will be backed by a spirit—"Dedication to the Motherland by Pursuing Excellence" which Haier persistently advocates. Therefore, everything deemed unbelievable and impossible can be real and possible, and the Billow of Haier will rush past everything on its way and roll on and on.

Thus, Haier should be like the sea—making contributions to mankind "sincerely forever." In so doing, it will exist forever for the good of all. Haier will be part of the whole society.

Haier is the sea.

reader, studied on his own, focusing particularly on Japanese and Western management techniques. By the beginning of the 1980s, Zhang had become the assistant manager of the city's Household Appliances Division, which oversaw the Qingdao plant, as well as a number of other city-owned appliance companies. After the Qingdao plant's managing director left the company in 1984, Zhang was placed as the factory's leader.

Zhang recognized that simply introducing Liebherr's technology would not be enough to turn the company around. The company's entire culture—marked by nepotism and indifference to quality—needed to be overhauled. One of Zhang's first moves was to turn to friends in Qingdao's outlying and cash-rich agricultural cooperatives for loans in order to pay some of the back wages owed to the company's workers. Zhang also bought a company bus and began providing transportation to workers in order to relieve commuting difficulties. Zhang himself began commuting with the company's workers.

Zhang's next move became the stuff of corporate legend. In 1985, one of the company's customers had brought back a refrigerator—then still a rare luxury item in China—he had bought because the refrigerator did not work. Zhang and the customer went through the available stock of refrigerators until they finally found a working model. Of the 400 or so finished refrigerators at the factory at that time, nearly 20 percent had failed Zhang's inspection.

In response, Zhang called his employees together and ordered that the 76 dud refrigerators be lined up on the factory floor. He then gave sledgehammers to the workers and ordered them to smash the refrigerators. As Zhang reportedly told workers: "Destroy them! If we pass these 76 refrigerators for sale, we'll be continuing a mistake that has all but bankrupted our company."

National Brand Leader in the 1990s

The refrigerators' destruction marked a new era for the Qingdao plant. The installation of Liebherr's equipment and technology was accompanied by a new and rigorous commitment to quality. Zhang also adapted new management techniques for the company, particularly the so-called "5-S Movement" developed by Japan's Masaaki Imai. The 5-S system established quality control through a five-step series of protocols: seiri (discard the unnecessary), seiton (arrange tools in the order of use), seisoh (keep the worksite clean), seiketsu (keep yourself clean), shitsuke (follow workshop disciplines). Zhang added a sixth "s"—"safety." Workers were expected to follow the protocols, at the risk of being exposed to public criticism—and ultimate dismissal, once a rarity in China.

By 1986, the transformation of the company was underway and the Qingdao plant had become profitable. Production had begun to rise steadily while sales began a remarkable climb, averaging some 83 percent per year. From sales of just RMB 3.5 million in 1984, the company's sales ultimately grew to more than RMB 40.6 billion in 2000—an increase of more than 11,600 percent.

Seeing the refrigerator company's success, the Qingdao government began asking the company to take control of a number of the city's other failing appliance makers. In 1988, the company took over Qingdao Electroplating Factory, which then became the Qingdao Microwave Electric Appliance Factory. Then in 1991, the company took over the Qingdao Air Conditioner Plant and Qingdao Freezer. Zhang quickly installed the company's corporate culture and commitment to quality at the new sites.

Having expanded beyond refrigerators, the company took on a new name in 1991, adopting an abbreviation of the phonetic spelling of Liebherr—written as Lieberhaier by the Chinese—to become Qingdao Haier Group. The German-sounding name also proved a useful marketing tool, inspiring confidence not only within the Chinese domestic market, but also later in the decade as the company imposed itself as a global appliance force.

The company adopted the simplified name, Haier Group, in 1992. By then, it had achieved the highly coveted ISO 9001 quality certification for its refrigerator production. By 1994, its air conditioner and freezer production had won ISO 9001 certification as well. The company's quality effort coincided with a drive to build Haier into a leading national brand. By the end of the decade, Haier had become the leading appliance brand in China, with clear dominance in many of its product categories.

Diversification in the 1990s

Although Haier, as a government-controlled body, was barred from the stock exchange, it found its way onto the Shanghai Stock Exchange through the listing of subsidiary

Key Dates:

1984: Zhang Ruimin is appointed general manager of nearly bankrupt Qingdao Refrigerator Co., and leads installation of new refrigerator technology and manufacturing equipment in partnership with Liebherr of Germany.

1986: Qingdao Refrigerator becomes profitable for the first time as new quality control commitment spurs sales.

1988: The company adds a new product group through the acquisition of Qingdao Microwave Electric Appliances Factory.

1991: The company acquires Qingdao Air Conditioner Plant and Qingdao Freezer General Plant; the brand name Haier is adopted.

1993: Qingdao Haier Refrigerator Co. is listed on the Shanghai Stock Exchange.

1995: The company builds its first foreign production plant in Indonesia.

1997: Production subsidiaries are opened in Malaysia and the Philippines.

1999: A production subsidiary is opened in the United States.

2002: A production facility is opened in Pakistan.

2003: Test production begins at a new plant in Jordan.

2004: The company acquires a controlling stake of the Haier-CCT Holdings joint venture in order to gain a backdoor listing on the Hong Kong Stock Exchange.

Qingdao Haier Refrigerator. The company raised nearly RMB 370 million in the offering, which it used to increase its production capacity—and especially to add capacity for production of refrigerators destined for the export market.

Indeed, the mid-1990s marked Haier's movement onto the global appliance scene. As part of its effort to establish itself as one of the world's top appliance makers, Haier opened a series of foreign production plants, starting with Indonesia in 1996. In 1997, the company opened new production subsidiaries in the Philippines and Malaysia. The company also had entered the U.S. market, identifying two potential, yet underdeveloped niche markets—that of small-sized refrigerators for dorm rooms, hotels, and the like; and electric wine cellars. Haier's imports of these appliances, coupled with a strong design and development team, helped the company rapidly impose itself, and by the beginning of the decade, Haier was one of the major players in both markets.

Haier's success in these niche categories encouraged the company to target the higher-end full-size refrigerator market in the United States. In order to break into that market, which remained dominated by the big four U.S. makers—GE, Whirlpool, Frigidaire, and Maytag—Haier decided to build its own manufacturing plant in the United States, which opened in Camden, South Carolina, in 1999.

During the 1990s, as well, Haier engaged in a diversification drive in order to protect itself from downturns in any of its core product categories. Part of the company's diversification came through a series of acquisitions of struggling Chinese companies,

often at the request of the municipal governments. Such was the case with the company's acquisition of its chief rival in Qingdao, Red Star Electric Appliance Factory, in 1995. That purchase was followed in 1997 by the takeover of failing Huangshan Electronics Group, a maker of televisions, in 1997. As with its earlier acquisitions, the company quickly worked to transform these companies' work culture, instilling them with its quality commitment.

Global Brand in the New Century

By the end of the 1990s, Haier's diversification, for the most part, was completed. With an array of products ranging from its core white goods to mobile telephones and personal computing systems, the company faced a degree of criticism from analysts, who wondered if the company had not diversified too widely. Nonetheless, the company continued to play a role as one of China's fastest-growing firms, with sales topping $2.3 billion in 1998. By then, the company had captured 40 percent of China's refrigerator sales, nearly 36 percent of washing machine sales, more than 47 percent of all freezer sales, and nearly 37 percent of air conditioners sold in China.

With its position in China relatively solid and highly profitable, Haier entered its third development phase, adopting a new strategy: that of transforming Haier into a globally recognized brand name. The company built a strong position in the Asia and Middle East markets, backed by new factories in Pakistan, opened in 2002, and in Jordan, which began test production in December 2003. By 2004, Haier had become one of the leading brands in those regions. The company also had succeeded in placing its products—although not necessarily its brand—in most of Europe's top retail chains.

The United States became the group's most ambitious target at the dawn of the 21st century. With sales of its electric wine coolers going strongly—the company already claimed a 60 percent share of that niche market—its effort to build brand status continued apace. By 2002, revenues from the group's U.S. operations topped $200 million—a drop in the bucket compared with the company's total of more than $7 billion. Nonetheless, Haier remained confident, announcing plans to build its U.S. position to more than $1 billion by mid-decade—and its intention to grab as much as a 10 percent market share in the country's full-size refrigerator market.

While observers remained skeptical of the company's chances in the United States—a notoriously difficult market for foreign brands—Haier's confidence remained bolstered by its success elsewhere. As the world's number two refrigerator maker, trailing only Whirlpool, Haier expected to be able to protect its dominant position in China, despite the increasing inroads made by foreign manufacturers into that market. In order to fuel its growth, Haier found its way onto the Hong Kong Stock Exchange through a so-called backdoor listing by acquiring a controlling stake in a publicly listed joint venture, Haier-CCT Holdings Ltd., in 2004. Under Zhang Ruimin, Haier had grown into a globally operating, diversified home appliance leader.

Principal Subsidiaries

Qingdao Haier Refrigerator Co., Ltd.; Haier Refrigerator Co., Ltd; Haier Refrigerator (International) Co., Ltd.

Principal Competitors

Siemens AG (SI); Matsushita Electric Corporation of America; Samsung Electronics Co. Ltd.; Electrolux AB; LG Electronics Investment Ltd.; Whirlpool Corporation; BSH Bosch und Siemens Hausgerate GmbH; GE Appliances; Siemens PLC; Daewoo Electronics Corporation.

Further Reading

Arndt, Michael, "Can Haier Freeze Out Whirlpool and GE?," *Business Week Online,* April 11, 2002.

Beatty, Gerry, "On a Haier Level," *HFN The Weekly Newspaper for the Home Furnishing Network,* March 8, 2004, p. 35.

"China's Haier Plans Backdoor HK Listing," *Asia Africa Intelligence Wire,* March 23, 2004.

Fonda, Daren, "Look Out, Whirlpool," *Time,* January 28, 2002, p. B9.

Grace, Robert, "When Far East Meets South," *Plastics News,* June 2, 2003, p. 1.

"Haier and Higher," *South China Morning Post,* June 22, 2001.

"Haier Group's Exports Soar," *China Daily,* December 21, 1999.

"Mainland Haier to Broaden Cooperation with Tsann Kuen," *Asia Africa Intelligence Wire,* May 19, 2004.

Roberts, Dexter, "Baby Steps for a Chinese Giant," *Business Week Online,* July 18, 2002.

Sprague, Jonathan, "China's Manufacturing Beachhead," *Fortune,* October 28, 2002, p. 192.

—M.L. Cohen

IDEO Inc.

100 Forest Avenue
Palo Alto, California 94301
U.S.A.
Telephone: (650) 289-3400
Toll Free: (800) 600-4336
Fax: (650) 289-3707
Web site: http://www.ideo.com

Private Company
Incorporated: 1991 as IDEO Product Development, Inc.
Employees: 380
Sales: $62 million (2003 est.)
NAIC: 334119 Other Computer Peripheral Equipment
    Manufacturing; 541330 Engineering Services; 541420
    Industrial Design Services; 541490 Other Specialized
    Design Services; 541512 Computer Systems Design
    Services; 541710 Research and Development in the
    Physical, Engineering, and Life Sciences; 541720
    Research and Development in the Social Sciences and
    Humanities; 541910 Marketing Research and Public
    Opinion Polling

IDEO Inc. is a leading design and innovation consultancy. Companies turn to IDEO to create and deliver innovative new products, services, and environments. IDEO is the design force behind such familiar products as the Palm V PDA, Humalog/ Humalin Insulin Pen, and the thumbs-up/thumbs-down innovation on TiVo's digital video recorder remote control.

The firm takes a multidisciplinary approach to design, including human factors experts, architects, linguists, and business and manufacturing specialists in its teams. IDEO has gone beyond developing leading edge products to designing customer ''experiences'' for clients such as lingerie manufacturer Warnaco.

IDEO's Palo Alto, California headquarters is furnished in true eclectic genius style with such ornaments as a DC-3 wing and a coin-operated hobby horse. IDEO also has offices in San Francisco, Chicago, Boston, London, and Munich; half of its work is done abroad. Office furniture giant Steelcase Inc. owns a majority holding in IDEO.

Origins

David M. Kelley was born in Barberton, Ohio. After graduating from Carnegie-Mellon he worked as an engineer for National Cash Register (NCR) and Boeing. Kelley then entered a graduate program in design at the Stanford University School of Engineering. (In addition to serving as IDEO's chairman, he is also the Donald Whittier Professor at Stanford and directs the school's unique design program. He was elected to the National Academy of Engineering in 2001.)

After earning a master's degree, Kelley formed his own design firm in 1978, partnering with fellow student Dean Hovey. Their first four employees were all friends from Stanford. The group's first studio, recalls Tom Kelley, David's brother, was a fly-infested office above a dress shop in nearby Palo Alto. They made their own furnishings and covered the floors with green patio carpet.

Kelley had met Apple Computer Inc. founder Steve Jobs at Stanford, and by 1983, the group had designed the first commercially available computer mouse for Apple's Lisa computer, later used on the first Macintosh. A butter dish and the ball from a bottle of roll-on deodorant were among the building blocks for the first prototypes.

In mid-1991, David Kelley Design merged with ID Two and Matrix Product Design to form IDEO Product Development, Inc. ID Two, led by Bill Moggridge in San Francisco, had nine years earlier designed the first laptop computer, the GRiD Compass. Moggridge had expanded his design business into the United States from the London office founded in 1969. Matrix Product Design, based in Palo Alto, was led by Mike Nuttall, another London designer who had amicably left ID Two. According to the *Independent* of London, both Moggridge and Nuttall had gone to Silicon Valley in the late 1970s as computer technology was emerging. The three companies had first collaborated on the second, award-winning ''Dove Bar'' mouse for Microsoft, Matrix priding industrial design, ID Two providing human factors expertise, and David Kelley Design providing engineering design.

Moggridge was the one who picked the name out of the dictionary, according to *The Art of Innovation.* ''IDEO'' is the combining form of the word ''idea,'' as in ''ideology'' or ''ideogram.'' The company had 125 employees in six offices in Europe and North America and clients in 19 countries. IDEO's multidisciplinary approach called on psychologists and manufacturing engineers as well as designers.

1990s Expansion

In 1990, offices opened in Boston and Chicago. Within a few years, the headquarters was spread across several buildings in Palo Alto, and IDEO had offices in San Francisco, Chicago, Boston, Tokyo, and London, as well as an affiliate in Tel Aviv.

Although the firm did have a president and CEO, David Kelley, the rest of IDEO's organization chart was pure flatland. There was virtually no hierarchy, no advancement, no promotions. Project management duties were rotated. A staff of ten was dedicated to administrative functions. To keep bureaucracy small, the size of each office was limited to about two dozen people.

There were five steps in IDEO's high-speed innovation process: understand, observe, visualize, implement, and evaluate. Extensive research began the process, followed by observations of end users. The visualization step leaned towards producing a series of inexpensive prototypes, rather than poring over lists of specifications. IDEO carefully researched consumer behavior through the eyes of its social scientists to find out what was truly required. The company also asked clients to participate in the role of their own customers, shopping for services and products from rival companies as well.

After implementation and evaluation, the trial-and-error cycle repeated. Speed was key: the company expected brainstorming sessions to produce 100 ideas per hour, one staffer told the *Boston Globe.* To stimulate creative thinking in the brainstorming phase, the offices maintained ''Tech Boxes,'' or cabinets of props containing innovative ideas: Hawaiian flip-flops, toothbrushes, holographic candy, etc.

In 1995, the company was developing 90 different products a year with a staff of just 180, reported *Research Technology Management.* Products ranged from electronics to medical equipment to toys. IDEO's Edge Innovations unit even produced a 3.5 ton mechanical orca whale for the movie *Free Willy.* The company's revenues at the time were between $40 million and $50 million.

In January 1996, office furniture manufacturer Steelcase Inc. made an equity investment in IDEO. At the same time, IDEO CEO David Kelley was designated Steelcase's vice-president of technical discovery and innovation. IDEO had been working with Steelcase companies on various projects since 1987. IDEO helped design the company's ergonomically advanced Leap Chair.

The company became known as simply IDEO, Inc. in 1998. IDEO was a huge force in the world of design throughout its first decade. Products it designed ranged from a stand-up Crest toothpaste tube for Procter & Gamble Co. to a portable defibrillator for HeartStream Inc. In 1999, 3Com tasked it with updating the Palm Pilot, which had already created a new category of portable computing devices. Including the 1980s output of David Kelley Design, IDEO had worked on thousands of products in all.

Nightline *in 1999*

The company picked up numerous design awards along the way and, according to *Business Week,* began to rival management consulting companies as it focused on its clients' interactions with their customers. ABC's *Nightline* news magazine profiled IDEO in a highly popular episode in 1999, giving the firm the assignment of redesigning the common shopping cart in four days.

In 2000, the firm formed ''IDEO U'' to teach clients to be more innovative. IDEO later designed Procter & Gamble's own innovation center, called ''The Gym.'' An office in Munich, Germany, opened at the end of 2000. IDEO had also added branches in Tokyo and Milan. IDEO opened an office in the tech center of Boulder, Colorado, in early 2001.

In April 2001, the company unveiled ''Dilbert's Ultimate Cubicle,'' created in partnership with that chronicler of corporate confinement, cartoonist Scott Adams. Features included a hammock and a ''boss monitor'' trained on the supervisor's door. Tim Brown of Great Britain, previously head of the San Francisco and then the London office, became IDEO's new president in July 2000, and CEO in January 2001.

In a 2001 interview with the *Boston Globe,* General Manager Tom Kelley, brother of the company's founder, described innovation as the next big wave for corporations to embrace

Key Dates:

1969: Bill Moggridge launches London design firm Moggridge Associates.
1978: David Kelley forms Silicon Valley design firm.
1983: Kelley's group designs first computer mouse for Apple.
1991: IDEO Product Development is formed by merger of David Kelley Design with ID Two (Moggridge's second, U.S.-based business) and Matrix Product Design.
1999: ABC's *Nightline* documents IDEO redesigning the shopping cart.
2000: IDEO U is formed.

after quality control and cost cutting. IDEO was extending its innovative process beyond product development to the design of consumer interactions. It set out to make the rail experience attractive again and relevant when hired by Amtrak to design interiors for its high-speed Acela train.

IDEO also ventured into the world of fashion, helping design a high-tech New York showroom for Prada Group NV. Revenues reached $72 million in 2002, reported *Business Week*, before the tech bust was felt. The magazine noted that Internet and other startups had accounted for more than a third of revenues in the boom years. Revenues slipped to $62 million in 2003. In 2004, IDEO was reorganized around "practices," or specific fields of expertise such as Technology-Enabled Experiences (TEX) and Smart Space. Health was the company's largest practice.

Principal Divisions

Health; Consumer Experience Design; Technology Enabled Experiences; Service Design and Innovation; Transformation Services; Zero20 (design for youth); Smart Space.

Principal Competitors

Design Continuum Inc.; frog design inc.; Lunar Design Incorporated; Ziba Design, Inc., McKinsey & Co.

Further Reading

Brown, Tim, "Nurturing a Culture of Innovation," *Financial Times* (London), November 17, 1997, p. 12.

Carrns, Ann, "Workspaces: Imagination's Playground," *Wall Street Journal*, October 18, 1996, p. B14.

Crainer, Stuart, "A Success in Design Minus the Capital D," *Times* (London), Features Sec., May 17, 2001, p. 4.

Eckhouse, John, "3 Product-Design Firms to Merge," *San Francisco Chronicle*, June 10, 1991, p. B1.

Grimes, Ann, "An Idea Firm Finds Growth in Recession," *Wall Street Journal*, March 7, 2002, p. B7.

Grothe, Sam, "Silicon Valley 'Secret Weapon' IDEO Drawn to County's High-Tech Surge," *Boulder County Business Report*, January 26, 2001, p. A1.

Hales, Linda, "Creating an Experience," *Washington Post*, Style Sec., May 12, 2001, p. C2.

Hamilton, Joan, "Now, That Didn't Hurt a Bit," *Business Week*, June 3, 1996, p. 84.

Hargadon, Andrew, and Robert I. Sutton, "Building an Innovation Factory," *Harvard Business Review*, May/June 2000.

——, "The Innovation Factory," *Australian Financial Review*, August 14, 2000, p. 30.

IDEO, Inc., *Extra Spatial*, San Francisco: Chronicle Books, 2004.

Johnson, Cecil, "Mouse Innovator Shares Secrets of Firm's Success," *Seattle Times*, May 21, 2001, p. E2.

Kazakoff, Lois, "Doctors of Design; Medical Market Is Booming for Industrial Designers," *San Francisco Chronicle*, November 15, 1997, p. D1.

Kelley, David M., "Performing Rapid Innovation Magic: Ten Secrets of a Modern Merlin," *Straight from the CEO*, Diane Publishing Co., 1998.

Kelley, Tom, "IDEO Was Wacky, But Got Things Done," *Washington Times*, January 7, 2002, p. D2.

Kelley, Tom, and Jonathan Littman, *The Art of Innovation: Lessons in Creativity from IDEO, America's Leading Design Firm*, New York: Currency, 2001.

Kirsner, Scott, "1. Come Up With Innovative Ideas. 2. Turn Them Into Cool Products. 3. Make Tons of Money. Apple and Ideo Excel in Steps 1 and 2. The Trick Is Getting to #3," *Boston Globe*, January 5, 2004, p. C1.

Koch, John, "The Interview: Tom Koch," *Boston Globe*, Magazine Sec., March 25, 2001, p. 8.

McGhee, Tom, "IDEO Has Designs on Boulder; Creative Firm Has Quirky Reputation," *Denver Post*, January 15, 2001, p. E1.

McGrane, Sally, "For a Seller of Innovation, a Bag of Technotricks," *New York Times*, February 11, 1999, p. G9.

Myerson, Jeremy, *IDEO: Masters of Innovation*, New York: Te Neues Publishing Company, 2001.

Nussbaum, Bruce, "The Power of Design; IDEO Redefined Good Design by Creating Experiences, Not Just Products. Now It's Changing the Way Companies Innovate," *BusinessWeek*, May 17, 2004, p. 86.

Perry, Tekla S., "Designing a Culture for Creativity," *Research Technology Management*, March 1995, pp. 14–17.

Peters, Thomas J., and Tom Peters, *Liberation Management: Necessary Disorganization for the Nanosecond Nineties*, New York: Knopf, 1992.

Pham, Alex, "At IDEO, Thinking Out of the Box Is Good Design," *Boston Globe*, May 29, 2000, p. C2.

Prendergast, Kimberly, "The Ideal Setting for Ideas: Brainstorming Sessions in Business Can Be Productive If Done the Correct Way," *Press-Enterprise* (Riverside, California), September 29, 2003, p. A7.

Reeves, Hope, "Building a Better Bra Shop," *New York Times Magazine*, November 30, 2003, pp. 44+.

Rosenberg, Ronald, "By Design, These Firms Take on Other Companies' Products," *Boston Globe*, May 11, 1997, p. C1.

Schupp, Katja, "IDEO's Product Development Is Second to None; Evanston-Based Firm Rakes in Design Awards," *Daily Herald* (Arlington Heights, Illinois), Bus. Sec., November 30, 2000, p. 1.

Sickinger, Ted, "Innovating Ideas," *Oregonian* (Portland), May 21, 2003, p. B1.

Teresko, John, "R&D Serves Dual Purpose; Steelcase Uses Its Innovations to Transform Its Own Practices As Well As Its Customers'," *Industry Week*, August 21, 2000, p. 103.

Trapp, Roger, "No Mystery Why IDEO Became the Home of Good Ideas," *Independent* (London), Bus. Sec., May 9, 2001, p. 4.

Vasilash, Gary S., "Developing (Manufacturing) Winning," *Production*, March 1995, pp. 8–9.

Ward, Sharon, "Scots Firms Must Do More to Innovate," *Scotland on Sunday* (Edinburgh), December 8, 2002, p. 5.

Watson, Lloyd, "Palo Alto Product Designer Finds Business Booming," *San Francisco Chronicle*, August 3, 1992, p. C3.

—Frederick C. Ingram

ILX Resorts Incorporated

2111 East Highland Avenue, Suite 210
Phoenix, Arizona 85016
U.S.A.
Telephone: (602) 957-2777
Fax: (602) 957-2780
Web site: http://www.ilxresorts.com

Public Company
Incorporated: 1986
Employees: 990
Sales: $65.4 million (2003)
Stock Exchanges: American
Ticker Symbol: ILX
NAIC: 531110 Lessors of Residential Buildings and
   Dwellings; 531210 Offices of Real Estate Agents and
   Brokers; 237210 Land Subdivision

While some still equate the word ''timeshare'' with fraud or scams, the concept of owning a small piece of a resort or hotel and being able to travel there once or twice a year has become increasingly attractive and profitable. Timeshare or flexible-stay vacation ownerships became big business by the late 1990s and have grown into a legitimate part of the billion-dollar hospitality industry. ILX Resorts Incorporated, based in Phoenix, Arizona, sells timeshares, operates resorts, and finances timeshare opportunities, throughout the United States and in Mexico. ILX has properties in Arizona, Colorado, Indiana, Nevada, and Mexico.

Timeshare Experiments: 1986–94

ILX Resorts was founded in 1986 in Phoenix, Arizona, by Joseph Martori. Martori established the company to sell timeshare or flexible-time vacation ownerships at resorts and hotels in the western United States. Martori, a director and CEO of the company, had worked for the Brown & Bain law firm in corporate real estate, and had been a senior partner at Martori, Meyer, Hendricks & Victor, P.A. He attended New York University, where he received both a bachelor's degree and an M.B.A. in finance. He then received his law degree from Notre Dame University in South Bend, Indiana, which would figure in the future of ILX.

ILX went public in 1987 and had a small offering of $2 million in shares in 1988. ILX began selling timeshare interests to a variety of upscale properties and soon realized that actually owning and operating its own resorts might provide additional benefits. The first ILX resort was acquired in Estes Park, Colorado, tucked among the Rocky Mountains. In 1989 the company bought the Los Abrigados Resort in Oak Creek, Arizona, in the beautiful Sedona region. Sedona would figure prominently in ILX's expansion, and prove to be one of the fastest growing travel destinations in the United States. By 1991 ILX was bringing in revenues of $6.1 million for the year; the firm was determined to extend its empire through both increased timeshare opportunities as well as owning and operating its own resorts. By the end of 1993 ILX had nine full-service resorts offering vacation ownership interests in Arizona and its neighboring states.

In 1995 the company made several pivotal moves, which included the acquisition of a historic lodge in Payson, Arizona, called Kohl's Ranch and the implementation of a new concept called Varsity Clubs of America. The Varsity Clubs were timeshares available in upscale, full-service accommodations located close to major colleges and universities. The first Varsity Club was in South Bend, Indiana, near Notre Dame University where Martori had received his law degree. The Club provided temporary housing to visiting alumni and parents of students for university events such as reunions and sports games. Accommodations were one- or two-bedroom suites with kitchenettes as well as a restaurant, lounge, fitness center, gift shop, pool, and even a playground. Also in 1995 was the arrival of Martori's son, Joseph II, who began working at ILX.

Major Expansion: 1996–99

By 1996 the timeshare concept had taken off; major hotel and resort chains had entered the timeshare market and established its legitimacy. Sales of flexible-stay vacation shares grew tremendously throughout 1996 and into the following year. ILX's sales increased from 1996's $31.6 million to $36.4 million in 1997. Industrywide revenues boomed, with record revenues of some $88 billion, according to *Hotel & Motel Management* magazine. The addition of such hospitality giants as Hyatt, Marriott, Hilton, Westin, and Four Seasons hotel chains did add stability to the timeshare market, yet also created major compe-

Company Perspectives:

ILX Resorts Incorporated was formed in 1986 to enter the Vacation Ownership Interest business. The Company generates revenue primarily from the sale and financing of Vacation Ownership Interests. The Company also generated revenue from the rental of its unused or unsold inventory of units at the ILX resorts and from the sale of food, beverages, or other services at such resorts. The company currently owns six resorts in Arizona, developable land adjacent to an existing resort in Arizona, one resort in Indiana, one resort in Colorado, 1,500 Vacation Ownership Interests in a resort in San Carlos, Mexico, and 1,326 (excluding 392 weeks purchased by Premiere Vacation Club but not yet annexed) Vacation Ownership Interests in a resort in Las Vegas, Nevada.

Key Dates:

1986: ILX Resorts is established in Phoenix, Arizona, by Joseph Martori.
1987: ILX becomes a public company.
1988: The first ILX public offering of $2 million in shares is made.
1995: The first Varsity Club, in South Bend, Indiana, is opened. 1997: ILX buys the development rights to the Roadhouse Resort in Arizona.
1998: A second Varsity Club is opened, this one in Tucson, Arizona.
1999: The Premiere Vacation Club Membership Plan is launched.
2000: ILX leases property near the Los Abrigados Resort in Sedona, and a parcel off the Las Vegas strip.
2001: ILX's Sea of Cortez property opens.
2003: ILX announces its first-ever dividend to common stockholders.

tition for a small company like ILX. In 1997 ILX acquired the development rights to the Roadhouse Resort in the White Mountains of Arizona and began selling timeshare opportunities in the popular property, which featured horseback riding and a wide range of outdoor activities.

While 1998 started out promising with the opening of ILX's second Varsity Club in Tucson, near the University of Arizona's main campus, and the inception of its new Premiere Vacation Club timeshare program, the end of the year heralded an end to the solid revenues and growth in the lodging market. ILX moved from the NASDAQ small-cap to the American Stock Exchange in February 1998 with a public offering in February. Chairman and CEO Martori told Steve Bergsman of *Hotel & Motel Management* in June 1998, "The American Stock Exchange will provide a more efficient market for ILX stock; the AMEX specialist system caters well to growing industries such as vacation ownership. We believe the AMEX will provide our stock with greater visibility and improved share liquidity." Soon after its offering, ILX bought a majority stake in the Sedona-based Timeshare Resale Brokers Inc., which built and operated timeshare properties in the western states. With the acquisition, ILX hoped to expand its vacation ownerships into resorts throughout the United States.

Yet poor sales near the end of 1998 forced ILX to reconsider its projected expansion. The firm began buying back its shares at depressed pricing (some two-thirds lower than its high) and managed to end the year with sales of $34.7 million and a profit of only $100,000. Timeshare sales remained stagnant in early 1999 when ILX's subsidiary Timeshare Resale Brokers launched an online listing service through a partnership with the Association of Timeshare Retail Agents. The new site listed available timeshares, auctions, and information related to the field. The market perked up a bit during the remainder of 1999 and ILX finished the year with sales topping $37 million and a profit of $700,000.

The New Century: 2000s

In 2000 ILX opened a sales office in Phoenix, which served as its fifth sales office in the United States. By the middle of the year ILX's sales had topped previous figures for the first and second quarters and the company leased a 44-acre parcel of land

off the Las Vegas strip with future plans for development. The Las Vegas parcel, at the corner of Tropicana and Paradise Road, had what ILX termed the "potential to be developed into a first-class mixed-use development," as quoted in Phoenix *Business Journal* in September 2000. Although the land was currently the site of the Las Vegas International Golf Center, ILX had secured the lease rights for the next 50 years if the company could find financing for its plans. ILX also leased a parcel adjacent to its Los Abrigados Resort in Sedona, Arizona, occupied by the Canyon Portal Motel. ILX planned to renovate the motel and create a sister property called Los Abrigados Lodge.

By 2001 the Sedona area was attracting much attention from developers, including ILX. The company already had its upscale Los Abrigados Resort & Spa, new plans for the soon-to-be Los Abrigados Lodge, as well as two additional purchases. The first was a $1 million parcel next to the Resort to open a sales office; the second was the $5.2 million purchase of the Bell Rock Inn, located in Oak Creek, just six miles from ILX's Los Abrigados properties.

On the Vegas beat, ILX continued with its plans for the $95 million parcel off the strip, envisioning a Varsity Club like those operated in South Bend and Tucson. The Varsity Club concept had proved quite successful, and the third would be close to the University of Nevada at Las Vegas. In addition, ILX gained access to Vegas by acquiring more than 600 timeshare intervals at the pricey Carriage House hotel in the summer of 2001. The 155-suite Carriage House was just off the Las Vegas strip and across from the flashy new Aladdin Hotel & Casino.

ILX's much anticipated Sea of Cortez resort in San Carlos, Sonora, Mexico, opened its doors by mid-2001. The company celebrated the property's grand opening by offering guests complementary scuba diving lessons. ILX pursued further expansion in Mexico by partnering with Consorcio Asag and Grupo Casa to develop additional timeshare opportunities in the San Carlos area.

By 2003 ILX was on a roll. The firm's stock had been touted by Dow Jones as one of its top ten performers for 2002 and

ILX's Sedona resorts were nestled in what *USA Today* called "the most beautiful place in America." ILX operated four resorts in the Sedona area's stunning landscape, and each was highly rated by its guests. In addition, ILX opened a sales office on the top floor of the luxurious Carriage House just off the Las Vegas strip, declared the company's first-ever dividend for common stockholders, and ended the year with its highest revenues yet of $65.4 million, more than 10 percent better than the previous year's figure. Each of ILX's three business segments did well in 2003, especially new sales in vacation ownership interests. According to a company profile of ILX in the *Wall Street Transcript* (April 2002), Martori had mentioned that only 3 percent of American families owned timeshares—which left an untapped market of the remaining 97 percent. Martori and ILX intended to pursue that market and make ILX a major player in the flexible vacation ownership industry.

Principal Subsidiaries

Timeshare Resale Brokers Inc.; VCA Nevada, Inc.; Varsity Clubs of America, Inc.

Principal Competitors

Cendant Corporation; Four Seasons Hotels & Resorts; Hilton Hotels Corporation; Hyatt Corporation; Marriott Ownership Resorts; Silverleaf Resorts, Inc.; Starwood Hotels & Resorts Worldwide; Walt Disney Company.

Further Reading

"AZ Inc.," *Arizona Republic* (reprinted by *Knight Ridder/Tribune News Service*), June 12, 1998.

"AZ Inc.," *Arizona Republic,* August 18, 1998.

"AZ Inc.," *Arizona Republic,* October 20, 1998.

"AZ Inc.," *Arizona Republic,* July 7, 1999.

"AZ Inc.," *Arizona Republic,* August 24, 2000.

Balzer, Stephanie, "Dealing in Vegas," *Business Journal* (Phoenix), August 3, 2001, p. 14.

——, "ILX Posts Best Results," *Business Journal* (Phoenix), May 5, 2000, p. 17.

——, "ILX Supporting Jazz," *Business Journal* (Phoenix), May 12, 2000, p. 18.

——, "ILX to Open in San Carlos," *Business Journal* (Phoenix), December 8, 2000, p. 14.

——, "Logging Some Success," *Business Journal* (Phoenix), August 4, 2000, p. 17.

Bergsman, Steve, "Companies Find REIT Status One Way to Maximize Stock Value," *Hotel & Motel Management,* June 1, 1998, p. 36.

Gilbertson, Dawn, "Arizona Stock Index Flat for 1998; Small Firms Bear Brunt of Big Losses," *Knight Ridder/Tribune Business News,* January 5, 1999.

"ILX Acquires Vegas Land," *Business Journal* (Phoenix), August 22, 2000, p. 55.

"ILX Buys Timeshare Broker," *Business Journal* (Phoenix), July 3, 1998, p. 4.

"ILX Resorts International: Company Profile," *Wall Street Transcripts,* April 8, 2002.

"ILX to Expand in Mexico," *Lodging Hospitality,* August 2001, p. 22.

Vandeveire, Mary, "ILX Resorts Reconsiders Strategy," *Business Journal* (Phoenix), October 23, 1998, p. 51.

—Nelson Rhodes

J. Alexander's Corporation

3401 West End Avenue
Nashville, Tennessee 37203
U.S.A.
Telephone: (615) 269-1900
Fax: (615) 269-1999
Web site: http://www.jalexanders.com

Public Company
Incorporated: 1971 as Volunteer Capital Corporation
Employees: 2,600
Sales: $107.1 million (2003)
Stock Exchanges: American
Ticker Symbol: JAX
NAIC: 722110 Full-Service Restaurants

J. Alexander's Corporation is a Nashville, Tennessee-based chain of 27 full-service, casual dining restaurants (as of December 28, 2003), located in a dozen states but mostly in Ohio, Tennessee, and Florida. The chain offers contemporary American cuisine, with an emphasis on high-quality products made from scratch. The menu features hardwood-grilled steaks, prime rib of beef, seafood and chicken, and pasta, as well as a variety of sandwiches, soups and salads, appetizers, and desserts. J. Alexander's also places a great deal of emphasis on architectural design and interiors. Exteriors are found in a variety of styles, some reminiscent of the work of Frank Lloyd Wright and others of a simple warehouse. Inside, the chain goes for an upscale feel and centers around an open kitchen. J. Alexander's is a public company, trading on the American Stock Exchange.

Founding the Company in 1971

J. Alexander's was founded in 1971 as Volunteer Capital Corporation by legendary entrepreneur Jack C. Massey, the principal shareholder, and two Nashville businessmen named Earl Beasley, Jr., and John Neff. Massey's story was one of a self-made man. He was only four years old when his father, a Georgia country lawyer, passed away, leaving his mother to scrape together a living and raise three children. Massey became a delivery boy for his uncle's pharmacy in Tennille,

Georgia, and because he liked the business, at the age of 17 he left home to become a pharmacist. He was only 25 when he bought a Nashville drugstore. Not only did he manage to keep the business running during the Depression, he was able to add four more drugstores. He sold his five-store chain in 1935 to become a wholesale distributor of surgical supplies to doctors and hospitals. He prospered when the economy rebounded with the advent of World War II and the boom that followed the war. In 1961, when he was just 56, Massey sold his medical supply company and retired a rich man. But after only six months in Florida, he was restless and returned to Nashville in search of a company to buy. By chance he became involved in the restaurant business.

A friend introduced Massey to Colonel Harlan Sanders, the founder of the Kentucky Fried Chicken (KFC Corporation) fast-food chain, then in his 70s. Sanders was impressed with Massey and offered him a $100,000 salary and half the profits if he would run the company for him. Massey declined but offered to find a buyer. According to company lore, the Colonel insisted that he wanted Massey to buy KFC, a decision he then confirmed by conferring with a horoscope. In 1964 Massey and an associate, John Y. Brown, who would one day be elected Kentucky's governor, paid $2 million for the chicken chain, which at the time was generating just $37 million in annual revenues. In seven short years Massey and Brown took KFC public, listing its shares on the New York Stock Exchange, expanded the number of franchised and company-owned restaurants from some 600 to more than 3,500 worldwide, and built KFC's sales to $700 million. In 1971 the business was sold to Heublein Inc., with Massey pocketing $45 million in the deal.

Focusing on Volunteer Capital Corporation in 1978

While he was leading KFC to new heights, Massey returned to his roots by helping to establish Hospital Corp. of America, a for-profit hospital chain. He devoted much of the 1970s growing the company, which he also would list on the New York Stock Exchange. He cut his ties to Hospital Corp. in 1978, but he did not have to worry about retirement and the boredom that accompanied it. He had another company, Volunteer Capital, to occupy his time.

Volunteer Capital was originally a Tennessee-based mutual fund that was not faring well. Earl Beasley, a junior associate, suggested that Massey acquire the fund, sell off the portfolio, and turn it into an operating company. Massey agreed and along with Beasley and John Neff started Volunteer Capital to enter the equipment leasing business, an area he knew from his days of leasing surgical equipment as well as chicken pressure cookers while with KFC. Beasley ran the company until Massey joined after his involvement with Hospital Corp. came to an end. When the leasing business became too competitive, as larger financial companies entered the field, Volunteer Capital switched gears and moved into Massey's other area of expertise, fast food. The company bought several Wendy's Old Fashioned Hamburgers franchises, but Massey soon steered the company toward the chicken sector. Massey believed there was an opening for a "family dining" chicken chain, an alternative to fast-food concepts like KFC and Church's Fried Chicken. In 1979 Volunteer Capital bought the Granny's of Atlanta chain of 21 restaurants, renamed it Mrs. Winner's Chicken & Biscuit, and relocated the headquarters to Nashville. Massey then took Volunteer Capital public two years later, thus becoming the first person ever to chair three companies listed on the New York Stock Exchange.

By the end of 1982 the Mrs. Winner's chain had grown to 64 units. Also in 1982, Volunteer Capital changed its name to Winners Corp. The chain grew to 96 stores in 1983 and reached a total of 184 (two-thirds of which were company owned) in 1984. Massey and his team hoped to build a 1,000-store chain, but the market for the concept proved less than expected and in the mid-1980s Winners was in trouble and losing money. In 1985 the company lost $3.6 million on $112 million in revenue. Following a difficult first quarter in 1986, President and CEO M.V. Hussung, Jr., resigned. He was replaced by 39-year-old Lonnie J. Stout II, who was quite familiar with the operation. Just two years earlier he had resigned as Winners' chief financial officer, a post he held from 1981 to 1984, to head Dinelite Corp., a D'Lites Franchisee. Soon, the chicken chain appeared to have stabilized and was producing a same-store increase in sales, due in large part to the introduction of new products. It was the 60 Wendy's franchises that management considered the major problem for the company. Nevertheless, in 1987 management tried to tinker with the Mrs. Winner's format. It converted six units to a cafeteria-style restaurant dubbed Mrs. Winner's Southern Café.

Winners found itself the object of an unwelcome suitor in 1988 when F.J. Spillman, the former head of the Pizza Inn chain, announced his desire to buy the Mrs. Winner's chain. Stout indicated that the business was not for sale, but in May 1989, after four years of losses that totaled $26.1 million, the company decided to sell Mrs. Winner's to RTM Inc., Arby's largest franchisee, for approximately $30 million in cash. Win-

ners, which reverted back to the Volunteer Capital name, would now concentrate on its Wendy's operations as well as the development of a new casual dinner-house concept, in the belief that the fast-food market was saturated and the dinner-house market offered strong growth opportunities for the next decade.

Massey died in February 1990 at the age of 85, replaced as chairman by Stout, and would not see the birth of the company's upscale dinner-house concept, J. Alexander's. The first unit was launched in Nashville in May 1991 on a street, White Bridge Road, known to local restaurateurs as Death Row, because so many restaurants on it had failed. Volunteer Capital Corp. acquired a restaurant named Rafferty's and considered adopting that name for its new concept, but in the end elected to use J. Alexander as its brand name. Unlike the Raffertys, Bennigan's, Red Lobster, and On the Border restaurants that had floundered on Nashville's Death Row, J. Alexander's flourished from the start, and management took steps to introduce the format on a national basis.

In 1992 two more restaurants opened, in Franklin, Tennessee, and Dayton, Ohio. To fund further expansion, Volunteer Capital made a secondary offering of stock in 1993, grossing close to $10 million. The company resumed opening new units in 1994, moving into Columbus, Ohio, and Oak Brook, Illinois. Volunteer Capital opened four restaurants in 1995, in Ft. Lauderdale, Florida; Birmingham, Alabama; Toledo, Ohio; and Overland Park, Kansas. Five units followed in 1996, in Plantation, Florida; Memphis, Tennessee; Cleveland, Ohio; Chattanooga, Tennessee; and Troy, Michigan. Clearly, the J. Alexander's chain was the future of the company, and so in November 1996 Volunteer Capital sold 52 of its 58 Wendy's restaurants to Wendy's International. In six months the remaining six units would either be closed or sold. In keeping with the company's commitment to its dinner-house format, Volunteer Capital changed its name to J. Alexander's Corporation in February 1997.

Four new restaurants opened in 1997, in Denver, Colorado; Tampa, Florida; San Antonio, Texas; and Livonia, Michigan. Management forecasted modest results for the year, but were caught off guard by the effects of rapid expansion, which—because of the divestiture of the Wendy's chain, and unsatisfactory sales performance in some of the new restaurants—could no longer be offset by another division. For the year, J. Alexander's recorded sales of $57.1 million, a significant decrease over the previous year's $90.9 million. After posting a profit of $7.2 million in 1996, the company now suffered a loss of nearly $6 million. According to a statement by Stout, J. Alexander's results "fell short of our business plan by a wide margin." As a result, the company cut back on its expansion plans to focus on improving sales in the existing 18 restaurants. In addition, management decided to focus on markets possessing a higher income population exceeding 200,000 people living within a five-mile radius. The chain added just two units in 1998—in Louisville, Kentucky, and Baton Rouge, Louisiana—and just one unit in 1999, located in West Bloomfield, Michigan.

Spurning O'Charley's 1999 Takeover Bid

J. Alexander's rebounded somewhat in 1998 and 1999, as management expressed satisfaction with the chain's growing sales momentum. In 1998 revenues grew to $74.2 million (for

Key Dates:

1971: The company forms to lease equipment.
1979: Mrs. Winner's Chicken & Biscuit is acquired.
1989: Mrs. Winner's is sold.
1991: The first J. Alexander's restaurant is opened.
1997: Wendy's operations are sold; the company is renamed J. Alexander's Corporation.
1998: Management rejects a bid by O'Charley's Inc. to buy the J. Alexander's chain.
2001: The company moves from the New York Stock Exchange to the American Stock Exchange.

53 weeks due to a change in the company's fiscal year), and the net loss fell to $1.5 million. Sales for a 52-week year in 1999 improved slightly, to $78.5 million, and the net loss narrowed further to $332,000. J. Alexander's also was dogged for several months in 1999 by an attempt by O'Charley's Inc. to buy the chain in a $30 million cash and stock deal. But management rejected the bid, expressing a commitment to pursue its strategic business plan, which now focused on measured rollout of new units in markets where the company already operated, in particular, Chicago, Detroit, and Miami.

The New York Stock Exchange implemented new listing requirements, mandating a minimum $50 million market capitalization and $50 million in total stockholders' equity. Because J. Alexander's could not meet these criteria, management met with representatives of both the NASDAQ and the American Stock Exchange. The company decided to apply for a listing on the American Stock Exchange and was approved. After 16 years of trading on the Big Board, J. Alexander's moved to the American Stock Exchange starting January 2, 2001.

J. Alexander's opened one restaurant in 2000, located in Cincinnati, Ohio, and two more in 2001, located in Atlanta, Georgia, and Boca Raton, Florida. In 2000 the company recorded its first profitable year since selling off its Wendy's division. For the year, sales totaled $87.5 million, resulting in a profit of $481,000. Despite difficult economic conditions that prevailed in 2001, J. Alexander's managed to remain profitable.

Revenues reached $91.2 million and net income fell slightly, to $271,000. The company added no new restaurants in 2002, during which sales approached $100 million and net income grew to more than $2.8 million (aided by a significant deferred tax benefit). The chain grew to 27 units in 2003 with the opening of three new restaurants. For the year J. Alexander's saw its revenues reach $107 million and net income grow to $3.8 million, which was again padded somewhat by a deferred tax benefit.

Management decided not to add any new restaurants in 2004, electing rather to concentrate on the growth of its existing units. The chain appeared to have turned the corner, and although expansion would likely take place incrementally, J. Alexander's was now well positioned for steady, long-term growth.

Principal Subsidiaries

J. Alexander's Restaurants, Inc.; J. Alexander's Restaurants of Kansas, Inc.; J. Alexander's of Texas, Inc.; JAX Real Estate, LLC.

Principal Competitors

O'Charley's Inc.; Outback Steakhouse, Inc.; P.F. Chang's China Bistro, Inc.

Further Reading

Coeyman, Marjorie, "A High-Wire Balancing Act," *Restaurant Business,* March 1, 1996, p. 108.
"Don't Try to Be Rich," *Forbes,* September 24, 1984, p. 222.
Henry, David, "The Virtues of Quitting While You're Ahead," *Forbes,* December 15, 1986, p. 64.
Howard, Theresa, "Volunteer Capital Dives into New Niche with J. Alexander's," *Nation's Restaurant News,* July 8, 1991, p. 4.
Louis, Arthur M., "The U.S. Business Hall of Fame," *Fortune,* April 13, 1987, p. 102.
Prewitt, Milford, "Volunteer Capital Sells Back Its Wendy Franchise," *Nation's Restaurant News,* July 22, 1996, p. 4.
Romeo, Peter, "Massey, Built KFC, Dead at 85," *Nation's Restaurant News,* February 26, 1990, p. 4.

—Ed Dinger

Jenkens & Gilchrist, P.C.

1445 Ross Avenue, Suite 3200
Dallas, Texas 75202-2799
U.S.A.
Telephone: (214) 855-4500
Fax: (214) 855-4300
Web site: http://www.jenkens.com

Private Company
Incorporated: 1951
Employees: 500
Sales: $272.0 million (2003 est.)
NAIC: 541110 Offices of Lawyers

With its home office in Dallas, Jenkens & Gilchrist, P.C. is one of the largest law firms in the United States, with more than 500 attorneys on staff. Additional offices are located in Austin, Chicago, Houston, Los Angeles, New York, Pasadena, San Antonio, and Washington, D.C. Jenkens is a full-service law firm, involved in more than 20 practice groups. Its intellectual property group is especially well regarded, as is the firm's work as a legal adviser in banking industry mergers. Jenkens' reputation is not without blemish, however. The firm has come under fire by the Federal Deposit Insurance Corporation (FDIC) for its involvement in the savings and loan scandal of the 1980s, and more recently the Internal Revenue Service has lodged a suit to force Jenkens to reveal the names of clients it advised on questionable tax shelter schemes.

Firm Grew Out of 1940s Legal Work for Texas Millionaire

Jenkens grew out of the legal needs of wealthy Texas oilman Clint Murchison, Sr. He was born in Tyler, Texas, the son of a banker. Despite having a prep school education, he defied his parents and refused to attend Trinity University. Instead, he went to work for his father's bank and began to dabble in cattle trading and other private ventures. After serving in the Army during World War I, he returned to Texas and along with a childhood friend, Sid W. Richardson, became involved in the new oil fields in the areas around Wichita Falls, Texas. He soon made a fortune in oil (and would later be credited with being a driving force behind the emergence of the natural gas industry). He then invested in a number of industries, becoming one of the first conglomerate makers. After serving in the military in World War II, his sons—Clint Murchison, Jr. (who would become best known as the first owner of the Dallas Cowboys professional football team) and John D. Murchison—became involved in the family's accumulation of a wide assortment of financial interests. These included the Holt Publishing Company, Easy Washing Machine Company, Virginia and Mississippi insurance companies, a Colorado amusement park, a California race track, bus lines, taxicab companies in both Dallas and Kansas City, a canning company, and worldwide construction contracts. In 1946 Murchison hired former Assistant Attorney General Holman Jenkens to become his personal lawyer, but his legal needs were so great that he had to hire a staff of lawyers and turn to outside law firms for help. One of those staff lawyers was William H. Bowen, who came to Dallas from Chicago and was strong in the area of financing.

The Murchisons decided to sponsor Jenkens and Bowen in setting up an independent law firm, which was formally organized on September 15, 1951. Although its primary purpose would be to service the family's business needs, Jenkens & Bowen would also be able to take on ''Non-Murchison Clients,'' as they were called. Joining the two principals of the firm were associates George C. Anson and Walter M. Spradley. This small group of attorneys set up shop at 1021 Main Street, a two-story remodeled bank building that housed the headquarters for the Murchison family business interests. Not only did Jenkens & Bowen have close business ties to the Murchisons, to reach the firm's offices on the second floor of the building visitors had to pass through the Murchison reception area.

Henry Gilchrist Joins Firm in 1952

Because of Murchison's diversified interests, Jenkens & Bowen was transaction-oriented from the outset, involved in all manner of business matters. With a secure base of work, the firm enjoyed steady growth and expanded its staff. In 1952 Henry Gilchrist joined the firm. After earning a degree in civil engineering from Texas A&M he graduated from the University

Company Perspectives:

At Jenkens & Gilchrist you'll find attorneys nationwide with industry-leading expertise in more than 20 areas of law. But we understand that our greatest insight comes when we work with you to define specific solutions that meet your circumstances and goals.

of Texas School of Law with honors in 1950. Involved in mergers and acquisitions and securities, he would become a strength of the firm for the next 50 years, and Jenkens would ultimately make him a name partner. In 1953 Wilson A. Hanna joined the firm, followed by Joe Gray in 1955.

Although the firm was located in the relatively small city of Dallas, which had a population of just 432,000 in 1951, its work extended well beyond the city limits during the 1950s. Jenkens was involved in a proxy fight for control of the New York Central Railroad; the purchase of a St. Louis subway car manufacturer; the formation of the Kirby Corporation, a Houston oil and gas company; the acquisition and operation of out-of-town banks; the creation of national chemical and steel companies; the establishment of the first publicly owned insurance holding company; the construction of a Denver office building; and even the financing of a John Wayne film, *The Alamo*.

There was so much work, in fact, that the firm had to decline some opportunities because it did not have enough attorneys. Thus, in the 1960s the firm began to expand its staff as well as its capabilities. Not only was Jenkens able to take on more business, it also became less dependent on the Murchisons—a wise move, given that the family would fall victim to falling oil prices in the 1980s and suffer a monumental collapse. Moreover, Dallas evolved into a major city and its economy grew and diversified, leading to even greater growth for Jenkens in the 1970s.

As the Texas economy expanded, Jenkens also broadened its operations, opening an office in Houston in 1983 during that city's boom period, followed by an office in the state capital of Austin. By 1986 Jenkens had 157 lawyers in its three offices and was ranked as the 113th largest law firm in the country. It took a major step in achieving further growth that year when it merged with another Dallas firm, Hutchison Price Boyle & Brooks, adding 28 lawyers. The merger filled out Jenkens' public law and municipal finance capabilities, while Hutchison added tax and banking expertise. Now with 185 attorneys in the fold, the combined firm became the second largest Dallas law firm, trailing only Akin, Gump, Strauss, Hauer & Fled, which had 271 lawyers. Jenkens' Christie Flanagan became managing partner and chief operating officer, and Hutchison's name partner, Ray Hutchison, became chief executive officer and chairman of the executive committee of the newly constituted Jenkens & Gilchrist.

Jenkens was drawn into the savings and loan scandal in June 1987 when the Federal Savings and Loan Insurance Company sued the firm for $100 million, charging the firm with malpractice in its work connected with two failed thrifts: Brownfield Savings and Loan Association and State Savings and Loan Association. Jenkens would agree to an $18 million settlement

in 1989, which released 44 partners from liability, but the matter would linger. After three years of discovery and the accumulation of a million pages of documents, federal regulators filed a new complaint in 1990, targeting four former partners in the firm, suing them each for $100 million. One would go to jail. These additional charges brought unwelcome publicity to the firm, especially because it was also involved in a securities lawsuit concerning a Texas oil company, which made a private stock offering in 1981 with Jenkens' help. In March 1990 a Dallas federal jury returned a $5.8 million verdict against Jenkens on this matter.

In 1989 David Laney became president and chairman of Jenkens. At the time, the firm had been reduced to 160 attorneys, involved in ten practice groups. Under Laney's leadership, Jenkens entered the 1990s very much growth oriented. Despite difficult economic conditions, he was also interested in expanding the firm nationally and actively scouted for merger candidates. In 1991 Jenkens grew its Texas operations. The Austin office merged with Shapiro, Edens & Cook, adding specialists in tax and corporate securities. All told, the Austin office expanded from 13 attorneys to 41. The Houston office, however, suffered a rapid decline. The firm was interested in merging the office with another Houston firm and in preparation restructured, reducing the number of attorneys from 34 to 25. This move led to several attorneys leaving to take jobs elsewhere, including the managing partner. By November 1991, the Houston office was reduced to just seven attorneys.

Jenkens did not begin to achieve the kind of growth Laney envisioned until the mid-1990s, as the U.S. economy began to pick up and Dallas emerged as one of the hottest legal markets in the country. The firm added offices in San Antonio, Washington, D.C., and Los Angeles. It hired new lawyers at a rapid clip, 180 of them from 1996 to 1998. In 1998 Jenkens hired 101 attorneys firmwide. Jenkens also added practices, such as construction law, a practice that had long been the province of boutique law firms but that Jenkens now used as a magnet to attract other business at all of its five offices. Altogether, Jenkens was now involved in 13 separate practice groups, and by the end of 1998 was ranked number 51 in the *National Law Journal*'s list of the largest law firms in the United States. In terms of the number of attorneys employed, Jenkens was now the largest law firm in Dallas. In terms of revenue, it only trailed Akin, Gump in the city.

Chicago Office Opens in 1999

In January 1999 Jenkens opened its seventh office, in Chicago, by cherry-picking five attorneys previously employed by area firm Altheimer & Gray. Over the next 18 months the Chicago office added more top Chicago attorneys, including almost 20 from Arnold, White, and Durkee, five from Houston-based Bracewell Patterson, five from Dallas-based Gardere & Wynne, and in June 2000 nine attorneys from the recently disbanded Hedlund Hanley & John. Jenkens made an even bigger move in 2000 when it entered the New York market by acquiring the firm of Parker Chapin, culminating a two-year search for a New York partner. Parker Chapin was founded in 1934 and added about 150 attorneys, bringing Jenkens' total to 600 attorneys firmwide. In addition to gaining a presence in the key New York market, Jenkens strengthened its corporate, intellectual property, and technology practices. The firm expanded so much that in 2000 it outgrew its Dallas offices, and the national management team moved to another building to open up another floor for lawyers.

After more than a decade as chairman, and instrumental in growing Jenkens from a firm with three offices and 160 attorneys to one with eight offices and more than 600 attorneys, Laney in January 2001 turned over his post to William Durbin, who had been with the firm since 1983. Laney stayed on as a Jenkens' partner, but two years later, in February 2003, elected to leave the firm after 26 years, assuming a non-managerial role at another Dallas law firm, Jackson Walker LLP. With Durbin in charge as CEO and chairman, Jenkens opened a new office in Pasadena and established a biotech consulting subsidiary, Connexon Life Sciences Consulting Inc., operating out of Washington, D.C. But Durbin also had to face some difficult times caused by a recession in the early years of the new century. After pursing a decade-long growth strategy, the firm in 2002 decided to step back and shrink its size in the belief that further expansion would simply dilute strength.

In 2003 Jenkens experienced a large number of defections, as more than 50 of its high-profile attorneys, including former chairman Laney, switched law firms. One contributing factor to this high turnover was the adverse publicity Jenkens was receiving from an IRS investigation on the part the Chicago office played in abusive tax shelters. (Laney, for one, denied that the IRS matter played any role in his decision to leave the firm.) Jenkins and Chicago law firm Brown & Wood (subsequently renamed Sidley Austin Brown & Wood) were accused of help-ing to develop highly technical tax shelters which they then "blessed" by issuing opinion letters that stated the shelters were "more likely than not" to be legal investments under the federal tax code. Such opinion letters were intended to aid taxpayers should they be challenged by the IRS, although there was no guarantee they would avoid penalties. The IRS demanded to know the names of Jenkens' clients who sought advice on tax shelters in order to conduct individual audits, but Jenkens and Sidley refused, citing client-attorney privilege. Jenkens also faced civil suits from clients alleging bad tax-shelter advice. The firm settled this matter by agreeing to pay $75 million. In 2004 Jenkens continued to fight the IRS over its demand that the firm turn over client names, but the firm's position was undercut when Sidley turned over the names of about 400 clients (although it maintained that it withheld the names of clients who asked not to be identified). The matter not only affected Jenkens, it held long-term implications about how individuals sought advice and how lawyers gave it.

In January 2004, Durbin stepped down as chairman and CEO and returned to the firm as a full-time fee-earner. He was replaced by Thomas H. Cantrill, who had served as the firm's chairman for a period some 15 years earlier.

Principal Competitors

Akin Gump Strauss Hauer & Feld LLP; Fulbright & Jaworski L.L.P.; Vinson & Elkins L.L.P.

Further Reading

Bryan-Low, Cassell, "Moving the Market: Jenkens & Gilchrist Agrees to Pay $75 Million in Tax-Shelter Case," *Wall Street Journal,* March 8, 2004, p. C3.

Hansard, Donna Steph, "2 Dallas Law Firms to Merge," *Dallas Morning News,* February 6, 1986, p. 1D.

Harland, Christi, "Jenkens Agrees to Settle Case of Malpractice," *Wall Street Journal,* August 11, 1989, p. 1.

Harland, Christi, and Paul M. Barrett, "Lawyers Are Sued in Dallas S&L Failure," *Wall Street Journal,* March 21, 1990, p. B8.

Maxon, Terry, "Chief Defends Dallas-Based Law Firm Jenkens & Gilchrist After Controversies," *Dallas Morning News,* July 25, 2003, p. 1.

"Texas Is New Wild West for Law Firms," *Salt Lake Tribune,* November 26, 1998, p. D2.

Whitley, Lisa M., "Jenkens & Gilchrist Has 'Never Been Strong,'" *Dallas Business Journal,* January 22, 1999, p. 6.

—Ed Dinger

Jet Airways (India) Private Limited

SM Center, Andheri-Kurla Road
Andheri East
Mumbai
India
Telephone: +91 (22) 2850 5080
Fax: +91 (22) 2850 1313
Web site: http://www.jetairways.com

Private Company
Incorporated: 1991
Employees: 6,500
Sales: $550 million (2003 est.)
NAIC: 481111 Scheduled Passenger Air Transportation

Jet Airways (India) Private Limited is India's leading private airline. It boasts a market share of about 45 percent. Jet operates a relatively young fleet of Boeing 737 jets and ATR72 turboprops. It carries about seven million passengers a year. Its reputation for punctuality and outstanding service attracts a large proportion of business travelers. Jet's founder and chairman is Naresh Goyal, an Indian expatriate living in London.

Origins

Company founder Naresh Goyal began his travel career in 1967 at the age of 18 as a general sales agent (GSA) for Lebanese International Airlines. In May 1974, he formed his own company, Jetair (Private) Limited, to market other foreign airlines in India. Jetair eventually grew to a network of 60 branch offices.

After three and a half decades of monopoly by Air India and Indian Airlines, the Indian government reopened the domestic aviation market to private carriers in April 1989. Goyal set up Jet Airways (India) Private Limited in 1991.

Initial investment was $20 million. Through an Isle of Man holding company, Tail Winds, company founder Naresh Goyal (then based in London) owned 60 percent of Jet Airways, with Gulf Air and Kuwait Airways dividing the remaining 40 percent.

Jet Airways began domestic flight operations with four new-generation Boeing 737s on May 5, 1993. The first flights were from Mumbai (Bombay) to Delhi and Madras and ten other destinations. (Jet was not the first private airline in the skies; that distinction went to East West Airlines, which launched in February 1992.) Jet Airways aimed to carry seven million passengers by the end of 1993, and to take in first year revenue in excess of $75 million (INR 2.4 billion).

The schedule was coordinated with that of Gulf Air to provide convenient connections. Gulf Air assisted the new airline with technical and marketing assistance. The Australian airline Ansett Worldwide also provided engineering expertise, and was the lessor for Jet's first four aircraft.

Malaysia Airlines System (MAS) provided technical and flight training and performed maintenance services, while a unit of British Airways educated cabin staff in customer service. Three of Jet's Boeing 737s were leased from MAS. Jet entered a comprehensive marketing agreement with KLM in 1995.

Surviving and Thriving in the Mid-1990s

Eight private airlines plied the skies over India in the mid-1990s. Jet Airways was the second largest. Revenues for the 1994–95 fiscal year were estimated at INR 360 crore ($120 million), with profits of more than INR 18 crore ($6 million), crore being a traditional term meaning 10 million.

Jet Airways claimed to be the only profitable privately owned airline in India. Indeed, by 1997, five of the seven that had been launched since 1992 were grounded. By another count, more than 20 start-up airlines had been launched in India since deregulation, reported *Airline Business*. Jet Airways was one of the very few survivors.

Jet's revenues rose 32 percent to $300 million in 1997, with profits of $11 million. During the year, Jet bought out the shareholdings of Kuwait Airways and Gulf Air after the Indian government banned foreign ownership in India's airlines. This also scuttled MAS's proposal to acquire a 9 percent stake in Jet Airways.

In 1997, Jet Airways was operating a fleet of one dozen Boeing 737s and was ordering ten more for $486 million. By this time, Jet was India's largest private carrier, and was flying to 20 destinations. Its market share was about 15 percent. Jet Airways Executive Director Saroj Datta (formerly of Air-India and Kuwait Airways) told Britain's *Financial Times* that the airline's choice of newer aircraft was a significant factor in its success. While they cost more to lease, they saved fuel and helped endear business travelers with their reliability. Datta added that Jet benefited from Goyal's background as a general sales agent; it had established interline agreements with 90 foreign carriers flying into India, accounting for 25 percent of revenues.

Late 1990s Price Wars

While the Tat industrial group was unable to secure government approval to create a proposed carrier with Singapore Airlines, the domestic aviation market remained competitive. As demand contracted, rivals engaged in a spirited price war, particularly on the Mumbai (Bombay) to Delhi route.

Nikos Kardassis, Jet's chief executive officer for five years, resigned in the summer of 1999. He was replaced by Executive Director Saroj Dutta, who had been with the airline since 1992.

In 1999, Jet Airways was flying 155 flights a day to 30 destinations. The fleet was up to 25 aircraft, and the airline employed 4,300 people. Jet estimated that it had a 32 percent market share and that 80 percent of its passengers were business travelers.

In October 1999, the airline launched a regional feeder network using leased 64-seat ATR 72 turboprop aircraft. Jet Airways unveiled new uniforms for its 270 cockpit crew members and 660 cabin staff about the same time as the ATR rollout. Designed by Ravi Bajaj, the new uniforms were a year in the making.

Changes in the Early 21st Century

Jet Airways got a new CEO in 2000, Steve Forte, formerly vice-president of marketing at the U.S. carrier TWA. Forte, a native of Italy, also had worked for Meridiana, a small Italian domestic airline, when its aviation market was undergoing liberalization. Forte left the airline in December 2002 to return to the United States. He was replaced by Wolfgang Prock-

Schauer, a former Star Alliance board member. In May 2003, Jet hired its first chief operating officer, Peter Luethi.

The air travel market in India was making up for lost time after being flat for a couple of years. Jet and other airlines were appealing to the government to reduce the tariffs on India's relatively expensive aviation fuel, as domestic carriers paid a $2 per gallon premium compared with foreign ones. Chairman Naresh Goyal told the *Hindu* the airline planned to connect to all of India's tourist destinations. Jet also was increasing frequencies on key routes.

According to *India Business Insight,* Jet Airways' share of domestic passenger traffic rose to 48.7 percent, or more than six million passengers, in 2002. Although the company had reportedly been profitable from its inception, it was now posting significant losses despite total revenue in 2003 of INR 2,876.41 crore ($550 million).

Business Today observed that interest costs had risen 50 percent during the year; fuel costs were also up sharply. The effects of the September 11, 2001 terrorist attacks on the United States, and, later, the SARS health crisis, took their toll on traffic for not just Jet Airways, but most airlines.

Controlling costs was CEO Wolfgang Prock-Schauer's primary agenda. The airline leased two of its Boeing 737s to a Japanese company, and implemented a number of workforce productivity measures. Prock-Schauer aimed for Jet to be posting a profit of $60 million by 2005.

The airline was introducing ultra-low "Super Apex" (advanced purchase excursion fares) tickets to lure passengers away from trains. Passenger demand fell slightly, however, and Jet reduced capacity on some routes and began assigning employees multiple roles and cutting capacity on various routes. A charge card for frequent flyers had been launched with Citibank in August 2000.

International in 2004

Jet Airways and rival private airlines in India were freed to begin flying outside the country on March 22, 2004. Colombo, Sri Lanka, was the first such international destination. Flights to Bangladesh and Nepal followed soon after.

Jet was poised to profit from an expected extension of flying rights throughout Asia. An initial public offering of 25 percent of shares, discussed since 1995, was also in the works. Jet had borrowed about $800 million to finance new aircraft.

Principal Competitors

Air Deccan; Air-India Limited; Air Sahara Limited; Indian Airlines Ltd.

Further Reading

"Air Sahara, Jet Record Losses in '02–03," *Business Standard,* April 13, 2004.

"Airlines' Market Share of Domestic Passenger Traffic," *India Business Insight,* May 31, 2003.

Almazan, Alec, "Indian Domestic Carrier to Add Two B737-400s to Fleet," *Business Times* (Singapore), July 13, 1994, p. 20.

Anand, Byas, "Jet Kicks Off Job Rationalisation," *Economic Times,* November 18, 2003.

——, "Penning a New Take-Off Plan," *Times of India,* June 3, 2003.

Baby, Soman, "Gulf Air to Help Launch Indian Airline," *Moneyclips,* April 19, 1993.

Ballantyne, Tom, "Jet Propelled into Action," *Airline Business,* December 1, 1997, p. 20.

Chatterjee, Purvita, "We Don't Believe Price Wars Are the Answer," *Business Line,* August 19, 1999.

Cuckoo, Paul, "Jet Setter," *Economic Times of India,* August 6, 1999.

"Domestic Airlines Vie for Market Share," *Hindu* (Chennai), September 6, 1999.

Endres, Gunter, "KLM Signs Up Indian Ally—Jet Airways," *Flight International,* September 6, 1995, p. 12.

Fernandes, Edna, "Jet Airways Set for IPO and Expansion," *FT.com,* August 5, 2002, p. 1.

Gupta, Nandini Sen, "High Market Power, Low Cost," *Economic Times,* March 17, 2000.

"India's Private Domestic Airlines," *Financial Times* (London), August 13, 1993, p. 3.

Ishmail, Fauziah, "Airline Eyes Stake in Jet Airways," *Business Times* (Malaysia), May 8, 1996, p. 1.

"Jet Airways CEO Clarifies on Quit Move," *Hindu* (Chennai), November 29, 2002, p. 1.

"Jet Airways Plans Public Issue," *Financial Express,* December 3, 2003.

"Jet Airways Plans to Go Public," *Business Standard,* April 13, 1995, p. 13.

"Jet Airways Will Sport a New Look from Today," *Times of India,* October 21, 1999.

"Jet Mulls Stake in AI to Fly Abroad," *Business Line,* August 23, 2000.

Kamath, Vinay, "Jet Airways Set to Expand Regional Feeder Network," *Business Line,* September 27, 1999.

Kripalani, Manjeet, "Look Who's Gaining Altitude in India," *Business Week,* September 14, 1998, p. 174.

Louden, David, "Fledglings Enter India's Open Skies," *Business Review Weekly* (Australia), June 4, 1993, p. 68.

Malhan, Sangita P. Menon, "Flying Is His Forte," *Times of India,* March 8, 2000.

Marcelo, Ray, "India Frees Up Private Airlines to Fly to South Asian Destinations," *Financial Times* (London), March 22, 2004, p. 5.

Mehta, Nina, "Jet Airways Considering IPO," *Hindustan Times,* November 25, 2003.

Parsai, Gargi, "Jet Airways Restrained from Bidding for Indian Airlines," *Hindu* (Chennai), September 30, 2000.

Phadnis, Ashwini, "New CEO of Jet Airways Targets $60M Profit," *Business Line (The Hindu),* July 16, 2003.

——, " 'Stabilisation, Market Research High on Agenda': Mr. Peter Luethi, Chief Operating Officer, Jet Airways," *Business Line,* May 19, 2003.

Prasad, Swati, and Ashish Gupta, "Can Jet Get Its Nose Back Up?," *Business Today,* December 21, 2003, p. 62.

Shankar, T.S., "Priority for Fleet Strength—Jet Airways Chief," *Hindu* (Chennai), August 7, 2000.

Sidhva, Shiraz, "Passengers Get a Choice—India," *Financial Times* (London), Survey of Business Air Travel, April 20, 1995, p. IV.

Slater, Joanna, "High-Flyer Seeks Airspace: India's Most Successful Airline Has Ambitions to Fly Beyond the Country's Borders, But the Government Wants to Protect the State Carriers," *Far Eastern Economic Review,* December 5, 2002, p. 37.

Tassell, Tony, "Jet Airways Leaves Its Indian Rivals Standing: Newer Aircraft Have Given Naresh Goyal's Carrier a Private-Sector Lead," *Financial Times* (London), Companies and Finance, January 4, 1997, p. 13.

Tay Han Nee, "Sky High Plans for Jet Airways," *Travel Trade Gazette Asia,* December 15, 2000.

Zaheer, Kamil, "Jet Airways CEO Kardassis Quits," *Economic Times,* July 7, 1999.

—Frederick C. Ingram

John Wiley & Sons, Inc.

111 River Street
Hoboken, New Jersey 07030-5774
U.S.A.
Telephone: (201) 748-6000
Fax: (201) 748-6088
Web site: http://www.wiley.com

Public Company
Incorporated: 1904
Employees: 3,500
Sales: $922.96 million (2004)
Stock Exchanges: New York
Ticker Symbols: Jwa; JWb
NAIC: 511120 Periodical Publishers; 511130 Book
 Publishers; 516110 Internet Publishing and
 Broadcasting

Founded in 1807, John Wiley & Sons, Inc. is a leading publisher of print and electronic products, including reference works and journals in science, technology, and medicine; textbooks and other educational materials; and professional and trade offerings in such areas as business and management, computers and engineering, architecture, culinary arts, and general interest. The company operates worldwide through its headquarters in Hoboken, New Jersey, and through foreign subsidiaries in Europe, Asia, Canada, and Australia. Roughly 35 percent of its total sales are derived from outside the United States, while about 25 percent of revenues come via Web-based products. John Wiley & Sons began as a publisher of American fiction writers, then moved into the science and technology segment of the publishing market after the Civil War. From the late 19th century on through the early 21st century, the company has continued to publish academic, professional, and scientific titles, achieving encouraging success as one of the oldest independent companies in all of American industry. Led by a succession of Wiley family members, John Wiley & Sons by 2002 had Peter Booth Wiley, a great-great-great-grandson of the company's founder, serving as chairman. Management of day-to-day operations, however, was in the hands of William J.

Pesce, president and CEO, a position held by a nonfamily member since 1971.

In the early 1980s, W. Bradford Wiley uttered the obvious when he told a reporter from *Publishers Weekly,* ''I guess you can say that we Wileys are survivors.'' In reference to a family whose business dated from the time of the presidency of Thomas Jefferson, this comment was an understatement. Chairman of John Wiley & Sons at the time, W. Bradford Wiley was the great-great grandson of the company's founder, who established a business during the dawn of the 19th century that would employ generation after generation of Wiley family members. Over the course of nearly two centuries the Wiley name has been closely linked to the publishing industry, a span of time that nearly encompasses the existence of the United States and charts the family tree of one of the oldest dynasties in American business. From the founder of the company to W. Bradford Wiley, to Peter Booth Wiley, a long line of Wileys—aided increasingly in later years by nonfamily members—has orchestrated the growth and perpetuation of a publishing empire.

Early History

The founder of John Wiley & Sons was not John Wiley, but his father Charles Wiley, the first of numerous Wileys to earn his money in the publishing business. In 1807 Charles Wiley opened a small printing shop alongside One Reade Street in New York City. Framed by a paperhanging shop on one side and a soapmaking shop on the other, Charles Wiley's business was a modest one, a trait of John Wiley & Sons that would continue to characterize the company for more than a century. Early on, however, the small shop on Reade Street played an integral role in the emergence of the American literary movement.

During its first years in a young country, Charles Wiley's small printing shop served as a bastion for the nation's struggling yet superlative writers. Among the roster of notable writers whose words went to print at the shop on Reade Street were Herman Melville, Edgar Allan Poe, Nathaniel Hawthorne, and James Fenimore Cooper. Each was an associate of Charles Wiley, who helped establish Cooper as perhaps the first major American novelist by publishing *The Spy* in 1821. (By 1820, Charles Wiley had refocused his business on publishing and bookselling, hiring outsiders to do the printing.) All of these famous authors outlived the instrumental Charles Wiley, however, who died in 1826, leaving the business he had founded to his son, John Wiley.

When he took control of the Wiley publishing business in 1826, John Wiley was only 18 years old, but his youth did not prevent the second generation of the Wiley publishing family from taking the company in new directions. John Wiley continued where his father had left off by bringing the words of American writers to the public, but he also embraced the English literary scene by shifting the company's geographic stance overseas, making the Wiley business the first American publisher to offer royalties to foreign authors. To a list that already included Melville, Hawthorne, Poe, and Cooper, John Wiley added such distinguished English literary figures as Charles Dickens, Samuel Taylor Coleridge, John Ruskin, Thomas Carlyle, and Elizabeth Barrett Browning. During his tenure, John Wiley also launched *Literary World,* a book trade weekly that was in publication from 1847 to 1853, representing a precursor to the influential *Publishers Weekly,* which held sway in the publishing world during the late 20th and early 21st centuries. Other business avenues were pursued as well, including John Wiley's foray into selling nonbook items. The sale of pencils, school slates, violins, and stereoscopic equipment and pictures was added to the Wiley business, lending a hint of diversification to the operations more than a century before such strategic moves would become a prevalent aspect of corporate existence. Also noteworthy during this period was the involvement of John Wiley's oldest son, Charles, starting in 1850, whereupon the business became known as John Wiley & Son.

The association the Wiley business had with the 19th century's greatest writers gave the company a unique and pivotal role in the development of the American publishing community. For the future of the company itself, though, the next Wiley to assume command of the company would direct the publisher toward one of the main paths it would pursue through the early 21st century. The years of disseminating the country's greatest literary works were over for the company. Ahead was the entry into a significant new segment of the publishing market for the company.

Post-Civil War Shift in Business Focus

Taking over during the years following the American Civil War was William Halsted Wiley, the second son of John Wiley and a former soldier for the Union Army (because of the latter, he was also known as ''the Major''). Aside from being the second son of John Wiley to join the business—accounting for a change in the company name to John Wiley & Sons in 1875—

William Wiley exerted a definitive influence on the firm. Trained as an engineer, the grandson of the company's founder instilled his passion for engineering and the sciences in the company he led, transforming John Wiley & Sons into a different type of publisher. Under William Wiley's stewardship, the company began publishing textbooks and professional books, a strategy that would fuel its growth for the remainder of the 19th century and carry John Wiley & Sons into the 20th century. In 1904, meantime, the company was incorporated.

By 1914, when annual sales exceeded $300,000, four decades of operating as a publisher focused on science and technology books had propelled the company forward. Between 1875 and the beginning of World War I, John Wiley & Sons' sales volume tripled, as did its payroll, which by the mid-1910s numbered 18 workers. Instead of publishing the novels of Melville and Dickens, the company was making its money in another field, earning its largest profits from publishing books on mechanical and electrical engineering. Such would be the future of the company, as it focused its efforts on the less glamorous, yet nevertheless profitable, science and professional side of publishing. In addition to this new core, John Wiley & Sons diversified into social sciences and business management publishing during the first few decades of the 20th century and gained a stronger presence in postsecondary educational publishing. By 1929, sales reached the $1 million mark for the first time, and then surpassed $2 million by 1941.

During World War II, John Wiley & Sons' business received a boost after several of the company's texts were adopted for use in training armed forces personnel, one of the lucrative markets opened up to the company as a scientifically and technologically oriented publisher. Another lucrative market for John Wiley & Sons expanded dramatically after the conclusion of World War II, when college enrollment swelled across the country, as veterans returned home and economic prosperity spread from coast to coast. Sales of textbooks climbed steadily as college enrollment rose in the United States, while in Asia and in Europe, where countries struggled to rebuild themselves in the postwar era, the demand for textbooks increased as well. John Wiley & Sons answered the call by exporting titles to Europe and Asia, substantially increasing the company's international business.

Post-World War II Growth

It was during this postwar upswing in business that W. Bradford Wiley, the great-grandson of John Wiley, rose to the top of John Wiley & Sons' executive ranks, becoming president of the company in 1956. The company's first overseas subsidiary was established three years later in London, touching off a period of international expansion that over a two-decade period would see John Wiley & Sons foreign subsidiaries established in Canada, Australia, Latin America, India, and Singapore. On the domestic front, John Wiley & Sons sidestepped the prevailing trend toward consolidations and takeovers that produced numerous conglomerate corporations during the 1960s. Despite eschewing the corporate maneuvers of the day, John Wiley & Sons did go public early in the 1960s, making its initial public offering of stock in 1962. It also executed several acquisitions during the decade, most notable of which was its 1961 purchase of Interscience Publishers, which substantially strengthened

Key Dates:

1807: Charles Wiley opens a small printing shop in New York City.

1820: Wiley shifts the focus of his business from printing to publishing and bookselling.

1826: Wiley dies, leaving the business to his son, John Wiley.

1850: John Wiley's oldest son, Charles, becomes involved in the business, which begins using the name John Wiley & Son.

1875: The company adopts the name John Wiley & Sons after John Wiley's son William Halsted Wiley comes onboard; W.H. Wiley is instrumental in the company's move into textbooks and science and technology publishing.

1904: The company is incorporated as John Wiley & Sons, Inc.

1959: The first overseas subsidiary is established in the United Kingdom.

1961: Interscience Publishers is acquired.

1962: The company makes its first public offering of stock.

1971: Andrew H. Neilly, Jr., becomes the first nonfamily member to serve as president and COO.

1996: John Wiley & Sons acquires a 90 percent interest in VCH Publishing Group, a German technical publisher.

1997: Professional book publisher Van Nostrand Reinhold is acquired.

1999: The company initiates the commercial launch of Wiley InterScience, offering online, subscription-based access to journals and reference works in science, technology, and medicine; the company acquires Jossey-Bass, the J.K. Lasser line of tax and financial guides, and a line of textbooks from Pearson PLC.

2001: Hungry Minds, Inc. is acquired in the largest acquisition in company history ($184.1 million).

2002: After 195 years in New York City, John Wiley & Sons relocates to Hoboken, New Jersey.

John Wiley & Sons' list of scientific titles and for the first time steered the company into the area of encyclopedia and journal publishing.

After serving as president for 15 years, W. Bradford Wiley ascended to the top of John Wiley & Sons' executive ranks in 1971, the year he was named chairman of the company, and then during the ensuing decade watched over the family business as it evolved into a thoroughly modern corporation. Also in 1971, Andrew H. Neilly, Jr., became the first nonfamily member to be named president and COO. After establishing a medical division in 1973, which a decade later would publish an average of 60 medical titles a year, W. Bradford Wiley took steps toward repositioning the company to compete in the future. Titles were grouped into product lines, and in 1978 John Wiley & Sons' business activities were restructured into four major groups, comprising the company's professional, educational, international, and medicine business areas.

By the beginning of the 1980s, as it had done for decades, John Wiley & Sons ranked as a leading publisher of textbooks and professional books in science and technology, with offices situated around the globe. In its 175th year of business, the company generated record high totals in sales and earnings, collecting $137 million in sales and earning slightly more than $10 million, fueling confidence that the years after 1982 would continue to bring robust growth. The company by this point in its lengthy history was publishing more than 1,000 titles, 50 percent more than a decade earlier, and with the groundwork laid for John Wiley & Sons' expansion into electronic publishing, expectations ran high, with company officials projecting $300 million in annual sales by 1987. The company's 175th year of business, however, marked the beginning of bad times. Quickly, confidence was replaced by consternation.

Faltering Steps During the 1980s

Amid the celebrations heralding the company's 175th year of business and its record financial highs, John Wiley & Sons acquired Wilson Learning Group, a company founded in 1965 by Larry Wilson, co-author of *The One Minute Sales Person*. A creator of training programs for businesses, Wilson Learning Group added a new facet to John Wiley & Sons' operations, giving the publishing company a new enterprise to help offset flagging book sales. Starting in the late 1970s, college enrollment in the United States began to ebb, causing the sales of college textbooks to drop as well. The sale of such books accounted for one-third of John Wiley & Sons' total annual sales, and as the growth of college textbooks fell from double-digit percentage figures, the Wiley publishing firm began to feel the pinch. By 1984, the growth rate of college textbook sales had dropped to 4.8 percent, significantly weakening one of John Wiley & Sons' chief markets. If help was expected from the 1982 acquisition of Wilson Learning Group, it did not materialize. The subsidiary had been given considerable autonomy, but that proved to be its undoing, as Wilson Learning Group recorded robust growth—expanding at a 30 percent clip—but posted paltry profits.

In 1986 Wilson Learning Group registered a $754,000 loss, prompting one John Wiley & Sons official to remark that the subsidiary was "growing in an undisciplined manner." Two years later, the subsidiary lost a deleterious $2.2 million, which, coupled with John Wiley & Sons' difficulties in the college textbook market, left the publisher hobbled. In 1988 John Wiley & Sons earned $4.7 million on $241 million in sales, totals that when compared with the record year of 1982 pointed to serious problems. In 1982 the company earned more than twice as much as it did six years later on slightly more than half the sales volume, a phenomenon that no one at John Wiley & Sons wanted to perpetuate.

Ruth McMullin, who was recruited from General Electric Company, was hired in 1987 as chief operating officer to lead John Wiley & Sons toward recovery. When McMullin was talking with a *Forbes* reporter two years after joining the publishing firm, she reflected on her assessment of the company at the time. "It was clear this company became complacent about its uninterrupted record of success," McMullin noted, "and complacency led to an inattention to being tough and disciplined." To bring back these qualities, McMullin reorganized John Wiley & Sons' businesses into three divisions—educational, professional and trade, and training—and sold much of the company's floundering medical division, as well as closing the company's West Coast distribution center. Further changes were in the offing, as John Wiley & Sons entered the 1990s and steadily moved toward complete recovery.

Recovery in the Early 1990s

A new management team took over during the early 1990s. Charles R. Ellis was named president and CEO in 1990; Bradford Wiley II, the son of W. Bradford Wiley and the great-great-great-grandson of the founder, succeeded his father as chairman in 1993. John Wiley & Sons began the decade with the launch of a sweeping strategic program aimed at restoring the company's profitability. The program called for the divestiture of poorly performing businesses, the strengthening of core businesses, and entry into new niches of the publishing market; its success restored the image of one of the country's oldest companies.

In 1991 the failing Wilson Learning Group subsidiary was sold, yielding John Wiley & Sons $30 million, and a medical book series was divested. A year that saw the company's college textbook sales record an encouraging gain also brought a new entity into John Wiley & Sons' fold. The law publications division of Professional Education Systems, Inc. was acquired, giving the company entry into a new publishing niche and marking the beginning of a concerted attempt to build John Wiley & Sons into a publisher of legal-oriented titles. Further gains were recorded in this area in 1992, when the company acquired Chancery Law Publishing Ltd. in the United Kingdom and the paralegal publishing line belonging to the James Publishing Group in the United States. By 1993, John Wiley & Sons' college division was recording double-digit leaps in revenues, concurrent with international expansion in Europe and Asia.

In a few short years during the early 1990s, John Wiley & Sons regained the luster lost during the middle and late 1980s. By 1995, after recording 14 consecutive quarters of earnings increases, the company was generating $331 million in sales and posting $18.3 million in net income, achieving performance levels company executives had projected to reach nearly a decade earlier. Despite the less-than-spectacular performance demonstrated during the 1980s, John Wiley & Sons was firmly positioned for strong growth during the later 1990s, its nearly 200-year-old presence in the publishing business and its resolute recovery during the early 1990s sparking confidence for the future.

Late 1990s, Early 2000s: Major Acquisitions, Electronic Initiatives

This confidence proved to be well placed, as John Wiley & Sons grew at an accelerating pace during the late 1990s and early 2000s. Sparking this growth was a multipronged approach encompassing organic growth, acquisitions, strategic alliances, and an increasing emphasis on electronic distribution. The first major acquisition of this era—and at the time of its completion, the largest in company history—was the 1996 purchase for $99 million of a 90 percent interest in VCH Publishing Group, a German technical publisher whose output included about 100 scholarly journals and more than 500 books annually. Many of the other major acquisitions, however, were completed by the company's professional/trade business unit. The first of these was the 1997 purchase of Van Nostrand Reinhold (VNR) from Thomson Corporation for about $28 million. VNR specialized in professional books in such areas as architecture and design, environmental and industrial science, culinary arts and hospitality, and business technology. Also in 1997 John Wiley & Sons sold its law publications division for $26.5 million, having decided it could not effectively compete with larger players in that field, and William J. Pesce was named COO. Pesce had joined the firm in 1989 as head of the educational publishing unit, leading it through the company's restructuring. In May 1998 Pesce was named president and CEO, succeeding Ellis.

The year 1997 also saw the first launch of Wiley InterScience, destined to become the centerpiece of the company's electronic distribution efforts. Initially offered free of charge, this online service was relaunched commercially in January 1999, providing access to more than 300 journals and major reference works in science, technology, and medicine on a subscription basis. By 2003, John Wiley & Sons was generating 25 percent of its revenues from Web-based products, principally from Wiley InterScience.

John Wiley & Sons made three more significant acquisitions in 1999, two of which involved the U.K.-based Pearson PLC. The company spent about $58 million to acquire more than 50 college textbooks and other instructional packages from Pearson Education. On the professional/trade side, John Wiley & Sons bought Pearson's Jossey-Bass unit for $82 million and the J.K. Lasser line of tax and financial guides from IDG Books Worldwide, Inc. for an undisclosed sum. San Francisco-based Jossey-Bass published books and journals for professionals and executives in the fields of business, psychology, education, and health management.

In mid-2001 John Wiley & Sons bought Wrightbooks Pty Ltd., an Australian publisher of personal investment books. The company followed up with its largest acquisition yet, the purchase of Hungry Minds, Inc. (the former IDG Books Worldwide) in September 2001 for $184.1 million in cash and assumed debt. Also based in New York, Hungry Minds was best known as the publisher of the ''For Dummies'' series of how-to books but also published the Bible and the Visual technological series for programmers, Cliffs Notes study guides, Frommer's travel guides, Betty Crocker and Weight Watchers cookbooks, and Webster's New World dictionaries. This acquisition significantly bolstered John Wiley & Sons' professional/trade division, increasing the division's portion of overall company revenues from one-third to significantly more than one-half. In 2001 this division also acquired Frank J. Fabozzi Publishing, publisher of finance titles for the professional and academic markets.

During 2002 Bradford Wiley II's brother, Peter Booth Wiley, was named chairman, with Bradford remaining on the board of directors. John Wiley & Sons also left Manhattan after 195 years in the city. Having outgrown its New York offices, the company was attracted to New Jersey by tax incentives that reward companies for creating jobs. About 800 employees moved into the new headquarters in Hoboken, New Jersey, in July 2002.

Thanks to the company's string of acquisitions, and its emphasis on strategic alliances and electronic distribution, John Wiley & Sons posted record revenues in 2003 of $854 million, a 16 percent increase over the previous year, and record net income (excluding unusual items) of $76.7 million, an 18 percent jump. Since 1993 the company enjoyed compounded annual revenue growth of 12 percent, while earnings had concurrently increased at a compound annual rate of 26 percent. Revenues grew another 8 percent in 2004, reaching $923 million—one or two years' growth away from the $1 billion mark. Net income surged another 16 percent, hitting $88.8 million. As it neared its bicentennial, John Wiley & Sons was expected to continue its reign as one of the oldest companies in the United States and as one of the preeminent publishers in American business history.

Principal Subsidiaries

John Wiley & Sons (Asia) Pte. Ltd. (Singapore); John Wiley & Sons Australia, Ltd.; John Wiley & Sons Canada Limited; John Wiley & Sons (HK) Limited (Hong Kong); Wiley Europe Limited (U.K.); Wiley Publishing, Inc.; Wiley-VCH Verlag GmbH & Co. KGaA (Germany).

Principal Competitors

Reed Elsevier Group PLC; The Thomson Corporation; Pearson PLC; Bertelsmann AG; The McGraw-Hill Companies, Inc.; Wolters Kluwer N.V.; Houghton Mifflin Company.

Further Reading

"Aggressive Marketing Helps John Wiley Book Steady Gains," *Barron's,* May 1, 1978, pp. 40+.

Anthony, Carolyn T., "John Wiley at 175," *Publishers Weekly,* September 24, 1982, pp. 42–46.

Baehr, Guy T., "Publisher Moving Its HQ to Hoboken," *Newark (N.J.) Star-Ledger,* August 10, 2000, p. 43.

Block, Valerie, "Wiley Writes Next Chapter: To Grow with Acquisitions," *Crain's New York Business,* June 21, 1999, p. 4.

Clendenning, Alan, "John Wiley Buying 'Dummies' Publisher," *Bergen County (N.J.) Record,* August 14, 2001, p. L7.

Denitto, Emily, "William J. Pesce: Getting a Read on Growth," *Crain's New York Business,* May 5, 1997, p. 13.

Milliot, Jim, "Pesce, New Wiley Chief, to Focus on Core Businesses," *Publishers Weekly,* July 27, 1998, p. 10.

——, "Revenues Jump 20% at John Wiley in Fiscal 2002," *Publishers Weekly,* July 1, 2002, p. 9.

——, "Wiley Posts Double-Digit Gains in Sales, Earnings," *Publishers Weekly,* June 23, 2003, p. 9.

Moore, John Hammond, *Wiley: One Hundred and Seventy-Five Years of Publishing,* New York: Wiley, 1982.

Poole, Claire, "Stubborn Patriarch," *Forbes,* February 6, 1989, p. 99.

Reid, Calvin, "Wiley Acquires VCH," *Publishers Weekly,* May 13, 1996, p. 22.

——, "Wiley Buys Hungry Minds," *Publishers Weekly,* August 20, 2001, p. 16.

"Unique Publishing Niche Pays Off in Impressive Way for John Wiley," *Barron's,* May 13, 1968, pp. 32+

"Wiley's Long March," *Forbes,* November 22, 1982, p. 155.

—Jeffrey L. Covell
—update: David E. Salamie

Kenmore Air Harbor Inc.

6321 Northeast 175th
Kenmore, Washington 98028
U.S.A.
Telephone: (425) 486-1257
Toll Free: (800) 543-9595
Fax: (425) 485-4774
Web site: http://www.kenmoreair.com

Private Company
Incorporated: 1946
Employees: 125
Sales: $12 million (2002 est.)
NAIC: 481111 Scheduled Passenger Air Transportation;
481211 Nonscheduled Chartered Passenger Air
Transportation; 487990 Scenic and Sightseeing
Transportation, Other; 336411 Aircraft Manufacturing

Kenmore Air Harbor Inc. is the largest seaplane-based airline in the world, offering flights from Seattle, Washington, to a variety of locations in the Pacific Northwest and British Columbia, Canada. Kenmore Air offers scheduled flights, charter service, and packaged excursions. The company's fleet of 22 aircraft, most of which are de Havilland Beavers and de Havilland Otters, carry more than 60,000 passengers annually, logging more than two million air miles. Kenmore Air also makes a substantial amount of its annual sales from repairing and restoring seaplanes. The company specializes in restoring and modifying de Havilland Beavers, stripping the aircraft down to the bare frame before restoring the seaplane and modifying it by increasing the aircraft's carrying capacity, climb rate, and cruising speed. In the aviation industry, these modified de Havilland Beavers are known as "Kenmore Beavers."

Origins

The largest seaplane operation in the world began on the shores of Lake Washington in Kenmore, a small community northeast of Seattle. The business was founded by three high school friends, Reginald Collins, Jack Mines, and Robert Munro, who combined their complementary talents to start an aviation business in the shadow of one of the world's premier aviation companies, Boeing Co. The three friends did not intend to create a rival to the behemoth Boeing; floatplanes could never match the commercial potency of airplanes. Instead, the business they started on Lake Washington was an extension of their passion for aviation, a hobby made into a business that, if successful, could only achieve modest growth. At the company's inception, Collins, Mines, and Munro were investing their time and money in a labor of love, but of the three founders, Munro demonstrated the greatest devotion. He spent more than a half-century nurturing Kenmore Air's development, leaving behind him a pioneering legacy and the world's largest seaplane operation.

Robert B. Munro was born in 1917 in Olympia, Washington, the state's capital located 60 miles south of Seattle. During the early years of World War II, Munro was living in Oakland, California, where he attended the Boeing School of Aeronautics, studying mechanics with his friend Reginald Collins. After completing their coursework, Munro and Collins worked for Pan American at the airliner's maintenance base at Boeing Field, located in Seattle. While working for Pan American, Munro and Collins bought their first seaplane, an Aeronca Model K that was in serious need of repair. "We found one that was turned upside down in Lake Union," Munro recalled in a June 1, 1996 interview with the *Seattle Post-Intelligencer*. "So we bought it for six or seven hundred dollars. Just for the fun of it we rebuilt it."

Collins and Munro's decision to spend their off-hours from Pan American rebuilding a floatplane spoke of their passion for aviation mechanics. Their high school friend Jack Mines had a similar passion, but his skills were expressed in flying planes rather than in fixing them. While Collins and Munro exercised their skills on the Aeronca Model K, Mines was using his talents in the Pacific, flying patrol planes for the U.S. Navy. After the war, the three high school friends were reunited in Seattle, where the two mechanics—in possession of a restored seaplane—and the pilot decided to turn their mutual interests and skills into a business. The trio searched for a location for their proposed flight service and found one in 1945 on the north shore of Lake Washington, where they purchased property occupied by a defunct lumber mill. The company was initially named "Mines Collins Munro," but the corporate title only

---

Company Perspectives:

Our airline is different. For starters, we build our own planes . . . our fleet is the envy of pilots worldwide. Tickets aren't necessary. Just tell your name. Don't look for departure gates. There aren't any. We'll direct you to a picnic table where you'll meet your pilot and fellow passengers. Feed the ducks 'til it's time to go.

---

existed for several months before the founders decided to affiliate their enterprise with the local community, renaming the fledgling concern ''Kenmore Air.''

The corporate life of Kenmore Air officially began on March 21, 1946, when the Aeronca Model K first lifted off Lake Washington in service of the company. Weeks later, the founders purchased three more seaplanes, giving the nascent Kenmore Air its first, modest-sized fleet of aircraft. During its early years, the company earned its money by accessing remote and sometimes dangerous locations. It was in such service that one of the founders died fours months after the company's first flight. In July 1946, Jack Mines lost his life flying supplies to a search and rescue team bivouacked in the Cascade Mountain Range east of Seattle. Mines's widow sold her late husband's interest in the company to Collins and Munro, who worked together briefly before Collins decided to accept a job offer in California. Collins sold his interest in the company to Munro, leaving Munro, by the late 1940s, as the sole proprietor of Kenmore Air.

An important part of Kenmore Air's business from the start was the company's involvement in seaplane repair and restoration. Although Munro obtained his pilot's license and earned recognition as a skillful aviator, his first passion was in fixing planes, a quality of his character that was reflected in his company. Kenmore Air gained its greatest global renown and a substantial amount of its revenue by repairing planes and, later, restoring planes. Munro's interest in airframe and engine mechanics prompted him to establish a parts department not long after Kenmore Air was formed. By the end of the 1950s, after a decade of servicing seaplanes for an expanding customer base, Kenmore Air became an official aircraft and parts dealer for Cessna Aircraft Company. During the 1960s, the company cemented its reputation for master mechanics and design with the de Havilland Beaver, an aircraft of singular importance to Kenmore Air. The company purchased its first Beaver in 1963 and shortly thereafter created a rebuilding and modification program for the seven-passenger seaplane. Kenmore Air built its fleet around the versatile Beaver, despite the fact that de Havilland ceased production of the model in 1967. After de Havilland stopped making Beavers, Munro and his team of mechanics stepped in, asserting themselves as expert refurbishers of the aircraft. The company modified and rebuilt the seaplanes to such an extent that throughout the global aviation community the aircraft were referred to as ''Kenmore Beavers.''

Against the backdrop of Kenmore Air's growing prowess in aviation mechanics, the flying side of its business developed. During the 1950s, the company began chartering flights, offering trips to fishing and hunting locations throughout the Pacific

Northwest. Kenmore Air also secured its first contract with the federal government early in the decade, leasing a restored plane that was used for a mapping survey in Alaska. The company's first contract with the federal government led to numerous other government-sponsored contracts, particularly with the U.S. Navy. The company attracted industrial customers during the 1950s as well, drawing business because of the unique capabilities of its growing fleet. In 1953, for example, a Canadian mining operation turned to Kenmore Air for help in establishing a mining camp north of Ketchikan, Alaska. The mining company wanted to establish a camp on Leduc Glacier, a massive operation that required the use of three Kenmore Air aircraft over a two-month period. The company's planes delivered several pieces of large equipment to the glacier, including diesel engines, railroad cars, and tractors.

Expansion: 1960s–70s

Kenmore Air established a stable business foundation in the 1950s, giving the company the opportunity to expand its base of operations during the 1960s and 1970s. As the company gradually expanded its fleet of de Havilland Beavers during the 1960s, concerns about the availability of space prompted Munro to expand Kenmore Air's physical operations. A new hangar was built as well as new office space, giving the company much needed room to accommodate its future growth. During the 1970s, as ''Kenmore Beavers'' entered the lexicon of the aviation community, Kenmore Air's aircraft flew for both institutional and private customers. In the early 1970s, the company strapped unarmed torpedoes to the floats of its seaplanes and hauled the weapons to a joint U.S.-Canadian test range facility near Vancouver Island, British Columbia. For a five-year period during the decade, Kenmore Air pilots transported scientists and supplies to the Olympic Mountain Range, located west of Seattle. The pilots' duties bordered on stunt work, requiring them to land on a glacier located at the 6,800-foot level of Mount Olympus. To take off, the pilots aimed their craft down the glacier and slid for 4,000 feet, pulling back on the flight stick just as the glacier dropped off to the valley below. The company's chartered flight service also expanded during the 1970s, when Kenmore Air offered roundtrip service through three- or five-day packages to fishing resorts in British Columbia.

By the late 1980s, Kenmore Air held sway as a nearly 50-year-old seaplane operation renowned for its mechanical repair and engineering, its chartered flights, and its service to commercial and government customers. Munro, in his early 70s by this point, continued to fly for his company, overseeing an operation that counted several of his children and grandchildren as employees. His fleet of aircraft, refitted, refurbished, and restored in large part by Kenmore Air mechanics, took on a measure of youthfulness with the addition of two de Havilland Turbo Beavers late in the decade. In the mid-1980s, Kenmore Air completed an acquisition when it purchased Otter Air. Otter Air offered scheduled service from Seattle to Victoria, British Columbia, routes Kenmore Air operated for two years before selling them to its main competitor, Lake Union Air, in 1988.

Kenmore Air in the 1990s

Expansion continued in the 1990s, as Kenmore Air solidified its position as the world's premier seaplane operator. The

Key Dates:

1946: Kenmore Air flies for the first time.
1951: Kenmore Air secures its first contract with the federal government.
1963: Kenmore Air purchases its first de Havilland Beaver.
1986: Kenmore Air acquires Otter Air.
1992: Kenmore Air acquires its principal competitor, Lake Union Air.
2000: Robert Munro dies after an extended illness.

company completed another acquisition in 1992, when it purchased its principal competitor, Lake Union Air. The acquisition brought Munro back to the site where he and Collins had purchased the submerged Aeronca Model K that became the company's first aircraft. Aside from eliminating Kenmore Air's only serious competition in the Pacific Northwest, the acquisition of Lake Union Air represented a valuable addition to Munro's operations for other reasons. The acquisition added significantly to the company's fleet and it gave Kenmore Air a terminal on Lake Union, a body of water close to downtown Seattle, that became Munro's second base of operations. A year after the acquisition, Kenmore Air converted one of Lake Union Air's de Havilland Otters into a turbine-powered aircraft, which, after the purchase of several Turbo Otters in 1994, gave the company the largest Turbo Otter fleet in the world.

Kenmore Air turned 50 years old in 1996, an anniversary that was celebrated at the northern end of Lake Washington on June 1. Those who attended the six-hour-long festivities came to pay tribute to Munro and his company, an organization that occupied a singular place in the Pacific Northwest's business community. The company's fleet of 22 aircraft, consisting of de Havilland Beavers and Otters, as well as several Cessnas, carried 50,000 passengers a year, logging two million miles on routes servicing Seattle, the San Juan Islands, and British Columbia.

As the company prepared for the late 1990s, it sought to expand its operations further to compensate for one economic development in particular. Canadian fishing areas, for years a popular destination for Kenmore Air's customers, fell under increasing restrictions during the first half of the 1990s, stripping the company of a mainstay source of business. To counter the decline in salmon-fishing tours, Munro proposed adding flights on Elliott Bay, a body of water that provided

access from Seattle's waterfront to the Puget Sound. In 1998, one year after Munro proposed the idea, Kenmore Air obtained a federal permit to float a 25-foot-square dock on Elliott Bay and to begin offering seaplane service. Munro intended to offer as many as 36 daily flights from the Elliott Bay float during the summer, but he still needed approval from Seattle's city council. Although the waterfront's business community welcomed the addition of Kenmore Air to Elliott Bay, the proposed venture sparked vigorous community resistance. In the fall of 1999, Munro decided to abort his plans for seaplane service from Elliott Bay. "It has been up and down for several years," he explained in an October 19, 1999 interview with the *Seattle Post-Intelligencer.* "I'm getting tired," he added. "I don't want to fight people. I want to be friends."

As Kenmore Air entered the 21st century, the family-run business suffered its greatest loss. After an extended illness, Munro died in October 2000, passing away at the age of 83. The challenge of continuing Munro's legacy of success fell to his family members, some of whom had been working for the company for years. Munro's son, Gregg, served as president, while Gregg Munro's sister, Leslie Banks, served as office manager, and was joined by her son Todd Banks, who served as general manager. In the years ahead, the task of maintaining Kenmore Air's premier stature fell to these principal figures.

Principal Subsidiaries

Kenmore Air Express.

Principal Competitors

Washington State Department of Transportation; Clipper Navigation Inc.; National Railroad Passenger Corporation.

Further Reading

Barber, Mike, "Council Gives Limited OK to Floatplanes in Elliott Bay," *Seattle Post-Intelligencer,* January 7, 1999, p. B3.
Brunner, Jim, "Robert Munro; Daring Pilot, Founder of Kenmore Air Harbor," *Seattle Times,* November 1, 2000, p. B5.
"Kenmore Air Drops Plan for a Base on Elliott Bay," *Seattle Post-Intelligencer,* October 19, 1999, p. B1.
"Kenmore Air Withdraws Bid to Offer Tours from Elliott Bay," *Seattle Times,* October 19, 1999, p. C2.
Lange, Larry, "Floatplane Base for Elliott Bay Hits Turbulence," *Seattle Post-Intelligencer,* September 3, 1998, p. B1.
Sell, T.M., "Many Happy Takeoffs and Returns," *Seattle Post-Intelligencer,* June 1, 1996, p. C8.

—Jeffrey L. Covell

Kirkland & Ellis LLP

Aon Center, 200 E. Randolph Drive
Chicago, Illinois 60601
U.S.A.
Telephone: (312) 861-2000
Fax: (312) 861-2200
Web site: http://www.kirkland.com

Private Partnership
Founded: 1908
Employees: 1,000
Sales: $611 million (2003 est.)
NAIC: 541110 Offices of Lawyers

Based on gross revenue of $611 million, Kirkland & Ellis LLP is the largest law firm in Chicago and the 12th largest in the United States, according to *American Lawyer* magazine, using 2002 financial results. It is also the fifth most profitable law firm in the country. In addition to its home office in Chicago, Kirkland maintains offices in Washington, D.C., New York, Los Angeles, London, and San Francisco. All told, the firm employs more than 1,000 attorneys, serving major national and international clients. The firm has ranked consistently within the top five most frequently used firms by *Fortune 250* corporations. Practice areas are divided into six groups: bankruptcy, intellectual property, interdisciplinary, litigation, tax and planning, and transaction. The firm has a reputation in the legal community for being extremely aggressive litigators. With the general public, however, Kirkland is best known for the notoriety generated by some of its attorneys: Robert Bork, whose failed nomination to the Supreme Court contributed to a widening gap between conservatives and liberals, and Kenneth Starr, the controversial special prosecutor whose investigations of President Clinton led to his impeachment.

Founding the Firm in 1908

Kirkland was established in 1908 by Chicago attorneys Stewart G. Shepard and Robert R. McCormick. Born to wealth, McCormick was by far the better known of the partners. His father's family made a fortune from manufacturing the McCor-

mick reaper, and his mother was the daughter of the founder and longtime publisher and editor of the *Chicago Tribune,* Joseph Medill. After attending English boarding schools, McCormick enrolled at Yale University, where he was no more than a mediocre student, graduating in 1903. Uncertain about career plans, he moved to Chicago at the behest of his father and enrolled in Northwestern University Law School. Although he never completed his studies, he was admitted to the bar in 1908. The law practice he formed with Shepard and another partner was originally housed in the Tribune Company building. McCormick's work with the firm was minimal because of his increasing interest in the *Tribune.* When his uncle, the managing editor of the newspaper, died in 1910, McCormick and his cousin, Joe Patterson, became joint publishers. By 1920 McCormick had severed his ties to the law firm he cofounded and would instead become an important client.

Kirkland's name partners—Weymouth Kirkland and Howard Ellis—both joined the firm in 1915. Kirkland, who was in his late 30s at the time and 15 years older than Ellis, would become the most significant attorney in the first half-century of the firm's history, especially well regarded for his work as a trial lawyer. Ellis, for his part, would assist Kirkland in some of his most celebrated cases. Together, Kirkland and Ellis were a formidable team.

Kirkland became chief counsel to the *Tribune,* which under McCormick's leadership adopted an aggressive outspoken attitude. The newspaper, which had been in decline when McCormick and Patterson took charge, having fallen to third place in Chicago's circulation wars, became a world famous publication—dubbed "The World's Greatest Newspaper" by the cousins—but the *Tribune* also became the object of defamation suits, which Kirkland and Ellis would litigate on McCormick's behalf. Henry Ford, for instance, sued the *Tribune* for $1 million for libel concerning a 1915 editorial. Although Ford actually won the case, Ford was only awarded six cents from the jury. The newspaper also was sued by a Chicago mayor who claimed that the *Tribune*'s campaign against him was in effect a libel against the city, a position the court rejected. The *Tribune,* represented by Kirkland & Ellis, also took the side of a small Minnesota newspaper that challenged a state "gag" law, which

Company Perspectives:

The Firm's goal is to be an instrumental part of each client's success.

limited the press's ability to criticize public officials. The case, *Near v. Minnesota,* was perhaps Weymouth Kirkland's greatest legal victory, and was without doubt one of the most important First Amendment cases in history. In 1931 the matter came before the United States Supreme Court, which ruled the Minnesota law unconstitutional. It was Ellis who was credited with developing the concept of "fair comment," which is today taken for granted as a fundamental right of free speech in the United States.

Hammond Chaffetz Joining the Firm in 1938

Ironically, the attorney that would have the greatest impact on the growth of Kirkland & Ellis into a top national law firm came to the attention of Weymouth Kirkland and Howard Ellis when he bested the seemingly unbeatable team—supplemented with legal all-stars—in the courtroom. The attorney was Hammond E. Chaffetz and the case in question was *United States v. Socony Vacuum, et. al.* Chaffetz graduated from Harvard Law School in 1930, a time when the country had descended into the Great Depression and jobs were difficult to find. Through the recommendation of a professor—Felix Frankfurter, who later became a Supreme Court Justice—Chaffetz was able to secure a position in the Justice Department's Antitrust Division, where over the next several years he became involved in trying a number of antitrust cases. In one, the Justice Department took on International Business Machines, challenging IBM's practice of "tying" the purchase of business machines with punch cards. Decades later, the underlying theories of this case would be used against Microsoft. But Chaffetz was a free-market Republican working in the Democratic administration of Frank Roosevelt. Because he felt his chances of advancement in the Justice Department were limited he decided to resign, but he agreed to take on one final case. In 1938 the 31-year-old Chaffetz headed a small team of Justice Department lawyers that took on 16 major oil companies and 30 executives, charging them with a price-fixing conspiracy in violation of the Sherman Antitrust Act. Chaffetz faced off against some of the country's leading corporate lawyers, including Weymouth Kirkland. Chaffetz won the case, and the ruling was upheld in a landmark Supreme Court ruling. Chaffetz's abilities were not lost on Weymouth Kirkland, who offered him a partnership in Kirkland & Ellis's Washington office, which had opened in 1930 and was little more than an outpost.

Chaffetz went to work in the Washington office, but his career soon was interrupted by World War II. He joined the Navy, served in the Pacific on the aircraft carrier Essex, and rose to the rank of Lieutenant Commander. Following the war, he continued to practice for Kirkland for several years in Washington, then in 1951 he moved to Chicago where most of the firm's major clients were located, and where he had recently met his future wife. After years of fighting against major corporations, Chaffetz now defended many of them, including oil companies accused of price fixing. He even defended a mobster,

Lucky Luciano of Murder Inc. fame, who along with publisher Moses Annenberg was accused of providing instant horse race results by telegraph to bookies. He argued a number of cases before the Supreme Court, including one that upheld the right of the Standard Oil Company to engage in competitive pricing. In the 1960s he represented General Motors, which faced charges of fixing the price of pollution control valves. He urged GM not to settle the matter out of court, then won the cases at trial. Moreover, when the plaintiffs promised not to appeal if they were paid $50,000 to cover legal costs, Chaffetz convinced GM to refuse, thus sending the message that litigation was not free. A lasting contribution Chaffetz made to the legal profession was his leadership in the development of the procedures and forms encompassed in the *Manual for Complex Litigation.* This effort grew out of an electrical equipment price-fixing case of the 1960s, when it was discovered that some equipment manufacturers had developed a scheme to allocate bidding rights to each other based on the phases of the moon. Utility companies around the country filed lawsuits against some 20 defendants, resulting in a tangled web of litigation unparalleled in the annals of the federal court system. Chaffetz was instrumental in determining a way to coordinate the handling of multiple lawsuits filed in different courts but involving related parties and issues. The guidelines that resulted from this effort would be relied on by federal judges in more recent cases involving asbestos, breast implants, and tobacco.

When Chaffetz moved to Chicago, he became a driving force in transforming Kirkland into a major law firm. He was a tireless recruiter of young legal talent, targeting the top students at the best law schools. He was known to take job candidates to dinner, capped off with a long walk and a sales pitch. Chaffetz convinced many of them to join Kirkland in Chicago, where he promised they would soon have a chance to work directly with clients, rather than becoming, in effect, the research assistant for a senior partner in a Manhattan law firm with a bigger name. After Weymouth Kirkland died in 1965, followed by Ellis in 1968, most of the firm's top lawyers had been brought in by Chaffetz. In addition to expanding the firm's roster of attorneys, he was also influential in setting the tone of Kirkland's culture. He was a major contributor, of time and money, to many of Chicago's most important civic, charitable, and educational institutions, including the Chicago Symphony, the Steppenwolf theater, United Way, The University of Chicago, and Northwestern Law Schools. In the early 1980s when he was in his 70s, Chaffetz began to cut back on his law practice but he never officially retired. In fact, he would come into the office for another 20 years, the last time the day before he died in January 2001 at the age of 93.

Washington Office Suffering Defections in 1983

Chaffetz was also influential in Kirkland's geographic expansion, as the firm moved into Denver, Los Angeles, New York, and London. Growth did not come without a few stumbles along the way, however. In 1983 the Washington office, which had a major communications law practice, underwent a significant change when the Chicago office landed a new client in Ameritech, the interests of which conflicted with many of the high-tech clients of the Washington office. As a result, partner Richard Wiley felt compelled to split off from Kirkland,

Key Dates:

1908: The firm is founded by Stewart Shepard and Robert McCormick.
1915: Weymouth Kirkland and Howard Ellis join the firm.
1930: The Washington office opens.
1938: Hammond Chaffetz joins the firm.
1965: Kirkland dies.
1990: The New York office opens.
2003: The San Francisco office opens.

forming his own law firm and taking with him about half of Kirkland's 80 Washington attorneys. Ten years later Kirkland lost five key Chicago and Denver attorneys in its lucrative litigation department. They formed their own law firm with offices in Chicago and Denver. A year later, Kirkland slashed its Denver operation, transferring most of the staff to the Los Angeles operation. The firm denied that the financial impact of losing its rainmakers played any role in the decision.

While Kirkland made its early reputation as a champion of the first amendment, over the years the firm became more associated with the protection of corporate interests. In fact, during the 1990s the managing partner of the Washington office, Tom Yannucci, became the scourge of news organizations, engendering both fear and respect for his success in defamation cases. His media law practice began in 1993 when he represented General Motors in its suit against "Dateline NBC," which was found to have used hidden explosives to spice up a crash test demonstration. Over the next several years he would take on the ABC, NBC, CBS, CNN, the *Wall Street Journal*, the *New York Times, USA Today, Consumer Reports*, and Reuters. His clients would include tobacco company Brown & Williamson and Chiquita Brands International.

In a 2002 profile of Kirkland, *American Lawyer* wrote, "Trial lawyers are, by nature, alpha dogs. But no big firm embraces that culture so jubilantly as Kirkland & Ellis. 'We love to try cases,' brags litigation partner Thomas Yannucci. 'The internal culture is that you're a wimp if your case is not tried.'" The firm was reluctant to work as a co-counsel, preferring a dominant role. According to one lawyer interviewed by the magazine, Kirkland was "unnecessarily aggressive." *American Lawyer* went on to say, "The firm is proud of its hard-nosed reputation, but Yannucci insists they don't go over the line. He suggests that any criticism leveled against the firm smacks of sour grapes. 'People will resent you if you make them look bad.'"

Kirkland also drew scrutiny during the 1990s because one of the firm's partners, Kenneth Starr, was named the Whitewater Independent Counsel to investigate past financial dealings of President Clinton, an office that took on a number of other cases, including the Paula Jones civil suit and the Monica Lewinsky investigation that eventually led to the President's impeachment. For a time, Starr continued to serve as a Kirkland attorney while pursuing his independent counsel duties, but under pressure eventually took an unpaid leave of absence. The firm was further entangled in the President's legal problems when a Kirkland attorney, Richard Porter, was found to have faxed an affidavit in the Jones case to the *Tribune* before it was officially filed in court. Porter was a former aide to President George H. Bush and Vice-President Quayle, overseeing opposition research on Vice-Presidential candidate Al Gore. Porter also was involved in directing Linda Tripp, who had secretly tape recorded conversations with Monica Lewinsky regarding her relationship with the President, to Starr's office. Kirkland maintained that Porter's activities were on his own time and did not represent a conflict.

Kirkland continued its growth into the new century. In 2001 it expanded its Los Angeles office by acquiring the small bankruptcy firm Wynee Spiegel Itkin. In January 2003 Kirkland established its second California location, and sixth worldwide, when it opened an office in San Francisco, a move that according to the firm was "driven by client demand."

Principal Competitors

Cravath, Swaine & Moore; Jones Day; Sidney Austin Brown & Wood LLP.

Further Reading

Beck, Susan, "Concert Masters: Litigators at Kirkland Always Expect to Call the Tune, Set the Beat, and Finish First," *American Lawyer,* January 2002, p. 76.

Johnston, David Cay, "H. E. Chaffetz, 93, Lawyer on Antitrust and Price Fixing," *New York Times,* January 17, 2001, p. A2.

Lennon, Robert, "Pushing the Envelope," *American Lawyer,* January 1, 2004.

Rosenberg, Geanne, "Tom Yannucci: On the Attack," *Columbia Journalism Review,* September/October, 2000.

Warren, James, "Law Firm Where Starr Was a Partner Says It Helped Group Backing Paula Jones, Court Papers Show," *Chicago Tribune,* November 10, 1998.

—Ed Dinger

Kroger

The Kroger Co.

1014 Vine Street
Cincinnati, Ohio 45202-1141
U.S.A.
Telephone: (513) 762-4000
Fax: (513) 762-4454
Web site: http://www.kroger.com

Public Company
Incorporated: 1902 as The Kroger Grocery and Baking
    Company
Employees: 290,000
Sales: $53.79 billion (2003)
Stock Exchanges: New York Cincinnati Chicago
Ticker Symbol: KR
NAIC: 445110 Supermarkets and Other Grocery (Except
    Convenience) Stores; 445120 Convenience Stores;
    447110 Gasoline Stations with Convenience Stores;
    448310 Jewelry Stores

Among companies that principally operate grocery stores, The Kroger Co. ranks first in the United States (discount retailer Wal-Mart Stores, Inc., through its supercenter outlets, is actually the leading seller of groceries in the country). Kroger runs more than 2,500 food stores in 32 states in the Midwest, South, Southwest, and West; these stores operate under about two dozen banners, including Kroger, Fred Meyer, Ralphs, Food 4 Less, Smith's, Fry's, Dillons, and King Soopers. More than 500 of the outlets include gasoline stations and nearly 1,900 feature pharmacies. Of Kroger's total sales, 95 percent is derived from these food retailing operations, with the remainder coming from the company's convenience stores, jewelry stores, and manufacturing facilities. Kroger operates nearly 800 convenience stores under six flags in 16 states, most of which also sell gasoline, and about 440 fine jewelry stores under the names Fred Meyer, Littman, Barclay, and Fox's. The company's 42 food processing facilities produce dairy products, bakery goods, deli items, and other grocery products.

Late 19th-Century Chain Store Pioneer

The Kroger Co. traces its roots back to 1883, when Bernard H. Kroger began the Great Western Tea Company, one of the first chain store operations in the United States. Kroger left school to go to work at age 13 when his father lost the family dry goods store in the panic of 1873. At 16, he sold coffee and tea door-to-door. At 20, he managed a Cincinnati grocery store, and at 24, he became the sole owner of the Great Western Tea Company, which by the summer of 1885 had four stores in Cincinnati. Kroger's shrewd buying during the panic of 1893 raised the number to 17, and by 1902, with 40 stores and a factory in Cincinnati, Kroger incorporated and changed the company's name to The Kroger Grocery and Baking Company.

Kroger Co. historians characterize B.H. Kroger as somewhat of a "crank," fanatically insistent upon quality and service. Profanity was called his second language; he often advised his managers to "run the price down as far as you can go so the other fellow won't slice your throat."

Part of Kroger's success came from the elimination of middlemen between the store and the customer. In 1901, Kroger's company became the first to bake its own bread for its stores, and in 1904, Kroger bought Nagel Meat Markets and Packing House and made Kroger grocery stores the first to include meat departments.

This important innovation, however, was not easy. It was common practice at that time for butchers to short-weight and take sample cuts home with them, practices that did not coincide with B.H. Kroger's strict accounting policies. When Kroger installed cash registers in the meat departments, every one of them inexplicably broke. When Kroger hired female cashiers, the butchers opened all the windows to "freeze out" the women and then let loose with such obscene language that the women quit in a matter of days. When Kroger hired young men instead as cashiers, the butchers threatened them with physical force. But Kroger was stubborn, and in the long run his money-saving, efficient procedures won out.

From the beginning, Kroger was interested in both manufacturing and retail. His mother's homemade sauerkraut and

197

Company Perspectives:

Our mission is to be a leader in the distribution and merchandising of food, health, personal care, and related consumable products and services. By achieving this objective, we will satisfy our responsibilities to shareowners, associates, customers, suppliers, and the communities we serve.

pickles sold well to the German immigrants in Cincinnati. In the back of his store, Kroger himself experimented to invent a "French brand" of coffee, which is still sold in Kroger stores.

Expansion Outside Cincinnati, Early 20th Century

The Kroger Grocery and Baking Company soon began to expand outside of Cincinnati; by 1920, the chain had stores in Hamilton, Dayton, and Columbus, Ohio. In 1912, Kroger made his first long-distance expansion, buying 25 stores in St. Louis, Missouri. At a time when most chains hired trucks only as needed, Kroger bought a fleet of them, enabling him to move the company into Detroit; Indianapolis, Indiana; and Springfield and Toledo, Ohio.

When the United States entered World War I in 1917, B.H. Kroger served on the president's national war food board and on the governor of Ohio's food board. His dynamic plain speech raised substantial amounts of money for the Red Cross and Liberty Bonds.

After the war, The Kroger Grocery and Baking Company continued to expand, following Kroger's preference for buying smaller, financially unsteady chains in areas adjacent to established Kroger territories. In 1928, one year before the stock market crashed, Kroger sold his shares in the company for more than $28 million. One of his executives, William Albers, became president. In 1929 Kroger had 5,575 stores, the most there have ever been in the chain.

Since the early 1900s, chain stores had been accused of driving small merchants out of business by using unfair business practices and radically changing the commerce of communities. In the 1920s, an anti-chain store movement began to gain momentum. Politicians, radio announcers, and newspapers talked about "the chain store menace." People feared the rapid growth of chains and their consequent power over their industries. Because the grocery industry was so much a part of most people's lives, food chains such as Kroger bore the brunt of public complaints.

Chain store company executives soon realized they would have to organize in order to prevent anti-chain legislation. In 1927 the National Chain Stores Association was founded and William Albers was elected president.

When Albers resigned as president of Kroger in 1930, he also resigned as president of the organization. Albert H. Morrill, an attorney who had served as Kroger's general counsel, was elected president of both in his stead. Morrill faced not only the economic challenges of the Great Depression but also the political challenges of the growing public distrust of chain stores.

With the limited transportation and communication systems of the time, the company had to decentralize in order to grow. Morrill established 23 branches with a manager for each branch, and hired a real estate manager to close unprofitable stores. He also implemented policies that guarded against anti-chain accusations, while encouraging customers to shop at Kroger stores.

Instead of going through the usual channels for buying produce, The Kroger Grocery and Baking Company began to send its buyers to produce farms so they could inspect crops to ensure the quality of the food their stores sold. This counteracted the frequent complaint that chain stores sold low-quality foods. The policy eventually resulted in the formation of Wesco Food Company, Kroger's own produce procurement organization.

Morrill also began the Kroger Food Foundation in 1930, making it the first grocery company to test food scientifically in order to monitor the quality of products. The foundation also established the Homemakers Reference Committee, a group of 750 homemakers who tested food samples in their own homes.

In 1930, one of the company's southern managers, Michael Cullen, proposed a revolutionary plan to his superiors: a bigger self-service grocery store that would make a profit by selling large quantities of food at low prices that competitors could not beat. But at this stage, Kroger executives were wary of the idea, and Cullen went on alone to begin the first supermarket, King Kullen, in Queens, New York.

Throughout the Depression, Kroger maintained its business; by 1935, Kroger had 50 supermarkets of its own. During the 1930s, frozen foods and shopping carts were introduced, and the Kroger Food Foundation invented a way of processing beef without chemicals so that it remained tender, calling the process "Tenderay" beef.

Morrill and Colonel Sherrill, vice-president of Kroger, became involved with the American Retail Association in 1935. A report of the organization's publicity release on the front page of the *New York Times* prompted controversy, because the headline stated that the organization would work as a "unified voice" in economic matters, which suggested a kind of "super lobby" to some people. This led to a congressional investigation and in 1938, a bill was introduced imposing a punitive tax against chain stores that would almost certainly force them out of business. Only after much controversy and public debate was the punitive tax bill defeated that year.

In 1942, Morrill died. Charles Robertson, formerly vice-president and treasurer, became president. The company's plans for growth were shelved during World War II, with about 40 percent of its employees serving in the armed forces. The Army Quartermaster Corps commissioned the Kroger Food Foundation to create rations that would boost the morale of soldiers, and the company produced individual cans of date pudding, plum pudding, and fruit cake. Other rations that came from Kroger included cheese bars, preserves, and "C-ration crackers."

Rapid Postwar Growth

After the war, in 1946, Joseph Hall, who had been hired in 1931 to close unprofitable stores, became president. He changed the company name from The Kroger Grocery and Baking Com-

Key Dates:

1883: In Cincinnati, Ohio, Bernard H. Kroger founds the Great Western Tea Company, one of the first chain store operations in the United States.

1902: With 40 stores and a factory in Cincinnati, the company incorporates as The Kroger Grocery and Baking Company.

1929: Store count peaks at 5,575.

1946: Company changes its name to The Kroger Co.

1952: Revenues surpass $1 billion.

1960: Kroger expands into the drugstore business.

1983: Company acquires Dillon Companies, Inc. and begins operating stores coast to coast; the Kwik Shop convenience store chain is also acquired.

1988: Kroger fends off hostile takeovers by awarding shareholders with a special dividend, pushing its debt load to $5.3 billion.

1999: In a deal valued at about $13 billion, Kroger acquires Fred Meyer, Inc.

2000: Revenues top $50 billion.

pany to The Kroger Co., in keeping with indications that the company was moving into a new period of growth. In 1947 Kroger opened its first egg-processing plant in Wabash, Indiana, in order to further ensure egg quality. Hall also saw that 45 private-label brands were merged into one Kroger brand, and introduced the blue-and-white logo with the name change.

Hall's new policy of consumer research was an important change for the company. Decisions about products and methods of selling were to come from the "votes" shoppers left at the cash register. During his years as president, the company moved into Texas, Minnesota, and California. Annual sales grew as small neighborhood stores were replaced with larger supermarkets. In 1952 Kroger's sales topped $1 billion.

This was a time of rapid growth for supermarkets. Between 1948 and 1963, the number of supermarkets in the country nearly tripled. Kroger was already testing the specialty shops that would later be integral to its "superstores." As competition in the industry grew increasingly fierce, Kroger joined with six other firms to found the Top Value Stamp Company, which tried to bring customers into the stores with stamp collecting promotions.

In 1960 the company began its expansion into the drugstore business, with an eye on the potential for drugstores built next to grocery stores. The company bought the small New Jersey-based Sav-on drugstore chain and made its owner, James Herring, the head of the drugstore division. The first SupeRx drugstore opened in 1961 next to a Kroger food store in Milford, Ohio.

Discount stores—strategically located stores that aggressively merchandised goods on a low margin basis with minimum service—were the retailing trend of the 1960s. By 1962, Kroger had also gone into discounting.

In 1963 Kroger's sales reached $2 billion. In 1964 Jacob Davis, a former congressman and judge and a vice-president of Kroger, replaced Hall as president and CEO. Davis concen-

trated on the manufacturing branch of Kroger. With the construction of the interstate highway system in the 1950s and 1960s, central manufacturing facilities could now serve larger territories, allowing Kroger to combine small facilities into larger regional ones.

Davis's experience in both retail and law became important to the company as the government began to clamp down on the food industry. During hearings for the 1967 Meat Inspection Act, several chains were exposed for selling adulterated processed meats. The U.S. Department of Agriculture revealed that Kroger was selling franks and bolognas with two to four times the legal amount of water or extender, and pork sausage treated with artificial colors to make it look fresh.

With the rapid growth of food chain stores, the government also began to concentrate on enforcing antitrust laws. Kroger was one of the companies the Federal Trade Commission (FTC) challenged on its mergers. In 1971 the FTC proposed a consent order that required the company to divest itself of three discount food departments, charging that Kroger stores would "substantially lessen" competition in food retailing in the Dayton, Ohio, area. Kroger settled without admitting any violation of antitrust laws, and sold the three food departments. The order also prohibited Kroger from buying any food store or department in nonfood stores in which the number of stores or sales accrued would indicate a lessening of competition in that city or county.

James Herring became president of The Kroger Co. in 1970 and began to take Kroger into the superstore age, closing hundreds of small supermarkets and building much larger ones with more specialty departments.

The 1970s were a turbulent time for the grocery industry in general, but both turbulent and productive for Kroger. The company perfected its "scientific methods" of consumer research, using the results in planning and advertising. In the early 1970s, at the request of consumer groups, Kroger led the industry in marking its perishable products with a "sell by" date. Kroger began to bake only with enriched flour to add nutrition to its bread products. Two years later, nutritional labels were put on Kroger private-brand products. In addition, food and nonfood products were stocked in twice the variety they had been in the previous two decades.

To increase the accuracy and speed of checkout systems, Kroger, in partnership with RCA, became the first grocery company to test electronic scanners under actual working conditions, in 1972. An invention borrowed from the railroad industry, the scanner was originally used as the electric eye that read symbols on the side of railcars. Kroger and other grocery chains decided to try to use it to read prices on products.

While the government controlled prices between 1971 and 1974, grocery stores suffered depressed profits, but by 1974, the net profits of the top food chains were up 57 percent. As food chains grew into ever larger and more powerful businesses and gained increasing control over the agricultural economy through their enormous wholesalers, there was another round of FTC hearings that revealed the illegal business practices of several chains. In 1974, Kroger settled out of court on an antitrust claim against Kroger and two other chains for fixing beef prices. In 1974 the FTC also sued Kroger for violations of its 1973 trade rule that all stores must stock a sufficient supply of specials to meet anticipated demand and must give rain checks if the supplies run out. In 1977 Kroger consented to the FTC order.

But the biggest battle Kroger faced in its tangles with the FTC concerned the company's use of "Price Patrol," an advertising promotion used in certain markets at different times between 1972 and 1978, in which Kroger advertisements compared Kroger prices with the prices of its competitors on 150 products a week. The figures were based upon surveys conducted among homemakers. The FTC ruled that slogans such as "Documented Proof: Kroger leads in lower prices" were unfair and deceptive because the items surveyed excluded meat, produce, and house brands. A controversy ensued when the Council on Wage and Price Stability expressed concern that tougher standards for Kroger might prevent the dissemination of food price information in the future, but the FTC decided that surveys must be conducted fairly and reliably and that their limitations should be made clear. Kroger appealed; the "Price Patrol" issue was not decided until 1983, when Kroger settled out of court with the FTC.

In 1978 Lyle Everingham, who began his career as a Kroger clerk, became CEO. The company sold Top Value Enterprises and opened Tara Foods, a peanut butter processing plant, in Albany, Georgia. As Kroger moved more toward the "superstore" concept of one-stop shopping, it began to test even more in-store specialty departments such as beauty salons, financial services, cheese shops, and cosmetic counters.

1980s: Acquiring Dillon and Kwik Shop, Fending Off Takeover Bids

The 1980s were a period of significant expansion for Kroger. In 1981 Kroger began marketing its Cost Cutter brand products. In 1983 Kroger merged with Dillon Companies, Inc. and began operating stores coast to coast. That same year, the company acquired the Kwik Shop convenience store chain. A year later, Kroger formed a nonunion grocery wholesaler for Michigan called FoodLand Distributors with Wetterau. In 1987, however, Kroger reduced its involvement in standalone drug stores when it sold most of its interests in the Hook and SupeRx chains.

In 1988 Kroger received several takeover bids, mainly from the Dart Group Corporation and from Kohlberg Kravis Roberts, whose highest bid topped $5 billion. Kroger rejected the bids and restructured, expecting that recapitalization would enhance its competitiveness. The reorganization expanded employee ownership to more than 30 percent of the company's shares. Kroger also awarded its shareholders with a dividend of cash and debentures worth $48.69 per share. Kroger financed the restructuring by selling $333 million worth of unprofitable assets and by assuming $3.6 billion in loan debt. Among the divested properties were 95 grocery stores, 29 liquor stores, its Fry's stores located in California, and the majority of its stake in Price Saver Membership Wholesale Clubs.

Following the restructuring, Kroger's debt load totaled $5.3 billion. For the next several years, the firm focused on paying down this debt and stayed away from major acquisitions and from significant expansion. Kroger did, however, purchase 29

Great Scott! supermarkets in Michigan in 1990 and add them to the Kroger chain.

Paying Down Debt and Improving Efficiency in the Early and Mid-1990s

During the recession of the early 1990s, Kroger felt the pressure of increasing competition in several of the markets it served. The geographic diversity of the firm's holdings, however, insulated it from serious trouble. Under the leadership of Joseph A. Pilcher, who became CEO in 1990, Kroger adopted a strategy of protecting market share at all costs, including sacrificing margins for the more important cash flow needed to pay off the debt. When faced with increased competition in a particular market—for example when Food Lion, Inc. expanded into Texas in 1991—Kroger would simply lower prices and accept the resulting reduced margins. In fact, Kroger lost money for a period in the early 1990s in Texas as well as in Cincinnati and Dayton, Ohio. The company was able to offset such losses to some degree by relying more heavily on higher margin markets, although such markets were becoming rarer thanks to the expansion of low-price competitors.

Kroger also had to face the consequences of its unionized workforce and had to compete with nonunion chains. In addition to the increasing competitive pressures, Kroger's sales and earnings were affected in 1992 by a ten-week strike in Michigan and another work stoppage in Tennessee. Although the Michigan strike ended with the workers essentially accepting the package initially offered them, 1992 sales increased only 3.7 percent over 1991 and the company margin remained in the 0.5 percent range where it had resided since 1990. Consequently, Kroger embarked on a major program to improve its efficiency through technological improvements. From 1992 to 1994, $120 million was spent to make checkout operations more efficient and accurate, to install a new management information system, and to improve direct-store delivery accounting.

By 1994 Kroger's debt load had been reduced significantly, to $3.89 billion. Kroger enjoyed savings of almost $23 million in 1994 alone from its technology investments. The company also benefited from the economic recovery during which interest rates fell, thus reducing the amount needed to spend servicing its debt whenever it could refinance its loans. Enough money could now be freed up for Kroger to shift its focus from debt maintenance to expansion. The timing of this expansion was critical in that Kroger now faced yet another and significant threat, this time from supercenters—such as those operated by Wal-Mart, Kmart Corporation, and Meijer Incorporated—which were combination food, pharmacy, and general merchandise stores. By 1994 more than one-quarter of Kroger's sales base competed directly with a supercenter. Kroger's plan was to continue using its combination food and drug store format—facilities that were about one-third the size of the supercenters—but to increase their number dramatically.

During 1994, Kroger spent $534 million on the expansion, which included 45 new stores, 17 expanded stores, 66 remodelings, and the acquisition of 20 stores. From 1995 to 1997, $600 million was to be spent each year on expansion projects. Overall, this would be the largest capital expansion in Kroger history.

To free up additional money for the program and further reduce the company debt, Kroger in early 1995 sold Time Saver Stores, a division of Dillon which included 116 convenience stores in the New Orleans area, to E-Z Serve Convenience Stores, Inc. of Houston, Texas. Later that year, David B. Dillon, CEO of the Dillon subsidiary, became president and COO of Kroger.

Early returns from the company's mid-1990s expansion were positive. Kroger's 1994 margin of 1.2 percent was its best in several years, and 1995 saw a healthy sales increase of 4.3 percent. By 1997, when Kroger's grocery store count was nearing 1,400, the company enjoyed its best year yet—net income of $444 million on sales of $27 billion, translating into a 1.6 percent margin—while total debt had dropped to $3.2 billion.

Late 1990s and Beyond: Acquiring Fred Meyer, Squaring Off Against Wal-Mart

Its improving fortunes emboldened Kroger to join—in a big way—the ongoing consolidation wave that was sweeping the grocery industry. In October 1998 the company announced that it planned to acquire Fred Meyer, Inc. in a stock swap valued at about $8 billion plus assumed debt of $4.8 billion. The deal closed in May 1999. The Portland, Oregon–based Fred Meyer brought to Kroger 800 grocery stores located in 12 western states—a good geographic fit given Kroger's presence primarily in the Midwest, South, and Southwest. The Oregon firm operated several chains: the flagship Fred Meyer stores, one-stop shopping superstores averaging 145,000 square feet and including more than 225,000 food and nonfood products arranged within dozens of departments; and the Smith's Food & Drug Centers, Ralphs Grocery, and Quality Food Centers supermarket chains—the latter two having been acquired by Fred Meyer earlier in 1998. Fred Meyer, which reported 1997 sales of $15 billion, was also the fourth largest fine jewelry retailer in the country, operating 381 stores under five names in 26 states. The Fred Meyer deal enabled Kroger to maintain its position as the largest supermarket operator in the United States, with annual sales of about $43 billion, although the company soon ceded its position as the largest U.S. food retailer to the hyperbolically growing Wal-Mart.

Kroger wrung out significant synergies from its huge acquisition, achieving annual cost savings of $380 million per year. By 2000, revenues had swelled to $49 billion, while net income hit $877 million, signifying another jump in the profit margin, to 1.8 percent. Also during 2000, however, a deal to purchase the 75 grocery stores operated by Winn-Dixie Stores, Inc. in Texas and Oklahoma was nixed by the FTC, which was concerned about the potential erosion in competition in the Fort Worth, Texas, market.

Combining to slow Kroger's growth to a crawl was the economic downturn of the early 2000s coupled with heady competition—particularly from Wal-Mart, which by undercutting prices charged at traditional grocery stores pressured the entire food retailing industry to keep prices down. Revenues only inched ahead, topping $50 billion for the first time in 2001, then reaching $51.76 billion the next year, an increase of just 5.6 percent over a two-year span. Profits, however, surged 37 percent, hitting $1.2 billion in 2002 (and representing a profit margin of 2.3 percent), as Kroger management reined in operating costs. Late in 2001, for example, the company launched a restructuring that involved the elimination of 1,500 jobs and the consolidation of its Nashville division into other divisional offices. During 2002 Kroger aimed to cut another $500 million in operating costs in part by shifting from a divisional buying structure to centralized, nationwide buying. At the same time, the company completed several small, fill-in acquisitions, adding 34 stores from Baker's, Furr's, and other grocers in 2001 and then buying 42 Raley's, Albertson's, and Winn-Dixie supermarkets the following year. By the end of 2002, Kroger was operating nearly 2,500 supermarkets and multi-department stores. About 350 of these outlets included gasoline stations, an initiative first launched in 1998 to generate additional revenue.

In June 2003 Pichler stepped down as CEO of Kroger and was succeeded by Dillon, who became chairman as well one year later when Pichler retired. The new leader's first year was a difficult one, punctuated particularly by labor disputes. Kroger's Ralphs chain, along with Albertson's, Inc. and Safeway Inc., endured a four-and-a-half-month strike in southern California—the longest grocery strike in U.S. history. That strike ended in late February 2004. Kroger was also hit by a two-month strike in West Virginia in late 2003 that temporarily closed 44 stores. The two disputes reduced the company's 2003 fourth-quarter profits by $156.4 million. Several other charges, including a $444.2 million pretax charge associated with goodwill impairment at the struggling Smith's chain, resulted in Kroger taking $801.3 million in after-tax charges for the year, reducing profits to just $314.6 million. Sales, however, increased 3.9 percent, to $53.79 billion.

Despite the disappointing results for 2003, Kroger seemed better positioned than the other major U.S. supermarket players to withstand the Wal-Mart onslaught. Its keen focus on curtailing operating costs was enabling it to hold the line on price increases, this in spite of the fact that its unionized workforce was better paid and enjoyed better benefits than the nonunion workers at Wal-Mart. Moreover, Kroger claimed to hold the number one or number two position in 43 of its 52 major markets. Future acquisitions and new store openings were likely to be designed to bolster the company's standing in these existing territories rather than to expand into new ones.

Principal Subsidiaries

Dillon Companies, Inc.; Fred Meyer, Inc.

Principal Divisions

Atlanta Division; Central Division; Cincinnati Division; Delta Division; Great Lakes Division; Mid-Atlantic Division; Mid-South Division; Southwest Division.

Principal Operating Units

City Market; Convenience Stores and Supermarket Petroleum; Dillon Stores; Food 4 Less; Fred Meyer Jewelers; Fred Meyer Stores; Fry's; Jay C; King Soopers; Kwik Shop; Loaf 'N Jug/MiniMart; QFC; Quik Stop; Ralphs; Smith's; Tom Thumb; Turkey Hill Minit Markets.

Principal Competitors

Wal-Mart Stores, Inc.; Albertson's, Inc.; Safeway Inc.; Royal Ahold N.V.

Further Reading

Benson, Eliot H., "Upswing in Kroger Results Reflects Expansion Effort," *Barron's,* September 16, 1974, pp. 24 + .

Berss, Marcia, "Cash Flow Joe," *Forbes,* June 6, 1994, p. 47.

"Big Marketplace, Big Stores," *Forbes,* December 10, 1979, p. 101.

Byrne, Harlan S., "Bigger Is Better," *Barron's,* February 28, 2000, p. 22.

Coolidge, Alexander, "Top of the Food Chain," *Cincinnati Post,* June 24, 2004, p. C6.

Cross, Jennifer, *The Supermarket Trap: The Consumer and the Food Industry,* Bloomington, Ind.: Indiana University Press, rev. ed., 1976, 306 p.

Gustke, Constance, "A Quiet Giant," *Progressive Grocer,* November 15, 2002, pp. 18–23.

Hackney, Holt, "Kroger Co.: Price Check," *Financial World,* June 7, 1994, p. 18.

The Kroger Story: A Century of Innovation, Cincinnati: The Kroger Co., 1983.

Lebhar, Godfrey M., *Chain Stores in America,* New York: Chain Store Publishing Corporation, 1963.

Lipin, Steven, "Kroger Agrees to Acquire Fred Meyer," *Wall Street Journal,* October 19, 1998, p. A3.

Nee, Eric, "Kroger Emphasis Is Shifting Away from the Sun Belt," *Supermarket News,* May 30, 1983, pp. 1 + .

Orgel, David, "Kroger Co. to Step up Expansion," *Supermarket News,* May 23, 1994, p. 1.

"Plain and Fancy: Supermarket Boutiques Spur Kroger's Gains," *Barron's,* May 25, 1981, pp. 37 + .

Saporito, Bill, "Kroger: The New King of Supermarkets," *Fortune,* February 21, 1983, pp. 74 + .

Tosh, Mark, "Kroger: Under Pressure," *Supermarket News,* January 18, 1993, p. 1.

Zwiebach, Elliot, "Kroger Faces Hurdles As It Consolidates Fred Meyer," *Supermarket News,* October 18, 1999, p. 1.

——, "Staying Power: Kroger Co. Is Putting a Familiar Face—David Dillon—at the Top and Sticking with Its Strategic Plan," *Supermarket News,* July 14, 2003, p. 14.

—Rene Steinke
—update: David E. Salamie

Landry's Restaurants, Inc.

1510 West Loop South
Houston, Texas 77027-9503
U.S.A.
Telephone: (713) 850-1010
Toll Free: (800) 552-6379
Fax: (713) 386-7707
Web site: http://www.landrysrestaurants.com

Public Company
Incorporated: 1993 as Landry's Seafood Restaurants, Inc.
Employees: 30,000
Sales: $1.11 billion (2003)
Stock Exchanges: New York
Ticker Symbol: LNY
NAIC: 722110 Full-Service Restaurants; 712130 Zoos
and Botanical Gardens; 721110 Hotels (Except Casino
Hotels) and Motels

Landry's Restaurants, Inc. is a major operator of full-service, casual-dining restaurants in the United States. The several chains run by the company mainly specialize in seafood and steaks, and Landry's ranks as the nation's second largest operator of seafood restaurants, trailing only Darden Restaurants, Inc., owner of the Red Lobster chain. By the end of 2003, the company was operating nearly 300 full-service restaurants in 36 states, including the flagship Landry's Seafood House and Willie G's Seafood and Steakhouse (a combined 41 units), Joe's Crab Shack (138 units), the Texas-Western-themed Saltgrass Steak House (29 units), the more upscale Chart House (26 units), the Amazon-themed Rainforest Café (26 units), Charley's Crab (15 units), and Crab House (11 units). Landry's Specialty Growth Division owns a number of additional properties. The largest of these is Kemah Boardwalk in Kemah, Texas (Galveston County), a 40-acre entertainment complex consisting of seven company-owned restaurants, retail shops, a hotel, amusement rides, and a marina. Landry's also owns and operates aquariums in Houston and Denver, hotels in Houston and Galveston, and the Galveston Island Convention Center. The extraordinary growth of Landry's since going public in 1993,

when it had only 11 restaurants, has been fueled mainly by acquisitions.

Launched by Landry Brothers in Early 1980s

The first Landry's restaurant, called Landry's Seafood Inn and Oyster Bar, was opened in 1980 in Katy, Texas, by brothers Bill and Floyd Landry. Bill and Floyd were sustaining a decades-old Landry family legacy of success in the restaurant business. In fact, Landry's was just one of several of the brothers' restaurant interests. They had started out working in Cajun-style restaurants that their father and two uncles operated. In 1976, when Bill was 38 and Floyd was 36, they opened their own restaurant, a seafood place dubbed ''Don's.'' By the mid-1980s they would be hands-on investors in five different restaurants, including The Magnolia Bar, Jimmy G's, Don's, and Willie G's. All of the outlets were located in east Texas and Louisiana, and sported seafood and Cajun fare. Furthermore, other Landry family members were operating more than 15 additional restaurants throughout the Southwest.

The Landry brothers profited from their restaurants primarily by offering excellent food, but also through economies of scale created by owning five seafood digs. They conducted most of the initial food preparation—cleaning, fileting, and shelling, for example—for all five establishments at a company-owned commissary operation called Creole Foods. Work at that center started at midnight and ended at eight in the morning, at which time the food was loaded onto trucks and delivered fresh to each kitchen. The brothers and other principal investors in the restaurant consortium kept food quality high by taking turns cooking at the different eateries.

Landry's Seafood Inn and Oyster Bar was among the smaller of the Landry restaurants by sales volume. Still, it was profitable. The average check was $12 to $16 per person, the 4,400-square-foot restaurant seated a maximum of 190, and the rent was only $3,500 monthly. The Landrys had created the eatery by purchasing an existing Cajun restaurant with only 85 seats, expanding it, and improving the menu. Landrys Seafood Inn offered a very casual dining atmosphere with a horseshoe bar, country-and-western music jukebox, and crayons for the kids. But it sported a somewhat upscale 101-item, dinner-only menu.

Company Perspectives:

Our objective is to develop and operate a nationwide system of restaurants that offers customers a fun dining experience, creates a loyal customer base that generates a high level of repeat business and provides superior returns to our investors. By focusing on the food, value, service, and ambiance of a restaurant, we strive to create an environment that fosters repeat patronage and encourages word-of-mouth recommendations.

Featured were catches from the Gulf of Mexico and the Louisiana coastal region, including various appetizers and seafood salads and soups. Main entrees, which ranged in price from about $5 to $15, included specialties such as snapper, broiled speckled trout, frog legs, and crab. The menu also featured steaks, chicken, sandwiches, and desserts such as ice cream and fresh fruit.

Late 1980s and Early 1990s: Beginning of the Fertitta Era

The most successful Landry operation was Willie G's, which had opened in 1981 and was bringing in $5 million annually by 1985. By that time, Landry's Seafood Inn was generating about $1.4 million in sales annually, while the family's other units were capturing about $3 million to $4 million per year. It was around this time that Tilman J. Fertitta became involved as one of several investors in the Landry brothers' restaurants. Fertitta was in his late 20s at the time, but had already made his mark as a successful developer during the Houston commercial real estate boom of the early 1980s. When real estate foundered in the mid-1980s, Fertitta began looking elsewhere for a challenge.

Fertitta had grown up in his father's seafood restaurant in Galveston, Texas, so he was not a complete newcomer to the industry. He was impressed with Landry's Seafood and believed that it had a lot of potential. A good restaurant concept coupled with his dealmaking skills, Fertitta reasoned, could be a powerful combination. "The original Landry's was a hole in the wall but it had great food," Fertitta recalled in the August 1994 issue of *Restaurant Hospitality*. "The basics were there, though, and I knew I could tweak it into a concept." In 1986 Fertitta purchased majority control of both Landry's and Houston-based Willie G's and then two years later became sole owner, buying out the Landry brothers and several other investment partners.

Fertitta's goal from the start was to transform the Landry's and Willie G's restaurants into regional, and eventually national, chains. That strategy sprang from observations that he had made about trends in the national restaurant industry. He noticed that the mom-and-pop restaurants were being phased out and that well-capitalized chains were increasingly dominating the business. He also saw that within the chain restaurant industry, seafood was poorly represented in comparison to burger, chicken, steak, and ethnic fare. With the exception of Red Lobster and a handful of regional operators, there were no major seafood restaurant operators. Furthermore, Americans'

consumption of seafood was rising faster than any other food segment.

To ply the full potential of Landry's and Willie G's, Fertitta scrutinized every aspect of the operations and hired a crack management team to help him start building a chain. Throughout the late 1980s and the early 1990s he added a few new outlets to the chain each year. The restaurants were geared for relatively casual dining, although the atmosphere was more polished than the original Landry's; for example, the waiters and waitresses wore white shirts, ties, and formal black pants. The menu offered similar fare with the average check running between $12 and $14. Fertitta wanted his restaurants to convey the feel of an old seafood house from the 1930s and 1940s, but with a more festive, brighter atmosphere. He also positioned most of the restaurants close to water to project a fresh seafood image, and typically shunned the overbuilt suburban sites pursued by other big chains.

Fertitta wanted to keep his outlets distinctive in order to avoid a repetitive, commercial look. Thus each restaurant was given a unique feel by the company's design team. Some of the units were converted from old family-owned seafood places that Fertitta's purchased and made into a Landry's. For example, Landry's put one of its restaurants in an old barge that had formerly housed a family-owned seafood place. The previous place had generated sales of more than $1 million per year, but still went belly-up. Landry's moved in and was able to make a healthy profit with its superior concept and operating strategy. Although each restaurant had its own unique flair, all of the outlets were similar in that they wore the same neon, movie-like marquee, which was designed to let people know that the restaurants were fun and entertaining.

By boosting per-unit sales and adding a few new units, Fertitta's venture managed to squeak out about $11.5 million in sales in both 1988 and 1989. The company posted losses in both years, however, as management invested for growth. Despite ongoing investments, Landry's managed to post a positive net income in 1990 of $419,000 from sales of about $15.5 million. Revenues bobbed up to $19.5 million in 1991 and then to roughly $22.5 million in 1992, as net income surged to a healthy $3 million. Improved profitability reflected the wisdom of Fertitta's operating strategy. Indeed, the Landry's restaurants were among the top in the industry with profit margins averaging more than 20 percent. High-margin menu items boosted that percentage. For example, more than 30 percent of the chain's orders were shrimp, which generated fat profits in comparison to most of the fare pushed in non-seafood restaurants. In 1993 Fertitta incorporated the venture as Landry's Seafood Restaurants, Inc.

Mid- to Late 1990s: Going Public, Acquiring Joe's Crab Shack, Developing Kemah Boardwalk

By late 1993 Landry's Seafood Restaurants was operating 11 units in Texas and Louisiana. The company was focusing on developing family-oriented Landry's Seafood Grill restaurants, but was still operating a few Willie G's, which were targeted more toward business patrons. Until 1993, Fertitta had been satisfied to grow slowly by funding expansion largely out of earnings. "I had the chance to go public several years ago,"

Key Dates:

1980: Brothers Bill and Floyd Landry open the first Landry's Seafood Inn and Oyster Bar in Katy, Texas.

1981: Landry brothers open the first Willie G's.

1986: Tilman J. Fertitta gains majority control of the Landry brothers' restaurants.

1988: Fertitta becomes sole owner of Landry's Seafood and Willie G's.

1993: The venture is incorporated as Landry's Seafood Restaurants, Inc.; company goes public.

1994: The Houston-based Joe's Crab Shack chain of three seafood restaurants is acquired.

1996: Bayport Restaurant Group, operator of 17 Crab House restaurants on the East Coast, is acquired.

1999: The Kemah Boardwalk officially opens in Kemah, Texas; a deal to acquire Consolidated Restaurant Cos., operator of several non-seafood chains, is scuttled.

2000: Landry's acquires Rainforest Café, Inc.

2001: Company shortens its name to Landry's Restaurants, Inc.

2002: Landry's acquires C.A. Muer Corporation and the Chart House and Saltgrass Steak House chains.

2003: Company opens its Downtown Aquarium in Houston; revenues surpass $1 billion.

Fertitta explained in the November 8, 1993, *Nation's Restaurant News,* "but I wanted to get my management team in place before I did that." Fertitta finally decided to go public with a September 1993 initial public offering of stock on the NASDAQ that brought $24 million into the company's war chest. The success of the offering was not surprising, given that Landry's sales per unit ($3.2 million in 1993) and cash flow were among the highest in the restaurant industry. Within two months the stock was trading at nearly 1.5 times the initial offering price.

A second stock offering captured $37 million more for Landry's, which Fertitta used to intensify expansion efforts. Rather than build new establishments, he preferred to purchase independent seafood places and convert them into Landry's. For instance, early in 1994 Landry's purchased two units operating under the Atchafalaya River Café banner in Dallas, and another in Memphis, Tennessee, named Captain Bilbo's. The basic goal was to purchase independents that were operating below their potential and convert them into 215-scat, 8,000-square-foot Landry's Seafood Grills. By mid-1994 the company was running 18 restaurants in Texas, Arkansas, Florida, and Louisiana, and was planning to expand into several other states including Tennessee, Georgia, Mississippi, North Carolina, Nevada, Arizona, and Colorado.

By the end of 1994 Landry's was operating about 25 restaurants. *Forbes* ranked the chain fifth on its list of the 200 best small companies in the United States in that year. Landry's store number increased to 35 units in 12 states by August 1995, helping to earn it a spot on *Business Week's* Top 100 Growth Companies list for the second consecutive year. Landry's sales

rose to $34 million in 1993 and then to $66 million in 1994. Net income, moreover, surged nearly 100 percent between 1992 and 1994 to about $5.8 million. Fueling profit growth was an increased emphasis on a trend sweeping the restaurant business in the early and mid-1990s: value. As Jeff Price, senior director of the National Restaurant Association, said in reference to Landry's in the August 22, 1995, *Knight-Ridder/Tribune Business News,* "When you have a meal sold at a good price and add a theme, you get traffic."

Landry's continued to rapidly expand its chain during 1995. Furthermore, the company was moving ahead with plans to diversify into the more casual spectrum of the seafood restaurant market. Early in 1994 Landry's had purchased Joe's Crab Shack, a Houston-based chain of three seafood restaurants. Fertitta had planned to convert them into Landry's Seafood Grills. Instead, Landry's managers tweaked the Joe's Crab Shack concept and came up with what they hoped would be a successful entry into the low-priced seafood eatery market. After the makeover, sales at the three units jumped 30 percent to average $3.2 million per unit. In 1995 Landry's opened a fourth Joe's in Dallas that achieved similar results.

While organic growth, particularly of the Joe's Crab Shack chain, continued in 1996, Landry's landed its second acquisition in August of that year, spending about $65 million for Hollywood, Florida-based Bayport Restaurant Group, operator of 17 Crab House restaurants on the East Coast. The Crab Houses, which averaged about $3.7 million in business per year and were described by Bayport management as having a "clean nautical motif," generated a collective $53.7 million in 1995 and net income of $1.5 million. The average check at a Crab House was $21, slightly higher than the $17 at Landry's and much higher than that of Joe's Crab Shack, $14. By the end of 1996 Landry's Seafood Restaurants owned more than 70 restaurants in 26 states, and its revenues had reached $232.6 million, more than double the year-earlier figure. Profits for the year, however, amounted to just $1.5 million because of $16.7 million in charges related to the acquisition of the Crab House chain.

In early 1997 Landry's bought every restaurant on the waterfront of Kemah, Texas, it did not already own. The company already operated Landry's Seafood House and Joe's Crab Shack units in Kemah, a small town on Galveston Bay about 20 miles from Houston. Landry's subsequently developed the extensive property it owned in the town into Kemah Boardwalk, which Fertitta hoped to expand into a major tourist attraction. Officially opened in January 1999, the Kemah Boardwalk, in addition to several company owned and operated restaurants, also featured retail and specialty shops, amusement rides, and the Boardwalk Inn hotel.

Although revenues were up 28 percent in 1998, falling just short of $400 million, Landry's suffered from declining same-store sales and sliding profits. Compounding matters were a succession of tropical storms that hit Landry's territory from May through October, temporarily closing some locations and cutting into sales at others. Many of Landry's restaurants were located on the waterfront, making the company unusually vulnerable to the vicissitudes of the weather. Investors lost faith in the company's stock for the first time since its initial public offering, sending it down nearly 70 percent for the year. By early 1999 Landry's halted a slide in sales by lowering the menu prices at its restaurants, and in March announced the closure of eight of its 122 restaurants and plans to close an additional three restaurants and to abandon more than 20 development sites. Associated with this restructuring, the company took a $37 million charge against 1998 earnings, resulting in a net loss for the year of $300,000.

Also in March 1999 Fertitta reached an agreement to acquire Consolidated Restaurant Cos., a privately held Dallas-based firm that owned the El Chico, Spaghetti Warehouse, and Good Eats chains. This $164 million deal to acquire Consolidated, which owned or franchised more than 150 restaurants in 21 states and Canada, represented a major move outside of seafood for Landry's. It was also structured as a reverse buyout, whereby Landry's would take over Consolidated but the executives of Consolidated would take over management of the combined company. Fertitta was slated to serve as chairman of the new firm, but in making the deal he had largely committed himself to turning over control of a business for which he had been the chief architect—if not the true founder. But Fertitta quickly developed second thoughts about giving up control, and less than a week after the deal was announced he scuttled it. In the aftermath of the aborted deal, Fertitta also took Landry's on a different path. Plans to open as many as 50 new restaurants per year were scaled back, and Fertitta began to take a more aggressive approach to acquisitions. Landry's ended 1999 with about 140 restaurants and revenues of $439 million. In December of that year the company's stock began trading on the New York Stock Exchange.

Shopping Spree in the Early 2000s

The organic growth at Landry's at this time centered on the Joe's Crab Shack chain, which opened its 100th location in June 2000. On the acquisitions side, Landry's began 2000 by more than doubling the size of its Kemah Boardwalk property by buying the adjacent Lafayette's Landing Marina, which was soon renamed Kemah Boardwalk Marina. The company's property in Kemah now totaled about 40 acres. Landry's next set its sights on Rainforest Café, Inc. Founded in 1994 with its first restaurant in the Mall of America in suburban Minneapolis, Rainforest Café by early 2000 was running 28 restaurants in the United States and had partial ownership in another ten cafes located overseas. Part of the dining entertainment trend, sometimes dubbed ''eatertainment,'' the Rainforest Cafés had a jungle theme complete with real and animatronic animals, tropical decor, and periodic ''thunderstorms.'' Although the company had run into problems during the expansion of the chain, its best locations had high volumes, generating annual sales as high as $20 million. The $8 million average sales volume per Rainforest restaurant was the highest such figure among U.S. eateries in 1999. Net income that year totaled $5.7 million on revenues of $262.7 million.

In February 2000 Landry's reached a deal to acquire Rainforest for $125 million in stock and cash. Two months later, however, Rainforest shareholders failed to approve the deal after Landry's stock started to fall, causing the value of the deal to fall below $100 million. In the wake of the failed bid, Rainforest's stock fell, affording Landry's another opportunity. In September, Landry's offered to buy Rainforest for $75 mil-

lion in cash, and with no competing bids in the offing, the deal was approved by Rainforest shareholders one month later.

By 2001 Landry's was operating more than 190 restaurants, and revenues had jumped to $746.6 million. Net income stood at $26.9 million. The expansion outside of the seafood niche prompted the shortening of the firm's name to Landry's Restaurants, Inc. Also during 2001 Landry's shifted its headquarters into a newly built, eight-story, company-owned building in Houston.

Three separate acquisitions highlighted developments during 2002. In February Landry's acquired Detroit-based C.A. Muer Corporation for about $28.5 million in stock. Muer, founded by Chuck Muer in 1964, had about $60 million in sales during 2001 through 21 restaurants, including nine Charley's Crab restaurants and four Big Fish Seafood Bistros. Operating in the Midwest and Florida, Muer also owned a number of fine-dining establishments located in historic buildings. These included the Gandy Dancer in Ann Arbor, Michigan; the Grand Concourse in Pittsburgh; and Engine House No. 5 in Columbus, Ohio. Several of the Muer restaurants were subsequently converted into other Landry's concepts, primarily Joe's Crab Shack.

A $45.5 million deal in August 2002 netted the Chart House chain of 39 restaurants. Acquired from Chart House Enterprises (subsequently renamed Angelo and Maxie's, Inc.), the Chart House chain was known for having prime waterfront locations on the both the East and West Coasts. With a history dating back to the early 1960s, the Chart Houses had started out as steakhouses but were eventually converted into seafood restaurants; they were positioned as more upscale than the Landry's Seafood House chain—as were the Muer restaurants—which provided Landry's Restaurants with an enlarged array of seafood concepts. As was the case with the Muer acquisition, Landry's converted about ten of the Chart Houses into Joe's Crab Shacks and also closed a handful of underperforming units.

Landry's landed its third catch of 2002 in October when it bought the Saltgrass Steak House chain in a stock deal valued at approximately $73 million. Founded in Houston in 1991, Saltgrass had grown to include 27 locations in Texas. Landry's bought it from MetroNational Corporation, a privately held investment company based in Houston. Saltgrass was slated to become Landry's second growth vehicle, along with Joe's Crab Shack, and as such was viewed as essential to the firm's goal of moving beyond the seafood niche. The three 2002 acquisitions helped boost the company's restaurant count to 275 (operating in 35 states), and revenues for the year surged ahead 20 percent, hitting $894.8 million.

During 2003 and 2004, it was Landry's Specialty Growth Division that grabbed headlines. This division was responsible for the company's developments outside of the restaurant sector. In January 2003 Landry's opened the Downtown Aquarium in Houston, a $38 million complex on six acres that in addition to a 500,000-gallon aquarium with about 200,000 fish and a train ride through a shark tank also featured two restaurants, a bar, and a miniature amusement park complete with a 90-foot-tall Ferris wheel and a 20-story observation tower. Landry's followed up just two months later with its $13.6 million acquisition of the bankrupt Colorado Ocean's Journey, a 17-acre aquarium complex in downtown Denver. Fertitta planned to redevelop the Denver aquarium into an entertainment destination similar to the one in Houston by adding a seafood restaurant and amusement rides. In January 2004 Landry's opened the Inn at the Ballpark in downtown Houston, a baseball-themed, 202-room boutique hotel adjacent to Minute Maid Park, home of Major League Baseball's Houston Astros. Landry's also developed a new beachfront convention center in Galveston, Texas, in partnership with the City of Galveston. The $32 million center, featuring 140,000 square feet of meeting and convention space, opened in May 2004 and was located adjacent to the high-end San Luis Resort, a property managed by Landry's. The Specialty Division was next looking at a site in downtown San Antonio for a proposed new entertainment complex that would feature an aquarium restaurant, a Rainforest Café, a boardwalk with a train ride, and a Ferris wheel.

Things were not entirely quiescent on the restaurant during this period. Landry's bought several well-known, upscale restaurants in Houston, including Pesce, Brenner's Steakhouse, Grotto, and La Griglia. The company also opened Vic and Anthony's, a steakhouse located adjacent to the Inn at the Ballpark in downtown Houston. These eateries, along with Willie G's, were placed within Landry's new Signature Group.

Now operating nearly 300 restaurants in 36 states as well as several other nonrestaurant ventures, Landry's Restaurants had its best year ever in 2003, achieving profits of $45.9 million on revenues of $1.11 billion. During 2004 the company planned to open approximately 20 new restaurants. About half of these would be Joe's Crab Shacks and three would be Saltgrass units. Other planned 2004 openings included a Rainforest Café in Atlantic City, New Jersey, and Aquarium Nashville, an aquarium/restaurant at Opry Mills. The growth-oriented Fertitta was sure to also have his eye out for further acquisitions to add to his seafood-based but diversifying empire.

Principal Subsidiaries

C.A. Muer Corporation.

Principal Divisions

Signature Group; Specialty Growth Division.

Principal Operating Units

Chart House; Crab House; Joe's Crab Shack; Landry's Seafood House; Rainforest Café; Saltgrass Steak House; Willie G's Seafood and Steakhouse.

Principal Competitors

Darden Restaurants, Inc.; Brinker International, Inc.; Outback Steakhouse, Inc.; Ruby Tuesday, Inc.; Applebee's International, Inc.; Carlson Restaurants Worldwide, Inc.; O'Charley's Inc.

Further Reading

Carlino, Bill, "Landry's Seafood: Not Just Another Fish in the Sea," *Nation's Restaurant News,* May 16, 1994, p. 74.

Davis, Michael, "Another Catch for Landry's," *Houston Chronicle,* April 20, 1996.

Davis-Diaz, Pamela, "Landry's Seafood House to Open Restaurant in Rocky Point," *Knight-Ridder/Tribune Business News,* August 22, 1995.

Elder, Laura Elizabeth, "Making a Splash on the Seafood Scene," *Houston Business Journal,* April 12, 1996, pp. 14A +.

Farkas, David, "Shopping Spree," *Chain Leader,* November 2002, pp. 54–56, 58, 60.

Hassell, Greg, "Landry's Led by Shrewd Big Fish," *Houston Chronicle,* April 16, 1995, p. E1.

——, "Tilman's Turnaround," *Houston Chronicle,* February 11, 2001.

Howard, Theresa, "Tilman Fertitta: Landry's Top Executive Wants to Be Nothing Less Than the 'King of Seafood,' " *Nation's Restaurant News,* January 1, 1997, p. 68.

Kaplan, David, "Beefing Up at Landry's: Empire Adds Saltgrass Chain," *Houston Chronicle,* September 12, 2002.

Lorek, L.A., "Visionary Ringmaster," *San Antonio Express-News,* April 18, 2004, pp. 1L, 5L.

Murphy, Kate, "From a Texas 'Trump,' Plans That Amaze (or Annoy)," *New York Times,* September 14, 2003, p. BU4.

Palmeri, Christopher, "Bill Clinton's Fish-House Friend," *Forbes,* November 18, 1996, pp. 126 +.

Prewit, Milford, "Casual Dinner-House Chains Tap Secondary-Brand Expansion (NRN Top 100)," *Nation's Restaurant News,* August 7, 1995, p. 120.

Reill, Howard, "Landry's Eyes Expansion of Cajun Food Restaurants; May Head for California, Chicago, New York," *Nation's Restaurant News,* February 17, 1986, p. 3.

Ruggless, Ron, "Landry's Enlarged Chain Portfolio Nets $1.1B in Revenue for 2003," *Nation's Restaurant News,* February 23, 2004, p. 4.

——, "Landry's Eyes Joe's Crab Shack As Possible 2nd Growth Concept," *Nation's Restaurant News,* June 12, 1995, p. 3.

——, "Landry's in Swim After Stock Sale," *Nation's Restaurant News,* November 8, 1993, p. 3.

——, "Landry's Nets C.A. Muer, Plans to Expand Seafood Concepts into Midwest," *Nation's Restaurant News,* March 4, 2002, p. 4.

——, "Landry's Surfs for Turf, Nets Chart House Chain for $45M," *Nation's Restaurant News,* June 3, 2002, pp. 1, 57.

Sanson, Michael, "The Man Who Would Be King Fish," *Restaurant Hospitality,* August 1994, p. 74.

Sit-DuVall, Mary, "Landry's Makes Another Run at Purchasing Rainforest Café," *Houston Chronicle,* September 27, 2000.

Wriggles, Ron, "Landry's Nixes Multichain Merger," *Nation's Restaurant News,* March 15, 1999.

—Dave Mote
—update: David E. Salamie

Laurus N.V.

Parallelweg 64
's-Hertogenbosch 5201 AD
Netherlands
Telephone: +31 73 622 36 22
Fax: +31 73 622 36 36
Web site: http://www.laurus.nl

Public Company
Incorporated: 1998
Employees: 27,282
Sales: EUR 4.1 billion ($4.5 billion) (2003)
Stock Exchanges: Euronext Amsterdam
Ticker Symbol: LAU
NAIC: 445110 Supermarkets and Other Grocery (Except Convenience) Stores

Laurus N.V. is one of the Netherlands' top food retailing companies. The 's-Hertogenbosch-based company boasts nearly 750 supermarkets throughout the country, grouped under three primary formats: discount-oriented Edah; large-scale Konmar, and mid-sized Super De Boer. The latter format includes the largest number of company locations, at 369 stores, of which 214 are owned by affiliated independent retailers. Edah is the group's next largest format, with 269 stores, all but 58 of which are directly owned and operated by Laurus. The 125 Konmar stores—including nearly 50 Konmar Superstores—are also primarily controlled by Laurus itself, with just four franchised stores in the network. Since late 2003, the company has been testing a conversion of its smaller Konmar stores to its Edah and Super De Boer formats. Following on the success of the conversions, the company plans to convert all of the smaller Konmar stores by the middle of 2004. Formed in 1998 through the mergers of Unigro and De Boer Winkelbedrijven, followed closely by the merger of the newly formed De Boer Unigro with Vendex Food Group, Laurus stumbled into the 2000s and was forced into a restructuring that included the sell-off of most of its foreign holdings. As part of its restructuring, the company also received a capital injection from French retail giant Casino, which in 2002 became

Laurus's largest shareholder at nearly 38 percent of its shares, with an option to raise its stake to 51 percent. By 2004, Laurus's restructuring, including its renewed focus on its three core formats, began to show signs of success. After losing nearly EUR 130 million in 2002, the company returned to profitability in 2003. Nonetheless, a brutal price war, led by Dutch market giant Albert Heijn, brought a drop in sales, to just EUR 4.1 billion ($4.5 billion) that year. Laurus is listed on the Euronext Paris stock exchange.

Dutch Grocers Group in the Early 20th Century

Laurus N.V. was formed through the mergers of three of the Netherlands' mid-sized supermarket groups in 1998. The merger of Unigro with De Boer Winkelbedrijven created Unigro De Boer. By the end of that year, the newly merged company had doubled in size, merging with the Vendex Food Group, the food retailing arm of Dutch department store heavyweight Vendex, to form Laurus. Yet the new company had roots in the early decades of the Dutch grocery retail industry and boasted such nationally recognized formats as Edah, Super De Boer, and Konmar.

Edah represented the oldest of the company's formats. The difficult economic climate in northern Friesland forced many in the region to move to the more industrialized south at the beginning of the 20th century. Among these were four Frisian grocers by the names of Ebben, Dames, Aukes, and Hettema who set up stores in the towns of Tilburg, Oss, Eindhoven, and Helmond. Much of the goods handled by these grocers came from the Dutch colonies, and by the end of the century's first decade, the four had banded together to increase their buying power. Taking the initials of their last names, they created a new cooperative, Edah. The cooperative's success soon led them to reincorporate as a public limited liability company, becoming NV Handel in Kolonie Waren Edah in 1917.

Edah began to expand following World War I as the Netherlands, which had remained neutral during the war, underwent an economic boom. The era saw the appearance of large numbers of new groceries—with little legislation codifying the establishment of grocery shops, the country saw the appearance of vast numbers of new, largely tiny grocers, reaching more than

70,000 by the end of the 1920s. At the same time, however, the first grocery chains, such as the Albert Heijn store chain, had already begun to form. These were joined by a growing number of cooperative grocery networks as well.

Edah itself grew strongly, in part through a series of acquisitions of other groceries and grocery chains in its Brabant region through the 1920s. The company's expansion also led it into the Limburg region as well, and by the beginning of the 1930s, there were already 100 stores within the Edah group. By the outbreak of World War II and the German occupation of the Netherlands, Edah had grown to nearly 130 stores. The war and the occupation severely restricted Edah's growth.

Following the war, however, Edah, like the rest of the Netherlands—and much of the world—became confronted with the grocery revolution pioneered by the United States earlier in the century. The appearance of the first self-service supermarket in the Netherlands in 1948 marked the beginning of a dramatic transformation of the Dutch grocery market. By the early 1950s, most of the country's grocery groups had already begun to experiment with their own supermarket formats. Edah itself joined this trend, opening its first supermarket in 1952 under the name Ziezo in the town of Heerlen. Edah also experimented with other formats, and especially became a pioneer in the discount segment in the early 1960s. By 1967, the company had begun to focus on the discount market, trimming back its network of stores to 87.

Forming the Vendex Food Group: 1970s

The 1970s marked a new period of growth for the company, which began a series of acquisitions, including the Brabant regio Andr van Hilst chain in 1972 and much of Coop Nederland in 1973. The latter acquisition in particular established Edah as one of the country's leading national supermarket groups. The company also expanded its range of formats, launching the Basismarkt and Torro chains, as well as the Dagmarkt and Autorama formats. In 1977, Edah itself was acquired, however, by department store group Vroom & Dreesmann (V&D). Edah then became that company's flagship supermarket brand.

At V&D, Edah was joined by another fast-rising supermarket format, Konmar. That company had been founded just a few years earlier by Henk van der Straaten and Jacques Koster, the former a market stall operator, the latter a grocer in the Hague. The two joined together in 1968 to launch their first deep discount store in Wateringen. That store's success led the partners to expand the format, and shortly after, the first Konmar (for Konsu-mentenMarkt) opened in the Hague. The large-scale, full-service format, which boasted among other features its own butcher, liquor store, drugstore, and baker, was an immediate success.

By 1970, Koster and van der Straaten had opened two more Konmars in the Hague, as well as a fourth property in Scheveingen. In the early 1970s, the company continued to improve and expand the Konmar format, becoming one of the first to deploy the superstore concept in the Netherlands. In 1977, Koster and van der Straaten sold the company to V&D, later Vendex International, with van der Straaten staying on to help guide Konmar's expansion into most of Holland's major urban markets.

By 1998, when Vendex spun off its grocery store operations into a new company, Vendex Food Group, there were nearly 100 Konmar stores in operation throughout the Netherlands. The new company, however, proved short-lived, however. By the end of 1998, Vendex Food Group had merged with another major supermarket force, De Boer Unigro, creating Laurus N.V.

Merging Unigro and De Boer in the 1990s

De Boer Unigro had been created just one year earlier through the fusion of southern Netherlands' Unigro and east Netherlands-based De Boer Winkelbedrijven. Both of these companies had their roots in the great Dutch grocery expansion years of the 1920s. Unigro's roots could be traced back to Theo Albada Jelgersma and son Ben Albada Jelgersma, who opened a wholesale grocery supplier in Breda in 1925. Their earliest products were such basics as coffee, tea, soap, and margarine. The Albada Jelgersmas' customer base grew strongly in its first decade—with more than 70,000 large and small grocers, many simply operating from their living rooms, in the country. New legislation in 1939 placed restrictions on grocery store ownership, and in the 1940s the number of grocers in the country dropped back to a still respectable 25,000.

The grocery market had also begun its first steps toward consolidation, in large part because of the appearance of a number of large-scale grocery chains, including Albert Heijn, Edah, and others. Grocers and wholesalers adopted the American innovation of forming independent affiliate groups, pooling their buying operations. The Albada Jelgersmas joined this trend, establishing their own buying partnership, called Verkoop Gemeenschap, or Végé. Other major buying groups included De Spar, formed in 1932; Centra, formed by the Schuitema family in 1934; and Vivo, formed in 1942. This last emerged as the country's strongest wholesalers association in the postwar period.

The rise of the self-service supermarket format, however, placed both wholesalers and their independent grocer customers under increasing pressure. During the 1950s and into the 1960s, the growing strength of the country's supermarket sector forced the wholesaler sector to consolidate. In 1966, a number of Vivo wholesalers decided to merge together to form a new, single operation, called Unigro, for Unie van Grossiers. Unigro grew strongly through the 1970s, in large part through the acquisition of more and more wholesalers and wholesaler associations.

In Breda, meanwhile, Eric Albada Jelgersmas had led the family's Végé group through its own acquisition drive. Végé initially concentrated on the Brabants and Limburg regions,

Key Dates:

1910: Grocery buying cooperative Edah is created.

1917: Edah is reformed as a public limited liability company, becoming NV Handel in Kolonie Waren Edah.

1925: Theo Albada Jelgersma and son Ben Albada Jelgersma open wholesale grocery supplier in Breda; Evert De Boer opens grocery store in Hoogeveen.

1932: Jan De Boer, brother of Evert, opens grocery store in Coevorden.

1967: Unigro is formed.

1969: Konmar supermarket format debuts.

1970: De Boer store chains merge to form De Boer Winkelbedrijven.

1977: Vroom & Dreesmann (later Vendex International) acquires Edah and Konmar.

1980: Eric Albada Jelgersma acquires control of Unigro.

1997: De Boer and Unigro merge to form Unigro De Boer; Vendex International spins off supermarket operations as Vendex Food Group.

1998: Unigro De Boer merges with Vendex Food Group, forming Laurus N.V., which institutes single format strategy under Konmar name.

2002: Casino of France acquires 39 percent of Laurus, which undergoes restructuring.

2003: Laurus completes disposal of Spanish holdings and returns to multi-format operations.

2004: Laurus rebrands most Konmar supermarkets as Edah and Super De Boer.

then expanded into Friesland and Belgium as well. In 1980, Végé acquired Unigro and its Vivo store format. Albada Jelgersma continued expanding the business through the 1980s, acquiring Kraan & Van Kuyk, another Végé wholesaler, in 1985, Spar wholesaler Van Silfhout as well as Coop Limburg two years later, and Verenignde Distributie Bedrijven in 1990.

In the 1980s, however, Unigro found itself under heavy pressure from the fast-rising Ahold group, and its Albert Heijn flagship. In response, Unigro decided to abandon both of its formats in favor of a new, larger self-service supermarket format, Super. The new format was an immediate success, and, backed by Unigro's string of acquisitions, established itself as a major name in the Dutch supermarket sector. Unigro nonetheless was forced to play catch up with the faster-growing Ahold concern. In 1997, however, Unigro moved into the country's top supermarket ranks with its agreement to merge with De Boer Winkelbedrijven. The new company, called Unigro De Boer, then launched a new store format, Super De Boer.

Three-Way Merger in the 1990s

De Boer had been founded by two brothers, Evert De Boer and Jan de Boer, who had gained experience as grocers in the Drente region within the Albino food store group active in the early 1920s. Evert de Boer left that group to open his own store in Hoogeveen in 1925, while Jan de Boer left the Albino group in 1932 to open a grocery store in Coevorden. The brothers each began opening new stores in the Drente region, yet operated as two separate and independent businesses until the 1970s.

Both De Boer operations launched their own self-service supermarket formats in 1952. In order to gain greater purchasing strength, they also helped form a new buying cooperative, ZICO. The Hoogeveen and Coevorden businesses also began working together directly in the 1950s and 1960s, coordinating advertising campaigns for the region. It was only after a fire destroyed the Hoogeveen De Boer's warehouse that the two companies decided to merge together, creating De Boer Winkelbedrijven in 1970. The De Boer family itself exited the company's direction by 1982.

De Boer expanded rapidly in the 1970s and early 1980s, at first by opening new stores. As the region became more and more saturated with supermarkets, however, the company began buying up a number of its ZICO partners. De Boer also launched a number of related retail formats, such as the Mitra liquor store in 1974 and the Trekpleister drugstore in 1980. De Boer fueled its expansion by a public offering in 1987. By 1995, the De Boer empire had topped 500 total stores, including 159 supermarkets. Two years later, the company merged with Unigro, and relaunched a combined supermarket format, Super De Boer. Yet the format barely had time to take hold—in 1998, the new management at Laurus N.V. decided to take a risk and convert all of its supermarkets under the single Konmar name. Laurus also moved to expand its foreign holdings in Belgium, but especially in Spain, where it began an aggressive series of acquisitions. By the early 2000s, the company already owned some 700 stores in that country.

Recovering in the New Century

The decision to focus on a single brand rapidly proved a disaster. By 2001, the Konmar concept had clearly failed to translate to the small and mid-sized supermarket formats which formed the largest share of the group's supermarket portfolio. At the same time, the company had expanded too quickly in Spain, and in Belgium as well, and its foreign operations had begun hemorrhaging badly. Adding to the company's woes was a brutal price war raging back home in the Netherlands. After Albert Heijn announced its decision to make permanent price reductions on a large number of products, Laurus was forced to follow suit. As a result, the company, which posted sales of more than EUR 6.5 billion in 2001, slid into losses, which mounted to EUR 128 million by 2002.

By 2001, the company was forced to seek help in shoring up its dwindling finances. Yet the EUR 250 million lifeline granted the company by its banks in 2001 proved unable to reverse Laurus's difficulties. Finally, in March 2002, the company agreed to a rescue package, in which 39 percent of its shares were transferred to France's retail powerhouse, Casino, in exchange for a new EUR 200 million capital injection. At the same time, Casino was granted the option to acquire a further 12 percent of Laurus in the future.

Under Casino's guidance, Laurus underwent a drastic restructuring. The company sold off the entirety of its Spanish holdings by September 2002, which were shortly followed by nearly all of its Belgian operations. Withdrawing to the Netherlands, the company's restructuring continued, with the shedding of a number of noncore holdings, including its Spar convenience store operations. By the end of 2002, the company's sales had been slashed back to just EUR 4.6 billion. Nonetheless, the company had successfully purged itself of its poorest performers.

Laurus has also reversed its single-format position and instead relaunched its popular Edah and Super De Boer formats. The company began testing a further conversion of much of its Konmar chain, retooling the smaller stores to the Edah and Super De Boer formats as well. Encouraged by an initial positive reaction, the company began a full-scale conversion, largely completed by mid-2004, leaving just 50 large-scale Konmar superstores. By then, Laurus's restructuring appeared to be succeeding—at the end of 2003, the company posted a profit of EUR 9 million on total revenues of EUR 4.1 billion. Laurus appeared prepared to continue making Dutch supermarket history in the new century.

Principal Subsidiaries

Assural BV; CV De Weerribben, Amsterdam (76.9%); CV Hijkerveld, Amsterdam (76.9%); De Boer Unigro Filialen BV; De Boer Unigro Groothandel BV; Echo SA (Belgium); Groenwoudt Food BV; Konmar BV; Laurus International BV; Laurus Nederland BV; Nieuwe Weme Supermarkten BV; Verenigde De Boer Unigro Beheer BV.

Further Reading

Bickerton, Ian, "Laurus Sells El Arbol," *Financial Times*, September 6, 2002, p. 28.

——, and Raphael Minder, "Casino Agrees Euros 200m Laurus Rescue Package," *Financial Times*, March 8, 2002, p. 29.

"Casino Gambles on Laurus for a Foothold in the Dutch Market," *Grocer*, March 16, 2002, p. 14.

"Casino Takes over at Laurus," *Grocer*, June 22, 2002, p. 16.

Dorens, Erven, "Laurus wil 'rotjaar' snel vergeten," *De Telegraaf*, March 21, 2001.

"Dutch Grocery Retailer Laurus to Concentrate on Core Business," *Europe Agri*, October 25, 2002, p. 500.

"Laurus Converts 79 Konmar Units," *MMR*, June 16, 2003, p. 110.

"Laurus komt met merkloze producten," *De Telegraaf*, February 2, 2004.

"Laurus Sale," *Grocer*, August 23, 2003, p. 13.

"Laurus zet nieuwe ombouwoperatie door," *De Telegraaf*, July 21, 2004.

—M.L. Cohen

Leroux S.A.S.

84 rue François Herbo
BP 28
59310 Orchies Cedex
France
Telephone: 33 3 (20) 64 48 00
Fax: 33 3 (20) 64 48 01
Web site: http://www.leroux.fr

Private Company
Incorporated: 1858
Employees: 250
Sales: EUR 40 million (2002 est.)
NAIC: 311230 Breakfast Cereal Manufacturing; 311423
Dried and Dehydrated Food Manufacturing; 311920
Coffee and Tea Manufacturing; 311930 Flavoring
Syrup and Concentrate Manufacturing; 311942 Spice
and Extract Manufacturing

Leroux S.A.S. is the world's leading producer of chicory; its output is 125,000 metric tons of chicory a year, which it ships to 50 countries. Popularized by the French as a coffee substitute in the days of Napoleon, chicory was pitched for its health benefits after World War II. Later, Leroux promoted it as the all-natural, "green" drink of the third millennium. Leroux supplies 95 percent of the chicory consumed in the United States, where it is best known for the distinctive flavor it adds to New Orleans-style coffee.

Ancient Origins

Related to salad plants such as endives, various parts of the chicory plant have been used since 4000 B.C. The ancient Egyptians and Romans prized chicory as a digestive aid. In modern times, it is the root of the plant that is chopped and roasted before being brewed as a beverage or used as an ingredient in other beverages, cereals, cosmetics, and medicinal compounds.

While coffee and chocolate became products of mass consumption during the 18th century, chicory did not yet meet the same widespread demand. After Napoleon blocked British shipping companies from carrying their Caribbean produce to Continental Europe in 1806, French citizens turned to chicory as a

coffee substitute, reports *La saga Leroux,* the definitive history of the company. The introduction of the railroad in the mid-1800s also helped spread chicory's success across France.

Acquiring Herbo in 1858

While on a business trip, on October 17, 1858, company founder Jean-Baptiste-Alphonse Leroux invested in Herbo Fils & Cie., a vendor of "colonial products"—chicory, chocolate, mustard, and tapioca. It had been founded in 1840 by François Herbo. Located near Orchies in the north of France, Herbo was conferred to the founder's son, Alphonse-Henri-François, and renamed Leroux. The company roasted its own "grains" from chopped chicory roots. At this time, the workshop had one foreman and six workers. Production was less than 100 metric tons a year.

In 1871, the company moved to be closer to the new Lille-Valenciennes railroad. The next year, Leroux abandoned its tapioca, mustard, and cacao business to focus exclusively on chicory. According to *La saga Leroux,* production more than tripled from 180 metric tons in 1872 to 750 tons in 1875. While Leroux shipped across France, it was as of yet virtually unknown in the industrial north, since each village in the region had its own chicory factory.

In 1876, Leroux began exporting, first to Spain. Via the port at Havre, Leroux was soon shipping its chicory across the seas; after 1881, Buenos Aires was an important early destination.

20th-Century Industrialization

After Alphonse-Henri-François Leroux died in 1895, his son Alphonse-Henri-Eugène Leroux took over the company he had begun working for 12 years earlier at the age of 17. While his father was known as having an inventor's soul, patenting machines for roasting chicory and other parts of the production process, Alphonse-Henri-Eugène was a driven industrialist. In fact, according to company literature, "Maison Leroux" was France's largest factory by 1914.

Leroux grew rapidly from 1900 to the beginning of World War I, becoming France's largest chicory producer. It had 160 employees by 1914, when it was making 7,000 metric tons of

Key Dates:

1840: François Herbo launches the firm, selling chicory, chocolate, mustard, and tapioca.
1858: Jean-Baptiste-Alphonse Leroux acquires Herbo Fils & Cie.
1871: Sales of other products are dropped to concentrate on chicory.
1895: Alphonse-Henri-Eugène Leroux takes over the company after the death of his father, Alphonse-Henri-François.
1927: The company is reorganized as a limited liability company, SARL Leroux.
1947: Alain and Robert Leroux become joint managing directors.
1992: Belgium's Chicobel is acquired.
1994: The company becomes Leroux S.A.; Michel Hermand is the sole chief executive.
1996: Spain's Molabe is acquired.
1997: Affiliated businesses are organized under the new Finaler holding company.
2003: Leroux becomes a simplified joint stock company, Leroux S.A.S.

chicory a year—one-tenth the entire country's production. In this period, the company began advertising and promoting "Leroux" as a brand name. A broad array of sub-brands targeted to particular markets followed.

The Great War devastated the North. Leroux's home village of Orchies was burned in 1914. During the war, Alphonse-Henri-Eugène set up shop in Havre and other locations. The factory was rebuilt after the war. In 1927, the company became a SARL (société anonyme à responsabilité limitée), or limited liability company: SARL Leroux. This structure facilitated the shared leadership of Alain and Robert Leroux after World War II.

Co-Managers After World War II

Alain and Robert Leroux took over management of the company in 1947. Alain gravitated toward operations, while Robert immersed himself in marketing. During the four decades the company was under their direction, notes *La Saga Leroux*, distribution was expanded while processing methods were refined. (Control of another chicory producer, Duroyon et Ramette, passed to Alain and Robert through an uncle. Duroyon had been established in Cambrai in 1873 and was also known for its chocolates.)

Leroux was the focus of a period of consolidation in the 1950s and 1960s, acquiring nearly two dozen related businesses, including Vilain, Les Arlatte, Bonzel, Lervilles, Lestarquit, and Montagne. In the 1950s, Leroux began selling instant and liquid concentrate forms of chicory. After the war, the company promoted chicory's health benefits; it was virtually caffeine- and fat-free and was rich in minerals and fiber.

Alain and Robert Leroux retired in 1989. They were succeeded by Michel Leroux and Michel Hermand, who had shared the top office with Alain and Robert for the previous three years, giving the company four chief executives. Hermand had first joined Leroux in the late 1960s and rejoined the company in 1978 after a five-year hiatus. In 1994, Hermand became the sole leader.

International Focus in the 1990s

Leroux pursued a strategy of global expansion in the 1990s (exports accounted for 25 percent of sales in 1986). A branch office opened in Montreal in 1989 and two years later the company set up a subsidiary in Belgium, a large producer as well as consumer of chicory. Leroux exported 9,000 metric tons of chicory in 1991, when it had revenues of FRF 220 million. Later in the decade, the company opened a branch office on Africa's Ivory Coast.

Leroux acquired Chicobel in January 1992. Chicobel was Belgium's largest supplier of chicory, which it sold under the Pacha brand. Chicobel, which sold a variety of other food products as well, had been formed by the 1975 merger of Van Lier, established in 1825, with Beukelaar à Anvers. It had a turnover of BEF 460 million in 1991 and employed 50 people when it was bought out.

The Chicobel buy gave Leroux a 40 percent share of the world market, according to *La saga Leroux*. Chicobel ceased chicory production after it was acquired by Leroux. Chicobel's Pacha brand, popular in Belgium, remained active, and work soon began on a new distribution center for Chicobel-Pacha products. At the time, Leroux also was partnering with Sopad-Nestlé in 1992 on a coffee-chicory blend.

In 1994, the firm changed its name from Chicorée Leroux to Leroux S.A. as it became a limited liability company. The next year, it began a new effort to market to institutions and restaurants.

Breakfast and snack food maker Union Biscuits was acquired in 1994, opening a new market to Leroux. Union Biscuits had revenues of FRF 30 million a year and 40 employees. In 1996, Leroux acquired Molabe, which accounted for 70 percent of Spain's chicory market, and had revenues of FRF 15 million. Trahe, another Spanish company, was acquired the same year.

Forming a Holding Company in 1997

Leroux and its affiliated businesses were reorganized under a holding company, Finaler (short for Financière Leroux), in 1997. Its five subsidiaries were Leroux S.A., Chicobel S.A. Belgique, Molabe S.A. Espagne, Union Biscuits, and SFD (Société française de déshydratation), which processed dehydrated foodstuffs.

Turnover reached FRF 380 million during the year. Also in 1997, Leroux launched a new cereal product, Chicoréal. Its product lines had been reorganized into three groups: Les Authentiques, or pure chicory in grains, grounds, or liquid form; Les Instants, flavored instant chicory for the breakfast market; and Les Trésors, new natural food products such as the cereal. Leroux also began making artificial sweeteners and in 1998 launched its Médicaler unit specializing in pharmacological products, which were to be distributed in Europe and North America with the assistance of ANVAR (Agence nationale pour la valorisation de la recherche). Leroux also marketed botanical toothpaste and mouthwash under the Acorea brand name.

Les Echos reported Finaler, Leroux's parent, achieved revenues of FRF 420 million (EUR 64 million) in 1999. Two new subsidiaries, Confiserie et Tradition S.A. and Finaler Tradition SCA, were established as the group prepared to enter the market for local produce through acquisitions. These plans were put on hold, however, a year later.

The Drink of the Third Millennium

In 2001, Leroux had 330 employees, two-thirds of them in Orchies. Sales were EUR 53 million, 40 percent of it from outside France. A joint venture was formed with Tufia to market chicory-based drinks in Tunisia.

Leroux was investing EUR 1.5 million in a research and development facility at its Orchies complex. The site was dedicated to finding new uses for chicory. Leroux was pitching chicory as an environmentally sound drink for the third millennium.

Turnover was EUR 40 million in 2002. The firm's structure changed again effective January 1, 2003, when it became a simplified joint stock company, Leroux S.A.S.

Principal Subsidiaries

Chicobel S.A. Belgique; Confiserie et Tradition S.A.; Finaler Tradition SCA; Leroux S.A.; Medicaler; Molabe S.A. Espagne; SFD (Société française de déshydratation); Union Biscuits.

Principal Competitors

Kraft Jacobs Suchard; Nestlé S.A.; Sara Lee Corporation.

Further Reading

"Chicobel to Cease Chicory Production from June 30," *De Financieel Economische Tijd,* March 10, 1992, p. 8.

Ducuing, Olivier, "Leroux investit dans un pole recherche-developpement (Leroux invests in R&D)," *Les Echos,* July 3, 2002.

"France's Leroux to Build New Distribution Centre in Belgium," *Agence Europe,* May 6, 1992.

"French Chicory Company Leroux Sets Up Subsidiary," *Les Echos,* April 18, 1991, p. 28.

"Leroux and Sopad-Nestlé Link Up with New Chicory-Coffee Blend," *Les Echos,* June 22, 1992, p. 7.

"Leroux Develops New Healthcare Products," *Pharmazeutishe Industrie,* October 19, 1998, p. 769.

"Leroux Group Intends to Diversify into Local Produce (Le groupe Leroux compte se diversifier dans les produits de terroir)," *Les Echos,* January 10, 2000.

"Leroux of France Acquires Chicobel," *L'Echo,* January 17, 1992, p. 6.

Maerten, Yves, Nathalie Duronsoy, and Valérie Leroy, eds., *Épopée d'une boisson : la chicorée dans le Nord-Pas-de-Calais,* Béthune, France: musée regional d'Ethnologie, 1993.

Neirynck, Dominique, *La saga Leroux,* La Tour d'Aigues, France: Éditions de l'Aube, 1999.

O'Neill, Robert, "Making a List, Checking It Twice. . . ," *National Journal,* July 29, 2000.

"Senior Management Changes and New Product Launches at Chicoree Leroux," *Les Echos,* September 6, 1994, p. 10.

"Striking Pacha Workers Reject Parent Company's Proposals," *L'Echo,* March 3, 1992, p. 5.

—Frederick C. Ingram

Lifeway®

Lifeway Foods, Inc.

6431 West Oakton Street
Morton Grove, Illinois 60053
U.S.A.
Telephone: (847) 967-1010
Fax: (847) 967-6558
Web site: http://www.kefir.com

Public Company
Incorporated: 1986
Employees: 55
Sales: $14.9 million (2003)
Stock Exchanges: NASDAQ
Ticker Symbol: LWAY
NAIC: 311999 All Other Miscellaneous Food
   Manufacturing

Lifeway Foods, Inc. is the largest manufacturer of kefir, a specialty dairy product, in the United States. Kefir is a milk-based drink of Turkish origin, long popular in Eastern Europe and the Middle East. Kefir is somewhat similar to drinkable yogurt in taste and consistency. Kefir is credited with a variety of health benefits because, like yogurt, it contains a plethora of live yeasts and bacteria thought to enhance digestion and boost the immune system. Lifeway sells kefir in a variety of fruit flavors. Other products include drinkable yogurt, farmer's cheese, a soy-based kefir called Soy Treat, and Basics Plus, a line of kefir enhanced with extracts of the dairy product colostrum. The company began as a niche marketer, selling to specialty food shops and health food stores. Lifeway gained national distribution of its products, and sells in mainstream groceries as well as niche food purveyors. The company also exports to Europe and Canada. While still a very small company in the early 2000s, Lifeway was notable for its rapid growth and for the fact that it held the kefir niche virtually without competition. Members of the founding Smolyansky family hold roughly half the publicly traded company's stock, while the French yogurt maker Groupe Danone owns 20 percent.

Starting Over in the United States in the 1970s

Lifeway Foods, Inc. was founded in 1986 by Michael Smolyansky. Smolyansky emigrated from the Soviet Union in 1976, during an era when few Soviet Jews were allowed out of the country. With his wife and small daughter in tow, Smolyansky arrived in Chicago with only the proverbial dollar in his pocket. Smolyansky had been trained as a chemical engineer, and in Chicago he found work as a draftsman in a machine shop. He worked there for almost ten years, while his wife opened her own small business, a Russian delicatessen.

It was his wife's business that sparked Smolyansky's venture into kefir. The family traveled to Europe in 1985, where they visited a German food show in search of new products for Mrs. Smolyansky's deli. At the food show, Smolyansky sampled kefir, a product he had grown up with but had never seen in the United States. Smolyansky became convinced that he could make and sell kefir in Chicago. Smolyansky incorporated Lifeway Foods in February 1986. It was a tiny business at first. Smolyansky made kefir in his basement and then made the rounds of area groceries, asking them to try stocking his new product. Early on the business went well, however, as Smolyansky got shelf space at the gourmet and health food outlet Treasure Island. In addition, numerous small groceries that catered to Chicago's large Eastern European immigrant community were happy to sell Lifeway kefir. The company soon moved to its own small manufacturing plant.

Although kefir was unknown in the United States, it had a very long history in other parts of the world. Kefir originated in the Caucasus Mountains region, where shepherds had been making and drinking it for some 2000 years. Marco Polo mentioned kefir in his records, and people in Eastern Europe had long consumed it as a particularly healthful food. It was commonly given to the sick, both in hospitals and at home, and it was a standard food for nursing mothers. Thus when Lifeway started making kefir in Chicago, there were two obvious markets. One was Eastern European immigrants like the Smolyanskys, who were already familiar with the product. Kefir also appealed to consumers of health food. The health food segment of the American grocery market had been expanding

215

since the 1960s. Dannon introduced yogurt to a very narrow market in the New York area in 1947, and it was only in the 1960s that that company was able to expand beyond urban areas on the East Coast. Yogurt had been marketed principally as a health food, before gaining more mass-market appeal. Kefir seemed likely to follow a similar trajectory. In terms of its claims to healthfulness, kefir had an even stronger argument than yogurt. It contained more types of live bacteria (the so-called ''good'' bacteria that flourish in the digestive tract) than yogurt, and also contained beneficial yeast organisms.

Taking the Company Public in 1988

Lifeway Foods did so well initially that it quickly outgrew its manufacturing plant. Smolyansky knew he needed a strategy to take the company to the next stage, but he was unsure how to proceed. Smolyansky's daughter Julie, who became president of the company in 2002, remarked to the industry journal *Dairy Foods* (May 2003) that her father's naiveté about business may have helped him at that early stage. Not fully understanding the risks he was taking, he was unafraid to take chances. Friends advised him to take the company public. ''Coming from the Soviet Union, and not having a business background, I'm not sure if he had any idea what they meant,'' Julie Smolyansky told *Dairy Food.* ''He went down to the library and found out that he could print these pieces of paper and sell shares in the company.'' Smolyansky reckoned that he needed to raise about $600,000 in order to expand the company.

Lifeway Foods debuted on the NASDAQ exchange in early 1988. The market was still shaky after its sudden plunge in October 1987, and the Lifeway initial public offering did not make much of a splash. But the stock offering raised the minimum Smolyansky had calculated the company could make do with, and he soon set up a new factory in the Chicago suburb of Skokie. The Skokie plant was twice as large as the earlier facility. Smolyansky himself acted as general contractor in equipping the new plant. The new plant opened in 1989. Lifeway had sales of $800,000 in 1988, and with the bigger facility, the company hoped to double that figure. Smolyansky told *Nation's Business* (July 1989) that he had only one regret about his new Skokie factory. ''I came to this country too late,'' he told the magazine. ''I came 12 years ago. If I'd come 20 years ago, I'd probably have five plants like this.''

Expansion in the 1990s

The company did indeed have an impressive record of growth. In 1990, Lifeway made an acquisition, buying up the drinkable yogurt business of Johanna Farms, Inc., a New Jersey company. Both sales and profits bounded upward as Lifeway's products moved into more markets. By 1991, the company

needed to build an addition to its plant, doubling its production space again. Sales for 1991 hit $2.4 million, an increase of more than 60 percent over the year previous. The figures for net income were even more astonishing, with an increase of more than 450 percent over 1990. By this time, Lifeway was placing its kefir in more supermarket chains and major food distributors, allowing the company to reach beyond ethnic markets and health food stores.

Lifeway was able to distribute kefir through the Jewel and Dominick's grocery chains, two major players in the Chicago area. Lifeway also got the rapidly expanding health food market chain Whole Foods to stock its line of kefir products. With more and more outlets stocking Lifeway products, sales continued to grow in double digits through the mid-1990s. By 1997, Lifeway Foods had sales of $6 million. It was still a small company, but it was also still the only manufacturer of kefir around.

New Products and New Leadership in the Late 1990s and After

Lifeway Foods began marketing more vigorously in the late 1990s, coming out with new products and emphasizing the health food aspects of its line. The company invested in a new facility in 1997, increasing its production capacity. In 1998, Lifeway introduced Basics Plus, a new variant of kefir that was billed as the nation's first ''functional food.'' So-called functional foods had been in the works for years from offshoots of both the food and pharmaceutical industries. A functional food was defined as providing a health benefit in addition to a nutritional benefit, and as such went a step beyond fortified foods such as calcium-enriched orange juice. Lifeway developed Basics Plus in a collaboration with GalaGen Inc., a small Minnesota biotech company that had been spun off from the dairy giant Land O' Lakes. GalaGen had patented a process for adding colostrum to dairy products. Colostrum is the milk an animal produces shortly after giving birth, and it is key to bolstering the newborn's immune system. Lifeway's new Basics Plus was fruit-flavored kefir blended with colostrum, and it was touted as boosting the human immune system. Lifeway had high hopes for the new product line, though it admitted it had few resources to back a major consumer education campaign.

Lifeway's sales rose roughly 13 percent in 1998, marking seven straight years of growth. Although milk prices had risen significantly that year, the company nevertheless continued to break its own profit records, with a rise of close to 30 percent over the year previous. Whether through its intriguing new product line or its impressive financial picture, the small Chicago company attracted the attention of the world's leading fresh dairy company, the French firm Groupe Danone. Groupe Danone manufactured the world's leading brand of yogurt, and its introduction of the Dannon brand in the United States had in some ways provided a parallel for Lifeway's kefir. Groupe Danone purchased 20 percent of Lifeway's stock in 1999. This still left half the stock in the hands of the Smolyansky family.

Lifeway came out with several more new products over the next few years. In 2000 the company introduced SoyTreat, which it advertised as the first organic soy kefir. SoyTreat came out in a different flavor array than Lifeway's kefir, with fruit flavors like

Key Dates:

1986: The company is founded by Michael Smolyansky.
1988: Lifeway goes public.
1998: The company debuts BasicsPlus, the nation's first "functional food."
1999: Groupe Danone buys 20 percent of the company.
2001: The company brings out the La Fruta line.
2002: The founder dies suddenly; daughter Julie Smolyansky becomes CEO.

apple and peach, as well as caramel, coffee, and English toffee. Like BasicsPlus, SoyTreat sold itself on its healthfulness, which included the proven benefits of soy protein in addition to the benefits of kefir itself. The next year, the company unveiled a new kefir line aimed at the Hispanic market. The Hispanic market was the fastest-growing customer demographic in the grocery industry, and Lifeway hoped to sell its new line in specialty grocery stores and in urban markets with large concentrations of Hispanic customers. It test-marketed its new kefir under the name Yogurito, and then brought it out as La Fruta.

By 2001, Lifeway was the largest, and only, manufacturer of kefir in North America. Its sales passed the $10 million mark that year. The company exported its goods to Eastern Europe and to Canada. In 2001 the company signed an exclusive agreement with a specialty grocery distributor in Canada, Jelian Foods. Jelian served natural food markets as well as specialty groceries and kosher food outlets and some mainstream grocery chains. The company seemed bound to continue its rapid growth in sales and profits for 2002, as its new La Fruta line was doing particularly well. The company had slightly more than 50 employees, and it still had room to grow, with much unused capacity at its manufacturing plant.

The company suffered an unexpected blow in 2002 with the sudden death of founder Michael Smolyansky. Smolyansky had a heart attack at age 55 and died with no warning. His daughter Julie then became president and chief executive. Julie Smolyansky had grown up with the company, and after completing a degree in psychology at the University of Illinois in 1996, she became Lifeway's director of sales and marketing. Julie Smolyansky's goal had been to bring Lifeway's kefir products to mainstream groceries, and she had overseen significant sales growth and the introduction of a new organic product line. At 27, Smolyansky was one of the youngest people to head a public company in the United States. Although Michael Smolyansky had not anticipated his early demise, he had named

Julie as his successor. She quickly gained the approval of Lifeway's board and of its investors, including major shareholder Danone. The company posted record gains for the quarter after Julie Smolyansky took over, which seemed to show that Lifeway would not falter under its new leadership. Julie Smolyansky's younger brother, Edward, was named Lifeway's financial director after the father's death.

The Smolyansky siblings were able to make big decisions for the company despite the loss of their father. The company made a major purchase in 2003, buying a new packaging system. The new packaging had more room on the label to print information about kefir, tailoring with Julie Smolyansky's desire to bring kefir to consumers in mainstream groceries. The company continued to show healthy financial results. In 2002, sales rose 14 percent, while profit rose by 25 percent over the year previous. Sales for 2003 climbed to almost $15 million, showing growth of more than 22 percent.

Up until 2003, Lifeway had held the kefir market alone in North America. That year, though, two large rivals began placing kefir on grocery shelves in the United States. Yoplait came out with a kefir line, as did Dannon Co., the U.S. subsidiary of Lifeway's major stakeholder Groupe Danone. The competition did not dampen Lifeway's sales, and the company's CEO was optimistic about future prospects. Lifeway was still too small to do a large-scale advertising campaign. But Smolyansky believed that if Yoplait and Dannon invested in marketing kefir, Lifeway also would benefit from increased public awareness.

Principal Competitors

Horizon Organic Holding Corporation; Stonyfield Farm; General Mills, Inc.

Further Reading

Barrier, Michael, "Liquid Gold," *Nation's Business,* July 1989, p. 14.
Buss, Dale, "Death in the Family, Daughter Takes Over," *Chief Executive,* October 2002, p. 14.
Kuhn, Mary Ellen, "Kefir Adds Soy," *Food Processing,* February 2000, p. 37.
Littman, Margaret, "Cheers! Here's to Your Health," *Crain's Chicago Business,* April 6, 1998, p. 4.
Phillips, David, "Life Goes On," *Dairy Foods,* May 2003, p. 28.
"Powerful Rivals Haven't Soured Lifeway's Strategy," *Crain's Chicago Business,* June 23, 2003, p. 16.
"Small Business Notebook," *Chicago Tribune,* June 26, 2002.

—A. Woodward

Martek Biosciences Corporation

6480 Dobbin Road
Columbia, Maryland 21045
U.S.A.
Telephone: (410) 740-0081
Fax: (410) 740-2985
Web site: http://www.martekbio.com

Public Company
Incorporated: 1985
Employees: 384
Sales: $114.7 million (2003)
Stock Exchanges: NASDAQ
Ticker Symbol: MATK
NAIC: 541710 Physical, Engineering, and Biological
    Research; 325411 Medicinal and Botanical
    Manufacturing; 325412 Pharmaceutical Preparation
    Manufacturing; 325414 Other Biological Products
    Manufacturing

Martek Biosciences Corporation develops and sells products derived from the microalgae it grows. Its Nutritional Products Group manufactures and sells two nutritional fatty acids, docosahexaenoic acid (DHA) and arachidonic acid (ARA). Martek sells its patented DHA and ARA oil blend, Formulaid, to infant formula manufacturers worldwide. The company also sells its DHA oil, Neuromins, to the nutritional supplement industry. The Fluorescent Products Group develops and sells a series of proprietary and non-proprietary fluorescent markers used in drug discovery and research applications.

1985–93: The Research Years

In 1985, Martin Marietta Corporation, saddled with debt from a complicated series of anti-takeover measures, engaged in streamlining its operations. As part of its restructuring, the aerospace giant decided to close its 25-member biosciences department. This department had earlier begun to research ways to use oxygen-producing algae as part of a closed life-support system in space in fulfillment of a contract with the National Aeronautics and Space Administration. Instead of shutting down operations, Dr. Richard J. Radmer, head of Martin's biosciences department, and his colleagues, David Kyle and Paul Behrens, arranged a subcontract with their former employer that allowed them to continue their research. Martin lent Radmer, Kyle, and Behrens most of the equipment they needed to operate the new spinoff in return for about 7 percent of its stock. Radmer, Kyle, and Behrens incorporated as Martek Biosciences Corporation. They rounded up $25,000 to finance Martek and moved themselves into a new laboratory.

Radmer, who held a doctorate in biology from Harvard University and was a member of the graduate faculty at the University of Maryland, became president of Martek. He and his partners were convinced that algae had untold potential uses and set about to collect, cultivate, and experiment with as many strains as possible. "There was all this genetic diversity . . . and it was virtually untapped," said Kyle in a 1997 *Knight Ridder/ Tribune Business News* article.

Grown in Martek's labs in 130-gallon vats of water surrounded by fluorescent bulbs and injected with a mix of nitrates, potassium, phosphates, carbon dioxide, and other elements, Martek's algae typically doubled its weight within five to 24 hours and was ready to harvest within a week. A single 130-gallon container yielded as much as $25 million of algae a year. Of the 10,000 to 30,000 strains of algae believed to exist, by 1988, Martek's scientists had worked with 50 to 100 purified strains, manipulating the cells' manufacture of fats, proteins, and other products to yield food colors, nutritional supplements, lubricants, and chemicals for use in medical diagnoses.

In January 1986, Suburban Capital Corp. led a team of outside investors to advance $750,000 to Martek in return for a 35 percent stake in the company. The company also received its first commercial contract in 1986 to help develop low-cholesterol eggs. (By studying algae's production of fat molecules, the company aimed to control cholesterol production in chickens.) At the time, Martek derived a portion of its revenue from research grants with various agencies under the Small Business Innovative Research Program. Funders included the National Sciences Foundation, the National Institutes of Health, and the Department of Energy.

Key Dates:

1985: Martin Marietta spins off Martek Biosciences Corporation.

1993: The company holds its initial public offering.

1994: Martek introduces Formulaid, its infant formula for low-birth weight infants, in Europe.

1995: Martek signs an agreement with the drug firm Neuromedica Inc.; acquires a fermentation plant in Winchester, Kentucky.

1998: Martek collaborates with SmithKline Beecham on research involving the use of Martek's patented Reconnaissance Probe technology.

2001: The Food and Drug Administration approves use of Martek oils in infant formulas.

2002: Martek acquires OmegaTech Inc. of Boulder, Colorado; Canada's government health agency, Health Canada, completes a favorable review of Martek's oils inclusion in infant formulas.

2003: The company acquires FermPro Manufacturing, L.P. and enters into an agreement with SemBioSys Genetics Inc. of Canada.

Martek moved into new offices in 1989. Four years later, in 1993, it held its initial public offering in the midst of a market skeptical about its future. Investors were wary; the typical biotech company spent about ten years and as much as $200 million to research and develop a new product with no guarantee of actual or commercial success. According to the company's chief financial officer, quoted in a 1994 *Baltimore Business Journal* article, Martek was different, however. It had "a little bit of an advantage because we're not the typical pharmaceutical 'wanna be' company. Our products are a lot closer to the market than others in our sector."

Martek also did not just burn cash in research and development; it sold its synthetically produced oils from the start. Revenues were small—$850,000 in 1988—but there was hope for more. In 1988, Martek was selling its oils in Japan to lubricate the bearings of gyroscopes which guided machines that dug tunnels for optical cables. The lubricant, made from the fats within the cells of algae, was 5 to 14 times more stable than petroleum-based products, and sold in small vials for as much as $2,000.

In 1989, Martek entered into a relationship with Oxford Partners of Stamford, Connecticut, and a group of five other investors. The venture capital syndicate gave Martek $2 million in return for ownership of about a third of the company. Martek used the money to move into new larger offices.

1994–99: Commercializing Its Discoveries

In late 1994, Martek introduced another product. Formulaid, its infant formula for low-birth weight infants, began to sell in Europe. Formulaid featured two known components of breast milk—DHA, docosahexaenoic acid, and ARA, arachidonic acid. In the 1980s and early 1990s, studies had begun to suggest that breast-fed babies had higher levels of DHA and ARA in their brain than their formula-fed counterparts, and, consequently, higher I.Q. and better visual acuity.

Martek had identified a species of algae rich in DHA and a fungus rich in ARA and developed a method of extracting the two fatty acids. Being a non-animal source of DHA, it did not contain the toxins or pollutants found in animal-source fatty acids. After raising cultures from the test tube to fermentation tank, the algae and fungi were dried, refined, and bleached, and the fatty acid removed and blended with sunflower oil. The resulting mixture could be added to infant formulas during their manufacture. Martek held three patents for the technologies employed to produce Formulaid. It began taking important steps to commercialize its DHA- and ARA-rich product worldwide in a bid to grab a piece of the then $5 billion worldwide market in infant formula.

However, Formulaid's appearance began a debate about adding fatty acids to infant formulas. While the European market went ahead and embraced Formulaid, the American market awaited the results of several studies to show whether Martek's nutritional boost was a safe and effective way to enhance infants' neurological development.

Meanwhile, there appeared other applications for DHA. In 1995, Martek signed an agreement with the drug firm, Neuromedica Inc., to combine DHA and dopamine into a treatment for tardive dyskinesia, a disorder that causes uncontrolled facial and other bodily movements and reduced intellectual functioning. The company also started selling DHA dietary supplements, under the name Neuromins, to supplement diets low in foods that contain DHA. General Nutrition Center, a U.S. chain, started selling Neuromins capsules nationwide in 1997.

By 1997, Martek had licensing agreements to provide it DHA- and ARA-rich oil to six infant formula manufacturers that together represented more than 40 percent of the infant formula market. These licensing deals brought in nearly $4 million in revenue in 1996 from sales of fatty acid-enriched formula in 24 countries. Still the company had yet to post a profit in its 12-year existence. In 1996, it had experienced a loss of $8.9 million. In 1997, it had a net loss of $15.4 million with revenues of $4.4 million.

By 1998, somewhere in the vicinity of 50 companies worldwide included Martek's oils in their pre-term infant formulas, and the company signed two more licensing agreements with companies in Australia to include its oils in full-term infant formulas. Iams Company added the DHA-containing nutritional oils to its Eukanuba brand formulas for puppies and kittens. The British Nutrition Foundation and the Joint Expert Committee on Human Nutrition of the United Nations Food and Agriculture Organization and World Health Organization recommended that DHA and ARA be included in all formulas for infants. The January 1998 issue of *Pediatrics* cited DHA as the "likely" breast milk component responsible for the improved academic outcomes and visual acuity of breast-fed children.

In a different vein in 1998, Martek collaborated with SmithKline Beecham Corporation on research involving the use of Martek's patented Reconnaissance Probe technology. The probe technology enabled scientists to map the binding sites where drugs interact with receptor-site proteins. Martek signed an agreement with Intergen Company for non-exclusive distribution of its line of ultrasensitive fluorescent products, expanding on a prior relationship it had with Intergen for distribution.

2000–03: Steady Growth

Another sale of stock to institutional investors in 1999 raised an additional $13.5 million in financing for Martek, and by 2000, about 60 countries had approved its oils for use in infant formulas. Martek also had licensing agreements pending with Wyeth-Ayerst Pharmaceuticals Inc., Mead Johnson & Co., and Royal Numico. When Abbott Laboratories signed a worldwide licensing agreement with Martek in April 2000, Martek gained access to 60 percent of the worldwide infant formula market. Its revenues hit $9.7 million in 2000, increasing 58 percent from 1999 totals. The company readied for even greater growth in 2001 when the Food and Drug Administration completed its favorable review of Martek's oils, deeming them safe for use in infant formula.

Putting in motion plans to increase production capacity five-fold, the company purchased a South Carolina fermentation plant. The facility was its second, Martek having purchased its first fermentation plant, located in Winchester, Kentucky, from Coors Brewing Co. in 1995. The addition of the second plant tripled its production capabilities. Martek also sold the assets of its stable isotope business to Spectra Gases in 2001 in order to concentrate on its other products.

Another breakthrough occurred for Martek in 2001 when researchers in its labs and at the Carnegie Institute of Washington figured out a way to make one species of single-celled algae grow without light. By inserting a single gene from either human red blood cells or a different single-celled algae, the researchers were able to make the algae grow in glucose fermenters. However, the company recorded a loss of $13.7 million for 2001 on revenues of $18.8 million due to the purchase of its new facility and extremely high production costs.

In 2002, Martek raised another $22 million through the private sale of common stock, some of which it used to acquire OmegaTech Inc. of Boulder, Colorado, an algal DHA producer. The acquisition allowed Martek to think about entering the $1 billion food and beverage industry with its nutraceuticals. Another step forward occurred when Canada's government health agency, Health Canada, completed its favorable review of Martek's oils inclusion in infant formulas. In addition, Bristol-Myers Squibb's Mead Johnson Nutritionals division and Abbott Laboratories' Ross Products division began to include Martek's oils in Enfamil Lipil and Similac Advance.

Wal-Mart introduced its DHA-enriched label infant formula line, Parent's Choice, in 2003 by which time Martek had li-

censees in more than 60 countries. Studies continued to provide evidence of the benefits of DHA and ARA, from contributing to higher I.Q. scores for four-year-olds whose diet had been supplemented with the fatty acids after birth to slightly longer gestation lengths for women on supplemented diets during pregnancy. In a final marketing coup, Martek signed a worldwide license with Nestlé, the only one of the major international infant formula companies it had not yet signed an agreement with. The company acquired FermPro Manufacturing, L.P. and entered into an agreement with SemBioSys Genetics Inc. of Canada to develop specialty oil products with potential pharmaceutical and nutraceutical applications.

As Martek looked to the future, it had reason to project continued growth. Although the evidence was as yet inconclusive, some researchers were beginning to believe that DHA- and ARA-enriched diets could prevent cardiovascular disease, Alzheimer's disease, and other dementias.

Principal Subsidiaries

Martek Biosciences Boulder Corp.

Principal Competitors

Cyanotech Corporation; Royal Numico NV; GE Healthcare Bio-Sciences.

Further Reading

Abel, Greg, "Beating the Odds on Wall Street: Martek, Guilford Poised to Benefit from Rebound in Biotech Market," *Baltimore Business Journal*, September 9, 1994, p. 13.

Brody, Jane E., "Experts Disagree on Adding Fatty Acid to Infant Formula," *New York Times*, November 6, 1996, p. C10.

"Columbia-Based Martek Biosciences Purchases a S.C.-Based Plant As U.S. Product Sales Near," *Baltimore Daily Record*, December 13, 2001.

Fountain, Henry, "Observation: Science Desk," *New York Times*, June 19, 2001, p. F5.

Frank, Peter, "New Biotech Concern Pins Hopes on Algae," *Sun*, May 26, 1988, pp. 1G-2G.

——, "Patience vs. Dollars and Cents: Investors Often Put Pressure on Young High-Tech Firms," *Sun*, May 11, 1988, pp. 1C, 3C.

Kaiser, Rob, "Martek Grows Overseas, but Struggles at Home," *Baltimore Business Journal*, December 19, 1997, p. 4.

Kleiner, Kurt, "Martek Secures $2 Million in New Capital," *Baltimore Business Journal*, January 30–February 5, 1989, p. 15.

Shaw, Donna, "Maryland's Martek Biosciences Has High Hopes for Algae," *Knight Ridder/Tribune Business News*, February 10, 1997, p. 3.

Whiteman, Lou, "BioNutrition Lands Healthy Round," *Daily Deal*, March 21, 2002.

—Carrie Rothburd

Matrix Service Company

10701 E. Ute Street
Tulsa, Oklahoma 74116
U.S.A.
Telephone: (918) 838-8822
Fax: (918) 838-8810
Web site: http://www.matrixservice.com

Public Company
Incorporated: 1989 as Matrix Environmental Company
Employees: 3,641
Sales: $288.4 million (2003)
Stock Exchanges: NASDAQ
Ticker Symbol: MTRX
NAIC: 236220 Commercial Institutional Building
   Construction

Matrix Service Company offers construction services, and repair and maintenance services related to aboveground storage tanks (AST) and related facilities used by the petroleum, petrochemical, power generation, power delivery, terminal, pipeline, utility, chemical, transportation, pulp and paper, food and beverage, heavy industrial, and industrial gas industries. The publicly traded company is based in Tulsa, Oklahoma, with regional facilities located in California, Delaware, Illinois, Michigan, Pennsylvania, South Carolina, Texas, Utah, and Washington, as well as Canada. Construction services include turnkey construction, handling projects from the design stage to decommissioning; heavy mechanical installations; electrical instrumentation construction in the Northeast, offering process control and instrumentation installation and fiber optic cabling; civil, concrete, steel erection, and structures construction services; erecting and replacing boilers; retrofits, expansions, and modernizations; plant dismantling and equipment relocation; AST construction; the installation of floating roof and seal systems used by many ASTs as an environmental precaution; secondary containment systems employed by ASTs to detect leaks and prevent groundwater contamination; and fabrication services for new tanks, new tank components, retrofits, floating roofs, and seals. The Matrix repair and maintenance services business segment provides routine ongoing maintenance of ASTs as well as emergency response maintenance, plant turnarounds, outages, and industrial cleaning. More than a quarter of the company's consolidated revenues come from two customers: Chevron and BP.

Founding the Company in 1984

Matrix was started in 1984 by former executives of Tank Service, Inc., a company involved in the repair and maintenance of tanks used in refineries and marketing pipeline terminals. The founders included Doyl D. West, former president of Tank Service; C. William Lee, vice-president, finance, at Tank Service; and Martin L. Rinehart, an executive vice-president with Tank Service. West became the CEO for Matrix, Lee became vice-president, finance, and Rinehart was appointed vice-president, operations. In 1988 the company formed a subsidiary, Petrotank Equipment Inc., and a year later Matrix Service Environmental Company was incorporated in Delaware as a holding company for the two units. In September 1990 the company adopted its present name, Matrix Service Company, and was taken public. PaineWebber Inc., Robertson, Stephens & Co., and First Analysis Securities managed an initial public offering (IPO) that sold 3.25 million shares of stock priced at $8 per share.

At the same time as the IPO, Matrix closed on the acquisition of Midwest Industrial Contractors at a cost of $22 million in cash, stock, and notes. Midwest Industrial provided maintenance and construction services to refineries and specialized in "turnarounds," the quick maintenance of a refinery's critical operating units. This transaction was just the first in a string of acquisitions Matrix made over the next four years, as part of a plan to diversify. In June 1991 the company paid $10.2 million for San Luis Piping Construction Co., Inc. and West Coast Industrial Coatings, Inc. to become involved in water storage tanks. San Luis Piping did fabricated plate work, and West Industrial provided sandblasting, coating, and other services in the maintenance of potable water storage tanks. In December 1992 Matrix completed a pair of acquisitions, picking up Colt Construction Company and Duncan Electric Company. Matrix looked north to Canada in 1993, acquiring Health Engineering. The Sarnia, Ontario-based company performed maintenance on oil storage tanks. Finally in 1994, Matrix bought Georgia Steel

Fabricators, Inc. and its principal operating subsidiary Brown Steel Contractors, Inc., which designed, fabricated, and erected aboveground water storage tanks for both industrial customers and municipalities.

During this period Matrix also looked overseas for new business. In 1993 it forged a joint venture in the Kingdom of Saudi Arabia with Al-Shafai & Sons Constructors to provide maintenance on oil refineries. For decades the Saudis had relied on the export of crude petroleum but were now pursuing a long-range strategy of becoming a producer of refined petroleum. As a result, the kind of services that Matrix provided in the United States would be needed in Saudi Arabia. Al-Shafai & Son supplied $2.5 million worth of equipment and buildings and took a 51 percent controlling interest in the venture, named Al Shafai-Midwest Constructors Ltd. For its part, Matrix put up $500,000 in cash and a pledge to invest another $1.5 million if needed. Matrix also controlled four of the joint venture's seven board seats.

During the first ten years of its existence, Matrix enjoyed steady growth, and at first its expansion program appeared to position the company to reach the next level. For the year ending May 31, 1992, revenues totaled $86.5 million and net income reached $5.6 million. A year later, sales topped $123 million and net income increased to $9.2 million. Business fell off the following year, with revenues dipping to $103.8 million and net income to $4 million. Acquisitions would boost sales over the next few years, but profits would suffer as the company's diversification plan began to unravel. The Saudi Arabia joint venture also succumbed to poor economic conditions in the Kingdom of Saudi Arabia, which led to Al Shafai-Midwest Constructors discontinuing operations in 1995. For the fiscal year ending May 31, 1994, Matrix posted sales of $133.5 million and net income of $2.7 million. Although revenues grew to $177.5 million the following year, the company lost $189,000, due in part to the lost investment in the Saudi joint venture. For fiscal year 1996 Matrix returned to profitability, recording net income of $2.4 million on revenues of $183.7 million. Although sales receded slightly in 1997, to $183.1 million, the company increased net income to $3 million.

Restructuring and Continuing Development into the 21st Century

In 1998 Matrix acquired General Service Corporation and affiliated companies, which provided similar services and products. In addition, Matrix began to enjoy the benefits of a five-year contract with Chevron Corporation to modify and repair its above-ground refining, fuel marketing, and pipelines across the country. It was a massive responsibility, given that Chevron maintained 900 ASTs in its pipeline operations alone.

Despite these positive developments, Matrix was almost sold during 1998. In December 1997, Iteq Inc., a Houston-based company that provided equipment, systems, and services to process, treat, store, and transport gases and liquids, agreed to pay $10 a share, or $94 million, to acquire Matrix. Several weeks later, however, the two parties terminated the deal "due to unanticipated difficulties in connection with the expected integration of personnel from divergent corporate cultures." Matrix now embarked on an effort to restructure its operation, to cut costs, close redundant facilities, and improve efficiencies. As a result of the General Service acquisition and Chevron contract, revenue jumped to $225.4 million in 1998, but the company recorded a net loss of $11.6 million, caused by costs associated with the restructuring and the operating losses incurred from discontinued operations.

Business conditions, particularly in the water tank segment, were poor in 1999, leading to a drop in revenues. Before the year was complete, the management team was replaced. Mike Hall became the chief financial officer and Bradley S. Vetal was named president and chief executive officer. Vetal graduated Cum Laude from the University of Michigan with a degree in Mechanical Engineering and had been with Matrix since 1987. For the past three years he had served as vice-president of the tank division, responsible for all AST operations. In the words of the *Tulsa World,* Vetal and Hall took over a company that had pursued "a series of fruitless ventures and investments in non-core areas such as municipal water storage. Those businesses, which led to losses in previous years, were quickly shed after Vetal and Hall took the helm." The operations of Midwest Industrial Contractors were discontinued, as were the operations of San Luis Tank and West Coast Industrial Coatings. The municipal water tank subsidiary, Brown Steel, was sold to Caldwell Tanks Inc. for $4.3 million. Matrix also adopted a poison-pill anti-takeover plan and hired the investor relations firm of Carl Thompson Associates to create a proactive investor relations program to help maximize shareholder value.

Because of some of the steps Matrix took in 1999, revenues slipped to $211 million and the company recorded a net loss of $12.6 million. But the new management team was also in the process of developing a five-year plan to double the size of the company despite the selling off and elimination of noncore assets. Although sales fell to $193.8 million in 2000 and $190.9 million in 2001, Matrix returned to profitability, earning $6.6 million in 2000 and $4.6 million in 2001. While it did make an effort to diversify somewhat—in 2002 it began manufacturing parts for power grids—the company was preparing to take advantage of stricter environmental regulations about to take effect that would raise standards on the use of storage tanks by the gas and oil industry. Matrix was well positioned in its field, boasting a solid reputation and maintaining offices in all of the major refining centers in the country. It was the second largest builder of ASTs and the top provider of AST maintenance and repair services.

Acquiring Hake Group in 2003

Revenues increased to $222.5 million in 2002 and net income grew to $5.9 million. In 2003 revenues exceeded $288 million and net income totaled $8.2 million. Matrix was making steady progress, but it now took a step that would eclipse its

Key Dates:

1984: The company is founded.
1989: A holding company, Matrix Environmental Company, is formed.
1990: The company is taken public as Matrix Service Company.
1999: Brad Vetal is named CEO.
2003: Hake Group is acquired.

five-year target in a single stroke. In February 2003 Matrix reached an agreement to buy Eddyston, Pennsylvania-based Hake Group, Inc. for $50 million, an acquisition that was the culmination of 18 months of work with Citigate Markowitz & McNaughton to identify companies that would provide a strategic fit for Matrix. All told, more than 240 companies were considered before Hake was singled out and its management expressed a willingness to sell to Matrix. In business since 1919, Hake provided industrial contracting services for the power generation, petroleum, chemical, and manufacturing industries. Not only did Hake's services nicely complement those of Matrix, the acquisition gave Matrix a major presence in the mid-Atlantic region and a strong relationship with high-quality customers. In essence, Matrix could now offer the same maintenance and construction services on the East Coast that it was already providing elsewhere in the country. The acquisition brought geographic balance as well as the addition of some capabilities the company did not previously possess. Moreover, Hake in its most recent fiscal year generated sales of $174.8 million and net income of $5.2 million. As a result, once the Hake assets were integrated, Matrix was in line to reach $500 million in annual revenues, an amount well above the five-year goal.

Wall Street showed its approval of the Hake acquisition by bidding up the price of Matrix stock. In October 2003 the company declared a one-for-one stock dividend on its common stock as demonstration of the board's confidence in the future of the company as well as to increase the number of Matrix shares in the marketplace and make it more attractive to investors. The company was enjoying strong business in fabrication and construction, but maintenance projects were unusually slow, as many energy companies, forced to spend money on upgrades to meet stricter environmental regulations that limited the amount of sulfur that oil refineries could include in gasoline, diesel fuel, and heating oil, were deferring preventive maintenance projects until cash became available. On the one hand, Matrix benefited from the stricter regulations because the company helped to clean emission from the smoke stacks of power plants and offered the equipment and expertise to help refineries in their efforts to cut sulfur levels. But because the maintenance and repair unit was saddled with high fixed costs, Matrix saw margins suffer. Management could still take comfort in knowing that repairs could not be delayed forever, and that the company would soon experience a significant rebound on the maintenance side of its business. Regardless, Matrix was well positioned to enjoy strong, sustainable growth for the foreseeable future.

Principal Subsidiaries

Matrix Service, Inc.; Hake Group, Inc.

Principal Competitors

Chart Industries, Inc.; Chicago Bridge and Iron N.V.; Denali Incorporated.

Further Reading

Alva, Marilyn, "This Firm Cleans Up, Thanks to EPA Regs," *Investor's Business Daily,* November 21, 2003, p. A04.

Russell, Ray, "Tulsa, Okla.-Based Storage Tank Specialist Aims to Maintain Good Reputation," *Tulsa World,* January 11, 2002.

Wilmoth, Adam, "Tulsa, Okla.-Based Petrochemical Services Firms Climbs on Acquisition," *Daily Oklahoman,* November 2, 2003.

—Ed Dinger

McMenamins Pubs and Breweries

1624 NW Glisan Street
Portland, Oregon 97209
U.S.A.
Telephone: (503) 223-0109
Fax: (503) 294-0837
Web site: http://www.mcmenamins.com

Private Company
Incorporated: 1983
Employees: 1,500
Sales: $60 million (2003 est.)
NAIC: 722110 Full-Service Restaurants; 312120
    Breweries; 721110 Hotels (Except Casino Hotels)

McMenamins Pubs and Breweries owns and operates more than 50 establishments in Oregon and the state of Washington and is the sixth largest producer of microbrewed beer in the Pacific Northwest. Unlike other breweries, McMenamins sells its ales only in its own pubs, restaurants, hotels, and movie theaters. A conscious anti-branding ideology permeates McMenamins: each business bears its own name and distinctive decorations, often reminiscent of the history of the building in which it is located. Several of the McMenamins businesses are in renovated buildings included in the National Historic Register of Places.

1974 to Mid-1980s: Evolving a New Kind of Pub

In 1974, after graduation from Oregon State University with a degree in political science, Mike McMenamin thought it would be fun to run a business. His past experience as a sandwich maker turned his thoughts to the food industry; so, along with two college friends-turned-business-partners, he bought the Produce Row Café, a pub famous for its all-night, high-stakes poker games, in Portland, Oregon's warehouse and wholesale district. The following year, Mike and brother Brian, an Oregon State graduate with a degree in business, bought Bogart's Joint, another Portland-area pub with backing from their father.

By 1980, the McMenamins had bought and sold a total of seven pubs. Looking back on these early ventures from the perspective of a 2004 *Chicago Tribune* article, Brian Mc-

Menamin would say, "Our kind of thing is learn by doing, and there's a lot of expense in that." Along the way, the brothers developed a prototype for a new kind of pub—one that departed from the dark, smoky, male-dominated, local tavern—and drew inspiration from the all-ages community hubs that characterized the urban and rural landscapes of England, France, and Italy.

"Our initial idea was to make our pubs into community centers, places for people in the neighborhood to gather and have a good time," said company President Mike McMenamin in a 2002 *Nation's Restaurant News* article. In 1983, the Mc-Menamins decided to try out their prototype at The Barley Mill Pub, a pub famous in Portland for its annual Grateful Dead anniversary party. At The Barley Mill, music became an essential ingredient in the McMenamin mix. "It's kind of like we are recreating the wheel all the time," according to Mike Mc-Menamin. "Part of the fun here is that things are always changing, and we do lots of experimentation. Energy is a large part of this company, energy combined with imagination."

1984 to Late 1990s: Ongoing Experimentation on a Theme

In 1984, Oregon passed a law that allowed small breweries to sell their product onsite and at a second location. The law also permitted minors in pubs during the hours when food was served. The McMenamins, taking advantage of the law, for which they had lobbied, opened the first brewpub in Oregon since Prohibition, the Hillsdale Brewery and Public House. "[H]aving beer on tap inspired us to make our own. We'd been offering a lot of imported and specialty beers, which sometimes seemed to have lost flavor because they'd been sitting on a boat too long. Making our own beers seemed like a natural move since we had some home brewers already working in the company," explained Mike McMenamin in a 2002 *Nation's Restaurant News* article. McMenamins establishments began offering their own Terminator Stout, a dark, heavy, English-style brew, and Ruby Tuesday, a light, raspberry-flavored beer. They later added their own Hammerhead Ale.

The brothers also began to allow their love of historic structures to direct their business growth. In 1986, they purchased a

125-year-old farmhouse in Hillsboro, Oregon, and turned it into the Cornelius Pass Roadhouse. Then in 1987, they converted the 1890s-vintage Swedish Tabernacle, a church-turned-union hall in northwestern Portland, into the state's first theater pub, which they called the Mission Theater and Pub. The Mission began showing classic movies and selling beer and snacks, but to limited success; so, in search of greater profits, the newest McMenamins venture began to serve burgers and pizza along with beer and to charge $1 admission to second-run movies. The new formula worked, and shortly thereafter, the McMenamins turned an old art deco theater slated for the wrecking ball into a second pub and movie house. The newly remodeled Baghdad Theatre had alternating rows of seats and long tables facing the movie screen.

By 1990, McMenamins had sales of about $10 million. In 1991, at a time when there were only 130 brewpubs nationwide, McMenamins, with ten, had twice as many brewpubs as any other company. The company owned a total of 24 taverns throughout the state of Oregon and sold close to 600,000 gallons of its own brew annually in addition to beer from other Oregon microbreweries, domestic beers such as Henry Weinhard, Budweiser, and Miller, and a sprinkling of foreign brews. By 1995, there were 30 McMenamins pubs throughout Oregon and Washington, the two leading states in terms of draft beer consumption. Twenty-seven percent of beer sold in these two states was on tap as compared with only 3 percent in nearby California.

Despite this growth, the company still relied solely on its existing network of pubs and theaters to cross-promote its properties. There were advertisements on everything from beer mats to movie screens. "[McMenamins exists] in the crease between neighborhood business and more formal businesses," according to Brian McMenamin in a 1995 *American Demographics* article. "Almost all of our advertising is word of mouth." The McMenamins prided themselves on their laid-back air and the company's open atmosphere where everyone did a little of everything. "We look for people as much as we do for properties," Mike McMenamin observed in a 2002 *Nation's Restaurant News* article. The company limited itself to promoting employees from within rather than recruiting from without to fill management positions.

In the late 1980s and early 1990s, the McMenamins put their profits back into the business, according to Brian McMenamin in a 1991 *Los Angeles Times* article. Much of that money went into the renovation and opening of the 25-acre Edgefield Manor in Troutdale, Oregon. Edgefield had once been the self-sufficient Multnomah County Poor Farm, complete with meatpacking plant, power station, large rooming house, and infirmary. The brothers purchased Edgefield, which was listed on the National Register of Historic Places, in 1987 for $560,000 and invested another $2.5 million over four years to transform the farm's 80-year-old buildings into a multi-utility complex. When the Edgefield Manor opened in 1991, the meatpacking plant had become a brewery; the power station a pub with a movie theater; the infirmary a winery; and the rooming house a 100-room lodge. There was also a meeting space, catering operation, a fine dining restaurant called the Black Rabbit, herb and flower gardens, four small liquor and cigar bars, a distillery, golf course, and an amphitheater.

One of the more outstanding things about Edgefield—and a feature that was to become the McMenamins' signature—was the art by 14 local artists that showed up in surprising places throughout the complex: on ceilings, exposed heating pipes, eaves, and fuse boxes. This art depicted local themes, images of former poorhouse residents, Northwest Indians, 19th-century brewers, and the Columbia River Gorge. A few years later, the company had a stable of 12 freelance artists that it kept employed working on its various new acquisitions. Another outstanding feature of McMenamins was its emphasis on recycling. "There was a lot of impetus within the company to recycle," said Brian McMenamin in a 1993 *Oregon Business* article. In 1991, the company set up a recycling program headed by a designated employee in each pub.

Throughout the mid-1990s McMenamins continued to evolve, as did the company's clientele. Portland's pubs were attracting fewer hard-core drinkers and more families than they had in the mid-1980s, in part in testimony to McMenamins' success. "There are more families now, and more people coming by to talk. . . ." Patrons were bringing their young children. "A lot of our pubs have toys and things for kids to do," said Brian McMenamin in the May 1995 *American Demographics*. There was also a growing demand in the pubs for local and regional foods. As a result, as much as 60 percent of the company's revenues began to come from food sales. By 1998, 70 percent of revenues came from food. McMenamins responded by developing menus that were eclectic and diverse enough to reflect the atmosphere of its various establishments with signature dishes at each of the pubs.

Late 1990s to Early 2000s: A Focus on Larger-Scale Operations

The company also began to focus on larger operations. It continued its practice of buying up old abandoned buildings with the 1997 purchase of the Crystal Ballroom in Portland. Built in the 'teens, the building—famous for its swaying dance floor on ball bearings—had stood vacant for 30 years. The newly rehabbed Crystal became a dance hall and concert facility that hosted national music acts and was filled with murals depicting the building's history; it had, of course, a brewpub and bar in its lower level.

Also in the late 1990s, McMenamins partnered with the Portland Development Commission and invested $4.5 million

Key Dates:

1974: Mike McMenamin opens his first tavern.
1983: The McMenamin brothers open their first pub, the Barley Mill Pub.
1985: The McMenamin brothers open their first microbrewery at the Hillsdale Brewery and Public House.
1986: The Cornelius Pass Roadhouse opens in Hillsboro, Oregon.
1987: The Mission Theater and Pub opens in Portland, Oregon.
1991: The Baghdad Theatre opens in Portland, Oregon; Edgefield Manor opens in Troutdale, Oregon.
1992: McMenamins earns the "Recycler of the Year" award from the Association of Oregon Recyclers.
1995: McMenamins purchases the Rock Creek Tavern in Hillsboro, Oregon.
1997: McMenamins purchases and rehabs the Crystal Ballroom in Portland, Oregon.
1999: McMenamins Hotel Oregon in McMinnville, Oregon, opens.
2000: The Grand Lodge in Forest Grove, Oregon, opens.
2001: McMenamins opens Centralia's Olympic Club Hotel in Centralia, Oregon.
2003: McMenamins reopens the Rock Creek Tavern in Hillsboro, Oregon.

in remodeling the Kennedy Elementary School in Portland. The once boarded-up neighborhood eyesore became a 35-room multi-use hotel with one pub, four bars, a movie theater, a jazz hall, cigar bar and soaking pool, and its own onsite brewery.

By 1998, McMenamins had 40 distinct units, or "destination places," as the company liked to call its establishments, half of which were brewpubs. Its business was increasingly successful at a time when experts were decrying the end of the brewpub craze. McMenamins employed 900 workers, 12 freelance artists, and brought in $30 million in annual sales, close to double what it had brought in just five years earlier. Although many thought the company should expand geographically, the McMenamin brothers were still interested only in focusing on the Northwest. "We're hands-on folks, and we're committed to the Northwest," they announced in a 1998 *Restaurant Business* article.

More growth came in 1999 when McMenamins opened the doors of McMenamins Hotel Oregon. The building in down-

town McMinnville, Oregon, listed in the National Register of Historic Places, had been in operation as a hotel since its first two stories were erected in 1905. Five years later, two more floors were stacked onto the hotel, which was renamed Hotel Oregon in 1932. The McMenamins renovation included completing the fourth floor, refurbishing guest rooms, and adding two bars—one on the rooftop, the other in the cellar. The company also added an art gallery that blended old photographs and paintings to depict the lore and history of the hotel and McMinnville. The next year, McMenamins took over the Grand Lodge in Forest Grove, Oregon.

Mike McMenamin was still saying, in 2001 in a *Portland Journal* article, "We never had a plan in our lives. This business is always evolving, and we do what makes sense and what fits us," when the company, with a workforce of 1,500, was ranked 132nd among Oregon's largest private companies. That year, McMenamins opened Centralia's Olympic Club Hotel and Theater, expanding upon its Olympic Club Pub in downtown Centralia, Washington. Overnight stays in the hotel's 27 restored rooms included admission to the movies and breakfast in the first floor café. By 2002, the company had 52 properties and annual sales of about $60 million and was targeting central Oregon for its next area of growth. In 2003, it reopened the Rock Creek Tavern in Hillsboro, Oregon, which it had purchased in 1995, when the old tavern there burned down. McMenamins also began branching out into other products for sale in its taverns, such as stout mustard in the early years of the new century. All signs were that the company would keep on growing.

Further Reading

Back, Brian J., "Hamblin Hattan Architects Hired to Renovate New Building Site," *Portland Business Journal,* October 29, 1999, p. 30.

Edmondson, Brad, "Beer's Best and Brightest," *American Demographics,* May 1995, p. 36.

Elder, Robert K., "Preservation Brotherhood: Oregon's Brian and Mike McMenamin Rescue Historic Properties and Give Them a Quirky Twist," *Chicago Tribune,* January 28, 2004, p. 1.

Green, Richard, "Oregon Brewers Thought Small and It Was the Start of Something Big," *Los Angeles Times,* December 15, 1991, p. B6.

Mayfield, Robert, "McMenamins Toasts the Earth," *Oregon Business,* February 1993, p. 26.

Stout, Heidi, "Tapping the Market," *Portland Business Journal,* June 22, 2001, p. 14.

Van Houten, Ben, "Bro Pubs," *Restaurant Business,* February 1, 1998, p. 20.

Weiss, Shari, "McMenamins: Prosperous Times for Company That Turned a Truck Stop into Profitable Pubs," *Nation's Restaurant News,* January 28, 2002, p. 130.

—Carrie Rothburd

Medical Management International, Inc.

dba Banfield, The Pet Hospital
11815 NE Glenn Widing Drive
Portland, Oregon 97220
U.S.A.
Telephone: (503) 256-7299
Toll Free: (800) 838-6738
Fax: (503) 256-7636
Web site: http://www.banfield.net

Private Company
Incorporated: 1955
Employees: 1,000
NAIC: 541940 Veterinary Services; 533110 Lessors of
  Nonfinancial Intangible Assets

Medical Management International, Inc., which prefers to be known by the name under which it does business, Banfield, The Pet Hospital, stresses "human quality medicine" and customer care for pets. The company still owns and operates its original animal hospital in Portland, Oregon, along with more than 300 other animal hospitals and more than 100 wellness clinics in 43 states, as well as a handful of clinics in the United Kingdom. Banfield, in addition, is a pioneer in the pet health insurance market and has embarked on plans to build teaching hospitals supported by two schools of veterinary medicine.

1985–93: Growth As a Neighborhood Animal Hospital

In 1955, Warren Wegert, a veterinarian, opened Banfield Pet Hospital, which he named after the area in Portland, Oregon, in which he located his business. Banfield was successful, and Wegert, a breeder and racer of greyhounds, operated the hospital continuously until he sold his practice to Scott Campbell in 1986.

Campbell, who had received his degree in veterinary medicine from Oregon State University in 1985, expanded Wegert's practice, adding a third veterinarian in 1987, and heavily promoting the business. Wegert continued to practice as a veterinarian at

Banfield until he retired in 2001 at the age of 82. In 1990, Campbell moved Banfield into a new 6,600-square-foot hospital across the street from the 2,000-square-foot hospital that Wegert had opened in the 1950s. According to Wegert in a 2003 *Oregonian* article, "Scott Campbell's a brilliant person—a genius at marketing [who] could foresee the future of veterinary medicine." The new hospital, open seven days a week, 365 days a year, with slightly limited hours on weekends, had a drive-up window, a closed circuit television system for monitoring sick patients 24 hours a day, a laboratory, low-radiation x-ray equipment, an operating room and five examination rooms, and a video system with tapes to educate pet owners about pet care. Wegert's old hospital, still owned by Banfield, was converted into a boarding and grooming salon capable of handling up to 100 pets.

The new Banfield stressed "human quality medicine" for pets. "We ask staff how they would like to be treated and try to treat the clients the same way," Campbell attested in a 1990 *Oregonian* article. "We certainly aren't the cheapest veterinary clinic. We have more staff, more equipment—but we practice a different quality of medicine and we think that is what people want." Unlike most veterinary practices, Campbell's did not require an appointment and practiced team-based medicine. Banfield also differed from other clinics in sales, generating more than twice as much revenue per veterinarian as the industry average.

Banfield stressed efficiency and responsiveness to its human customers. Staff tracked activities performed and the length of time each customer spent in the clinic—on average, 29 minutes, 19 of those with a vet. The hospital handled 60 to 120 pets a day. When a pet was hospitalized, staff called at least twice a day to keep the owner informed of the pet's progress. The hospital also called everyone whose pet had not been in for more than a year or had missed vaccinations or checkups. Beginning in 1986, Banfield hired a research company, Bardsley & Neidhart Inc., to call and survey 200 of its clients monthly and about 350 once a year. In 1987, it began to offer an HMO-type plan, its Optimum Wellness Plan, to customers. It also marketed this plan to 12 other veterinary hospitals.

Banfield's emphasis on customer care was very timely. With a concurrent development in the sophistication and cost of

Company Perspectives:

Today our hospitals provide the same medical systems, procedures and client service that made our original hospital a critical part of its neighborhood for half a century. And, we continue to be driven by the same goal that has always inspired us: making life better for families. We do this by giving Pets the same care we want for ourselves, making Pet health affordable, strengthening the value of Pets in families, teaching how better Pet care maximizes lives, and stopping euthanasia by keeping Pets healthy. Put simply, treating your Pet like family.

veterinary medical and surgical services, procedures once reserved for humans, such as ultrasound, chemotherapy, and blood transfusions, had made their way into veterinary medicine. There were veterinary specialists in fields as diverse as neurology, cardiology, ophthalmology, dermatology, dentistry, and surgery. By the mid-1990s pet owners were spending about $5 billion a year on healthcare for pets in the United States and wanted to be sure that their money was well-spent. In fact, to accommodate and encourage this trend, veterinary clinics around the country picked up on the new practice of pet HMOs.

1993–2003: Developing a Partnership with PETsMART

Banfield's success did not go unnoticed. In 1993, PETsMART, a Phoenix-based pet supply chain, decided to open stores in Washington and Oregon, and approached Campbell to propose that he open additional veterinary practices inside individual PETsMART stores. Store research had shown that about half of PETsMART's customers did not have veterinarians. Campbell agreed, and by the end of the first year, there were 37 Vetsmart hospitals owned by Banfield in stores across the country. PETsMART, meanwhile, retained ownership of its own chain of pet clinics in stores without a Vetsmart veterinarian. These clinics, called PETsMART Veterinary Services, offered vaccines, therapeutic diet sales, and neutering for dogs and cats, but were generally not full-service pet hospitals.

In the summer of 1995, Vetsmart Pet Hospital introduced its own Optimum Wellness Plan. Pet owners paid a one-time membership fee ranging from about $70 to $100, followed by monthly payments of about $10 to $35. The lowest-cost plan covered vaccinations, two physical exams per year, and several blood tests. The next plan up also included surgical fees for sterilization, de-worming, and blood and thyroid tests. The more expensive plans added in higher-priced dental services and chest x-rays and electrocardiograms.

In 1998, Banfield started to franchise hospitals in PETsMART stores to individual veterinarians; these practices, which bore the Banfield name and branding were referred to as "Charter Practices." Then, in the summer of 2000, Banfield bought all of PETsMART's 118 clinics. At the time, fewer than 5 percent of the 18,000 pet hospitals nationwide were owned by large corporations. Banfield upgraded the PETsMART Veterinary Services clinics to full-service hospitals and changed the

name of all of its hospitals to Banfield, The Pet Hospital. The reason for the name change was that a study that Banfield had conducted showed that people associated Vetsmart with PETsMART and assumed that the veterinary hospitals were a part of the pet supply chain. The name Banfield, on the other hand, connoted high-quality independent veterinary care and allowed the practice to capitalize on its long history.

But many independent vets were critical of the services provided by Banfield and objected to the image the franchiser wanted to create for its practices. According to one veterinarian quoted in a 1996 issue of the *Chicago Tribune,* the veterinarians at Banfield were "on limited salaries, often inexperienced, and commonly transient." Another offered that "[t]he strongest lure of the corporate organizations is convenience for the pet owner. He buys dog and cat food and inoculates his pet at the same location. . . . Corporate apparently doesn't solicit the long-term veterinary patient or the long-term veterinarian." The implication here and elsewhere was that the quality of care Banfield vets provided was questionable.

However, at least some customers felt otherwise. Pet owners' pocketbooks were not keeping up with the advances in veterinary care and the cost of this care. At the same time, a shift was occurring in the way in which many Americans were treating their pets, with more and more willing to regard companion animals as members of the family. According to a survey of small animal veterinarians published in the July issue of *DVM Newsmagazine,* the average amount pet owners spent before deciding to end a pet's treatment or choose euthanasia was $576 in 1997. Veterinarians also were changing. In 1980, more than 90 percent of graduating veterinarians were male and most owned their own practice. By 1985, the number of female and male veterinarians was roughly equal, with female veterinarians much less likely to own their own practice.

By 2000, there were more than 200 full-service Banfield hospitals in 27 states throughout the nation, and Banfield had partnered with PETsMART to increase the number of its franchises. By 2001, Banfield's 260 hospitals were caring for 60,000 pets each week. Banfield took action to dispel the image attributed to it of the corporate, impersonal vet. In the fall of 2000, it began national promotions to introduce itself to pet owners by offering free weight evaluations for pets along with food measuring cups and nutrition guides. By early 2002, its hospitals and Wellness Clinics had increased to number more than 300 in 38 states, making it the largest veterinary practice in the world. It cared for an estimated 50,000 pets per week, or a total of almost two million per year.

By 2000, although fewer than 1 percent of the nation's estimated 120 million pets were insured, more than 260,000 pet owners had purchased Banfield's Optimum Wellness Plan. Campbell took his company's involvement in preventive pet care one step further and founded BluePaws Pet Health Insurance. BluePaws, with access to two million pet health records from Banfield, created the only actuarial tables ever created for pets and offered a more sophisticated rate schedule than other pet insurances. It also created a streamlined online claims system that greatly reduced claims processing costs. Veterinarians went online to determine their client's share of the bill and to submit claims.

Key Dates:

1955: Warren Wegert opens Banfield Pet Hospital in Portland, Oregon.
1985: Scott Campbell receives his degree in veterinary medicine from Oregon State University.
1986: Scott Campbell purchases Banfield Pet Hospital.
1990: Banfield moves into a new 6,600-square-foot hospital across the street from the original hospital.
1993: Banfield enters a partnership with PETsMART.
1998: Banfield begins to franchise its hospitals in PETsMART stores to individual veterinarians.
2000: Banfield buys PETsMART's 118 clinics, upgrades them to full-service hospitals, and changes the name to Banfield, The Pet Hospital.
2003: Banfield has become the largest veterinary practice in the world, operating more than 300 hospitals and 100 clinics in 38 states and employing more than 800 veterinarians.

BluePaws ran into branding problems, however, with Blue Cross and Blue Shield. The health insurance provider for humans alleged "infringement of trademark" in 2001 on the basis of the similarity between the two companies' names. BluePaws changed its name to TruePaws and modified its signature color and logo from blue to maroon and black. It continued test marketing its services in Portland, Oregon, and Austin, Texas, until the end of 2001. Then, at the end of 2001, it closed.

2003: Entering the Field of Veterinary Education

By 2003, Banfield was operating more than 300 hospitals and more than 100 Wellness Clinics in 38 states and employing more than 800 veterinarians. Banfield vets saw approximately 2.5 million cats and dogs a year, or 2 percent of the nation's pet population, and delivered about 5 percent of the veterinary care provided in the United States. Since all Banfield hospitals used the same computer programs and data systems that were backed up regularly to central computers in Portland, Banfield's records offered exciting opportunities for research. Epidemiologists at Purdue University's School of Veterinary Medicine began to develop software to allow them to review Banfield's data to look for unusual clusters of symptoms, which might signal early signs of biological or chemical threat. Anthrax, plague, and tularemia all affect animals in the same way they do humans, but animals feel the effects more quickly because they are smaller.

Banfield also initiated a collaboration in 2003 with Western University of Health Sciences College of Veterinary Medicine to create a primary teaching hospital for first- and second-year veterinary students where they would have the chance to learn about routine veterinary care as part of the school's new problem-based curriculum. Construction began on the new hospital, located in Pomona, California, in 2003. Plans for the facility included five exam rooms, a large surgical suite, an x-ray room, isolation facilities, and two conference rooms.

Banfield expanded in another direction as well in 2003, partnering with mypetstop Pet Resort & Care Centers to open its first hospital overseas in Manchester, England. It also made plans for its second small animal teaching hospital at the Universidad Nacional Autonome de Mexico (UNAM). These plans included a full-service hospital with nine exam rooms, in-house laboratory, three surgical suites, and overnight accommodations to house residents. Campbell described the relationship with UNAM in the October 2003 issue of *DVM.* "They need a hospital and we can help them obtain practical training and they can help us with the shortage of veterinarians."

Principal Competitors

Veterinary Centers of America Inc.

Further Reading

Baumgartner, Kathy, "Banfield Plunges into International Waters," *DVM,* October 2003, p. 42.
Brinckman, Jonathan, "Pet Care and Wares," *Oregonian,* September 11, 2003, p. B1.
Golin, Marlene, "Pet Stores in a Dogfight: Competitors Have to Get More Creative Than Selling Just Collars and Kibbles," *Chicago Tribune,* March 3, 1996, p. 1.
Goranson, Eric, "Pet Clinic to Move to New, Larger Quarters," *Oregonian,* April 5, 1990, p. 8.
Jaques, Susan, "The Pet Policy: As Care Costs Rise, Owners Have One More Option—Insurance," *Los Angeles Times,* May 12, 1995, p. E3.
Trevison, Catherine, "The Cost of Puppy Love," *Oregonian,* March 29, 2001, p. C1.
Verdon, Daniel R., "Western University to Build Primary Care Teaching Hospital Courtesy of Banfield," *DVM,* September 2003, p. 10.

—Carrie Rothburd

Mediolanum S.p.A.

Via Francesco Sforza 15, Palazzo
Meucci-Milano 3
20080 Basiglio, Milano
Italy
Telephone: +39 02 90491
Fax: +39 02 90492401
Web site: http://www.mediolanum.it

Public Company
Incorporated: 1982 as Programma Italia
Employees: 995
Total Assets: $660.7 million (2001)
Stock Exchanges: Borsa Italiana
Ticker Symbol: MED.MI
NAIC: 524113 Direct Life Insurance Carriers

Holding company Mediolanum S.p.A. offers a broad range of private banking and related financial services, including assets management, insurance, brokerage, mutual fund investment, and related products. While not the biggest bank in Italy, group holding Banca Mediolanum is one of the country's fastest growing, in part due to its business model—the company specializes in providing personalized door-to-door and ''virtual'' banking services. Customers gain access to their accounts through the Internet, over the telephone, and through an exclusive television-based teletext service, as well as home visits from Mediolanum's army of more than 5,000 sales affiliates, nearly all of whom sell exclusively Mediolanum's products. The company's operations are based primarily in Italy. In the 2000s, however, the company has begun an effort to develop into a pan-European bank, acquiring businesses in Germany and Austria (Bankhaus August Lenz and Luxembourg-based Gamax), in Spain (Fibanc), and Monaco (Compagnie Monegasque du Banque). The company also has plans to expand into France and Poland, and ultimately expects to have operations throughout all of Europe, including much of Eastern Europe. While developing its own financial products and services for a customer base of nearly 15,000, Mediolanum has teamed with Italian banking giant Mediobanca to attract a higher-end market. In 2002, the two banks formed the joint venture

Banca Esperia, which targets wealthier investors with assets of more than EUR 5 million ($4 million) to invest. Mediolanum also has launched a mid-range investment vehicle for foreign investors, Mediolanum Private, which offers traditional private banking services to individuals with at least EUR 350,000 to invest. Mediolanum is led by founder Ennio Doris, who holds a 35 percent stake. The company, listed on the Borsa Italiana, enjoys strong business connections: Silvio Berlusconi, Italian premier and media magnate, is Doris's silent partner, maintaining a share of 35 percent through his family's Fininvest vehicle.

Rags to Riches in the 1980s

A native of Tombolo, a poor village in Italy's Padua region, Ennio Doris built one of Italy's fastest-growing financial empires in less than 20 years and a personal fortune of more than EUR 4 billion—making him one of Italy's ten richest people in the early 2000s. The secret behind his success lay in his ability to combine his early work experience both in the banking industry and as a salesman for an insurance company.

Doris started out his career working for a local bank, Banca Antoniana (later Antonveneta), based in the regional capital of Padova. Then he was offered a job working for an engineering company run by one of the bank's directors. Doris accepted the position, becoming the manager of the firm in his mid-20s. Yet Doris's ambitions ran higher. As Doris explained to *Personal Wealth Management:* ''As a general manager of a firm at the age of 28, I thought my career was in good shape, until one day I had a meeting with the boss. We had to go to Padova to the headquarters of the bank in his car, a huge Citroën Palace. When I got in the car, I made a comparison between his luxury Citroën and my small Fiat. I was sitting behind my boss, who was driving. As the back seats are lower than the front, he appeared to be sitting on a throne. I thought: 'This is the kind of car I want to have. He is driving my car and my life.' I wanted to drive my own life.''

Soon after, a friend approached Doris with the proposition that they begin selling mutual fund and insurance products for a new company, Fideuram. Doris agreed to join on as a salesman, accepting to be paid in commission, rather than a straight salary. Doris spent the better part of the 1970s on the road, gaining experience as a door-to-door salesman.

By the beginning of the 1980s, Doris had formulated a plan to adapt the personalized, door-to-door sales approach to a broader spectrum of financial services, including traditional assets management and other private banking services. With just the equivalent of $50,000 in savings, Doris needed a stronger financial backer for his plan. An interview with an up-and-coming young entrepreneur—Silvio Berlusconi, then building his first business empire in the real estate sector—caught Doris's attention.

As Doris explained to *Euromoney:* "In the interview, Berlusconi said young people with entrepreneurial ideas should not go to Gianni Agnelli or Carlo De Benedetti as these men would not receive them but he would." Doris arranged a meeting with Berlusconi in Portofino on the Italian Riviera—according to legend, the pair met by chance in the town square. Doris suggested that his idea for a door-to-door financial services company could be expanded to include sales of Berlusconi's real estate products, providing the future media magnate with the cash flow he needed in order to make his first entry into the Italian media sector.

Berlusconi agreed, and in 1982 the partners set up Programma Italia. Backed by the equivalent of $350,000 from Berlusconi, the new company became a 50–50 partnership, with Berlusconi, through his holding firm Fininvest, acting as a silent partner. The partnership was later credited with forming the basis of Berlusconi's business empire, prompting some observers to suggest that, without Programma Italia and Ennio Doris, Berlusconi might never have achieved his position as Italy's wealthiest person.

Programma Italia began offering savings and mutual fund products that same year. In 1984, the company moved to achieve the full scope of its original business plan, that of providing an entire range of financial products, with the acquisition of two insurance companies, Mediolanum Vita and Mediolanum Assurasione. Programma Italia's customers were now able to arrange nearly all of their financial services needs through a single sales contact.

Multi-Channel Service Provider in the 1990s

In 1985, Programma Italia expanded its range of products again. Joining with Fininvest, the company created Gestione Fondi Fininvest. This move enabled Programma Italia to begin offering investment trust products and other assets management services to the company's growing number of customers.

Doris's financial services model struck a chord with Italy's households, and by the mid-1990s, the company was one of the fastest-growing in Italy's financial services sector. A key element of the group's success came with its insistence on developing an in-house sales culture, training its steadily expanding army of independent sales affiliates—the majority of whom began selling Programma Italia products exclusively.

In the mid-1990s, Doris and Fininvest began preparations to steer their partnership into a new banking era. Efforts to streamline and modernize Italy's notoriously inefficient banking system, coupled with increasing levels of cross-border European competition ahead of the adoption of the euro, convinced the companies to develop a new holding company structure. In 1995, the partners formed a new company, Mediolanum S.p.A., to oversee its existing operations. The new entity also provided a structure through which the company could launch new services and operations into the next century.

Mediolanum's steady growth also encouraged the partners to begin planning a public offering. In June 1996, Mediolanum S.p.A. went public on the Borsa Italiana. In the process, both Doris and Berlusconi, through Fininvest, reduced their holdings to just 35 percent—although Doris retained right of first refusal in the event that Fininvest should seek to sell its part of the company. The company immediately joined the Borsa Italiana's MIB 30 blue chip index.

The success of its public offering also led Mediolanum to take the next step in its range of financial services offerings. In 1997, the company established Banca Mediolanum, enabling the company to offer full-scale banking services for the first time. Yet, rather than establish a network of bricks-and-mortar branches, Mediolanum opted to establish itself as a "multi-channel service provider"—providing its range of products and services through the Internet, over the telephone, as well as through its traditional direct sales force. Mediolanum went a step further, rolling out its own television-based teletext service giving customers access to account and product information on television screens.

International Banking Group for the New Century

Having struck a chord with the Italian consumer market, Mediolanum now began seeking out new frontiers. In Italy, the company moved to expand its customer base into the upper income brackets. In 1997, Banca Mediolanum acquired a 2 percent stake in Mediobanca, which in turn took a 2 percent stake in Mediolanum. Mediobanca, Italy's largest investment bank, had recently broken off its relationship with Banca Commerciale Italiana and needed a new partner for its private banking operations.

With Doris taking a seat on Mediobanca's board of directors, the two companies launched a joint venture in 1997. The new banking service, called Esperia, enabled Mediolanum to expand its services into a higher-end bracket, targeting customers with more than ITL 10 billion ($4.7 million) in assets. Whereas Esperia targeted primarily Italian citizens, who might otherwise have transferred their funds outside of the country, Mediolanum also sought to attract another customer segment, wealthy foreigners with at least EUR 350,000 to invest. As part of that effort, the company formed a new subsidiary, Mediobanca Private, in 1997 as well.

Mediolanum now turned to expansion beyond Italy. The company's first foreign move came in 1997, when it created a

Key Dates:

1982: Ennio Doris founds Programma Italia in 50–50 partnership with Silvio Berlusconi.
1984: Programma Italia acquires Mediolanum Vita and Mediolanum Assuransione.
1995: Mediolanum S.p.A. is created as a holding company for group operations.
1996: Mediolanum goes public on the Borsa Italiana.
1997: Mediolanum International Funds is formed; Banca Esperia is formed in partnership with Mediobanca; Banca Mediolanum and Mediolanum Private are formed.
2000: Fibanc, in Spain, is acquired, which also adds an office in Argentina.
2001: Gamax Holding and Bankhaus August Lenz are acquired to enter German and Austrian markets.
2002: Majority control of Monaco's Compagnie Monegasque du Banque is acquired.
2003: Doris announces plans to expand Mediolanum as a pan-European banking network.

new subsidiary, Mediolanum International Funds, in Dublin, Ireland. In 2000, the company acquired a 66 percent stake in the Spanish private bank Fibanc for a price of $112 million. The acquisition not only gave Mediolanum several offices in Spain's major cities, but also Fibanc's branch in Argentina. Mediolanum then began adapting the Spanish operation to match its model, including training Fibanc's 300-strong sales force.

The German market became Mediolanum's next expansion target. In 2001, the company acquired two firms, Gamax Holding for EUR 70 million and Bankhause August Lenz for EUR 12.5 million. Luxembourg-based Gamax operated primarily in Germany, through Gamax Finanzdienste Vermittlungs, and in Austria, through Gamax Austria, and also brought to Mediolanum its assets management operation, Gamax Management. The smaller August Lenz, a private banking specialist, gave Mediolanum a foothold in that sector in Germany.

Both purchases fit into Mediolanum's strategy of entering new markets through small-scale acquisitions. In this way, the Italian bank was better able to impose its own corporate culture and sales methods on its new operations. As Doris told *Euromoney:* ''We purposely aim at very small acquisitions because we want to recreate our model that does not exist anywhere else

and you have to change mentality and approach and you cannot do that if the company is large.''

In the early 2000s, Doris began making plans to base a pan-European banking network around the Mediobanca Private model. The company began seeking acquisition targets in Belgium, The Netherlands, France, and elsewhere. The bank also became interested in the Eastern Europe market, particularly Poland. In the meantime, the company found its next acquisition candidate closer to home. After establishing a 17 percent stake in Monaco's Compagnie Monegasque du Banque, the company paid Commerzbank EUR 190 million to acquire its 34 percent stake, giving Mediolanum majority control in 2002.

Mediolanum expected to achieve its pan-European ambitions as early as the mid-2000s. Doris also began predicting a later expansion onto a global scale, with particular interest in the Americas and the Chinese market. In the meantime, Mediolanum began searching for a new business partner, as Berlusconi faced increasing pressure to shed a number of his assets, including his stake in Mediobanca, in order to resolve a number of conflict of interest issues surrounding Berlusconi's presidency. With right of first refusal for Fininvest's stake in the bank, Doris suggested a possible future linkup with a foreign partner.

Principal Subsidiaries

Bankhaus August Lenz AG (Germany); Compagnie Monegasque du Banque (Monaco; 51%); Gamax Holding (Luxembourg); Gamax Austria; Fibanc SA (Spain; 66%); Mediolanum International Funds (Ireland).

Principal Competitors

Gruppo Credem; Gruppo B. Pop. Milano; Gruppo RAS; Gruppo Generali; Bancoposta; Azimut.

Further Reading

Bender, Yuri, ''Doris Dreams of Pan-European Sales Network,'' *Professional Wealth Management,* March 2, 2003.
Galbraith, Robert, ''Italian Firms Ally in Private Banking Venture,'' *Private Banker International,* May 2000.
''Mediobanca in Monaco Buy,'' *Private Banker International,* June 2002.
Semler, P.K., ''Mediolanum Runs Political Risks,'' *Retail Banker International,* August 22, 2001, p. 3.

—M.L. Cohen

The Midland Company

7000 Midland Boulevard
P.O. Box 1256
Cincinnati, Ohio 45201-1256
U.S.A.
Telephone: (513) 943-7100
Fax: (513) 943-7111
Web site: http://www.midlandcompany.com

Public Company
Founded: 1938 as Midland Discount Corporation
Employees: 1,200
Sales: $718.2 million (2003)
Stock Exchanges: NASDAQ
Ticker Symbol: MLAN
NAIC: 524126 Direct Property & Casualty Insurance
    Carrier; 524113 Direct Life Insurance Carrier; 483211
    Inland Water Freight Transportation

The Midland Company generates the vast majority of its revenue through specialty insurance, targeting loss types that occur with more frequency but less severity than other types of coverage. Subsidiary The American Modern Insurance Group, offers nearly a half-century of experience to its core business sector, manufactured housing. In an effort to diversify, the company has tapped into the motorcycle, watercraft, recreational vehicle, collectible automobile, and snowmobile markets. A much smaller subsidiary operates in the river transportation business and produces just 4 percent of total revenues. The family of one of the original founders leads the company and controls much of the stock.

Finding Their Niche: 1930s–80s

J. Page Hayden, Sr., and J.R. LaBar founded Midland Discount Corporation as an automobile finance company in 1938. The company began broadening its business three years later with the addition of consumer finance. As the 1940s drew to a close, Midland entered the mobile home finance arena. In 1956, the company dropped out of the auto finance sector entirely.

To fuel dreamed-of expansion, Midland began trading over the counter in 1961. The American Modern Home Insurance Company was formed in 1965 and M/G Transport Inc., a specialized river transportation concern, followed in 1968. As the 1960s wound down, Midland Company began trading on the American Stock Exchange and took a stab at the mobile home manufacturing and retailing businesses.

In 1980, the consumer finance business was dropped, putting the specialty insurance and river transportation operations in the spotlight. The last mobile home receivables and five retail branches were sold in 1984 for $70 million in cash, ending Midland's direct involvement in the financing of manufactured housing, according to *American Banker*. The company continued other finance activities and made plans for new endeavors.

The insurance business continued to grow: American Modern Home Group topped $100 million in premiums written in 1987. In the river transportation end of the business, MGT Services Inc. was formed, in 1989, as M/G Transport's freight brokerage operation. Finally, the company shifted gears yet one more time, when it established CS Crable Sportswear that year.

Weathering the Storms: The Early 1990s

American Modern was hit by more than $2.3 million in losses related to Hurricane Andrew in 1992. Despite the devastation, the company produced record results for the year. The waterway transportation subsidiaries suffered under depressed pricing conditions, according to the *Cincinnati Business Courier*. Expenses related to litigation settlements—one for dumping waste into the Ohio and Mississippi Rivers and another related to insurance licensing—added additional downward pressure on Midland.

Moreover the sportswear division, with sales of $33 million, was in the midst of the construction of a new facility.

''On a brighter note, the company's 1994 decision to broker shipping deals, rather than operate a shipping company, is paying off, with M/G now 'very nicely profitable,' '' CEO Michael Conaton told *Cincinnati Business Courier* in October 1996. His predictions of a turnaround for the sportswear division proved

Company Perspectives:

Our Mission: To enhance shareholder value by being an Indispensable Partner to customers in chosen markets by providing value-added specialty insurance products and services. Our Vision: We will create sustainable competitive advantage by providing our policyholders, associates, and business partners with products, services and relations they value more than those offered by our competitors. Our Values: Integrity, WinWin Solutions, Teamwork, Personal Growth, Humility, Creativity, Propriety, Sharing/Caring, Strong Work Ethic.

to be premature, though; the company would sell off the unprofitable business in 1997.

Midland experienced the doldrums from 1993 through 1996. Earnings growth was weak and the stock lost nearly 10 percent of its value during the time period. The 1996 hurricane season was particularly tough on the company. Earnings fell to around $1 million, down from $9.6 million in 1995.

Brighter Outlook: Late 1990s

The situation improved in 1997, operating results were strong, the company received more coverage by financial analysts, and the weather was less inclement. The stock price made impressive gains in response, growing 136 percent from the beginning of 1997 to May 1998, according to the *Business Courier*.

"Investors could see the stock coming around from its '96 problems," analyst John Roberts of Hilliard Lyons Inc. in Louisville told the *Business Courier*. "They started to push it up, but it's still very attractive now. When you're looking at small, well-managed insurers, Midland is very cheap."

The insurance business continued to drive the company in 1999. Nearly 70 percent of premium volume was generated by the sale of manufactured housing insurance. In a move to diversify its revenue stream American Modern bought businesses providing loan facilitation, warranty, insurance sales and telemarketing services to its core customers. The Michigan-based companies would help bump up its fee revenue and expand its services to dealers.

A 3-for-1 stock split and a switch to NASDAQ from the American Stock Exchange in 1999 was intended to increase Midland Company stock visibility and the number of shares outstanding. While the company shined performance-wise, and even outpaced others in its core industry, its stock had not been able to keep up.

An insider stock sale, planned to dilute the 62 percent Hayden family stake in the company, was set aside in September, when the company deemed it was undervalued. Insurance stocks in general were experiencing a slump at the time.

Although the company had added other insurance lines such as homeowners, lower valued homes, dwelling fire, mortgage fire, collateral protection, watercraft, specialty auto, recrea-

tional vehicle, long-haul truck, commercial, and excess and surplus, insurance for manufactured housing still produced the lion's share of written premiums.

Change was in the works by means of partnerships and acquisitions. A managing general agency and two insurance service businesses had been acquired and agreements to underwrite specialty insurance for Countrywide and GEICO had been struck.

Insurance industry consulting firm Ward Financial Group recognized American Modern as one of the nation's "top 50" property and casualty insurers in 2000. The rating period covered the years 1995 to 1999. It was the second consecutive year for the specialty insurer to make the list. American Modern had been found to outperform the industry in a number of areas, including premium growth rate.

Fine Tuning: 2000–04

Rising interest rates cut into manufactured housing industry sales during the first half of 2000, but Midland Company's manufactured housing insurance business continued to produce solid margins. Moreover, while the majority of companies trading on NASDAQ took a hit as the stock exchange tumbled in the second half of 2000, Midland Company was one of a few that posted new highs. Thus, despite the deteriorating climate, for a fourth straight year the company celebrated record results: 2000 net income was $35.5 million and gross written premiums amounted to $541 million.

The company entered into a strategic alliance with Amica Mutual Insurance Company in 2001. The deal, which allowed Amica to sell Midland's manufactured housing policies, gave American Modern a new distribution outlet.

Assets topped $1 billion during the year and Midland Company was named to the *Forbes* "200 Best Small Companies" list. But the highlights were accompanied by some challenges. After a decade of offering the service, American Modern stopped writing commercial liability coverage. Ended were unprofitable manufactured housing park and dealership programs. All open claims were reviewed and reserves were strengthened. During 2001, the company also saw an increase in its fire loss ratio in manufactured housing programs. The upward trend historically had been tied to deteriorating economic conditions. American Modern countered with rate increases and reviews of underwriting.

Midland faced additional concerns, the insurance environment was increasingly competitive, the bond market would yield lower rates cutting into investments, and claims were up. The developments would dampen both premium growth and earnings.

Midland Company's next income fell to $27.2 million in 2001, down from $35.5 million in 2000. Net operating income was off due to commercial-liability line losses and higher-than-normal fire losses in personal line business. Total revenue grew to nearly $592.3 million, up from $538.9 million. Midland succeeded in creating diversification in its products and distribution during the year.

An early 2002 deal with the U.S. subsidiary of London-based broker Bell & Clements Ltd. was struck to provide excess and surplus (E&S) coverage in the states. The September 11,

Key Dates:

1938: Midland Discount Corporation is formed as an auto finance company.
1941: The company adds consumer finance business.
1949: The company enters mobile home finance.
1961: The company begins trading over the counter to fund expansion.
1965: American Modern Home Insurance Company is formed.
1968: M/G Transport Inc. is established to operate in river transportation.
1989: CS Crable Sportswear is formed.
1999: The company moves from the American Stock Exchange to the NASDAQ.
2000: The company enjoys its fourth straight year of record results.
2001: Assets top $1 billion.

2001 attacks on New York and Washington, D.C., had stimulated growth in the E&S market, which had already experienced an upward tick.

Premium growth outside manufactured housing climbed in excess of 20 percent in 2003, but the improvement was offset by problems within the motorcycle line. In other areas, the watercraft line was solid, the collector car line was promising, and the recreational vehicle line was being fine-tuned.

The core manufactured housing segment had been strengthened over the year, producing growth despite a drop in new shipments, an increase in repossessions, and a tightening of lending standards. Dwelling fire product for site-built homes, an increasingly significant business area gaining a national presence, met needs not offered by standard insurance carriers. But California brush fires prevented the niche from turning a profit for the year.

M/G Transport continued to operate in a small geographic area, the lower Mississippi River below Baton Rouge and the Gulf Inter Coastal Waterway, but in 2003 it opened an office in St. Louis, Missouri, to sell fee-based management for other companies' barges. MGT moved only dry commodities, primarily petroleum coke, barite, sugar, and coal.

Principal Subsidiaries

American Modern Insurance Group.

Principal Competitors

AIG; Danielson Holding; State Farm Insurance Companies.

Further Reading

Bender, Roxanne, "PSFS Unit Pays $70 Million to Acquire Mortgage Package," *American Banker,* December 19, 1984, p. 3.

De Lombaerde, Geert, "Berg-Berry Buys Atlas Insurance Retail Division, *Business Courier Serving Cincinnati-Northern Kentucky,* November 26, 1999, p. 2.

——, "Boom Times Disappear for Midland, Competitors," *Business Courier Serving Cincinnati-Northern Kentucky,* November 16, 2001, p. 6.

——, "Mario Gabelli," *Business Courier Serving Cincinnati-Northern Kentucky,* April 20, 2001, p. 12.

——, "Midland Branching into New Insurance Avenues," *Business Courier Serving Cincinnati-Northern Kentucky,* July 14, 2000, p. 30.

——, "Midland Endures Sector Downturn, Branches Out," *Business Courier Serving Cincinnati-Northern Kentucky,* December 8, 2000, p. 35.

——, "Midland Hits Stride, Stock Price Soars," *Business Courier Serving Cincinnati-Northern Kentucky,* May 8, 1998, p. 1.

——, "Midland Striving to Draw Wall Street's Attention," *Business Courier Serving Cincinnati-Northern Kentucky,* August 6, 1999, p. 27.

"Hitched at Midland?," *Business Week,* October 30, 2000, p. 207.

"Midland Co.," *Cincinnati Business Courier,* August 23, 1993, p. S39.

"Midland Stock Begins Trading," *National Underwriter Property & Casualty-Risk & Benefits Management,* June 7, 1999, p. 22.

Monk, Dan, "Midland Aims to Overcome Weather, Lawsuits," *Cincinnati Business Courier,* October 21, 1996, p. 25.

—Kathleen Peippo

MNS, Ltd.

dba ABC Stores
766 Pohukaina Street
Honolulu, Hawaii 96813
U.S.A.
Telephone: (808) 591-2550
Toll Free: (888) 703-4ABC
Fax: (808) 591-2471
Web site: http://www.abcstores.com

Private Company
Incorporated: 1955
Employees: 900
Sales: $150 million (2003 est.)
NAIC: 453220 Gift, Novelty, and Souvenir Stores;
    454110 Electronic Shopping and Mail-Order Houses

MNS, Ltd. is the parent company for ABC Stores, a chain of 67 convenience stores based in Honolulu. If you have visited Hawaii, odds are good that you have seen one of them, especially on the island of Oahu, where there are 39 locations. The chain also has locations in Las Vegas, Guam, and Saipan. ABC Stores (no relation to the Alcoholic Beverage Control stores found in some states) provides convenient shopping for travelers. *Chain Store Age Executive* reported that tourists comprise up to 90 percent of ABC's customers. The emphasis is indeed on convenience; most of the stores are open 365 days a year.

Founded in the mid-1960s to provide an alternative to high-priced hotel stores, the chain is owned by members of the Kosasa family. The concept of cannibalism does not seem to exist to this chain, which has 37 stores in Waikiki alone. Nevertheless, the company has expanded geographically to help weather the ups and downs of the Hawaiian economy. Stores in Guam and Saipan, other popular destinations for residents of Japan, opened in the mid-1990s. In December 2001, ABC opened the first of its locations in Las Vegas, the top tourist destination for Hawaii residents.

Origins

Sidney Kosasa was born the son of first-generation Japanese immigrants who owned a grocery store in Honolulu. In 1942 he graduated from the pharmacy program at the University of California at Berkeley.

In 1949 Kosasa launched Kaimuki Pharmacy with his wife, Minnie. *Chain Store Age Executive* reports Kosasa borrowed $50,000 against his house to launch the venture, while his parents already owned the land where the store stood.

Kosasa opened the Medical Arts Pharmacy in 1954, and the next year launched the Thrifty Drugs of Hawaii chain, which included five shops, three of them inside Gem department stores. Kosasa's Thrifty chain was not related to a similarly named business based in California. MNS, Ltd., which would be the parent company of ABC Stores, was incorporated in Hawaii on June 17, 1955. It merged with Sidko Sundries, Inc. on April 30, 1965, and with SMK, Inc. on December 27, 1991.

According to the *Pacific Business News,* Kosasa was inspired by the success of convenience stores he saw in Miami as an alternative to expensive hotel shops. The Kosasas brought the idea to the heart of Waikiki, opening the first ABC Discount Store there in 1964. This location, reported *Chain Store Age Executive,* stocked prescription drugs as well as healthcare and beauty items.

Kosasa acquired a grocery store in 1968, broadening ABC's offerings. The mix was tweaked further by dropping the prescription drugs (and the pharmacist) from the stores, while liquor and touristy gifts were added. The name was also abbreviated to simply ABC Stores (dropping the ''Discount''). When the chain expanded, new ABC Stores sprouted within blocks of each other.

New Leadership, New Horizons in the 1980s and 1990s

The Kosasas' son Paul had worked at the stores since the first grade, reported *Hawaii Business.* After earning an engi-

236

Company Perspectives:

Just another chain of convenience stores?
Not really!

Like most convenience store chains ABC Stores has multiple outlets; sixty-seven stores that span the Pacific from Hawaii to Guam and Saipan, along with our newest location—Las Vegas, Nevada.

Owned by Sidney and Minnie Kosasa, ABC Stores had its genesis in the 30s. Sidney grew up working in his parents' grocery store in Honolulu and earned a pharmacist's degree at the University of California at Berkeley in 1942.

In 1949 the Kosasas opened their own drug store, and a chain of drug stores followed shortly. On a trip to Miami Beach Kosasa watched visitors shopping local convenience stores instead of the high priced hotel shops. He envisioned that Waikiki would someday be packed with visitors, like Miami Beach, and the ABC concept was born: stores conveniently located for visitors with merchandise sold at fair prices.

Drawing upon his experience in drug and grocery stores, Kosasa opened the first ABC outlet, on Waikiki Beach in 1964. It stocked groceries, souvenirs, drugs and cosmetics and anything else a visitor would need. He decided to stay away from a fancy moniker and settled on ABC as a name that everyone could remember.

Today there are ABC Stores on every major island in the State of Hawaii and the ABC concept has been exported to Guam and Saipan. ABC Stores employs more than 900 Associates. Almost all the stores open 365 days a year from 6:30 AM to 1 AM. Ranked 37th among Hawaii businesses, ABC Stores sells more macadamia nuts, suncare products, souvenirs and other visitor-related products than anyone else in the state.

Just another chain of convenience stores? Not really. Making your vacation a bit more enjoyable is what ABC is about!

Key Dates:

1949: Sidney Kosasa opens Kaimuki Pharmacy.
1954: Medical Arts Pharmacy opens.
1964: The first ABC Discount Store opens in Waikiki.
1968: A small grocery store is acquired.
1996: The company opens a store in Guam.
1997: The mail-order division opens.
1998: The web site is launched.
1999: Paul Kosasa, son of the founders, becomes company president.
2001: A flagship store opens in Wailea, Maui; the first mainland store opens in Las Vegas.

catalog in March 1998, beginning with just 50 items (this increased tenfold in the next few years). The ABC Stores web site was featured in national advertising for the company's e-commerce vendor, IBM.

Hawaii Business Magazine reported ABC Stores had revenues of $155 million in 2000, when the company had 600 employees. The company continued to tweak its product mix, adding jewelry and cosmetics at certain locations.

On the Mainland in 2001

A new 5,500-square-foot flagship store opened on Maui in February 2001 in The Shops at Wailea. The nautical-themed store won its Honolulu-based architects a national award. Observers felt confident ABC could ascertain and meet the needs of this upscale locale.

ABC opened its first store in the mainland United States in December 2001, inaugurating a 6,500-square-foot location on Freemont Street in Las Vegas. The resort center seemed well suited to the ABC Stores concept. Las Vegas, which hosted 30 million visitors a year, was the favorite tourist destination for Hawaii residents and had a sizable population of former residents, many of whom congregated at the nearby California Hotel. Two more stores opened in Las Vegas toward the end of 2002, one of them in the colossal Fashion Show Mall, which was anchored by eight department stores and was undergoing a $1 billion expansion. ABC Stores' sales rose about 2 percent to $143 million in 2002, according to one source.

Another dozen stores were planned for Las Vegas, according to the Associated Press. "We are always interested in expanding," company President Paul Kosasa told *Pacific Business News* in 2004. Existing stores also were being continually updated.

The relaxing of city rules requiring new parking to accompany retail construction prompted the makeover of a half-dozen ABC Stores along Waikiki's Kalakaua Avenue, a major pedestrian thoroughfare, reported *Pacific Business News*. This included a $1 million renovation of a 3,500-square-foot store at the corner of Kuhio Avenue and Kanekapolei Street. The renovation of the outdated building was comprehensive; three of the store's four walls were torn down in the process.

neering degree at the University of Michigan in 1979, he worked for a time at a Los Angeles supermarket, studying the business while stocking shelves. He rejoined ABC Stores in 1980 as an assistant manager trainee. After successive managerial positions and extensive time as a buyer, he became company president and chief executive officer in 1999. The Ernst & Young consulting firm dubbed Sidney Kosasa an Entrepreneur of the Year in 1997. These two decades were a period of great growth for ABC Stores until the Hawaiian economy slowed down in the late 1990s.

ABC Stores-Guam Inc. and ABC Stores-Saipan Inc. were incorporated in March 1995. These were tourist markets with a lot of visitors. The first Guam store opened its doors in 1996; one in Saipan followed a couple of years later. The two islands were closer to Japan than Hawaii and more attractive to young Japanese tourists, noted *Pacific Business News.*

A mail-order division opened in 1997, allowing ABC to communicate with its customers after they left the Islands. Volume, however, was small. The company launched an online

After opening a new site at the Waikiki Marriott, ABC Stores had 55 locations in the Hawaiian Islands (37 in Waikiki alone), seven in Guam, two in Saipan, and three in Las Vegas, where it was planning to add more. The company had more than 900 employees, most of whom were full time; this was a rarity in the convenience store industry, noted the Associated Press.

ABC Stores considered its employees ambassadors not just for the company, but for Hawaii, Paul Kosasa told *Hawaii Business.* A secret shopper service was used to monitor the courtesy and sales skills of its clerks. The chain tried to keep repeat customers interested by mixing up its selection of souvenirs. Kosasa told *Pacific Business News* the company employed special staff to accommodate Hawaii's Japanese-speaking guests, who made up a little less than a third of ABC's business.

Principal Competitors

7-Eleven Hawaii Inc.; Food Pantry Ltd.; Longs Drug Stores Corporation; Outrigger Enterprises, Inc.

Further Reading

"AM Partners Wins Design Award," *Pacific Business News,* February 7, 2002.

Cho, Frank, "Guam to Get ABC Stores," *Pacific Business News,* June 5, 1995, p. 1.

Choo, David K., "Stocking Up; ABC Stores' Paul Kosasa Says the Key to Successful Retail in Waikiki Is to Remerchandise," *Hawaii Business,* Road Ahead Sec., July 2004.

Cruz, Cathy S., "All Blocks Covered," *Hawaii Business Magazine,* Top 250 Family Businesses, August 1, 2001, p. 46.

Danninger, Lyn, "ABC Rolls the Dice in Las Vegas; The Hawaii-Based Retail Chain Is Set to Open Its First Store on the Mainland," *Honolulu Star-Bulletin,* March 22, 2001.

Engle, Erika, "Cinnamon on a Roll," *Honolulu Star-Bulletin,* September 19, 2002.

Higa, Carrie Lyn, "Humble Beginnings," *Hawaii Business,* August 1997, pp. 19+.

Jones, Chris, "The Lei of the Land; Hawaiian Retailers Add Stores in Las Vegas, Targeting City's Tourist-Heavy Clientele," *Las Vegas Review-Journal,* August 8, 2002.

Paiva, Derek, "ABC Stores Meets Big Blue's Hawaii," *Hawaii Business,* January 1, 2000, p. 18.

"Sidney S. Kosasa," *Chain Store Age Executive,* December 1997, p. 80.

Sokei, Debbie, "Hawaii Businesses Find Fertile Ground in Las Vegas," *Pacific Business News,* October 24, 2003.

Song, Jaymes, "ABC Taps What Tourists Need," *Honolulu Advertiser,* May 31, 2004.

Warner, Gary A., "Vegas Goes Hawaiian; The California Hotel & Casino Is a Slice of Aloha in the Gambling Mecca," *Orange County Register* (California), Travel Sec., April 7, 2002.

Wilson, Marianne, "ABC Puts Upscale Spin on Convenience Retail," *Chain Store Age Executive,* October 2001, pp. 116+.

Wu, Nina, "ABCs of Retailing Pay Off for Family-Owned Chain," *Pacific Business News,* March 15, 2004.

——, "Relaxed Rules Spur Waikiki Retail Growth," *Pacific Business News,* July 2, 2004.

Youn, Jacy L., "Does the Customer Come First?," *Hawaii Business,* April 2002.

—Frederick C. Ingram

Monarch Casino & Resort, Inc.

1175 W. Moana Lane, Suite 200
Reno, Nevada 89509
U.S.A.
Telephone: (775) 825-3355
Fax: (775) 825-7705
Web site: http://www.monarchcasino.com

Public Company
Incorporated: 1993
Employees: 1,792
Sales: $115.95 million (2003)
Stock Exchanges: New York
Ticker Symbol: MCRI
NAIC: 713990 All Other Amusement and Recreation
 Industries

Monarch Casino & Resort, Inc. owns and operates the Atlantis Casino Resort in Reno, Nevada, through its lone subsidiary, Golden Road Motor Inn, Inc. The Atlantis is a tropically themed hotel and casino adorned with such tropical décor as giant artificial palm trees, thatched roof huts, and waterfalls. The property includes three high-rise hotel towers, containing 831 rooms and suites, as well as a low-rise motor lodge with 149 rooms that appeal to value conscious guests. The 51,000-square-foot casino offers nearly 1,500 slot and video poker machines, 37 table games, and a sports book operation run by an outside party. The Atlantis also provides several restaurants, a health spa, indoor and outdoor pools, a full-service salon for men and women, retail establishments, a family entertainment center, and banquet, convention, and meeting room space. Monarch owns 16 acres of adjacent land that is available for further development, but in the meantime is used for parking, which is connected to the Atlantis by the "Sky Terrace," supported by two 100-foot-tall Grecian columns. The Sky Terrace also maintains a tropical look and contains banks of slot and video poker machines, a comfortable lounge, oyster bar, and sushi bar. While clearly appealing to leisure travelers, the Atlantis also caters to area gaming customers by offering more slot and video poker machines with higher than average payout rates and liberalized rules at blackjack. Much of the success of the Atlantis is due to its location, several miles from Reno's downtown casinos and the only hotel within walking distance of the Reno Convention Center, which supplies a steady stream of fresh customers. Monarch is 48 percent owned by brothers John Farahi, Bob Farahi, and Ben Farahi. All three are co-chairs of the company, with John serving as chief executive officer and chief operating officer, Bob as president, and Ben as chief financial officer.

Establishment of Legalized Casino Gambling in Reno in 1931

Reno, Nevada, named after Union Civil War General Jesse Reno, was founded in 1868 when the Central Pacific Railroad established a depot. The area already had become an important agricultural center and transportation hub supporting the mining of the legendary Comstock silver mines, but the railroad depot ensured that Reno would not suffer the fate of other boomtowns that disappeared once the gold and silver deposits ran out. In addition to being an important freight and passenger center, Reno also gained a reputation for providing less savory services, earning the moniker "Sin City." Reno was known for its brothels, underground gambling dens, prize fights, and easy divorces. Reno eventually became known as the divorce capital of the world. With the deepening of the Depression of the 1930s, Nevada decided to legalize casino gambling and it was Reno that set the stage for the casino industry on which Las Vegas would capitalize. With the building of highways, Reno became a tourist destination and the casinos flourished. The city decided in 1947 to prohibit casinos outside of a designated downtown area, but that "redline" legislation was repealed in 1972, making the area where The Atlantis now stands available for casino gambling.

Monarch traces its history to 1972, when the father of the company's co-chairmen, David Farahi and his brother-in-law, Isaac Poura, bought a rundown 142-room motel called the Golden Door Motel located on four acres of leased property on the southern edge of Reno. It was well removed from the bulk of the tourist trade that frequented the downtown casinos. The facility's only tangible asset was its close proximity to the city's convention center, which provided enough business, along with overflow guests from downtown hotels during peak times, to barely keep the enterprise afloat. The Golden Door was a two-story low-rise structure with an adjoining building that housed the lobby, a coffee shop, banquet room, and lounge. Because it was part of the Golden Door chain, the name was changed to the Golden Road Motel. John Farahi, a political science graduate from California State University, Hayward, soon went to work for the motel and during summer vacations from college he was helped by his brothers. Bob would earn a biochemistry degree from the University of California at Berkeley, and Ben received a mechanical engineering degree from the University of California at Berkeley as well as an M.B.A. degree in accounting from California State University, Hayward. Over the next several years all three sons would eventually come to work for the business on a full-time basis. Poura would not be with the company, however. The two brothers-in-law proved incompatible business partners and in mid-1973 David Farahi bought out Poura. In 1976, with his sons having taken on so much of the responsibility for running the business, he transferred ownership to them and their sister Jila.

Switching to Travelodge in 1983

The problems that troubled the Golden Door did not dissipate with a name change. The motel struggled through the 1970s, and the three Farahi brothers filled in doing every conceivable job at some point. It was not until the early 1980s, when Reno finally grew large enough to bring the Golden Road well within the orbit of the city's developed section, that the motel began to truly prosper. In 1983 the Farahi brothers began taking steps to improve the motel's image by making it a Travelodge franchise. In addition, they took back the coffee shop, which had been leased to outsiders, remodeled it, and opened the Cooper Kettle restaurant, which proved popular and helped to bring in more local business and outside traffic. The next major step in the development of the business came in 1986 when it seized an opportunity to buy 15.8 acres of nearby property, within walking distance of the convention center, which the Farahi brothers believed would become highly valuable as this area of Reno continued to enjoy rapid growth. It was a costly, risky investment, but they bought the parcel and then successfully petitioned the city to have the site zoned for use as a hotel casino. Also in 1986, they remodeled all of the rooms of the Travelodge, another step in transforming a once dilapidated motel into an upscale accommodation.

The use of the newly acquired property, however, would not matter greatly to the company's immediate plans, because in 1987 the Farahi brothers were successful in buying the land on which the Travelodge was situated plus several acres adjoining

it. After receiving permission from the city to operate 50 slot machines on the site, they began a further remodeling of the motel. It now became a Quality Inn, and the renovated restaurant and lounge would one day form a building block for the Atlantis complex. The upgraded motel, restaurant, and combination nightclub and lounge became very popular with area residents, prompting the owners to take their most ambitious step to date: to transform the Quality Inn and its eight acres of land into a major hotel casino. Finding financial backing was not an easy task, given that many bankers failed to accept the Farahi brothers' contention that being located away from the downtown area was actually desirable. First Interstate Bank of Nevada finally agreed to fund the project to the tune of $18 million, a syndicate was formed, and the project was launched in mid-1989. Soon the venture received an unrestricted gaming license from the state. Already half of the motel units had been moved to the outskirts of the property in preparation for the major construction. Working with the Farahi brothers was Peter Wilday, an experienced architect who had designed several of Reno's most successful hotel casinos. They decided on a tropical motif, featuring waterfalls, palm trees, and thatched roof huts. In 1990 the rest of the motel units were relocated and construction began on a 160-room high-rise hotel tower along with another 16,000-square-foot structure that would house 500 slot machines, 21 table games, a restaurant, several bars, an outdoor pool, and a health club. Work was completed in just eight months and within 2 percent of the projected budget.

A licensing agreement with Choice Hotels International was reached, so that when the project was completed it opened in April 1991 as the Clarion Hotel Casino and was an immediate success. Less than a year later, more casino space was added, as well as a fashionable restaurant and nightclub. During the first full year in operation, the Clarion generated $23.2 million, a significant increase over 1990's $5.2 million. Business was so strong that by the end of 1992, the Farahi brothers began making plans for further expansion. This time they looked to the stock market for funding, after a number of gaming companies had enjoyed recent success in floating offerings. Because the company owned just one gaming property, however, they met with some resistance from investment banks. Finally Volpe, Welty & Company agreed to underwrite an initial public offering of stock. In preparation, Monarch Casino & Resort, Inc. was formed in 1993 for the purpose of acquiring Golden Road Motor Inn, Inc., the legal name of the business. Then in August 1993, 2.4 million shares in Monarch were sold to the public, raising $17.1 million.

With the necessary cash in hand, Monarch launched the next phase of expansion in October 1993, constructing a second high-rise hotel tower, which added 283 rooms and suites, a buffet restaurant, an 8,000-square-foot family entertainment center, 10,000 square feet of banquet and meeting space, and an additional 14,000 square feet of casino space, able to accommodate 450 more slot machines and 14 table games. In less than a year, and on budget, the new facilities were opened to the public, which once again expressed its approval through its business. Within six months occupancy rates exceeded 90 percent.

Failed Attempts at Riverboat Gambling in the 1990s

Monarch, in the meantime, attempted to become more than a single gaming property company. In 1993 it formed a subsid-

Key Dates:

1972: The original property, Golden Door Motel, is acquired by David Farahi and his brother-in-law.
1976: Ownership is transferred to Farahi's children.
1991: The Clarion Hotel Casino opens on the site of the original motel.
1993: Monarch Casino & Resort, Inc. is formed and taken public.
1996: Clarion is renamed Atlantis Casino Resort.

iary, Dunes-Marina Resort and Casino, Inc., and looked to become involved in the riverboat gambling business that was opening up in midwestern states. Monarch sought to develop such a project in Gary, Indiana, hoping to win one of the first gaming licenses issued by the state. Monarch won approval from the city, prevailing over a dozen rivals, including the likes of Donald Trump, Aztar Resorts International, and Carnival Cruise Lines. In anticipation of winning a gaming license, Monarch in March 1994 bought the Muskegon Clipper, which at 345 feet long and 65 feet wide, was one of the nation's largest riverboats. But the vessel would not be needed. Despite winning the endorsement at the city level, Monarch was beat out at the state level by two other bidders. The venture was written off, as was a 1995 attempt to secure a lease on a riverboat casino project in downtown St. Louis. The Dunes Marina Resort and Casino subsidiary finally would be dissolved in 1999, as Monarch decided to focus on its Reno property.

In the mid-1990s Monarch looked to build up its middle and upper-middle income clientele. As of 1994 the customer mix for the Clarion was 60 percent local, but the expansion helped to move the mix closer to 50–50. Marketing efforts were concentrated in the northwest, on northern California, Oregon, Washington, and British Columbia, but going forward Monarch looked to grow its customer base beyond these traditional markets. Another important factor in growing the tourist side of the business would be the opening of the National Bowling Stadium in Reno, a massive bowling complex that would host major tournaments and was expected to draw tens of thousands of visitors to Reno each year. In 1995, the first full year following the most recent expansion, Monarch saw revenues rise to $53 million. With future prospects looking bright, the Farahi brothers wasted no time in developing a master plan for expansion, which could be accomplished in phases and was approved by the city of Reno.

In April 1996 Monarch terminated its licensing agreement with Choice Hotels International and changed the name of the Clarion Hotel Casino to the Atlantis Casino Resort. Conditions in the Reno gaming industry were becoming highly competitive; during a 17-month stretch in 1995 and 1996 the city added some 3,500 hotel rooms. Changing names in that environment was risky, but the owners believed it was in their best interest

long term and they were able to rebrand the hotel casino with only a short-term loss in business.

Monarch decided to proceed with the first phase of its master plan in May 1998, taking the unusual step of funding the $75 million project entirely out of operating cashflow and an available line of bank credit. In June 1999 construction was completed, resulting in a second hotel tower, 28 stories high, containing 388 rooms and suites, as well as 1,500 square feet of new meeting space. Rooms on the top seven floors of this structure were larger, featuring more luxurious accommodations, a private concierge service, and private elevator access. The Sky Terrace was also part of this expansion phase.

As Monarch entered the new century, it continued to invest in upgrading the Atlantis. In 2001 the company spent $4.5 million to renovate suites in the third tower, acquire new slot machines, and improve the facility's computer information systems. Another $6.5 million was spent in 2002 to renovate the first hotel tower, a restaurant, the front desk, and VIP services area, as well as further upgrades to gaming equipment. In 2003 Monarch spent $8.4 million to build a new sushi bar and salon, conduct renovations on the second hotel tower, and continue the effort to acquire and upgrade gaming equipment. As a result of continued expansion, Monarch experienced steady growth on the balance sheet. For 2003 revenues totaled $116 million and net income amounted to $9.6 million.

Monarch stood at a crossroads by 2004. It had an option to purchase property in South Reno for the development of a new hotel casino. It also had approval to expand the Atlantis by 520 hotel rooms and 500 more slot machines. Moreover, it could choose to build another resort casino or entertainment facility on the adjoining 16-acre parcel. For the time being, the Farahi brothers decided not to develop any of these properties, electing instead to adopt a wait-and-see strategy, gauging industry trends and consumer demand before taking the next step in the hotel casino's development.

Principal Subsidiaries

Golden Road Motor Inn, Inc.

Principal Competitors

Boomtown, Inc.; Caesars Entertainment, Inc.; MTR Gaming Group, Inc.

Further Reading

"CEO Interview: Monarch Casino & Resort Inc.," *Wall Street Transcript,* March 28, 1994.
"Former Clarion Casino Resort in Reno Cuts Ties to Choice Hotels," *Travel Weekly,* June 17, 1996, p. 66.
Land, Barbara, and Myrick Land, *A Short History of Reno,* Reno: University of Nevada Press, 1995.

—Ed Dinger

Moody's Corporation

<table>
<tr><td>

99 Church Street
New York, New York 10007
U.S.A.
Telephone: (212) 553-0300
Fax: (212) 553-7194
Web site: http://www.moodys.com

Public Company
Founded: 1900 as John Moody & Company
Employees: 2,300
Sales: $1.25 billion (2003)
Stock Exchanges: New York
Ticker Symbol: MCO
NAIC: 514191 On-Line Information Services; 541611
    Administrative Management and General Management
    Consulting Services; 511120 Periodical Publishers

</td></tr>
</table>

While almost everyone in the world has heard of Moody's Investors Service and its ratings and research reports, fewer know that it is a wholly owned subsidiary of Moody's Corporation. The Moody name has been synonymous with securities for more than a century, adapting to the ever changing needs of Wall Street and financial markets worldwide. A trusted name in an often volatile business, Moody's reaches thousands of financial institutions and has more than 20,000 global subscribers. Moody's KMV, a sibling to Moody's Investors Service, provides credit risk management to large financial institutions.

Starting Small: 1900–13

John Moody was born in 1868. He was considered an intelligent, primarily self-taught man with a strong sense of right and wrong. Moody was also an astute businessman and set out to make his mark in the growing investment community of New York. His first major undertaking was the creation of an information source for investors called *Moody's Manual of Industrial and Miscellaneous Securities.* Moody established an eponymous business (John Moody & Company) and published the first issue of *Moody's Manual* in 1900. The *Manual* was filled with data and statistics about the day's trading companies, from financial institutions and government agencies to mining and manufacturing firms.

Within a few months of its conception, *Moody's Manual* had amassed a following and sold out its print run. By 1903 both *Moody's Manual* and Moody Publishing Company, as the firm was now called, had national reputations. *Moody's Manual* had become indispensable to investors and John Moody decided to publish other financially themed books under Moody Publishing Company. His first title, *The Truth About Trusts: A Description and Analysis of the American Trust Movement,* was published in 1904. Ironically, this very book would be reprinted by Greenwood Press 64 years after its initial printing.

Financial doom, however, was around the corner; Moody and many of his loyal readers faced ruin after the stock market crash of 1907. Moody was forced to sell his business, including the *Manual.* Within two years, however, Moody was back with a new approach—to provide wary investors with not just information about companies but to go a step further and evaluate their performance and assets. He decided to tackle the burgeoning rail industry and wrote a book entitled *Moody's Analyses of Railroad Investments* in 1909.

Moody's in-depth reporting on the railroads included a rating system composed of letters, the very same method used by credit reporting agencies of the day. An updated 4,000-page version of *Moody's* came out in 1911, even touted by the *New York Times,* followed by *How to Analyze Railroad Reports* in 1912. By 1913 Moody extended his expertise from railroads to general financial ratings.

Lessons Learned and Rebirth: 1920s–80s

Like his initial success, Moody's business acumen once again brought him to the forefront of the securities industry. His ratings were sought out by investors and Moody responded with a new company, Moody's Investors Service, incorporated in July 1914. Moody expanded his coverage, rating stocks as well as bonds, and within a decade of his new firm's creation covered the entire U.S. bond market. Moody also wrote several books for Yale University Press, including *The Masters of Capital: A*

Chronicle of Wall Street and *The Railroad Builders: A Chronicle of the Welding of the States,* both published in 1919 and reprinted several times.

When the stock market crashed in 1929 and ushered in the Great Depression, John Moody did not lose his business like before. He survived and so did his thriving ratings service. Moody continued to write his evaluations and publish his findings despite the collapse of much of the financial community. He also wrote his memoirs, beginning with *The Long Road Home: An Autobiography,* published by Macmillan in 1933, which was followed by a sequel called *Fast By the Road* (Macmillan, 1942).

In February 1958 John Moody died at the age of 89. Within four years of his death, in 1962, Moody's was bought by credit reporting and information collection giant Dun & Bradstreet Corporation (D&B). Moody's expanded its rating services in the 1970s and began charging fees to the companies it covered. The time-consuming, meticulously researched reports done by Moody's proved invaluable to both investors and the covered companies; companies soon realized that a good rating from Moody's was like money in the bank. For many corporate clients, Moody's ratings increased investor confidence and in turn helped add stability to the marketplace.

Dominating the Market: 1990s

The last decade of the century was a roller coaster ride for Moody's. In 1994 the company failed to make a profit and in 1995 and 1996 there were rumors of a corporate overhaul. In January 1996 D&B announced its intention to divide into three public companies to better serve its shareholders and market segments. Moody's was to remain part of the ''new'' Dun & Bradstreet information services company. Soon after news of D&B's upcoming split came the resignation of Moody's president, John Bohn, Jr., in March, followed by rumors of a Department of Justice (DOJ) inquiry concerning possible antitrust violations. The DOJ investigation, which targeted only Moody's ratings service, contacted both its chief rivals—Standard & Poor's Corporation (S&P) and Fitch Investor Services—to provide information.

In the midst of the DOJ probe, Moody's reorganized its domestic operations and stepped up plans for international expansion. In 1998 Moody's bought a 10 percent stake in Korea Investors Service (later increased to more than 50 percent) and began investing in Argentina the following year. In 1999 the DOJ investigation into Moody's alleged antitrust violations was closed, and no charges were filed. D&B, still fighting poor performance and stagnant sales, announced it would spin off

Moody's within a year. Moody's sales for 1999 had reached $564.2 million, with net income just shy of $156 million.

A New Era: The 2000s

The new millennium brought independence for Moody's when it was spun off from Dun & Bradstreet at the end of September 2000 and became a publicly traded company. This provided a bit of irony; since Moody's could now be rated by others according to its performance. While this gave some ammunition to those who believed Moody's wielded too much power in the industry, the company finished the year with $602.3 million and then for its first complete year as a stand-alone company (2001) raked in $797 million in revenues and $212 million in net income. Moody's commanded a 37 percent share of the corporate bond rating market according to *Investor's Business Daily,* while rival S&P's had 45 percent and Fitch the remaining 18 percent. Despite S&P's bigger chunk of the market, Moody's maintained the distinction of being named the top credit rating firm for five consecutive years by *Institutional Investor* magazine.

Because of its value to investors, Moody's became a powerful entity unto itself. Along with its top rival, S&P, the two dominated the corporate bond rating services field and exercised enormous influence. This power, however, was like a double-edged sword. As Bethany McLean pointed out in a *Fortune* profile of Moody's and S&P in December 2001, ''The weight their opinions carry make their judgments critical—but also complicated. The agencies cannot just be observers but active participants in the course of events. ... If the rating agencies act too rashly, they could be accused of causing a bankruptcy. Yet if they deliberate too long, they'll simply be stating what everyone already knows.''

In 2002 Moody's bought the San Francisco-based KMV (renamed Moody's KMV), a loan risk assessment agency, for

$212.6 million and followed the acquisition with a 20 percent stake in Moscow's Interfax Rating Agency. Moody's international sales had increased to a third or about $343 million of the firm's $1.02 billion in sales in 2002.

By 2003 Moody's had become the top structured finance rating service controlling 37 percent (amounting to $460.6 million for the year) of the worldwide market, besting even S&P. Domestically, a third of Moody's revenues was from its subscription clients and structured finance accounted for another third. One of Moody's most attractive assets was its most famous investor—Warren Buffett's Berkshire Hathaway—which owned a 15 percent stake in the firm. Buffett's ownership was an endorsement in and of itself and lent the company considerable clout. Would this clout keep the company safe from further competition? In 2003 the SEC (Securities and Exchange Commission) gave Toronto newcomer Dominion Bond Rating Service Ltd. official status as a nationally recognized statistical rating organization (NRSRO). Dominion's formal admittance as a NRSRO, forced S&P, Moody's, and Fitch to reevaluate their status as the top three bond ratings services. While it would take the privately owned Dominion years to overtake either S&P (number one in the market) or Moody's (second), it was conceivable the company could give Fitch a run for its money.

By the end of 2003, Moody's Corporation had offices in 18 countries including Argentina, Australia, Germany, Hong Kong, Singapore, South Africa, Spain, and Taiwan; covered $30 trillion in debt from 100 countries; and brought in revenues of $1.25 billion and net income of $364 million.

Principal Operating Units

Moody's Investors Service; Moody's KMV.

Principal Competitors

Standard & Poor's Corporation; Fitch, Inc.; Dominion Bond Rating Service Ltd.

Further Reading

Eaton, Leslie, "Judge Dismisses Lawsuit Against Moody's Service," *New York Times,* May 10, 1996, p. D2.

Gasparino, Charles, "Probe into Moody's Could Spur Curbs on Rating Agencies," *Wall Street Journal,* March 28, 1996, p. C13.

Gilpin, Kenneth N., "Dun & Bradstreet to Split into Three Public Companies," *New York Times,* January 10, 1996, p. D1.

——, "Federal Antitrust Inquiry Has Begun Against Moody's," *New York Times,* March 28, 1996, p. D4.

——, "Justice Dept. Inquiry on Moody's Is Over with No Charges," *New York Times,* March 13, 1999, p. C3.

——, "Moody's Combining Two Units in First Big Shift in Years," *New York Times,* May 29, 1996, p. D2.

McLean, Bethany, "The Geeks Who Rule," *Fortune,* December 24, 2001.

"Moody's Corporation: Company Interview," *Wall Street Transcript,* June 2003.

Rossi, Josephine, "Money Machine," *Kiplinger's Personal Finance,* August 2002.

Watkins, Steve, "Overseas Funding Shift Creates Bullish Market," *Investor's Business Daily,* May 14, 2001.

Wayne, Leslie, "In a Surprise Move, President of Moody's Ratings Service Steps Down," *New York Times,* March 23, 1996, p. 37.

——, "Moody's Names Ex-President to Head Its Operations Again," *New York Times,* April 9, 1996, p. D4.

White, Lawrence, "Credit and Credibility," *New York Times,* February 24, 2002, p. 4.

—Nelson Rhodes

MWH Preservation Limited Partnership

RR 302
Bretton Woods, New Hampshire 03575
U.S.A.
Telephone: (603) 278-1000
Fax: (603) 278-8828
Web site: http://www.mtwashington.com

Limited Partnership
Incorporated: 1991
Employees: 1,000
Sales: $41 million (2002 est.)
NAIC: 721110 Resort Hotels Without Casinos

The Mount Washington Hotel, the oldest frame building in New Hampshire, was built in 1902. One of five original grand hotels in the state, the Mount Washington Hotel has been restored beyond its former grandeur under the ownership of MWH Preservation Limited Partnership. The partnership also owns several adjacent properties that now make up the largest ski resort in New Hampshire. The hotel is known beyond the state's borders and has been host to presidents, diplomats, and financial luminaries in its 100-year-old history.

A Mountain and a Hotel: Prior to 1991

Before MWH Preservation Limited Partnership made its purchase of the Mount Washington Hotel, the property had experienced a turbulent history. In 1881, Joseph Stickney, railroad tycoon and New Hampshire native, purchased 10,000 acres of land around Mount Washington, the highest mountain in New Hampshire. In 1902, construction of The Mount Washington Hotel was completed. From the beginning, the grand project was criticized, with many believing that it was foolhardy to build a hotel at the location. On its opening night Joseph Stickney toasted to "the damn fool who built this white elephant."

In December 1903, Joseph Stickney died, leaving the hotel to his widow Carolyn and beginning a long history of ownership changes. Carolyn remarried Prince Lucinge of France and con-

tinued her ownership of the hotel until her death. Her nephew Foster Reynolds ran the hotel for the next ten years and sold it to a Boston syndicate in 1944. That year the most historic event of the hotel's history occurred when the International Monetary Conference met in the hotel. The meeting of financiers from 44 countries organized the World Bank and the International Monetary Fund, which set the price of gold at $35 per ounce and selected the U.S. dollar as the standard of international exchange.

The Boston syndicate sold the hotel to Morris J. Fleisher and his wife, of Philadelphia, Pennsylvania, in 1955. The Fleishers then sold the hotel to the Mount Washington Development Company in 1969. It was sold again to Bretton Woods Corporation in 1975. During the 1980s, the hotel fell into disrepair, despite being named a National Historic Landmark by the U.S. Department of the Interior, and was purchased in 1987 by a new partnership. In 1989, 63 employees of the hotel lost their jobs due to the decline in bookings. The partnership, which owned the hotel, was a subsidiary of the Eliot Savings Bank of Boston, and in 1991, the bank failed as part of the collapse of the savings and loan system. That left the hotel under the control of the Federal Deposit Insurance Corp. (FDIC), which put the hotel up for auction in June 1991.

A New Era of New Hampshire Leadership: 1991–95

When the auction for the Mount Washington Hotel began, the auctioneer, Wayne Mock, opened the bidding with this statement, according to the *New York Times,* "This is not a bell tolling for the grande dame of the White Mountains," he said. Five bidders and news media attended the auction for the property offered by the FDIC. The agency had already spent $1.2 million on the hotel and had refused an earlier offer to purchase the hotel by MWH.

A group of New Hampshire investors formed a partnership in 1991, the Mount Washington Hotel (MWH) Preservation Limited Partnership, to bid on the historic hotel. The partnership included Joel Bedor, CPA and president of the partnership; Cathy Bedor, Joel's wife and a marketing professional; Wayne Presby, an attorney and chairman of the board; John and Jere

---

Company Perspectives:

Our future lies not in growth for growth's sake. Our future abides rather in respecting the past and adhering to the values that helped the Crawfords survive—generous hospitality. Our future abides in the values that Joseph Stickney expressed when he imagined this magnificent structure—as an integral part of the landscape, as natural and appropriate as a glacier carved hill.

Eames, brothers whose family had been in the hospitality business for many generations, and Robert Clement, the resort's general manager. The Bedors and Presbys had purchased the Mount Washington Cog Railway in 1983 under a different partnership, the Mount Washington Railway Company. The bidding began in quarter million increments and according to an article in *American Profile*, Joel Bedor felt as if his small group was not going to be able to compete. After the bidding halted at $3 million, partner Wayne Presby bid $3.15 million, and the sale was made. The hotel was once again owned by New Hampshire residents marking the first time since Joseph Stickney had died that the hotel was locally owned. Bedor recalled that his initial reaction was "Oh my God, what have I done?"

That question was a good one for Bedor, president of MWH, to have asked. The new owners now had a large task awaiting them. The hotel needed more than $10 million in renovations, 225 guest rooms had been gutted but not repaired, paint was peeling, and the building did not meet fire codes. The partnership was determined to renovate the hotel and make it profitable, even in the first year. Their careful renovations were planned to bring modern conveniences into the hotel while still preserving the historical elements.

In a speech to The Newcomen Society in 2003, Joel Bedor described the goals and mood of the investors after the purchase of the hotel. "We vowed that the days of real estate gimmicks were over. We agreed to preserve and restore the grand resort, confident that the end of the Cold War would result in a new demand for classic vacation experiences. We had seen that the Hotel was no opportunity for a quick profit—its future depended on re-investing every penny of operating revenue in refurbishing the magnificent structure—and quietly preparing it for winter operations," he said.

After focusing their efforts on restoring the hotel, the owners' next goal was to bring back under their ownership other segments that had been part of the hotel properties but had been sold piecemeal decades earlier. The original purchase in 1991 included the main hotel and the 83 acres surrounding it; The Breton Arms, a 34-room country inn; The Lodge of Bretton Woods, a 50-room hotel; and Fabyans, a restaurant converted from a train depot. In 1993, the partnership bought back the 27-hole PGA Championship golf course adjacent to the property.

In 1994, the hotel was host to presidents once more when former President George Bush was the keynote speaker at Citicorp's international banking convention. After years of disrepair, the hotel was again considered for conferences of national and international importance.

Expansion and Improvements: 1996–2000

MWH Preservation Limited Partnership purchased 950 acres of land that bordered the hotel in 1996. In 1997, the partnership acquired the Bretton Woods downhill and cross-country ski areas, again uniting the 730-acre ski area with the hotel's 1,200 acres of land. Bretton Woods was purchased for an undisclosed amount. "It has been a long-term dream of our company to have a fully integrated resort at Bretton Woods," said Wayne Presby in an interview with the *Union Leader* after the purchase. "Today's acquisition is the culmination of that dream."

The Mount Washington Hotel was open for its first winter season in 1999. Bretton Woods ski area was renovated in time for the 1999–2000 winter season. The expansion included 24 new trails; The Zephyr, a high-speed quad lift; and a new base camp lodge that included a Family Learning Center. In 1999, the hotel was named the "Hospitality Business of the Decade" by *Business NH Magazine*. The 1999 expansions to the ski area made it the largest ski area in New Hampshire and the third largest in the Northeast. The partnership spent over $2 million getting the hotel ready for its first winter season. Condos were also built on the property to add more options for overnight guests.

The hotel had to undergo several major improvements to be open during the winter, including the replacement of 800 windows with double-pane insulated glass, the addition of thermostats and a backup generator, as well as winterization of the hotel's water-treatment system. The hotel's general manager, Anthony Ferrelli, and his wife lived in the hotel during the winter of 1998–99 to ensure livability. Wayne Presby, chairman of the board, stated in a profile by the Mount Washington Observatory's quarterly bulletin, *Windswept,* that he did not expect the hotel to be 100 percent occupied in its first winter but reservations were strong. Chairman Wayne Presby, in an article in *Travel Weekly,* said that the improvements were part of a $25 million, five-year project that would include additions to the resort and hotel.

A Century of Hospitality: 2000 and Beyond

On September 11, 2001, terrorists attacked the United States, destroying the World Trade Center towers in New York City and damaging the Pentagon. The attacks were carried out with commercial airplanes, and afterwards, the tourism industry was badly affected when consumers canceled hotel rooms, airline reservations, and cruises. The Mount Washington Hotel was also affected.

After opening for its first winter season in 1999–2000, the hotel and resort area experienced a great amount of success, but for the few years after September 11, 2001, the hotel's reservations were down. Many more people waited until the last minute to make vacation plans, said Bonnie MacPherson, the hotel's director of Public Relations in the *Union Leader* on July 28, 2003. For example, the Fourth of July was usually fully booked well in advance of the holiday. In 2003, the hotel sold out its rooms for the weekend but did so much later than usual.

In 2002, the hotel celebrated its centennial on July 28 with a series of events, including a fireworks display. The hotel was one of two finalists considered to host the 2004 G8 summit with

Key Dates:

1902: Hotel is built by Joseph Stickney.
1903: Joseph Stickney dies.
1986: Mount Washington Hotel is recognized as a National Historic Landmark.
1991: MWH Preservation Limited Partnership is formed to purchase the Mount Washington Hotel.
1993: Mount Washington Golf Course and Mount Pleasant Golf Course are acquired.
1997: Company acquires 950 acres adjacent to the hotel, including the Bretton Woods Sports Club and Ski Area.
1999: Company opens for the first year-round season in hotel's history.
2003: World-class skier Bode Miller joins staff.

leaders from the world's major industrial nations. The G8 countries (the United States, Great Britain, France, Germany, Japan, Italy, Canada, and Russia) were planning their annual meeting to discuss economic and political issues facing the world. However, Sca Island, Georgia, was named as the location in July 2003.

In October 2003, MWH announced that Bode Miller, the world's top-ranked skier, would be working to promote skiing and other sports at the Mount Washington Hotel and Bretton Woods. The skier agreed to a seven- to ten-year commitment to the resort area and hotel. Wayne Presby, MWH chairman, said that Miller approached the hotel with the idea of working with them. Miller's title was director of skiing, and, though he would be skiing competitively in Europe during most of the winter, he would reside at Bretton Woods.

"I'm in for the whole program," said Miller in an interview with the *Union Leader* on October 4, 2003. "They have my three favorite sports here: skiing, golf and tennis. I am looking at being able to exploit all three and activate more interest." Miller also said that while he received celebrity treatment in Europe, he felt most at home in the eastern United States citing it as a healthier environment.

Besides the addition of Bode Miller to the staff, 12 new trails were added to Bretton Woods and the second phase of an expansion to the base lodge. The lodge area expansion included the addition of a general store, Slopeside Restaurant & Pub, and a new TreeTop Sports alpine shop. The Mount Rosebrook Summit Express high-speed detachable quad was also added, opening new trails on Mount Rosebrook.

Over the past decade, MWH restored and expanded the hotel and resort area. Now as other investors decided to restore other grand hotels, the partnership's success served as a positive case study. In a 2002 interview with Mike Recht of The Associated Press, Joel Bedor said, "I think people, investors, have seen what we have been able to do, and they're trying to replicate it. You can leave your car and never have to drive anywhere; everything is here. You can relax and forget about the rest of the world."

In his speech to The Newcomen Society in 2003, MWH President Joel Bedor said that the progress for MWH Preserva-

tion Limited Partnership was still moving forward. Plans included a new spa, golf course renovation, and ski area expansion. The partnership was committed to continuing its improvements to this century-old hotel and surrounding resort area. "To express the spirit of this enterprise on its 100th anniversary," said Bedor. "There is no more appropriate word that I can summon than 'optimism.'"

Principal Competitors

Berkshire East Ski Resort; Mountain Sports Inn.

Further Reading

Ashworth, Jon, "New Deal for Bretton Woods," *Times*, May 20, 1991.

Bedor, Joel, *The Mount Washington Hotel & Resort: A Heritage of Optimism*, Exton, Pa.: Newcomen Society of the United States, 2003.

Biggs, Marcia, "Ski Trails Lead to Landmark Hotel in New Hampshire," *Tampa Tribune*, September 17, 2000, p. 1.

Calta, Marialisa, "Grand Survivor of Another Age," *New York Times*, May 4, 1997, p. 8.

Colquhoun, Lorna, "Drummond Name Has Strong Link to Hotel," *New Hampshire Sunday News*, July 28, 2002, p. B7.

——, "Grand Times: The Mount Washington Hotel," *Union Leader*, July 28, 2003, p. A1.

"Economic Heartbreak at Mount Washington Hotel," *Independent*, July 21, 1991, p. 28.

Flaim, Denise, "New Hampshire Hotel As Grand As Era It Embodies," *Ottawa Citizen*, July 8, 1995, p. J5.

Goldberg, Randi, "A Return to Grandeur for Mt. Washington Hotel," *News Standard*, September 11, 1997.

Goodwin, Nadine, "Mount Washington Hotel Expands Reach, Grasp," *Travel Weekly*, March 10, 2003.

Harbord, Trisha, "Holiday: In Bed with a President: Sumptuous Hotel That Is a Genuine Washington Monument," *People*, August 10, 2003, pp. 44–45.

"Historic Hotel Is S&L Victim," *New York Times*, May 14, 1991, p. D6.

"Historic New Hampshire Hotel for Sale," *Washington Post*," May 28, 1991, p. A10.

Houston, Jourdan, "Abstracts," *New York Times*, July 22, 1997, p. 3.

Kaplan, Mitch, "White Mountain High," *Record*, November 2, 2003, p. T1.

Kostrzewa, John, "Today's Global Economy Born at Bretton Woods in 1944," *Providence Journal-Bulletin*, July 20, 2003, p. F1.

Lash, Rochelle, "Resort Returns to Its Splendorous Past: Renovated Mount Washington Hotel Shifting into Winter Mode with Shuttle Rides to Ski Areas," *Gazette*, November 6, 2003, p. D7.

Miller, Nancy, "S&L Collapse Claims Resort," *USA Today*, May 17, 1991, p. 4B.

"Mount Washington Hotel up for Bids Today," *Boston Globe*, June 26, 1991, p. 69.

Muther, Elizabeth, "Mount Washington Hotel: The Place to Enjoy Fall Colors," *Christian Science Monitor*, August 31, 1982, p. 16.

Nemethy, Andrew, "Saving a Landmark on Nothing but Faith," *American Profile*, September 22, 2001.

O'Connor, Michael, "Mount Washington Hotel Becomes a Four-Season Resort," *Boston Herald*, April 1, 1999, p. 64.

——, "NH Hotel Mounts Grand Plans to Open for Winter Season," *Boston Herald*, July 30, 1998, p. 45.

Pitcher, Rosemary, "Mount Washington Hotel Offers a Glimpse of Shangri-La," *Toronto Star*, September 24, 1988, p. F19.

Recht, Mike, "Grand Hotels: An All-But-Extinct Species Making a Comeback in New Hampshire," *Bryan-College Station Eagle*, August 14, 2002.

"Resort Jobs Cut," *Boston Globe*, July 30, 1989, p. 15.

Rifkin, Glenn, "Saving a New England 'Grand Dame'," *New York Times*, June 27, 1991, p. D1.

St. John, Kent E., "The White Mountain's Grande Dame," *http://www.gonomad.com*, June 6, 2003.

Talbot, Roger, "NH Grand Hotel May Play Host to Next G8 Summit," *Union Leader*, June 22, 2003, p. A1.

Tracy, Paula, "Bretton Woods to Get a Boost from Bode," *Union Leader*, November 7, 2003, p. C1.

——, "Grand Hotel Buys Bretton Woods, Mount Washington Owners Will Operate Downhill, Cross-Country Ski Areas," *Union Leader*, September 10, 1997, p. A1.

——, "Snow Welcomes North Country Ski Ambassador," *Union Leader*, October 4, 2003, p. A8.

Waters, Paul, "Historic Hotel Opens All Year," *Gazette*, December 4, 1999, p. H1.

—Melissa Rigney Baxter

Nash Finch Company

7600 France Avenue South
P.O. Box 355
Minneapolis, Minnesota 55440-0355
U.S.A.
Telephone: (952) 832-0534
Fax: (952) 844-1234
Web site: http://www.nashfinch.com

Public Company
Incorporated: 1896 as Nash Brothers Wholesale Produce
 Co.
Employees: 10,570
Sales: $3.97 billion (2003)
Stock Exchanges: NASDAQ
Ticker Symbol: NAFC
NAIC: 422410 General Line Grocery Wholesalers;
 445110 Supermarkets and Other Grocery (Except
 Convenience) Stores

One of the largest food wholesalers in the United States, Nash Finch Company serves more than 1,800 supermarkets and institutional customers in more than two dozen states—mainly in the Upper Midwest and East—as well as more than 100 military commissaries and distribution centers located in the United States (primarily in the Mid-Atlantic region), Puerto Rico, Cuba, Europe, and Iceland. The company's wholesale operations, which generate about three-quarters of total revenues, are supported by 15 distribution centers. Retail operations, centering on the Upper Midwest, contribute the remaining one-quarter of sales. These encompass about 80 traditional supermarkets under the Econofoods, Sun Mart, and Family Thrift Center names and three deep-discount supermarkets under the Wholesale Food Outlet banner. In addition to nationally branded and unbranded products, Nash Finch supplies its company-owned stores and its affiliated independent stores with the private label brands Our Family, Value Choice, and Fame, which together represent approximately 2,500 dairy, meat, grocery, frozen food, beverage, health and beauty, and paper and household products.

Early History

Nash Finch Company began in 1885 when Vermont native Fred Nash, after traveling west and toiling at several unpromising jobs, invested $400 and established a candy and tobacco shop in Devil's Lake, a Dakota Territory boomtown. Nash soon enlisted his two younger brothers, Edgar and Willis, to join him. All three benefitted from having worked in their parents' general store back East, and they shared a determination to live frugally so that their business might succeed. By the time North Dakota achieved statehood in 1889, the brothers had opened three additional stores, suffered the loss of one and severe damage to another from separate fires, and, finally, consolidated their operations in the emerging urban center of Grand Forks.

The year 1889 proved pivotal to the company for two reasons. The first stemmed from the serendipitous arrival in Grand Forks of a boxcar of peaches for which no buyer existed. Although primarily retailers, the Nash brothers had conducted some fruit wholesaling and quickly decided to secure a bank loan for the peaches. The venture was a large gamble—the brothers' only collateral was the Grand Forks store—but it paid off when sales were made to retailers throughout the region. Two years later the Nashes became wholesalers exclusively and earned the distinction of founding both the first and largest of the state's wholesaling firms. The second turning point came when Edgar contracted tuberculosis and moved to California for health reasons. While Edgar's new contribution as West Coast fruit buyer aided the growth of the company, a replacement was needed at the Grand Forks headquarters. That person was 14-year-old Harry Finch, who several decades later became president of the company. (A legacy of Finch management continued in the hands of Finch's grandson, Harold B. Finch, Jr., who was the company's chief executive officer and chairman of the board in the early 1990s.)

Expansion in the Early 20th Century

Although 1896 was overshadowed by the death of Edgar Nash in January, later that year the company celebrated its first expansion beyond North Dakota with the acquisition of the Smith Wholesale Company of Crookston, Minnesota. Harry Finch, still relatively young but now with seven years of experi-

Company Perspectives:

Nash Finch is a high performance organization specializing in the wholesale and retail distribution of supermarket products. Our wholesale operation is sales driven and relentlessly focused on premier service and low cost. In retailing, Nash Finch dominates its primary trade areas through convenience, consistently excellent execution and superior service. Individual success will be based upon contribution and performance.

ence in clerking and sales, was placed in charge of the Crookston operation, which was renamed Finch-Smith Company. Also in 1896, the company incorporated under the name Nash Brothers Wholesale Produce Co. By the early 1900s, Nash Brothers solidified its position as North Dakota's leading wholesaler with the successive purchases of Minot Grocery Company and Grand Forks Mercantile Company. A 1905 partnership forged with a budding Red River Valley produce brokerage named C.H. Robinson Company—to which Finch was elected vice-president—further broadened Nash's service base. After Nash Brothers acquired control of Robinson in 1913, branch offices were established in Minneapolis, Sioux City, Milwaukee, Chicago, Fort Worth, and virtually everywhere else the parent company had sprouted its own warehouse facilities. Until 1966, C.H. Robinson served as the produce procurement branch of Nash Brothers/Nash Finch, because, at that time, the Federal Trade Commission (FTC) succeeded in limiting Nash's broker-buyer monopoly. Ten years later, C.H. Robinson became independent and has since blossomed into a leading third-party logistics firm headquartered in Eden Prairie, Minnesota.

From 1907 to 1918, Nash acquired 54 fruit wholesalers spread throughout the northwestern United States and Canada. Highlights of this era included the establishment in Lewiston, Idaho, of White Brothers and Crum, the company's first fruit growing and shipping venture; the creation of the Randolph Marketing Company in Los Angeles to package citrus fruit; and the formation of Nash DeCamp Company, a California-based produce growing and marketing concern that would prove to be one of the company's most prized concerns. By 1919 Nash Brothers had become so vast that it required a more centralized headquarters. The logical choice was Minneapolis, which had developed into the nation's 17th largest city, a premier milling center, and the wholesaling hub of the Northwest. According to historian Bruce Gjovig in *Boxcar of Peaches: The Nash Bros. & Nash Finch Company,* ''Although the loss of the Nash Bros. headquarters was a blow to Grand Forks, the move made good business sense. . . . [In] Minneapolis, the Nash Bros. had joined the ranks of the Pillsburys, Cargills, and Hills.'' Two years later, the firm reincorporated under the name Nash Finch Company and consolidated its more than 60 businesses, which had previously functioned as separate units with independent officers. Canadian operations were united under Nash-Simington Ltd. while C.H. Robinson Company and Nash Shareholders became the corporation's primary subsidiaries. As the corporation's first president, Fred Nash oversaw the complex consolidation process, which was completed in 1925. His death the following year resulted in Harry Finch's elevation to president. Willis Nash remained as corporate

treasurer and also served as president of the Nash Company, the Nash family's own investment corporation.

At the onset of the Great Depression in 1929, Nash Finch ranked as one of the foremost food distributors in the Midwest, with sales of more than $35 million. Because of its firm foothold within a recession-proof industry, Nash weathered the 1930s better than most U.S. manufacturers. The only year in which the company failed to turn a profit was 1932, generally considered the worst year of the Depression. During the 1930s, one of the most significant advances for the company came with its large-scale promotion of the Our Family private label brand, which was first introduced in 1904 and later became a symbol of the company's operating philosophy and a favorite of Nash consumers by the 1940s.

Rising Revenues in 1960s and 1970s

During the early 1950s, Nash Finch reentered food retailing with the purchase of 17 supermarkets in Nebraska. The move proved crucial to the company's future health, for it allowed Nash to remain competitive with much larger food concerns, including Eden Prairie-based wholesaler and retailer Super Valu Stores, Inc. From 1960 to 1969 Nash saw its sales grow from $91 million to $248 million. As the company increasingly diversified within its industry and offered a greater variety of services to its retailers, growth in overall revenues became even more impressive during the 1970s and 1980s.

By the mid-1980s, Nash ranked as the nation's tenth largest grocery wholesaler, with sales of $1.3 billion. Its geographic sphere of influence, however, was still confined largely to the rural Midwest, which at the time represented a conspicuously slow-growth market. This, and just a 5 percent compound increase in earnings over a ten-year period (Super Valu's increase, over the same period, was 23 percent), had perpetuated what Dick Youngblood termed the company's ''comparative anonymity.'' In an effort to improve his company's rankings within the food industry, Chairman Harold Finch, Jr., announced a sweeping expansion plan designed to nearly triple earnings and double revenues by the end of the decade.

The 1985 acquisition of M.H. McLean Wholesaler Grocery Company effectively inaugurated the plan. A North Carolina distribution facility serving approximately 60 Hills Food stores, the McLean Company signified additional wholesale revenues of roughly $100 million. More important, though, was Nash's consonant commitment to the South, with its higher-than-average population growth. A series of purchases, including that of Georgia's second largest food wholesaler as well as that of Colorado's largest wholesaler, highlighted the next few years. Yet, the Nash Finch Company entered the 1990s somewhat precariously; quick profits had not followed quick expansion. Instances of store closings and margin problems related to three separate acquisitions led to notable charges against shares, and, although revenues and book value climbed steadily, net income stagnated in 1988 before it plunged by 27 percent in 1989.

Growth Through Acquisition, Early to Mid-1990s

In the early 1990s, Nash Finch continued its strategy of achieving expansion through acquisition and improving profit-

Key Dates:

1885: Fred Nash establishes a candy and tobacco shop in the Dakota Territory boomtown of Devil's Lake; brothers Edgar and Willis soon join the venture.

1889: Operations are consolidated in Grand Forks; wholesaling begins; Harry Finch joins the firm.

1891: The Nash brothers become wholesalers exclusively.

1896: Company is incorporated as Nash Brothers Wholesale Produce Co.; company expands outside North Dakota for the first time through the acquisition of a Crookston, Minnesota wholesaler.

1904: The Our Family private label brand makes its debut.

1905: Partnership is forged with produce brokerage C.H. Robinson Company.

1919: A more centralized headquarters is established in Minneapolis.

1921: Firm reincorporates as Nash Finch Company and consolidates its more than 60 businesses.

1950s: Company reenters food retailing with purchase of 17 supermarkets in Nebraska.

1985: North Carolina-based M.H. McLean Wholesaler Grocery Company is acquired.

1992: Position as a leading distributor to the U.S. military is enhanced through the purchases of Virginia-based Tidewater Wholesale Grocery and a division of Maryland-based B. Green & Company.

1993: Nash Finch acquires Easter Enterprises, a retail chain with 16 stores in Iowa, Illinois, and Missouri.

1996: Company purchases Military Distributors of Virginia; Dayton, Ohio-based Super Food Services, Inc.; and T.J. Morris Company, a wholesale distributor in Georgia.

1998: Charges related to a major restructuring result in a net loss of $61.7 million.

1999: Nash Finch consolidates its supermarkets under the banners Econofoods, Sun Mart, and Family Thrift Center; 18 Erickson's Diversified supermarkets in Minnesota and Wisconsin are acquired.

2000: The 14-unit Hinky Dinky Supermarkets chain in Nebraska is purchased.

2004: Company announces it will close 21 underperforming stores.

ability through broadened services and updated facilities. Following a slight dip in net sales from 1990 to 1991 (during which time profits increased by 7 percent), the company topped the $2.5 billion mark in 1992 revenues while posting its highest earnings ever—more than $20 million. Two mid-Atlantic acquisitions in 1992, Virginia-based Tidewater Wholesale Grocery and a prominent division of Maryland-based B. Green & Company, fortified Nash's position as one of the largest distributors to the U.S. military. That same year, the company sought overseas growth by participating in a group venture to acquire 75 percent of Hungary's largest wholesale food company, Alfa Trading Company. The December 1992 loss of an account with Lunds Inc., a $120 million upscale Minnesota retail chain, seemed hardly to hinder the company; within four months it had reached an agreement to acquire Easter Enterprises, a 16-store chain with

sales of $250 million. Headquartered in Des Moines, Easter consisted of 11 stores in Iowa, three in Illinois, and two in Missouri. Perhaps the sweetest part of the deal was the lost business that it represented for Easter's former provider, Supervalu Inc. (the former Super Valu Stores). The purchase also served notice that Nash had no intention of abandoning its bread-and-butter Midwest market, which estimates in the early 1990s placed at approximately 70 percent of sales.

In 1994 Chairman and CEO Harold B. Finch, Jr., died in an automobile accident. The grandson of Harry Finch, he had followed in his grandfather's footsteps and those of his father, Harold B. Finch, Sr., who had been president from 1939 to 1961. Finch, Jr., was initially succeeded in both positions by Al Flaten, who had been with the company since 1961 and had served as president and COO since 1991. Breaking with typical U.S. business practice, Flaten soon decided to split the CEO and chairman positions, with an independent director, Donald R. Miller, taking the latter spot. Flaten told Ann Merrill of the *Minneapolis Star Tribune* that having the same person in both positions was like "putting a fox in charge of the hen house."

The company's acquisitions continued into the mid-1990s. In 1994 Nash Finch bought Food Folks, a grocery store chain headquartered in North Carolina with 23 stores. The following year the company boosted its presence as a supplier to U.S. and European military commissaries by agreeing to acquire Norfolk-based Military Distributors of Virginia, a purchase it completed in January 1996. By the end of 1995, the company was supplying 120 of its own stores in 16 states and 5,700 independent stores in over 30 states.

But Nash Finch's share of the market took an even bigger leap in 1996 through the company's acquisition of Super Food Services, Inc. By spending about $247 million for the Dayton, Ohio-based wholesaler, Nash Finch went from the fifth largest food wholesaler in the United States to the third largest. Super Food not only added $1.2 billion in revenues, it also expanded Nash Finch's territory into areas of Ohio, Michigan, Kentucky, Indiana, Tennessee, and West Virginia that the company did not previously serve. In addition, Nash Finch planned to use Super Food's strength in gourmet foods to supply its company-owned stores, eliminating the need to buy such products from other wholesalers. Nash Finch also planned to sell produce, one of its own strengths, to Super Food's customers, who could not previously buy produce through Super Food.

Another acquisition in 1996 extended the company's geographical reach. Nash Finch purchased the wholesale distributor T.J. Morris Company, which supplied over 100 independent grocery retailers in Georgia. The company closed its warehouse in Macon and consolidated it with T.J. Morris's distribution facility in Statesboro. The newly enlarged warehouse cost-effectively served existing T.J. Morris and Nash Finch customers in Georgia.

These acquisitions helped raise Nash Finch's revenues to $3.38 billion in 1996, up more than 16 percent from 1995. Net earnings rose as well, to $20 million, from $17.4 million in 1995. Expansion did not result only from acquisitions, however. The company's independent supermarket customers rose 16 percent to 767, not including new customers from Super Food and T.J. Morris.

Restructuring in the Late 1990s

During 1997 Nash Finch bolstered its wholesale operations in the Midwest by acquiring United-A.G. Cooperative Inc., a firm based in Omaha, Nebraska, serving about 100 member-owned co-op stores in Nebraska, Kansas, Iowa, Colorado, and South Dakota. Revenues in 1996 for United-A.G. were approximately $200 million. Sales at Nash Finch were a record $4.39 billion in 1997, but the firm posted a net loss of $1.2 million.

Following Flaten's retirement in June 1998, Ron Marshall was named CEO, becoming the first CEO to come from outside the company. Marshall had most recently served as executive vice-president and CEO of Pathmark Stores, Inc., a major grocery chain in the Mid-Atlantic region. In February 1999, eight months after joining Nash Finch, Marshall launched a major restructuring in an attempt to restore profitability, streamline the wholesaling operation, and overhaul the company's information systems. The company closed three of its distribution centers and earmarked 12 underperforming corporate-owned retail stores for sale or closure. Two more distribution centers were closed later in 1999, reducing the total number to 13. Marshall also scrapped a $30 million information systems project that was not equipped to handle the Y2K rollover issue, spending another $20 million to get the company ready for Y2K. He also centralized a range of operations, including such functions as buying, finance, information technology, and human resources. Despite the store closures, Marshall aimed to grow the retail side of the business, which at the time generated 20 percent of sales. Through acquisitions and organic growth, the new leader hoped to eventually increase this share to 50 percent. Nash Finch took a pretax charge of $106 million in relation to the restructuring, leading to a net loss for 1998 of $61.7 million.

During 1999 Nash Finch overhauled and expanded its retail operations. Stores that once operated under 17 different names were consolidated under three banners: Econofoods, Sun Mart, and Family Thrift Center. The company bought 18 supermarkets in Minnesota and Wisconsin from Erickson's Diversified Corp. in 1999 and soon converted most of them to Econofoods outlets. In January of the following year Omaha-based Hinky Dinky Supermarkets, Inc. and its 14 stores in Nebraska were acquired; most of these soon began sporting the Sun Mart name. Nash Finch's supermarkets also began placing greater emphasis on convenience, service, and selection of perishables in order to distinguish them from Wal-Mart Stores, Inc.'s Supercenters, which were beginning to encroach into Nash Finch territory. Moreover, the company began testing two other retail concepts: Buy-n-Save, a deep-discount, limited-assortment store aimed at low-income consumers, and Wholesale Food Outlet, which targeted Hispanic consumers. By mid-2001 there were four Buy-n-Saves in Minnesota, while Wholesale Food Outlet stores had been opened in Greeley, Colorado; Muscatine, Iowa; and Omaha.

In July 1999, meantime, Nash Finch completed two deals to divest noncore operations. Nash-De Camp, the California-based produce growing and marketing subsidiary, was sold to Agriholding Inc., while Nash Finch's dairy operations—consisting of Rapid City, South Dakota–based Gillette Dairy of the Black Hills, Inc. and Nebraska Dairies, Inc.—were bought by the Minneapolis firm Marigold Foods Inc., which at the time

was a subsidiary of Koninklijke Wessanen nv of the Netherlands. In November 1999 Nash Finch reached an agreement to acquire Fairway Foods of Michigan Inc., a grocery wholesaler with annual sales of $160 million, but the deal later fell through.

Nash Finch returned to profitability in 1999, reporting net income of $19.8 million on sales of $4.12 billion. Company Chairman Miller retired in May 2000 and was succeeded by longtime board member Allister P. Graham, who was the retired chairman and CEO of The Oshawa Group Limited, a Canadian food distributor.

Refocusing on Wholesaling in the Early 2000s

Marshall began the new century continuing with his plan to bolster the firm's retail side. In August 2001 U Save Foods, Inc., which operated 14 supermarkets in Nebraska, Kansas, and Colorado, was acquired for approximately $145 million, and most of the stores were soon operating under the Sun Mart banner. In 2002 Nash Finch launched a new concept called Avanza. Like Wholesale Food Outlet, Avanza was aimed at Hispanic consumers, but the newer concept was to be located mainly in major cities rather than smaller towns. The first Avanza opened in Denver in May 2002 and was following by additional locations in Denver, Chicago, and Pueblo, Colorado. Wholesale Food Outlet was subsequently repositioned as a more traditional deep-discount supermarket. In the meantime, Nash Finch refocused its retail operations strictly on the Midwest as it sold its supermarkets in North and South Carolina in 2001.

As the 2000s continued, however, Nash Finch's retail operations felt increasing pressure from the fierce competition that stemmed from the aggressive growth of Wal-Mart and other discounters. The company faced the added burden in late 2002 and early 2003 of a Securities and Exchange Commission (SEC) investigation of its accounting practices, which led to the departure of two outside auditing firms and the delayed filing of the company's third- and fourth-quarter reports for 2002. The SEC probe sent the company's stock down more than 75 percent, seemingly an overreaction given that the government agency did not take any immediate action against the company. Nevertheless, the financial results for 2003 prompted another change in direction. Nash Finch's wholesale operations enjoyed strong growth—aided particularly by business picked up following the demise of Fleming Companies, Inc., which at one time was the largest food wholesaler in the country—while the retail side showed a sharp decline in sales.

In May 2004, then, Marshall announced that 21 underperforming stores would be closed, and the Buy-n-Save and Avanza concepts would be jettisoned. A special pretax charge of $36.5 million was taken in relation to this pullback. This left Nash Finch with about 85 stores, the bulk of which were traditional supermarkets operating under the Econofoods, Sun Mart, and Family Thrift Center banners. Most of these were located in markets where Nash Finch held the number one or two spots, positions that Marshall intended to defend from encroaching competitors. While expansion on the retail side was put on hold—and Marshall's aim of a 50–50 split between wholesale and retail was quietly abandoned—Nash Finch hoped to find additional opportunities for growth in wholesaling, particularly from former Fleming customers.

Principal Subsidiaries

Erickson's Diversified Corporation; GTL Truck Lines, Inc.; Hinky Dinky Supermarkets, Inc.; Nash Finch Funding Corp.; Piggly Wiggly Northland Corporation; Super Food Services, Inc.; T.J. Morris Company; U-Save Foods, Inc.; NFCG, LLC.

Principal Competitors

Supervalu Inc.; Hy-Vee, Inc.; McLane Company, Inc.; H.T. Hackney Co.; Purity Wholesale Grocers, Inc.; Spartan Stores, Inc.; Wal-Mart Stores, Inc.; The Kroger Co.; Albertson's, Inc.

Further Reading

Byrne, Harlan S., "Nash Finch Co.: It Puts Recent Acquisition Stumbles Behind It," *Barron's,* March 26, 1990, p. 40.

Cochran, Thomas N., "Nash Finch Co.: A Food Wholesaler Succeeds in the Retail End of the Business," *Barron's,* June 6, 1988, pp. 65–66.

Gelbach, Deborah L., *From This Land: A History of Minnesota's Empires, Enterprises, and Entrepreneurs,* Northridge, Calif.: Windsor Publications, 1988.

Gjovig, Bruce, *Boxcar of Peaches: The Nash Bros. & Nash Finch Company,* Grand Forks, N.D.: Center for Innovation and Business Development, 1990.

Kennedy, Tony, "Lunds to Drop Nash Finch in Favor of Fairway Foods," *Minneapolis Star Tribune,* December 23, 1992, p. D3.

——, "Nash Finch Acquires Wholesaler," *Minneapolis Star Tribune,* January 8, 1993, p. D3.

Lambert, Brian, "Nash Finch Celebrates 100 Years of Business," *Corporate Report Minnesota,* March 1985, p. 19.

Lee, Thomas, "Nash Finch Plans to Close 21 Stores; Two Chains Will Be Jettisoned," *Minneapolis Star Tribune,* May 20, 2004, p. 1D.

——, "Time to Punt: Edina Food Distributor's Retail Outlets Struggling Against Wal-Mart's Supercenters," *Minneapolis Star Tribune,* March 16, 2004, p. 1D.

Lewis, Len, "Rebuilding Nash Finch," *Progressive Grocer,* August 2001, pp. 12–14, 16, 18.

Marcotty, Josephine, "Nash Finch to Buy Midwest Supermarket Chain," *Minneapolis Star Tribune,* April 8, 1993, p. D3.

Merrill, Ann, "An Appetite for Growth: Nash Finch Becomes Bigger Fish in the Grocery Wholesaling Pond," *Minneapolis Star Tribune,* January 20, 1997, p. 1D.

——, "Deadlines Closing in on Nash Finch," *Minneapolis Star Tribune,* February 15, 2003, p. 1D.

——, "Shopping for Growth: Nash Finch, Faltering Badly Two Years Ago, Is Making Major Changes Under New Management," *Minneapolis Star Tribune,* August 13, 2000, p. 1D.

"Nash Finch Invests in Hungarian Firm," *Minneapolis Star Tribune,* November 18, 1992, p. D3.

"Nash Finch to Buy 16 Easter Stores," *Supermarket News,* April 12, 1993, p. 4.

"Nash Finch to Buy Supermarkets," *Wall Street Journal,* April 8, 1993, p. B5.

Sansolo, Michael, "Nash Finch: A New Horizon," *Progressive Grocer,* November 1985, pp. 40, 42.

Schafer, Lee, ed., "Super Valu Stores Inc.; Nash Finch Company," *Corporate Report Minnesota,* June 1991, pp. 147–48.

"Super Food Services Agrees to $174 Million Acquisition," *Wall Street Journal,* October 9, 1996, p. B3.

Tosh, Mark, "The Marshall Plan," *Progressive Grocer,* April 1999, p. 9.

——, "Nash Finch to Capitalize on Strength," *Supermarket News,* June 1, 1992, p. 9.

Youngblood, Dick, "Grocery Giant Nash Finch Still Keeps a Low Profile," *Minneapolis Star Tribune,* June 9, 1986, pp. M1, M8.

Zwiebach, Elliot, "Nash Finch Examines Viability of Low-Price Format," *Supermarket News,* June 14, 2004, p. 60.

——, "Nash Finch Eyes Southeast Buys As Way of Boosting Profitability," *Supermarket News,* May 27, 1991, p. 52.

——, "Nash Finch Shifts from Restructuring to Growth," *Supermarket News,* February 28, 2000, p. 1.

——, "They Will Succeed," *Supermarket News,* December 11, 1995, pp. 12–16, 79.

—Jay P. Pederson
—updates: Susan Windisch Brown, David E. Salamie

National Financial Partners Corp.

787 Seventh Avenue, 49th Floor
New York, New York 10019
U.S.A.
Telephone: (212) 301-4000
Fax: (212) 301-4001
Web site: http://www.nfp.com

Public Company
Incorporated: 1998
Employees: 1,450
Total Assets: $671.6 million (2003)
Stock Exchanges: New York
Ticker Symbol: NFP
NAIC: 523930 Investment Advice

National Financial Partners Corp. (NFP), formed to bring small independent financial services firms beneath one umbrella, hopes to succeed where others have failed. By maintaining an entrepreneurial spirit among its member firms, NFP expects to drive growth internally as well as through acquisitions. NFP targets high-net-worth individuals and small- to mid-sized companies for its product sales.

High Expectations: 1998–99

National Financial Partners' $125 million in seed money came from Apollo Management LP. The leveraged buyout firm, based in New York, received 125 million shares of NFP for its investment. For its part, NFP planned to begin its own buying spree, attempting to consolidate independent companies in the business of advising the nation's richest individuals as well as entities offering financial services and products to mid-sized corporations.

NFP offered a combination of cash and stock for 100 percent ownership of the financial planning firms and independent insurance brokers it sought to buy. Once under the NFP umbrella, the owners were promised continuing autonomy and access to a broader range of products and services for their clients and technological upgrades for their offices.

"Robert L Rosen, founder and chairman of the six-month-old NFP, described his firm's concept as a producer group with the added element that member firms have an equity share in NFP and will be able to obtain capital infusions from it, if needed," wrote Carole Ann King for *National Underwriter Life & Health* in April 1999.

Thus far, NFP had spent $87 million for 28 companies with combined yearly earnings topping $15 million. NFP expected to complete 20 more deals by the end of May. During its first five years of operation, NFP predicted, a total of 300 firms would join the fold.

NFP received a cut of each firm's revenue stream, 40 to 50 percent of earnings. According to *Best's Review*, NFP was wooing firms with a loyal customer base, strong local ties, good renewal rates, and asset gathering ability.

In April 1999, Rosen tapped Jessica Bibliowicz, the daughter of his former boss, to lead NFP. "Bibliowicz gives the firm star power," wrote Theresa Miller for *Best's Review*. Much had been written about her father, Citigroup CEO Sandford Weill, and Bibliowicz had been etching out her own presence on Wall Street.

Her introduction to the world of finance began at home, listening to her father recount his business deals. As a teenager, she worked the summer months for his company, then graduated from Cornell University, her father's alma mater. Work connections with her father continued after college, first, with American Express Co., where Weill served as president.

Marriage and a stint with Shearson's asset management division followed—Shearson Loeb Rhoades, Weill's company, had been purchased by Amex. At Prudential Securities Inc., which was headed by a family friend, she rose to director of sales and marketing for mutual funds but left after failing to move further up the ranks.

Back with one of her father's operations, Smith Barney, she ran the mutual fund business, later adding insurance and estate planning, but she exited over a conflict with Weill's heir apparent.

Prior to joining NFP, Bibliowicz landed positions as president and chief operating officer for New York investment advising firm

John A. Levin & Co., but she wanted more of a challenge. When the job offer came to build a new company, she took it.

Challenging Path: 2000–01

Bibliowicz believed smaller independent financial firms would benefit from their affiliation with NFP. The ever changing world of technology burdened their budgets. Moreover, big name competitors had the upper hand in name recognition. As part of NFP, some of that load would be lifted.

By early 2001, NFP held 85 firms and a market value of about $219 million. But, Bibliowicz was behind schedule. To boost acquisitions, NFP offered a finders fee for leads on firms interested in selling out. During the first six months of her tenure, she brought in 23 firms, though maintaining that pace would prove difficult.

Companies declining the offer cited loss of independence, dissatisfaction with the monetary rewards, and possible risk to their name from association with other member companies that might be involved in improprieties, according to *American Banker*. The business environment also played against Bibliowicz's cause. Predictions of sweeping changes in the financial services industry following the Gramm-Leach-Bliley Act of 1999 had not panned out. Furthermore, the stock market slumped, putting a damper on initial public offerings (IPOs); and with the economy lagging so did the growth of wealth.

Although Bibliowicz had an IPO in her sights, other possibilities existed. Larger financial companies interested in attaining high-net-worth clients might very well look to NFP itself as a potential target for acquisition, something Bibliowicz had not ruled out.

"Yet, selling National Financial Partners to a bank, insurer, brokerage, or any other company would not only be less lucrative than an IPO, it may also make her someone else's employee—perhaps even her father's—again. And even that scenario may be optimistic," wrote Jacqueline S. Gold for *American Banker*.

NFP's plans for a public offering went forward, but a bid by Citigroup Inc. to underwrite was scuttled by an investigation, in the later half of 2002, by New York Attorney General Eliot Spitzer over the possible influencing of a research analyst's opinion by Weill. The situation, combined with the father/daughter connection, threatened to taint the small company's entrance on Wall Street.

While NFP touted the benefits for smaller companies entering the network, some companies appeared to fare better than others under the system. Fee-based advisers, for example, were at a disadvantage to commission-based advisers, due to NFP's vision of being a "conduit for products," according to *Investment News*. Financial planners and advisers represented 25 percent of member companies. Estate planners and insurers made up 40 percent and corporate benefits and executive benefits planners the remaining 35 percent.

Out in Public: 2003–04

By around mid-year 2003, NFP had acquired about 138 firms for about $375 million. More than a dozen companies had failed to do what Bibliowicz was attempting, to successfully group independent financial advisers, observed *Business Week*. "The problem, says Dennis Gallant, of consultants Cerulli Associates, Inc., is that advisers tend to be fiercely independent entrepreneurs who like to work for themselves. 'It's like herding cats,' he says." Bibliowicz helped keep member firms on a growth track with financial incentives and disincentives.

NFP closed at $26.25 at the end of its first day of trading, September 18, 2003.

The financial services industry brought forth nearly half of the IPOs introduced on the year; they were among the first to benefit from an upswing in the economy, according to the *New York Times*.

Goldman Sachs, Merrill Lynch, and J.P. Morgan took the company public, with Citigroup out of the picture. A "preferred relationship" with Citigroup division, Travelers Life, continued. NFP had product agreements with some of the country's largest financial concerns, including her father's company.

Bibliowicz held 1.4 percent of the company she had brought from $10.5 million in losses to its first profitable year, 2002. The IPO raised $239 million from 10.4 million shares at $23 per share. The company's market value was $850 million. With the number of independent estate advisers, benefits consultants, and financial planners in the United States an estimated 4,000, NFP was afforded a significant growth potential. The company predicted 20 percent annual gains in profit per share via acquisitions and internal growth. But with its member companies' worth less than the selling price of NFP stock, the company looked overvalued, according to *Barron's*.

Bibliowicz rejected the term roll-up when applied to NFP. Roll-ups were viewed as companies whose ongoing growth largely depended on acquisitions. Bibliowicz maintained NFP's structure and encouraged continuing internal growth. During the first half of 2003, internal revenue grew by 13 percent; for prior years, 25 percent in 2000, 14 percent in 2001, and 6 percent in 2002.

Internal growth depended on member firms pulling in business as aggressively as they had when they were independent operations. Bibliowicz, according to *American Banker*, viewed client relationships to be the industry's best asset. Therefore, principals of acquired companies were required to stay with their companies for a minimum of five years following acquisition. Owners were to be in the middle rather than end of their careers, seeking an exit strategy.

Consequently, NFP had no plans to market NFP as a brand, preferring to allow member companies to maintain their propri-

---

Key Dates:

1998: Apollo Management LP finances move to consolidate small financial services firms under National Financial Partners umbrella.
1999: Well-connected executive Jessica Bibliowicz is hired to lead company.
2000: Bibliowicz presses hard to bring firms into network.
2002: Company records its first profitable year.
2003: NFP makes public offering.

---

etary brands while accessing the products of others in the network. Boutique firms had historically dominated the high-net-worth market, observed Robert Julavits in *American Banker*.

Revenue in 2003 grew 33 percent over 2002, reaching $479.6 million. "NFP did a couple things right," Mark Tibergien, a principal with Moss Adams LLP in Seattle told *Investment News*. "It got funded early, acted quickly and executed its plan."

By March 2004, NFP had paid $418.5 million in cash and stocks to acquire small firms for its network. Future purchases would lean toward insurance agents and corporate- and executive-benefits firms and away from financial planners and investment advisers, according to *Investment News*.

The investigative spotlight of New York Attorney General Eliot Spitzer was turned on NFP in 2004. Spitzer was already examining the agreements between insurers and commercial brokers of the three largest brokerages in the country, March & McLennan Inc., Aon Corp, and Willis Group Holdings. NFP's property and casualty operations licensed in New York, which contributed less than 5 percent of 2003 revenue, was the focus of the probe.

Principal Competitors

Aon Corporation; Marsh & McLennan Companies, Inc.; Willis Group Holdings Limited.

Further Reading

Altas, Riva D., "A Proud Father, His Daughter and Her Financial Baby," *New York Times*, September 19, 2003, p. C1.

Bary, Andrew, "Betting on Bibliowicz," *Barron's*, September 29, 2003, p. 40.

Elstein, Aaron, "Stock Watch: Roll-Up Firm's Fast Growth Obscures Several Faults," *Crain's New York Business*," September 29, 2003, p. 43.

"Full Speed to $1 Billion?," *Business Week*, November 15, 1999, p. 106.

Gold, Jacqueline S., "Stakes Higher in Weill Scion Solo Bid," *American Banker*, February 23, 2001, p.1.

Goldsmith, Margie, "Like Father, Like Daughter," *Chief Executive*, October 2001, p. 36.

Henry, David, "Bibliowicz's Tricky Pitch," *Business Week*, July 21, 2003, p. 64.

Hoffman, David, "Investors Hot for IPO, Targets Cool to NFP," *Investment News*, June 9, 2003, p. 3.

Julavits, Robert, "Bibliowicz Assembles a Growth Machine at NFP," *American Banker*, December 4, 2003, p. 10A.

Kelly, Bruce, "Growth Gambit: NFP Continues to Make a Splash," *Investment News*, March 1, 2004, p. 24.

Kelly, Kate, "Leading the News: Salomon Withdraws Bid to Underwrite Hotly Pursued IPO," *Wall Street Journal*, November 29, 2002, p. A3.

King, Carole Ann, "Agency Consolidator Scoops Up 30 Firms," *National Underwriter Life & Health*," April 19, 1999.

Lehmann, Raymond, "Compensation Probe Expands to National Financial Partners," *A.M. Best Newswire*, May 6, 2004.

Lohse, Deborah, "Apollo Management Invests in National Financial," *Wall Street Journal*, April 7, 1999, p.1.

Maldonado, Rosemarie, "For Little Guy, Challenges Are Getting Even Bigger," *Investment News*, May 15, 2000, p. 32.

Miller, Theresa, "Opening a Corporate Umbrella," *Best's Review Life/Health Edition*, May 1999.

Moore, Michael O., "Insurance: Start-Up Distributor Buys Agencies, Hires 'Name' CEO," *American Banker*, April 13, 1999.

Wirth, Gregg, "Will Bibliowicz Return to Street Stage? Weill's Daughter's NFP May Be Ripe for a Merger or IPO," *Investment Dealers' Digest*, August 13, 2001, p. 1.

—Kathleen Peippo

Nebraska Book Company, Inc.

4700 S. 19th Street
Lincoln, Nebraska 68501-0529
U.S.A.
Telephone: (402) 421-7300
Fax: (402) 421-0510
Web site: http://www.nebook.com

Private Company
Founded: 1915
Employees: 2,900
Sales: $398.7 million (2004)
NAIC: 424920 Book, Periodical and Newspaper
   Merchant Wholesalers

With its headquarters in Lincoln, Nebraska, Nebraska Book Company, Inc. is involved in the college bookstore industry. Its college bookstore division operates more than 110 on-campus and off-campus bookstores, where in addition to books, other merchandise, such as apparel bearing a school's name and mascot, is sold. Nebraska Book's textbook division sells new textbooks to more than 2,500 college bookstores, and the division also buys and sells used textbooks. Finally, Nebraska Book's complementary services division offers several services and solutions for college bookstores, including Prism software for inventory control; CampusHub, an e-commerce solution that allows local college bookstores to sell over the Internet; specialty books used by students in distance learning and non-traditional courses; Connect2One, an alliance of independent college bookstores; marketing services geared toward independent bookstores; college store design, to help college bookstores better utilize space in an esthetic manner; and NBC graphics, which produces silk-screen and embroidered apparels for colleges as well as high schools, service clubs, and other groups. Nebraska Book is a private company majority owned by investment firm Weston Presidio.

Founding the Company in 1915

The origins of Nebraska Book date back to 1915 with the opening of a small college bookstore in Lincoln, Nebraska,

home of the University of Nebraska. The owner was a young man named E.H. "Red" Long, who had learned the business by working in his brother's bookstore located in Columbus, Ohio, while attending The Ohio State University. Long's venture had an inauspicious start. After the first year, the store was hit by lightning and burned to the ground. Long replaced the structure with one made of brick only to have one of the sides collapse. Long made the best out of the situation by moving back the wall to increase the size of the building, which not only housed books and supplies but also the Silver Moon Luncheonette.

Long owned the bookstore until 1937, when he sold it to a former employee, Johnny Johnsen, who would transform Long's single bookstore into the Nebraska Book Company. Johnsen had worked part time for Long while attending college, then managed the textbook department for a year. At that point, Long suggested that Johnsen find employment with a textbook jobber that could afford to pay him the money he was worth. Heeding his mentor's advice, Johnsen took a position with the College Book Company of Ohio and furthered his education in the field. Three years later he returned to Lincoln and bought Long's business. Long, who would launch another store devoted to high school textbooks, along with his family would live above the Nebraska Bookstore building until his death in 1959.

Johnsen took over a store that was only 50 feet by 90 feet in size. One of his first moves was to open a wholesale department that dealt in used college textbooks. Then in 1939 he brought back the supply business that Long had sold seven years earlier. But just as the business was starting to grow, World War II intervened and Johnsen lost his most important employees. Nevertheless, Nebraska Book managed to survive, only one of three college textbook jobbers that would still be in business by the end of the decade. Because of the war, the production of new textbooks was curtailed, which led to a rising market for used textbooks, an area that Nebraska Book was quick to exploit. It was during the postwar years that the company really began to grow. Many returning servicemen used the G.I. Bill to attend college and Nebraska Book developed a strong business in providing books and supplies to them. Also during the final years of the 1940s the used textbook market experienced rapid growth, and in response the wholesale department began to expand beyond the area surrounding Lincoln, eventually covering the entire country. Nebraska Book would either purchase books directly from students, with buyers paying a two-day visit to a campus, or take over a bookstore's overstock or excess merchandise. Nebraska Book's most experienced buyers then gathered for a ten-day meeting to set the prices for used textbooks, which would be published in an annual buying guide. In 1964 Nebraska Book acquired California-based College Book Company, which became the West Coast extension of its used textbook business and gave Nebraska Book a national reach. The wholesale division outgrew its space in the Nebraska Book building, and in 1967 moved into a new 110,000-square-foot warehouse in Lincoln.

Launching Branch Store Operations in 1948

In 1948 a branch store operation, supervised by the wholesale department, was launched when Nebraska Wesleyan decided to lease its bookstore operations to Nebraska Book. Soon the company added other textbook stores at Nebraska colleges, including Doan, Hastings, and Dana Colleges. The addition of these bookstores increased Nebraska Book's buying power, which further fueled the growth of the company. Over the next few years, stores were added at Washburn University, Baker University, Union College, Concordia College, Norfolk Jr. College, and McCook Jr. College. In 1965 three stores were opened and the branch store operation became a separate division. A year later, three new stores were added, bringing the total number of textbook stores to 12. Before the decade closed, Nebraska Book added two more stores.

In 1973 Nebraska Book was sold to George Lincoln, owner of Lincoln Grain, Inc., who had no experience in the textbook business. He was raised on a farm in Missouri and moved to Lincoln in 1959 to manage two grain elevators, which he would buy and merge in 1961 to form Lincoln Grain. While he built up this business he decided to take on Nebraska Book, which by this point owned or leased 42 bookstores. Lincoln closed all but the ten most profitable stores. In the 1980s the company began to build up the chain again, adding a dozen units to bring the number back up to 22. In 1987 Elders Grain, an Australian company, acquired Lincoln Grain, and George Lincoln devoted all of his time to the management of Nebraska Book, which was owned through another company he controlled, Lincoln Industries, Inc.

The bookstore business changed significantly during the time George Lincoln owned Nebraska Book, mostly due to technology, which replaced pencil and clipboard in filling orders. In the mid-1980s the College Book Company's Cypress, California, warehouse operation of College Book Company was restructured so that it mirrored the Lincoln operation, featuring the same inventory and systems so that customers around the country could expect to receive the same product and service from both facilities. To upgrade the business, Nebraska Book first automated the billing process. The next revolutionary step took

place in the 1990s with the advent of online inventory sales, which led to a remodeling of the warehouse and shipping process automation. As a result of implementing these new technologies, Nebraska Book greatly reduced the amount of time it took to fill a customer's order, while achieving greater accuracy.

In 1985 Nebraska Book offered its first computer software product, PC Text, to help college bookstores automate their operations. Out of this effort emerged the company's current PRISM and WinPRism support software programs geared toward the specific management needs of a college bookstore, including the integration of inventory control with point-of-sale systems. Nebraska Book became involved in all aspects of college bookstore management systems, from design and development to installation, training, and support.

On the bookstore side of the business, Nebraska Book became increasingly involved in retail, focusing on "spirit" apparel featuring the local college's colors and logo as a way to make money between the peak periods of book buying that preceded the start of classes each semester and to prevent the store from becoming little more than a warehouse. Local managers were given a great deal of latitude in the planning of the store to suit the community. In universities with major football and basketball programs, for example, a store might devote more retail space to school apparel and souvenirs. In the early 1990s Nebraska Book began a push to expand its bookstore holdings, with the goal of opening five new stores each year for the next five years.

The expansion program would be continued by a new owner in 1995. In January of that year, Lincoln Industries announced that Nebraska Book was on the block. In August 1995 Olympus Partners, a private equity fund, bought the business for approximately $100 million. Based in Stamford, Connecticut, Olympus was founded in 1989 by Robert S. Morris, a former executive with General Electric Investment Corporation, where he managed General Electric Pension Trust's $1.6 billion private equity portfolio. Olympus took on a limited number of investments each year, ranging from $10 million venture capital deals to buyouts in the $150 million range.

Olympus owned Nebraska Book for little more than two years, during which time the company opened or acquired 17 new college bookstores, expanding its network of retail stores to 54. Cash flow during this period increased from $17 million to $29 million. The company also acquired Collegiate Stores Corporation (CSC), a buying service serving more than 500 independent college bookstores. In addition to textbook purchasing, CSC's programs included a supply program, providing some 3,000 school, office, computer, and art supplies that accounted for three-quarters of the inventory most college bookstores carried. CSC also offered reference materials, shopping bags, an apparel and giftware program, candy and nuts, credit card processing, security programs, store catalog production capability, and freight discounts. CSC would later be renamed Connect2One.

Acquired by Haas Wheat in 1998

Shortly after the CSC acquisition, in February 1998, Olympus sold Nebraska Book to Haas Wheat & Partners Inc. for $245 million, thereby realizing a sizable return on its initial invest-

Key Dates:

1915: The company is founded by E.H. Long.
1937: Johnny Johnsen acquires the business.
1948: A branch store operation is launched.
1973: Lincoln Grain acquires the company.
1995: Olympus Partners acquires the company.
1998: Haas Wheat acquires the company.
2004: Weston Presidio acquires the company.

ment. Haas Wheat was a Dallas, Texas-based private equity firm founded by Robert B. Haas and Douglas D. Wheat in 1992. The new owners expressed a commitment to invest the funds necessary to expand Nebraska Book even further. In June 1999 Nebraska Book completed a major deal by acquiring TRIRO Inc., a College Station, Texas-based company that owned 18 bookstores in Texas, New Mexico, and Arizona. Nebraska Book also broadened its business by becoming involved in e-commerce, establishing CampusHub to help independent college bookstores to sell books and merchandise online 24 hours a day.

In August 2002 Weston Presidio, a San Francisco-based investment partnership, acquired a 33 percent stake in Nebraska Book. Weston Presidio was founded in 1991 by Michael Cronin and Michael Lazarus. The firm's investments exceeded $2.2 billion, covering a range of opportunities, from venture capital for high-growth start-ups to buyouts of mature companies. Nebraska Book fell into the latter category, attracting the interest of Weston Presidio because it was the clear leader in its field. Moreover, with the number of college students increasing, Nebraska Book was well positioned to enjoy continued growth. The cost of textbooks also was rising, with the average price now exceeding $100. A primary reason for this increase was caused by publishers who now brought out new editions of a textbook more frequently. Some 20 years earlier, a textbook was updated every seven years, but now in some cases new editions were separated by as little as 18 months. Nebraska Book's used book buyers found their jobs more challenging but because of the high cost of new books, more students were interested in buying used books, which played to the company's strength.

In 2003 Nebraska Book posted sales of $370.5 million, a 9.3 percent improvement over the prior year, with all three operating divisions enjoying sales increases, while net income soared by 45.5 percent to $23 million. A year later, revenues approached the $400 million mark, as the company added three more bookstores. In March 2004 Weston Presidio bought out Haas Wheat's position and assumed majority control of Nebraska Book, with management owning an 11 percent stake in the business. Weston Presidio's managing partner, Michael Cronin, expressed his satisfaction with the acquisition and support for management's long-term vision for the business.

Principal Subsidiaries

College Book Company; Connect2One; The CampusHub.com; Speciality Books, Inc.; NBC Textbooks.

Principal Competitors

Barnes & Noble College Bookstores, Inc.; Follett Corporation; Varsity Group Inc.

Further Reading

"California Group Acquires Stake in Lincoln, Neb.-Based Textbook Supplier," *Omaha World-Herald,* August 6, 2002.
"The College Store: A Textbook Case," *Retail Store Image,* July 1, 1995, p. 54.
Dunn, Robert, "Haas Wheat Buys Nebraska from Olympus," *Buyouts,* March 23, 1998.
"Looking Back," *Nebraska Branch Stores Central Newsletter,* April, 1968, p. 2.

—Ed Dinger

Newfield Exploration Company

363 N. Sam Houston Parkway East, Suite 2020
Houston, Texas 77060
U.S.A.
Telephone: (281) 847-6000
Fax: (281) 847-6006
Web site: http://www.newfld.com

Public Company
Incorporated: 1988
Employees: 375
Sales: $1.01 billion (2003)
Stock Exchanges: New York
Ticker Symbol: NFX
NAIC: 211111 Crude Petroleum and Natural Gas
    Extraction

Newfield Exploration Company, based in Houston, Texas, is one of the most successful independent crude oil and natural gas exploration and production companies in the United States. Its performance has been used by many independents as a benchmark for gauging their own success. Newfield's areas of operation include both the shallow and deep waters of the Gulf of Mexico, the onshore U.S. Gulf Coast of Texas and Louisiana, the Anadarko and Arkoma Basins, the North Sea, and China's Bohai Bay. At the close of 2003 the company had proved developed and undeveloped reserves of oil totaling 37.8 million barrels and 1.09 trillion cubic feet of gas. About 60 percent of these reserves were located onshore, with the balance in the Gulf of Mexico. Newfield is a public company trading on the New York Stock Exchange.

Chairman and Founder Launching Tenneco's Business in the 1960s

Newfield's chairman, Joe B. Foster, was the man most responsible for the founding of the company. He was born and raised in the Texas oil patch, the son of an oilman. He attended Texas A&M University and graduated first in his petroleum engineering class while simultaneously earning a business ad-

ministration degree. He went to work for a new oil company that would become known as Tenneco Oil Exploration & Production. In the 1960s he and some colleagues spearheaded an effort to get Tenneco involved in offshore drilling in the Gulf of Mexico. Foster became manager of exploration and distinguished himself by aggressively acquiring leases, so that in the aftermath of the 1973 oil embargo Tenneco was well stocked with properties and in a position to prosper. Foster was also responsible for establishing a team concept with a multidisciplinary approach that was unusual for the day. As a result, he built employee loyalty, a factor that would become important in the creation of Newfield and its subsequent success.

Foster became a director and executive vice-president, in charge of Tenneco's worldwide operations in oil and gas, and eventually became president of the company. Then in May 1988, in what was considered a shocking move, Tenneco decided to sell its oil and gas properties, despite Foster's objections. Foster took steps to develop a leveraged buyout plan to acquire some of Tenneco's Gulf of Mexico properties, recruiting key employees and enlisting the help of investment banker Shearson Lehman Hutton. After bidding began on the properties, however, the price of oil dropped by four dollars a barrel, dealing a psychological blow to Foster's effort to raise adequate funds, which also was hindered because so many of the properties were undeveloped and banks were reluctant to gamble on mere potential. In the end, the bidders with greater resources—the likes of Arco, Amoco, Chevron, Mesa, and British Gas—acquired Tenneco's properties for an aggregate $7.3 million. It was a major disappointment for Foster, and the several million dollars he received in severance was inadequate consolation. Nevertheless, he considered his treatment by Tenneco as "fair and generous." He told *Oil & Gas Investor* in July 1989, "They gave me my day in court and an opportunity to make the LBO attempt."

Incorporating Newfield in December 1988

Some 300 people in Foster's Lafayette, Louisiana, division office were also out of work, so that when Foster decided to launch a start-up oil and gas company, he was able to recruit the top two dozen people, who all agreed to invest some of their severance pay to fund the venture as well as to take major pay cuts until the business caught on. The new company was incorporated in December 1988 as Newfield Exploration Company. It started out with $9.1 million in the bank, $1.3 million coming from Foster himself, plus funding from two investor groups: the Houston investment firm of Duncan Cook & Co., headed by Charles W. Duncan, Jr., and The University of Texas Systems Permanent University and Common Trust funds, which until this time had only been allowed to invest in dividend-paying stocks and bonds. All told, about a third of the seed money came from the employees, a third from Duncan Cook, and a third from The University of Texas (which also pledged to provide another $3 million in loans). Foster and his team had a tremendous amount of experience and record of success in finding oil. They and their backers were banking on their ability to replicate what they had done at Tenneco. As part of the business plan, Newfield concentrated on one segment of the market: the shallow waters of the Gulf, 100 yards offshore in a stretch of the Louisiana coast that was known to produce gas. The company also was devoted to being a low-cost producer, one able to weather difficult times. Because employees had a financial stake, they were personally committed to the idea of saving money wherever possible. This commitment was even reflected in the way the company chose to furnish its offices. Newfield's new controller, who during the previous decade had done Tenneco's purchasing, picked up Tenneco's old desks and chairs for 25 cents on the dollar. One area where Foster would not stint, however, was on technology and information. The company spent more than a third of its start-up funds, $3.5 million, to procure seismic data on 30,000 acres of the Gulf of Mexico.

After analyzing the seismic data, the Newfield team located desirable leases. The company drilled its first well in the Gulf in August 1989 but it came up dry, as did two more wells drilled between then and February 1990. A fourth well had the misfortune of capsizing because strong currents knocked the foundation out from under the rig. When Newfield finally succeeded in drilling the well, it also proved to be a dry hole. By the end of March 1990, the company had just $100,000 of its initial funds remaining, nine of the ex-Tenneco employees had left, and Foster was taking care of payroll out of his own bank account. Due to falling gas and oil prices and rising exploration costs, it was not the most opportune time to be operating in the Gulf of Mexico. Moreover, most of the reserves in the Gulf had already been tapped, leaving just leftover pockets that were not large enough for the majors to bother with and too difficult to locate without seismic data and a lot of engineering expertise. An investment bank that was planning to make a private placement of Newfield stock was now ready to back out, and only intense lobbying by Foster saved the deal. In April 1990 Newfield received a much needed infusion of cash, $37 million, from such investors as Yale and Duke Universities, Dartmouth College, and Warburg, Pincus Investors, L.P. Finally, on Memorial Day weekend 1990 Newfield located its first discovery, 300,000 barrels of oil and 20 billion cubic feet of gas. Days later

Newfield bought its first property, adding 250,000 barrels of oil and 24 billion cubic feet of gas. More leases would soon be acquired, adding another 39 billion cubic feet of natural gas.

The start-up had turned the corner and would soon erase the losses accumulated during the first year. Late in 1990 it made its first operated exploratory discovery, which led to a drilling program of six wells in 1991. Because of a dropoff in activity in the Gulf, Tenneco, by drilling 18 wells in 1991, became one of the most active drillers in the area. Newfield's ability to control overhead costs was a key factor in its success. The company spent an average of $2 million per well, about half as much as many rivals.

From the beginning, Foster intended to take Newfield public, in large part to provide a way for the investors, both institutional and employees, who had been so instrumental in launching the company, to gain liquidity. In 1991 the company posted income of $2.2 million, followed by $11.2 million in 1992. Believing the time was now right to go public, Newfield completed an offering in November 1993, underwritten by Goldman, Sachs and PaineWebber, netting $57.3 million. Because the company had no debt to pay down, the proceeds were earmarked to fund drilling in 1994 and be available should an acquisition opportunity arise. Shares of Newfield stock began trading on the New York Stock Exchange.

Moving Onshore in 1995

Newfield continued to successfully drill offshore in the Gulf of Mexico. Revenues reached $69.7 million in 1994 and net income totaled $14.4 million. A year later revenues improved to $94.6 million and income topped $16.2 million. It was in 1995 that Newfield expanded beyond the shallow waters off the Louisiana coast, moving onshore in Louisiana for the first time. In this way, should offshore rig rates increase, the company would still have a place to drill economically. The fields chosen were similar to the geology and geophysics with which the company was familiar offshore. In addition, Newfield could apply its expertise in 3D seismic technology to an area that had not been studied as systematically as the Gulf. The first significant onshore success came in 1998 with the drilling of an exploratory well in the Lafayette area of Louisiana. But Newfield remained active in the Gulf. In 1995 it was the 17th largest producer in the Gulf of Mexico. The company drilled 16 exploratory wells, of which ten resulted in discoveries, making it the seventh most active driller in the region.

Revenues grew at a steady clip in the mid-1990s, reaching $149.3 million in 1996 and approaching $200 million in 1997. Net income grew to $38.5 million in 1996 and $40.6 million in 1997. Commodity prices fell in 1998, hurting everyone in the oil and gas business. Newfield saw its revenues decline slightly to $195.7 million, but it recorded a net loss of $57.7 million. Prices did not rebound until the spring of 1999, and when they did, Newfield resumed its pattern of strong growth. Revenues increased to more than $265.6 million and net income totaled $32.2 million in 1999. The year also was marked by a continued effort to diversify. The company expanded its area of focus by entering into joint ventures to drill in new areas of the Louisiana and Texas Gulf coasts. Newfield also made an international move, acquiring a pair of offshore oilfields in Australia. (Two

Key Dates:

1988: The company is incorporated.
1990: The company drills its first successful well.
1993: The company is taken public.
1995: The company engages in its first onshore drilling.
2001: Lariat Petroleum is acquired for approximately $333 million.
2002: EEX Corporation is acquired through a $280 million stock transaction and the assumption of $360 million in debt.

years earlier the company had made its first overseas acquisition when it picked up a 35 percent interest in a property in Bohai Bay, offshore China, as part of the purchase of Huffco International.) In addition, there was a change in the management ranks at Newfield announced in November 1999: Effective in February 2000 Foster would step down as chief executive officer, replaced by David A. Trice. Foster would stay on as chairman, however, and remain very much involved in Newfield's affairs.

Newfield became a serious player onshore in 2000 when it paid $139 million for three producing gas fields in south Texas. It was by far the largest acquisition in the company's history, but it would soon be eclipsed by the purchase of Lariat Petroleum, an independent exploration and production company, in a deal that closed in January 2001. The total cost of approximately $333 million included $265 million in cash and $68 million in stock. Not only did Newfield significantly bolster its onshore drilling program, further reducing risk to a downturn in the offshore sector, it added a new area of focus—Oklahoma's Anadarko Basin—as well as Lariat's team of experienced employees. Another significant event in 2000 took place in offshore China, where in August Newfield's joint venture drilled a successful well, capable of producing 2,700 barrels of oil a day.

Revenues reached $480 million in 2000 with net income soaring to $132.4 million. A year later revenues continued to grow to $714 million and profits were again strong, totaling $119 million. In 2002 Newfield completed another major deal, acquiring EEX Corporation in an exchange of stock valued at $280 million, plus the assumption of $360 million in debt and existing obligations. The addition of EEX was important for a number of reasons. Its onshore properties located in Newfield's area of concentration in south Texas were highly complemen-

tary, transforming Newfield into one of the largest independent gas producers in the basin. EEX also afforded Newfield an opportunity to become involved in the deep waters of the Gulf of Mexico. For some months, the company had been assembling a deepwater team and the EEX addition gave it an impressive slate of properties and a running start. EEX had become involved in deep water some 20 years earlier but was unable to exploit its deepwater acreage, much of which had gone untested.

After experiencing a dropoff in revenues in 2002, dipping to $626.8 million, and a decrease in net income to $73.8 million, Newfield experienced a record-breaking year in 2003, topping the $1 billion mark in revenues while recording net income of $199.5 million. The company enjoyed deepwater success in the Gulf and took steps to transfer the knowledge it gained there to another part of the world: the North Sea. At the same time, it sold off its Australian holding. All told, Newfield was well stocked with promising properties, both onshore and offshore, both domestically and internationally. Given the company's track record of consistent success, there was every reason to expect Newfield to maintain a strong pattern of growth for the foreseeable future.

Principal Subsidiaries

Newfield Explorations Mid-Continent Inc.; Newfield International Holdings Inc.; Newfield Gulf Coast Inc.; EEX Exploration and Production Company LLC.

Principal Competitors

BP p.l.c.; The Houston Exploration Company; Royal Dutch/Shell Group of Companies.

Further Reading

Calkins, Laurel Brubaker, "Tenneco Exes Team Up to Form New Energy Firm," *Houston Business Journal,* January 23, 1989, p. 11.

Cederberg, Wendy, "Reunited and Ready to Roll," *Oil & Gas Investor,* July 1989, p. 43.

Poruban, Steven, "Newfield Balances Experience, Technology for Success in the Gulf of Mexico Region," *Oil & Gas Journal,* February 22, 1999, p. 18.

Snow, Nick, "Deeper Roots," *Oil & Gas Investor,* July 2002, p. 57.

Solomon, Caleb, "Oil Firm's Best Find: Penny-Pinching," *Wall Street Journal,* September 30, 1992, p. B1.

—Ed Dinger

Neyveli Lignite Corporation Ltd.

Neyveli House
135 Periyar EVR H
Chennai 600 010
India
Fax: 91 44 2825 5499
Web site: http://www.nlcindia.co.in

Public Company (94% Government-Owned)
Incorporated: 1956
Employees: 22,200
Sales: $601.1 million (2003)
Stock Exchanges: Bombay
Ticker Symbol: NELG.BO
NAIC: 212111 Bituminous Coal and Lignite Surface
    Mining; 221122 Electric Power Distribution; 325311
    Nitrogenous Fertilizer Manufacturing

Neyveli Lignite Corporation Ltd. (NLC) is India's largest lignite mining company, and is also one of the country's leading power generation companies. The company operates three open cast mines in Neyveli, in the state of Tamil Nadu at the southeastern tip of India, producing some 24 million tons of high-grade lignite per year. Mine I, the company's original mine, is operated over an area of nearly 17 square kilometers and offers a reserve of nearly 300 million tons. Mine II, first tapped in early 1984 and expanded in the early 1990s, features a reserve of nearly 400 million tons. The total reserves in the Neyveli field are estimated at more than two billion tons. Most of that production is used in NLC's two thermal power generation plants, which combine for a total capacity of 2,070 megawatts. After shutting down its fertilizer and briquette and carbonization plants in the early 2000s, NLC has begun a drive to expand its power generation capacity. In 2003, the company began construction of a greenfield power generation facility in Tuticorin, in Tamil Nadu, with a proposed capacity of as much as 1,000 megawatts. In 2004, the company received approval to expand beyond its home state, and is beginning preparations to build a 250 megawatt facility in Bikaner, near Rajasthan. NLC has also been tapped to restart the nearly 4,000-megawatt plant in Hirma, originally developed by a Mirant-Reliant partnership. Owned at 94 percent by the Indian government, NLC has as its primary customer the Tamil Nadu Electricity Board. In 2003 the company posted revenues of INR 2,681.48 crore ($601.1 million).

Powering the Economy in the 1950s

The vast Indian subcontinent had always offered an abundant supply of natural resources. Particular interest was placed on exploring for fossil fuel sources in what was later to become the Tamil Nadu region along the country's southeastern tip. Among the first to be discovered were the peat fields in Calimere, in 1828. The first lignite deposits, a still more valuable fuel source, were located along the coast region near Cannanore in1830. This initial deposit was followed by the discovery of others in the region, at Beypore, Pondicherry, and elsewhere. French engineers began drilling bore holes in then French-dominated Bahoor, and succeeded in locating significant lignite deposits in Kasargod and in the region around Cuddalore, near Neyveli, in 1884.

Attention again focused on the region around Neyveli in the 1930s. Neyveli was then a small village in Tamil Nadu; its chief resources at the time were its cashew and jackfruit forests. The earliest discovery of exploitable lignite deposits in Neyveli was attributed to Jambulingam Mudaliyar, a prominent local landlord who controlled some 600 acres across Neyveli, Cuddalore, Mandarakuppam, and Virudhachalam. Farms covered only a small part of Mudaliyar's land. In the early 1930s, Mudaliyar began sinking well holes, searching for a source of water in order to transform more of his holdings into cultivatable land. Water proved easy to find—but brought with it pieces of a black substance that local workers called ''black clay,'' which were thrown away. Yet, once dried by the sun, the ''black clay'' proved highly combustible.

Mudaliyar brought the existence of lignite to the attention of the British authorities, hoping to convince them to launch a lignite mining operation in Neyveli. Mudaliyar began drilling new bore holes in 1935, discovering large quantities of the substance. Samples were sent to the governor of Madras for testing, yet the British colonial government remained un-

Company Perspectives:

Neyveli, home of the Neyveli Lignite Corporation, is India's energy-bridge to the 21st century and a fulfillment of Pandit Nehru's vision. Incidentally, Nehru and NLC share a common birthday (14.11.1956). Nehru launched the mining operations with his golden touch in May 1957. Ever since, there has been no looking back. NLC has achieved the objectives it has set for itself, fulfilling its corporate mission to be the leader in the industry.

interested in pursuing the project. Instead, Madras-based Binny & Co. began sinking bore wells in Aziz Nagar, near Neyveli, in 1941. That company succeeded in discovering a significant lignite deposit, but, lacking the equipment to pursue further drilling operations, the company withdrew.

The colonial government's Geological Survey of India at last began drilling in Neyveli in 1943. Over a three-year period, more than 30 bore wells were sunk, confirming the region's lignite potential. Following India's independence, the new government appointed H.K. Ghosh—who later earned the nickname "Lignite Ghosh"—to oversee further lignite exploration activities. Ghosh began sinking a new series of wells in 1947. Initial wells were abandoned, however, after they became blocked with water and sand. By 1948, Ghosh had discovered the first viable site, and succeeded in drawing out samples of lignite.

Ghosh revealed the ambitiousness of his project in 1949, when he drafted plans to establish a vast open-cut, mechanized mine covering an area of some 14 square kilometers. Ghosh began coordinating bids for the project that year. Preparations were made to drill a more extensive series of bore wells in the proposed area, and under Ghosh's direction, the drilling of 175 bore wells began in 1951. A second series of 150 wells was also launched that year, this time in Vriddhachalam under the auspices of the Tamil Nadu government. Ghosh's efforts were crowned with success—by the end of the drilling project, Ghosh had revealed potential lignite reserves of some two billion tons.

Approval for a pilot quarry was granted in 1952. By 1953, Ghosh had succeeded in mining the first 100 tons of lignite. The development was all the more significant because of the high quality of the field's lignite, which had a relatively high moisture content compared to other lignite deposits. A visit by Indian President Nehru in 1954 brought government backing to the lignite mining project, and in 1955, the Tamil Nadu state government transferred oversight of the project to the central government.

Neyveli Lignite Corporation was created as a government-owned enterprise in 1956 in order to launch the full-scale exploitation of the lignite field. NLC's mandate was to produce lignite, and to construct and operate a lignite-burning thermo-electric plant providing electrical power to the state of Tamil Nadu. Construction on Neyveli Mine I began in 1957, using technology and equipment brought in from Germany. The mine by then extended over an area of nearly 17 square kilometers, with an estimated reserve of 287 million tons. Mine I was constructed to produce a capacity of 6.5 million tons per year.

With an "overburden" varying from 70 to 95 meters, the Neyveli field's first lignite seam—with a thickness ranging from ten to 23 meters—was exposed only in 1961. Full-scale lignite mining was launched in 1962. That year saw the commissioning of the first stage of NLC's Thermal Plant Station I. Built with technology and assistance from the Soviet Union, TPS-1's initial capacity stood at just 50 megawatts. By the end of the decade, however, NLC had commissioned a total of six 50 megawatt units and three 100 megawatt units. All of NLC's power production was then taken up by the Tamil Nadu Electricity Board.

In the mid-1960s, however, NLC diverted some of its lignite production to fuel its extension into two new areas. The first was the launch of its Fertilizer Plant, producing urea, a byproduct of its lignite mining operations. The second was a Briquetting and Carbonization Plant, established that same year to produce more than 3.25 million tons of charcoal and 2.6 million tons of coke per year. That plant also produced such byproducts as carbolic acid, xylenol, phenol, and neutral oils and other chemicals.

As India began its industrialization program in the 1970s, demand for electrical power rose steadily. By the late 1970s the decision was made to extend NLC's operations to include a second mine, which in turn provided support for a new thermal power station. The new mine, Mine II, was located some five kilometers south of the original mine, on a 26 square kilometer site that exploited the same lignite seam. The total exploitable lignite deposits at the site were estimated at 398 million tons. Construction of the open pit mine, with an overburden reaching up to 103 meters and a lignite seam between eight and 22 meters in thickness, was launched in 1978. Mine II's initial production capacity was placed at 4.7 million tons per year.

Mine II's lignite seam was exposed by September 1984, and full-scale lignite production began in 1985. By then, NLC had already been granted authorization to increase the scale of the Mine II project to 10.7 million tons per year. The mine reached full capacity in 1991. Mine II's production fueled NLC's Thermal Power Station II. Construction began on the new plant in 1978, with an initial capacity of 630 megawatts. With the increase in Mine II's production levels, TPS II's capacity was expanded as well, to 1,470 megawatts. The first 210-megawatt unit was commissioned in 1986, and the plant reached full capacity in 1993. Also in 1986, the Indian government converted NLC to a public company, selling shares to institutional investors as well as placing a small number of shares on the Bombay Stock Exchange. Nonetheless, the government's control of NLC remained at more than 94 percent.

Emphasizing Power Generation in the New Century

By that time the company had launched a Life Extension Project on TPS I, intended to extend the plant's viability by another 15 years. The project, launched in 1992, was completed in 1999. In the meantime, NLC had also been granted authorization to expand the capacity of the Mine I site, raising total annual production to 10.5 million tons. As part of that effort, the company also launched an extension of TPS-1 in 1996, adding an additional 420 megawatts to the plant's total capacity.

In 1998, the government authorized NLC to expand its lignite production yet again, with the construction of an exten-

megawatts. These projects were expected to be completed by 2006.

At the same time, NLC began plans to develop a new 250-megawatt power generation plant at Rajasthan, which was activated in 2002. That project was approved in 2004. The company also launched development of a new greenfield site at Tuticorin. Initially planned for a capacity of 500 megawatts, in 2003 NLC announced its intention instead to build a 1,000 megawatt plant on the Tuticorin site. By 2003, NLC also appeared likely to revive a 2,000 megawatt plant in Orissa, part of the Hirma project initially developed by a partnership between Mirant and Reliant. In that year, the company also received an invitation from the Madhya Pradesh state government to construct and operate a 1,000-megawatt plant there, a tribute to NLC's technological and operational expertise. With plans in place to increase its total power generation capacity to more than 6,000 watts by the end of the decade, NLC appeared to be redefining itself, from a lignite mining concern to one of India's leading self-sufficient energy producers.

Key Dates:

1956: Neyveli Lignite Corporation is established to exploit lignite deposits in Neyveli area in Tamil Nadu state in India.
1957: Construction begins on Mine I and Thermal Power Station I (TPS 1).
1962: Lignite mining operations begin; TPS I is commissioned.
1966: Fertilizer Plant and Briquette & Carbonization Plant open.
1978: Second lignite mine and thermal power station are launched.
1983: Mine II begins operations.
1986: TPS II is commissioned.
1992: Life Extension Project on Mine I begins.
1996: Mine II and TPS II are expanded.
2000: Construction begins on Mine IA.
2002: Mine II and TPS II expansions are completed; shutdown of Briquette & Carbonization Plant.
2003: Shutdown of Fertilizer Plant; company begins development of new power plant at Rajasthan.
2004: Company launches greenfield power plant at Tuticorin.

sion to its original mine as a new site, Mine IA. Construction of the mine began in 2000, with production of lignite expected to begin by the mid-2000s. The company also began preparations for the expansion of Mine II and the proposed construction of a Mine III, launching an exploration and drilling operation in 1999.

Low demand for fertilizer products led the company to close its fertilizer plant in 2003. By then, NLC had already shut down its outdated Briquetting & Carbonization operations as well. Instead, NLC focused on expanding its power generation operations. In 2002, the company announced its intention to expand production of Mine II to 15 million tons per year in order to fuel the extension of its TPS-2 facility to nearly 2,000

Principal Competitors

Fushun Coal Mine Bureau; RWE AG; Pingdingshan Coal Group Company Ltd.; Rostovugol; American Electric Power Company Inc.; Kreka Coal Mine; Mono Bobov Dol AD; Coal India Ltd.

Further Reading

"Indian State Co to Double Capacity of Proposed Power Project," *AsiaPulse News*, April 14, 2003.
"India's PFC Inks MOU with NLC to Provide Financial Support," *Asia Pulse News*, April 26, 2004.
"PIB Clearance for Barsingsar Power Project," *India Business Insight*, April 26, 2004.
Rajkumar, Deeptha, "Neyveli Lignite on Expansion Mode," *India Business Insight*, November 28, 2002.
Ramesh, M., "New Plant Will Solve Surplus Lignite Problem," *Business Line*, March 12, 2003.
Sundar, Sowmya, "Nevyeli Lignite: Buy," *Business Line*, March 16, 2003.

—M.L. Cohen

North Atlantic Trading Company Inc.

257 Park Avenue South
New York, New York 10010-7304
U.S.A.
Telephone: (212) 253-8185
Fax: (212) 253-8296
Web site: http://www.zigzag.com

Private Company
Incorporated: 1988 as National Tobacco Corporation
Employees: 89
Sales: $101.6 million (2003)
NAIC: 312229 Other Tobacco Product Manufacturing

North Atlantic Trading Company Inc. is a New York City-based holding company for several subsidiaries involved in the tobacco industry. National Tobacco Company, L.P. is the third largest loose-leaf chewing tobacco company in the United States. Its most famous brand is Beech-Nut. North Atlantic Operating Company, Inc., under an agreement with Bollore, S.A., sells cigarette papers, tubes, loose tobacco, and cigarette-making machines under the world famous Zig-Zag brand. North Atlantic Cigarette Company, Inc. markets and distributes Zig-Zag Premium Cigarettes. North Atlantic's chairman and chief executive officer, Thomas F. Helms, Jr., owns 49 percent of the privately held company.

Formation by Helms in 1988

Helms started his business career at Revlon Inc. He held a number of sales and marketing positions from 1964 to 1979 before becoming general manager of Revlon's Etherea Cosmetics and Designer Fragrances Division. In 1983 he was named president of Helme Tobacco Company, the smokeless tobacco subsidiary of Culbro Corporation that manufactured and marketed Navy and Railroad Mills dry snuff; Gold River, Wilver Creek, and Redwood moist snuff; and chewing tobacco under the Mail Pouch, Chattanooga Chew, and Lancaster brands. Two years later, in September 1985, Culbro announced that Helme was up for sale. Several weeks later Helms resigned in order to put together a leveraged buyout proposal. In the end, however,

the business was sold to Swisher & Son. Inc., the cigar subsidiary of American Maize-Products Co.

Despite failing to buy Helme, Helms decided to remain in the tobacco business. In 1988 he and an investor group led by Lehman Brothers formed National Tobacco Corporation to acquire the smokeless tobacco division of Lorillard Tobacco Company. Lorillard was the oldest tobacco manufacturer in the country, launched in 1760 by French immigrant Pierre Lorillard in New York City to make pipe tobacco, cigars, plug chewing tobacco, and snuff. The company would become a pioneer in marketing, paying farmers for painted signs on the sides of their barns, initiating the use of trading cards, and according to some, introducing the cigar store Indian. In the 1890s Lorillard introduced Beech-Nut chewing tobacco. It was also during this period that it became part of American Tobacco Co., the massive tobacco trust created by legendary James Buchanan Duke, who parlayed the rights to a cigarette-making machine into the creation of a corporation that at one point controlled 90 percent of the U.S. market in cigarette sales. In 1911 the trust was ruled in violation of the Sherman Anti-Trust Act and dissolved. Lorillard along with R.J. Reynolds and Liggett & Meyers became products of the breakup.

While Helms remained in New York City to manage the company, National Tobacco took over Lorillard's manufacturing facilities in Louisville, Kentucky, where it produced loose-leaf chewing tobacco under a variety of labels. The next major step for the company came in 1997 with the acquisition of North Atlantic Trading Co. Inc., which had been formed by investors in 1993 to make the $39 million acquisition of Zig-Zag's distribution rights from UST Inc. To finance the Zig-Zag purchase and restructure its debt, National Tobacco negotiated a $300 million high-yield bond issue and loan package assembled by a group of European Investors with Natwest, the U.S. investment branch of Britain's National Westminster PLC, leading the effort. Upon completion of the acquisition, National Tobacco gained the exclusive rights to market and distribute Zig-Zag cigarette papers in the United States, Canada, and other international markets. It also took on the North Atlantic Trading Company name as part of a plan to invest in other tobacco-related areas. The Louisville facility was using only about one-third of its capacity, leading management to think about taking on new product lines. The most likely addition was dry snuff, but there was also talk at this stage of introducing a new blend of loose-leaf tobacco for "make-your-own" (MYO) cigarettes, and even the possibility of applying the Zig-Zag name to a new brand of cigarettes.

Zig-Zag Origins Dating to the 1890s

The Zig-Zag brand had strong name recognition, although generally associated with marijuana use in the 1960s and 1970s. In fact, Zig-Zag rolling papers had been in the marketplace since the 1890s. According to lore, the cigarette was conceived by a French soldier during the battle of Sevastopol in the mid-19th century, at a time when tobacco smokers used a pipe. Because the soldier's clay pipe was shattered by a bullet, he rolled some loose tobacco in a scrap of paper torn from a bag of gunpowder. This makeshift way to smoke tobacco was improved upon by Maurice and Jacque Braunstein, who in 1894 perfected the process of interleaving papers in a zig-zag manner to produce a slower, smoother burn; hence they called their papers Zig-Zag. In 1900 the rolling papers gained international fame when they were awarded a gold medal at the Universal Exposition in Paris. UST obtained the distribution rights to Zig-Zag from French manufacturer Bollore in 1938.

North Atlantic faced some difficulties entering the MYO field. It had to contend with counterfeit Zig-Zag cigarette papers, the sale of which the company estimated cost it $10 million in sales and another $7 million in out-of-pocket expenses investigating and litigating counterfeiting claims. North Atlantic also became embroiled in litigation with a competitor, Republic Tobacco, L.P., which sold cigarette papers under such brand names as Drum, Job, and Top. In 1998 Republic launched an incentive program to its wholesale and retail customers. According to North Atlantic, Republic pasted its advertising materials over Zig-Zag point of purchase vendor displays. North Atlantic responded by writing letters to Republic's wholesale and retail customers, maintaining that some of Republic's trade promotions might violate antitrust and unfair competition laws. In one letter, North Atlantic disparaged Republic's rebate program as little more than "smoke and mirrors," and stated that North Atlantic's lawyers had initiated legal action, alleging that Republic had infringed on Zig-Zag's patent and trademark rights. In truth, North Atlantic had not filed suit. On June 30, 1998, Republic was first to file a complaint, claiming unfair competition, defamation, false advertising, and violations of Consumer Fraud Acts, among other charges. North Atlantic countersued on July 15, 1998, claiming that Republic's use of activities such as exclusivity agreements, rebates, incentive programs, and buy-backs violated state and federal antitrust and unfair competition laws.

Republic's antitrust claims were dismissed before discovery was completed. Then over the course of the next few years all of the charges by both parties were dismissed, with the exception of Republic's defamation claim. A four-day trial was conducted in July 2003 in Illinois and a jury ruled in favor of Republic, awarding it $18.6 million, of which $8.4 million was general damages and $10.2 million punitive damages. Later in 2003 the court reduced the award by 60 percent to $7.44 million and Republic accepted the change. But in January 2004 North Atlantic appealed the judgment, including the finding of liability, ensuring that the matter would continue to wend its way through the court system.

Another challenge facing North Atlantic was the diminishing number of tobacco chewers. Not only was the demographic of the core user aging, but moist snuff products were luring away customers. As a result, chewing tobacco sales dropped 4 percent each of the last three years of the 1990s. In 2000, in an effort to concentrate on the growing MYO cigarette market, North Atlantic agreed to sell its four chewing tobacco brands—Beech-Nut, Durango, Trophy, and Havana Blossom—to Stockholm-based Swedish Match and its North American subsidiary for $165 million. Swedish Match was North America's leader in smokeless tobacco sales and owned the top-selling chewing tobacco, Red Man, which controlled about one-third of the premium segment of the chewing tobacco market, compared with Beech-Nut's 12 percent. The deal did not, however, pass muster with the Federal Trade Commission, which ultimately quashed the deal on antitrust grounds.

In 2003 North Atlantic was on the other end of a failed acquisition, as it attempted to enter the cigarette business. In February of that year the company reached an agreement to purchase Star Tobacco, a Star Scientific Inc. subsidiary, for $80 million. Based in Chester, Virginia, Star made deep-discount, low-toxin cigarettes under four brand names using a tobacco-curing process that substantially reduced the number of cancer-causing toxins, nitrosamines, in tobacco leaf. But in July 2003 the parties agreed to terminate the deal, citing "uncertainties in the tobacco industry." Star experienced a 22 percent drop in sales during the first quarter and one of its key markets, Minnesota, increased its excise tax by 35 cents per pack, factors that likely caused North Atlantic to have second thoughts about the deal. Scuttling the acquisition cost North Atlantic $2 million in earnest money it had placed in escrow, as well as another $1.3 million in related expenses.

In 2003 North Atlantic decided to enter the cigarette business, taking advantage of its Zig-Zag brand by launching an all-natural premium cigarette under its name. The idea appeared sound on a number of levels. There was little chance of cannibalizing Zig-Zag papers, since the MYO customer was not the kind to buy packaged brands, let alone higher-priced cigarettes. The Zig-Zag line was being positioned between popular brands such as Marlboro, Camel, and Winstons, and the more expensive brands such as Natural American Spirit. The target customers were people 25 to 45 years old with an average income of $35,000. North Atlantic also hoped to leverage Zig-Zag by focusing on the cigar shops and tobacconists that already sold the rolling papers, eschewing convenience stores where the bulk of cigarette sales were made. Despite these advantages, it remained a difficult time to enter the cigarette business, due in large part to the 1998 settlement of tobacco litigation that cost tobacco companies hundreds of billions of dollars and resulted in the price of cigarettes increasing by 85 percent over the next several years.

"In lieu of a share of the damages for past misdeeds," according to *Forbes* in a June 2004 profile, "newcomers like Zig-Zag must pay deposits into escrow accounts to cover potential tort claims. So far, legal costs to set up these accounts have come to $750,000 for the 22 markets North Atlantic can now sell in. 'Having to deal with each state, whose legislatures are constantly changing laws, is like guerrilla warfare,' says [cigarette division head Lawrence] Wexler." Zig-Zag cigarettes premiered in Dallas, Los Angeles, Miami, and Seattle.

Acquiring Stoker Inc. in 2003

In November 2003 North Atlantic succeeded in completing an acquisition, paying $22.5 million for Dresden, Tennessee-based Stoker, Inc. The addition of Stoker's product lines strengthened both North Atlantic's MYO cigarette business and smokeless tobacco business. Focusing on the value-oriented niche, Stoker was the fifth largest manufacturer and distributor of loose-leaf chewing tobacco, sold under the Stoker, Our Pride, and numerous other brand names. It also offered moist snuff and pipe tobacco brands, as well as five brands of MYO tobacco. Of particular importance was Stoker's strong position in the 16-ounce value-oriented bag category. In addition, Stoker brought with it a catalog operation, devoted mostly to tobacco products.

After acquiring Stoker, North Atlantic informed Louisville city officials that it intended to consolidate its operations, either in its new Dresden facility or in Louisville. Both the city—which was preparing for the departure of Brown & Williamson Tobacco Corp. and a Philip Morris USA plant—and the state of Kentucky were determined to keep North Atlantic's operation and worked together to fashion an incentive package to encour-

age the company to consolidate its tobacco manufacturing operations in Louisville. In June 2004 North Atlantic agreed to stay, accepting a package worth $3.8 million if the company met hiring goals. North Atlantic's plan was to invest as much as $24.6 million over the next three years as it closed the Tennessee manufacturing operation and incorporated it into the Louisville plant. Only about a dozen employees would remain in Dresden to run the catalog and fulfillment operations.

In little more than a year, North Atlantic had expanded its operation to include a brand of premiere cigarettes and value-priced smokeless tobacco and MYO cigarette products. Yet what was likely to drive growth over the next few years was the MYO business. With taxes continuing to rise on manufactured cigarettes, the number of smokers electing to roll their own was growing steadily. In 1989 MYO cigarettes accounted for just 0.5 percent of the market. By 2004 that number had grown to 2 percent and was continuing to rise.

Principal Subsidiaries

National Tobacco Company, L.P.; North Atlantic Operating Company, Inc.; North Atlantic Cigarette Company, Inc.; National Tobacco Finance Corporation; Stoker, Inc.

Principal Competitors

Conwood Sales Co., L.P.; Swisher International Group Inc.; UST Inc.

Further Reading

Green, Marcus, "Loose-Tobacco Maker May Grow," *Courier-Journal,* December 5, 2003.

Hill, Toya Richards, "National Tobacco Considers Expansion," *Business First of Louisville,* December 4, 2003.

Kamuf, Rachael, "Zig Zag Purchase May Boost Jobs at National Tobacco," *Business First of Louisville,* August 25, 1997, p. 10.

Sachdev, Ameet, "War of Words Over Tobacco Gets Ugly," *Chicago Tribune,* July 11, 2003.

Smillie, Dirk, "Slow Burn," *Forbes,* June 21, 2004, p. 177.

Wolfe, Bill, "Leaf Plant May Grow Hiring," *Courier-Journal,* June 16, 2004.

—Ed Dinger

NTL Inc.

76 Hammersmith Rd.
London
W14 8UD
United Kingdom
Telephone: (44) 2079673338
Fax: (44) 2079673322
Web site: http://www.ntl.com

Public Company
Incorporated: 1993 as International CableTel
Employees: 15,130
Sales: $3.27 billion (2003)
Stock Exchanges: NASDAQ
Ticker Symbol: NTLI
NAIC: 551112 Offices of Other Holding Companies;
    515210 Cable and Other Subscription Programming

NTL Inc., based in London but registered in the United States and listed on the NASDAQ, has survived the global telecom crash at the beginning of the 21st century by refocusing itself as one of the United Kingdom's top cable-based broadband communications providers. The company is the leading provider of broadband Internet and related services in the United Kingdom, with nearly one million customers. Backed by its own hybrid fiber optic-coaxial network, built at a total cost of more than £12 billion during the 1990s, NTL is able to offer cable television programming; local, national, and international telephone services; and high-speed Internet access to customers through a single line. The company also operates the United Kingdom's national network of broadcast towers, providing analog and digital transmission services for the country's broadcast and satellite-based television networks. The tower network, featuring more than 2,300 broadcast towers and land sites throughout the United Kingdom, has not only provided NTL with a natural backbone for the deployment of its cable-based network, but also provides it with unique opportunities for the deployment of wireless transmission services, both for itself and for third-party providers. NTL operates through five primary divisions: ntl: home, its consumer division, which represents more than 63.5 percent of group sales; ntl: business, providing voice, data, and Internet services to the corporate and community markets, and representing 27 percent of sales; ntl: broadcast, which oversees the group's transmission tower operations, representing 9.5 percent of total revenues; and ntl: networks and ntl: carrier services, which operate the group's network infrastructure and carrier telecommunications services, respectively. Crippled by debt garnered during its rapid growth sprint made during the late 1990s, NTL was forced to file for bankruptcy protection in 2002, yet emerged from its Chapter 11 restructuring at the beginning of 2003. As part of its restructuring, the company split off its non-U.K. operations, and, during 2003 announced its intention to sell off its loss-making cable television operations in Ireland in order to focus exclusively on the U.K. market. Cofounder Barclay Knapp, who survived the group's financial collapse, turned over the CEO spot in the company to Simon Duffy that year.

British Cable Consolidator in the 1990s

NTL was launched in the early 1990s under the name International CableTel by two American businessmen, George Blumenthal and J. Barclay Knapp. The pair had met in the early 1980s when Blumenthal, a wealthy investor who had inherited his father's seat on the New York Stock Exchange, hired Knapp to help him prepare applications for U.S. cellular telephone licenses. Knapp, a former mathematics student at Johns Hopkins University and then enrolled in Harvard Graduate School, instead went into business with Blumenthal. In 1983 the pair established Cellular One, which grew into the highly successful Cellular Communications Inc.

Blumenthal and Knapp sold most of Cellular Communications to AirTouch, later known as Vodaphone, in 1996 for $2.5 billion. By then, Blumenthal and Knapp had already focused their business interests on a new market: the cable television industry in the United Kingdom. Lagging far behind its U.S. counterpart, the U.K. cable television sector had failed to achieve significant penetration levels, which hovered at around the 20 percent mark into the 1990s. Expensive, and burdened by over-large channel offerings, the cable industry was also under imminent threat from the emerging satellite television sector.

In the early 1990s, however, Blumenthal and Knapp came across the case of a U.K.-based cable television operator that had

---

Company Perspectives:

We are people who are passionate about broadband. Imagine the Internet working hundreds of times faster than it does now. And imagine being able to use the phone and watch a film at the same time as you're surfing the Internet. Now imagine an office where you can phone, send e-mails, transfer vast amounts of data, run e-commerce and have videoconferencing all through one simple connection. If you like, think of it as a big fat pipe coming into your home or office, capable of carrying huge amounts of different information at once, backwards and forwards, at a speed unknown until now. And broadband is at the heart of our operations. It brings you the emergency services. It brings you business systems. It brings you home services. It comes through wired or wireless networks, to your choice of device. It brings you freedom.

---

succeeded in selling telephone services to some 30 percent of its customers. The news inspired the pair, who recognized the potential for bundling services via a cable-based platform. As Blumenthal told the *Independent:* ''It changed everything. If you could break the hold of [British Telecom], this is a business model.''

In 1993, Knapp and Blumenthal put up $25 million to establish a new company, International CableTel—registered in the United States—and started bidding for a cable television license in the United Kingdom. The company quickly succeeded in acquiring Insight Communications, which held a license covering nearly one million homes. By forming partnerships, CableTel managed to extend its range to nearly 1.5 million homes by the end of the year. Blumenthal and Knapp also quickly took CableTel public, listing it on the NASDAQ in 1993.

With more than $400 million raised from the public offering, CableTel set out to build the infrastructure it needed to fulfill its ambitions. By 1994, the company had already laid more than 1,500 kilometers of state-of-the-art hybrid fiber optic and coaxial lines. Through the rest of the decade, CableTel would spend more than £4 billion ($6.5 billion) on constructing its fiber optic network. The company's range was also expanding steadily, boosted by the acquisition of the licenses from a number of dormant cable companies. As such, CableTel established a presence in Glasgow, Scotland, and in Cardiff, Wales, among other markets.

By 1995, CableTel had extended its coverage to 2.3 million homes, making it the United Kingdom's third largest cable television provider. Yet the company had already begun to extend itself into the telecommunications market, setting up its business service that year, providing voice and data transmission support. At the same time, CableTel became the first U.K. cable provider to offer Internet access services, with the launch of Cable Online.

By 1996, CableTel had signed up nearly 170,000 customers for its Internet service. The company also sold bandwidth to partners for the creation of ''virtual'' Internet Service Providers, such as VirginNet, launched by Virgin Communications, and Which? Online, created by The Consumers' Association. In October of that year the company at last prepared to test

its bundling concept. The company launched a new service in the test market of Luton, offering telephone services combined with a smaller array of television channels—at a low price. Indeed, at £9 per month, the company's subscribers received 12 stations—including seven cable channels—and local and long-distance telephone services. Corresponding offers from the group's competitors paled in comparison.

The results of that test encouraged CableTel to launch the bundled service across its network by the beginning of 1997. The company's new bundled service proved an instant success, and by the end of the 1990s, CableTel boasted the highest sign-up rate in the industry, with customer penetration rates of nearly 50 percent in some regions.

By then, the company had become a truly major player in the British telecommunications market. In June 1996, CableTel acquired National Transcommunications Ltd., otherwise known as NTL. That company had been formed as a spinoff during the breakup of Britain's Independent Broadcasting Authority (IBA) at the beginning of the 1990s. NTL took over the IBA's operation of the country's independent television transmitter network, which provided national coverage through more than 2,000 broadcast towers. Following the completion of the acquisition, CableTel took over NTL's name and logo as its own, becoming NTL Inc.

NTL now went on a buying spree—gaining, along the way, credit for the consolidation of the United Kingdom's fragmented and underdeveloped cable industry. In February 1998, the company bought Comcast UK Cable Partners, paying $600 million to acquire the operator's license for a region serving more than 1.1 million homes. The Comcast acquisition also added more than 6,500 corporate customers to NTL's business branch.

NTL followed that purchase with two more in mid-1998, paying a total of $1.1 billion for ComTel, with a base of 1.1 million homes in the Midlands and South East regions, and Diamond Cable Communications, which served the East Midlands and more than 1.2 million homes. By the end of that year, NTL boldly positioned itself as a major rival to media giant Rupert Murdoch, whose BskyB had already dominated the British satellite television market and who had recently acquired a stake in the Manchester United football club, as well as its Premier League broadcasting rights. NTL responded by acquiring a stake in Newcastle United, grabbing that team's broadcasting rights, then going on to strike similar deals with other Premier League clubs.

NTL also displayed international expansion ambitions. In 1996, the group bought Northern Ireland's Ulster Cablevision, outbidding its closest rival by more than three to one. In 1999, the company moved into Ireland proper, buying Cablelink, the leading cable provider in that country, then traveled to Australia, where it bought that country's National Transmission Network. By the end of the year, NTL had moved onto the European continent, paying $3.7 billion to acquire Switzerland's leading cable television provider, Cablecom. The following year, NTL acquired France's IG Networks, giving it a 27 percent stake in Noos, one of the country's leading cable television providers, for EUR 563 million ($500 million).

By then, however, NTL had stunned the U.K. cable industry by snapping up one of its major rivals, Cable & Wireless

Key Dates:

1983: George Blumenthal and J. Barclay Knapp establish Cellular Communications, which gains a number of U.S. mobile telephone licenses, then sells the business in 1996 to AirTouch (Vodaphone) for $2.5 billion.

1993: Blumenthal and Knapp launch International Cable-Tel in order to acquire cable television licenses in the United Kingdom; company acquires Insight Communications, then goes public with listing on the NASDAQ.

1995: Company acquires licenses in Wales, Scotland, and Northern Ireland; launches first U.K. cable Internet access service.

1996: Company acquires National Transcommunications Ltd. (NTL).

1997: Company changes name to NTL Inc.

1998: NTL acquires Comcast UK, ComTel, and Diamond Cable Communications; acquires stake in Newcastle soccer team.

1999: NTL acquires Cablelink (Ireland), Cable & Wireless Communications, and Cablecom (Switzerland) in a bid to become a global cable and Internet provider.

2000: Company gains 27 percent stake in French cable operator Noos.

2002: With debt of more than £10 billion, NTL files for Chapter 11 bankruptcy protection; spins off foreign holdings into separate company, NTL Europe.

2003: NTL emerges from bankruptcy protection, and launches new Premium Broadband services at the end of the year.

Communications (CWC), then in the midst of drawn-out negotiations with another rival, Telewest, in 1999. Yet NTL moved more quickly, outgunning Telewest with a bid worth £6.3 billion ($9 billion), as well as the promise to take over some £1.9 billion in CWC debt. The acquisition—only fully completed in 2000 after withstanding scrutiny from the British Mergers and Monopolies Commission—established NTL as the outright leader in the U.K. cable television market.

Fall and Rise in the New Century

Joining NTL in that purchase was France Telecom, itself eager to expand beyond its home market, which agreed to buy a 25 percent stake in NTL for $5.5 billion. France Telecom was not NTL's first powerhouse partner—the company had earlier sold a stake to Microsoft Corporation for $500 million in a 1999 agreement that enabled NTL to step up its rollout of its broadband offering. With France Telecom, on the other hand, NTL—and through it Blumenthal and Knapp—sought a re-entry into the mobile telecommunications sector. In 2000 the partners tendered a bid of more than £4 billion ($6.4 billion) to acquire one of the United Kingdom's "3G" high-speed mobile telephone licenses.

Instead, BT snatched up the license, and the partners were forced to withdraw their bid—fortunately for NTL. By then, the company had financed its expansion drive almost entirely through debt. With its debt levels topping £10 billion ($16

billion), NTL was finding it more and more difficult to meet even its interest payments, despite the steady growth of its bundled services offerings—and despite the launch and rapid growth of its new broadband service. The company was struggling in other areas as well—by 2001, when it became apparent that its efforts to become a Premier League broadcaster could not be profitable, the company was forced to back out of its agreements, leaving a number of teams with no television coverage.

The collapse of the telecommunications sector at the start of the 2000s proved NTL's undoing. The company's share price went into a nosedive, blocking access to more investment capital. NTL attempted to rein in its costs, reducing much of its capital expenditures—at the same time, the group weathered criticism for a number of somewhat lavish expenditures, such as the $25 million per year cost of its U.S. "headquarters."

Yet the company's efforts came too late. By the beginning of 2002, NTL was forced to default on a $96 million loan payment. The company entered negotiations with its bondholders, eventually working out an agreement giving the bondholder group control of the company, which then began a massive restructuring and recapitalization program under Chapter 11 bankruptcy protection in May 2002. While Blumenthal was forced out of the company, Knapp himself remained at the helm—at least temporarily.

As part of its restructuring, nearly all of NTL's non-U.K. holdings, with the exception of the group's operations in Ireland, were spun off into a separate entity, NTL Europe. NTL cut back on its marketing, instead focusing on improving customer service—successfully reducing its "churn" rate by more than a third by the end of the year, while continuing to sign up more customers. By the end of 2002, the company had grabbed nearly 50 percent of the U.K. broadband market.

NTL came out of bankruptcy protection at the beginning of 2003. With its hands freed, the group once again began a push to win new customers, boosting its entry level broadband product to 150K—compared to rivals' 128K. By April of that year, NTL boasted nearly 700,000 broadband customers. NTL expected that number to rise even more strongly with the rollout in November 2003 of its Broadband Plus content service, available to its higher-speed customers.

NTL had revealed itself as a survivor in a European telecommunications market littered with the corpses of its rivals. Barclay Knapp, however, proved less resistant—in August 2003, Knapp agreed to step down from the company's leadership, turning over the CEO spot to Orange veteran Simon Duffy. At least Knapp, and Blumenthal, could be comforted by the thought of knowing that NTL's ability to survive—and prosper—rested as much on their vision of bundling telecommunications, television, and Internet access services into a single cable.

Principal Subsidiaries

NTL UK; NTL Ireland; NTL Europe.

Principal Divisions

ntl: home; ntl: business; ntl: broadcast; ntl: networks; ntl: carrier services.

Principal Competitors

Vodafone Group Plc; British Telecommunications plc; News Corporation Ltd.; Cable and Wireless PLC; Global Crossing Ltd.; Datatec Ltd.

Further Reading

Bulkley, Kate, ''The Cable Guy,'' *Independent*, February 9, 2000, p. 3.

Hodgson, Jessica, ''Sun Sets on Cable Man Who Reached for Sky,'' *Observer*, August 17, 2003, p. 9.

Holmes, Mark, ''Barclay Knapp: How Will History Judge NTL's Departing CEO?,'' *Inside Digital TV*, August 20, 2003.

Waxler, Caroline, ''Telecom à la Carte,'' *Forbes*, July 27, 1998.

Webdale, Jonathan, ''NTL Emerges from Chapter 11 Following US Restructuring,'' *New Media Age*, January 16, 2003, p. 15.

''The Yank Who's King of British Cable,'' *Business Week*, August 9, 1999, p. 46.

—M.L. Cohen

BETTER LENSES, BETTER CARE

Ocular Sciences, Inc.

1855 Gateway Boulevard, Suite 700
Concord, California 94520-3200
U.S.A.
Telephone: (925) 969-7000
Fax: (925) 969-7118
Web site: http://www.ocularsciences.com

Public Company
Incorporated: 1985 as O.S.I. Corporation
Employees: 2,591
Sales: $310.6 million (2003)
Stock Exchanges: NASDAQ
Ticker Symbol: OCLR
NAIC: 339115 Ophthalmic Goods Manufacturing

Ocular Sciences, Inc. manufactures a wide range of soft contact lenses and markets them under different brand names to private eyecare practitioners, retail optical chains, and mass-merchandising optical shops. Products include daily lenses, a full line of disposable lenses, toric lenses for wearers with astigmatism, and bifocal, colored, aspheric, and sports lenses. Brands are assigned according to distribution channel. Independent practitioners sell products under the Biomedics, Hydrogenics60, EdgeIII, ProActive, and SmartChoice labels. The UltraFlex brand is reserved for retail chains. National brands sold to all channels are Subsoft, Lunelle, Rythmic, and Hydron. Ocular's corporate headquarters is located in Concord, California, with manufacturing facilities found in Albuquerque, New Mexico; Juana Diaz, Puerto Rico; Eastleigh, United Kingdom; and Ligny-en-Barrios, France. In addition, the company maintains sales and distribution operations in Australia, Canada, France, Germany, Hungary, Japan, The Netherlands, Switzerland, and the United Kingdom. Ocular relies on a dry-cast molding process, which is both highly consistent and scalable, allowing the company to ramp up production levels as conditions warrant. Ocular has succeeded in carving out a niche in the contact lens industry by focusing its marketing efforts on

eyecare professionals rather than consumers, and its ability to make decisions quicker than its much larger rivals.

Incorporating the Company in 1985

Ocular was founded by its chairman, John D. Fruth, in 1983 and incorporated in California two years later as O.S.I. Corporation. He brought with him considerable experience in the optical trade. He worked for Bausch & Lomb, Inc. from 1972 to 1976, serving in a variety of sales and marketing positions. He then went to work for contact lens manufacturer CooperVision, Inc., at first involved in regulatory affairs and later becoming president of the contact lens division. In 1983 Fruth struck out on his own and launched O.S.I.

In the beginning O.S.I. acted as a contact lens distributor. At the time contact lenses were designed to be replaced every one to two years and required that customers adhere to a time-consuming daily and weekly cleaning procedure. A major change in the industry took place in the late 1980s with the introduction of disposable contact lenses that eliminated much of the cleaning burden and led to a sharp increase in the global demand for soft lenses. Due to the higher volumes, and because bulk packaging for a supply of disposable lenses was cheaper, manufacturers could achieve economies of scale, lower prices, and make disposable lenses a more economical choice for consumers—which spurred even greater sales and led to greater economies of scale. A further benefit to consumers in changing lenses more frequently was the reduction in health risks associated with dirty lenses.

O.S.I. became a contact lens manufacturer in September 1992 when it traded stock to acquire its primary supplier, a U.K. company called Precision Lens Laboratories Ltd. (PLL). Of particular importance was PLL's recently developed patented lens molding technology. A month later O.S.I. completed an even larger purchase, paying $24.5 million for American Hydron, the North and South American contact lens business of Irvine, California-based Allergan, Inc. For Allergan the divestiture was part of an effort to concentrate on core businesses, such as contact lens care products, ophthalmic surgical devices, skin care products, and specialty pharmaceuticals. O.S.I., in turn, added a second manufacturing plant (located in Puerto Rico), another line of contact lens products, and a greatly expanded customer base.

Entering the Weekly Disposable Market in 1993

The next major step for O.S.I. came in the summer of 1993 when it entered the weekly disposable contact lens market. Prior to this time, the company derived the lion's share of its sales from annual replacement lenses and a smaller portion from monthly disposables. With the new weekly disposables leading the way, O.S.I. would now see most of its growth coming from disposables. The weekly disposables initially contained 38 percent water. In 1995, in order to better compete with Johnson & Johnson's Acuvue line of contact lenses, O.S.I. introduced 55 percent water content lenses. These new weekly replacement lenses allowed greater volumes of oxygen to be transmitted, thereby providing increased comfort for overnight wear.

O.S.I. recorded steady sales increases after becoming an integrated contact lens company. In 1993 sales totaled $38.5 million, as the company posted a $4.4 million loss. The next year revenues improved to $48.5 million and the company regained profitability, posting net income of $5 million. In 1995 O.S.I. generated sales in excess of $68 million and net income grew to 8.8 million. The following year sales reached $90.5 million and profits totaled $10.2 million. All told, during this period O.S.I. enjoyed a compound annual growth rate of 81 percent. Moreover, profits were enhanced because the company also was able to cut its per-unit product costs by approximately 64 percent, a factor that also allowed an average price reduction of 50 percent, spurring greater sales volumes.

In July 1996 O.S.I. was reincorporated in Delaware as Ocular Sciences, Inc. in preparation for becoming a publicly traded company. Ocular's initial public offering was conducted in August 1997, underwritten by a syndicate that included Morgan Stanley Dean Witter; Bear, Stearns & Co.; and Cowen & Co. The company grossed nearly $120 million and much of the proceeds were earmarked to pay down debt as well as expand and automate plant facilities.

After four full years of producing disposable weekly lenses, Ocular by 1998 enjoyed a 16 percent market share in the category. Although the U.S. contact lens market was highly competitive, leading to price cutting and thinner margins, Ocular with little debt and $40 million in cash on hand was well positioned to maintain its growth trajectory. The company's private branding strategy also was providing an edge. As explained by the *Wall Street Journal* in a 1999 profile, the goal was "to build customer loyalty: If the wearer likes the lens, he or she will keep going back to the place that sells it, giving the seller reason to

promote it. Ocular also tries to keep its lenses out of the hands of Internet and toll-free telephone sellers, to protect the air of exclusivity and the price." Another important factor in the company's success was its second-to-market strategy. Rather than spend a great deal of money on research and development, Ocular only entered a market segment once it was established. It was then able to take advantage of its dry-cast molding manufacturing process to enter with high production volumes and stake out a low-cost position. The effectiveness of the business model was reflected on the company's balance sheet. Sales topped the $100 million mark in 1997, totaling $118.6 million, with net income exceeding $20.6 million. In 1998 the company generated nearly $152 million in sales, and net income grew by a third to $30.6 million. Ocular also had a great deal of unrealized potential in overseas business. International sales in 1998 reached $33 million, a 31 percent increase over the prior year but accounted for only a fifth of Ocular's total sales.

Ocular endured a difficult two-year stretch during 1999 and 2000. Aside from a general slowdown in the contact lens market, it had to contend with a product recall in 1999, involving a packaging-seal problem. Although there were few lenses affected and no harm done to patients, Wall Street nevertheless punished the company stock, which quickly tumbled in price by 15 percent. Next, in March 2000 Fruth attempted to sell Ocular to Wesley Jessen VisionCare Inc. as a way to take the company to the next level. It was a $413 million stock deal that would have left Fruth as nonexecutive chairman of the combined company and Wesley Jessen's chairman and CEO, Kevin Ryan, staying on as president and CEO. Wesley Jessen made its mark in the colored soft contact lens market as well as specialty lenses. But almost immediately Bausch & Lomb made an unsolicited bid of $600 million to acquire Wesley Jessen, contingent upon the scuttling of the Ocular acquisition, and made it clear that it might pursue a hostile takeover attempt. Bausch & Lomb had been courting Wesley Jessen for some weeks and its management maintained that the latter had "embraced emphatically" the idea of a sale in the days before the Ocular deal transpired. Bausch & Lomb was not alone in thinking that Wesley Jessen was better off aligned with the larger company, but the Wesley Jessen board of directors unanimously rejected the $600 million offer, or $34 per share, which it deemed far too low. Weeks later, another giant, the Swiss pharmaceutical company Novartis and its Ciba Vision eyecare unit stepped in with an offer of $38.50 per share. This bid was accepted and Wesley Jessen's acquisition of Ocular was terminated.

A $25 million termination fee Ocular received provided cold comfort. A number of key executives had left the company, including the chief financial officer, head of U.S. sales, and director of international marketing. To make matters worse, the company had to contend with a stagnant U.S. market for soft contact lenses. As a result, Ocular suffered through three consecutive quarters of year-over-year earnings reductions. Once the deal with Wesley Jessen had fallen through, Ocular moved quickly to rebuild its management infrastructure and take on the challenge of meeting internally the goals it hoped to achieve in concert with Wesley Jessen. To improve domestic sales, it added a second telemarketing operation in Phoenix. Moreover, an outside sales force was brought in to supplement efforts in both the United States and the United Kingdom. Distribution efforts also were expanded in both Europe and Asia, and the

---

Key Dates:

1985: The company is incorporated.
1992: Manufacturing operations are acquired.
1997: The company is taken public.
2000: The Wesley Jessen merger falls through.
2001: Essilor International is acquired.

---

company looked to spur further growth by way of new product introduction, such as a monthly disposable toric contact lens. This product represented Ocular's first attempt to enter the higher-margin, higher-growth specialty contact lens market. A further step in realizing the company's goals was taken in February 2001 with the $48.3 million cash purchase of Paris-based contact lens manufacturer Essilor International S.A. Because the U.S. market was mature, increasing European sales was a top priority, and Essilor greatly enhanced Ocular's sales structure in the market. The new subsidiary already sold its products in Austria, Belgium, France, Germany, Italy, Scandinavia, Switzerland, The Netherlands, and the United Kingdom. Moreover, Essilor brought with it a number of specialty product lines: the SunSoft line of toric lenses and multifocals; the Lunelle line of soft toric contact lenses; and the Variations line of soft multifocals.

Appointing Stephen Fanning CEO in 2001

Another important development in 2001 occurred in August with the appointment of Stephen J. Fanning as Ocular's new president and CEO. Fruth, who had been serving as CEO on an interim basis for the previous year, continued on as the chairman of the board. Fanning came to the job with 25 years of experience at Johnson & Johnson. He joined Ocular in October 2001 and began immediately to shift the company's focus from standard contact lenses to the higher-margin specialty lenses. At the same time, Fanning made it clear that he wanted Ocular to remain nimble in the marketplace and to avoid the spread of bureaucracy, the effects of which he knew all too well from his quarter-century at giant Johnson & Johnson.

Fanning was interested in increasing Ocular's market share in Japan, especially regarding toric lenses used to correct stig-

matism, a condition with a higher frequency among Asians than other ethnic groups. To bolster its position in Japan and gain a direct sales channel in the country, Ocular acquired assets from Seiko Contact Lens, a contact lens distributor, in 2002 at a cost of $21.7 million. The companies had already been working together, with Ocular products accounting for 65 percent of Seiko's sales.

Ocular experienced a revival in revenues and profits in the early years of the new century. Revenues grew from $225 million in 2001 to $310.6 million in 2003. Net income rebounded from a low of $6.5 million in 2001 to $26.6 million in 2003. The company also appeared to be well positioned to enjoy further growth. The demographics favored the business. The teenage echo boom resulted in millions of new contact lens wearers, many of whom needed vision correction because of the eyestrain they endured from heavy consumption of television, video games, and computers. Ocular also was reaping the benefits of new manufacturing technologies that once again gave Ocular a competitive edge, allowing it to shave price points and improve margins. To ensure that it had the new products necessary in the pipeline to sustain growth, the company also doubled its R&D spending in 2004.

Principal Subsidiaries

SunSoft, Inc.; O.S.I. Puerto Rico Corporation; Precision Lens Manufacturing & Technology, Inc.

Principal Competitors

Bausch & Lomb Inc.; Novartis AG; Vistakon.

Further Reading

Linecker, Adelia Cellini, "Concord, California Rebuilt Lens Maker Eye Better Days Ahead," *Investor's Business Daily,* November 27, 2001, p. A10.

Moore, Brenda L., "Ocular Sciences, Once Spurned, Is Being Viewed in a New Light," *Wall Street Journal,* August 25, 1999, p. CA3.

Shinkle, Kirk, "Lens Maker Cashes in on Young Customers," *Investor's Business Daily,* June 10, 2004, p. A08.

Silber, Judy, "Pleasanton, Calif.-Based Contact Lens Maker Taps into Rich Teen Market," *Contra Costa Times,* April 12, 2004.

—Ed Dinger

Office Depot
DEPOT

Office Depot, Inc.

2200 Old Germantown Road
Delray Beach, Florida 33445-8223
U.S.A.
Telephone: (561) 438-4800
Toll Free: (800) 937-3600
Fax: (561) 438-4001
Web site: http://www.officedepot.com

Public Company
Incorporated: 1986
Employees: 46,000
Sales: $12.36 billion (2003)
Stock Exchanges: New York
Ticker Symbol: ODP
NAIC: 453210 Office Supplies and Stationery Stores;
    454110 Electronic Shopping and Mail-Order Houses

Office Depot, Inc. ranks as the second largest operator of office supplies superstores in the United States, trailing only category leader Staples, Inc. The company operates about 870 retail stores in 44 states and the District of Columbia, offering a full range of office supplies and office furniture, business machines and computers, and computer software. Most of the stores also include a copy and print center offering multiple services, such as printing, reproduction, mailing, and shipping. These stores principally serve consumers and small to medium-sized businesses. Besides retail, Office Depot's distribution channels include direct mail, contract delivery, Internet web site, and business-to-business e-commerce. Office Depot also owns Viking Office Products, Inc., a wholly owned subsidiary and one of the leading direct-mail marketers of office products in the world. International operations, involving a full array of distribution channels, extend to 23 countries, including Canada, where there are more than 30 retail stores; France, 42 stores; Japan, 19 stores; Spain, six stores; and Hungary, four stores. In addition, Office Depot has joint venture and licensing agreements for approximately 130 stores in Mexico, El Salvador, Guatemala, Costa Rica, Israel, Poland, and Thailand. Nearly one-quarter of the company's revenues are generated outside the United States.

Mid-1980s Origins

Along with rival companies Staples and Office Club, Inc., Office Depot was a pioneer in the field of office supplies discount retail. The three companies were founded within months of each other in 1986 in three different corners of the United States—Office Depot in Florida, Staples in Massachusetts, and Office Club in California. All of them saw opportunities in selling office supplies to small businesses at bulk discount rates that had previously been the privilege of larger companies. Since small businesses had never purchased supplies in quantities large enough to receive bulk discounts, they had been at the mercy of conventional retailers who, in the absence of price competition, could sell at manufacturer's suggested retail prices and take markups of as much as 100 percent. Buying directly from manufacturers instead of wholesalers and keeping overhead low, a discount retailer could offer goods from 20 to 75 percent off of full retail. Another trend that proved advantageous for these three companies was the advent of warehouse-style discount retailers in the 1980s; what Price Club had done for general merchandise and what Circuit City had done for consumer electronics, Office Depot, Office Club, and Staples sought to do for ballpoint pens and legal pads.

Office Depot was founded in Boca Raton, Florida, by entrepreneur F. Patrick Sher and two partners, Jack Kopkin and Stephen Dougherty. The company opened its first retail store in Fort Lauderdale in October 1986, and it proved successful enough that two more Office Depot stores appeared in Florida by the end of the year. The company continued to grow rapidly; in 1987 it opened seven more stores in Florida and Georgia and sales topped $33 million. Sher did not have long to savor his success, however, for he died of leukemia scarcely a year after his first store had opened. He was succeeded as CEO by David Fuente, an experienced retail executive whom Office Depot lured away from Sherwin-Williams, where he had been president of the paint stores division.

Fuente's strategy was to have Office Depot continue to grow at a breakneck pace, to trap market share before copycats got into the act. He planned to enter ten new markets a year and add 50 stores a year. Although Office Depot opened only 16 stores in 1988, expanding into Kentucky, North Carolina, Tennessee, and

Texas, Fuente met his goal in 1989 and 1990. Sales topped $132 million in 1988, and Office Depot went public in June with an initial offering of more than 6 million shares at $3.33 per share. Office supply discount retail as a whole was proving wildly successful; although they accounted for only a small fraction of office supply retail sales by the end of the decade, at least one analyst predicted in 1989 that discounters would form the fastest growing specialty-retail segment for several years to come.

Office Depot gained the distinction of being the first of the three original discount chains to turn a profit for a period of four consecutive quarters, which it did during the last two quarters of 1988 and the first two of 1989. The company achieved its success with stores that resembled nothing so much as warehouses. Their decor was functional and unassuming, in a style described by a reporter for *Fortune* as "plain pipe rack," with merchandise stacked floor-to-ceiling on steel shelves. As David Fuente explained it, "Customers pick only from the first six feet of 'shelf' space anyway. So we use the area above 'for storage.' " By 1989, Office Depot stores were averaging $150,000 in sales per week. Of course, lack of concern for the aesthetics of interior design characterized the company's competitors, as well. Office Depot held an edge in that commercial rents were lower in the South than elsewhere in the United States, allowing the company to build exceptionally large stores and still keep overhead costs relatively low.

Rapid Growth in the Early 1990s

Office Depot continued to grow dramatically in 1989 and 1990, expanding beyond its regional base in the South into the Midwest. By the end of 1990 the company boasted 122 stores scattered across 19 states and sales of $625 million. Much of that expansion was financed by the sale of 3.6 million shares of stock for $41 million to Carrefour, a French chain-store concern with subsidiaries throughout Europe.

The office supply discount field became more crowded and competitive in the early 1990s as other companies, including OfficeMax and BizMart, joined the lucrative industry. With the struggle for market share becoming more vigorous, Office Depot and Office Club decided to merge in 1991. The move solidified Office Depot's position on the Pacific Coast in one swoop by eliminating a major competitor and giving it a substantial number of new stores in a regional market where the company previously had only a slim presence. For its part, Office Club had not fared quite as well as its fellow discounting pioneers; during the four quarters that constituted Office Depot's first profitable one-year period Office Club lost $2.7 million, compared to Office Depot's gain of $5.1 million and Staples' narrower loss of $1.9 million. The merger, therefore, proved advantageous to Office Club as well.

Office Club had been founded in northern California in 1986 by Mark Begelman—previously an executive with British American Tobacco—in partnership with a friend who had been selling office products to Price Club. They reasoned that the same marketing principles that allowed Price Club to retail office supplies at deep discounts would work for stores specializing in that kind of merchandise. The first Office Club store opened in January 1987 in Concord, California. Office Club grew quickly, though not as frantically as Office Depot. By the end of 1987 Office Club had opened five stores. At the time of the merger, it operated 59 stores, most of them in California, and had posted annual sales of $300 million.

The merger was approved by Office Depot shareholders in April 1991. As a result of the agreement, which entailed a stock swap worth $137 million, Mark Begelman became president and chief operating officer of Office Depot, with David Fuente remaining chairman and CEO. Over the next 13 months, all Office Club stores were either closed or converted into Office Depot outlets, and the membership fee that Office Club had been charging its regular customers was dropped.

Even after the merger, Office Depot continued to expand. In June 1991 it sold another 1.8 million shares of stock to Carrefour for $40 million to finance expected growth, making Carrefour an 18 percent owner. In addition to the outlets acquired from Office Club, the company opened 57 new stores in 1991. At the end of the year, Office Depot had 229 stores and posted sales of $1.3 billion.

At about the same time, Office Depot saw its sales of office machines, including personal computers, begin to grow by leaps and bounds, and the company began to emphasize this side of its business more strongly. In December 1992, Begelman claimed in an interview that 10 percent of all fax machines sold in the United States were sold by Office Depot. Store layouts were redesigned so that more machines could be put on display. The company began selling not only PC clones by Packard-Bell and Compaq, but also the real thing—in August 1991 IBM agreed to let Office Depot sell its PS/1 computers and around that time Apple gave permission for them to sell the Macintosh Performa line as well.

In 1992 Office Depot went international, acquiring HQ Office International, the parent company of the Great Canadian Office Supplies Warehouse chain, which operated seven stores in western Canada. HQ Office International, Inc. had been founded in 1990 by Robert McNulty as a Canadian extension of his unsuccessful California-based HQ Office Supplies Warehouse chain, which was carved up and bought out by Staples and BizMart in 1990. Office Depot immediately replaced the HQ Office International name with its own and began expanding its presence in Canada, opening two stores in Manitoba. Office Depot's entry into the Canadian market set the company up for an eventual confrontation with Business Depot, a small chain based in eastern Canada, in which Staples held a minority stake.

In addition to expanding into new geographic areas, Office Depot began expanding its customer base. Originally catering to businesses with 20 or fewer employees, Office Depot decided to attract larger business by acquiring contract stationers and integrating them into its retail business. In May 1993 Office Depot acquired the office supply operations of contract stationer Wil-

Key Dates:

1986: F. Patrick Sher and two partners found Office Depot, Inc. in Boca Raton, Florida, and open their first store in Fort Lauderdale.

1987: Sher dies of leukemia and is succeeded as CEO by David Fuente.

1988: Company goes public.

1991: Office Depot acquires Office Club, Inc. and its 59 stores, mostly in California.

1992: Company acquires Canadian firm HQ Office International, Inc. in first move outside the United States.

1997: Federal Trade Commission blocks proposed acquisition of Office Depot by Staples, Inc. on antitrust grounds.

1998: Company's first web site, www.officedepot.com, is launched; direct-mail marketer Viking Office Products, Inc. is acquired.

2000: Bruce Nelson succeeds Fuente as CEO.

2001: Major restructuring involves the closure of 70 stores and an exit from several markets.

2003: Office Depot acquires the French firm Guilbert S.A., a leading European contract stationer.

son Stationery & Printing, a subsidiary of Steelcase Inc. The deal was valued at $16.5 million. In the next year the company bought three more contract stationers.

Having successfully moved into the established retail office supply market, Office Depot was confident they could challenge the existing system that served larger businesses. CEO David Fuente told *Forbes* in May 1994, ''We're all selling the same stuff; we're all selling legal pads and pens and pencils, and we all buy from the same place. The real difference in performance is going to be: Are you pricing them better? Giving better service? Delivering better? The difference is not in the strategy but in the execution.'' Staples and OfficeMax clearly felt Office Depot was on the right track: they both followed suit by acquiring their own contract stationers. Two years later, however, Office Depot had yet to see big returns on its investment. Integrating the contract stationers into their core retail business had cost more than expected, but Office Depot remained confident that the more diverse customer base should make the investment worth it in the long run.

The company saw $2.6 billion in sales in 1993, with $63 million in profit. By 1994 Office Depot had grown to 362 stores, which still followed the company's original concept—warehouse-like buildings that stocked office supplies at 30 to 60 percent off manufacturer's list prices. The company's closest competitor, the Kmart Corporation subsidiary OfficeMax, was only half its size. Not satisfied, Office Depot planned to double the number of its stores in the next five years.

Mid- to Late 1990s: Failed Staples Takeover, International Expansion, Viking Acquisition

In September 1996 Office Depot agreed to be acquired by Staples, its largest competitor, in a deal estimated at $4 billion.

As these companies were number one and two, respectively, among discount chains, questions about antitrust violations were quickly raised. The Federal Trade Commission (FTC) found that the combined company would control prices in many metropolitan areas and that in cities where Office Depot and Staples competed head to head, prices might be expected to rise 5 to 10 percent. The FTC sought a court order to stop Staples from buying Office Depot. In response, the two companies agreed to sell 63 stores to OfficeMax to open competition in certain areas, a proposal that had to be approved by the FTC. They also argued that, with only 5 percent of the office supply market, their merger was not threatening. Unappeased, the FTC argued that office superstores are a market to themselves and that Office Depot and Staples controlled 75 percent of that market. The FTC sued to stop the deal, and in late June 1997 a federal judge granted a preliminary injunction to block the transaction. At this point, Staples and Office Depot abandoned their merger plans, conceding defeat.

Aside from this failed merger, the mid- to late 1990s were noteworthy for Office Depot's steady expansion of its overseas operations. From 1995 to 1998 the company opened stores in Poland, Hungary, and Thailand under licensing agreements, and in Mexico, France, and Japan through joint ventures. In 1998 Office Depot bought out its joint venture partner in France and it did likewise in Japan the following year. Also important to this international push was the August 1998 acquisition of Viking Office Products, Inc. for about $2.7 billion in stock. Based in Torrance, California, Viking was the largest direct-mail marketer of office products in the world. Of Viking's $1.29 billion in 1997 revenues, 60 percent was generated outside the United States. It operated 11 delivery centers in Europe and Australia.

Also in 1998 Office Depot added to its growing channels of distribution with the launch of its first web site, www.officedepot.com, in January. The company's first European e-commerce site, www.viking-direct.co.uk, was launched in the United Kingdom one year later. Also in 1999 Office Depot entered into a partnership with United Parcel Service, Inc. (UPS) in order to begin offering UPS packaging and shipping services at its U.S. stores. That year, revenues surpassed the $10 billion mark for the first time, hitting $10.2 billion, while profits were a record $257.6 million. Office Depot ended the decade with 825 stores in the United States and Canada, and 32 overseas.

Early 2000s: Struggling to Regain Momentum

Despite the record results for 1999, all was not well at Office Depot. As the ill-fated Staples deal unfolded, Office Depot had placed its expansion plans on hold. Then when the deal died, the company scrambled to make up for lost time, opening new stores rather haphazardly—entering new markets, where competitors were already entrenched, with just a couple stores, and making some poor choices in regard to specific store locations. Office Depot was also hurt by heightened competition from warehouse discounters, particularly Costco Wholesale Corporation and Wal-Mart Stores, Inc.'s Sam's Club, who made aggressive moves into some of the most profitable office supplies categories, including computer paper, toner, and ink—forcing price cuts. Sales and profits were negatively affected, and Office Depot began missing some analysts' projections. After second-quarter 2000 earnings dropped 22 percent, the company's board reacted by easing Fuente out of the CEO slot and into the position of nonexecutive chairman. Bruce Nelson was promoted to CEO from his previous position as international president. Nelson had joined Office Depot as the president of Viking Office Products, and earlier in his career had garnered more than two decades of senior management experience at Boise Cascade Office Products.

Nelson spent the next several months making changes to top management and launching a thorough review of the firm's operations to identify underperforming outlets and weak markets. In January 2001 he announced that Office Depot would close 70 of its 888 North American stores, leaving the following markets altogether: Cleveland; Columbus, Ohio; Phoenix; and Boston. Expansion for 2001 was pared back to 50 new stores, with the new outlets being about 20,000 square feet each, about 5,000 square feet smaller than the average existing store. Nelson also aimed to refocus the stores on small and medium-sized businesses by eliminating a great deal of consumer-oriented merchandise, such as DVD players and children's computer software. In all, about 1,800 products were to be cut; these represented about 20 percent of the total number of products but generated only about 2 percent of sales. In connection with this restructuring, Office Depot recorded an after-tax charge of $260.6 million for the fourth quarter of 2000, leaving profits for that year to stand at a much reduced $49.3 million.

Continuing its ongoing overseas expansion, Office Depot in early 2001 acquired Sands & McDougall, an office products firm that was the largest contract stationer in Western Australia. The company also expanded its business services operations into Ireland, the Netherlands, and France that year. In December 2001 Nelson was named to the additional position of chairman, succeeding Fuente, who nevertheless remained on the company board. The Viking direct-mail business expanded into Switzerland, Spain, and Portugal during 2002, and Office Depot's business services division expanded into Italy. Through its Mexican joint-venture partner, Grupo Gigante, S.A. de C.V., the company expanded into Central America that same year, opening stores in Guatemala and Costa Rica.

In early 2003, however, Office Depot elected to exit from the Australian market in order to concentrate its international attention mainly on Europe. It sold its Australian operations to Officeworks, a subsidiary of Coles Myer Ltd. that was the leading office supplies retailer in Australia. It took little time for Office Depot to make a major move that nearly doubled its European operations. In June 2003 the company acquired the France-based Guilbert S.A. from Pinault-Printemps-Redoute S.A. for $945.2 million. Guilbert was one of the largest contract stationers in Europe, with operations in nine European countries and 2002 revenues of $1.6 billion. The acquisition of Guilbert, based in Senlis (outside Paris), not only accelerated Office Depot's penetration of the market for large business customers in Europe, it also gave the company the number one position among the continent's office supply firms. Office Depot subsequently, in April 2004, gained its first wholly owned operations in Eastern Europe by acquiring its licensee in Hungary, which had been operating three Office Depot stores in that nation. The company planned to use its Hungarian subsidiary as a base for expansion into the ten countries in the region that had recently joined the European Union.

After nearly four years of declines in quarterly same-stores sales (sales at stores that have been open for more than one year), Office Depot appeared to have turned the corner during the first half of 2004 when it posted two consecutive quarters of 3 percent increases in same-store sales. The company was also busy with a number of new initiatives. In February it rolled out its first-ever customer loyalty program, Office Depot Advantage, which rewarded customers who spend as little as $200 in a three-month period with a gift certificate good for future purchases. To help ramp up expansion efforts, the company agreed to buy 124 former Kids "R" Us stores from Toys "R" Us, Inc. for $197 million in cash. The deal was later reduced to 109 stores, and Office Depot planned to resell or sublet about half of the total, but 45 to 50 of the stores were to be converted to the Office Depot format. Many of the acquired stores were in the Northeast, and the company announced an aggressive expansion into that region, a stronghold for its two main rivals, Staples—now the number one U.S. operator of office supplies superstores—and OfficeMax. Overall, in an attempt to close the gap with Staples, which had 1,400 stores, the 900-unit-strong Office Depot aimed to open 80 new stores in 2004 and then 100 new stores in each of the following three years. The new stores were to feature a new store format called Millennium 2. Nelson told the *Palm Beach (Fla.) Post:* "We worked to create a store that was easier to shop, less expensive to open and more efficient to operate. This serves as our foundation to enter a new era." The format emphasized grouping product categories together in the way customers use them and also featured increased cross-merchandising. Also significant was that the stores began showcasing a new line of fashion-forward furniture created by Emmy Award–winning designer Christopher Lowell.

Principal Subsidiaries

Eastman Office Supplies, Inc.; Guilbert SAS (France); OD International, Inc.; The Office Club, Inc.; Office Depot of Texas, L.P.; Office Depot International (UK) Limited; Viking Office Products, Inc.; Office Depot International BV (Netherlands).

Further Reading

"The Big Interview: Mark Begelman—Office Depot," *Office Products International,* December 1992.

Brooks, Rick, "Office Depot to Buy Viking in Stock Deal," *Wall Street Journal,* May 19, 1998, p. A3.

Caminiti, Susan, "Seeking Big Money in Paper and Pens," *Fortune,* July 31, 1989.

Davids, Meryl, "Pushing the Envelope at Office Depot," *Journal of Business Strategy,* September/October 1998, pp. 25+.

Dieckmann, Heike, "Buckled Wheels?," *Office Products International,* November 2003, p. 40.

Hirsh, Michael, "But Nary a Trust to Bust," *Newsweek,* June 2, 1997, pp. 44–45.

Kaye, Steven D., "Out with the Old, In with the New," *U.S. News and World Report,* March 24, 1997, p. 60.

La Monica, Paul R., "Office Depot: Stock Up," *Financial World,* January 30, 1996, p. 24.

Libbin, Jennifer, "Office Depot CEO Outlines Future," *DSN Retailing Today,* May 21, 2001, pp. 4, 59.

Liebeck, Laura, "Office Depot Ventures into Canada, Magazine Business," *Discount Store News,* February 3, 1992.

Milstone, Erik, "Office Depot on the Fast Track," *Palm Beach (Fla.) Post,* March 29, 1992.

Moukheiber, Zina, "A Lousy Day for Golf," *Forbes,* May 9, 1994, pp. 60, 64.

Ostrowski, Jeff, "Office Depot Closing 70 Stores," *Palm Beach (Fla.) Post,* January 4, 2001, p. 1D.

Owers, Paul, "Acquisition to Put Office Depot on Top," *Palm Beach (Fla.) Post,* April 9, 2003, p. 8B.

——, "Office Depot Replaces CEO Fuente," *Palm Beach (Fla.) Post,* July 19, 2000, p. 6B.

Pascual, Aixa M., "Can Office Depot Get Back on Track?," *Business Week,* September 18, 2000, p. 74.

Rawls, Linda, "Office Depot's New Store Style Set," *Palm Beach (Fla.) Post,* July 1, 2004, p. 1D.

Selz, Michael, "Office Supply Firms Take Different Paths to Success," *Wall Street Journal,* May 30, 1991.

Terhune, Chad, "Office Depot, Shifting Selling Strategy, to Post a Charge of Up to $300 Million," *Wall Street Journal,* January 4, 2001, p. B13.

Troy, Mike, "Change Is in the Air at Office Depot," *DSN Retailing Today,* August 7, 2000, pp. 3, 88.

——, "Expansion and Renovation on Agenda at Office Depot," *Discount Store News,* June 8, 1998, pp. 7, 134.

——, "Moving Beyond No. 1: Office Depot Gets Better, Not Bigger," *Discount Store News,* October 26, 1998, p. 43.

——, "Office Depot Churning Up Change," *DSN Retailing Today,* March 22, 2004, pp. 1, 43.

——, "Office Depot Resurges amid Merchandising Makeover," *DSN Retailing Today,* June 7, 2004, pp. 20, 24.

——, "Office Depot Shifts Store Expansion to M2 Format," *DSN Retailing Today,* July 19, 2004, pp. 4, 21.

—Douglas Sun
—updates: Susan Windisch Brown, David E. Salamie

Onex Corporation

161 Bay Street, 49th Floor
P.O. Box 700
Toronto, Ontario M5J 2S1
Canada
Telephone: (416) 362-7711
Fax: (416) 362-5765
Web site: http://www.onexcorp.com

Public Company
Incorporated: 1984
Employees: 98,000
Sales: CAD 17.0 billion ($13.21 billion) (2003)
Stock Exchanges: Toronto
Ticker Symbol: OCX
NAIC: 551112 Offices of Other Holding Companies

Onex Corporation, one of Canada's largest companies, operates on a global level. Founder Gerald Schwartz built his empire by making timely acquisitions of struggling businesses. Highly diversified, the investment firm holds ownership in companies involved in businesses ranging from electronics manufacturing and auto products to healthcare services and movie theaters.

Early History: 1970s

The history of Onex Corporation is actually the biography of one man, Gerald Schwartz. A young man with ambition and bold ideas, Schwartz graduated from the University of Manitoba with degrees in commerce and law. Upon graduation, he headed for Harvard University and earned a degree in business administration in 1970. Schwartz then took a job in Europe, working for Bernard Cornfield, a rather eccentric and flamboyant international financier based in Switzerland. When Cornfield's company, Investors Overseas Services, was investigated for fraud and then collapsed in 1973, Schwartz moved on to the United States, seeking work in the financial caverns of Wall Street in New York City. Hired by Bear Stearns & Company, Schwartz learned the intricacies of hostile takeovers and corporate mergers. Two of his most renowned and notorious colleagues included Henry Kravis and Jerome Kohlberg.

After a stint of four years in the United States, Schwartz decided to return to his hometown of Winnipeg. There, he formed a partnership with a lawyer, Israel Asper, an astute and driven entrepreneur, and together they founded CanWest Capital Corporation, the forerunner of CanWest Global Communications Corporation, which would own numerous broadcasting businesses throughout western Canada. The partnership first acquired several small to mid-sized Canadian firms during the late 1970s and early 1980s, and seemed to be heading in a promising direction. Yet Schwartz and Asper began to quarrel about strategic issues surrounding acquisitions, venture capital, and timing, and before long decided to end their partnership.

A New Company: 1980s

In 1983, Schwartz relocated to Toronto and, with the financial backing of former investors at CanWest, formed Onex Capital Corporation, which he intended to use as a holding company for widely diversified acquisitions. The first such acquisition was Onex Packaging, the Canadian subsidiary of the American Can Company based in Connecticut. With a purchase price of approximately $220 million, the acquisition was the largest leveraged buyout in the history of Canada.

Schwartz was not afraid of debt and had learned his lessons well while working at Bear Stearns in New York. His *modus operandi* was to use debt or other innovative financing to purchase undervalued companies, and then initiate a comprehensive restructuring of the company purchased. He would then sell either parts of the company or the whole at a profit. Onex Packaging, a manufacturer of rigid packing materials, offered an initial public sale of its stock in 1987, to cover the costs of the restructuring and to raise additional funds for the expenses incurred in modernizing the company. Unfortunately, by 1987, Onex Packaging was losing money and Schwartz decided to take the company private once again. Not long afterward, he sold Onex Packaging for less than he had originally anticipated.

Having learned a hard lesson about economies of scale in the North American market with Onex Packaging, Schwartz was not about to make the same mistake twice. During 1987, as Onex Packaging began to flounder, Schwartz acquired both

Company Perspectives:

Fundamental to our business is an entrepreneurial philosophy based on ownership. Each member of the Onex management team has a meaningful personal financial interest in Onex and the companies we own. Our focus is squarely on building value.

Norex Leasing, a leading leasing company owned and operated by Citibank, and Purolator Courier Ltd., the leading overnight delivery service in Canada. At the same time, Schwartz made a conscious decision to make more acquisitions in the United States and began to decrease his holdings in Canada, although his company would always remain based in his native country. This strategy led him to one of the most important acquisitions during the late 1980s: the purchase of the airline catering company called Sky Chefs.

Growth Through Acquisition: 1990–99

One of the first huge successes of Schwartz's acquisition strategy was Beatrice Foods Canada, Ltd. Purchased in 1987 when its parent firm was in the course of being dismantled in Chicago, Schwartz paid a bargain-basement cash price of $21.9 million for the company, although it was valued at a purchase price of slightly more than $300 million. In 1991, the entrepreneur resold the company for $475 million, after a complicated but productive restructuring plan that involved merging Beatrice Foods Canada with two other Canadian dairy firms. Additional acquisitions followed at a quick pace, including ProSource Distribution, a foodservice distributor in both the United States and Canada, and Dura Automotive Systems and Tower Automotive, two high-quality automotive parts manufacturers.

Schwartz's goal with Sky Chefs was to transform it into a leader in the in-flight catering industry. The first step in this direction was an alliance formed between Sky Chefs and LSG Lufthansa Service in 1993. The alliance was formed to give Sky Chefs access to international airline customers that it did not previously have. Revenues for Sky Chefs remained relatively the same from 1991 through 1994, hovering around $470 million annually. During this time, however, Sky Chefs was transformed into the leading low-cost producer of in-flight meals for the airline industry. A policy of cycle-time reduction was implemented in 1992 and resulted in a 30 percent labor production increase over a three-year period.

Although many innovative alliances and policies had been implemented at Sky Chefs during the early 1990s, it was not until 1995 that the company developed a worldwide reputation. Much of this was due to the takeover of Caterair International Corporation, one of the preeminent in-flight catering companies. Funded entirely by third-party lenders, the acquisition of Caterair International propelled Sky Chefs to the top of the industry with slightly less than 50 percent of the American domestic airline catering market and 30 percent of the international airline catering market. The acquisition of Caterair International and the earlier alliance with LSG Lufthansa gave Sky Chefs access to airline customers around the world, including new contracts in

Central and South America, as well as in Australia. As the consolidation of in-flight catering services continued through 1995, additional contracts were signed with British Airways, Delta Airlines, USAir, and Midway. By the end of 1995, Sky Chefs counted more than 250 airline customers located in every part of the world, while revenues shot up to $739 million, an increase of 58 percent over the previous year.

ProSource, Onex Corporation's foodservice distributor for restaurant chains, was the largest in North America. Starting in 1992 with a single customer, Burger King, the company expanded to provide services for more than 22 different types of restaurants and fast-food establishments. In 1993, ProSource acquired Valley Food Services, and in 1994 Malone Products, but the most significant addition was the acquisition of the National Accounts division of the Martin-Brower Company in 1995. These three acquisitions expanded and diversified the ProSource Distribution customer base, so that instead of relying exclusively on quick-serve restaurants, there was more of a balance, with distribution to quick-serve establishments comprising 75 percent and distribution to casual dining restaurants totaling 25 percent of ProSource business. Revenues in 1995 for ProSource were reported at $3.5 billion, compared with the 1994 figure of $1.6 billion. Much of the increased revenue was derived from the acquisition of the National Accounts division of Martin-Brower, but a significant portion of the increase was due to implementing highly successful cost-effective distribution techniques. One such technique involved "rolling shelving," wherein carts used by ProSource delivery trucks could also be used for instant in-store shelving at restaurants. Another cost-effective distribution method involved the company's electronic ordering system, which reduced time and effort. These innovations helped ProSource develop into one of the leading-edge distributors in the foodservice industry.

Hidden Creek Industries was formed as a partnership by Onex Corporation to manage the operations of Dura Automotive and Tower Automotive. Dura Automotive, purchased in 1990, became the largest supplier of parking-brake systems to original equipment manufacturers (OEMs) in North America. In 1994, Dura acquired the Orscheln Company, to increase its market share of the parking-brake systems industry. With the purchase of Orscheln, Dura achieved its goal; revenues increased 34 percent from 1994 to 1995, jumping from $189.7 million to $253.7 million. Tower Automotive was purchased in 1993 and transformed by management into one of the leading developers and manufacturers of structural metal stampings and various other assemblies for original equipment manufacturers. In 1994, Tower purchased Edgewood Tool and Manufacturing, as well as Kalamazoo Stamping and Die, and the following year added the Trylon Corporation to its holdings. These acquisitions not only increased revenues from 1994 to 1995 by 35 percent, but complemented Tower Automotive's already existing line of products. While Dura Automotive's major customers included Ford, Chrysler, General Motors, and Toyota, Tower Automotive negotiated lucrative contracts with Ford and Honda motor companies.

As a holding company, one of Onex's top priorities was to enhance the value of shareholder equity. During 1995, this goal was pursued by a number of strategic investments, made primarily under the direction of Gerald Schwartz. Onex invested $20 million in Phoenix Pictures, a brand new film production

Key Dates:

1983: Gerald Schwartz forms Onex Capital Corporation with the intention of using it as a holding company.
1987: The company acquires Beatrice Foods Canada, Ltd.
1995: In-flight catering company Sky Chefs attains global status.
1996: The company buys a controlling interest in IBM Canada subsidiary Celestica.
1999: The Onex name gains notoriety with a failed takeover bid.
2001: Holdings in the entertainment industry are expanded.
2003: The company enters the healthcare services business.

company owned by Onex, Sony Pictures Entertainment, and Britain's Pearson PLC. The company also purchased Vencap Equities Alberta, Ltd., a promising venture capital fund located in western Canada. Finally, management at Onex formed Rippledwood Holdings, an acquisition fund developed to hold the 52 percent of the company's interest in Dayton Superior Corporation. Other continuing strategic investments included a 19 percent share of Purolator Courier (down from majority ownership a few years earlier), 16 percent of Scotsman Industries (a manufacturer of ice machines, freezers, food preparation workstations, and refrigerators), and an 8.1 percent share in Alliance Communications, the leading producer and distributor of television entertainment in Canada.

In the spring of 1995, Gerald Schwartz decided to launch a $2.3 billion hostile takeover of John Labatt Ltd., one of the most prominent brewers in Canada. Located in Toronto, Labatt had a long and distinguished history starting as a brewer of fine beers in London, England, in 1847. Controlling approximately 45 percent of the Canadian beer market in North America, second only to Molson, by 1995, Labatt also had diversified into businesses unrelated to the brewing industry. At the time of Schwartz's attempted takeover, Labatt owned The Sports Network, Le Reseau des Sports, an 80 percent interest in The Discovery Network, a 42 percent interest in Toronto's SkyDome, and a 90 percent stake in the Toronto Blue Jays baseball team.

Unwilling to join the Onex Corporation holdings, management at Labatt began looking for a ''white knight'' to foil the hostile takeover attempt. After meetings with a number of possible suitors, Labatt finally arranged a deal with Interbrew S.A., a Belgian-based brewery that had been attempting to break into the North American beer market for years. Interbrew cooked up a deal that amounted to $2.7 billion, successfully outbidding Onex Corporation for control of Labatt. After the acquisition was finalized, Interbrew began to sell off Labatt's nonbrewing operations, which had been the sole purpose of Schwartz's attempted takeover of the company.

Although Schwartz was frustrated in his attempt to acquire Labatt, he continued to seek out undervalued companies for acquisition. Although committed to running his company from Canadian headquarters, he was reportedly increasingly interested in looking south toward the United States to expand his operations.

To appease the markets, many conglomerates shed companies to concentrate on core businesses. But Onex stayed the course. In September 1996, the company announced it was buying a controlling interest in a subsidiary of IBM Canada Ltd. Celestica Inc., a maker of electronic components for computer and telecommunications systems, had sales of about CAD 3 billion in 1995. Onex joined forces with Celestica management in the $700 million transaction, putting up $199 million for a 43 percent equity interest and voting control. Celestica's new circumstances put it in position to sell to competitors of IBM and thus broaden its customer base.

The stock market liked the move and drove up Onex's price per share. The company had spent more time than not trading at a level below its initial asking price. Despite the positive outlook, Onex's earnings were being dragged down by the continued integration of purchases by ProSource and Sky Chefs.

In 1997, Onex broadened its vehicle business with the acquisition of Trim Systems. Additional purchases in the interior components supply segment of the OEM heavy truck market were made the following year.

Celestica completed its initial public offering (IPO) in 1998. With a total value of $610 million, it was the largest offering by an electronics manufacturing services (EMS) company and the largest IPO by a technology company in Canadian history.

In another 1998 deal, Onex purchased Sofbank Services Group Inc., an American outsourced customer care and fulfillment company. Joining with Canadian contact center North Direct Response, Onex would form ClientLogic.

During 1999, Celestica expanded its capabilities in Europe and South America. With 18 acquisitions over three years and a spate of new global customers, Celestica was the fastest growing EMS provider in its industry. Onex purchased J.L. French Automotive Castings, a leading supplier of aluminum die-cast components to the automotive industry. In addition, Onex established MAGNATRAX as a growth platform, following the purchase of American Building Company, the third largest U.S. producer of metal building systems. At year end, Onex and several of Canada's largest pension funds and financial institutions joined together to form ONCAP, to support small- to midcap investments.

All in all, 1999 was a stellar year for growth. Revenues climbed 69 percent to $14.9 billion. Earnings were up 66 percent to $293.9 million. But it was a failed deal that planted the name Onex in the mind of the public. Schwartz bid $1.2 billion to take over and merge Canada's two national airlines—Air Canada and Canadian Airlines. The move was contentious, pulling the Canadian government into the row. Ultimately, the courts assisted Air Canada in blocking the Onex purchase.

New Challenges Arising: 2000–04

In order to sustain returns Schwartz had to up the ante dealwise. ''Net of fees, Onex's annual returns on its 17 deals have averaged 35% over the past 15 years. That's double the average rate of all private equity outfits and better than KKRs,'' wrote Bernard Condon for *Forbes* in March 2000.

Onex differed from other buyout companies in some significant ways, such as reliance on public capital to fund deals and retention of purchased companies as a base for consolidation. Onex still held 47 percent of Sky Chefs 13 years after buying into the company. Over the nine years it held Dura Automotive, 13 car parts businesses had been added to the fold.

Moreover, ten top managers put their money where their mouths were when it came to investment. "They not only own 21% of Onex but must personally contribute up to 9% of whatever the company agrees to invest in deals. Each of them has been anteing up between two and six times his salary each year for years. So the grilling over proposed buyouts at Monday meetings at Onex's headquarters overlooking Lake Ontario occasionally turns fierce," wrote Condon.

Although the company remained headquartered in Canada, the majority of its revenues were generated elsewhere. Due to its nature, Onex had no true counterpart in Canada. Furthermore, since Onex purchased businesses in a number of industries, the competition shifted from deal to deal.

In April 2000, Onex withdrew a planned IPO of ClientLogic, citing market instability. Onex and the Ontario Municipal Employees Retirement System (OMERS) took part in a $105 million equity financing of the company in September. ClientLogic had 36 facilities in nine North American and European countries. Revenues for the customer management services provider had been growing from new business and through acquisitions, but the company's net in 2000 was hurt by infrastructure investment, particularly in Europe.

Other businesses needed some tweaking. In the building sector, MAGNATRAX was not getting expected results from its early 2000 acquisition of Jannock Limited. J.L. French's integration of Nelson Metal Products—an aluminum casting company purchased in late 1999—also failed to go as hoped.

The commercial vehicle sector was expanded with the addition of Bostrom, a leading North American and European producer of seat systems for heavy truck, bus, and worldwide construction and agricultural markets.

Celestica, though, set new earnings and revenue records in 2000. In addition, the acquisition of home meal replacement businesses boosted Sky Chefs' results. This helped Onex's revenues climb 65 percent to $24.5 billion, placing it among the largest Canadian companies. The company posted net earnings of $188 million, its second best on record.

Onex bought LeBlanc Ltd. and BMS Communications Services Ltd. in February 2001. Combined, the pair was the largest full-service provider of wireless infrastructure in Canada. Onex formed Radian Communication in the wake of the acquisitions.

Other deals in 2001 included the sale of Sky Chefs to Lufthansa—Onex sold Lufthansa 23.5 percent of the business in 1999 with a promise to sell the remainder before 2003. Onex achieved a compound annual return of 30 percent over its 16 years of ownership.

Troubled economies hurt some of Onex's business segments in 2001. North American car and light truck as well as building construction industries declined. The high-tech sector also was in trouble. Celestica's growth slid dramatically due to a steep decline in customer demand. In response, the company eliminated jobs and manufacturing plants and turned to low-cost regions for its new acquisitions.

During 2001, Onex prepared for an expansion in the entertainment industry. The company invested in the debt of and developed a restructuring plan for one of the largest owners of movie theaters in North America. Onex and partner Oaktree Capital completed the acquisition of Loews Cineplex following its emergence from bankruptcy in 2002. Onex and Oaktree also purchased a leading theater exhibition company in Mexico, engaged in a Spanish joint venture, and made theatrical purchases in South Korea and Michigan.

Although economic conditions dogged Onex businesses, the company Schwartz founded earned high marks. "Indeed, when it comes to smartly timed acquisitions, no other Canadian private equity player can hold a candle to Onex, which has made billions in a wide range of industries, including auto parts, airline catering, sugar and electronics, running companies such as Celestica, Sky Chefs and Lantic Sugar," wrote Thomas Watson for *Canadian Business* in May 2003.

Lantic Sugar was the largest sugar refiner and marketer in Canada. Onex entered the industry in 1997 with a $74 million investment in BC Sugar. As it had in other businesses it entered, Onex worked to build the value of the companies it bought. Thus, in the case of the sugar business, Onex poured in capital to cut production costs. The expansion and modernization of Lantic Sugar's Montreal refinery took more time and cost more than expected and disrupted production in 2000. During 2002, Lantic Sugar merged with Rogers Sugar and operated under Rogers Sugar Income Fund.

Onex moved into a new line of business in 2003. Maryland-based Magellan Health Services, market leader in behavioral managed healthcare, needed a bailout. Onex Partners LP, a new Onex fund, invested $101 million for approximately 24 percent ownership and controlling interest in the company. Magellan's 2002 revenue was approximately $2.8 billion. Customers included health plans, corporations, unions, and government agencies. Magellan offered administrative services, risk-based services, and employee assistance program services.

Other activity in 2003 included the merging of Loews Cineplex Group with another Onex entity, Galaxy Entertainment. Under a new income fund, the pair would account for 30 percent of Canada's box office revenues.

Onex exited two business areas in 2003, bringing in $230 million in earnings for discontinued operations. Of that, $66 million was from the sale of Rogers Sugar Income Fund trust units. A $164 million accounting gain came from the disposition of MAGNATRAX, which had gone into bankruptcy.

Onex posted a net loss of CAD 332 million for 2003, compared with a net loss of CAD 145 million in 2002. Revenues for the year were CAD 17 billion, down from CAD 21 billion the previous year. The decrease in revenues was primarily due to continuing weak demand for Celestica's products, but some areas of the automotive business also contributed to the declining numbers.

Principal Subsidiaries

Celestica Inc.; ClientLogic Corporation; Magellan Health Services, Inc.; Dura Automotive Systems, Inc.; J.L. French Automotive Castings, Inc.; Performance Logistics Group, Inc.; Bostrom Holdings, Inc.; Radian Communication Services Corporation; InsLogic Corporation; Loews Cineplex Entertainment Corporation.

Principal Competitors

Counsel Corporation; HEICO Corporation; Thomas H. Lee Co.

Further Reading

Bagnell, Paul, "Conglomerate No Longer a Dirty Word," *Financial Post,* January 4, 1997, p. 21.

Condon, Bernard, "Kravis of the North," *Forbes,* March 6, 2000, p. 76.

Dalglish, Brenda, "A Private Play: Onex Bids $2.3 Billion to Take Over Labatt," *MacLean's,* May 29, 1995, p. 44.

De Santis, Solange, and Martin Du Bois, "Labatt Agrees to White Knight Deal with Belgium's Interbrew, Foiling Onex," *Wall Street Journal,* June 7, 1995, p. A3.

Fanelli, Christa, "Onex and Ontario Boost CRM," *Buyouts,* September 11, 2000.

Henry, John, "Canadian Firm Buys Windsor Door Parent," *Arkansas Business,* April 19, 1999, p. 10.

"Holding Company Agrees to Buy Vencap Equities," *Wall Street Journal,* October 26, 1995, p. A19.

Jereski, Laura, "Can-do Canadian," *Forbes,* September 7, 1987, p. 124.

McMurdy, Deirdre, "Predators on Parade," *MacLean's,* May 29, 1995, p. 49.

——, "Sacred Pensions in Play," *MacLean's,* June 12, 1995, p. 36.

——, "Southern Accent," *MacLean's,* August 2 1993, p. 26.

"Onex Closes on Magellan Health Services," *Canadian Corporate News,* January 9, 2004.

"Onex Corporation," *Wall Street Journal,* May 11, 1995, p. C18.

"Onex Hopes for Better 2004 After Troubles at Celestica, Auto Units," *AP Online,* February 16, 2004.

Pearce, Ed, "Gerry Schwartz of Onex," *Ivey Business Journal,* July 2000, pp. 18 +.

Piotrowski, Julie, "Sailing with Magellan," *Modern Healthcare,* June 2, 2003, p. 14.

"Top 10 Wealth Creators: 9 and 10," *Canadian Business,* August 7, 2000.

Watson, Thomas, "The Countdown Continues: 49 Onex," *Canadian Business,* May 26, 2003.

Willis, Andrew, "Eye for the Prize," *MacLean's,* May 29, 1995, p. 46.

——, "The Winning Brew," *MacLean's,* June 19, 1995, p. 44.

—Thomas Derdak
—update: Kathleen Peippo

Par Pharmaceutical Companies, Inc.

One Ram Ridge Rd.
Spring Valley, New York 10977
U.S.A.
Telephone: (845) 425-7100
Fax: (845) 425-7907
Web site: http://www.parpharm.com

Public Company
Incorporated: 1978 as Par Pharmaceutical, Inc.
Employees: 500
Sales: $661.7 million (2003)
Stock Exchanges: New York
Ticker Symbol: PRX
NAIC: 325412 Pharmaceutical Preparation Manufacturing

Par Pharmaceutical Companies, Inc., formerly Pharmaceutical Resources, Inc., develops, manufactures, and distributes a broad line of more than 170 generic drug products (an assortment of doses of 71 prescription drugs) through its principal subsidiary, Par Pharmaceutical. The focus is on antiinflammatory, cardiovascular, and central nervous system drugs. About half of these products are manufactured by other companies, including GlaxoSmithKline, Dr. Reddy's Laboratories, and Merck KGaA. In addition, Israel-based subsidiary FineTech Laboratories, Ltd. produces complex synthetic pharmaceutical ingredients. Through an agreement with Bristol Myers Squibb, Par also markets a small number of mature brand name drugs. Par customers are drug distributors, wholesalers, and retail pharmacy chains.

Founding of Par Pharmaceutical: 1978

Par Pharmaceutical was incorporated in New York in September 1978 and became operational in 1979. Its founders included R.K. Patel, Ashok H. Patel (unrelated), and Perry Levine, who became the company's chief executive officer. Par grew into a high flyer in the fast growing generic drug industry. In the mid-1970s generics accounted for just 9.5 percent of U.S. prescription drug sales, but over the next decade that number would top 15 percent and continue to grow. Par capitalized on the trend, going public in 1983. In essence, the company targeted brand drugs that would soon lose their patent protections, performed required testing for the Federal Drug Administration, and then accumulated enough inventory so that when the brand drug lost its protection Par was able to quickly establish a beachhead in the market before other competitors arose and price cuts inevitably occurred.

After going public, Par enjoyed several years of strong growth. In 1985 it paid nearly $1.2 million in cash to acquire an 80 percent stake in another publicly traded generic firm, bankrupt BetaMED Pharmaceuticals, Inc. Based in Indianapolis, BetaMED was founded in 1979 by Gregory and Judith Buckley, along with Martin Sweeney, a former Eli Lilly & Co. executive. The company underwent a number of management changes and endured a string of losses before seeking Chapter 11 bankruptcy protection in June 1984. Par renamed it Quad Pharmaceuticals, Inc. Less than a year later, Par bought the remaining 20 percent interest for $560,000 in cash and stock. A new management team was brought in and the business began to post strong results. To support its growing business in generics, Par in 1987 established an in-house advertising agency, Generic Innovations, Inc., and Par Printing Enterprises, Inc., to provide printing services. In that same year, Par began trading on the New York Stock Exchange.

Par and the generic drug industry, however, were soon mired in scandal, with allegations that Food and Drug Administration (FDA) officials were paid off to approve drugs and that test results had been fabricated. Quad in particular drew attention, given that in just its second year under the control of Par it received approval for more products than any other drug company in the history of the FDA. Moreover, Quad's CEO, Dilip Shah, was a former FDA employee and maintained close ties to the agency's generic supervisor, Charles Chang. Congress took up the matter, with a House Energy & Commerce oversight and investigations subcommittee conducting hearings and preparing legislation that could very well close down Par. According to *Business Week,* "In July 1989, a fired Par researcher named Satish Shah had threatened to report senior officials to the FDA if they didn't pay him off. When they didn't, Shah called Washington. He claimed that Par had submitted different formulations of a hypertension drug called triamterene in order to pass both clinical

Company Perspectives:

The company has focused on developing products with limited competition and longer life cycles. Par's strategy of aggressive business development including creative alliances and acquisitions, has successfully complemented its steadily increasing investment in internal research and development.

and analytical tests. The drug passed the agency's scrutiny, but only one version went into production. (The FDA requires that the same formulation pass both sets of tests.)'' Executives also faced criminal charges, stemming from a grand jury investigation launched by the U.S. attorney's office in Baltimore, initiated by evidence offered by another generic drug maker, Pittsburgh-based Mylan Laboratories Inc. Shah ultimately pleaded guilty to giving approximately $1,000 to Chang, and Ashok Patel also pleaded guilty to providing $500 to Chang.

Intervention of Kenneth Sawyer: 1989

By August 1989 Par was in difficult straits. Not only was it in the crosshairs of prosecutors, it also faced civil suits from enraged shareholders, who had helplessly watched their investment in Par crumble. Moreover, 68-year-old Perry Levine, not implicated in any wrongdoing, was advised by his physician to retire as soon as possible because of a long-term illness that had already prevented him from testifying before the House subcommittee. His son, Jeffrey Levine, an executive vice-president, was forced by outside directors of the company to take a leave of absence because they believed he had failed to look into the company's problems in a timely manner. At this point Perry Levine sought outside help, turning to Kenneth I. Sawyer, who was uniquely qualified to intervene.

After graduation from law school at Temple University, Sawyer worked five years in the Philadelphia district attorney's office. Then in 1975 he relocated to Fort Lauderdale, Florida, for the law office of Hodgson, Russ, Andrews, Woods & Goodyear, representing generic drug companies. Four years later he became an executive in the industry, accepting the presidency of a Goldine Laboratories Inc. subsidiary, Purge. He later became general counsel and vice-president at drug manufacturer Orlove Enterprises Inc. A few months before being summoned by Perry Levine, Sawyer had launched a private law practice. His tenure as a private attorney, however, would be short-lived, as he would spend the next 14 years as the head of Par, preoccupied with salvaging the business.

According to *Business Week,* ''Sawyer's first taste of Par's corporate culture came soon after he arrived. He says Perry Levine offered a full-time job—with a Ferrari as a sweetener. Sawyer says the implicit message was: 'Help us, don't hurt us.' '' Sawyer turned down the offer, but following Levine's ensuing resignation he became interim president and CEO, and a month later accepted the role on a permanent basis. (He would become chairman in 1990.) He faced a daunting task. ''Problem was,'' in the words of *Business Week,* ''the state and federal officials bearing down on Par didn't trust him any more than

they did former management. ... To keep regulators at bay, Sawyer made them a deal: Not only would he cooperate fully with their investigations, but he would also launch his own and report back with any evidence of wrongdoing. If necessary, he promised to close the company down.'' While he conducted his own probe, Sawyer also took steps to shore up Par's finances, quickly terminating two-thirds of the company's 450 employees. As reported by *Business Week,* Quad was Par's only bright spot: ''But when Sawyer tried to make an initial audit, some Quad managers blocked him. 'If you come in here, you'd be shooting yourself in the foot,' he recalls being told. Sawyer sued to gain access, and what he found, investigators say, was a pattern of phony submission for FDA approvals. ... Sawyer's findings led to indictments of three of the four owner-managers. Par bought them out and shut Quad in 1990.'' Sawyer also provided investigators with other key evidence. ''As executives left the company under fire,'' according to *Business Week,* ''Sawyer made it a practice to search their offices. Snooping around one night he found a set of keys to R.K. Patel's office credenza and looked inside. Incredibly, he found a bottle marked triamterene.'' The substance turned out to be the missing sample that Shah had called Washington about, and it was instrumental in the two Patels pleading guilty to charges of conspiracy to obstruct the regulatory functions of the FDA. Shah was still very much a player in the unfolding story at Par. *Business Week* reported that ''in January 1990, Satish Shah had surfaced again—this time demanding that Sawyer pay him $300,000 or face more disclosures about Par's former practices. Sawyer agreed to meet with Shah, but he alerted the FBI.'' The hotel room where they met was bugged and Shah was soon arrested and charged with conspiracy to defraud the FDA in June 1992. While Shah was out on bail, Sawyer received a number of threats in the mail, and also came into the Par offices one day to find the walls plastered with news articles about workplace shootings. The U.S. attorney advised Sawyer to retain a bodyguard and he even took to wearing a bulletproof vest, a disconcerting sight for his wife, who also had to be escorted to and from her car by armed guards when she came to visit him at the office. According to *Business Week,* ''The threats ended after Shah was convicted of conspiracy and jailed.''

While concerned about the safety of his family and dealing with Par's legal problems, Sawyer cleaned house, ultimately dismissing 35 managers. The company itself pleaded guilty to ten felony counts and paid some $2.5 million in fines. Sawyer, in the meantime, looked for a way to get the company back to business. He improved the company's reputation with the FDA, voluntarily recalling some drugs and imposing a set of protocols for manufacturing and quality control that eventually became standard in the generic drug industry. Although subject to external audits, Par was permitted to once again sell some of its products, but it was banned for five years by the FDA from receiving new drug approvals. Sawyer concluded that the company's best chance to generate revenues was to take advantage of its distribution network. He was able to convince some drugmakers to let Par act as a distributor. He also engineered a restructuring of the business in 1991, creating Pharmaceutical Resources, Inc. (PRI) to act as a holding company for Par. In this way, PRI would be able to seek financing and pursue new opportunities without being subject to the pending lawsuits that continued to beset Par.

Forging an Alliance with Merck: 1999

After losing more than $42 million in 1991 on $34.2 million in revenues, PRI staged a comeback in the early years of the decade. Revenues peaked at $74.5 million in 1993, and the company posted four consecutive years of profit. A difficult stretch followed, however, as PRI endured several years of net losses: $8.3 million in 1996, $8.9 million in 1997, and $9.6 million in 1998. In fiscal 1999 the company laid off 50 employees and discontinued some disappointing product lines, but it was also during this year that Sawyer formed a key alliance with major European drug manufacturer Merck KGaA, which became PRI's largest shareholder, paying $2 a share to own a 42.5 percent interest. All told, Merck, in an effort to gain a presence in the U.S. market, invested more than $20 million in PRI. PRI, for its part, was able to share in the U.S. profits of 40 of Merck's high-margin generic products and jumpstart its drug pipeline in anticipation of the lifting of the FDA ban on new drug approvals.

In August 2001, Merck decided to cash in on its investment in PRI, selling its shares for $27 each, a total of $366 million, which represented a tidy profit on the investment. The distribution and manufacturing agreements forged between the two companies, however, remained in effect. Merck believed that the money it realized in the sale of PRI stock could be better utilized in some other way, and for PRI it was advantageous to cut the cord. The company had turned the corner and was in the midst of recording a comeback year. In 2001 PRI booked sales in excess of $271 million, a major jump over the previous year's $85 million, and it also reported net income of $53.9 million after losing $1.65 million the year prior. Also in 2001 PRI received six first-to-file drug applications from the FDA, allowing a six-month window of exclusivity to produce and market the drugs. Moreover, the company's pipeline included 20 drugs that were pending FDA approval and another 30 in different stages of development. PRI had reached the point where its relationship with Merck was in some ways holding back its growth. Because of conflicts of interest with Merck, PRI had been forced to shy away from ventures with other drug manufacturers. In the words of Westchester's *Journal News,* "Merck wanted to lead a subdued waltz while Pharmaceutical wanted to move along in a high-energy tango."

PRI's relationship with Merck was far from severed, however. In May 2002 it licensed to PRI the rights to 11 generic drugs under development and projected to enter the market between 2003 and 2006. Another significant alliance struck in 2002 involved Rhodes Technologies Inc. A joint venture with PRI called for the development and marketing of specialty pharmaceutical products. Also in 2002 PRI paid $32 million to acquire Fine Tech Ltd. from International Specialty Products. Adding the synthetic chemical process company provided some diversity for PRI, allowing it to develop proprietary pharmaceutical products and giving it the ability to offer drug development services to outside companies. The company enjoyed another year of impressive financial results, with net income in 2002 of more than $70 million.

In June 2003 Sawyer announced his retirement after heading Par and PRI for nearly 14 years. Following a three-month search, his replacement was selected: Scott Tarriff. He had been working for a PRI subsidiary since 1998. Prior to that, he spent 12 years at the Apothecon division of Bristol-Myers Squibb. The company, which had renamed itself Par Pharmaceutical Companies, Inc. by 2004, hoped to continue to follow its successful formula of allying itself with foreign drug manufacturers to market drugs in the U.S. market. Yet it also wanted to make a greater commitment to product development, with the goal of achieving a balance between licensed products and those developed internally. Tarriff told *Drug Store News* in November 2003, "As we look to the future, we are trying to build a specialty pharmaceutical section to our business, having some branded drugs that we will ultimately promote directly to physicians along with our business on the pharmacy side."

Principal Subsidiaries

Par Pharmaceutical, Inc.; PRX Distributors, Ltd.; Fine Tech Ltd.

Principal Competitors

Barr Pharmaceuticals, Inc.; Perrigo Company; Teva Pharmaceuticals Industries Limited.

Further Reading

Alva, Marilyn, "After Rocky Past, Drug Firm Heals Its Wounds," *Investor's Business Daily,* July 12, 2001, p. A10.

Harton, Tom, "Quad Investigated: Generic Drug Maker, Parent Firm Targets of Grand Jury Probe," *Indianapolis Business Journal,* October 31, 1988, p. 1A.

Stodghill, Ron, II, "Red Ink, Wiretaps, and Death Threats," *Business Week,* February 21, 1994, p. 80.

Stricharchuk, Gregory, "House Panel Says Par Pharmaceutical Problems Are More Extensive Than Said," *Wall Street Journal,* September 11, 1989, p. 1.

—Ed Dinger

Paul Mueller Company

1600 W. Phelps Street
Springfield, Missouri 65801
U.S.A.
Telephone: (417) 831-3000
Fax: (417) 831-3528
Web site: http://www.muel.com

Public Company
Incorporated: 1946
Employees: 966
Sales: $116.76 million (2003)
Stock Exchanges: NASDAQ
Ticker Symbol: MUEL
NAIC: 332313 Plate Work Manufacturing

Based in Springfield, Missouri, Paul Mueller Company is a global manufacturer of stainless steel tanks and equipment used in the dairy, food, brewery, beverage, pure water, and pharmaceutical industries. In addition to a manufacturing facility in Springfield, the publicly traded company maintains a plant in Osceola, Iowa. Mueller's business is divided into four segments. Industrial equipment, the largest segment, custom designs and builds processing, biopharmaceutical, heat transfer, commercial refrigeration, and thermal-storage equipment. Generally, the dairy farm equipment segment has been Mueller's most profitable segment, producing milk-cooling equipment, storage equipment and accessories, refrigeration units, and heat-recovery equipment for dairy farmers. These products are sold around the world through approximately 270 independent dealers. The company's field fabrication segment assembles onsite large stainless tanks and vessels built and shipped from the factory. Finally, Mueller operates a trucking subsidiary through its transportation segment. With a fleet of 15 tractors and 40 specialized trailers, the company delivers industrial equipment and dairy farm equipment, as well as components to be installed by the field fabrication segment.

Incorporating the Company in 1946

Paul Mueller Company was founded by Paul K. Mueller in Springfield, Missouri, in 1940 and was incorporated in Missouri in 1946. The original facility was a 900-square-foot single-garage shop involved in general sheet metal work and heating, primarily serving the building industry. With the United States' entry into World War II in 1941, the company became involved in producing stainless steel components to help in the war effort. Then, to serve the population boom that followed the war, it branched out to become involved in the manufacture of stainless steel cheese-making vats used in dairy plants and poultry processing equipment. To support its growing business Mueller built a new 23,720-square-foot manufacturing plant in Springfield in 1950. The additional space would be sorely needed by mid-decade when the company started making stainless steel milk coolers for dairy farms. In 1960 the company began manufacturing stainless steel storage tanks. By now it was clear that Mueller's manufacturing operations were the key to its future and the original sheet metal business was discontinued.

Mueller went public in 1969, fueling further growth. By the end of the 1970s the company had outgrown its space, requiring that an addition of 14,000 square feet be made to the original plant. During this period, there was a change in leadership, as Paul Mueller, who stayed on as chairman, turned over the chief executive officer position to Lawrence P. Mueller in 1976. In April 1982 Lawrence Mueller resigned, citing personal reasons, and was replaced on an interim basis by Daniel C. Manna, vice-president of engineering. Instead of hiring someone else, however, the board of directors during its annual meeting several weeks later decided to retain Manna, who would remain at the helm into the mid-2000s.

Over the years, Mueller spawned a number of stainless steel fabricating companies, making Springfield in the eyes of some "Tank Town U.S.A." One of Paul Mueller's first employees, Milo Letsch, launched his own stainless steel company, Letsch Corp., in 1968. After selling that business he started another company in 1976 called Letco Inc. Art Rude, who worked for both Paul Mueller and Letsch, along with a pair of Letsch employees, launched Custom Metal Craft in 1976. Two Paul Mueller employees then bought Letsch in 1984, and renamed it Precision Stainless Inc. to compete with Mueller in the custom stainless steel business. Another Springfield company, Stainless Fabrication Inc., would compete with Mueller in the field fabrication market.

Having other stainless steel companies in the community proved beneficial to all concerned. Having Springfield so closely associated with stainless steel helped Mueller and the other companies in their marketing efforts. Springfield also attracted a pool of specialized craftsmen that would not have developed had it not been for so many potential employers. Moreover, the companies bought components and contracted out work to one another, taking advantage of each other's specialized equipment and personnel. During times of overload, they often shared each other's burden. By and large, Mueller and the other Springfield stainless steel companies did not conflict because each branched off into specialty areas.

Significant Changes in the Late 1980s and the 1990s

Mueller experienced a number of significant changes during the late 1980s. In January 1987 the company acquired a water purification product line. It was also in that year Mueller opened a plant in Osceola, Iowa, adding 200,000 square feet of manufacturing space. Yet 1987 also brought with it labor problems, as Mueller endured a 16-week strike by the Sheet Metal Workers' International Association, Local 208. As a result, the company lost money in 1987. During the early months of 1988 the company rebounded, due in large part to increased international demand for its products. Investors became attracted to the company, bidding up its stock price to more than $23, a remarkable rise given that the stock had posted a high of $22 before the October 1987 stock crash. Yet there was another factor to investor enthusiasm: Paul Mueller was now 72 years old, and many believed he was interested in selling his 20 percent stake in the company. A management-led buyout was a possibility, as was a takeover attempt. The book value of the company was approximately $22 a share, but Mueller also carried an overfunded pension plan worth another $4.75 a share. Mueller disappointed the speculators, however. He did not sell out and despite his advancing years stayed on as chairman for another 16 years.

In 1990 Mueller posted $77.8 million in annual sales, while earning more than $5.6 million. A recession cut into business over the next three years and revenues sagged, to $75 million in 1991, $74.6 million in 1992, and $73.8 million in 1993. Net income during this period bottomed out at $2.2 million in 1993. Business improved in 1994, with sales growing to $79.5 million and net income to $3.5 million. During this period, the company expanded its product offering. In 1992 it negotiated a license agreement for the rights to manufacture and market water distillation equipment, and in 1994, Mueller acquired the rights to make evaporator assemblies used in liquid-ice systems for gas turbines, HVAC (heating, ventilation, and air conditioning), the process cooling of food and chemicals, and concentration of milk, fruit juices, and acid solutions. Manufacturing and marketing for evaporator assemblies began in 1995. In addition, in 1994 Mueller extended a license agreement with a Dutch company to manufacture and sell its dairy farm equipment in Europe.

Mueller experienced another strike in 1995, after the labor contract with the Sheet Metal Workers expired in June 1994 and the two sides were unable to reach an agreement. A strike was launched in July 1995, with a varying number of workers out on strike at any particular time, as the union chose not to prevent nonstriking employees from working. Nevertheless, the company's level of production suffered, adversely impacting the balance sheet for the year. Revenues in 1995 declined to $78.4 million and net income fell to $1.96 million. Aside from the strike, the sale of dairy farm equipment was down, and it was becoming clear that this important part of the company's business had seen its best days and that if Mueller wanted to prosper in the future it would need to seek new opportunities.

In February 1997 Mueller acquired property in downtown Springfield to build a microbrewery and brewpub, which opened in December of that year as the Springfield Brewing Company. Although the operation was intended to succeed on its own, more important was that it served as a showcase for Mueller's brewing systems to show visiting customers how the system worked and to allow them to get a feel for what equipment might fulfill their needs. The showcase brewery soon drummed up business both in the United States and overseas. Great Lakes Brewing in Ohio contracted Mueller to develop a brewing system, and a Japanese brewer launched an $8 million project with the company to design, build, and install a brewing system. The Japanese contract was indicative of an increasing emphasis Mueller placed on its international business. In 1991 the international division accounted for $5 million in revenues. That amount would exceed $17 million in 1997. The company's top markets overseas were the United Kingdom, Japan, and Mexico.

Launching Field Operations in 1998

Another important development was the 1998 launch of a field operations subsidiary, part of an effort to transform Mueller from a manufacturer of components to one that offered systems using the components it manufactured. Essentially, the company had little choice but to change, because the industry began moving toward field fabrication to serve customers who no longer wanted to put together components themselves. In fact, because of consolidation in the beverage and dairy industries, and elsewhere, customers, to realize economies of scale, wanted to build much larger processing plants, which meant larger tanks. Because such equipment was too large to transport, it had to be fabricated in the field, meaning that Mueller in order to compete had to establish a field operation, as well as a trucking fleet, to economically transport the components to a job site. Aside from the necessity of expanding its operation in this way, Mueller also saw opportunity in its new approach. Because dairy farm equipment, the company's traditional product line, was a mature sector, much of Mueller's growth would have to come from its three other business segments.

As a result of transforming its business, Mueller enjoyed steady growth in the late 1990s, leading to an expansion of the Springfield manufacturing facility. In 1996 the company posted sales of nearly $84 million and net income of $4.4 million. Sales grew to $86.7 million in 1997, $89.7 million in 1998, and $95.2 million in 1999. Net income during this period ranged from $1.9 million to $3.1 million. In 2000 the company was once again at odds with the Sheet Metal Workers union. Owning 90 shares

Key Dates:

1940: The company is founded as a sheet metal operation.
1946: The company is incorporated.
1960: The sheet metal business is discontinued.
1969: The company is taken public.
1976: Paul Mueller steps down as CEO.
1998: The field fabrication operation is launched.
2004: Paul Mueller retires as chairman.

of stock, the union, with support from an institutional investor, attempted to elect a dissident member to the company's board of directors. It also attempted to have a shareholder rights plan, a "poison-pill provision" adopted in 1991, put to a vote. Although the union was defeated on both initiatives, it did make it clear to management that some investors desired to see an independent voice on the board. Management, on the other hand, expressed displeasure in the distraction of a proxy fight, which required spending money and time that could have been put to better use in running the business.

Mueller topped the $100 million mark in annual sales in 2000, totaling $105.3 million, while recording net income of $3.8 million. In 2001 the company finally reached a new agreement with the Sheet Metal Workers union, but because of a number of factors the company suffered a setback. A strong U.S. dollar and the effects of hoof-and-mouth disease in Europe were all key factors in a significant erosion in dairy farm equipment, resulting in a 22 percent decline domestically and 30 percent internationally. Sales of milk cooler units were also lower by 31 percent domestically and 34 percent internationally. As a result, revenues for the year fell to $94.3 million, and the company recorded a net loss of $1.4 million.

Mueller rebounded in 2002, due in large part to a jump in sales in the industrial equipment segment, in particular the biopharm systems product line, which enjoyed a 260 percent increase in orders over the previous year. Sales of dairy farm equipment also improved over 2001. As a consequence, sales grew to $114.1 million and net income improved to $1.9 million.

In 2003 the industrial equipment segment again led the way, with sales for the year approaching $92 million, a significant improvement over the $78.2 million recorded the prior year. Still, the sale of dairy farm equipment during this period fell from $20.3 million to $14.3 million, the lowest amount the company had achieved since 1987. The main factor was the low price of milk, the average of which from July 2002 through June 2003 was the lowest level in 25 years. Dairy farmers, therefore, simply could not afford to increase their milk-cooling and storage capacity.

Paul Mueller finally stepped down as chairman in January 2004, replaced by Director William R. Patterson. He assumed the position during a challenging period for the company. The biopharm product line, which had been so instrumental in the company's recent success, suffered a setback, as major customers refrained from launching major projects. In addition, the price of stainless steel was rising, which hurt profitability. More than likely these problems would prove temporary, and Mueller would continue its transformation from a stainless steel components manufacturer to one that provided total solutions.

Principal Subsidiaries

Mueller Transportation, Inc.; Mueller Field Operations, Inc.

Principal Competitors

FMC Corporation; mg technologies ag; Spectris PLC.

Further Reading

Cantrell, Patty, "Springfield Stainless Steel Mecca," *Springfield News-Leader,* July 19, 1993.

Culp, Karen E., "Paul Mueller to Go Global," *Springfield Business Journal,* October 6, 1997, p. 1.

Flemming, Paul, "Strange Currencies," *Springfield News-Leader,* November 12, 2000, p. 11A.

Marcial, Gene G., "There's a Pot of Gold in Steel Vats," *Business Week,* May 9, 1988, p. 134.

—Ed Dinger

Q.E.P. Co., Inc.

1081 Hollard Drive
Boca Raton, Florida 33487
U.S.A.
Telephone: (561) 994-5550
Fax: (561) 241-2830
Web site: http://www.qep.com

Public Company
Incorporated: 1979
Employees: 441
Sales: $143.3 million (2004)
Stock Exchanges: NASDAQ
Ticker Symbol: QEPC
NAIC: 332212 Hand and Edge Tool Manufacturing

Q.E.P. Co., Inc. is a publicly traded company based in Boca Raton, Florida, that manufactures, distributes, and markets some 3,000 flooring tools and accessories for both the do-it-yourself and professional installer markets in the United States and approximately 50 other countries. The company has carved out a unique niche in the home improvement field and has no serious challengers. Its products are used in surface preparation and the installation of carpet, ceramic tile, vinyl, and wood flooring. They are sold under several brand names—Q.E.P., Roberts, Q-Set, Elastiment, Vitrex, Fresh, and O'Tool—and include trowels, tile cutters, wet saws, spacers, nippers, carpet trimmers and cutters, flooring adhesives, seaming tape, tack strip, knives, dry set powders, and grouts. Although Q.E.P. manufactures many of its own products, it also relies on 250 different suppliers to provide the rest. Most of the company's sales come from two customers, Home Depot, accounting for 46.4 percent of sales in 2004, and Lowe's with 13.2 percent. Q.E.P. is headed by its founder, Lewis Gould, who along with his family owns about half of the company.

Company Founding in 1979

By his own admission, Gould, who preferred to spend his spare time as a ham radio operator, stumbled into the home improvement industry. As a businessman he was more familiar with decorative telephones, an area he came to know while serving as vice-president of Saxton Products, a New York wire and cable company that decided to diversify. In 1979 Gould struck out on his own to sell electronics, forming a company he named Q.E.P., which stood for Quality Electronic Products. Instead of going high-tech, however, he decided, along with his wife Susan, to spend $10,000 for a new bathtub-edging company, which sold a kit to cover the grout around the edge of a bathtub. He converted his one-car garage in New City, New York, 20 minutes north of Manhattan, into a makeshift assembly line to package the edging kit. Gould traveled on sales calls, leaving his wife and 10-year-old son, Leonard, to package the kits and box the orders. UPS provided the shipping, but the driver, according to Leonard's recollection, refused to carry the boxes to the truck, making the wife and son do the heavy lifting. It was a humble beginning, but the bathtub-edging kit proved popular.

Distributors began asking Gould if he could supply them with tile tools, needed by floor installers. Having no idea what tile tools were, Gould began to educate himself, learning what was needed to do ceramic tiling: wet saws, tile cutters, trowels, spaces, sponges, and tile nippers. Thus Q.E.P. moved even further away from electronics as Gould began meeting customer demand by adding more and more flooring tools and accessories. The most significant break for the company came in 1982 when Home Depot, which would revolutionize the home improvement industry, made Q.E.P. its flooring products supplier. Home Depot asked Q.E.P. to produce a tile tools kit in a package with instructions. Gould tried to comply with the request but lacked the necessary funding. Home Depot's founder, Bernie Marcus, stepped in and helped the company secure a loan that provided the working capital Q.E.P. needed in order to grow and keep pace with Home Depot's needs in flooring products. In 1993 Q.E.P. added another giant customer in the home improvement industry, Lowe's, which became the company's second largest account. In 1996 Q.E.P. added Builder's Square, a Kmart division, as a full distribution customer.

Q.E.P., which relocated to Boca Raton in the 1980s, also began to make acquisitions to fill out its product lines and fuel further growth. In 1994 it paid $580,000 for O'Tool Company, a Henderson, New York, company that offered concrete, ma-

Company Perspectives:

QEP strives to supply our customers with the most comprehensive flooring installation products available and our broad product line sets us apart from the competition. Whether you are a professional floor covering installer or a "weekend warrior," QEP has the right tools for quality installations.

sonry, stone, plaster, and drywall tools, and accompanying supplies. Later in the year Q.E.P. added Marion Tool Corporation, based in Marion, Indiana, paying $425,547, and early in 1995 it acquired Andrews Enterprises at a cost of $67,500.

Taking the Company Public in 1996

In 1996 Q.E.P. was at a crossroads and needed to decide how to fund further growth. Gould told *South Florida Business Journal* in a 1998 company profile, "I thought the best way was to have a well-funded public company, so that our customers could see we had made a commitment over a long period of time to grow with them and have access to capital markets." The offering, lead underwritten by Irvine, California-based Cruttenden Roth Incorporated, was completed in September 1996. All told, one million shares offered by the company and 200,000 shares by the principal shareholders were sold at a price of $8.50 per share. Some of the money raised was soon put to use consolidating three locations into a single Boca Raton facility, which would serve as the new corporate headquarters, a manufacturing plant, and distribution center serving the eastern United States. As a result of improved efficiency, Q.E.P. would be able to achieve lower per-unit costs.

In 1997 Q.E.P. completed its most significant acquisition to date, paying $12.35 million in cash and stock for Roberts Consolidated Industries, Inc. of City of Industry, California. Roberts, founded in 1938, was a leading manufacturer and marketer of flooring installation tools and related supplies, specializing in such soft surfaces as carpeting as opposed to Q.E.P.'s strength in hard-surface flooring tools. The businesses complemented one another and allowed both entities to take advantage of the other's distribution channels and broaden their customer bases. The Roberts brand name also was highly valuable to Q.E.P. In addition Q.E.P. added operations in Mexico, Missouri, and Toronto, Canada. In January 1998 Q.E.P. followed up with the purchase of the outstanding shares of Roberts, Holland BV, at a cost of $1.6 million and the assumption of approximately $1.5 million in debt. The Rotterdam-based company held a license to market flooring tools and supplies in 49 countries under the "Roberts" trade name. It also operated subsidiaries in France, Germany, and the United Kingdom, affording Q.E.P. an opportunity to expand its customer base in Europe and other international markets. According to Gould, the Roberts deal gave Q.E.P. "critical mass." According to the *Palm Beach Post,* the acquisition "rounded out Q.E.P.'s product line and made it the monster of flooring-tool products."

Q.E.P. had now established itself as a major consolidator in its niche and was starting to gain some recognition. It made the 1997 Florida 100 List as well as the "Top 100 Hot Growth Small Corporations" list compiled by *Business Week.* Wall Street, on the other hand, had yet to warm up to the company, preoccupied with high-tech and Internet ventures. Q.E.P. stock traded below its initial offering price, and was so close to book value that the company could not effectively make use of it in acquisitions, forcing it to be a cash buyer. Some suggested that Q.E.P. should change its name, taking advantage of the far more recognizable Roberts brand, but Gould believed that all that was necessary was more of a public relations effort. He told the *South Florida Business Journal* in February 1998, "We have to get our story out and do the road shows. The difficulty is you still have to run the business at home. That's hard to manage."

Over the next few years, Q.E.P. continued to pursue its consolidation strategy. In July 1998 it closed on the acquisition of Novafonte, Limitada, a Santiago, Chile-based manufacturer, distributor, and installer of ceramic tile and ceramic tile accessories. The addition of Novafonte helped Q.E.P. in the South American market and provided more momentum in the company's quest to become the world's dominant player in flooring installation products, as well as to establish a presence in all of the markets where Home Depot, Lowe's, and its other major customers operated. Days later Q.E.P. completed a deal halfway around the globe, acquiring two Australian flooring companies: Neon Australia Pty. Ltd. and Accessories Marketing Pty. Ltd. Neon Australia served the carpet industry and was a major producer of flooring tapes and metals. Accessories Marketing supplied the Australian marketplace with a wide variety of tools and installation products for all types of flooring. The two companies were combined as Q.E.P. Australia and instantly became a dominant company in Australia for flooring products. The business was supplemented later in 1999 with the acquisition of Trade Mates Pty, Ltd., an Australian distributor of ceramic tile tools. Another significant development in 1999 was the acquisition of Boiardi Products Corp., a Little Falls, New Jersey, company with nearly 40 years of experience in such flooring products as thin-set mortars, grouts, self-leveling concrete toppings, and crack-suppressing waterproof membranes. In addition to supplying products and expertise to projects in the United States, Boiardi did work in the Middle East and Far East. In December 1999 Q.E.P. also acquired Zocalis S.R.L., a Buenos Aires, Argentina-based company that manufactured and distributed ceramic tile, metal and plastic trims, and profiles to the Argentinean flooring market.

More Acquisitions in 2000

Several more acquisitions followed in 2000. In March Q.E.P. added to its Australian business by picking up Southern Tile Agencies Ltd. Pty., maker of ceramic tile installation products such as trowels and kneepads. In that same month, Q.E.P. bought Stone Mountain Manufacturing Company of Georgia, a Calhoun, Georgia, manufacturer of dry set powders and grouts needed for ceramic tile installation. Several weeks later, Q.E.P. added Stone Mountain Manufacturing Company of Florida, a Fort Pierce, Florida, company that made dry set powders and adhesives of ceramic tile installation. Another significant development in 2000 was the decision to close an outdated distribution center in City of Industry, California, upon the expiration of a lease, and to move into a modern 117,000-square-foot facility

---

Key Dates:

1979: The company is formed.
1982: Home Depot becomes a customer.
1993: Lowe's is added as a customer.
1996: The company is taken public.
1997: Roberts Consolidated Industries, Inc. is acquired.
2003: The company adds do-it-yourself interactive manuals to its web site and launches a new product line, Fresh, geared toward women do-it-yourselfers.

---

located in Henderson, Nevada. The new site would serve as the primary distribution center for the western United States and would also support manufacturing to help Q.E.P. keep pace with its domestic growth.

In 2000 Q.E.P. posted sales of $113.6 million, which produced a profit of $3.2 million. Business would flatten out over the next two years, and the company refrained from making further acquisitions during this time. Sales fell slightly to $113 million in 2001, and dropped to $109.7 million in 2002, with net income totaling $1.4 million in 2001 and $2.1 million in 2002. Reduced profits in 2001 were the result of charges taken after closing the City of Industry facility and downsizing a Dutch subsidiary. Although the economy was struggling, Q.E.P. would begin to benefit from a trend that saw people foregoing vacations but showing an increased interest in investing money to improve their homes, which for most people was their biggest asset. Investors were beginning to take notice of a company that was still able to make money when so many other businesses were suffering severe losses. In the summer of 2003 shares of Q.E.P., which had been trading around $5 more than doubled, due mostly to the decision of institutional investors for the first time to recognize Q.E.P.'s potential. The company held a dominant position in a unique niche in the home-improvement market, one that was not likely to be challenged. According to Larry Rader, a partner in LAR Management, which bought a stake in the company, "In technology, there's always some idiot in a garage who can make something better than you. But who's going to design a new trowel or go into the trowel business?"

In 2003 revenues totaled $129.3 million and grew to $143.3 million in 2004. Net income increased to nearly $3.5 million in fiscal 2004. Q.E.P. also began to renew its consolidation efforts. In January 2004 it acquired two companies: Vitrex Ltd., a British maker of ceramic tiles, tools, and protective equipment,

and Dublin, Ireland-based Purchistics, which distributed ceramic tools throughout Europe. In March 2004 Q.E.P. added Crestwin Trade Supplies Pty, Ltd., an Australian distributor of flooring tools. Q.E.P. also was taking steps to stimulate sales internally. To take further advantage of a home-improvement trend, and to help address customer questions about how to use the tools Q.E.P. sold, the company added a do-it-yourself interactive manual for laying carpets and tiles to its web site. Included were the stock numbers for the tool needed to complete a project, in the hope that visitors to the site would then seek out those items at a Home Depot, Lowe's, or elsewhere. Moreover, in 2003 Q.E.P. launched a new product line called Fresh, geared toward women do-it-yourselfers. The line was initially composed of 11 different kits of tools to complete painting and wallpapering projects. Each tool featured an ergonomic handle and bright colors. What was especially important to the company was that by focusing on women, Fresh opened up a new distribution channel, that of mass-market retailers including supermarkets. After 25 years in operation Q.E.P. retained an entrepreneurial spirit and gave every indication that it was just beginning to realize its true potential.

Principal Subsidiaries

Roberts Consolidated Industries, Inc.; Q.E.P.–O'Tool, Inc.; Boiardi Products Corporation; Marion Tool Corporation; Q.E.P. Stone Holdings, Inc.; Q.E.P. Zocalus Holding L.L.C.; Q.E.P. Aust. Pty. Limited; Roberts Holland B.V.

Principal Competitors

The Black & Decker Corporation; Cooper Industries, Ltd.; Danaher Corporation.

Further Reading

Pounds, Stephen, "Flooring Tool Maker's Stock Builds Momentum," *Palm Beach Post,* July 8, 2003, p. 6B.
——, " 'I Like Being Low-Tech. It's Predictable,' " *Palm Beach Port,* February 3, 2003, p. 1D.
——, "QEP Chief Rapped for Modest Earnings Forecast," *Palm Beach Post,* July 10, 2003, p. 1D.
——, "Record Sales Push Q.E.P. Stock to High Mark," *Palm Beach Post,* January 9, 2004, p. 4D.
Varma, Kavita, "Throwing in the Trowel: Boca Raton's Q.E.P. Goes from Family Business to World Leader," *South Florida Business Journal,* February 20, 1998, p. 1A.

—Ed Dinger

Raleigh UK Ltd.

Church Street, Eastwood
Nottinghamshire NG16 3HT
United Kingdom
Telephone: 01773 532 600
Web site: http://www.raleigh.co.uk

Private Company
Incorporated: 1888 as The Raleigh Cycle Company
Employees: 200
Sales: £35 million (2003 est.)
NAIC: 336991 Motorcycle, Bicycle, and Parts
   Manufacturing

Raleigh UK Ltd. is Britain's leading bike producer. The brand has also been well regarded in the United States and other countries. Raleigh was the world's largest bicycle manufacturer for much of the 20th century. A competitive marketplace led the company to shift all of its manufacturing to Asia by 2002. Entrepreneur Alan Finden-Crofts owns 42 percent of parent company Raleigh Cycles Limited.

Origins

Mechanic R.M. Woodhead, engineering and design expert Paul Angois, and financier William Ellis formed a bicycle shop on Raleigh Street in Nottingham, England, in 1886. The next year, they met Frank Bowden, a British lawyer who had moved to San Francisco after making his fortune in Hong Kong.

Bowden had taken up bicycling for health reasons. He was eager to help Woodhead, Angois, and Ellis promote their improved version of the "safety cycle," an alternative to the "penny farthings" of the day. In 1888 Bowden invested £2,000 in the business, buying out Ellis's share and becoming a half owner of the business. The company was incorporated as a limited company in January 1889, when local businessmen were invited to invest.

Before Bowden joined the firm, its dozen or so employees in three workshops rolled out perhaps 150 bicycles a year. Bowden soon moved the firm to a five-story former lace factory

on Nottingham's Russell Street, raised employment to 200 people, and had the company producing 3,000 bikes a year. According to *Raleigh and the British Bicycle Industry,* another 200 workers and 400 sales agents were added by 1892.

The number of different designs also proliferated, such as a new, lightweight (64 pounds) safety bicycle. Raleigh introduced a number of innovations that would remain part of bicycle design for another hundred years. Participation in the globally popular sport of bicycle racing kept the name in front of spectators around the world.

Raleigh bikes were priced at the top end of the market, from £18 up. The company sold £7,148 worth of products in 1889, resulting in a net profit of £1,862. Annual revenues more than doubled for the next three years; in the fiscal year ended August 1892, the firm had sales of £45,633 and a net profit of £7,072.

Bowden brought in more investors with a small private offering in 1889 and a public flotation in 1891. He bought out the shares of Woodhead and Angois by 1894.

A new factory opened in Lenton a few miles away from the original site in 1896. George Pilkington Mills, formerly works manager at another cycle firm, Humber & Company, was in charge of running Raleigh's operations. Under Mills, Raleigh incorporated automation and other American-style manufacturing practices.

Early 20th-Century Brands

Raleigh accumulated large debts and the existing Raleigh Cycle Company was reorganized around another business, the Gazelle Cycle Company, in 1899. Bowden had set up Gazelle as a budget brand two years earlier. Another low-priced brand, Robin Hood Cycles, was acquired in 1906.

A very important subsidiary, Sturmey Archer Gears Limited, was launched in the early 1900s. This unit would be known for its three-speed internal hub gears throughout the 20th century; they were used exclusively in Raleigh bikes for decades.

Frank Bowden acquired Raleigh outright in 1907. He died in 1921, and his son Sir Harold Bowden took over as managing director. The firm grew to 2,500 employees by 1926, when

Harold Bowden introduced a profit-sharing plan at the Raleigh Cycle Company, as it was then known.

Raleigh produced motorcycles in the 1920s; these were priced at about £130 for the most deluxe (5/6 hp) model with a sidecar, with more basic versions running at half that. The company even expanded into automobiles (the three-wheeled variety).

A new holding company, Raleigh Cycle Holdings Company Limited, was incorporated on February 13, 1934. Raleigh had recently built new offices and had more than 4,000 people on the payroll. There were about 300 other makes of bike in Britain in the early part of the 20th century; most of these were eliminated in the interwar years.

In 1938, Raleigh rolled out a line of budget bikes under the re-introduced Gazelle name, adding to the Raleigh and Humber brands. Raleigh sold nearly 400,000 bikes that year. The Gazelle line was renamed Robin Hood to avoid confusion with an unrelated bicycle manufacturer in Holland of the same name. Raleigh's bicycle sales slipped to about 130,000 in 1942.

During World War II, the company produced armaments, particularly artillery fuses and cartridge cases for the 20mm cannon rounds used by some fighter aircraft. Employment swelled to 9,000 during the war. In 1946, the holding company's name was changed to Raleigh Industries Limited.

Postwar Dominance

After extensive postwar retooling, cycle production soon recovered. Production exceeded one million cycles in 1951; up to 70 percent of these were exported (compared to less than 40 percent before World War II). However, notes historian Tony Handland, newly affluent consumers began turning to the automobile in droves, halving British bike sales. To compete, in the late 1950s Raleigh again began producing motorized vehicles: mopeds and motor scooters.

A second, £1.25 million factory was built in 1952, according to *The Emergence of the British Bicycle Industry.* A £5 million expansion in 1957 brought the size of the Raleigh compound to 64 acres; however, the third factory went unused for several years.

The company was renamed Raleigh Industries Limited after the war. A number of international trading or manufacturing subsidiaries were formed, in the United States (1947), East Africa (1951), South Africa (1952), India (1952), Canada (1954), Holland (1957), and West Germany (1957). Acquisitions included J.B. Brookes (Saddles) Ltd. (1958) and Carlton Cycles Ltd (1959) in the United Kingdom and Irish Bicycle Industries Ltd. (1959) and Consolidated Cycle Industries (1960) abroad.

In addition, Raleigh bought rivals Triumph and Three Spires in 1954 and BSA in 1957. Three years later, in 1960, Raleigh merged with British Bicycle Corporation, a division of Tube Investments (TI). These transactions involving the company's closest rivals brought Raleigh complete dominance of the British bicycle industry, producing 80 percent of the cycles made in Britain. Both deals added brand names to Raleigh's stable. These included New Hudson and Sunbeam from BSA, and Sun, Norman, Phillips, and Hercules from TI.

Production peaked in the late 1970s at four million bikes per year. However, in spite of the popularity of such models as the Chopper, by 1981 market share had slipped to 40 percent.

Straddling an industry trend, Raleigh launched its Maverick mountain bike in 1985. In the same year Huffy Corp. launched Raleigh Cycle Co. of America to build Raleigh bikes under license near Seattle. Derby International bought back the U.S. rights in 1988.

Acquired by Derby in 1987

According to the *Financial Times,* Raleigh lost money throughout the 1980s until it was acquired by Luxembourg-based Derby International Corp. SA in April 1987. The Derby Cycle Corporation, led by former Dunlop Slazenger chief Alan Finden-Crofts and attorney Ed Gottesman, acquired Raleigh from Tube Investments (TI) for £18 million plus £14 million in assumed debt. At the same time, the investors also bought TI's venerable Royal Worcester tableware group, which was managed under a separate holding company.

Raleigh maintained a one-third share of the £300 million British bike market in the mid-1990s. A group of New York investors including Thayer Capital and Perseus Partners bought the company in 1998 just as the mountain bike craze was winding down.

In December 2000, the famous Sturmey Archer gears company was sold to British management firm Lenark. Soon after, investor George Soros and others brought £21 million in rescue funding to Derby. Alan Finden-Crofts was brought back to lead a turnaround. Derby Cycle sought U.S. bankruptcy protection on August 20, 2001, first selling its Gazelle Rijwielfabriek unit in the Netherlands for EUR 142.5 million (US$122 million).

2001 Management Buyout

On September 28, 2001, a management group led by Alan Finden-Crofts acquired Derby Cycle Corporation in a deal worth about $73 million, including more than $50 million in assumed debt. At the same time, Germany's Wiener Bike Parts and Derby South Africa were sold off. Finden-Crofts then owned 42 percent of Derby Cycle, which was renamed Raleigh Cycle Limited.

Raleigh sold its Triumph Road site to the University of Nottingham in 2001. Environmental protection issues complicated a planned move to a nearby location. Management decided to shift manufacturing to lower wage countries in the Far East and Raleigh's British production line closed in November 2002. The Nottingham factory had employed 600 people and was producing 500,000 bikes a year before it was closed, though it had stopped making its own frames in 1999. In addition, the management team was replaced and a new com-

Key Dates:

1887: Frank Bowden acquires bike frame shop in Nottingham.
1888: The Raleigh Cycle Company is founded.
1902: Sturmey-Archer gears business is acquired.
1932: Humber Cycles is acquired.
1934: Raleigh is reorganized as Raleigh Cycle Holdings Limited.
1938: Budget "Gazelle" brand is relaunched.
1954: Raleigh acquires Triumph and Three Spires.
1957: BSA's bike business is acquired.
1960: Tube Investments (TI) buys Raleigh.
1987: Raleigh is acquired by Derby International.
2001: Management acquires Derby Cycle Corporation and renames it Raleigh Cycle Ltd.
2002: U.K. production ceases as manufacturing is shifted to the Far East.

puter system installed. Raleigh's sales and design operations moved from the original location on Triumph Road, Nottingham, to Eastwood in December 2002.

After four years of losses, Raleigh UK managed a small profit on sales of £35 million in 2003. It then had about 200 employees. Raleigh America had sales of about $75 million. In a bit of nostalgia, Raleigh brought back its 1970s-era Chopper in the spring of 2004.

Principal Subsidiaries

Derby Cycle Werke (Germany); Raleigh America (U.S.A.); Raleigh Canada; Raleigh China; Raleigh Taiwan; Raleigh UK Limited.

Principal Competitors

Moore Large & Co. Ltd.; Tandem Group PLC; Universal Cycles.

Further Reading

Ballard, Mark, "Raleigh Gets on Its Bike," *Sunday Times* (London), Bus. Sec., May 23, 2004, p. 15.
Berke, Jonathan, "Judge OKs Derby Cycle's Liquidation Plan," *Daily Deal* (New York), February 1, 2002.
Bowden, Sir Harold, "Raleigh Cycle Holdings; Great War Effort; Sir Harold Bowden on the Outlook," *Times* (London), January 17, 1946, p. 10.
Buckingham, Lisa, "Raleigh—Soros Rides In," *Mail on Sunday,* December 17, 2000.
Burns, Mairin, "Corporate Restructuring Takes a Transatlantic Turn," *High Yield Report,* November 5, 2001.
Cope, Nigel, "Raleigh Hears the Wheels of the Pack," *Independent,* March 7, 1994, p. 25.
Gibbs, Geoff, "Raleigh Reaches End of Assembly Road," *Guardian* (Manchester), March 16, 2002, p. 28.
Gillis, Cydney, "Kent Firm Rebounds from Bankruptcy," *Associated Press Newswires,* August 8, 2003.
Handland, Tony, "Raleigh in the Last Quarter of the 20th Century," 11th International Cycle History Conference, Osaka, August 2000.
International Business Machines Corporation, "The Evolutionary Cycle," *Vision,* Winter 2003, pp. 8–11.
Johnson, Bruce, "Raleigh Pedals Against the Tide," *American Shipper,* September 1985, pp. 16+.
Lloyd-Jones, Roger, and M.J. Lewis, *Raleigh and the British Bicycle Industry: An Economic and Business History, 1870–1960,* Aldershot, United Kingdom: Ashgate, 2000.
"Profit-Sharing at Nottingham: Raleigh Cycle Company's Scheme," *Times* (London), April 26, 1926, p. 9.
"Raleigh Bikes in Major Marketing Department Rejig," *Marketing,* February 6, 2003, p. 4.
Rosen, Paul, *Framing Production: Technology, Culture, and Change in the British Bicycle Industry,* Cambridge, Mass. and London: MIT Press, 2002.
Seaton, Matt, "Here Comes the Chopper," *Guardian* (Manchester), Feature Sec., May 10, 2002, p. 2.
"A Sporting Chance: After His Success in Turning Around Dunlop-Slazenger Alan Finden-Crofts Is All Lined Up to Give Raleigh Cycles the Same Treatment," *Management Today,* June 29, 1987, p. 11.
"Success Recycled," *Financial Times,* March 13, 1996, p. 20.
"This Article Looks in Detail at the Unexpected Purchase of This Company by Derby International from London International," *Financial Times,* June 25, 1988, p. 7.
Tressider, Richard, "Raleigh's on the Road to Stability," *Nottingham Evening Post,* August 22, 2001.
——, "Raleigh's Owner to Close Offices," *Nottingham Evening Post,* January 8, 2001.
"Turn of the Last Wheel . . . ," *Nottingham Evening Post,* November 29, 2002, p. 6.
Wiebe, Matt, "Management Team Takes Over Derby," *Bicycle Retailer,* November 1, 2001, p. 1.
——, "Raleigh Cycle Restructures to Compete," *Bicycle Retailer,* December 1, 2001, p. 1.
Wilhelm, Steve, "Build a Better Bicycle, and Buyers Come to You," *Puget Sound Business Journal,* September 10, 1990, pp. 4+.
——, "Kent Raleigh Bike Plant Gears Up for Export Sales," *Puget Sound Business Journal,* October 10, 1988, p. 14.

—Frederick C. Ingram

Rinker Group Ltd.

Level 8 Twr. B, 799 Pacific Hwy.
Chatswood
NSW 2000
Australia
Telephone: + 61 2 9412 6600
Fax: +61 2 9412 6666
Web site: http://www.rinker.com.au

Public Company
Incorporated: 2003
Employees:
Sales: $3.94 billion (2003)
Stock Exchanges: Australian New York
Ticker Symbol: RIN
NAIC: 212312 Crushed and Broken Limestone Mining
and Quarrying; 212313 Crushed and Broken Granite
Mining and Quarrying; 212321 Construction Sand and
Gravel Mining; 327121 Brick and Structural Clay Tile
Manufacturing; 327123 Other Structural Clay Product
Manufacturing; 327310 Cement Manufacturing;
327320 Ready-Mix Concrete Manufacturing; 327331
Concrete Block and Brick Manufacturing; 327390
Other Concrete Product Manufacturing; 327420
Gypsum and Gypsum Product Manufacturing; 551112
Offices of Other Holding Companies

Rinker Group Ltd. is one of the world's top ten heavy building materials groups, with emphasis on cement, concrete, aggregate, and other construction and infrastructure materials, such as asphalt, cement pipes, and prestressed concrete products. Rinker Group was formed by the breakup of Australia's CSR Limited, which performed a demerger in 2003, separating into specialized sugar (CSR) and building materials (Rinker) companies. Although Rinker remains headquartered in Australia, that country accounts for less than 20 percent of its total sales, primarily through its Readymix and Humes concrete and concrete pipe businesses. The United States, where Rinker ranks among the industry's top five, is the group's largest market, generating some 80 percent of its revenues of more than $3.9 billion in 2003. Florida, the home base of the original Rinker operation and where the company is market leader, represents by itself more than 43 percent of the company's sales. Las Vegas and Arizona are also major markets for Rinker, and the company has also built a strong presence in the Midwest. Rinker has grown rapidly through acquisition in the highly fragmented heavy building materials market, in which high transportation costs force companies to establish local operations. The company has also established a foothold in China, acquiring two cement plants in anticipation of the expected building and infrastructure boom in that country. Nonetheless, China represented only 1 percent of the group's sales in 2003. Rinker Group is listed on the Australian and New York Stock Exchanges and is led by David Clarke.

Sugar Scrap Beginnings in the 1930s

CSR Limited originated as the Colonial Sugar Refining partnership in Sydney, Australia, in 1855. That company quickly grew into one of Australia's leading sugar companies. As the company grew, it became interested in making use of the large amount of sugar cane scrap left over from the sugar production process. In 1936, CSR began developing a method to transform the sugar cane fiber scrap into wallboard. By the end of the decade, the company was ready to launch production, and in 1939 CSR acquired a chemicals plant to begin manufacturing the Cane-ite wallboard brand.

Building materials became a major company focus during World War II, with the launch of a plaster mill in Sydney in 1942. The company began producing plasterboard in 1948, and extended its construction materials operations with the launch of a floor tiles unit that year as well. These were placed under a new subsidiary, CSR Chemicals. CSR developed a number of other interests during this time, including asbestos mining. By the late 1950s, CSR had begun manufacturing insulation materials as well.

CSR's introduction to the cement and concrete markets came in the mid-1960s when, in partnership with Blue Metal Industries, the company bought a 50 percent share of Readymix Concrete. That company had been founded in 1939 in Glebe,

Australia, in order to produce Readymix-branded concrete. Readymix began delivering concrete using its own fleet of truck-mounted tumblers. Following World War II, Readymix began its national expansion, opening plants in Melbourne in 1945 and Brisbane in 1946. Other locations opened during the 1950s included Botany, Glanville, and Brompton.

In 1952, Readymix began its international expansion, opening a subsidiary in the United Kingdom—and promptly buying up its existing Readymix rival in that country. Readymix also entered Brazil in 1953, then, through its U.K. subsidiary, Germany in 1955. Readymix's European presence grew rapidly, especially in the United Kingdom. By the mid-1960s, Readymix had opened nearly 60 plants throughout the United Kingdom and had captured one-fourth of the market. Growth was slower in Germany, as the company more or less introduced ready-mix concrete to that market; yet by the 1960s, Readymix had established itself as a leader.

In the meantime, Readymix had not neglected its domestic market, where it added quarrying operations at mid-decade, starting with the purchase of the Styles quarry in Sydney in 1957. The company also acquired its own sand and gravel reserves in Penrith, in New South Wales, that year. In 1958, Readymix boosted its quarrying division with the acquisition of ABM, which operated quarries in Adelaide, Perth, Melbourne, Hobart, and Sydney.

After CSR acquired 50 percent of its capital, Readymix divested its foreign holdings, which included spinning off its U.K. and European branch as a separate, publicly listed company, Readymix (UK), which later became known as RMC.

CSR placed Readymix within its building materials division, boosting it in 1966 through the acquisition of a stake in Goliath Cement Co., based in Tasmania. That purchase enabled the company to enter the cement market for the first time, and gave it terminals in Sydney and in Melbourne. The company further expanded its cement operations through a joint venture with Pioneer International to buy Australian and Kandos Cement. The company also acquired slightly more than half of another prominent concrete and cement products group, Farley and Lewers Pty.

In 1976, CSR restructured its construction and building materials operations into three divisions: minerals, building materials, and construction materials. The restructuring came ahead of CSR's further diversification into the oil and gas industries. Nonetheless, CSR continued building up its construction materials division, acquiring full control of both Readymix and Farley and Lewers in 1981. These were then combined into a single subsidiary, Readymix Farley, which was then renamed CSR Readymix in 1987.

Moving into America in the 1990s

By the middle of the 1980s, CSR was forced to abandon its attempt to build a presence in the oil industry. Instead, in 1987, the company sold off its oil interests and refocused around a dual core of sugar and building and construction materials.

CSR then began a drive to step up its building and construction materials component. A key part of the group's strategy involved returning to the international market. This time the group turned to the vast and highly fragmented U.S. market, buying Florida's Rinker Materials Corp. in 1988 for $515 million.

Rinker had been founded in 1926 by Marshall E. "Doc" Rinker, who started in business hauling sand and rock with a single dump truck—which was subsequently repossessed in 1929. Yet Rinker was able to buy back the truck, and then went on to found a fleet of trucks serving a network of cement, concrete, and other construction materials plants throughout Florida. By the late 1980s, Rinker had grown into the largest heavy building materials company in Florida—then one of the fastest-growing markets in the United States, with sales approaching $500 million.

David Clarke was placed in charge of developing CSR's new American unit—which took the name of CSR America in the early 1990s. After restructuring Rinker's management—which had been closely controlled by its founder—Clarke began adding new businesses to the fold, building one of the first of the large-scale construction materials groups in the fragmented market. Growth in the sector nonetheless required establishing a physical presence in potential new markets—the high transportation costs of the materials made local production and delivery imperative.

CSR America made its first major acquisition in 1990, buying ARC America for nearly $700 million. That acquisition gave the company a significant quarrying business in the United States, and also enabled it to expand its construction materials operation beyond Florida. Among the companies included in the ARC purchase were Associated Sand & Gravel, adding four ready-mix, two concrete pipe, and four aggregates plants in Washington state; American Aggregates, based in Indianapolis, with 41 plants in Indiana, Ohio, and Michigan; and WMK Materials, with five plants serving the Las Vegas market, as well as ready-mix and block operations in Arizona.

The company supplemented those acquisitions with a long series of bolt-on acquisitions supporting its positions in the Las Vegas and Florida markets, but also in other markets, such as Baltimore and Albuquerque. The purchases helped boost the company's total U.S. construction materials revenues past $1 billion. At the same time, CSR made its first move into another potentially huge foreign market, China, buying a cement operation in Tianjin in 1994.

Yet the company's growth inspired competitors and, by the late 1990s, CSR America appeared to have lost its momentum, slipping from a fourth place position to fighting to maintain its spot in the top ten. After selling off most of its aggregates operations in 1997, the company began plans to launch a new acquisition drive in order to reclaim a spot among the top-ranking building and construction materials companies.

Key Dates:

1855: Colonial Sugar Refining (CSR) is formed.
1926: Marshall E. "Doc" Rinker founds sand-and-rock hauling business in Florida.
1936: CSR begins developing means of producing wallboard using scrap from sugar cane refining operations.
1939: Readymix Concrete is established in Sydney; CSR begins production of wallboard based on sugar cane scrap.
1952: Readymix establishes U.K. operations.
1965: CSR acquires 50 percent of Readymix, which then spins off its U.K. operations as a separate, public company.
1981: CSR acquires remaining 50 percent of Readymix, which is combined with Farley and Lewers to form Readymix Farley.
1988: CSR restructures around dual core of sugar and construction materials; acquires Rinker Materials Corp. in Florida, which becomes CSR America.
1990: CSR America acquires ARC America, adding materials operations in Nevada and elsewhere.
1994: CSR acquires concrete business in Tianjin, China.
1998: CSR America begins new acquisition program, adding 28 companies over five years.
2000: Company acquires Florida Crushed Stone for $350 million.
2001: CSR America makes biggest purchase to date, paying $540 million to acquire Kiewit; company changes name to Rinker Group.
2003: CSR demerges, spinning off Rinker Group as separate, public company; Rinker acquires second Chinese concrete plant.
2004: Rinker announces plans to spend $120 million on new acquisitions and greenfield development.

Focused Building Materials Group in the New Century

By 2003, the company had made some 28 acquisitions, spending more than $1.17 billion. Among CSR America's most notable acquisitions was its purchase of Florida Rock Industries, adding that company's quarry operations in 1999.

The following year marked CSR's return to the top five. In 2000, CSR bought Florida Crushed Stone for $348 million. The company next bought South Culvert, a manufacturer of concrete pipes, also in Florida. These acquisitions were joined by the $42 million purchase of American Limestone in 2001, with operations in Kentucky and Missouri, helping the company capture the number three position in the U.S. ready-mix market, number six in crushed stone, and the leading share of the concrete pipe market.

CSR America changed its name to Rinker Materials Corp. in 2001 in an effort to build a brand position in the U.S. market. The company continued to make bolt-on acquisitions, paying, for example, $42 million to Cemex in order to acquire five quarries complementing its American Limestone operations in Kentucky and Missouri—both states were earmarked for sub-

stantial federal infrastructure spending into the first half of the next century. The company also paid Hanson Plc $24 million to acquire its quarry and concrete operations in Las Vegas that year. In 2001, also, Rinker boosted its U.S. presence through the purchase of Mid-Coast Concrete Co.

At the beginning of 2002, CSR announced its plans to spend upwards of $1 billion on new acquisitions in order to solidify its U.S. operation. In July of that year, CSR announced its largest U.S. acquisition to date, with an agreement to purchase Kiewit Materials, the largest aggregates producer in Arizona, for $540 million. That purchase helped boost the share of heavy building materials to more than two-thirds of CSR's total sales—and more than three-quarters of its profits—sparking recommendations that CSR split itself into its two component companies in order to enhance its share value.

By the end of 2002, CSR agreed, and the company announced a spinoff of Rinker Materials Group for 2003. That move was completed at the end of March, with the creation of Rinker Group Ltd. The newly independent company was then listed on the Australian Stock Exchange. A listing on the New York Stock Exchange, in recognition of the preponderance of Rinker's U.S. operation in its sales, followed at the end of 2003.

In the meantime, Rinker appeared to have maintained its acquisitive nature. The company made its first post-demerger acquisition in May 2003, paying $8 million in order to buy Calloway Concrete, a supplier of concrete for swimming pools as well as a maker of precast burial vaults. The company then announced plans to spend more than $300 million over the next year or so on further acquisitions.

While most of the group's acquisition efforts targeted the United States, it nonetheless remained open for growth elsewhere. In mid-2003, for example, the company paid $5 million to acquire the second largest premix concrete plant in Qingdao, in China's Shandong province. That market appeared attractive given the presence of such major global manufacturing groups as Mitsubishi and Lucent.

After successfully listing its shares on the New York Stock Exchange in December 2003, Rinker began looking for new growth opportunities. In February 2004, the company announced plans to spend $120 million on acquisitions, as well as on greenfield expansion, to bolster its core U.S. holdings. By then, the United States accounted for some 80 percent of Rinker's total sales, which topped $3.4 billion in 2003. Yet the company remained committed, at least for the short term, to maintaining its status as an Australian company.

Principal Subsidiaries

Rinker Materials, Inc. (U.S.A.).

Principal Competitors

Lafarge Group; CRH Plc; Holcim Ltd.; RMC Group; Heidelberg Cement; Cemex SA; Hanson Plc; Italcementi SpA; Lafarge North America.

Further Reading

"Australia's Rinker Group Looks to Expand Via Acquisitions," *Asia Africa Intelligence Wire,* February 20, 2004.

Drake, Bob, "A Closer Look: Rinker Materials Builds Solid US Foundations for CSR," *Pit & Quarry*, January 2002, p. 20.

Easdown, Geoff, "Spin-Off by CSR to Result in World Giant," *Courier-Mail*, February 11, 2003, p. 23.

Owers, Paul, "Heavy Building Materials Firm Seeks NYSE Listing," *Palm Beach Post*, October 7, 2003.

"Rinker Acquires Calloway," *Pit & Quarry,* August 2003, p. 69.

"Rinker Group Arrives on Wall Street," *Concrete Products*, November 1, 2003.

"Rinker on Stock Exchange," *Pit & Quarry,* December 2003, p. 103.

"Rinker's US Takeover Really One to Die For," *Daily Telegraph*, April 9, 2003, p. 55.

Scholz, Nathan, "Soaring Aussie Hampers Rinker," *Courier-Mail*, February 20, 2004, p. 35.

—M.L. Cohen

Sandals Resorts International

4950 SW 72nd Ave.
Miami, Florida 33155
U.S.A.
Telephone: (305) 284-1300
Toll Free: (888) 726-3257
Fax: (305) 667-8996
Web site: http://www.sandals.com

Private Company
Founded: 1981
Employees: 1,500
Sales: $600 million (2003 est.)
NAIC: 721110 Hotels (Except Casino Hotels) and
　　Motels; 721199 All Other Traveler Accommodation

Sandals Resorts International is world-renowned for its luxurious all-inclusive resorts dotting the Caribbean. The company's primary hotel brands are Sandals and Beaches, fittingly named given their location along some of the most sought-after stretches of sand in the world. With more than a dozen properties open or under construction in Jamaica, the Bahamas, St. Lucia, Antigua, and elsewhere, Sandals continues to take its properties to a higher level of service, truly earning the many awards bestowed on its brand of "Ultra All-Inclusive" resorts.

Entrepreneurial Experiments: 1970s–81

Gordon Stewart was born in Kingston, Jamaica, on July 6, 1941. The playground of his youth consisted of stunning stretches of coastline, including the white sand beaches running along the northern coast of Jamaica. As a young man, Stewart began his career in sales for the Dutch-owned Curacoa Trading Company. After working his way up to sales manager, Stewart departed in 1968 to start his own company called Appliance Traders, Ltd.

Appliance Traders was initially formed as a service and distribution company for air conditioners, but soon came to include other cold-air appliances such as refrigerators and freezers. Stewart faced a major challenge when Jamaica's government turned to socialism in 1970, severely restricting the import of goods into the struggling country. The young entrepreneur, however, soon found a way to work within the confines of the government's tightened controls: he segued into manufacturing.

By the dawn of the 1980s the Jamaican government had relaxed some of its strictures and turned its attention to promoting tourism. A government-owned, "all-inclusive" resort opened in Ocho Rios and Appliance Traders won the contract to supply the property's kitchen appliances and air conditioners. By this time, Stewart had crafted an unofficial motto for his business enterprises, always believing "We can do better." In this sense, Stewart decided to outdo the Jamaican government by creating his own all-inclusive resort.

The all-inclusive concept (originated by Club Med) met with high praise by vacationers around the world. Early all-inclusive packages included airfare, accommodations, and meals; as the notion caught on, other items were added such as premium alcoholic beverages, transportation to and from the airport, tips, and as part of Stewart's package, even water sports and activities. Later, some excursions, free transportation to other resorts, massages, and spa treatments were added.

Stewart found a property in Montego Bay called the Bay Roc Hotel. It was old and in desperate need of renovation yet situated directly on one of Montego Bay's loveliest beaches. Stewart believed the coastline alone was worth the price of the hotel and bought the property in 1981. He then turned it into a beautiful all-inclusive resort for couples. Although he had no direct experience in the travel or hospitality industry, Stewart followed a simple philosophy of not only giving clients (in this case, travelers) what they desired but to offer them more than they even expected or thought they might need.

Location, Location, Location: 1981–91

The Bay Roc Hotel was transformed into Sandals Montego Bay over several months with $4 million in refurbishing costs. Sandals Montego Bay was more than just all-inclusive, offering its guests water sports and a host of other extras all for the same price. The resort's rooms were a notch above competitors with upscale furnishings and service, and Sandals was the first Caribbean destination to place Jacuzzis, satellite television, gourmet dining, and swim-up bars at its resorts.

By the end of the 1980s Sandals had become a favored destination for weddings and honeymoons. Many of the company's guests were "repeats" who had visited a resort and come back to stay again at one of the four Jamaican properties (Sandals Montego Bay and Sandals Royal Caribbean in Montego Bay, Sandals Ocho Rios, and Sandals Negril). In actuality, there were five different Sandals hotels—if the smaller, more intimate Carlyle on the Bay was included in the count. The Carlyle was not considered a "resort" because it was not only small (52 rooms) but also because the inn was not a full-service facility like its siblings with several restaurants, bars, pools, and expansive beaches. The hotel, however, was renamed Sandals Inn and renovated over the next few years and included as one of the company's Montego Bay "Stay at One, Play at All" properties.

By 1990 Sandals had married its 1,000th couple and maintained an occupancy rate of more than 90 percent at its four full-service resorts. Funds from this phenomenal occupancy rate fueled expansion and Sandals bought another property to refurbish. Eden II, located in Ocho Rios by the Dunn's River waterfall, was set to undergo $20 million in renovations to become Sandals Dunn's River. Around the same time, Sandals initiated its first television advertising campaign, spending more than $3 million to inform television audiences about the firm's luxurious romantic getaways and to spotlight the "Stay at One, Play at All" concept.

The ad campaign (featuring three separate commercials filmed in Montego Bay, Ocho Rios, and Negril) in late 1990 was not only a first for Sandals, but for Jamaica as well, since no other resort in the country's young tourist trade had ever advertised on international television. With the launch of the Dunn's River resort in April 1991, Sandals not only celebrated ten years in business but reached two impressive milestones: First, of having 1,000 well-appointed rooms available at its resorts; and second, of becoming the Caribbean's largest operator of all-inclusive resorts (its number one rival, SuperClubs, had five).

Sandals ventured off its home turf to open its sixth all-inclusive resort on the Caribbean island of Antigua. The former Divi Anchorage Beach Resort, located on 11.6 acres of coastline at Dickenson Bay, was renovated and trebled in size for its rechristening as Sandals Antigua in July 1991.

Major Expansion: 1992–96

By mid-1992 Stewart had departed from his couples-only caveat by announcing construction of a property for families, to be called "Beaches." Families would be offered the same amenities as couples—several dining establishments, large pools, beachfront activities, as well as babysitting services and family-oriented fun. Beaches, like sibling Sandals resorts, would also be all-inclusive for a no-worry vacation. Another new approach was to build environmentally friendly resorts, working around a property's natural beauty as much as possible. This became particularly important at the Beaches construction site, after several native artifacts were found. According to *Travel Weekly,* the National Trust, the Institute of Jamaica, and Caribbean Environmental Consulting Services were all involved in the resort's construction to preserve as much of the natural environment as possible.

By 1993 Sandals had bought four new properties (one in Barbados, three in St. Lucia) to renovate and expand as future resorts. Two of the St. Lucia properties were combined to create Sandals St. Lucia, a luxuriously designed resort appealing to honeymooners and couples seeking top-notch, upscale accommodations. Sandals St. Lucia opened in April and the other St. Lucia property, Sandals Inn St. Lucia (later renamed Sandals Halcyon), opened the following year.

In addition to its buying spree Sandals adopted a new marketing concept as the only "Ultra All-Inclusive" resorts in the Caribbean. The new campaign was partially in response to Super-Clubs calling itself "Super All-Inclusive" and for Sandals to differentiate itself from the all-inclusive imitators who were not all-inclusive and charged guests for airport transfers, baggage handling, taxes, premium alcoholic drinks, water activities, and other items. With many resorts calling themselves "all-inclusive" without actually embracing the concept, Sandals feared vacationers would think all resorts were the same. While Club Med had created the concept and SuperClubs had introduced it to Jamaica, Sandals believed it had perfected the art of all-inclusives—and set out to prove it one guest at a time.

In 1994 and 1995 Sandals launched a new advertising campaign ("Sandals is for Lovers"), updated and rebuilt Sandals Antigua (damaged by a hurricane), refurbished three of its Jamaican resorts, and worked on the renovation of a recently acquired Barbados property. Sandals Barbados was slated to open in April 1995 but was put on hold after the Barbadian government balked at granting the company incentives similar to those granted to visiting cruise ships. While the Barbados property languished, Sandals Royal Bahamian Resort and Spa debuted in 1996 to much fanfare. Located on Cable Beach on the island of Nassau, the newest Sandals was part of the company's new "Royal" scheme, denoting even more luxurious appointments than other properties. By this time the company had a 40 percent "return" guest rate (repeat customers) with about two-thirds of its overall guests from the United States and the remainder from other countries.

As Sandals awaited results from its "Royal" branding, SuperClubs had launched its "Lido" upgrades in Ocho Rios and Negril, featuring better food, rooms, and spa services. Club Med, the more mature of the three leaders, had started the trend with its "Finest" brand a few years earlier and made plans to renovate several of its less upscale resorts to Finest specifications. Regardless of how a Sandals, Club Med, or SuperClubs resort was titled, they all offered the concept of "worry-free" vacations to travelers willing to spend a little more to receive a lot more in amenities and services.

Key Dates:

1981: Gordon "Butch" Stewart renovates the Bay Roc hotel in Jamaica and renames it Sandals Montego Bay.

1982: Sandals receives good press from a Montego Bay newspaper and a second hotel is acquired in the area.

1986: Sandals unveils the "Stay at One, Play at Two" concept with Sandals Montego Bay and Sandals Royal Caribbean.

1988: Sandals Negril opens along the Seven Mile Beach in Jamaica.

1989: Another resort is opened, Sandals Ocho Rios, a few hours from Montego Bay.

1991: Sandals Dunn's River resort, also in Ocho Rios, opens for business.

1992: Sandals buys the Upton Golf Course in Ocho Rios and offers golf to its resort guests.

1993: A new resort in St. Lucia debuts.

1994: Sandals launches wedding packages and a second St. Lucia resort, Sandals Halcyon, opens its doors.

1996: Sandals Royal Bahamian Resort & Spa opens in Nassau, the Bahamas.

1997: The first "Beaches" resort in Negril is opened.

2000: Beaches Grande Sport opens in Ocho Rios.

2002: Two additional resorts open, a Beaches in Ocho Rios and another Sandals in St. Lucia.

2004: Sandals combines two Ocho Rios properties while sibling company Beaches adds a spa and water park to its Negril property.

All-Inclusives for Everyone: 1997–2001

For Butch Stewart, with no experience in the hospitality industry whatsoever, business acumen had paid off in spades. He was not only one of Jamaica's most famous entrepreneurs but by 1997 his holding company, ATL Group, was the country's largest private corporation. Stewart had parlayed his Sandals success in several directions, such as buying into Air Jamaica, the country's primary airline, and turning it around. Stewart was behind the addition of Montego Bay as an Air Jamaica hub, which of course helped bring vacationers to his Sandals resorts.

Milestones in 1997 were the opening of Beaches Negril and Beaches Turks and Caicos. Beaches Sandy Bay (in Negril) opened the following year. Sandals and sister company Beaches were the hottest properties in the Caribbean marketplace. In 1998 came a new marketing campaign to attract more European vacationers to the company's Caribbean resorts. The company also began offering its clients a new travel pledge or "Blue Chip Hurricane Guarantee," to reschedule guests free of charge when hurricanes interrupted travel or forced the closure of any Sandals or Beaches property. Near the end of 1999, Sandals bought another Ocho Rios property called the Plantation Inn, slated to become the new Beaches Royal Plantation—a hybrid of Sandals and Beaches—for adults and kids 16 years and older.

In the new century, Sandals and its rivals experienced a bit of a slowdown as travelers tightened their belts. With the terrorist attacks in the United States on September 11, 2001, travel declined dramatically, impacted by fears of further terrorist activity. Airlines, travel agencies, and the entire hospitality industry suffered significant losses; but amazingly, business picked up at most Sandals resorts within several weeks. As 2001 came to a close, travelers were already returning to the Caribbean.

Travel Making a Comeback: 2002 Onward

In the summer of 2002 the fourth Beaches property, called Beaches Boscobel Resort & Golf Club, was opened in Ocho Rios. Beaches Boscobel became the third family-themed resort in Jamaica, with the other two, Beaches Negril and Beaches Sandy Bay, located several hours away in Negril. Beaches Boscobel was the first Beaches to offer families free golf in addition to its other amenities. Sandals inked a deal with Weddings.com for an online honeymoon registry, while Beaches pitched a "familymoon" concept for parents and kids.

In 2004 Sandals began several ambitious renovation programs, including the merger of two of its properties in Ocho Rios, Sandals Ocho Rios and the Grande Sport Villa Golf Resort & Spa. The new property, reopened in late 2004, was called Sandals Grande Ocho Rios Beach & Villa Resort and had undergone more than $10 million in refurbishing. Major changes were also on the drawing table for Beaches Negril, with the addition of a huge spa facility for adults and a water park for kids. The property's name was changed to Beaches Negril Resort & Spa to reflect these upgrades. Renovations and the addition of a new "Mediterranean Village" also were put in the works for Sandals Antigua, along with the opening of two additional Sandals resorts in Jamaica: Sandals Whitehouse (Westmoreland, opened in late 2004) and Sandals Dragon Bay (Port Antonio, opening in late 2005).

For Sandals, a sunny sky was literally the limit for the luxury resort operator. With more than a dozen popular properties and more due to open in the near future, the Sandals name had become synonymous with all-inclusive luxury. According to an April 2004 Zagat's survey of the best international hotels, resorts, and spas there were only three factors to which travelers paid attention when scheduling their plans: 35 percent said the fluctuating economy influenced whether or how much they would travel, while 17 percent had some concerns over terrorism or SARS. Since neither terrorism nor SARS had much impact on the Caribbean isles Sandals called home, travelers apparently ignored their economic fears and continued to come to paradise for a Sandals-styled respite.

Principal Competitors

Allegro Resorts; Club Méditerranée S.A. (Club Med); Super-Clubs International; Hilton Hotels; Holiday Inn Sunspree Resorts; Sunscape Resorts.

Further Reading

Acohido, Byron, "He Turned Web Site in the Rough into Online Jewel," *USA Today,* October 20, 2003, p. 5B.

"Barbados Prime Minister Dismisses Incentives for Sandals Resort," *Caribbean News Agency, Knight Ridder/Tribune News Service,* October 16, 2001.

Blum, Ernest, "Sandals Jockeys for Market Position," *Travel Weekly,* July 28, 1994, p. 40.

Elster, Judy, "Sandals Resorts to Launch First Television Advertising Campaign," *Travel Weekly,* October 15, 1990, p. C24.

Ingram, Leah, "Life's a Beach," *Entrepreneur,* April 1994, p. 98.

"Major Chains Introduce Brands to Capture Upscale Market," *Travel Weekly,* November 11, 1996, p. 91.

"Sandals Gears Up for Season with New Features, Renovations," *Travel Weekly,* December 4, 1995, p. 62.

"Sandals Jamaica Resort to Be Custom Designed for Families," *Travel Weekly,* July 30, 1992, p. 12.

"Sandals Opens Its First Resort Outside Jamaica," *Travel Weekly,* October 17, 1991, p. C16.

"Sandals to Buy Three Resorts," *Travel Weekly,* October 8, 1992, p. 45.

Seldon, W. Lynn, Jr., "Sandals Marks 10th Anniversary with New Ocho Rios Property," *Travel Weekly,* April 11, 1991, p. C20.

Sidron, Jorge, and Christopher Elliott, "Sandals to Adopt 'Ultra-Inclusive' Concept," *Travel Weekly*, May 20, 1993, p. 18.

Weeks, Scott, "Cool Operator," *Latin Finance,* May 1997, p. 61.

—Nelson Rhodes

Select Medical Corporation

4716 Old Gettysburg Road
Mechanicsburg, Pennsylvania 17055
U.S.A.
Telephone: (717) 972-1100
Fax: (717) 972-1042
Web site: http://www.selectmedicalcorp.com

Public Company
Incorporated: 1996
Employees: 20,800
Sales: $1.4 billion (2003)
Stock Exchanges: New York
Ticker Symbol: SEM
NAIC: 621610 Home Health Care Services

Based in Mechanicsburg, Pennsylvania, Select Medical Corporation specializes in two niches of the hospital and rehabilitation care business. The company operates a network of more than 80 "hospitals within hospitals," located in some 25 states. Using leased spaced in hospitals, Select Medical provides specialty and long-term acute care for patients with complex medical conditions, such as kidney, cardiac, brain and spinal cord injuries, and neuromuscular disorders. After patients have been stabilized in the host hospital, they are moved to these long-term units, thus freeing up beds for the host hospital while providing patients with better specialty care. Select Medical also operates approximately 800 outpatient rehabilitation clinics in about 30 states. In addition, the company does contract work, providing rehabilitation services to hospitals, nursing homes, assisted living and senior centers, as well as school and worksites. The 2003 acquisition of Kessler Rehabilitation Corporation also has positioned the company to become a player in the inpatient rehabilitation industry. Select Medical is publicly traded on the New York Stock Exchange.

Cofounder a Physical Therapist in 1950

Select Medical was founded by Rocco A. Ortenzio and his son Robert A. Ortenzio. Rocco Ortenzio had previously launched three publicly traded healthcare companies and gained legendary status in the rehabilitation field. Ortenzio, whose father worked in a Bethlehem Steel mill, grew up one of six children in Steelton, Pennsylvania. His first intention was to become a football coach, but he became sidetracked because of his interest in physical therapy. After earning a bachelor's degree from West Chester University, he graduated from the University of Pennsylvania School of Physical Therapy in 1956. He now decided to go on to medical school. He finished up some pre-med coursework at Dickinson College and was accepted to medical school, but because he had to wait a year to enroll, he elected to put his training as a physical therapist to use as a way to "test the waters." He took a job with Carlisle Hospital in Carlisle, Pennsylvania, but soon realized he preferred to work for himself. In 1958, with $10,000 borrowed from his brother, the 26-year-old Ortenzio launched his own physical therapy practice in Harrisburg, Pennsylvania. A solo practitioner was a rarity at the time because physical therapists could only work with patients with a direct referral from a physician. Thus physical therapists aligned themselves with hospitals and other institutions. Ortenzio tried a different approach, using direct mail and other ways to market his service directly to physicians. A main selling point was his promise to write detailed reports on each patient, a service that hospital therapists did not provide. Within just four months Ortenzio was turning a profit and he soon added a second office located in Mechanicsburg.

Ortenzio never enrolled in medical school, but he was far from content with his solo physical therapy practice, however prosperous it may have been. He developed a bigger dream. All too often he saw patients at his office come in for a 30-minute session, knowing that what they truly needed was five or six hours of therapy a day. In 1969 Ortenzio envisioned a chain of rehabilitation hospitals where cardiac patients and others could receive more in-depth rehabilitation services, but the concept was well ahead of its time. It was not certain that the state would license such a hospital, nor was it certain that insurance companies would pay for such care. As a result, one bank after another turned him down. According to Ortenzio, "They thought I was from another planet." He refused to give up and finally found a backer in Pennsylvania National Mutual Casualty Insurance Co., which provided $400,000—after he had helped the wife of the insurer's chairman rehabilitate a sore ankle. Ortenzio forged ahead and built Rehab Hospital of Mechanicsburg even though he had no state license for the facility. It came through the day before the facility was set to open. Out of this hospital grew Rehab Corp.

Starting a Second Company in 1979

In 1972 Ortenzio took Rehab Corp. public and two years later it merged with American Sterilizer Co. Ortenzio started his second company, Rehab Hospital Services Corp., in 1979. The purpose of this company was to open rehabilitation hospitals in underserved locations. Over the next five years, this company also went public and grew into a six-hospital chain. Helping him to run the business was his son, Robert, a 1982 graduate of Dickinson Law School, who started out as legal counsel. Rehab Hospital Services would be acquired by National Medical Enterprises Inc. in 1985. In the meantime, Ortenzio endured some medical problems of his own. He underwent heart-bypass surgery in 1982, but it did not sideline him for very long. After the sale of Rehab Hospital Services, he wasted little time in starting his third company, launching Continental Medical Systems (CMS) in 1986. With a solid reputation in the field, Ortenzio no longer had problems finding backers: Within two weeks he raised $26 million. He also was able to take the company public in its first year. CMS grew into a chain of rehabilitation hospitals that offered community-based rehabilitation programs and services for patients suffering from the effects of strokes, head and spinal cord injuries, orthopedic problems, neurological problems, and work-related disabilities. Again, Robert joined his father at this new venture, becoming chief operating officer and later president of the company.

CMS was sold in 1995. Rocco Ortenzio made an attempt to retire, but he soon grew restless. He decided to start yet another company, Select Medical, but only if he could meet three conditions. First, he wanted Robert involved. After his son came on board, he then wanted to make sure they could recruit key employees from past endeavors. He finally wanted to make sure the new company had sufficient seed money. Two venture capital firms that had worked with him in the past—New York's Welsh, Carson, Anderson & Store and Chicago's Golder, Thoma, Cressey, Rauner Inc.—each put up $25 million. The company was incorporated in December 1996. According to the *Patriot News*, "With the people and money in place, the only remaining issue was finding a niche for their health-care operations." It was hardly surprising that Ortenzio would decide to work within the rehabilitation field.

In February 1997 Select Medical made the first of many acquisitions, acquiring Sports and Orthopedic Rehabilitation

Services, a central Florida full-service, outpatient rehabilitation company that grew out of a therapist-owned practice founded in 1988. Three months later Select Medical attempted to make a much larger acquisition, the $565 million purchase of Las Vegas-based Transitional Hospitals Corp., which operated long-term-care hospitals. An agreement was signed, but at the 11th hour Vencor Inc. offered $650 million for the business and Transitional Hospitals backed out of the deal with Select Medical, which received $20 million in compensation. Nonetheless, the aggressive bid at the very least announced to the world that Rocco Ortenzio was once again a player to be reckoned with.

Select Medical's first major deal came in June 1998 when it acquired American Transitional Hospitals, a subsidiary of Beverly Enterprises Inc., America's largest nursing home operator. At a cost of $62.8 million in cash and the assumption of $15 million in liabilities, Select Medical in one stroke became a significant force in the long-term, acute-care hospital industry. Select Medical picked up 15 long-term acute-care hospitals located in eight states: Arizona, Georgia, Indiana, Mississippi, Ohio, Oklahoma, Tennessee, and Texas. Only two were free-standing facilities, with the rest operating as hospitals within hospitals. They mostly handled complicated treatment programs on both an inpatient and outpatient basis. Long-term acute care was a promising field, filling a void in the hospital industry. Although the average stay in a hospital intensive-care unit was around five days, patients who moved to a long-term acute hospital remained much longer. To be certified by Medicare, in fact, a facility had to demonstrate that on average patients stayed at least 25 days. Moreover, studies indicated that all parties benefited from long-term acute hospitals: They were 10 percent to 40 percent less expensive than hospital intensive-care units, and they could provide more focused care.

Select Medical added a 16th hospital, located in its home state of Pennsylvania, but before the end of 1998, it also would complete another major acquisition, paying $103.6 million in cash, plus the assumption of $56.5 million in liabilities, for St. Louis-based Intensiva HealthCare Corporation. Intensiva was founded in 1994, went public two years later, and now generated more than $100 million in annual revenues from 22 long-term, acute-care hospitals. With 38 hospitals in its network and another 13 contracted to open, Select Medical had established a strong base, which was a key in the hospital industry. Rocco Ortenzio commented to the press, "Critical mass is of paramount importance in today's health-care environment." In 1998, Select Medical generated revenues of close to $150 million, but that amount would grow at a strong clip over the ensuing years.

The next major step in the development of Select Medical came in November 1999 with the acquisition of NovaCare Physical Rehabilitation and Occupational Health Group, a division of King of Prussia, Pennsylvania-based NovaCare Inc. At a cost of $160.4 million in cash and the assumption of $64.7 million in liabilities, Select Medical entered the outpatient rehab business, picking up 500 clinics and in the process becoming the second largest player in the industry, trailing only HealthSouth Corporation. As a result, Select Medical was now well established in two branches of the healthcare industry.

In 2000 Select Medical added ten hospitals to the fold, a yearly rate that the company hoped to maintain. The target was

Key Dates:
1996: The company is incorporated.
1998: American Transitional Hospitals and Intensiva Healthcare Corporation is acquired.
1999: NovaCare Physical Rehabilitation and Occupations Health Group is acquired.
2001: An initial public offering of stock is made.
2003: Kessler Rehabilitation Corporation is acquired.

hospitals with at least 250 beds, serving markets of more than 500,000 people. Revenues during 2000 improved to $806 million, almost double the $456 million posted in 1999. To achieve that growth, the company took on considerable debt, which climbed to about $335 million. To help pay down that amount, as well as to fund further acquisitions, the company began taking steps in 2000 to make an initial public offering (IPO) of stock. With Wall Street heavy hitters Merrill Lynch, Credit Suisse First Boston, and J.P. Morgan managing the offering, Select Medical launched a road show in March 2001 to promote the company. What made the company an attractive opportunity to many investors was the aging of the American population. As the Baby Boom generation became seniors, the need for Select Medical's services would only grow. The hope was to sell 12.5 million shares for $11 to $13 each, but the stock market staggered after a series of losing sessions, putting a damper on all IPOs. Select Medical postponed its offering, lowered its price range to $10 to $11 per share, then seized upon a momentary rebound in the market to conduct the sale, priced even lower at $9.50. At the end of the day, the company netted approximately $85.5 million.

A changing of the guard also took place in September 2001, when Rocco Ortenzio stepped down as chief executive officer in favor of his son Robert. After working closely together for more than 20 years in three start-up companies, they felt the time was right for the 44-year-old Ortenzio to step up to the next level. His father, however, remained chairman of the board and very much involved in the affairs of Select Medical. Rocco Ortenzio stated at the time: "We have a common vision for Select Medical's strategic direction and its approach to building shareholder value. This appointment recognizes Bob's knowledge, experience and leadership ability and does not reflect any significant change in my duties."

After adding another ten long-term acute-care hospitals and 35 outpatient rehabilitation clinics in 2001, Select Medical saw its revenues in 2001 improve by 19 percent over the previous year to $959 million, with a net profit of $29.7 million. The company continued to grow in 2002, adding eight new hospitals and 20 rehabilitation clinics. Revenues topped the $1 billion mark, reaching $1.3 billion, and net income totaled $44.2 mil-

lion. The company also was paying down the debt it incurred while building its base of operations. The debt load now stood at slightly more than $200 million, a significant improvement over the amount the company owed in 1999. Moreover, cash flow from operations grew at an impressive rate, from $22.5 million in 2000 to $120.8 million in 2002. The company also was recognized by *Business Week* magazine, which ranked it among the nation's top 100 "hot growth companies" in its annual listing of smaller public corporations.

Select Medical had not completed a major acquisition since 1999, but because of its strong financial position it was able to add a major asset in 2003, paying $230 million for Kessler Rehabilitation Corporation. As a result, Select Medical added 92 outpatient clinics in Delaware, Florida, Georgia, Illinois, Massachusetts, New Jersey, North Carolina, Pennsylvania, and Virginia. In addition, it picked up four rehabilitation hospitals in New Jersey and a rehabilitation hospital joint venture in Maryland—moving Select Medical into the inpatient rehab business as well as supplementing its offsite contract therapy services. Kessler also added about $225 million in annual revenues. Furthermore, in 2003 Select Medical added seven new hospitals and 53 rehabilitation clinics. Revenues for 2003 grew to nearly $1.4 billion, and net income improved to $74.5 million. With its specialty hospitals and outpatient rehabilitation businesses well established, and having gained a platform in the inpatient rehabilitation industry through the Kessler acquisition, Select Medical was now well positioned to continue its record of strong growth.

Principal Subsidiaries

American Transitional Hospitals, Ltd.; Intensiva Healthcare Corporation; Kessler Rehabilitation Corporation; NovaCare Rehabilitation, Inc.

Principal Competitors

HCA Inc.; HealthSouth Corporation; Kindred Healthcare, Inc.

Further Reading

Dochat, Tom, "Father-Son Team to Take Fourth Health-Care Business Public," *Patriot News,* August 2, 1998.

Gupta, Udayan, "Rocco Ortenzio Succeeds in a Field Filled with Pitfalls," *Wall Street Journal,* June 28, 1990, p. B2.

Slavinsky, Cheryl, "Rocco Ortenzio: Ortenzio Leads CMS to Phenomenal Heights," *Central Penn Business Journal,* March 1, 1991, p. 1.

Vadum, Matthew, "They're Back: Ortenzios Buy Hospitals in 8 States from Beverly Chain," *Central Penn Business Journal,* June 12, 1998, p. 1.

Warner, Mary, "Ex-Therapist Led Rehabilitation Revolution," *Harrisburg Patriot,* October 17, 1988, p. 2.

Zweig, Jason, "Rocky III," *Forbes,* July 20, 1992, p. 45.

—Ed Dinger

Severstal Joint Stock Company

Mira Street 30
Cherepovets
Vologda 162600
Russia
Telephone: +7 (8202) 568009
Fax: +7 (8202) 571276
Web site: http://www.severstal.ru

Public Company
Incorporated: 1993
Employees: 53,000
Sales: $2.8 billion (2003)
Stock Exchanges: RTS (Moscow)
Ticker Symbol: CHMF
NAIC: 331111 Iron and Steel Mills

Severstal Joint Stock Company, also known as OAO Severstal, is one of Russia's largest steel mills and the center of the steel industry in the northwest of the country. The company's facilities in the centrally located city of Cherepovets encompass all stages of the metallurgical process, including production of coke, production of pig iron in blast furnaces, the manufacture of raw iron into steel, and the production of finished steel products using both hot-rolled and cold-rolled methods. The company also has electric arc furnaces for the processing of steel scrap. Severstal's annual output is around 9.6 million metric tons of steel. Its major customers include both foreign and domestic automobile companies and oil and gas concerns. The first steel producing facilities were built in Cherepovets after World War II, and the mill grew to be one of the more technically advanced facilities in the Soviet steel industry. In the 1990s, General Director Aleksey Mordashov guided Severstal through the transition to a market economy and won the company a reputation as one of the better-managed firms in Russian industry.

Developing Steel Capacity Under Soviet Leadership

The raw materials for the steel industry in northwest Russia were first discovered between 1930 and 1933. Iron ore deposits were found above the Arctic Circle on the Kola Peninsula and coal was discovered in the Pechora River region of the far north. Traditionally, steel mills were built either close to iron or close to coal, but since these new deposits were located in such remote and inhospitable territory, Soviet planners decided to construct the mill in a central area near the intersection of trade routes for ore, coal, and finished products. The chosen site was near the small town of Cherepovets, equidistant from Moscow and St. Petersburg and 1,500 to 2,000 kilometers away from iron and coal sources.

On June 20, 1940, the government of the U.S.S.R. approved the resolution "On the Organization of a Metallurgical Base in the Northwest of the USSR," calling for the construction of a steel mill near Cherepovets. Dozens of scientific institutes began testing the raw material deposits and drawing up plans for the mill, but the USSR's involvement in World War II temporarily halted progress. Construction was resumed in early 1948. In 1951 a metal prefabrication shop was finished, followed by a heating and electrical power center in 1954. On August 24, 1955, the blast furnace—which transforms iron oxide ore into molten iron—was ready for operation. Blast furnace operator F.E. Drozdov drilled a tap hole at 3:25 p.m. and the first molten iron ran out of the furnace. This date was considered the birthday of the Cherepovets Steel Mill.

Additional components were added to the mill over the next five years. In February 1956 an oven began processing coal into coke, a source of pure carbon used to reduce iron ore in the blast furnace. The first steel ingot was cast on May 1, 1958. In 1959 rolling mills began processing semi-finished steel into finished sheets. The Cherepovets mill now had all the pieces of a full metallurgical cycle. Skilled steel workers were recruited from other regions to train Cherepovets residents, and their training mixed with onsite experience to produce a distinctive smelting process. In particular, the Cherepovets mill prided itself on its ability to optimize payload volumes in the blast furnace and on the high output of the blooming mill.

In the 1960s the Cherepovets mill became a leader in domestic steel production, implementing more advanced technology than the nation's much older steel mills in the Ural Mountains region. In 1963 the mill produced its first cold-rolled steel,

Company Perspectives:

Severstal aims at being a world steelmaking leader and an attractive place of work. The Company's Mission: To be the best partner for all interested parties; to create competitive advantages for its customers; to generate growing and sustainable demand for suppliers; to guarantee an attractive income to shareholders and a decent level of salaries to Company employees; to contribute to the development of employees' creative potential.

allowing for secondary finishing after the hot-rolling mill. The first twin-hearth furnace in the USSR was put into operation in 1965. The following year the mill was awarded the Order of Lenin. In 1969 the Cherepovets mill began operating an electric arc furnace, which uses electric power to efficiently produce steel from scrap rather than from molten iron. A section bending mill began operation in 1972. In 1975 a Model 2000 continuous hot-rolling mill began producing extra-thin strip to meet domestic demand for more sheet steel. The 100 millionth metric ton of steel was produced at Cherepovets in 1979. The Cherepovets mill also took on many social responsibilities in addition to steel production since it was the only major employer in town. Under the socialist system the steel mill provided for the needs of its workers by maintaining city apartments, operating public transportation, supporting schools, and building an airport.

Nationwide steel production was growing steadily from the 1950s to the 1980s, but it was not enough to keep up with the demands of the domestic machine building industry. According to Boris Rumer, the steel industry in the USSR was characterized by quantitative rather than qualitative improvements; consumption of raw materials and electricity per ton of steel produced was high by international standards. The Cherepovets mill was a major producer of thin sheet steel, which was chronically in short supply. But Cherepovets was not able to produce enough semi-finished steel slabs on its own to keep its rolling mills operating at full capacity, so millions of tons of raw steel had to be brought in from other sites every year. In November 1980 the commissioning of a new oxygen converter helped remedy some of this imbalance. Oxygen converters transformed iron into steel more efficiently than the traditional open-hearth furnaces already in use at Cherepovets. Smaller oxygen converters had been tested at other sites in the USSR starting in the 1960s; the converter now built at Cherepovets was a larger and more efficient version of those.

In 1983 the Cherepovets Steel Mill was reorganized into the Cherepovets Iron and Steel Complex in recognition of the complex nature of its operations. In April 1986 the "Severyanka" blast furnace No. 5 cast its first iron. With a capacity of 5,580 cubic meters, this furnace could produce 20 times as much pig iron as the furnaces built at the start of the century in the Ural Mountains.

The national shortage of steel was a central concern at the 27th Congress of the Communist Party in 1986. Iron and steel production had leveled off after 1980 and was holding back production in the oil, gas, and automotive machine building industries. Cherepovets began testing a continuous casting machine near the end of the decade that was expected to eliminate the need to ship raw slabs from other enterprises. But in late 1989 a month-long strike at the Vorkuta coal mine, which had been established to exploit the Pechora coal, nearly depleted the steel mill's coal reserves and held back production. In 1991 the Soviet Union fell apart, bringing an end to the usual way of operating at the Cherepovets mill.

Making the Transition to a
Private Enterprise: 1992–95

The sudden collapse of the Communist system created chaos in Russian industry. Formerly, all payments bypassed individual companies and were processed at the state bank; now companies began billing each other directly, but they had no infrastructure to manage payments. Aleksey Mordashov became finance director at the Cherepovets mill in 1992 and set about trying to develop an efficient cash flow system. Mordashov was a native of Cherepovets who had studied at the Leningrad Institute of Economics & Engineering and was then hired as an economist at the steel mill. He was sent to Austria for training, where he experienced a radically different way of doing business—responding to customer demands rather than to the production targets of central planners. He was only 26 years old when Cherepovets General Director Yuri Lipukhin, prizing youthful flexibility over Soviet-era experience, appointed him to the finance director position.

On September 24, 1993, a presidential decree transformed the Cherepovets mill into the joint stock company OAO Severstal ("Northern Steel"). Early in 1994 shares in the firm were distributed to workers and Lipukhin was elected general director. The exact details of transfer of ownership during this tumultuous period are unclear. Mordashov apparently began buying shares personally and through the holding company Severstal-Invest. In the end he controlled 16 percent of the company directly and up to one-half indirectly, making him one of the richest men in Russia by the end of the decade.

Severstal's first few years as a private company were full of turmoil. In the spring of 1994 workers held a strike demanding cost-of-living wage increases as well as the resignation of the Russian government. Management begged the workers to be patient as the company waited for payments. Many of the payments Severstal did receive were barter rather than cash. The union that led the strike was working with the semi-fascist organization Russian National Unity; many workers were sympathetic with their nationalistic ideas of giving precedence to ethnic Russians. The union also contacted the Vorkuta coal miners, who threatened to strike if they were not paid for shipments. In the end, Severstal made payments to the coal miners and managed to get its own facilities running again after a short stoppage. In the fall of 1995 the Soviet press reported that President Boris Yeltsin had signed a decree including the Cherepovets facility in a new state-controlled metallurgical enterprise, but the decree was not signed by other government officials and did not take effect. Severstal's output fell more than 20 percent from 1989 levels during this period. Meanwhile, the Severstal group was expanding vertically to include longtime iron ore suppliers such as the Karelsky Okatysh mine and the Olenogorsky mining and processing plant in the Karelia region.

Key Dates:

1940: A Soviet resolution calls for the creation of a steel mill at Cherepovets.

1947: Construction of the mill is resumed after a hiatus during World War II.

1955: The Cherepovets blast furnace produces its first molten iron.

1969: The first electric arc furnace begins operation.

1980: An oxygen converter begins producing steel as part of a plan to replace inefficient open-hearth furnaces.

1986: The very large Severyanka blast furnace begins producing pig iron.

1994: The Cherepovets mill is privatized as Severstal.

1996: Alexey Mordashov becomes general director and implements reforms at Severstal.

2002: Severstal's raw material and automotive operations are spun off into separate companies.

2003: Severstal acquires Rouge Steel Co. of Michigan.

Reform and Expansion
Under Mordashov: 1996–2004

Severstal's operations improved after 1996, when Mordashov was elected general director. He was more of a marketwise manager than many Russian oligarchs and pulled together a team to reform the company's operations. Mordashov brought in international consultants, cut thousands of jobs, and established cost and profit centers to make managers more accountable. At the same time, he tried to motivate Severstal's demoralized workforce by offering respectable wages and incentives. He also started phasing out the inefficient open-hearth furnaces in favor of oxygen converters. In 1996 output increased for the first time since the transition, reaching 7.4 million metric tons of finished steel.

Because the domestic economy was suffering, Severstal sought business in foreign markets. In 1996 about 60 percent of production was exported to North America, Southeast Asia, and China. Russian mills were able to produce steel at such low costs that the United States and the European Union accused them of dumping; opposition to Russian imports caused Severstal to turn its attention to domestic markets after the start of the new millennium.

In 2000 Severstal expanded into new markets through acquisitions. It purchased a Model 5000 rolling mill from the Izhorskiye Zavody near St. Petersburg in April with plans to modernize the factory and use it to produce pipes for the natural gas monopoly Gazprom. This facility became known as the Izhorsky Pipe Factory. That fall Severstal moved into the steel-consuming sector for the first time when it acquired a controlling interest in the off-road vehicle manufacturer Ulyanov Automobile Factory (UAZ). In 2001 Severstal acquired the coal mining concern Kuzbassugol and, after a protracted battle with Siberian Aluminum, the engine builder Zavolzhsky Motor Plant. That year low worldwide steel prices, a drop in demand from Southeast Asia and the imposition of steel quotas in the United States led to a $466.9 million net loss on sales of $1.79 billion after a $452.7 million profit the year before. But production remained steady and the company returned to profitable operation when steel prices rose in 2002.

During this time, Severstal also was spinning off many of the side enterprises that had sprung up during the Soviet period. Mordashov already had reduced Severstal's involvement in social services such as housing, transportation, and education. Now he hoped that the establishment of independent side enterprises would generate more diverse opportunities for job growth in a town that was still dependent on the steel mill. Mordashov put market-minded young people in charge of the furniture division Severstal-mebel and the kitchenware division Severstal-emal. Severstal's repair and maintenance division became an independent engineering and machine building concern and the catering division became a food company in charge of a brewery, restaurants, and a meat processor.

Severstal's restructuring became even more extensive in late 2001 when the company's activities were divided into three major divisions: steel production, raw materials, and the automotive industry. In mid-2002 these divisions became the independent companies OAO Severstal, OAO Severstal-Resurs, and OAO Severstal-Avto; shares in them were distributed in lieu of a dividend. The three companies became part of the loosely connected Severstal Group, of which OAO Severstal, or Severstal Joint Stock Company, was the largest and most profitable part.

Severstal's production capacities continued to develop. A new electric arc furnace had begun operation in 1999; in 2002 a continuous casting steel billet machine was added at this shop. Severstal signed an agreement with Arcelor S.A. in April 2002 for the joint production of galvanized steel. The venture, known as Severgal, was 75 percent controlled by Severstal and would produce zinc-coated steel sheet for the automotive industry when a continuous galvanizing line was completed. Also in 2002, Mordashov became chairman of the board and was replaced as general director by A.N. Kruchinin, who had been working at Severstal since 1982.

In 2003 Severstal began pursuing opportunities for foreign acquisitions. That fall it bid on the privatization of Krivorozhstal, the largest steel producer in Ukraine, but the tender was awarded to a firm controlled by the Ukrainian president's son-in-law even though Severstal's bid was higher. The company also bid on the Hungarian steel mill Dunaferr, but in December 2003 it transferred its attention to the bankrupt U.S. firm Rouge Industries, Inc., parent of Michigan-based Rouge Steel Co. In a deal valued at around $285 million, Severstal beat out United States Steel Corporation to gain control of this company, which became part of its new subsidiary Severstal North America Inc. Severstal considered shipping steel slabs to be rolled and finished in Michigan, but it was unclear what would happen to the American plant's melting shop. In the spring of 2004 Severstal also declared an interest in the Czech state-owned steel mill Vitkovice and secured Citigroup as an adviser for this investment. With a 2003 profit of $892 million, it appeared that Severstal had successfully transformed itself into a stable private enterprise. The company's domestic operations were now secure enough to allow for expansion beyond Russia's borders.

Principal Subsidiaries

OAO Cherepovets Steel Rolling Mill; ZAO Izhorsky Pipe Factory; OAO Orlovskii Steel Rolling Mill; Severstal-mebel; OOO Severstal-emal; OOO ZAO Severgal (75%); Severstal North America Inc. (U.S.A.).

Principal Competitors

Magnitogorsk Iron and Steel Works Joint Stock Company; Novolipetsk Metallurgical Group Joint Stock Company; United States Steel Corporation; LNM Group.

Further Reading

"Alexei Mordashov: Chairman, Severstal, Russia," *Business Week,* July 7, 2003, p. 48.

Baker-Said, Stephanie, "Steel Mill Begins Crawl to Productivity," *Moscow Times,* July 2, 1997.

Beglyak, Sergei, "Will Fascism Take Over Cherepovets Steel Mill?," *Current Digest of the Post-Soviet Press,* June 8, 1994, p. 5.

Dunne, Nancy, "Russians in Talks on US Steel Quotas," *Financial Times,* September 18, 1997, p. 7.

Forster, Harriet, "Russian Steelmaker Buys Big Stake in UAZ," *American Metal Market,* October 20, 2000, p. 5.

McChesney, Andrew, "Severstal Acquires Steel Mill from Izhorsk," *Moscow Times,* April 18, 2000.

"A Model for Putin?," *Business Week,* May 22, 2000, p. 20.

Nicholson, Alex, "Severstal Warns Kiev Over Major Sell-Off," *Moscow Times,* May 14, 2004.

Ostrovsky, Arkady, "Inside Track: Economist Takes to the Blast Furnace: Profile Alexei Mordashov," *Financial Times,* October 19, 2000, p. 18.

Robertson, Scott, "Severstal Wins Rouge; What It Keeps Is Issue," *American Metal Market,* December 24, 2003, p. 1.

Rumer, Boris Z., *Soviet Steel: The Challenge of Industrial Modernization in the USSR,* Ithaca: Cornell University Press, 1989, pp. 1–6, 51–57.

"Russian Metallurgical Companies Lost the Tender for Sale of a 93% Stake in Ukrainian Krivorozhstal Metal Works," *Russian Business Monitor,* June 16, 2004.

"Russian Steelmaker Severstal Declares Interest in Vitkovice Steel," *Czech Business News,* May 20, 2004.

Savvateyeva, Irina, "Socialism Is Being Restored in Russia's Metallurgical Industry," *Current Digest of the Post-Soviet Press,* October 25, 1995, p. 16.

"Soviet Coal Strike Starts to Hit Steel Production," *Financial Times,* November 15, 1989, p. 2.

—Sarah Ruth Lorenz

Sonatrach

Djenane El Malik, Hydra
160335 Algiers
Algeria
Telephone: 213-2154-8011
Fax: 213-2154-7700
Web site: http://www.sonatrach-dz.com

Government-Owned Company
Incorporated: 1963 as Société Nationale de Transport et
de Commercialisation des Hydrocarbures
Employees: 36,558
Sales: DZD 1.53 billion ($19.58 million) (2002)
NAIC: 211111 Crude Petroleum and Natural Gas
Extraction; 211112 Natural Gas Liquid Extraction;
213111 Drilling Oil and Gas Wells; 213112 Support
Activities for Oil and Gas Operations

Sonatrach, formerly Entreprise Nationale Sonatrach, is the
Algerian state-owned oil and gas company. It has control—both
direct and indirect—over all aspects of the country's hydrocarbons and has guided Algeria toward its present status as the
second largest global supplier of liquefied natural gas.
Sonatrach produces about 90 percent of all Algerian export
income. It was the fourth largest exporter and producer of gas in
the world in 2003. The company hopes to become a major
international oil and gas company in the 21st century.

Assuming Control of Algerian Gas and Oil
During the Early Years: 1960s–70s

The original governmental decree of December 31, 1963,
which created the Algerian state oil company, gave it the title
Société Nationale de Transport et de Commercialisation des
Hydrocarbures. This was the origin of the acronym Sonatrach.
The role of transportation and marketing was given to the company at the date of its creation and was extended on September
22, 1966, making the title of the company still longer in an
attempt to summarize all its activities: Société Nationale pour la
Recherche, la Production, le Transport, la Transformation et la

Commercialisation des Hydrocarbures. In other words, it was a
state-owned company with responsibility for all oil activity in
Algeria. This responsibility grew during the 1960s and 1970s
with the nationalization of many of the country's foreign-held oil
assets, though the adoption in July 1981 of a rather less cumbersome title—Entreprise Nationale Sonatrach—coincided with a
reduction in the company's direct control over these assets.
Sonatrach continued to be responsible for the central features of
the Algerian oil and gas industry, but it effectively spun off
certain of its operational areas to a number of subsidiaries, with
Sonatrach retaining overall coordination for their activities.

The first three decades of Sonatrach's existence divide
neatly into three stages of development. The 1960s saw the
establishment of the company, with the nationalization of foreign interests and the acquisition of much of the necessary
infrastructure, such as pipelines. The 1970s was a decade of
consolidation, with Sonatrach embarking on several joint ventures with foreign partners in an effort to increase its exports of
liquefied natural gas (LNG). The 1980s saw the company entering into full bloom, reaping the rewards of its previous labors
and becoming one of the world's major suppliers of LNG.

When the original Sonatrach was established in 1963 by the
government of the newly independent Algeria, its role was
essentially limited to building a third export pipeline from Hassi
Messaoud to the Arzew oil terminal on the Mediterranean. The
gaining of political independence, however, had thrown up the
question of how far the economic ties with France should be
maintained, and Sonatrach came to play a central role in the
course of these discussions. The result of the protracted negotiations was the Franco-Algerian Oil Agreement of 1965, which
provided for the Algerian state to take effective part in the
exploration and exploitation of the country's hydrocarbons,
while also raising the income tax on oil from 50 percent to 55
percent, thus effectively gaining for Algeria a substantial increase in revenues from its oil and gas operations. In recognition
of the part played by Sonatrach's representatives in these negotiations, the company's role was extended by a new decree in
September 1966 to cover all aspects of the Algerian oil industry.

Over the next two years Sonatrach turned its attention
toward those U.S.-owned companies that had petroleum inter-

Key Dates:

1963: The Algerian government creates Société Nationale de Transport et de Commercialisation des Hydrocarbures.
1966: The name is lengthened to Société Nationale pour la Recherche, la Production, le Transport, la Transformation et la Commercialisation des Hydrocarbures.
1971: The Algerian government nationalizes all natural gas fields in Algeria.
1981: The name is changed to Entreprise Nationale Sonatrach.
1988: Sadek Boussena is named head of Sonatrach.
1995: Sonatrach forms joint venture In Salah Gas with British Petroleum (BP), the company's first major gas venture with a foreign company.
2001: Minister of Energy and Mines Chakib Khelil becomes CEO of Sonatrach.
2003: Sonatrach forms a joint venture with BP to distribute liquefied natural gas to the United Kingdom.

ests in Algeria. In August 1967 the company took over the Algerian assets of the Esso and Mobil companies, and in October 1968 it acquired a 51 percent participation interest in the Getty Oil Company. Sandwiched between these two events was the nationalization in May 1968 of all foreign interests in the Algerian distribution sector, thus establishing a monopoly for Sonatrach in this field.

One of the effects of these decisions was that Sonatrach's share in the Algiers refinery, in which Esso and Mobil had originally held 40 percent, Compagnie Française des Pétroles (CFP) 32 percent, and Shell 24 percent, rose from 4 percent in early 1967 to 56 percent in 1968. The Esso and Mobil interests were taken over in 1967, and the others bought out by 1969. In addition to establishing an infrastructure by nationalizing existing foreign-held assets, Sonatrach also acquired majority stakes in three major oil and gas pipelines between 1963 and 1965. While Algeria's oilfields became the exclusive preserve of Sonatrach, the company also acquired majority participation interests in foreign companies engaged in businesses allied to its central activities, for example, drilling, construction, geophysics, and pipe-laying.

Relations with France worsened steadily in the second half of the decade, however, though France was still buying more than half of all Algerian oil output. The tension came to a head in 1971 when, on February 24, the government completely nationalized all natural gas fields and allied installations and took over all rights to the associated gas—natural gas that overlies and contacts crude oil in a reservoir—from producing oil wells. It brought under state control 51 percent of all of the activities of French petroleum companies, namely 51 percent of the shares, rights, and interests in Algerian oil concessions belonging to these companies. At the same time, it brought its stakes in other foreign companies up to 51 percent. All pipelines that did not already belong to Sonatrach also were nationalized. The French retaliated by banning all imports from Algeria, although this action did not have the expected effect on the

Algerian economy, since rising world energy demand had sufficiently opened markets elsewhere.

The main problem that remained, however, was exploration. Since foreign companies were understandably reluctant to invest in exploration when they might not be allowed to reap the rewards, they stayed away, and Sonatrach had not yet built up a stock of technical expertise in its indigenous workforce to do the work itself. The impasse was settled when Sonatrach decided that since the concession agreements had now lapsed a new set of rules would have to be introduced, which would once more encourage foreign companies to put their money and their expertise back into Algerian exploration.

The result was the Fundamental Law on Hydrocarbons, which was promulgated by the Algerian government on April 12, 1971. This law had two main purposes. The first was that it formally abolished the system of concessions and established that all mining titles, as well as the control of all petroleum reserves that might be discovered in the future in any part of Algeria, were transferred to Sonatrach. The second was that it made provision for foreign companies to enter into service contracts or joint ventures with Sonatrach, provided that 51 percent of the assets were held by the state company.

The area in which joint ventures were to be particularly encouraged was exploration, and many foreign companies soon entered into such agreements, notably CFP and Elf Aquitaine of France, Amoco and Sun Oil of the United States, Hispanoil of Spain, Petrobras of Brazil, and Deminex of West Germany.

In addition to the requirement that 51 percent of the share capital be held by Sonatrach, the other conditions under which the joint ventures were signed were fairly straightforward. All gas found was to belong to Sonatrach. If oil was found, 15 percent of the foreign company's exploration costs would be refunded, and Sonatrach would become responsible for 51 percent of future development costs. Foreign partners would be entitled to 49 percent of the crude output after paying taxes, royalties, and other duties, though their term of exploration was limited to 12 years.

In the 1970s, having established its dominant role in the Algerian oil and gas sector, and having come to terms that were acceptable to its joint venture partners, Sonatrach formulated a guiding policy for its development. It saw its future prosperity lying in the exploitation of its natural gas, and thus set itself the task of developing these resources: this would involve subduing foreign demand for crude oil and persuading its clients to purchase its gas instead, while also requiring a great deal of exploration work to be done in the country. Such thinking was based on the fact that Algeria had the fifth largest gas reserves in the world, compared with relatively small and shrinking reserves of oil.

The achievement of the second of these aims, increased exploration activity, continued to elude Sonatrach. For example, of the 447,600 meters drilled in 1977, only 25 percent was for exploration; the main reason for this was the continuing diversion of resources to the development of the two major Saharan drilling fields, the Hassi Messaoud oil and Hassi R'Mel gas fields.

On the other hand, Sonatrach was managing to agree to terms with foreign buyers for its natural gas, and by 1977 several major supply contracts were already in place. The single most important of these was the contract signed in October 1977 with Ente Nazionale Idracarburi (ENI) of Italy, which provided for the export to Italy of some 12 billion cubic meters per year (cm/year) of gas over 25 years through the Trans-Mediterranean pipeline. The cost of the project was estimated at $2.5 billion, and deliveries through the pipeline—which was to run some 1,770 miles from Hassi R'Mel to Bologna in northern Italy— were expected to commence some four years from the signing of the contract.

Another consideration borne in mind by Sonatrach was that Algerian oil reserves, though scarce, were cheaper and easier to export than gas, and so the Algerian government began a policy in the 1970s of using gas wherever possible in its industrial infrastructure, involving the conversion of factories and hospitals to the use of gas. Two other policies initiated by the government—to bring electricity to every home by the year 2000, and to construct a substantial gas grid to supply these homes with gas—also fit in well with Sonatrach's own aims, since the power stations that supplied the Rural Electrification Project were gas-fired. By 1986 it was reported that 83 percent of Algerian homes had electricity, and 35 percent had gas.

A Focus on Refining and Natural Gas: 1980s

Sonatrach's declared exploration and production policy was not successful in practice. Sonatrach consolidated its position in refining. By 1980 it controlled the Algiers refinery, and during the 1980s it developed facilities at Hassi Messaoud, Arzew, and Skikda, making full use of foreign technical expertise, mainly Italian and Japanese. By developing refining capacity Sonatrach was able to reduce the amount of crude exported and to increase the value of the country's trade. By 1984–85, export revenues from oil and gas provided Algeria with $13 billion and accounted for 95 percent of total export earnings.

After 1985, when the shape of the oil and gas markets worldwide altered dramatically, Algeria revised its energy policy in favor of reducing dependence on oil reserves and focusing instead on its natural gas reserves, reckoned to be two-thirds of Algeria's total energy resources.

Until the mid-1980s Algeria found itself in difficulties with respect to its pricing policies, insisting on maintaining contract prices that were way in excess of current market prices, especially Soviet and Dutch prices. Until late 1987 the government insisted that LNG prices be related to crude oil prices and not products, as in most other cases. This worked reasonably well until the price of crude collapsed in early 1986, after which Algeria found itself in dispute with a number of its contract customers. At the same time it saw its revenues falling.

One of the consequences of this was a restructuring of the law governing energy policies at the end of 1986, considerably liberalizing the terms under which foreign companies could participate in exploration projects. The old laws dictated that foreign companies could form joint ventures, but Sonatrach held the majority stake and furthermore held title to the oil or gas. The foreign companies had "operator only" status. If gas was found it was treated as the result of an unsuccessful search for oil, and Sonatrach took 100 percent of the field. One of the

consequences of this was that companies of the standing of Texaco and Amoco ceased exploration activities in Algeria.

This kind of intransigence was reflected in the way in which Sonatrach negotiated its major contracts. Despite the need for supplies of LPG (liquefied petroleum gas) and LNG by a variety of countries, including Italy, Yugoslavia, and the United States, contracts repeatedly hit problems in the late 1980s as Algeria attempted to maintain its upper hand in a falling market.

This led to what was seen as a fundamental reversal in Algerian export policy. By the end of 1987, a number of changes were becoming apparent. The most interesting was reflected in a contract finally signed with the U.S.-registered Trunkline LNG Company, a subsidiary of Panhandle Eastern Corporation, in which Sonatrach held a 12 percent stake, which was understood to have incorporated the most flexible terms seen out of Algeria. In effect there was no contract price; rather, prices were to be determined on the basis of conditions in the end-use markets with the proceeds being split on a predetermined basis between Sonatrach and Trunkline. To a large extent, this deal was seen as evidence of Sonatrach's deep concern over its position in the international gas market, its substantial surplus in LNG capacity, and its desire to develop new markets to utilize this spare capacity more fully.

By 1988 there was a widespread belief that Algeria had decided to accept commercial reality after years of sticking to a high price strategy, which had resulted in the loss of markets. Early that year it became apparent that the country was going to be marketing LNG on a worldwide basis and with some intensity. One consequence of this was the opening of branches in the United States and London, as well as the development of a Tokyo office.

Until the summer of 1988 more than half its LNG capacity of 30.8 billion cubic meters a year was idle as a result of difficulties with export contracts. Since then Sonatrach dropped its insistence on treating existing customers less favorably than new ones, a practice that caused a long dispute with Boston-based Distrigas, and revived exports to the United States at competitive prices. Sonatrach also reopened the world's first commercial LNG trade, between Algeria and the United Kingdom, with spot cargoes—cargoes sold at the going rate, not a forward price. In addition, it developed a new and potentially exciting relationship with Japan and redefined its relationship with its largest customer, Gaz de France.

The government appointed a new head of Sonatrach, Sadek Boussena, in the summer of 1988—appointed minister of energy as well in November 1988—and his influence was felt in the new methods noted in negotiations. Part of this change of policy had—as always in Arab nations—a political basis. With LNG grossly overpriced, a number of customers, including U.S. utilities and Gaz de France itself, simply paid some 83¢ per million British thermal units less than they were invoiced, arguing that they would not pay over the accepted market price. The 1988 riots in Algiers underlined the high price the country was paying for the austerity induced by the sharp decline in its foreign income—more than 90 percent of which derived from its oil and gas income.

Since then, the Algerians managed to restore a number of crucial relationships in the United States and Europe and seemed set on a course of action that would make Sonatrach a crucial element in several nations' LNG stockpiles. During 1989 Sonatrach exported a record 17.2 billion cubic meters (cm) of gas as LNG, or about 12.3 million tons. Export capacity stood at around 25 billion cm, but Sonatrach's deputy general manager, Mustapha Faid, announced that this was to be substantially expanded during the 1990s, to 33 billion cm by 1992, and to between 60 billion and 80 billion cm by 2000.

By the end of 1990 Algeria had about 3.25 trillion cm of natural gas reserves, placing it among the top seven in the world. As part of this expansion Sonatrach planned to construct a new LNG unit of about five billion cm capacity. Meanwhile, it would also be expanding the country's LPG capacity to allow exports of seven million tons annually, up from the 1990 level of about four million tons. In addition, a new, fourth pipeline to mainland Italy via Tunisia and Sicily was being planned, while there was a more tentative plan to build a pipeline through Morocco and across the Strait of Gibraltar to the Iberian Peninsula.

Faid also announced impending contracts with U.S. and French companies to refurbish and expand gas liquefaction plants at the ports of Arzew and Skikda. In February 1990, a cooperation agreement was signed between Sonatrach and Total Compagnie Française des Pétroles (formerly CFP) covering upstream and downstream work, and in November 1989 these companies signed two production-sharing contracts for liquid hydrocarbons at the same time as Shell and Sonatrach signed a deal to study cooperation in the natural gas sector. The main thrust of Sonatrach's expansion plans, however, became apparent in 1991, with Sonatrach running a campaign to attract both producing and consuming companies to participate in joint ventures for the production and separation of around four million tons a year of LPG, which would double the production capacity.

Cooperation with Other Countries Leading to Growth: 1990s

Sonatrach, in its quest to become one of the top oil and gas producers in the world, adopted an aggressive growth campaign in the 1990s. In April 1996 the Algerian government implemented a program designed to increase the country's crude oil production capacity to 1.5 million barrels per day by 2001. To reach this goal the government planned to allow for the drilling of 300 exploration wells, half of those allotted to Sonatrach and the other half to foreign investors.

Cooperation with foreign companies rose steadily in the 1990s, and by 1999 Algeria had 25 foreign companies conducting business in the country. Among these companies were Anadarko Petroleum Corporation, which had discovered two oilfields, Atlantic Richfield (Arco), Phillips Petroleum, Occidental Petroleum Corporation, and Mobil. Sonatrach was involved in a joint venture with Anadarko, Lasmo, and Maersk Oile of Denmark to develop the Hassi Berkine South oilfield, and Block 404 of the field came onstream in May 1998, producing 65 million barrels per day by 2000. In addition, Sonatrach formed a joint venture with British Petroleum in 1995 to develop seven gas fields in the In Salah region. The joint venture, In Salah Gas, marked Sonatrach's first major gas partnership with a foreign company and was set to come onstream in 2002.

Other joint ventures in which Sonatrach was involved by the late 1990s included an exploration agreement with Oryx Energy Company worth $28.8 million, a deal with Compañia Española de Petróleos, S.A. (CEPSA) of Spain to develop the Ourhoud oilfield, and a production-sharing agreement with Arco and Elf Aquitaine of France to produce oil at Rhourde El Baguel, the second largest oilfield in Algeria. In the summer of 1998 Amoco, prior to its merger with BP, made a $900 million deal with Sonatrach to develop gas fields in In Amenas in southern Algeria.

Sonatrach also was involved in pipeline joint ventures in the 1990s: with Spain's Enagas, Sonatrach built the Maghreb-Europe Gas (MEG) line to Spain. Construction began in the early 1990s, and the portion to Portugal came onstream in March 1997. Sonatrach also worked on the Trans-Mediterranean (Transmed) line linking Algeria's Hassi R'Mel field, Algeria's largest natural gas field, to Mazzara del Vallo in Sicily, Italy.

On the Road to Globalization in the New Millennium

As Sonatrach headed into the new millennium, it had hopes of boosting its presence and becoming a major player in the global oil and gas market. The company entered into a five-year development plan worth $19.2 billion and planned to spend 62 percent on oilfield development, 17 percent on pipeline construction, 13 percent on exploration, and the rest on other projects, including gas liquefaction.

One key to Sonatrach's success, according to Chakib Khelil, Algeria's minister of energy and mines since 1999 and Sonatrach's head since 2001, was to change Sonatrach's status and to free the state-run company from complete government control. Khelil championed the hydrocarbons law that would have put an end to the government's monopoly of Sonatrach, but the law was placed on hold in early 2003, making energy reform unlikely. Still, the government claimed it hoped to liberalize Sonatrach and set up Alnaft, an agency with the responsibilities of negotiating energy contracts with foreign companies and offering exploration and development deals.

The Ourhroud field came onstream at the beginning of 2003, bringing Sonatrach closer to realizing its goal of becoming an international powerhouse. Initial production was at 75,000 barrels of oil per day, but the company expected to boost output to 230,000 barrels per day within a month or two. Total oil production capacity was expected to increase from 1.1 million barrels to 1.3 million barrels per day with Ourhroud.

Joint ventures continued and were among Sonatrach's strategies for diversifying its holdings and expanding internationally. In 2000 Sonatrach entered a major joint venture with CEPSA and others to build MedGaz, a 450-kilometer gas pipeline running from Algeria to Spain. The pipeline was set to begin distributing gas in 2006. MedGaz would greatly increase the export possibilities of Algerian gas to members of the European Union. In 2002 Sonatrach and Shell formed a partnership to explore and develop oil and gas interests, and in March 2003 Sonatrach formed the joint venture Helison with Germany's Linde Engineering. The venture's plan was to construct a helium plant in Algeria. Construction was estimated at $87 million.

In October 2003 Sonatrach formed a joint venture with BP to distribute LNG to the United Kingdom. Under terms of the agreement, shipment would begin in 2005, with the possibility of extending distribution to other markets, including the United States. Import capacity was estimated at 3.3 million tons per year over the course of 20 years. The bulk of the LNG would come from Algeria, which was prepared—the Ohanet project, a joint venture with BP Billiton, came onstream in October and had the capacity to pump 7.3 billion cubic meters per year; the In Salah venture was to be operational in 2004; and In Amenas was to come onstream in 2006.

Sonatrach dabbled elsewhere in the world as well. In Peru the company was a member of a consortium along with Argentine firms Techint and Pluspetrol to sell and distribute gas in Peru. The venture was known as the Camisea project. Sonatrach also had plans to develop the Tuba field in southern Iraq, and it had dealings in Sudan and Yemen in the early 2000s. In 2003 Sonatrach entered into an agreement with China National Oil and Gas Exploration and Development Corporation to construct a new refinery in Algeria. The company also exported oil to Asia, and in October 2003 it began shipping Saharan Blend crude oil to China and Thailand, bringing its shipments to Asia up to three million barrels in October.

In May 2003 Sonatrach gained a new CEO with the appointment of Djamel Eddine Khene. Khene had worked at Sonatrach since 1971 and as vice-president of exploration and production prior to his promotion. Khene took over for Khelil, who continued in his position as minister of energy and mines. Unfortunately, Khene died two months later, in July. In October Sonatrach veteran Mohamed Meziane was appointed CEO. Meziane had been with Sonatrach since 1967.

Exploration brought positive results. In the spring of 2003 Sonatrach, along with partners Anadarko, Lasmo, and Maersk, made an oil discovery near Hassi Messaoud. Sonatrach reported that initial tests yielded output of 2,689 barrels of oil and 4.72 million cubic feet of gas per day. Another significant discovery was made in November 2003, this time in the Berkine North East field of the Berkine Basin. Other Berkine Basin discoveries included wells in Hassi Berkine North East and Sif Fatima South West.

Sonatrach reported a net income of DZD 175 million for 2002. For the first six months of 2003, Sonatrach earned $12 billion, and its export earnings rose 46 percent compared with the same period in 2002.

Growth and expansion remained Sonatrach's goals, and the company hoped to double production and exports by 2020. By 2010 Sonatrach wished to elevate its reserves by 20 percent and to increase gas liquefaction capacity by a quarter. In 2003 Sonatrach's oil output was some 1.2 million barrels per day. Capacity was expected to increase to 1.5 million barrels per day by 2005 and two million barrels per day by 2010. Part of Sonatrach's strategy was to make foreign investments to boost its reserves. CEO Khene told *Middle East and North Africa Today* in July 2003, "Sonatrach is pursuing a change in strategy. It does not want to be limited to one source of hydrocarbons, regardless of how reliable and promising they may be." In 2002 Algeria was the 11th biggest supplier of oil and gas; the company hoped to work its way into the top ten by the end of the decade.

Principal Subsidiaries

Société de Transport du Gaz Naturel d'Hassi-Er-r'Mel Arzew (SOTHRA); Société Algérienne de Géophysique (ALGEO); Société de la Raffinerie d'Alger; Sonatrach International Holding Company (British Virgin Islands); Helison (49%); Galsi SpA (40%); ENAGEO; Entreprise National de Forage; Entreprise Nationale d'Industrie Petrochimique; NAFTEC; Reganosa (Spain); ENAFOR (Algerian National Enterprise for Drilling); GCB; ENSP (National Enterprise for Well Services).

Principal Competitors

BP p.l.c.; Compañia Española de Petróleos, S.A.; Repsol YPF, S.A.

Further Reading

"Algeria's Sonatrach Announces 2020 Development Goals," *Middle East and North Africa Today,* July 4, 2003.

"Algeria—Triumph of the Old Guard," *Middle East Economic Digest,* January 24, 2003.

Buckman, David, "Algeria—New Search Gets Under Way," *Petroleum Economist,* July 1989.

Leblond, Doris, "The Dual Pattern of Algeria's Gas Contracts," *Petroleum Economist,* May 1988.

Moran, Jacinta, "Khelil Maps Algeria's Oil Production Growth," *Platts Oilgram News,* July 7, 2003, p. 3.

Shirkhani, Nassir, "Old Hand to Take Reins," *Upstream,* May 16, 2003.

Wright, John, "Sonatrach—Key to Algeria's Future," *Petroleum Economist,* January 1977.

—Adam H. Seymour
—update: Mariko Fujinaka

The Source Enterprises, Inc.

215 Park Avenue South
New York, New York 10003
U.S.A.
Telephone: (212) 253-3700
Fax: (212) 253-9344
Web site: http://www.thesource.com

Private Company
Incorporated: 1988
Employees: 100
Sales: $30 million (2000 est.)
NAIC: 511120 Periodical Publishers

The Source Enterprises, Inc. publishes *The Source* magazine, which covers hip-hop music and culture and is one of the largest-selling music monthlies on newsstands. The company also sponsors an annual hip-hop music awards ceremony and a syndicated radio show, and lends its name to a clothing line and compilations of hit songs and videos, among other activities. The firm is run by CEO and cofounder David Mays.

Beginnings

The magazine known as *The Source* was founded by two Harvard students, David Mays and John Shecter. While undergraduates, the two fans of rap and hip-hop music had begun hosting "Street Beat," a radio show on Harvard's student station WHRB, while Mays promoted rap concerts in the Boston area. In August 1988 the pair published a two-page newsletter they dubbed *The Source.* The simple publication, which contained a concert calendar and hip-hop news items, was produced with a budget of $250, and sent out to 1,000 fans of their radio show. The response was so favorable that the next issue was six pages long, and by the third the duo were selling advertisements and laying plans to create a magazine that they could sell regionally or even nationally.

Over the next two years, publication of *The Source* continued while Mays and Shecter completed their undergraduate degrees. During their senior year they borrowed $10,000 to keep the magazine going, and after graduating in 1990 they moved the operation to New York. At this time they also took on two new partners, Harvard Law School graduate James Bernard and *New Republic* magazine associate publisher Ed Young.

By 1991 *The Source* had become a 68 page, four-color publication, and advertising space was being sold to the major rap record companies. An estimated 50,000 copies were being distributed via record stores and newsstands, as well as 2,000 to subscribers. The firm's annual revenues were $1 million, two-thirds of which came from ad sales. Mays held the titles of CEO and publisher, while Shecter served as editor-in-chief.

In contrast with many magazines devoted to popular culture that included mainly photographs and stories about the stars, *The Source* took a more serious tack and covered the social and political issues that mattered to rappers, as well as more controversial topics including sexism in rap. It was officially dedicated to covering "Hip-hop music, culture and politics," a mission directly inspired by rock music's *Rolling Stone* magazine.

Formation of Source Entertainment & Marketing: 1993

In 1993 the company created a new division, Source Entertainment & Marketing, to take charge of and expand an existing fax newsletter, *The Source Weekly,* that was sent to radio stations, record stores, and music writers. The unit also began publishing the *Hip-Hop Music Directory,* an ad-supported industry source book, and issued a quarterly compilation of new music videos, *Slamming Jams.* Ad buyers in *The Source* now included Nike, Reebok, and Bugle Boy, and the 75,000 circulation magazine's staff had grown to 20. The firm had also recently begun sponsoring a touring "Source Van" that visited urban areas and college campuses, giving away promotional items and sometimes hosting personal appearances by rap performers.

In April 1994 the first Source Awards ceremony was held at the Paramount Theater in New York. Awards were given in 14 categories that included artist of the year, best album, and best video, with winners determined by the magazine's readers. The event was modeled on the more mainstream Grammys, which had paid scant attention to hip-hop. The magazine's circulation was now growing rapidly, and by mid-year stood at 125,000. Annual revenues were estimated at between $3 million and $4 million.

In September James Bernard, who had been elevated to co-editor-in-chief with Shecter, clashed with Mays over the publisher's use of *The Source* to promote a band he had managed in Boston. A three-page spread on the relatively unknown Almighty RSO, which Mays had allegedly penned under a pseudonym, was inserted into the magazine without Bernard's knowledge, and the furious editor wrote a public letter asking him to resign. Bernard had earlier been threatened by RSO leader Ray Scott with bodily harm if he did not give the group more coverage, and had banished them from its pages as a result. After his letter became public Bernard was suspended by Mays, which led most of the magazine's staff, including cofounder Shecter, to walk out in support. The December issue was put together with freelancers, and Mays subsequently hired new staff to replace the striking workers, including Bernard and Shecter.

In the spring of 1995 the second Source Awards ceremony was held, this time packaged by the company as a syndicated television program. It was picked up by only a few stations, and the firm lost several hundred thousand dollars on the endeavor. The failed television broadcast and recent staff firings had little impact on the magazine's circulation, however, which continued to grow over the next several years.

Newsstand Sales Top Rolling Stone in 1997

The latter half of 1997 saw *The Source* reach a new plateau when its single-copy sales topped those of the venerable *Rolling Stone*, making it the best-selling music magazine on newsstands in the United States. Its total paid circulation now stood at

357,000, of which nearly 90 percent was derived from newsstand sales, though the total amount was still dwarfed by the heavily subscribed *Rolling Stone*'s 1.25 million. The end of 1997 also saw the first compilation album issued under the Source banner on Def Jam Records, as well as publication of the magazine's 100th edition.

A typical issue now ran to nearly 300 pages, of which ads constituted almost half. Readers were mostly male, with 60 percent African American and 80 percent under 25 years of age. An increasing number of major corporations were now buying advertisements, though record and fashion firms still led the pack. *The Source* refused cigarette and alcohol ads, however, because of the young age of its readers. The company's annual revenue was now estimated at $15 million.

In the spring of 1998 the firm introduced a new magazine, *Source Sports,* which covered its subject in an edgier, more "hip-hop" fashion than category leader *Sports Illustrated.* Later in the year an Internet portal, TheSource.com, was launched as well. It offered news, video clips, and concert listings, along with merchandise and ticket sales. The Source Enterprises was now also sponsoring a college fashion show/rap group concert tour, in association with Mountain Dew and more than a dozen clothing and shoe companies including Lee Jeans and Reebok.

In 1999 The Source Hip-Hop Music Awards show was revived after an absence of several years. Broadcast on the UPN network, it boasted strong ratings among younger viewers. The company had also recently founded The Source Youth Foundation, to help nonprofit organizations that performed outreach to young people.

In the fall of 1999 Source editor-in-chief Selwyn Seyfu Hinds quit the magazine after Mays allegedly "sweetened" a review of an album recorded by his friend Ray Scott's new group Made Men. Hinds subsequently joined Russell Simmons' Internet venture RS1W.com.

In April 2000 The Source Hip-Hop Music Awards made headlines when it was cut short by L.A. police after fistfights and bottle-throwing broke out in the auditorium. Several days later the ending was restaged and a sanitized version of the show was broadcast as scheduled, to solid ratings. Soon afterward, TheSource.com posted unaired footage of the fights online.

In the fall of 2000 two new television programs, dance show *The Source Soundlab* and news magazine *The Source All Access,* debuted on UPN. The Source Enterprises, which was also exploring the possibility of making feature films, had recently begun marketing a DVD called *The Source All Access: Volume 1* which featured videos and interviews with rap and R&B stars. Meanwhile, the company's sports magazine, which was not performing up to expectations, was folded. Revenues for the year had grown by more than 20 percent, to $30 million, with profits estimated at $10 million. *The Source*'s circulation was now edging close to 450,000, and CEO Mays declared his firm's goal to be "the Time Warner of the hip-hop generation."

In July 2001 the company's awards show, now moved to Miami, featured increased security from a Nation of Islam affiliate, and a smaller, invitation-only audience. Some 900,000 copies of a $4.99 companion publication were printed for news-stand sale. Though the show, which featured performances by such stars as P. Diddy and Eminem, went off without a hitch, there was a stabbing outside the official post-show party, and the next day Ray Scott, now known as "Benzino" and listed on *The Source*'s masthead as a co-owner, was arrested for reckless driving, possession of marijuana, and assaulting a police officer. Miami Beach police later alleged that CEO Mays had pressured them to drop the charges, while he countercharged that the arrest was an example of "racial profiling."

2002: Earl Graves Buys $17 Million Stake in Firm

During 2001 Mays had unsuccessfully sought buyers for the magazine, reportedly asking $100 million, but in early 2002 he sold a $17 million stake to Earl Graves' Black Enterprise/Greenwich Street Corporate Growth Partners. In the spring The Source Enterprises joined with Reebok and Interscope Records to sponsor a national rap talent contest, while David Mays returned to radio as co-host of *The Source Street Beat,* a weekly three-hour syndicated program. Over the course of the year *The Source*'s advertising page count fell by nearly 22 percent, due in part to the changing U.S. economic climate.

The world of hip-hop was famous for squabbles between rappers, and *The Source* itself had become a target of such rival publications as *XXL,* whose editor Elliot Wilson criticized the magazine in almost every issue. In the February 2003 *Source* a two-sided foldout poster was included that showed Wilson being crushed by a hulking figure on one side, and Ray "Benzino" Scott holding Eminem's severed head on the other. Though *The Source* had at one time supported the white rapper, it had turned on him and Scott had labeled him "a rap Hitler," apparently because Eminem's success appeared to be undercutting the impact of African American rappers including Scott. The issue of race had always been a sensitive one at *The Source,* which had been founded by privileged whites to cover the music and culture of mostly lower-class blacks. It had for some time been written and edited by a largely black staff, however.

Following the poster's publication Wilson shot back in print, while Eminem's label Interscope pulled its ads from *The Source,* and Eminem recorded an anti-Scott rap. The incident further eroded the magazine's credibility in some quarters, and the March issue of *XXL,* which featured Eminem, 50 Cent, and Dr. Dre on its cover, outsold *The Source* on the newsstand for the first time ever.

In September 2003 the company added a French language edition which contained a blend of translated articles and locally-written ones. Some 80,000 copies were printed by the French firm Arcadia, which paid Source Enterprises a licensing fee. The company was now also preparing to launch a line of branded clothing in conjunction with AST Sportswear which would be targeted toward such mass-marketers as J.C. Penney, while David Mays and Ray Scott had opened a hip-hop nightclub in Miami's South Beach area.

In the fall the magazine's campaign against Eminem heated up when Mays and Scott held a press conference to play decade-old recordings in which the white rapper disparaged African American women. The tapes were also made available on TheSource.com. Eminem apologized, saying he had been young and foolish at the time, and a number of members of the hip-hop community voiced their support for him. A plan by *The Source* to include a compact disc of the recordings in its February 2004 issue was met by a lawsuit, which was resolved when a judge allowed the inclusion of 20-second snippets of the songs and the printing of eight lines of text from the lyrics. The issue, which featured Eminem's photo on the cover and a long article on his alleged racial insensitivity, was seen by some pundits as more of an attempt to boost *The Source*'s flagging newsstand sales than a serious journalistic effort. Eminem responded with a "mixtape" rap, and through an interview in *XXL.* For 2003 the magazine's ad pages had dropped by almost 2 percent, and newsstand sales by nearly 10 percent. Challenger *XXL*'s circulation, meanwhile, had increased by more than a third during the same period.

In just over 15 years The Source Enterprises, Inc. had grown from humble beginnings to publishing the leading magazine covering hip-hop and rap. Though it faced stiff competition from several new challengers, *The Source* was still viewed by many as the most important magazine on its chosen subject, while the company's other endeavors gave it a strong presence in a variety of other media.

Principal Subsidiaries

The Source Clothing Company; Source Entertainment & Marketing.

Principal Competitors

Harris Publications, Inc.; Miller Publishing Group, LLC; Rap Sheet.

Further Reading

Arango, Tim, "Rap Bible Bashed: The Source Hit Hard on Newsstand by Rival XXL," *New York Post*, May 19, 2003, p. 35.

Carter, Kelly, "Hip-Hop Heat," *Tulsa World*, January 16, 2004, p. S12.

Dam, Julie, "Taking Rap Very Seriously," *Dallas Morning News*, July 4, 1991, p. 5C.

Farber, Jim, "Benzino Vs. Eminem: Principles or Publicity?," *New York Daily News*, January 16, 2003, p. 36.

Hedges, Chris, "Public Lives: His Beat Goes On, As a Hip-Hop Empire," *New York Times*, February 20, 2001, p. 2.

Horovitz, Bruce, "Hip-Hop: More Than Hype—Gritty Magazine Goes Mainstream," *USA Today*, September 16, 1997, p. 1B.

Manly, Lorne, "Flurry of New Products from The Source," *Folio*, October 1, 1993, p. 20.

McLeod, Harriet, "Source Gives Voice to Hip-Hop Culture," *Richmond Times-Dispatch*, April 21, 1994, p. D6.

Ogunnaike, Lola, "War of the Words at Hip-Hop Magazines," *New York Times,* January 29, 2003, p. 1.

"Police: Awards Sponsor Asked Chief to Fix Felony Arrest," *Associated Press Newswires*, August 23, 2001.

Potter, Maximillian, "Getting to the Source," *GQ: Gentlemen's Quarterly*, December 1, 2001, pp. 144–51.

Rich, Cary Peyton, "They Don't Teach This at Harvard," *Folio*, May 1, 1991, p. 60.

Tilove, Jonathan, "True Colors: White Role in Rap Is Questioned," *New Orleans Times-Picayune*, November 1, 1992, p. A6.

Tyrangiel, Josh, ''A Source of Discomfort,'' *Time*, January 12, 2004, p. 74.

Warner, Melanie, ''The Source of Conflict: Publisher and Editor Grapple Over Gangsta Group Article,'' *Inside Media*, October 5, 1994, p. 5.

Wartofsky, Alona, ''Ink-Splattered Hip-Hop Rivalry,'' *Washington Post*, February 25, 2003, p. C1.

Wilson, Steve, ''The Source Plays on Despite Editorial Scratches,'' *Folio*, May 1, 1995, p. 19.

Zook, Kristal Brent, ''In Source Awards Fracas, 'Old Beef' in New Battles,'' *Washington Post*, August 25, 2000, p. C1.

—Frank Uhle

SOUZA CRUZ

Souza Cruz S.A.

Rua Candelaria 66
Rio de Janeiro
20092-900 RJ
Brazil
Telephone: +55 21 3849 9000
Fax: +55 21 3849 9643
Web site: http://www.souzacruz.com.br

Public Subsidiary of British American Tobacco PLC
Incorporated: 1903 as Souza Cruz & Cia
Employees: 4,843
Sales: BRL 6.8 billion ($1.2 billion) (2003)
Stock Exchanges: Sao Paulo
Ticker Symbol: CRUZ
NAIC: 312221 Cigarette Manufacturing

Souza Cruz S.A. is Brazil's leading producer and distributor of tobacco and tobacco products, including cigarettes and cigars. In Brazil, the company controls nearly 78 percent of the total tobacco market, while worldwide the company sells almost 82 billion cigarettes through 200,000 sales outlets. A subsidiary of British American Tobacco, Souza Cruz is one of the world's largest exporters of tobacco and tobacco products, with sales of cigarettes and other products to more than 180 countries—and holds the leading share in more than 50 markets. Souza Cruz markets its own brands, including Derby and Free, the number one and two-selling brands in Brazil. Other brands, include Hollywood, Hilton, and such BAT brands as Carlton, Kent, Viceroy, Pall Mall, and Lucky Strike. The company also manufactures and distributes a number of licensed brands, such as Camel. Altogether, the company produces some 300 brands, including six of the top ten Brazilian brands. The company's production facilities include a state-of-the-art site in Cachoerinha, inaugurated as part of the company's centennial celebration in 2003, the world's largest cigarette manufacturing facility. Together with its factory in Uberlandia, Souza Cruz has a total production capacity of more than 100 billion cigarettes per year. The company also operates a number of leaf processing facilities in Brazil, including its facility in Santa Cruz do

Sul. Souza Cruz also works in close partnership with its pool of tobacco farmers, providing technological guidance and equipment, as well as seeds and fertilizers. Beyond Brazil, the company operates the Brascuba joint venture with the Cuban government to produce cigarettes incorporating that country's black tobacco. Souza Cruz's sales topped BRL 6.8 billion ($1.2 billion) in 2003, making it one of Brazil's top five corporations.

Founding a Brazilian Tobacco Giant in the 1900s

Souza Cruz was founded in Rio de Janeiro, Brazil, by Portuguese immigrant Albino Souza Cruz, who immigrated to the then-young republic in 1885. Cruz, then just 15 years old, went to work for a local cigar producer, Famosos Fumos Marca Veado, and remained there for some 18 years. In 1903, however, Cruz decided to leave Veado and set up his own business producing cigarettes using the recently developed cigarette rolling machine.

Souza Cruz & Cia was the first to produce machine-made, ready-rolled cigarettes in Brazil. The company launched its first brands in 1903, as well, including the popular Dalila, which became a company best-seller for the next two decades. Other cigarette and cigar brands launched in the company's early years were Três Misturas (1903), Hamburgueses (1903), Boccacio (1905), and the French-inspired Coquelin (1905) and Petits Cigarettes n. 45 (1909).

The rising popularity of cigarette smoking caused the company to seek an expansion of its production capacity. In 1910, the company acquired the Imperial Fabrica owned by Paulo Cordeiro in Rapé. The company then imported new German machinery, which enabled the company to further mechanize its operations, increasing production.

Souza Cruz remained an independent company until the beginning of World War I. In 1914, however, the company agreed to be acquired by British American Tobacco, then in the midst of its massive global expansion. Nonetheless, Albino Souza Cruz continued to lead the Brazilian company's operations, debuting a new and successful version of Dalila in 1915. Other highly popular new brands including Pavlova, named for the Russian ballerina, in 1918, and Yolanda, which went on to inspire a notable song of the period. That cigarette remained a company best-seller for some 45 years.

Meanwhile, Souza Cruz's association with BAT gave it access to the most modern tobacco technologies and techniques. In 1918, for example, the company began working closely with tobacco farmers, forming partnerships to ensure its tobacco supply. The company also became the first to begin processing tobacco using new tobacco shed production techniques in 1918. In the 1920s, the company's Odalisca brand became the first in Brazil to feature aluminum-backed paper wrappers, helping to preserve the freshness of cigarettes. Also during the 1920s, Souza Cruz stepped up its association with its tobacco farmers, providing new fertilizer techniques, and importing tobacco seeds from all over the world in order to improve the country's tobacco output. During this period, the company led its pool of farmers to begin planting Virginia and Burley varieties from the United States.

Long-Lasting Brand Success in the 1930s

Cigarette smoking became more and more popular in Brazil, spreading beyond Rio de Janeiro to other areas of the country in the 1920s. In response, Souza Cruz began adding new facilities and subsidiaries around Brazil. In 1924, the company created its first subsidiary in Porto Alegre, followed by the opening of a new factory in Santo Angelo in 1926. That year, also, the company acquired Litograficao Ferrerira Pinto, allowing it to expand its packaging and marketing efforts. A new sales subsidiary opened in Salvador in 1927. That year the company added a production facility in Brós as well. In 1930, the company opened a new factory, in Recife.

The year 1931 marked a new success for the company, with the launch of the hugely successful Hollywood brand. Hollywood became the company's longest-lasting success, and remained in production at the turn of the 21st century. The success of Hollywood and the company's other brands enabled it to gain control of one of its chief rivals, Companhia de Cigarros Castelloes, in 1935. The Castelloes business remained a separate operation at first, but was finally absorbed into Souza Cruz in 1955.

By then, Souza Cruz had marked a number of new expansion efforts, including the opening of a new subsidiary in Rio de Janeiro in 1936 and a new factory in Belo Horizonte in 1938. These were kept busy by the launch of another highly successful cigarette brand, Continental, which emerged as the country's top seller, accounting, by the end of the 1950s, for more than 63 percent of all of Souza Cruz's sales. Following World War II, the company stepped up its production capacity to meet the surging demand for the Continental brand. In 1946 the company inaugurated two new tobacco leaf processing facilities in Lajeado and Blumenau in 1946.

During the 1950s, the company added another subsidiary in Belém do Pará, and a third tobacco leaf processing facility in Tubarao, in 1954 and 1955, respectively. Souza Cruz also responded to the growing popularity of U.S. blonde tobaccos, used in particular in parent company BAT's brands, by beginning processing and sales of cigarettes incorporating these tobaccos. The company also created a new in-house graphics department, which took over from the Ferrerira Pinto operation. At the beginning of the 1960s, the company expanded again, opening a new leaf processing facility in Rio Negro in 1961. The following year, Souza Cruz retired from the head of the company he had founded at the age of 91 years. By then, Souza Cruz had already claimed the place as Brazil's leading cigarette company.

A new factory, dedicated to producing cigarillos and cigarettes, was created in Inducar in 1967. Meanwhile, Souza Cruz had begun plans to extend its business beyond Brazil for the first time. The company's low-cost tobacco production made it a prime candidate for the foreign export market. In 1969, the company sent out its first exports shipment, a 25-ton order to the United Kingdom.

To fuel its growing exports—which later topped 100,000 tons per year—Souza Cruz invested in new production facilities. In 1974, the company began construction of a new plant in Uberlandia. That site, completed in 1978, became the largest cigarette production facility in Latin America, and, with a total capacity of 65 billion cigarettes per year, one of the largest in the world. During this period, as well, the company went on a brief diversification drive, changing its name to Companhia Souza Cruz Indústria e Comércio to mark its move into paper production and fruit growing, among other industries.

Tobacco remained at the heart of the company's business, nonetheless. After modernizing its production and processing facilities at the beginning of the 1980s, the company prepared to step up its tobacco exports, as well as its overseas sales of its own cigarette brands. As part of its expansion effort, the company created a new subsidiary, Companhia de Cigarros Souza Cruz, which became the holding company for all of its cigarette operations.

Tobacco Leader in the 21st Century

Throughout its history, Souza Cruz continued developing new brands. In 1979, the company had a new hit with the launch of its first low-tar cigarette, Advance. Meanwhile, the 1980s marked a huge boom in the company's tobacco exports, as cigarette manufacturers from around the world—hit hard by rising taxes on cigarettes—stepped up the demand for the country's relatively low-cost tobaccos. At the same time, the country's cigarettes, dominated by Souza Cruz's brands, underwent a huge boom in demand, in part serving to fuel a new emerging market for discount cigarettes. If Souza Cruz and Brazil's other tobacco producers already exported more than 600 million cigarettes at the beginning of the 1980s, by the mid-1990s cigarette exports topped 63 billion.

Another factor lay behind Souza Cruz's growing export success. In the early 1980s, Brown & Williamson, another BAT subsidiary, had developed a genetically modified tobacco plant

Key Dates:

1903: Albino Souza Cruz founds first modern cigarette production plant in Rio de Janeiro and launches popular Dalila brand, among others.

1910: Souza Cruz acquires Imperial Fabrica de Rapé Paulo Cordeiro in Tijuca and imports new German production equipment.

1914: Souza Cruz is acquired by British American Tobacco.

1918: Company launches Yolanda brand, which remains a best-seller for 45 years.

1919: Company begins processing tobacco with new shed production techniques.

1931: Hollywood brand is launched.

1935: Souza Cruz acquires Companhia de Cigarros Castelloes.

1936: Souza Cruz begins marketing Continental brand, which later represents 63 percent of all company cigarette sales.

1946: Leaf processing facilities open in Lajeado and Blumenau.

1962: Albino Souza Cruz retires at the age of 91.

1969: Company begins exports of tobacco, starting with the United Kingdom.

1973: Company changes name to Companhia Souza Cruz Indústria e Comércio.

1977: Cigarette production facility in Uberlandia begins operations.

1981: Companhia de Cigarros Souza Cruz is created as holding company for cigarette operations.

1996: Brascuba cigarette manufacturing joint venture is formed with Cuban government; inauguration of new leaf processing plant at Santa Cruz do Sul.

2003: State-of-the-art cigarette production plant begins operations in Cachoerinha, near Porto Alegre.

that not only grew faster than the natural plant, but also contained twice the nicotine levels. Since the company was barred from growing the crop in the United States, seeds for the plant were smuggled into Brazil in the 1980s and provided to Souza Cruz's pool of farmers. By the 1990s, the crops had matured, and Souza Cruz began exporting the tobacco, much of which became incorporated into BAT's cigarettes destined for the United States and other markets. A still larger part was reserved for the fast-developing Asian nations, as well as the Middle East, where smoking rates were rising rapidly. By 1994, Souza Cruz had shipped more than eight million pounds of the leaf, which became known as "wacky tabacky."

By the mid-1990s, Souza Cruz had captured nearly 80 percent of Brazil's cigarette market. The country had also emerged as the world's fourth largest tobacco producer, as well as the largest leaf tobacco exporter and the sixth largest cigarette producer. Souza Cruz itself ranked in the top ten of the world's tobacco companies. By 1998, the company's cigarette exports alone topped 73 billion pieces. Fueling the company's growth was the success of its international brand, BAT-owned Lucky Strike. At home, the company had new brand hits with its Derby and Free brands, which rose to become the domestic market's number one and two top-selling brands by the early 2000s.

In response to its strong growth, Souza Cruz inaugurated a new state-of-the-art leaf processing facility in Santa Cruz do Sul in 1996. The new plant began production at 70,000 tons per year, with plans to nearly double capacity to 150,000 tons per year by the next decade. Also in 1996, Souza Cruz launched a joint venture with the Cuban government, creating Brascuba in order to produce cigarettes for the Cuban market, as well as export cigarettes containing Cuba's black tobacco to other markets.

By the year 2000, Souza Cruz found its domestic operations under pressure. New legislation had placed new restrictions on the company's marketing efforts, while at the same time stiffening taxes—which rose to account for as much as 80 percent of the price of a package of cigarettes. This in turn stimulated the growth of a cigarette black market and by the early years of the 2000s, smuggled cigarettes were estimated to account for as much as one third of all cigarettes in the country.

Nonetheless, Souza Cruz remained one of Brazil's industrial powerhouses—with sales of BRL 6.8 billion ($1.2 billion), the company ranked as the country's fourth largest company. In 2003, the company celebrated its centennial in style, inaugurating a new state-of-the-art cigarette production facility in Cachoerinha, near Porto Alegre, that was expected to reach its full capacity of 45 billion cigarettes per year by 2005. Despite the difficulties faced by the global tobacco industry—in 2004, the company lost a new class-action lawsuit brought against it in Brazil—Souza Cruz remained committed to remaining a force in the cigarette and tobacco market, and a pillar of the British American Tobacco empire.

Principal Competitors

Bulgartabac Holding PLC; Societatea Nationala "Tutunul Romanesc"; Limbe Leaf Tobacco Company Ltd.; DIMON Malawi Ltd.; Philip Morris International Management S.A.; Altria Group Inc.; Loews Corp.; Djarum, PT; Japan Tobacco Inc.; Shanghai Tobacco Group Corporation; International Tobacco Company Ltd.

Further Reading

Barham, John, "Souza Cruz Hit by Smuggling," *Financial Times*, February 5, 1999, p. 26.

Knight, Patrick, "Factories Closed As Exports Collapse," *World Tobacco*, March 2000, p. 23.

——, "New Brazilian Plant Built for the Long Run," *World Tobacco*, March 1997, p. 34.

Luxner, Larry, "Souza Cruz Says Cuban Cigarette Venture Is Thriving," *CubaNews*, January 2002, p. 4.

Morais, Fernando, *Souza Cruz 100 Anos: Um Seculo de Qualidade*, Rio de Janeiro: DBA, 2003.

Schaffler, Rhonda, "Souza Cruz Turns over BRL 6.8 Bil," *Valor Economico*, February 2, 2004.

"Souza Cruz Announces BRL 300 Mil Investment," *Gazeta Mercantil*, April 14, 2004.

"Souza Cruz Launches Small-Sized Cigarette," *Valor Economico*, June 3, 2004.

Townsend, Abigail, "BAT Faces Legal Barrage After Brazil Blow," *Independent*, February 22, 2004, p. 3.

—M.L. Cohen

SRAM Corporation

1333 North Kingsbury, Fourth Floor
Chicago, Illinois 60622
U.S.A.
Telephone: (312) 664-8800
Fax: (312) 664-8826
Web site: http://www.sram.com

Private Company
Incorporated: 1987 as OLLO Bicycle Components, Inc.
Employees: 1,000
Sales: $150 million (2003 est.)
NAIC: 336991 Motorcycle, Bicycle, and Parts
   Manufacturing

SRAM Corporation is a leading producer of bicycle components. Started around a single product—the Grip Shift gear shifter—the company, through acquisitions and research and development, has extended its product line to more than 100 different items. (The Grip Shift name has since been dropped.) Two notable recent acquisitions have been Sach Bicycle Components (1997) and RockShox, Inc. (2002). SRAM has several factories in Europe, North America, and Asia.

Origins

SRAM Corporation was started in Chicago in 1987 by Stanley R. Day, who hated fumbling for the gearshift on his bike while training for triathlons on weekends. Day came from an entrepreneurial family; his father was chairman of Champion Home Builders. After earning his M.B.A., Day worked three years at Molex Inc., a maker of electronic components. He serendipitously met Sam Patterson on a 1987 ski trip in Park City, Utah. As the *Chicago Sun-Times* reported, Day had attended business school at Northwestern University with Sam's brother, Art.

Most gear shifters until then used little levers that required the rider to momentarily move one hand away from the handlebars to change gears. This was an extra nuisance while bike racing or negotiating treacherous mountain trails, when the rider often was holding on for dear life with both hands.

Sam Patterson, then living in San Diego and working for an engine manufacturer, was a precociously talented designer. A native of Erie, Pennsylvania, he graduated from an accelerated program at the University of South Carolina's engineering school. Within weeks of the fateful ski trip, Patterson designed a new gear shifter, one that wrapped around the handlebars. Although this configuration was not an entirely new innovation in itself, Patterson's design was indexed, meaning it easily clicked to numbered positions corresponding with specific gears.

Day assembled a group of investors in the summer of 1987 and set up an office in the Fulton-Carroll entrepreneurial incubator building run by the Industrial Council of Northwest Chicago. The company ended 1988 with about a dozen enthusiastic employees, some culled from Day's former employer Molex.

Day became the company's president while Patterson served as head of research and development. The name SRAM was reportedly made up of letters from the names of its founders, including attorney Scott Ray King. (The company was originally incorporated as OLLO Bicycle Components, Inc., then renamed a couple of months later, according to filings with the Illinois secretary of state.)

Scott Molina, 1988 Ironman champion, was among the triathletes who enthusiastically embraced the product, originally called the DB shifter. Its location at the end of the handlebars proved troublesome, however, and it was repositioned between the grips and the center of the handlebars. The DB shifter originally was packaged as an aftermarket accessory kit and priced at about $120. The product later evolved into the Grip Shift.

Taking on the World in the 1990s

Cannondale began using the CX model of the shifter on its mountain bikes in 1989. A couple of years later, after being hounded by SRAM for years at trade shows, Trek and Specialized Bicycle Components finally introduced Grip Shift as standard equipment on their hybrid bikes, a smaller market.

The bike components business was then dominated by Japan's Shimano Inc., which had an 85 percent market share. Shimano

sold its shifters and derailleurs to bike manufacturers as complete
sets until a California antitrust lawsuit by SRAM, which was
settled in 1991 for an estimated $3 million to $5 million.

SRAM opened a plant in Taiwan in 1991, and the Chicago
operation grew to 60 people. The company shipped more than
300,000 of its SRT 300 shifter sets to leading bike brands. An
office opened in Dortmund, Germany, in 1992 and moved to
The Netherlands the next year.

Revenues were about $25 million in 1994. The company
shipped two million shifters for the 1994 model year, reported
Crain's Chicago Business, and five million for the next.

By the mid-1990s, Grip Shifts were specified on half of the
bicycles sold at independent bike shops in the United States and
dominated the U.S. cross-country racing circuit. SRAM also
had made substantial progress in the European market, attaining
a 30 percent market share for nonmass-market bikes.

SRAM's factories in Taiwan and China were going full tilt.
The company opened a 43,560-square-foot manufacturing plant
near Chicago in 1994. In 1995, SRAM set up its first European
plant in Carrick-on-Suir, County Tipperary, Ireland. The Irish
government provided incentives for building the IEP 5 million
factory there. After opening the new factory, SRAM had 600
employees, half of them in Asia.

SRAM began selling its own derailleur—the device that
moves the change between the different cogs—in the spring of
1995, intensifying its competition with Shimano in the upper
end of the market (SRAM's was priced at $200).

Acquiring Sachs in 1997

SRAM bought Sachs Bicycle Components from Mannesmann Sachs AG, a unit of German telecommunications group
Mannesmann AG, in November 1997. It specialized in internal
gear hubs and bicycle chains, both new product lines for
SRAM. Based in California, Sachs had 1,250 employees and
annual revenues of more than $125 million. The acquisition
made SRAM the world's second largest bicycle components
company, and a leader in the European market for comfort (or
''trekking'') bicycles.

Sachs had been founded in Germany in 1895 as Schwein-
furter Praezisions Kugellagerwerke Fichtel und Sachs. The firm
was a pioneer in ball bearings as well as bicycle wheel hubs,
including the legendary Torpedo freewheel hub. Mannesmann
had acquired control of Sachs in 1987.

Globalization After 2000

By 2000, reported the *Chicago Sun-Times,* SRAM had 1,000
employees around the world and facilities in Taiwan, China,

The Netherlands, Portugal, Germany, Ireland, and Mexico
(opened in Chihuahua in 1997). New offerings included
sprocket cassettes and the SPARC electrical assist system.
Products in development included an integrated handlebar system for leisure bikes called SmartBar (designed by Inspire
Design Group, LLC of Wisconsin). A new internal gear hub
factory opened in Schweinfurt, Germany, in 1999.

In 2001, SRAM's German subsidiary filed an anti-dumping
complaint with the European Union against rival Shimano. At
the time, SRAM Deutschland GmbH accounted for 85 percent
of the EU's production of gear hubs and employed 1,200 people
in Europe, according to *European Report.*

SRAM moved into a new 100,000-square-foot manufacturing and headquarters complex in Chicago's near north side in
2001. By this time, its product line had expanded into brakes,
handlebars, and battery-powered motors.

Acquiring RockShox in 2002

SRAM bought RockShox, Inc. for $5.6 million in March
2002. RockShox of Colorado was known for the shock
absorber-equipped front forks it supplied to the mountain bike
industry. Sales were $65 million in 2002. RockShox' line of
mountain bike suspension products was well respected in the
market and complementary to SRAM's other components.

RockShox went public in 1996 in an offering that raised $72
million. Its shares were traded on the NASDAQ exchange and
later over the counter under the ticker symbol RSHX. The
company had become the undisputed leader in bike suspen-
sions, with a 60 percent market share. RockShox rode the
mountain bike boom to sales of $106 million for the fiscal year
ending March 1997. Then, according to *Business Week,* fewer
than one in five mountain bikes was equipped with shocks,
leaving room to grow. The mountain bike market crashed, however, in the late 1990s.

RockShox had been started by two motorcycle aficionados.
Paul Turner was an employee of Honda R&D North America
Inc. and Stephen Simons had his own motorbike suspension
business, reported *Business Week.* RockShox was formed in
North Carolina in 1989 and moved to California three years
later. Its June 2000 move to Colorado saved it an estimated $5
million a year. RockShox had about 300 employees at its Colorado Springs plant at the time of the acquisition. The company
had lost more than $10 million in 2001, and its manufacturing
operations were moved to Taichung, Taiwan, in 2002 to take

advantage of lower labor costs and to be closer to the host of American bike brands that had set up plants there. (RockShox retained a small base in Colorado Springs for testing mountain bikes.) In less than ten years, the annual U.S. output of finished bikes had fallen from five million to 500,000. SRAM had opened its first plant in Taiwan in 1991 and also had two factories in the People's Republic of China.

SRAM entered the road bike market in 2003 with cassettes and chains. Sales were about $150 million for the year; the company's catalog included 100 different products. The company dropped the Grip Shift name from its shifters, focusing on the SRAM brand.

Principal Subsidiaries

RockShox, Inc.; SRAM Deutschland GmbH; SRAM Europe (Netherlands); SRAM France (IRCOS); SRAM Taiwan.

Principal Competitors

Daiwa Seiko Inc.; Falcon Cycle Parts; LDI, Ltd.; Shimano Inc.; SR Suntour Inc.; Sun Race Sturmey-Archer Inc.

Further Reading

Beebe, Paul, "Owner of Colorado Springs, Colo.-Based Bicycle Parts Maker Completes Transfer," *Gazette* (Colorado Springs), June 11, 2003.

Brokaw, Leslie, "Shifting Gears," *Inc.,* February 1989, p. 24.

Crown, Judith, "Getting a Grip; Tiny Firm Whips Japan Biking Titan," *Crain's Chicago Business,* May 15, 1995.

"EU/Japan: Commission Rides Tightrope Over Bike Hub Dumping Case," *European Report,* October 6, 2001.

Gurwell, Lance, "Bicycle Parts Maker to Relocate for Cheaper Labor," *Colorado Springs Business Journal,* May 17, 2002.

Hamilton, Joan, "RockShox: Cycling's Easy Riders," *Business Week,* May 26, 1997, p. 96.

Ivey, Mike, "Raising the Bar: Local Design Firm Gaining National Notice," *Capital Times & Wisconsin State Journal,* Bus. Sec., February 28, 2001, p. 1E.

Light, Larry, "Where Are They Now?," *Business Week,* May 31, 1999, p. 98.

"MCIT PLC—Re Flotation of RockShox, Inc.," *Regulatory News Service,* September 27, 1996.

Moore, Patricia, "Gripping Tale with a Twist," *Chicago Sun-Times,* Financial Sec., November 28, 1988, p. 37.

"Recycling Resources: Tenants Shunning Build-Outs to Save Money," *Crain's Chicago Business,* October 15, 2001.

Saint, Steven, "Bike-Part Maker to Buy Colorado Springs, Colo.-Based Shock-Absorber Producer," *Gazette* (Colorado Springs), February 21, 2002.

——, "Maker of Bike Shock Absorbers to Move Manufacturing to Taiwan from Colorado," *Gazette* (Colorado Springs), May 14, 2002.

Tita, Bob, "SARS Roils Area Manufacturers; Companies Recall Far East Execs, Delay Deals," *Crain's Chicago Business,* April 14, 2003, p. 1.

"US Cycle Plant to Open in Tipperary," *Irish Times,* Bus. Sec., February 28, 1995, p. 12.

Wiebe, Matt, "RockShox Revolutionized Mountain Biking, Then Quickly Bottomed Out," *Bicycle Retailer,* April 1, 2002, p. 24.

Williams, Kevin M., "Geared Up," *Chicago Sun-Times,* Financial Sec., July 27, 2000, p. 48.

—Frederick C. Ingram

Suntory Ltd.

Dojimahama 2-1-40, Kita-Ku
Osaka 530-8203
Japan
Telephone: +81 6 6346 1131
Fax: +81 6 6345 1169
Web site: http://www.suntory.co.jp

Private Company
Incorporated: 1907 as Kotobukiya Liquor Shop
Employees: 18,059
Sales: ¥1.32 trillion ($12.19 billion) (2003)
NAIC: 312140 Distilleries; 111421 Nursery and Tree
    Production; 312111 Soft Drink Manufacturing;
    312120 Breweries; 312130 Wineries; 325131
    Inorganic Dye and Pigment Manufacturing; 325412
    Pharmaceutical Preparation Manufacturing; 424810
    Beer and Ale Merchant Wholesalers; 424920 Book,
    Periodical and Newspaper Merchant Wholesalers;
    484121 General Freight Trucking, Long-Distance,
    Truckload; 493110 General Warehousing and Storage
    Facilities; 721110 Hotels (Except Casino Hotels) and
    Motels; 722110 Full-Service Restaurants

Suntory Ltd. is Japan's leading alcoholic and nonalcoholic beverage company, with a leading position in that country's whiskey market, and strong positions in the beer, wine, and soft drink and other beverage segments as well. The company's sales of more than ¥1.3 trillion (US$12.19 billion) also places it among the world's top drinks companies. Whiskey remains the company's strongest product area—Suntory is credited with introducing Scotch-style whiskey to Japan—and production of the group's 18 different bottled blends and single malts are concentrated at its Yamazaki Valley and Hakushu distilleries. The company also produces a number of other alcohol varieties, such as the melon-flavored liqueur Midori, and the distilled alcohol, Shochu. Suntory also acts as distributor for a long list of international brands in Japan, including Beefeater, Courvoisier, Jack Daniels, Campari, and Drambuie among nearly 150 brands. In addition to its Japanese operations,

Suntory manages Scotland's Morrison Bowmore Distillers, France's Chateau Lagrange and Chateau Beychevelle, and Germany's Weingut Robert Weil. In the United States, Suntory operates Pepsi Bottling Ventures LLC, and is that country's third largest mineral water distributor through subsidiary Suntory Water and brands including Hinckley & Schmidt. Other operations in the diversified group, which counts nearly 180 subsidiaries, include restaurants, health food, publishing, and botany—in 2004, the company flower development division debuted the world's first successful blue rose. Suntory remains controlled by the founding Saji family, and is led by President Nobutada Saji.

Wine and Whiskey Pioneer in the Early 20th Century

Into the beginning of the 20th century, Japan's alcoholic beverage market remained dominated by two traditional Japanese recipes, sake, a fermented rice-based alcohol, and shochu, a distilled variation of sake. The opening of the company to Western influences in the early part of the 20th century, however, introduced a number of Japanese drinkers to Western-style alcoholic beverages, including wine and whiskey. For the most part, however, these beverages remained unsuitable to the Japanese palate.

The revolution in Japan's drinking habits that occurred during the century—giving rise to the famous image of the whiskey-drinking "salaryman"—began through the efforts of Shinjiro Torii. Born to an Osaka money-changer in 1879, Torii originally apprenticed to a drug wholesaler at the age of 13, and later worked for a paint and dye wholesaler as well. By the turn of the century, however, Torii had discovered Western alcoholic beverages, and especially wine. Torii started studying Western wine-making techniques. His first professional effort, however, was to start up his own wine wholesaling business in 1899, importing wines from Spain. The company's original name was Kotobukiya Liquor Shop.

The Spanish wines did not, however, appeal to Japanese tastes, and Torii's first business failed. Instead, Torii recognized that he would have to develop his own wine adapted to Japanese preferences, and he began experimenting with recipes and blends of Spanish wines with flavorings and sweeteners. By

1907, Torii had perfected his recipe and launched the first Japanese-style wine, which he called Akadama Port Wine.

Torii began contracting with wholesalers to distribute his wine. He also exhibited a flair for marketing, becoming one of the first in Japan to employ Western advertising and marketing techniques. In another skillful move, Torii adopted wine marketing techniques from France as well, such as transforming the decasking of the year's wine into a media event. In 1910, Torii began touting the Kotobukiya company's wines for their medicinal virtues as well.

The success of Akadama led Torii to guide Kotobukiya into a wider array of products, such as black tea, curry powder and other spices, soy sauce, and even toothpaste. The company also began brewing beer. By the 1920s, however, Torii had found a new target for his ambitions: the production of Japan's first whiskey.

While Torii himself had developed a taste for Scotch whiskey, he remained a rarity among Japanese consumers. Torii's interest in establishing his own distillery—and developing a whiskey that would be acceptable for Japanese drinkers—came in 1920. In that year, Masataka Taketsuru, who had been sent to Scotland by one of Torii's competitors to study Scotch whiskey-making techniques, returned to Japan after a two-year stay. Taketsuru initially intended to build his own distillery but was unable to do so due to the poor economic climate of the time. Instead, Taketsuru went to work for the Kotobukiya company, applying his technical knowledge to Torii's plans to build a distillery.

Taketsuru initially proposed building the distillery in Hokkaido, which had a terrain and climate similar to that of Scotland. Torii, however, saw more potential in establishing the distillery in Yamazaki, situated between the major Kyoto and Osaka markets. The Yamazaki site nonetheless benefited from its extremely pure well water.

The Yamazaki distillery started production in 1923 and Torii and Taketsuru began work on perfecting a whiskey blend suitable to Japanese drinking habits. Among other features, the pair sought a whiskey capable of maintaining its flavor when mixed with water, satisfying the Japanese preference for drinking during meals. This style of whiskey became known as Mizuwari, literally ''water cut'' whiskey.

Kotobukiya's first whiskey debuted in 1929. Known as Suntory Shirofuda, the whiskey initiated the Suntory brand. The whiskey, considered Japan's first domestic-produced whiskey, later became known as Suntory White. Yet the first whiskey was reputedly more akin to ''firewater'' than the Scotch whiskies it sought to emulate. Torii and Taketsuru continued work, seeking a flavor closer to their Scotch inspiration.

Building the Postwar Whiskey Culture

Taketsuru left Kotobukiya in 1934 in order to found his own distillery, in the town of Yoichi, on the island of Hokkaido, considered by Taketsuru to resemble more closely the climate of the Scottish Highlands. Taketsuru's company, which later became known as the Nikka Whiskey Company (and still later became part of the Asahi Brewing empire), developed into a major Japanese whiskey maker in its own right.

In the meantime, Torii persevered with developing a new blended whiskey through the 1930s. During that decade, Torii decided to focus the company's efforts solely on its alcoholic beverage production, shutting down its general foods business. The difficulty in obtaining foreign wine imports during the Depression Era and the Spanish Civil War in the 1930s encouraged Torii to branch out into a new area, however: that of the production of a domestic Japanese wine. Torii began planting a vineyard in Yamanashi, near Mt. Fuji, founding the Suntory Tomi-no-Oka Winery in 1936. Using French grape varieties such as Cabernet Sauvignon and Chardonnay, Torii developed a domestic version of the Akadama sweet wine, as well as a number of other wine varieties.

The year 1937, however, marked what many consider as the beginning of the great Japanese whiskey culture—destined to become the world's second largest whiskey market. In that year, Kotobukiya released a new whiskey blend, dubbed Kakubin. Considered Japan's first authentic ''Scotch'' whiskey, the blend was highly successful and launched the Suntory brand as the country's leader.

Torii continued developing new blends, launching ''Old'' in 1940. Production became more difficult during World War II, especially as Torii refused to use substitute ingredients, such as artificial sweeteners for the company's sweetened wine. Torii's commitment to quality also was evident in the company's research and development efforts. Through the 1930s and into the 1940s, the company installed onsite laboratories, which grew into a dedicated research and development center in 1943.

Rebuilding the company and its market following World War II, Torii was joined by son Keizo Saji. Born in 1919, Saji had studied chemistry at Osaka University before joining Kotobukiya in 1945, where he became the chief architect of the group's later diversification and growth into Japan's dominant whiskey group.

Through the reconstruction effort of the 1950s, Kotobukiya developed strongly, in part because of the presence of U.S. troops in Japan. The company also continued to develop unique advertising campaigns, such as the début of a ''literary'' campaign featuring texts from known Japanese writers.

An important factor in the company's continued growth was the rise of the so-called ''salaryman'' group. Shouldering the burden of rebuilding the country's economy and dedicated to raising Japan into the top ranks of the world's economy, the salaryman became synonymous with whiskey drinking. Suntory whiskey quickly became the salaryman's whiskey of choice. This was in large part because of the launch of a new bar concept, devised by Keizo Saji, called Torys. Launched in the 1950s, the Torys chain became a national phenomenon, with more than 1,500 bars in operation at its peak.

Key Dates:

1899: Shinjiro Torii founds a wine import business in Osaka, then begins developing a sweetened wine for the Japanese market.

1907: The popular Akadama sweetened wine debuts.

1923: The company builds a distillery in Yamazaki and begins developing a whiskey blend.

1929: The company launches its first whiskey, Suntory Shirofuda.

1937: The company launches the successful Suntory Kakubin, considered the first authentic Japanese whiskey.

1945: Son Keizo Saji joins the company.

1950s: The company develops the Torys bar chain, which grows into more than 1,500 bars.

1963: The first Suntory beer is launched.

1968: The first Suntory draft beer is launched.

1970: The company enters into a distribution agreement to import Brown-Forman whiskey brands into Japan.

1973: The company builds a second distillery in Hakushu.

1980: The company forms the Pepcom bottler for PepsiCo in the United States.

1981: The company builds a third distillery, also in Hakushu.

1984: The company enters China, brewing beer through the China Jiangsu Suntory Foods Co. Ltd. joint venture.

1990: The company begins acquisition of Florigene in Australia and begins development of ''blue rose.''

1995: The company enters the Shanghai beer market with subsidiary Suntory Brewing (Shanghai) Co. Ltd.

2003: Yamazaki 12-year-old single malt wins top prize at the International Spirits Challenge in London.

2004: Suntory introduces the world's first successful blue rose.

Global Group in the New Century

Keizo Saji took over as president of the company, renamed as Suntory Ltd., in 1961. At that time, the company's sales represented the equivalent of some $100 million. The company by then had become interested in extending its operations into other beverage categories, a move begun in 1963 with a return to beer brewing for the first time since the 1930s.

Suntory initially brewed heat-treated beer, which then commanded the largest share of the Japanese beer-drinking market. In 1968, however, the company launched its first draft beer, a style of beer that soon imposed itself as a major part of the domestic beer market. The company's Penguin Boy and other beer brands ultimately enabled it to capture a 10 percent share of the Japanese beer market.

Suntory continued to develop and diversify its portfolio during the 1970s. The company began acting as a distributor for foreign brands into the heavily restricted Japanese market in the early 1970s, starting with an agreement to import the whiskey portfolio of the United States' Brown-Forman in 1970. In this way, Suntory was able to capture a still larger share of the domestic whiskey market. Nonetheless, Suntory's own brands remained dominant—in part because of the high tariffs placed on whiskey imports.

The growth in demand for Suntory's whiskey led the company to build a new distillery in Hakushu in 1973. To these the company added a third distillery, also located in Hakushu but called Hakushu Higashi (''West''), which began developing its own distinctive single-malt and blended whiskeys. Hakushu Higashi originally operated as a separate entity. During the 1990s, however, the company combined the two distilleries into a single operation.

In the meantime, Suntory had begun to make inroads on the global market. Part of the group's efforts was inspired by a slowdown in the domestic whiskey market, as the salaryman culture began to be hit by the country's growing economic difficulties. Suntory's globalization effort was coupled with continued diversification. In the United States, for example, the company launched Pepcom Industries, which, later replaced by the joint venture Pepsi Bottling Ventures, grew into one of PepsiCo's major bottling partners.

In 1984, Suntory entered China, forming the joint venture China Jiangsu Suntory Foods Co. Ltd. to produce beer for that market. That company soon captured a major share of the Jiangsu market. In 1995, the company moved into Shanghai, forming Suntory Brewing (Shanghai) Co. Ltd. The company's Suntory Beer became that market's top-selling beer brand by the end of the decade.

Suntory's expansion effort—the privately held company returned as much as one-third of its profits to new investments each year—took it to France, where it bought up Medoc-region's Chateau Lagrange, and entered partnerships to manage a number of other wine chateaus, including Bordeaux's Chateau Beychevelle. The company also bought a California vineyard, Chateau St. Jean, in 1984, and later turned to Germany, buying Weingut Robert Weil, based in Rheingau.

Suntory's diversification continued through the 1990s. The company launched its own international chain of Japanese restaurants, opening restaurants throughout the Asian region. In 1992, the company formed a joint venture to introduce the Subway fast-food chain into Japan. In that year, also, Suntory created its Consumer Health Products division, which was supplemented by the group's Health Food Division in 1999, and the Suntory Institute for Health Care Science in 2001.

Other diversified company interests included the launch of a publishing business, starting with a Japanese version of the *Encyclopedia Britannica* in 1986, followed by Japanese-language versions of *Newsweek* and France's *Figaro*; Tipness, a 32-branch chain of health clubs, launched in 1987; the Mac-Gregor Golf Japan manufacturing franchise; and the launch of a biotechnology division concentrated on the development of new flower varieties. Among the company's successes in that field are the Surfinia petunia, introduced in 1989, and, backed by its acquisition of Australia's Florigene Pty. Ltd. starting in 1990, the début of the world's first successful blue rose. These diversified operations nonetheless remained a small part of the group's sales, dominated by its drinks operations.

Keizo Saji died in 1999, leaving his son Nobutada Saji in charge of the family-held company. Saji had built Suntory into one of the world's largest drinks companies, with sales of more than $12 billion at the end of 2003, and Japan's leading drinks group. The efforts of Keizo Saji and father Shinjiro Torii were crowned in 2003 when the company's 12-year-old Yamazaki single malt won the top prize at the International Spirits Challenge in London. Backed by this success, Suntory's thirst for growth remained strong as it moved into the new century.

Principal Subsidiaries

Cerebos Australia Ltd. (Australia); Cerebos Gregg's Ltd. (New Zealand); Cerebos Pacific Ltd. (Singapore); China Jiangsu Suntory Foods Co., Ltd.; Chiyoda Kogyo Co., Ltd.; Chugoku Pepsi-Cola Bottling K.K.; Country House., Inc. (Taiwan); Eastern Viva Co., Ltd.; Gold Knoll Ltd. (Hong Kong); Hokkaido Pepsi-Cola Bottling Co., Ltd.; Iwanohara Vineyard Co., Ltd.; Kanbaku Co., Ltd.; Kinki Pepsi-Cola Bottling K.K.; Minami Kyushu Pepsi-Cola Bottling K.K.; Morrison Bowmore Distillers, Ltd. (U.K.); Nihon Pepsi-Cola Bottling K.K.; Okinawa Pepsi-Cola Beverage K.K.; Princeville Corporation (U.S.A.); Shanghai Suntory-Maling Foods Co., Ltd. (China); Suncafé Ltd.; Sungrain, Ltd.; Sunlive, Ltd.; Suntory (AUST) Pty. Ltd. (Australia); Suntory (China) Holding Co., Ltd.; Suntory (Shanghai) Marketing Co., Ltd. (China); Suntory (Thailand) Ltd. (Thailand); Suntory Allied, Ltd.; Suntory Brewing (Kunshan) Co., Ltd. (China); Suntory Brewing (Shanghai) Co., Ltd. (China); Suntory Europe PLC (U.K.); Suntory Food Manufacturing Co., Ltd.; Suntory Foods, Ltd.; Suntory France S.A.S. (France); Suntory Guangzhou Foods LTD. (China); Suntory International Corp. (U.S.A.); Suntory Ltd. (France); Suntory Ltd. (Italy); Suntory Ltd. (China); Suntory Ltd. (Spain); Suntory Ltd. (Taiwan); Suntory Mexicana, S.A.De C.V. (México); Suntory Pharmaceutical, Inc. (U.S.A.); Suntory Water Group, Inc. (U.S.A.); Tokaj Hetszölö R.T. (Hungary); Touhoku Pepsi-Cola Bottling K.K.; Weingut Robert Weil (Germany).

Principal Competitors

Asahi Breweries Ltd.; Sichuan Yibin Wuliangye Distillery.

Further Reading

Beauchamp, Marc, "Buy American," *Forbes,* October 6, 1986, p. 74.

Carpenter, Susan, "Sipping Sound," *Inside/Outside Japan,* February 1992.

"Japan Beverage, Whiskey Maker's Net Profit Almost Doubles in Jan-June Term," *Knight Ridder/Tribune Business News,* August 8, 2003.

Koch, Neal, "Small Beer," *Forbes,* August 1, 1983, p. 158.

"Whiskey Leader with Taste for Fine Life," *Financial Times,* November 4, 1999, p. 29.

—M.L. Cohen

Superior Energy Services, Inc.

1105 Peters Road
Harvey, Louisiana 70058
U.S.A.
Telephone: (504) 362-4321
Fax: (504) 362-1430
Web site: http://www.superiorenergy.com

Public Company
Incorporated: 1991 as Small's Oilfield Services Corp.
Employees: 3,150
Sales: $500.6 million (2003)
Stock Exchanges: New York
Ticker Symbol: SPN
NAIC: 213112 Support Activities for Oil and Gas Operations

Superior Energy Services, Inc. is a Louisiana-based oilfield services and equipment rental company, serving oil and gas companies operating in the Gulf of Mexico. Operations include well intervention services, marine services, and rental tools. Superior's well intervention services help oil and gas producers to stimulate wells by a variety of nondrilling methods. In addition, the company provides permanent and temporary plug and abandonment services for wells. (According to both state and federal laws nonproducing offshore wells must have their holes plugged with concrete and their rig and piping removed as far as 15 feet below the sea floor.) Superior also has begun acquiring mature shallow water oil and gas properties, with the intent of using the group's expertise to develop remaining reserves and then plug and decommission the wells. Superior's marine services is centered around a fleet of more than 50 liftboats, representing about one-quarter of all liftboats operating in the Gulf of Mexico, which can be used in conjunction with the company's well intervention services. Liftboats are self-propelled, self-elevating work platforms that also provide living accommodations. In addition, Superior manufactures, sells, and rents specialized equipment used in oil and gas well drilling, both onshore and offshore. The company maintains 36 rental tool operations in the Gulf of Mexico, located in all major staging points, offering such items as pressure control equipment, specialty tubular goods, connecting iron, drill pipe, tongs, power swivels, and stabilizers. Further, Superior maintains tool rental operations, offering a smaller range of equipment, in Venezuela, Trinidad, Canada, the United Kingdom, The Netherlands, and the Middle East. Superior also offers a variety of other oilfield services, such as platform and field management services, nonhazardous oilfield waste management and environmental cleaning services, and the manufacture and sale of specialized drilling rig instrumentation, electronic torque, and pressure control equipment.

Founding the Corporation in 1991

Superior's corporate lineage can be traced back to April 1991, with the incorporation of Small's Oilfield Services Corp., the predecessor of which had been founded by Carl W. Small some 25 years earlier. In conjunction with its incorporation, the company, based in Big Spring, Texas, traded stock to acquire Small Fishing and Rental, Inc.; Rentco Pipe and Tool Corp.; Curry Fishing and Rental, Inc.; and KCK Pipe Rentals Corp. Specializing in the rental of oil well equipment and fishing tools in west Texas and New Mexico, the company was taken public in 1992. It fared poorly, though, leading to its founder stepping down as president and chief executive in October 1993. In 1995 Small's lost $1.6 million and negotiations were begun to merge it with Superior Group of Belle Chasse, Louisiana.

Founding of Superior Group: 1984

Superior Group consisted of Superior Well Service, Inc.; Connection Technology, L.L.C.; Superior Tubular Services, Inc.; and Ace Rental Tools. Superior was founded by New Orleans attorney Terence E. Hall, who started out as a consultant in the oil and gas industry, and then in 1984 started Connection Technology, which manufactured computer monitoring systems to test drilling pipelines. Over the next five years he diversified into other oilfield services, forming Superior Tubular Services to manufacture and install tubing, and Superior Well Services Inc., a plug and abandonment company. In 1989 the three independently operated companies came under the common ownership of Superior Group.

Unlike Small's, Superior prospered in the early 1990s, producing strong results. Hall was attracted to Small's, believing he could turn around the business in a short period of time. Moreover, because Small's was a public company he would also be able to convert Superior into a public company through a reverse merger, and by way of a secondary stock offering he could raise cash he needed to support an aggressive expansion effort. The reverse merger was complicated and after more than a year had passed it finally was completed in December 1995. The owners of the Superior subsidiaries exchanged their holdings for shares in Small's and in the process gained a majority interest in the resulting company, which was subsequently renamed Superior Energy Services, Inc. Simultaneously, the company made a public offering of stock, netting $9.3 million. Some of that money, $2 million, along with 1.8 million shares of stock, was put to quick use in the acquisition of Oil Stop Inc., which made inflatable offshore oil cleanup booms. Superior also took immediate steps to rectify matters with Small's. A joint venture was forged with Abilene, Texas-based G&L Tool Co., whereby G&L bought Small's land for $300,000 and took over its rental equipment through a monthly payment agreement: $110,000 each month for two years, followed by three years of $80,000 monthly payments. After five years G&L had the option to buy Small's.

In the two years following the merger with Small's, Superior pursued its strategy of growth through acquisition, paying particular attention to the rental field as a way to lower dependence on plug and abandonment activities, which accounted for more than 80 percent of the company's revenues at this stage. Long term, the company's goal was to become a general "workover and remediation" company, able to provide the full range of services and equipment needed to restore wells. Both equipment rental and plug and abandonment capabilities were important facets of the plan. Superior also implemented a strategy of allowing acquired companies to operate as wholly owned subsidiaries, keeping their names and generally most of their management, thereby retaining name recognition, customer contacts, and goodwill accumulated over the years. Hall told *New Orleans City Business* in a June 1997 company profile, "We just try to lend some management expertise and help them run their business."

In July 1996 Superior completed the purchase of Baytron, Inc., paying $1.1 million in cash and 550,000 shares of stock, in a deal worth approximately $2.6 million. The Gretna, Louisiana-based company designed, manufactured, sold, and rented computerized rig data acquisition systems to monitor drilling activities in oilfields, a business that nicely complemented the activities of Connection Technology. Later in 1996 Superior added Dimensional Oil Field Services, Inc. in a deal valued at $3.5 million. The Louisiana company was a plug and abandonment services company that was a direct competitor of Superior Well Service, and its acquisition helped Superior to gain a majority position in the Gulf of Mexico plug and abandonment market. Next, Superior bolstered its Ace Rental Tools,

Inc. division by acquiring the assets of Advance Oilfield Rental Tools, Inc., a Houma, Louisiana, company that provided customers in south Louisiana with specialized high-pressure hoses, manifolds, and valves. For the year, Superior posted $23.6 million in sales and a $3.9 million profit.

Superior picked up the pace of acquisitions in 1997. It added to its oilfield tool rental business with the purchase of Concentric Pipe & Tool Rentals, another Houma, Louisiana, company that served the Gulf of Mexico market. It also bought Nautilus Pipe & Tool Rental, Inc. and Superior Bearing & Machine Works, Inc. The company then enhanced its well intervention services with the acquisition of F&F Wireline Service, Inc., which provided production wireline services on land and the Gulf of Mexico. Next, Superior grew the rental side of its business, paying cash and stock totaling $11 million for Tong Rental and Supply Inc. With offices in Lafayette, Louisiana, and Houston and Alice, Texas, Tong Rental was one of the Gulf's largest rental companies for power swivels, power tongs, and related tools. Later in 1997 Superior paid $25 million in cash and notes to pick up Stabil Drill Specialties, Inc., which manufactured, for sale and rental, tools used in the bottom hole assembly, such as stabilizers, hole openers, and drill collars. At the same time, Superior completed the $7.4 million purchase of Fastorq, Inc., which provided hydrostatic test pump rentals as well as such oilfield services as hydraulic nipple up, wrench bolting, bolt turning, nut splitting, bolt removal, and mechanical pipe cutting. A further expansion of the rental business resulted from the $25 million purchase of Sub-Surface Tools, Inc., a Morgan City, Louisiana-based company that specialized in the rental of tubulars, tubular handling tools, and pressure control equipment. As a result of its rapid growth, Superior saw revenues increase in 1997 to $54.3 million and net income to $9.5 million.

Industry conditions were poor in 1998, leading Superior to slow down the acquisition pace, and the company even decided to sell off one of its subsidiaries, Baytron, to Tuboscope Inc. Over the course of the year, Superior added just three companies to its portfolio. It acquired Tong Specialty, Inc. and Lamb Services, Inc., both Lafayette companies that provided tubing and casing running services and drilling and rental tools. In addition, Superior acquired Hydro-dynamics Oilfield Contractors, Inc. Rather than always being the buyer, Superior was almost acquired itself in 1998. In October it reached a tentative agreement to be purchased by Tulsa, Oklahoma-based Parker Drilling for approximately $168 million in stock and assumed debt. Hall expressed his belief that the deal was in the best interests of Superior's shareholders. "But more importantly," he said in prepared remarks, "it will allow our existing business lines to grow by accessing Parker's well-established international platform." Parker, founded in 1934, offered drilling service and oil tool rentals in 14 countries. But the sale would not be completed, with the parties deciding in January 1999 to terminate the merger. The major problem was Parker's fluctuating stock price, which made it almost impossible to fix the value of Parker's offer. Despite difficult industry conditions, Superior improved its sales in 1998 to $91.3 million, although it suffered a net loss of $4.1 million.

Acquiring Cardinal Holdings in 1999

Superior remained well positioned to benefit from an industry rebound and completed a pair of significant acquisitions in

---

Key Dates:

1989: Superior Group is formed.
1991: Small's Oilfield Services Corp. is formed.
1992: Small's is taken public.
1995: Small's acquires Superior in a reverse merger, and Superior Energy Services is created.
1999: Cardinal Holdings Corp. is acquired.
2003: Subsidiary SPN Resources, LLC is formed.

1999 to strengthen its base. It used $197 million in stock to acquire Cardinal Holdings Corporation, a liftboat company with related well-servicing operations. By contributing $45 million of equity, Cardinal shareholders, led by First Reserve Corporation, a private equity firm, gained a 51 percent stake in the merged operation. Not only did Superior double its revenues in one stroke, it greatly enhanced its long-term strategy of becoming a start-to-finish oilfield services provider to oil and gas producers. The other acquisition completed in 1999 added a further key component. For stock and cash valued at $5.7 million Superior picked up Production Management Companies Inc., a Harvey, Louisiana, company that provided contract operating and supplemental labor services for offshore drilling operations, offshore construction and maintenance services, offshore and dockside environmental cleaning services, and sandblasting and platform coating services. Superior now possessed a competitive edge over other service companies. Cardinal liftboats could deliver the wide range of oilfield services Superior had to offer. For the year Superior generated sales of $113 million and recorded a net loss of $6.6 million, but with conditions improving in the oil and gas industry the company was poised to enjoy strong results going forward.

Superior completed several important purchases in 2000. It bought six liftboats from Trico Marine Services, Inc. for $14 million, expanding the company's fleet to 48 liftboats at an opportune time, with dayrates on the rise. In June 2000 Superior acquired HB Rentals, L.C., and its subsidiary Eagle Rentals Co., Inc., which served both the onshore and offshore oil and gas markets with onsite housing units. Later in the year Superior paid $9.5 million in cash to supplement its well intervention capabilities by acquiring assets of AMBAR, Inc.'s Production Services Division, which provided coiled tubing, pumping, stimulation, nitrogen, pipeline remediation, and related services to restore lost production from oil and gas wells in the Gulf region. Finally, Superior added International Snubbing Services, Inc. (ISS) and its affiliated companies, international providers of leading-edge well services such as hydraulic workover, drilling, and well control services. ISS operated offshore of the United States as well as Australia, Europe, Trinidad, and Venezuela. As a result of improved conditions, the addition of Cardinal and Production Management, and the centralization of operations, Superior posted impressive numbers in 2000. Sales more than doubled to $257.5 million and net income totaled $18.3 million. Also of importance was the company's increased exposure to the production side of the industry.

In 2001 Superior continued to grow by external means. It paid $80.5 million to acquire the assets of Power Offshore Service and Reeled Tubing, adding seven liftboats, 21 coiled tubing units, and 20 nitrogen units. Superior also bought Workstrings, LLC and its related company Technical Limited Drillstrings, Inc., which provided rental tubulars, accessories, and services. Once again, Superior reported excellent year-end results, with revenues improving to $449 million and net income soaring to $53.8 million. But in the fourth quarter activity in the Gulf of Mexico began to fall off, a situation that would have an impact on 2002. Sales were flat, receding to $443.1 million, and net income dropped to $21.9 million. Activity in the Gulf, however, began to pick up by year's end.

Superior enjoyed a strong year in 2003. It completed a major acquisition that offered international growth, adding Premier Oilfield Services, Ltd., a United Kingdom-based provider of oilfield equipment rentals, serving the North Sea, other European markets, northern Africa, and the Middle East. Also during 2003 Superior formed a new subsidiary, SPN Resources, LLC, to expand on its well intervention business by acquiring mature drilling properties, managing them until the end of their productive life, then decommissioning them. The focus was on wells with five or more years of reserve life located in the shallow waters of the Gulf of Mexico. In 2003, despite what was considered a soft year for the energy sector in the Gulf of Mexico, Superior reported record revenues, topping $500 million, and net income grew by almost 40 percent, to $30.5 million. Having taken steps to grow internationally and to move into the production side, Superior was well positioned to enjoy even greater long-term results.

Principal Subsidiaries

Ace Rental Tools, L.L.C.; Connection Technology, L.L.C.; H.B. Rentals, L.C.; International Snubbing Services, L.L.C.; Production Management Industries, L.L.C.; SPN Resources, L.L.C.

Principal Competitors

Baker Hughes Incorporated; Parker Drilling Company; W-H Energy Services, Inc.

Further Reading

Darce, Keith, "Superior Is Off to a Running Start," *New Orleans City Business,* May 27, 1996, p. 1.

Slaton, James, "Superior Reacts to Oil Field Changes with Acquisitions," *New Orleans City Business,* June 16, 1997, p. 1.

Slawsky, Richard, "Superior Energy Overcomes Soft Gulf Biz Climate," *New Orleans City Business,* June 21, 2004, p. 1.

Stuart, Stephen, "Oil Services Merger a Good Fit, Analysts Say," *New Orleans City Business,* September 13, 1999, p. 2.

——, "Superior Energy Services Inc., Superior Flexing Newfound Muscle," *New Orleans City Business,* June 18, 2001, p. 31.

——, "Superior Seeks Stock Rebound As It Digests New Acquisitions," *New Orleans City Business,* April 3, 2000, p. 9.

—Ed Dinger

Taro Pharmaceutical Industries Ltd.

14 Hakitor Street
Haifa Bay 26110
Israel
Telephone: +972 9 971 18 00
Fax: +972 9 955 74 43
Web site: http://www.taro.com

Public Company
Incorporated: 1950
Employees: 364
Sales: $315.46 million (2003)
Stock Exchanges: NASDAQ
Ticker Symbol: TARO
NAIC: 325412 Pharmaceutical Preparation
   Manufacturing; 325411 Medicinal and Botanical
   Manufacturing; 541710 Research and Development in
   the Physical Sciences and Engineering Sciences

Taro Pharmaceutical Industrials Ltd. is one of Israel's leading pharmaceutical companies. The company's major focus has long been on providing generic medications and pharmaceutical preparations—the company is the leading producer of topical medications (ointments, gels, etc.) for the North American market. Other company specialties are the fields of cardiology, pediatrics, and neurology. The company also develops its own proprietary formulations and medications, under its TaroPharma division, such as its Ovide head lice treatment, the Topicort line of topical corticosteroids, and Elixsure, introduced in 2003, which provides a spill-resistant preparation for liquid cough, cold, and other children's medicines. Although based in Israel and founded by Israeli pharmacists, Taro has long had an American connection: the company is listed on the NASDAQ stock exchange and North America remains its largest market, accounting for 90 percent of the company's sales. In the 2000s, however, Taro has begun expanding its geographic scope, targeting especially the European market. As part of that effort, the company bought a pharmaceutical production facility in Ireland and established a U.K. marketing subsidiary in 2003. The company also operates research and production facilities in Israel,

Canada, and the United States. Taro boasts an impressive growth record, with sales rising from less than $50 million in the mid-1990s to more than $315 million at the end of 2003. Leading the company is Chairman Barrie Levitt, M.D.

Founding Israel's Pharmaceuticals Industry in the 1950s

Just two years after the founding of the state of Israel, a number of pharmacists and physicians in Israel and in the United States sought to make use of the new country's large pool of highly educated researchers and scientists. In 1950 a team of Israeli pharmacists joined in founding a new company in Haifa, called Taro Pharmaceutical Industries (the name Taro was derived from the Hebrew words for "pharmaceutical industry"). Two years after its founding, Taro found firm financial footing when it was acquired by U.S. investors. The company's development was led by Dr. Daniel Moros, and his nephews Dr. Barrie Levitt, and Andrew Levitt.

Taro initially sought to build an Israeli pharmaceutical industry in order to produce drugs and medications for Israel itself, while also developing the expertise to market to the global pharmaceutical industry. The company started out by producing pain relievers, launching its own Rokal and Rokacet brands in the early 1950s. Both products remained mainstays in Israeli pharmacies into the 2000s.

The next phase in Taro's development came through the acquisition of licenses to produce third-party products for the Israeli market. In 1957, the company launched production of its first three licensed products, including Coumadin, also known under its generic name, Warfarin, one of the world's most widely prescribed medications. The company also started manufacturing two other important drugs under license, Percodan and Percocet, adding to Taro's array of pain relievers.

Through the 1950s, Taro relied on imports for the active pharmaceutical ingredients (APIs) of its products. Yet the political situation following the Suez War in 1956 severely restricted Taro's ability to procure its APIs. Instead, the company decided to begin producing its own active ingredients. In 1960, the company instituted a new chemical synthesis operation that

---

Company Perspectives:

Taro is a multinational, science-based pharmaceutical company dedicated to meeting the needs of its customers through the discovery, development, manufacturing and marketing of the highest quality healthcare products.

---

enabled it to achieve a stronger degree of independence in its pharmaceutical formulations. The company then became capable of ensuring the quality of its products by producing both the API and the completed dosage formulation.

Generics Leader in the 1990s

Taro went public in 1961, listing its stock on the over-the-counter market in the United States. Nonetheless, through the 1970s and into the early 1980s, Taro remained focused on the Israeli market. It was only at the beginning of the 1980s that the company became interested in moving into the North American market, in part because of the impending opening of the U.S. generics market through the passage of a new law then in preparation. The legislation, known as the Hatch-Waxman Act, was passed in 1984 and provided a framework for the production and marketing of off-patent drugs in the United States. Among other features, the act opened up the U.S. market to greater competition, which significantly reduced prices of a number of important drugs.

In preparation for this opening, Taro shifted its listing to the NASDAQ stock index in 1982. At that time, the company's market valuation was less than $5 million. Yet the listing helped Taro raise the investment capital it needed to move into the North American market. By 1984, Taro had found its foothold—buying up Toronto, Canada-based K-Line Pharmaceuticals Ltd. K-Line specialized in generic topical medications, that is, gels, creams, and ointments used especially for dermatological applications. This niche market then became Taro's primary focus in the North American market.

Exports to the United States began soon after the K-Line purchase, centered around the company's generic version of Lidex, a dermatological medication originally developed by Syntex. At first Taro relied on a distributor to introduce its products into the United States. In 1988, however, the company founded a dedicated import and distribution subsidiary for its U.S. sales.

Taro's sales grew steadily through the 1980s, based on its successful entry into the United States. By the late 1980s, the company's sales had already topped $11 million. Expansion into the United States had cut into the company's profits, yet by 1991, with sales of more than $20 million, Taro posted a profit of $1.4 million.

By then, North America had clearly become the company's primary target market, as the company took advantage of the loosening of control over generic medications. By targeting the niche market of topical applications, Taro was able to gain scale rapidly, and by the end of the decade had captured the leading share of that segment. An important early product in the com-

pany's success was its generic version of the antifungal product Lotrimin, developed by Schering-Plough. In the early 1990s, that product alone accounted for some 30 percent of Taro's revenues, which reached $32 million by 1994. The North American market already accounted for more than three-quarters of Taro's sales.

Research-Driven for the New Century

Part of Taro's success in North America came from the adoption of a new business model in 1991 that established a new research-driven strategy. The company now diverted a significant share of its revenues—as much as 12 percent of sales or more, doubling the industry average—into its research and development operations. Supporting the company's strategy was the creation of a new unit, the Taro Research Unit, that year.

The company's commitment to research enabled it to step up the rate of its new product applications, especially its submission of Abbreviated New Drug Applications (ANDAs), used for introducing generic medications. By the early 2000s, Taro had succeeded in developing 80 ANDA-approved medications for the U.S. market, as well as a number of applications in Canada, Israel, and elsewhere. The company also boosted its API capacity, with more than 20 approved by the FDA in the United States. This allowed Taro to broaden its operations to include the manufacture of medications for the third-party channel, as well as developing its own proprietary formulas. To promote its international sales, the company established a new subsidiary, Taro International Ltd., in 1992.

Nearly all of Taro's product line, which topped more than 60 in the mid-1990s, targeted the topical applications market, such as the generic versions of Diprosone and Synalar, both introduced in 1994. In 1996, however, Taro achieved its first approval for an oral dosage drug, based on the anti-seizure medication carbamazepine, used to control epilepsy. That product also enabled Taro to move beyond North America. In 1998, the company was granted approval to introduce its carbamazepine formulation into the United Kingdom.

The following year, the company's Warfarin Sodium Tablets received FDA approval in the United States. The company enjoyed a distinct advantage as it entered this new generic market, since it had been manufacturing the API for Warfarin, marketed as Coumadin in Israel, for more than 30 years. Approval for the sale of Taro's Warfarin in Canada followed in 2000; by 2002, the company had received permission to sell its Warfarin preparation in the United Kingdom as well. The success of Warfarin enabled Taro to extend beyond its core topical medications line to develop an expertise in oral dosage drugs for the fields of cardiology and neurology.

Taro's sales began to skyrocket in the early 2000s. From sales of $100 million in 2000, the company jumped to $150 million just one year later. By 2002, sales had topped $211 million—and soared past $315 million just one year later.

In support of this group, Taro made a number of significant investments. In 2002, the company, which continued to operate two manufacturing facilities in Canada, turned to the United States. In that year, the company bought up the privately held New York company, Thames Pharmacal, Inc. The purchase was made in part to allow Taro to expand its range of products.

Key Dates:

1950: A team of pharmacists and physicians found Taro in Haifa, Israel, in order to create the Israeli pharmaceutical industry.

1952: Taro is acquired by U.S. investors and begins marketing Rokal and Rokacet pain relievers.

1957: Taro begins producing Coumadin, Percodan, and Percocet under licenses.

1960: Taro begins production of APIs, including Warfarin.

1961: Taro goes public on the U.S. over-the-counter market.

1982: The company shifts its listing to the NASDAQ.

1984: The company acquires Canada's K-Line Pharmaceuticals Ltd. in order to enter the U.S. generics market, focusing on topical formulations.

1991: Taro Research Institute is established as part of its new research-driven strategy.

1996: Taro receives FDA approval to market carbamazepine, the company's first oral dosage formulation.

1998: The company begins marketing carbamazepine in the United Kingdom.

1999: The company receives approval to market Warfarin in the United States.

2000: The company launches Warfarin in Ireland.

2002: Thames Pharmacal in New York is acquired; the company launches Warfarin in the United Kingdom.

2003: Taro acquires a manufacturing and research facility in Ireland and forms the Taro Pharmaceuticals Ireland subsidiary; TaroPharm is formed to market proprietary products in the United States; the company acquires the license for four drugs from Medicis.

2004: The company launches the Elixsure spill-resistant medication formulation in the United States.

That expansion came in January 2003, when the company reached an agreement with Medicis to license four of its branded products, Topicort, A/T/S, Ovide, and Primsol, for sale in the United States and Puerto Rico. Soon after, Taro created a new division for its proprietary products in the United States, called TaraPharma, which began directly marketing to U.S. physicians using a team of medical sales representatives hired from Elan Pharmaceutical Products.

Having gained leadership in its topical application niche in the United States, and with rising strength in both its proprietary and generic products, Taro's attention turned toward deepening its entry into the European market. In 2003, the company established a new subsidiary, Taro Pharmaceuticals Ireland, and bought up an idled multipurpose pharmaceutical manufacturing and research and development plant in Ireland. That plant had formerly been owned by Miza Pharmaceuticals before being placed in liquidation.

Toward the end of that year, Taro launched a new proprietary product line called Elixsure, which enabled the preparation of liquid medications, especially children's medications such as cough and cold medicines, in a spill-resistant form. The company began marketing a number of Elixsure formulations as over-the-counter preparations in 2004. Taro had grown from a tiny generics-based company into an increasingly innovative, multinationally operating niche pharmaceuticals player in the new century.

Principal Subsidiaries

Taro Pharmaceuticals Inc. (Canada); Taro Pharmaceuticals Ireland Ltd.; Taro Pharmaccuticals (UK) Ltd.; Taro Pharmaceuticals U.S.A., Inc.

Principal Competitors

Pfizer Inc.; Procter & Gamble Co.; Johnson & Johnson; Bayer AG; GlaxoSmithKline PLC; Merck and Company Inc.; Alpharma Inc.; Altana Inc.; Barr Laboratories Inc.; Teva Pharmaceutical Industries Ltd.

Further Reading

Benjamin, Jeff, "Israel: New Deal for Taro," *IPR Strategic Business Information Database,* May 14, 2002.

Greenberg, Shlomo, "No Rush on Taro," *Israel Business Arena,* November 16, 2003.

"Introducing TaroPharma," *R&D Directions,* March 2003, p. 10.

"Taro Acquires Plant in Ireland," *Chemical Week,* March 5, 2003, p. 22.

"Taro Clarifies Production Expansion Plans," *Israel Business Arena,* October 20, 2002.

"Taro Receives FDA Approval for Ammonium Lactate Lotion, 12% ANDA," *Chemical Business NewsBase,* June 1, 2004.

"Taro to License Four Branded Pharmaceutical Product Lines from Medicis," *Chemical Business Newsbase,* January 15, 2003.

—M.L. Cohen

Thomsen Greenhouses and Garden Center, Incorporated

29756 156 Avenue
St. Joseph, Minnesota 56374
U.S.A.
Telephone: (320) 363-7375
Fax: (320) 363-0025
Web site: http://www.tgreenhouses.com

Private Company
Incorporated: 1981
Employees: 30
NAIC: 444220 Garden Centers, Nurseries

Thomsen Greenhouses and Garden Center, Incorporated (Thomsen's), with more than 62,000 square feet of indoor growing space, is the largest retail greenhouse under glass in Minnesota. The greenhouse provides gardeners throughout the central Minnesota region with a host of plant materials, including trees, shrubs, annual and perennial flowers, vegetable plants, landscape materials, and garden novelties. The garden center houses more than 5,000 hanging baskets, 10,000 flats of annuals and more than 800 varieties of perennial plants in the spring and summer growing season.

Staking a Claim in Collegeville Township: 1960s–70s

Tucked in the rolling hills of Collegeville Township, Minnesota, Thomsen's began its history rooted in the personal interests of its founders, Bob and Bonnie Thomsen. But, having an interest in a given area and enjoying what you do is not always sufficient to grow a successful business. Fortunately for the Thomsens there were two other favorable factors at work when they established Thomsen's in 1981. First there was an emerging market of home gardeners spurred on by the do-it-yourself television home shows and magazines and, perhaps more important, there was a commitment and dedication on the part of the Thomsens to a lot of hard work.

In the late 1960s Bob and Bonnie Thomsen were young recent graduates of St. Cloud State University. Bob had majored in political science and sociology and Bonnie pursued a degree in education. They met while students, then married and settled in St. Cloud.

After a few years of city living the Thomsens found land in rural Collegeville, Minnesota, and began to build a home. In the fall of 1973 the couple found a dismantled old log cabin for sale and began to reassemble it on their property. It turned out to be no easy task. The parts were not marked and needed to be puzzled together. To make things even more difficult the property was without electricity, so primitive hand tools were required for construction projects.

The Thomsens eventually settled in the newly built cabin and homesteaded without running water, refrigeration, or electric lights for an entire year. Relying on kerosene lanterns for light, an outhouse for bathroom facilities, and a stream for cold storage, Bob and Bonnie led a Henry David Thoreau-like lifestyle the first year. The following summer the couple added a garage and lean-to greenhouse and brought electrical wiring to the garage. An extension cord running from the garage to the cabin enabled the couple to have electric lights the second year. In the coming years they added a second cabin to their home and brought in plumbing and electricity.

Bob Thomsen worked at a variety of jobs during the early years of their marriage. He eventually settled on starting a small excavation business of his own. Bonnie had become certified in special education. Her first years teaching were spent in a parochial school in St. Cloud. In 1975, she was offered a position in the nearby Rocori school district.

Embracing the frontier lifestyle the two had carved out for themselves, the Thomsens began building their homestead throughout the 1970s. Their interest in gardening led them to build a small lean-to greenhouse off of their cabin, where they began growing vegetables from seed. The Thomsens often had a surplus of seedlings and sold the remainder to friends, colleagues, and neighbors.

It was fortuitous that the interest in their seedlings coincided with a lag in the new business Bob had begun. Bob had bought a bulldozer, truck, and trailer, and was trying to get his company established, but the record high interest rates of the late 1970s had slowed the demand for excavation work. Thomsen had decided to sell the business and put the money they made from the sale of his equipment into a new business venture.

The Thomsens had been toying with the idea of greenhouse gardening when a serendipitous trip to Utah sealed the deal. While rafting down the Colorado River, the Thomsens met a couple from Wisconsin who owned and operated a wholesale greenhouse. The Thomsens followed up on the chance meeting by visiting the couple at their Milwaukee greenhouse. Armed with the advice gleaned from their meetings the Thomsens turned to books and the Minnesota Extension Service horticulturist to continue to hone the concept of beginning their own commercial greenhouse into a plan of operation.

The 1980s and 1990s: Building the Business

In the fall of 1981 Bob and Bonnie Thomsen built a 30- by 100-foot hoop-style greenhouse and began to prepare for their first season of commercial growing the following spring. The undertaking was on a fairly modest scale at the outset, but in the summer of 1982 Thomsen's added a second hoop house, doubling its growing space and anticipating future sales. The following year the greenhouse expanded again when a four-bay, gutter-connected greenhouse was added and the head house was built.

Thomsen's Greenhouses' early years were focused on growing vegetable seedlings and a small variety of plants such as potted geraniums and assorted container plants. Bob traveled the area grocery store circuit selling his plants to retailers and building accounts. For a time the greenhouse operated three satellite retail outlets in St. Joseph, Buffalo, and Monticello, Minnesota. The wholesale area that Thomsen's serviced ran from St. Cloud to Minneapolis and as far west as Long Prairie, Minnesota. Soon word began to spread about the charming greenhouse in Collegeville Township.

Thomsen's had introduced itself as a wholesale grower, growing solely for commercial retailers, but the retail market was expanding and the absence of a large, quality retail greenhouse in the region led the Thomsens to rethink the company's direction. In 1987 Thomsen's opened its retail outlet full-time. According to a 1996 article in the *St. Cloud Times* the Thomsens

decided to transition to a retail business after experimenting with retail sales for one weekend a year.

"We kept getting busier each year," Bob said. Customers would flood the greenhouse for its annual retail sale. It was a gamble that paid off when the store opened regularly to retail customers and the early annual turnout turned out to be a good prediction of future demand. In order to get the new business off the ground Bonnie Thomsen took a five-year leave of absence from the school district. The following year in 1989 Thomsen's purchased Lord and Burnam Glass Houses and the company spent two years reconstructing the greenhouses and setting up two Quonset huts in the back of the new buildings.

Throughout its years of operation Thomsen's has held a series of special events and activities designed to promote itself to the local community. In an effort to draw people to the greenhouse and extend the season beyond the typical spring and summer garden center focus, Thomsen's hosted an annual winter celebration it called, "Christmas Under Glass." The company sold Christmas trees and poinsettias and held special festive activities for customers. Christmas Under Glass featured choirs singing traditional carols, horse-drawn trolley rides, a reindeer and sleigh team, cookie decorating, and story telling. The celebration ran annually from 1990 though 1994.

In a 1990 article in the local *St. Joseph Newsleader* Bob Thomsen described the growth of the business, particularly the retail end of the operation: "The people who come out the first weekend in May are absolutely spellbound by all the stuff we have in here." He continued to recount the spring rush and Mother's Day madness when thousands of loyal customers frequent the aisles at Thomsen's to purchase gift certificates, hanging baskets, and garden merchandise. For many locals Mother's Day was incomplete without a visit to the garden center. Braving the crowds to enjoy the sights and smells of spring and encounter friends and neighbors had become a tradition for many in St. Cloud and its surrounding towns.

In 1996, in a collaborative effort under the direction and design of landscape architect Stacy Kalthof the staff at Thomsen's added its Backyard Gardens. Built around the focal point of an existing pond, a small walking path wound its way around lush gardens marked with plant tags so customers could identify plants they liked. The space was similar to a small-scale landscape arboretum and the inviting area brought many weekend visitors to Collegeville. The garden featured a pond shop run by Scenic Specialties from 2000 to 2003 and a Cabin Creek Coffee shop complete with freshly brewed coffee and baked goods in 2004.

Fine-Tuning the Operation: 1990s and Beyond

In 1997 Thomsen's added a 90- by 100-foot Perennial House. An assortment of perennial plants were always available at the greenhouse but the expansion made possible the addition of greater plant offerings. There was space for more than 800 varieties of perennial plants. An assortment of popular woodland flowers and bulbs also filled the space.

Throughout the late 1990s and early 2000s the company installed many labor-saving devices that helped the greenhouse staff keep up with the growing customer demand. A trolley system that allowed greenhouse staff to move plants through the buildings without having to push cumbersome carts was installed in 1998. In 2000, a mechanized flat and pot filler allowed staff to make quick work of filling the multitude of planting trays and pots for seeding, transplanting, and potting. Seasonal workers also were engaged to assist with planting and transplanting. The company's seasonal employment included hiring temporary workers to keep up with the spring rush and hiring adult handicapped workers through a local agency to help during peak transplanting time.

Throughout the spring Thomsen's was a favorite destination for a number of school children. Local area schools took advantage of the beautiful setting with its acres of blooming plants and its outdoor garden for field trips. Children toured the buildings and were taught basic horticultural facts and encouraged to plant a flower and take it home to care for it. A free kids garden club was organized by the greenhouse in 1997. Children participated in growing an outdoor vegetable and flower garden, worked on craft projects, learned about the environment and horticulture, and celebrated the harvest with an end of the season cookout.

In 1996 Thomsen's began its Best Yard Contest. Amateur gardeners were called on to submit photos for judging with gift certificates ranging from a $200 first prize to a $50 third prize. The contest ran for several years annually.

In addition to the Best Yard Contest the staff at Thomsen's initiated a self-directed garden tour each summer. Picturesque gardens were selected throughout the area by Thomsen's master gardener Diane Hansgen. Ticket buyers received a map with garden descriptions for the self-directed tour with proceeds benefitting the United Arts of Central Minnesota, an area nonprofit organization. The tour sold as many as a thousand tickets in a given season.

In addition to its philanthropic work with the garden tour, the greenhouse sponsored local arts productions for children through two area colleges, The College of St. Benedict and St. John's University, and made many in-kind charitable donations that helped local nonprofit organizations through plant sales and assorted fundraisers.

The staff at Thomsen's helped customers over the years with their landscape and garden plans. Customers could request a landscape planner sheet provided free by the greenhouse. The client could then schedule a meeting with a landscape designer from Thomsen's with the first hour free of charge. Design services were by appointment and were not available during the greenhouse peak month of May. The company web site also provided garden designs that could be replicated by homeowners. The web site garden categories included plans for shade, cottage, sun, butterfly, mailbox or lamppost, and fence and border gardens.

Each year the business maintained a presence at the St. Cloud Home and Garden show. The booth for Thomsen's Greenhouse was introduced to answer questions, help with design work, and promote the greenhouse to the public.

Thomsen's had continued to flourish in the years since its inception. The greenhouse had grown at a steady rate and Thomsen's had captured a good part of the market in its geographical region. People from rural areas all around the state and into Wisconsin still made annual pilgrimages to buy the quality plants for their own yards and gardens. The need for premium landscaping plants had remained steady. New home construction in the region also remained strong, bringing an increased demand for landscape needs. In addition, home and garden TV shows as well as special interest magazines continued to promote and respond to the trend for home improvement and home makeovers featuring garden transformations. All the focus had helped Thomsen's establish and continue to grow its business. The company seemed assured of realizing its mission to be an area leader in assisting gardeners in their outdoor beautification projects.

Principal Competitors

Gertens Greenhouse; Linders Greenhouse.

Further Reading

DuBois, John, ''Business Is Blooming,'' *St. Cloud Times,* May 1994 p. 1C.
Goldschen, Stuart, ''Thomsen Greenhouses Debut Half a Million Plants,'' *St. Joseph Newsleader,* April 27, 1990.
''Thomsen Greenhouses in Rural St. Joe Keeps on Growing,'' *St. Cloud Times,* April 5, 1990, p. 3.

—Susan B. Culligan

Tomy Company Ltd.

7-9-10 Tateishi 7-chome, Katsush
Tokyo 124-8511
Japan
Telephone: +81 3 3693 9033
Fax: +81 3 3693 2472
Web site: http://www.tomy.co.jp
Public Company
Incorporated: 1953
Employees: 1,850
Sales: ¥73.78 billion ($688.4 million) (2003)
Stock Exchanges: Tokyo
Ticker Symbol:
NAIC: 339932 Game, Toy, and Children's Vehicle Manufacturing

Tomy Company Ltd. is Japan's second largest toy manufacturer and the fifth largest toy company in the world. The Tokyo-based company has been producing toys since 1924, including its long-running Tomica series of miniature cars and related fixtures. Tomy is also the producer of the hugely popular Pocket Monsters, the Microtecs toy line. The company holds the exclusive license for toys and other products based on Disney characters for the Japanese market. The company has a number of other licenses as well, including those for the Teletubbies, Star Wars, and Thomas the Tank Engine in the United Kingdom. Tomy also operates a distribution partnership with Hasbro in the United States and Japan. In addition to its Japanese production and development facilities, Tomy has built a global presence, with subsidiaries in the United Kingdom, France, the United States, Hong Kong, and Thailand. Tomy is listed on the Tokyo Stock Exchange and is led by Kantaro Tomiyama, grandson of the company's founder. In 2003, Tomy recorded revenues of ¥73.78 billion (US$668 million).

Pioneering the Modern Japanese Toy Industry in the 1920s

Eiichiro Tomiyama began producing toys in 1924. His original designs were tin-based toys, a material the company was to

favor into the 1950s. At its start, Tomiyama's company was only one of many turning out cheap-to-manufacture products. Yet Tomiyama recognized early on that Japan had the opportunity of becoming a major player in the worldwide toy market. This would happen only if its toymakers ended the often cut-throat competition among them and instead banded together to produce higher-quality, and innovative products.

In 1929, Tomiyama brought together a group of small-scale toymakers into a common association, founding the so-called "Omocha no machi," or Toytown. This was to become the heart of the Japanese toy industry. Tomiyama took his vision a step further in 1935, establishing a dedicated research and development center to create new types of toys using new manufacturing techniques, materials, and technologies. From a staff of 20, Tomiyama's R&D team eventually grew to more than 200, located worldwide, a commitment that enabled the company to react quickly to consumer trends and preferences.

World War II cut short the company's toy development as key materials were shifted to support the Japanese war effort. The rapid growth of the Japanese economy in the postwar era, however, and the country's emergence onto the global market as an industrial and technological powerhouse, provided new opportunities for the toy company. Production of toys resumed, and in 1953 Tomiyama formally incorporated the company as Tomy Company.

The 1950s saw the launch of the Tomy brand, soon to become one of the world's major toy brands. An important component of the company's success was its early shift to a new and exciting toy material: plastic. The development of more supple forms of plastic—coupled with an overall consumer enthusiasm for the "modern" material—offered an entirely new range of toy possibilities. From simple tin models, Tomy's toys achieved an increasing complexity of shapes and forms.

One of the group's early toy hits was, paradoxically, a model of the B-29 bomber, released in 1951. The company followed that toy with a B-50 model in 1953. With these toys, Tomy discovered the lucrative export market, and became responsible in part for establishing Japan as one of the major centers of the global toy industry. Yet the company's first brand-name success came with a more whimsical creation. In 1957, the company launched a figure of an elephant capable of blowing soap bubbles. The marriage of cuteness with mechanical intricacy, a hallmark of Japanese design, not only captivated children and parents in Japan, but worldwide. The elephant broke all of the company's previous sales records, with more than 600,000 copies sold.

Defining Eras in the 1960s

As much as, and perhaps more than any other toy company, Tomy played a role in defining entire toy eras. Such was the case with its release in 1959 of its "sky ping pong" set. Riding on the wave of popularity for ping pong in Japan—which during the period dominated world table tennis championships—the set, which consisted of basket-like, spring-loaded cups for catching and launching the ping pong ball, became one of the world's most ubiquitous toys. That toy was also the first Tomy toy to be made almost entirely of plastic.

Throughout the 1960s, Tomy continued to marry its gift for whimsy with a dedication to exploring new technical possibilities. The company became one of the first to investigate uses of new electronic capabilities offered by the development of transistors. Tomy released a new electromotive train set in 1961, and, in 1964, a talking doll powered by electronics. By then, too, the company had begun developing its first robots, a class of toy that remained a central part of Tomy's business into the next century. Tomy's first "mecha-tronics"–based robot appeared in 1962. This led to the development of another huge international success for the company, a space expedition set launched in 1969, which sold more than two million units worldwide.

In the 1970s, Tomy developed a new specialty, that of hand-held skill-based toys. At first mechanically based—the company is responsible for such global standards as the so-called Waterfall games, which used water jets to provide game play—Tomy increasingly became interested in electronics and the use of newly developing microchips and liquid-crystal displays. Tomy now became a pioneer in the hand-held console market, at first wedding electronics to mechanical movement to produce such favorites as Hit and Missile, Blip, and Digital Derby. Before long, the company had begun to develop entirely electronic-based toys, winning licenses to produce handheld versions of such global arcade hits as Pacman in 1980.

That success led Tomy to make a foray into the home computer and console market, launching its own Pyuuta (literally "computer dude") in 1982. Known as the Tomy Tutor on the international markets, the device enjoyed some success, particularly through the winning of a license for Disney's hit film Tron. Unable to match the success of such video game greats as Atari and Commodore, Tomy returned to its core toy development. Yet the company's sense of innovation remained intact, leading to the launch of such hit toys as its "watch man golf," an electronic golf game housed in a wristwatch, and a robot, released in 1984, capable of speech recognition.

In the meantime, Tomy had been developing another hugely successful toy category. In 1970, the company released a new series of model cars that reproduced in detail popular automobile models of the day. Called Tomica, the first line sported just six models, based on Japanese cars. The enthusiastic reception of the cars, in Japan at least, encouraged the company to step up production of the Tomica line. By 1976, the Tomica line had expanded to include more than 180 models. In that year, the company turned to the worldwide market, launching a new series based on foreign (for the Japanese) car models. The U.S. and European vehicles enabled the Tomica name to build a strong following around the world, and particularly in Europe. By the beginning of the 1980s, the Tomica range had grown to more than 280 models. Although subsequently scaled back to a core of just 120 models, Tomica inspired the creation of a wide range of ancillary products, such as track, buildings, and other fixtures, all of which became known as Tomica World.

By the mid-1980s, Tomy had firmly established itself as a leader in the worldwide toy market. A large part of the company's success was its willingness to move closer to its core markets. Tomy's first international move came in 1970 with the establishment of a manufacturing base in Hong Kong, then at the very beginning of its own development into a major world manufacturing and financial center. The move helped Tomy lower its production costs. Three years later, the company entered the United States, the world's largest single toy market, establishing a sales subsidiary there.

From the United States, the company turned to Europe, where its Tomica line, as well as its electronics toys, were meeting with great success. The company opened a subsidiary in the United Kingdom in 1982, which took over its sales and marketing activities for all of Europe. The specificity of the French and Belgium markets, where Tomy rapidly became one of the top toy brands, encouraged the company to launch a dedicated sales and marketing subsidiary in France in 1985. Beyond supporting sales of existing Tomy products, the company's new international subsidiaries grew into full-fledged research and development centers. In this way, Tomy was able to respond quickly to shifting consumer trends and tastes, as well as tailor products for specific domestic markets.

Global Toy Leader in the 21st Century

Tomy continued to expand its international network in the late 1980s and into the 1990s. In 1987, the company opened a

Key Dates:

1924: Eiichiro Tomiyama begins producing tin toys.

1929: Tomiyama leads founding of Japanese toy makers association, improving quality and design and helping establish the country as a worldwide toy center.

1935: Tomiyama establishes research and development center.

1953: Company incorporates as Tomy Company Ltd. and begins producing toys using plastic.

1970: Tomy establishes first foreign manufacturing facility in Hong Kong.

1973: Company enters United States with launch of sales subsidiary.

1982: Tomy forms first dedicated European sales and design subsidiary in the United Kingdom.

1985: Company creates dedicated sales and design facility in France, which takes over operations in France and Belgium.

1987: Company constructs new manufacturing plant in Thailand.

1992: Company opens manufacturing and engineering plant in Shenzhen, China.

1998: New sales, marketing, and development subsidiary opens in the United States.

1999: Tomy Company goes public with listing on Tokyo main board; signs partnership agreement with Hasbro Inc.

2002: Company wins license for Disney characters in Japan and forms Tomy Link joint venture with Disney.

2003: Glow-Tec International joint venture is formed as part of a shift toward the development of lifestyle products.

manufacturing center in Thailand, which, together with the company's Hong Kong plant, took over much of the group's production capacity. Then, in 1992, Tomy entered the newly liberalized Chinese market, opening a manufacturing and engineering site in Shenzhen.

The 1990s marked a new era for the company, which played a formative role in the development of cross-media and cross-marketing tie-ins. The company's Tron franchise in the early 1980s had been a representative of this emerging toy industry trend. Where toys were once inspired by other media formats, such as book, film, and video game and cartoon characters, in the 1990s the toys themselves provided inspiration for media products. Ultimately the two currents merged in the late 1990s, inspiring a new breed of programming created specifically to support new toy launches, which themselves were created to sell more programming. At the same time, cross-marketing of toy characters—placing characters on a huge array of items, from food to clothing and even household goods and equipment—became an industry mainstay.

Tomy quickly gained a number of prominent licenses. One of the group's most lucrative licenses was for the Pocket Monster series created by Nintendo in the late 1990s. Known as

Pokemon on the international market, the series enjoyed enormous success worldwide. In 1999, the company snared another important license, for the production of toys based on the hugely popular Teletubbies series. That license also encouraged Tomy to step up the design and production of toys for the infant segment, which became one of Tomy's core product lines in the 2000s. Another strong selling license gained during this period was that for the Thomas the Tank Engine series, also developed in the United Kingdom.

Tomy went public in 1999, listing its stock on the Tokyo main board. The Tomiyama family, now headed by Chairman and CEO Kantaro Tomiyama, grandson of the founder, remained the company's largest shareholder. By then, the company had begun a shift toward a new trend in the toy world, that of international partnerships.

As part of this move, Tomy disbanded its former U.S. sales subsidiary and instead founded a new U.S. subsidiary, Tomy Direct Company, which, as its name suggested, began operating directly in the U.S. market—rather than receiving direction from its Japanese parent—in 1998. At first, Tomy Direct provided direct sales support to the country's largest retailers, such as Wal-Mart and Toys 'R' Us. Then the subsidiary emerged as a toy developer in its own right. This became especially true with the signing of a strategic partnership with Hasbro Inc. in 1999.

In 2002, the Hasbro partnership resulted in Tomy taking over development and production of toys and other products based on the popular Star Wars films. At the same time, Tomy Direct became focused on supporting the Tomy-Hasbro partnership. By then the company had also won another extremely important license, that for the Disney characters and brands. These licenses permitted the company to step up development of new product segments, and especially candy bonus toys and capsule toys. In 2002, the two companies set up the Tomy Link joint venture, which began preparing new products related to the Disney brand, and its resorts and retail stores.

Despite the successful launch of its new Micropets series in 2002, Tomy faced a slump leading to losses. In 2003, the company responded by developing a strategy to add a new lifestyle component to its operations. In support of that effort, the company formed a joint venture called Glow-Tec International Company Ltd., beginning development of electric luminescence-based lifestyle products—such as youth-oriented telephones and cameras, as well as stationery and related products—and toys. After more than 75 years in business, Tomy had emerged as Japan's number two toy company, and held a solid position among the world's top ten.

Principal Subsidiaries

Creston Investments Ltd.; P&P Company, Ltd.; Play Kingdom Company, Ltd.; TOMNIC Company, Ltd.; TOMY (Hong Kong) Ltd.; TOMY (Thailand) Ltd.; TOMY Corporation; TOMY Creative Company, Ltd.; TOMY Direct Company, Ltd.; TOMY Do Brasil Ltda. (Brazil); TOMY Engineering Service Company, Ltd.; TOMY France S.A.R.L.; TOMY Kasei Company, Ltd.; TOMY Kohsan Company, Ltd.; TOMY Ryutu Service Company, Ltd.; TOMY System Design Company, Ltd.;

TOMY Tec Company, Ltd.; TOMY UK Ltd.; TOMY Yujin Corporation; U-Ace Company, Ltd.; U-Mate Company, Ltd.; Yujin Company, Ltd.

Principal Competitors

Mattel Inc.; Hasbro Inc.; Lego A/S; Little Tikes; Smoby International SA.; Giochi Preziosi SpA; Simba Toys GmbH und Co.; Top-Toy A/S; Milton Bradley Co.; Berchet SA.

Further Reading

Davey, V., and Danny C.Y. Chan, *The Complete World of Tomy Diecast*, Hong Kong: Northcord, 1997.

''Tomy Moves into the Black with Help from Little Friends,'' *Japan Toy and Game Software Journal*, June 25, 2003.

''Tomy Stationery Push,'' *Office Products International*, November 2003, p. 32.

''Tomy Strengthens Commercialization Rights on Toys,'' *Japan Toy and Game Software Journal*, July 25, 2002.

—M.L. Cohen

U.S. PHYSICAL THERAPY, INC.

U.S. Physical Therapy, Inc.

1300 W. Sam Houston Parkway South, Suite 300
Houston, Texas 77043
U.S.A.
Telephone: (713) 297-7000
Toll Free: (800) 580-6285
Fax: (713) 297-7090
Web site: http://www.usphysicaltherapy.com

Public Company
Incorporated: 1990
Employees: 1,276
Sales: $105.6 million (2003)
Stock Exchanges: NASDAQ
Ticker Symbol: USPH
NAIC: 621498 All Other Outpatient Care Centers

U.S. Physical Therapy, Inc. is one of the only major players in the physical therapy clinic market, operating a chain of approximately 250 clinics across the United States. The company's clinics are each owned in partnership with a trained physical therapist. The company in most cases builds new clinics from the ground up. Its markets are principally small towns and suburban areas where there is little competition. Its clinics offer standard physical therapy treatments for occupational and sports injuries and postsurgical care. The vast majority of its services are paid for by insurers, health maintenance organizations, or Medicare. The company also operates some physical therapy clinics for third parties.

An Entrepreneur Taking a New Direction in 1990

U.S. Physical Therapy, Inc. was founded by Texas businessman J. Livingston Kosberg. Kosberg grew up in Texas and had a varied career by the time he began U.S. Physical Therapy in 1990. He founded a chain of nursing homes called National Living Centers, which had grown from three homes to 300 when it was acquired by another company in 1973. Kosberg had interests in television stations and the insurance industry as well, and in 1983 he became chairman of the Texas Board of Human Services, a state governing body. He also had interests in the

banking industry. In 1981 he and several partners sold the Houston savings and loan Centennial Holding Co. to First Texas Savings Corp. The next year, Kosberg and an investment group bought First Texas outright. The savings and loan industry had been deregulated by an act of Congress in 1982, and First Texas, which had been losing money steadily, was now eligible to take on potentially valuable commercial real estate loans. First Texas got in at the beginning of a boom in commercial real estate development in the area. In 1984, Kosberg, as chairman of the bank, arranged a massive takeover of the largest Texas savings and loan, Gibraltar Savings of Houston. Kosberg's bank became First Texas Gibraltar. By mid-1985, the commercial real estate boom started to bust in Texas, and one year later, the state was overrun with federal bank regulators as savings and loans began to fold under an avalanche of bad debts.

First Texas Gibraltar was eventually taken over by federal regulators. Kosberg was accused of several offenses, and he settled the case against him by paying $2.5 million in restitution and agreeing not to work in the banking industry again. Revlon Chairman Ronald O. Perelman bought First Texas in 1989. That year Kosberg was attacked by a man who shot mace at him, whipped him with a pistol, and attempted to abduct him in handcuffs. The man turned out to be a condominium developer foreclosed on by First Texas. He was arrested after a further attempt on Kosberg, when he demanded $6 million.

By that time, Kosberg had already settled on a new business plan. Kosberg had made his first million building a chain of nursing homes, and after his foray into banking, he returned to the healthcare arena. In 1990 he founded U.S. Physical Therapy (USPH), with the idea of forming a chain of physical therapy clinics. He also established another company, at first called T.U. Management Inc., which provided temporary staffing for rehabilitation therapy clinics at hospitals and nursing homes. This company was renamed CareerStaff Unlimited. It went public in 1994 and was acquired by a larger company in 1995. Meanwhile, U.S. Physical Therapy began with just a handful of clinics, and it hoped to expand rapidly by acquiring existing clinics. The company went public on the NASDAQ exchange in 1992. That year it had revenue of $2.4 million, and only four clinics.

Company Perspectives:

U.S. Physical Therapy, Inc., which was founded in 1990, is a publicly held company which operates 244 outpatient physical and/or occupational therapy clinics in 35 states across the United States as of December 31, 2003. The Company's clinics provide post-operative care for a variety of orthopedic-related disorders and sports-related injuries, treatment for neurologically-related injuries, rehabilitation of injured workers and preventive care. In addition to owning and operating clinics, the Company manages several physical therapy facilities for third parties, including physician groups.

Changing Strategy in the Early 1990s

A few other firms owned groups of physical therapy clinics, but U.S. Physical Therapy was the only one operating solely in that field. NovaCare and Healthsouth Rehabilitation were other companies in the physical therapy niche, but their interests were more diversified. USPH went public only two years after its debut, and at a time when it had still not earned any money. But its plan for growth seemed solid: buy up successful clinics and run them at low cost. Yet the company had to change its strategy after a more thorough exposure to economic reality. Buying existing clinics turned out to be simply too expensive. Although the company could take on clinics that already had a thriving business and a high likelihood of success, the price tag for such an acquisition could be as high as $2 million. The company had revenue of only slightly more than that, at $2.4 million, in 1992, and it had lost $1.2 million that year. In 1994, Kosberg hired a seasoned physical therapy executive to be CEO of U.S. Physical Therapy, and the two mapped out a new course for the young company.

Roy Spradlin had gotten his physical therapy license in 1978 and opened his first clinic in 1980. By 1988, Spradlin's business had grown to a chain of three clinics, North Kansas City Physical Therapy. Then he sold the chain to a larger firm, Pinnacle Rehabilitation. Spradlin went to work for Pinnacle, eventually overseeing 30 clinics as president of the firm's outpatient clinic division. When he came to USPH, he helped the company revamp. The company announced that instead of buying clinics, it would build them. This meant that U.S. Physical Therapy would have to pay money up front to get each new store going, and the new clinics would naturally take some time—estimated at four to six months—to become profitable. Thus the company might continue losing money for the time being. Still, it seemed like a more workable way to get ahead than making expensive individual deals with successful clinic proprietors.

By the close of 1994, U.S. Physical Therapy had grown to about 55 clinics, and it had built most of these itself. Its formula was to find a physical therapist who was ready to run his or her own clinic. This person made a minimal investment and became a USPH partner. Partners were usually people who had run a hospital's physical therapy unit or had had a similar level of managerial control. The partner got a 20 percent interest in the new USPH clinic, which could increase to 35 percent. The clinic's success was dependent on the get-ahead spirit of the partner. The clinic carried the name of the partner, not USPH.

The therapist partners could increase their income through bonuses for good performance. The parent company managed the clinics to run at low cost, which was quite different from the way some other physical therapy clinics were run. The federal program Medicare reimbursed clinics on what was called a "cost-plus" basis, meaning it paid the clinic's costs, and then added an amount so that the clinic could make a profit. Under this system, a clinic had little incentive to hold down expenses. However, USPH clinics followed a traditional business model, and kept costs in line as a matter of course. CEO Spradlin described his company's clinics to a reporter from *Equities* (November 1994). "The equipment in our clinics is low-tech and not high dollar," he said. Yet the clinics also offered extras that hospital units generally did not, such as late hours, quick appointments, and hand-delivery of evaluations within 48 hours. The USPH clinics emphasized customer service, something else that probably set them apart from hospital-run clinics.

USPH finished 1994 with revenues of $17.2 million. It opened 27 clinics in 1994, and as expected, it took some time for the new shops to become profitable. When they did, results were good. The new clinics brought in more revenue as the number of patient visits per day increased. Yet it did not cost substantially more to run a busy clinic than an empty one. Eventually a successful clinic had a profit margin Spradlin described as "huge." USPH finally saw black ink in the second quarter of 1995, and the company began a run of year-by-year increases in sales and net income, often at spectacular rates.

Profitability in the Late 1990s

In 1997, the company changed its stock listing from the NASDAQ Small Cap Market to the NASDAQ National Market System. Sales had grown to roughly $40 million that year. By the close of the next year, the company had just under 100 clinics operating. USPH did well in the late 1990s, continuing to open new clinics across the country. The company's formula seemed to make sense, as it spent only some $200,000 to build and develop a new clinic, whereas other companies were spending upward of $600,000 to buy existing physical therapy practices. USPH also picked its markets carefully. It did well in smaller cities or in suburbs. These areas tended to have patients with fuller insurance coverage (as opposed to coverage by managed care), which meant higher revenue per patient, and less competition. USPH did not concentrate on one region of the country, though it had a pocket of clinics in Texas and another large group in Michigan. New clinics in 1998, for example, were all over the map, in such smaller cities as Portland, Maine, and Brookings, South Dakota, and suburban areas such as Tenafly, New Jersey.

The company presented a very pleasant profit picture for much of the late 1990s into the early 2000s, in spite of a new federal law that changed the way physical therapy clinics were compensated. Revenue rose as the company opened more clinics, and although some quarters produced a loss as new clinics were starting up, other quarters showed sharp increases in profits. With an increase of almost 25 percent in patient visits in the third quarter of 2000, profits rose 64 percent. Every quarter did not show such a high rate of increase, but by 2001, U.S. Physical Therapy could boast six straight years of profitability. This looked especially good in light of a major revision to

```
┌─────────────────────────────────────────────┐
│                Key Dates:                    │
│                                              │
│  1990:  The company is founded.              │
│  1992:  The company goes public on the       │
│         NASDAQ Small Cap Market.             │
│  1994:  A new CEO heads the company.         │
│  1997:  The company moves its stock listing  │
│         to the NASDAQ National Market        │
│         System.                              │
│  2002:  Founder Kosberg resigns.             │
│  2004:  Chairman and CEO Spradlin resigns;   │
│         Kosberg returns.                     │
└─────────────────────────────────────────────┘
```

Medicare in 1999. The Balanced Budget Act of 1997 took effect on January 1, 1999, and outpatient clinics were no longer compensated on the "cost-plus" basis. The change in law prompted a surge in bankruptcies among some healthcare facilities, particularly nursing homes. Yet USPH had always reined in its costs and tried to avoid low-priced managed care contracts, so the new law did not force the company to make any drastic changes. The company did lower the typical amount it paid its therapists, as the whole industry settled salaries downward. "We were running our business as you should run a business—not on a cost-plus basis," Spradlin told *Investor's Business Daily* (May 29, 2001), and so USPH was in good shape to manage the change in compensation.

USPH attracted more patients through 2001 and 2002, resulting in rising profitability. Earnings in the second quarter of 2001 were double what they had been for the same period a year earlier, while patient visits rose more than 20 percent for both the first two quarters of that year. By the third quarter of 2001, revenue was more than 70 percent greater than for the same time a year earlier. USPH seemed to be benefiting from a demographic pattern where the aging baby boomers were still very active physically and brought their sports-related injuries to physical therapists. When the financial magazine *Kiplinger's* profiled USPH (February 2002), it described the phenomenon as a "demographic sweet spot that should fuel growth for years to come." The company planned accordingly, hoping to increase its number of clinics by 20 percent in each of the next several years. USPH also continued to hold its costs down, with operating costs as a percentage of revenue falling between 1999 and 2001.

In early 2002, one analyst covering the company expected to see an earnings increase of 30 percent each year into the middle years of the decade. The company seemed to be able to achieve a high growth rate in spite of some uncertainty about the overall U.S. economy. Because almost all of its billings were covered by insurers, and not by the patients directly, the company expected patients to keep filling its clinics even as the recession that began in the final months of 2000 dragged on.

Management Changes in the 2000s

By the middle of 2002, USPH had grown to a chain of 162 clinics in 31 states. Founder J. Livingston Kosberg resigned in March 2002, as the company was releasing record figures for 2001. The company showed an increase in profit of an astonishing 89 percent for 2001, and an increase in revenue of 28 percent, to almost $81 million. President and CEO Roy Spradlin took Kosberg's place as chairman of the company, while Kosberg said he would continue as a consultant to the firm he got off the ground 12 years earlier.

The company rolled out more new clinics, passing the 200 mark in 2003. Business started to slow at the end of 2002, though, and the company was forced to reduce its profit estimates. Typically business was slow in the summer, and the number of patient visits to USPH's clinics picked up in the fall. Yet patient visits remained slow after the summer of 2002. By the spring of 2003, USPH decided that its earnings would probably grow in the range of 10 to 17 percent for the year, instead of the 17 to 22 percent it had projected earlier. Although overall patient visits climbed, the average number of visits per clinic per day fell slightly. By 2003 the company also admitted that the generally sluggish economy was affecting USPH. It had thought that its business was more or less recession-proof, as consumers did not pay directly out of their own pockets for their physical therapy appointments. Yet it seemed that even people with health insurance to pay for therapy were sometimes reluctant to schedule clinic appointments. Worried about job security, they seemed to be preferring to stay at work rather than take time off for a physical therapy session.

USPH hired a new chief operating officer in late 2003, as well as a new vice-president of operations. Both had backgrounds as practicing physical therapists, along with extensive business management experience. But USPH had run out of good news by late 2003. In September it lowered its profit outlook for the second time that year, as once again patient visits did not pick up strongly after the summer vacation lull. Nevertheless, the company had a strong cash balance and no debt, and it continued to open new clinics. By 2004, the chain had grown to close to 250 clinics. In July 2004, Chairman and CEO Roy Spradlin resigned. He had led the company for ten years, and had overseen the building of almost 100 clinics. The company offered no reason for Spradlin's resignation except that he wished to pursue other interests. At that point, company founder J. Livingston Kosberg returned to USPH as interim CEO and instituted a search for a new leader.

Principal Competitors

Healthsouth Corporation; NovaCare Rehabilitation; RehabCare Group, Inc.

Further Reading

"Co-Founder Resigns from Board of Houston-Based U.S. Physical Therapy," *Knight Ridder/Tribune Business News*, March 1, 2002.

Dodge, Robert, "Hands on Deck, Full Steam Ahead," *American Banker*, August 20, 1985, p. 26.

Fromson, Brett Duval, "The Screwiest S&L Bailout Ever," *Fortune*, June 19, 1989, p. 114.

Hayes, Thomas C., "Talking Business with Kosberg of First Texas," *New York Times*, May 6, 1986, p. D2.

Hoffman, Tony, "U.S. Physical Therapy: Building Partnerships One Clinic at a Time," *Equities*, November 1994, p. 18.

——, "U.S. Physical Therapy: Partnerships, Pure Play and Profitability," *Equities*, November/December 1995, p. 39.

"Houston Developer Jailed in Kosberg Kidnapping," *Austin American Statesman*, August 5, 1989, p. B4.

Kreimer, Susan, "U.S. Physical Therapy Reports Strong Profits," *Houston Chronicle,* August 3, 2001, p. C2.

Lau, Gloria, "Cost Controls Get Firm Over Medicare Hurdle," *Investor's Business Daily,* May 29, 2001, p. A10.

McGrath, Courtney, "No Pain, No Gain," *Kiplinger's Personal Finance,* February 2002, p. 60.

Pybus, Kenneth R., "CareerStaff Will Take Temps to Wall Street with New IPO," *Houston Business Journal,* May 23, 1994, p. 1.

Schlegel, Darrin, "Physical Therapy Earnings Limp Along," *Houston Chronicle,* May 1, 2003, p. 2.

——, "U.S. Physical Therapy Says Earnings Down," *Houston Chronicle,* September 25, 2002, p. C2.

——, "U.S. Physical Therapy Trims Projection," *Houston Chronicle,* September 23, 2003, p. B2.

—A. Woodward

Van's Aircraft, Inc.

14401 NE Keil Road
Aurora, Oregon 97002
U.S.A.
Telephone: (503) 678-6545
Fax: (503) 678-6560
Web site: http://www.vansaircraft.com

Private Company
Incorporated: 1983
Employees: 60
Sales: $30 million (2004 est.)
NAIC: 336411 Aircraft Manufacturing; 541710 Research
and Development in the Physical, Engineering, and
Life Sciences

Van's Aircraft, Inc. is the world's largest producer of kitplanes. The company ships the equivalent of 650 full kits a year for completion by home builders. The company has developed a half-dozen new models in addition to the original RV-3, including a four-place version.

More than 3,800 RV kits have been assembled since the company began offering them in 1973 (even more have been delivered but not yet completed).

Flying magazine reports that kits for two-place RV models average around 1,600 hours to build and require an average investment between $50,000 and $60,000. The time spent building the kits can be nearly halved by paying an extra $8,000 for a partially completed QuickBuild kit.

Van's is based at Aurora Municipal Airport in Oregon, where it operates a 63,000-square-foot factory. Founder Dick VanGrunsven commutes there from his fly-in community and pilots the first prototype of each new model.

Exports account for around 15 percent of sales, reports the *Oregonian.* The kits have been shipped to more than 40 countries around the world; Nigeria formed a local enterprise to assemble them as primary trainers for its air force. Another company, in Malaysia, partially assembles QuickBuild kits for sale throughout the world.

Oregon Origins

At the age of 16, Richard E. VanGrunsven learned to fly on his family's farm near Cornelius, Oregon. While a teen, VanGrunsven visited experimental aviation pioneers George Bogardus and Hobie Sorrell via their private landing strips.

He joined the Air Force in 1961 after earning an engineering degree from the University of Portland. VanGrunsven aimed to become a fighter pilot but a vision test led instead to a three-year stint as a communications officer.

Upon returning to civilian life, VanGrunsven worked as a designer for Hyster, an Oregon manufacturer of lift trucks. He acquired a kit aircraft—the diminutive, aerobatic Stits Playboy—and began making his own performance-enhancing modifications. He replaced the original wood and fabric wings with aluminum ones of his own design. The result, dubbed the RV-1 after VanGrunsven's initials, was completed in 1965. This plane was sold three years and 550 flight hours later.

A subsequent model, the RV-3, first flew in August 1971. The next year, VanGrunsven flew the prototype to the Experimental Aircraft Association (EAA) Convention in Oshkosh, Wisconsin, where its high performance generated interest from pilots who wanted a hot rod of their own.

With a narrow fuselage and bubble canopy, visibility was excellent. The low wing, aluminum skin, and taildragger configuration were reminiscent of World War II fighter aircraft.

Kits for Sale in 1973

The first kits were made available to the public in 1973. The company's first product was the single place RV-3. It was a sport airplane designed to fly mostly in good weather. It could pull 6 Gs, compared to the standard Cessna 150's 3.8 Gs, and was capable of some basic aerobatic maneuvers.

According to *Oregon Business,* the enterprise grossed about $72,000 in the first year, when the company sold 35 kits. Van's was originally based in the garage at VanGrunsven's home in Forest Grove, Oregon, and moved to the Aurora Airport in 1990.

Company Perspectives:

Total Performance, a term coined to describe the RVs, refers to their wide performance envelope and sporty handling qualities. While the RVs are excellent cross-country airplanes, they are not simply "go-fast" machines. They are also aerobatic (except RV-9A) and have outstanding low speed characteristics and short-field capabilities; a rare combination. First and foremost, though, they are fun to fly. Their controls are light, responsive, and beautifully harmonized. Chances are that you have never flown an airplane that offers anything approaching the exhilarating sensation of an RV.

Michigan builder Art Chard became the first to complete an RV-3 in 1975. (A later model of Chard's own design would provide some ideas for the subsequent RV-6.) VanGrunsven's next kit, first flown in August 1979, was the RV-4, which added a second seat behind the lead pilot.

While they required hundreds of hours of assembly before they could be flown, kitplanes became popular due to their low cost and high performance. While other kit makers embraced composite materials, however, Van's Aircraft's planes retained many similarities to conventionally produced aircraft. They were largely constructed of aluminum, and the panels were riveted on.

Gaining Acceptance in the 1980s and 1990s

As product liability lawsuits grounded virtually all conventional aircraft manufacturers in the United States in the 1980s, kitplane makers swept in to fill the void. With kits, builders assumed legal responsibility as manufacturers. (There have always been home builders in the aircraft industry; before the availability of kits they drew up planes themselves or purchased them from others.)

In the mid-1980s Van's introduced the RV-6, a two-seater with a side-by-side configuration. Though designed for touring rather than performance, it was only fractionally slower than the RV-4, whose wing design it shared. All of Van's Aircraft's planes to this point were taildraggers, with two main landing gear under the wings and a small tailwheel. The RV-6A derivative offered tricycle gear instead (incorporating a steerable nosewheel rather than a tailwheel). The RV-6/A series would become Van's Aircraft's best-selling model. Incorporating years of refinements, the tandem seat RV-8 began testing in 1995. It offered a wider cockpit and more luggage room.

The total kitplane market was estimated at $200 million in the early 1990s, noted the *Oregonian*. Van's employed 31 people and had sold an estimated 3,500 kits by then.

Van's began introducing partially completed quick-build kits, which cut construction time by a third or half (anything more than 49 percent completed would not be considered an amateur experimental aircraft). In late 1995, Tong Kooi Ong, CEO of Malaysia's Phileo Allied Group, established PhileoAviation Sdn Bhd to assemble RV-6A QuickBuild kits for

sale in the United States, Malaysia, and around the world. (Tong, a "brash" and "impish" young entrepreneur, was one of Malaysia's fastest rising elites, according to the *Asian Wall Street Journal*.) The first of these kits, priced at $11,000 (MYR 27,940), were delivered in November 1996. Separately, Nigeria ordered 60 RV-6As as primary trainers for its air force, and a local company was established there to assemble them.

Van's began testing the RV-9A in 1997 and offered the first kits for sale about two years later. The entry-level RV-9A, which had side-by-side seats and tricycle landing gear, was designed to use lower-powered engines. The controls were also more forgiving.

Van's passed several milestones in the 1990s. It delivered more than 550 kits in 1994. By 1995, more than 1,000 RVs had been completed and were flying in 20 countries. Annual sales reached $25 million by the late 1990s. Van's was believed to have sold more aircraft kits than any other company.

Around this time, reported *Fortune Small Business,* Van's embraced computer-aided design and manufacturing (CAD/CAM). The company began offering pre-drilled panels, or matched hole construction, making placement of each plane's 14,000 rivets much simpler.

Flying High Beyond 2000

The two-seat, side-by-side RV-7 and RV-7As became available in the spring of 2001. These newly designed aircraft boasted more legroom and headroom and more fuel capacity.

A profile of Van's in the May 2002 *Oregon Business* included a survey of the kitplane industry. The number of manufacturers had grown from one to 210 in the nearly 30 years Van's had been in business. Van's Aircraft's closest competitor, geographically at least, was Lancair, based in Redmond, Oregon (though Lancair had begun to build fully completed aircraft as well).

More than 3,100 RV kits had been completed by the end of 2002. *Oregon Business* reported revenues were about $20 million at the time, when the company employed 60 people.

While Van's had no competition among conventional aircraft makers for its two-place aircraft, a number of them had continued to make larger, four-place aircraft. As the values for these planes went up, Van's entered the four-place market in 2003 with the RV-10, priced at $35,000 for the kit alone.

In 2004, *Fortune Small Business* reported Van's had annual sales of $30 million. The best-selling RV-7 was priced at $17,000 (the engine and other parts cost another $40,000). According to the *Oregonian,* exports accounted for about 15 percent of sales.

The EAA awarded VanGrunsven its Freedom of Flight award in June 2004. By this time, more than 3,600 of his kitplanes had been completed and flown. VanGrunsven told *Flying* magazine that the key to his success was the attention given to the RVs' control systems: "Flying an RV is more an extension of the pilot's thought process, instead of manhandling

<table>
<tr><td colspan="2" align="center">**Key Dates:**</td></tr>
<tr><td>**1973:**</td><td>Van's Aircraft's first kit, the single-seat RV-3, is introduced.</td></tr>
<tr><td>**1981:**</td><td>Two-place RV-4 debuts.</td></tr>
<tr><td>**1985:**</td><td>Best-selling RV-6 first flies.</td></tr>
<tr><td>**1995:**</td><td>First flight of RV-8 occurs.</td></tr>
<tr><td>**1998:**</td><td>RV-8A is introduced.</td></tr>
<tr><td>**1999:**</td><td>Less demanding RV-9A is introduced.</td></tr>
<tr><td>**2001:**</td><td>Two-seat side-by-side RV-7 series is introduced.</td></tr>
<tr><td>**2003:**</td><td>Van's enters the four-place market with the RV-10.</td></tr>
</table>

a machine through the air.'' *Flying* praised the stable handling characteristics on even the fastest planes in the series.

Principal Competitors

Cirrus Design Corp.; Lancair International Inc.

Further Reading

Alexander, Julie, ''On a Wing and a Prayer; Hobby Becomes Business for Plane Builder,'' *Tulsa World,* January 31, 1996, p. 4.

Boone, Jerry F., ''Firm Landing at Aurora Airport,'' *Oregonian* (Portland), September 21, 2000, p. E2.

Butler, Mary, ''North Plains, Ore., Company's Home-Built Kit Airplanes Gain Popularity,'' *News Tribune,* February 1, 2000.

Colby, Richard N., ''Doctor's Home-Built Plane Not First to Fail,'' *Portland Oregonian,* November 5, 1995, p. C1.

Gaffney, Timothy R., ''Plane Market's Homebuilts Hit New Highs,'' *Dayton Daily News* (Ohio), February 25, 2004, p. D1.

Gitman, Mitch, ''Wing It Yourself: Home-Built Aircraft Boom Has Fliers on Cloud Nine,'' *Arizona Daily Star,* June 2, 1997, p. 8D.

Goyer, Robert, ''1000+ RVs Flying,'' *Flying,* October 1995, p. 38.

——, ''RV-8 Sales Sizzle,'' *Flying,* March 98, p. 30.

——, ''RV-6 Successor,'' *Flying,* June 2001, p. 31.

——, ''Van's Eliminates RV-8 'Restrictions','' *Flying,* February 1999, p. 39.

——, ''Van's Flies RV-10,'' *Flying,* September 2003, p. 34.

——, ''Van's Tops 2,000 Kits Built and Flying,'' *Flying,* p. 36.

——, ''Van's Working on Four-Seater,'' *Flying,* March 2002, p. 32.

Hamburg, Ken, ''Kitplane Makers Get a Piece of the Sky,'' *Oregonian* (Portland), Bus. Sec., February 23, 1992.

Jacobs, Jennifer, ''Recreational Planes Ready for Sale in June,'' *Business Times* (Malaysia), November 29, 1995, p. 1.

Kadera, Jim, ''Plane-Kit Maker Soars,'' *Oregonian* (Portland), August 25, 2003, p. D2.

Katauskas, Ted, ''In Character: Flying Solo; Do-It-Yourself Aviators Turn to Richard VanGrunsven to Get Airbornes,'' *Oregon Business,* May 2002, pp. 34–35.

''Malaysia's PhileoAviation Hopes to Make 100 More Kitplanes,'' *Asia Pulse,* August 12, 1999.

McCool, Lewis, ''Durango Man's Hobby in Rarefied Air,'' *Associated Press Newswires,* April 24, 2002.

Nobbe, Thomas A., ''Kitplanes: High Tech in a Box,'' *Machine Design,* March 22, 1990, p. 70.

''Phileo Aviation Poised for Take Off,'' *Sun* (Christchurch, New Zealand), January 8, 1999.

''PhileoAviation Sells First Plane for Use in Malaysia,'' *Star* (Malaysia), December 4, 1998, p. 1.

Pura, Raphael, ''Phileo's Brash Boss Starts to Draw Flack—Tong's Fast-Growing Malaysian Financial Empire Stirs Resentment,'' *Asian Wall Street Journal,* December 21, 1995, p. 1.

''QuickBuild Takes Flight,'' *Aviation Week & Space Technology,* January 12, 1998, p. 420.

Wallace, Lane, ''Conventional Wisdom: The Success of Van's Aircraft,'' *Flying,* August 2004, pp. 51, 53.

Wise, Jeff, ''Plane Dealer; How Digital Manufacturing Helped an Aviator Take Off,'' *FSB: Fortune Small Business,* July/August 2004, pp. 83+.

Yeow, Jimmy, ''PhileoAviation Ships QuickBuild Kits to US,'' *Business Times,* November 9, 1996, p. 1.

Yunus, Kamarul, ''Kitplanes Maker Set to Venture into Local and Regional Markets,'' *Business Times,* August 6, 1997, p. 20.

—Frederick C. Ingram

Walgreen Co.

200 Wilmot Road
Deerfield, Illinois 60015-4620
U.S.A.
Telephone: (847) 940-2500
Toll Free: (800) 289-2273
Fax: (847) 914-2804
Web site: http://www.walgreens.com

Public Company
Incorporated: 1916
Employees: 154,000
Sales: $32.51 billion (2003)
Stock Exchanges: New York Chicago
Ticker Symbol: WAG
NAIC: 446110 Pharmacies and Drug Stores

Walgreen Co. is the largest drugstore chain in the United States in terms of sales, more than 60 percent of which derives from retail prescriptions. During 2003 Walgreen filled 400 million prescriptions, representing about 13 percent of all retail prescriptions in the country. It operates more than 4,400 Walgreens drugstores in 44 states and Puerto Rico. About 80 percent of these outlets are freestanding locations, more than three-quarters have drive-through pharmacies, and nearly all of them offer one-hour photofinishing. In addition to the flagship Walgreens, the company also runs Walgreens Health Initiatives, a prescription benefit manager serving small and medium-sized employers and managed care organizations. Walgreen's century-plus history has been marked in more recent years by explosive growth fueled almost entirely by the opening of new stores—a sharp contrast with the firm's main rivals, CVS Corporation and Rite Aid Corporation, both of which have led a wave of industry consolidation through acquisition. By 2004, more than half of Walgreens outlets were less than five years old.

Early Years of Rapid Growth

The company had its origin in 1901, when Charles R. Walgreen bought the drugstore, on the south side of Chicago, at which he had been working as a pharmacist. He bought a second store in 1909; by 1915, there were five Walgreen drugstores. He made numerous improvements and innovations in the stores, including the addition of soda fountains that also featured luncheon service. Walgreen also began to make his own line of drug products; by doing so, he was able to control the quality of these items and offer them at lower prices than competitors.

By 1916, there were nine Walgreen stores, all on Chicago's South Side, doing a business volume of $270,000 annually. That year, the stores were consolidated as Walgreen Co. with the aim of assuring economies of scale.

By 1919 there were 20 Walgreen stores, 19 of which were on Chicago's South Side while the other was on the near north side. Also in 1919, the company opened its first photofinishing studio; it promised faster service than most commercial studios.

The 1920s were a booming decade for Walgreen stores. In 1921 the company opened a store in Chicago's downtown, its first outside a residential area. Walgreen stores introduced the malted milkshake at their fountain counters in 1922. To meet the demand for ice cream and to assure its quality, Walgreen established its own ice cream manufacturing plants during the 1920s. The company continued to add to its number of stores, and by mid-1925, there were 65 stores with total annual sales of $1.2 million. Fifty-nine of the stores were in Chicago and its suburbs, with others in Milwaukee, Wisconsin, and St. Louis, Missouri. Before the year was out, the company had expanded into Minneapolis and St. Paul, Minnesota.

The company opened its first East Coast store, in New York's theater district, in 1927. That year, the company went public. By the end of 1929, there were 397 Walgreen stores in 87 cities; annual sales were $47 million with net earnings of $4 million.

Great Depression Years

At first, the company suffered little from the 1929 stock market crash and the subsequent Great Depression. Sales actually rose in 1930, to $52 million. The same year, the company opened a 224,000-square-foot warehouse and laboratory on Chicago's southwest side. Early in the 1930s, the company expanded on a project begun in 1929 setting up an agency system by which independent drugstores could sell Walgreen products.

By 1934, 600 Walgreen agency stores were functioning in 33 states, mostly in Midwestern communities with populations of less than 20,000. By 1932, however, the company was feeling the Depression's pinch. Sales dipped to $47.6 million, and wage cuts were instituted; the company also set up a benefit fund to assist retirees and needy families inside and outside the company. The company continued promoting itself, however; in 1931, it had become the first drugstore chain in the United States to advertise on radio.

There were several major events for Walgreen in 1933. The company paid a dividend on its stock for the first time, its concessions at Chicago's Century of Progress exposition helped boost sales, and Charles Walgreen, Jr., became a vice-president of the company. With the repeal of Prohibition late that year, Walgreen Co. acquired liquor licenses and soon was selling whisky and wine in 60 percent of its stores.

In 1934 the company opened its first Walgreen Super Store, in Tampa, Florida. At 4,000 square feet, the store was nearly double the size of the typical store, and it had a much larger fountain and more open displays of merchandise than an average store. Other Super Stores followed in Salt Lake City, Utah; Milwaukee, Wisconsin; Miami, Florida; and Rochester, New York. Also in 1934 the company's stock began trading on the New York Stock Exchange.

Walgreen's business recovered in the mid-to-late 1930s; 1938 sales totaled $69 million. By 1939 the founder's health was failing; Charles Walgreen, Sr., resigned the presidency of the company in August. His son was named to succeed him, and Justin Dart, who had been with the company in various capacities since 1929, was named general manager. Dart had been married to and divorced from Ruth Walgreen, the founder's daughter. Charles Walgreen, Sr., died in December 1939 at the age of 66.

Continued Expansion in the 1940s

The company began the 1940s with the opening of a superstore in downtown Chicago. The store was the 489th in the chain and featured a two-way high-speed escalator to provide access between the two floors of the store, the first of its kind in any drugstore in the world. The store also contained a full-service restaurant-tea room. In April 1940 the Marvin Drug Co., which operated eight stores and a warehouse in Dallas, merged with Walgreen Co. At year-end, Walgreen Co. announced the establishment of a pension plan, with an initial contribution of more than $500,000 from the proceeds of Charles Walgreen, Sr.'s life insurance policy.

In 1941 there was a split between Charles Walgreen, Jr., and Justin Dart. Dart's unorthodox management style made others in the company uncomfortable; he was arbitrary in determining bonuses to store managers and critical of the company's conservative approach to business. Board members considered him erratic and extravagant. They called for his resignation in July 1941. In November of that year he resigned and joined United Drugs Inc., where he built a substantial career and diversified beyond the drug business.

Walgreen Co. put continued growth and expansion on hold with the United States' entry into World War II after the Pearl Harbor attack in December 1941. The company felt the war's impact in a variety of ways; certain foods became scarce, as did film and tobacco products. More than 2,500 Walgreen employees served in the armed forces; 48 did not survive. Walgreen stores sold war bonds and stamps. In 1943 the company opened a store in the Pentagon, in Washington, D.C.

After the war, expansion was once again possible. In 1946 the company acquired a 27 percent interest, later increased to 44 percent, in a major Mexican retail and restaurant company, Sanborns. More Walgreen Super Stores were opened in the late 1940s, including one on Chicago's Michigan Avenue, a street of elegant shops and restaurants. In 1948 the company expanded its corporate headquarters in Chicago. That year, sales were up to $163.6 million, and Walgreen began advertising on television.

Transition to Self-Service Beginning in 1950s

The 1950s ushered in the era of self-service in drug retailing, a concept Walgreen had tried on an experimental basis at three stores in the 1940s. In 1949 the company canceled plans for a merger with Thrifty Drug Co., a California chain, largely because Thrifty's clerk-service style would hamper a conversion of the entire company to self-service. In the course of the merger negotiations, however, Charles Walgreen, Jr., had researched Thrifty's competitors and had been impressed by the self-service Sav-on chain, which fueled his interest in taking his stores in that direction.

The first self-service Walgreens opened on Chicago's South Side in June 1952; the second followed in a few months at Evergreen Plaza, Chicago's first major shopping center. The self-service stores offered lower prices than traditional stores but often actually required more employees, because the stores were larger and carried more products. By the end of 1953, there were 22 self-service Walgreens. Self-service continued to grow throughout the 1950s; the company built many new self-service units and converted conventional ones. It also closed some older conventional stores because they either were too small or in locations that had become undesirable. While the number of stores grew to only 451 in 1960—from 410 in 1950—sales grew from $163 million to $312 million over the course of that decade, thanks largely to the increased size and wider selection of the self-service stores.

Key Dates:

1901: Charles R. Walgreen buys the drugstore on the south side of Chicago where he had been working as a pharmacist.
1909: Walgreen opens his second store, which features a soda fountain.
1916: Now operating nine drugstores, the founder incorporates his business as Walgreen Co.
1925: Walgreen has more than 65 stores in Chicago, Milwaukee, St. Louis, and Minneapolis-St. Paul.
1927: Company goes public.
1952: Walgreen begins transition to self-service with the opening of its first self-service drugstore.
1975: Sales surpass the $1 billion mark.
1984: The 1,000th Walgreens store is opened.
1986: Company completes its largest-ever acquisition, the 66-unit Medi Mart chain.
1992: First freestanding Walgreens store opens; drive-through pharmacies make their debut.
2003: The 4,000th Walgreens store opens.

With the opening of a self-service store in Louisville, Kentucky, at the end of 1960, self-service units outnumbered traditional ones. Another major event of 1960 was the opening of the first Walgreens in Puerto Rico.

Diversifying Beyond Drugstores in 1960s and 1970s

In 1962 Walgreen Co. entered the discount department store field by paying about $3 million for the assets of United Mercantile Inc., which owned three large Globe Shopping Center stores and seven smaller Danburg department stores, all in the Houston, Texas, area. The company expanded the Globe chain throughout the South and Southwest; by 1966, there were 13 Globe stores generating annual sales of more than $120 million.

Operating Globe gave Walgreen Co. experience in running larger stores, and the company began to open ever larger stores under the Walgreens name. The first Walgreens Super Center opened in 1964 in the Chicago suburb of Norridge. By 1969 there were 17 Super Centers around the country.

Walgreen Co. changed and diversified its restaurant operations in the 1960s. A detailed analysis early in the decade showed that the return on investment of Walgreen's fountains and grills was generally less than that of the rest of a store. Therefore, the company decided not to include fountains and grills in new stores and began closing them in others. Instead of getting out of foodservice altogether, however, the company went into full-scale restaurants; the first of these was the Villager Room, located within a Walgreens in Oak Park, a Chicago suburb. Also added during the 1960s were the fast-food chain Corky's and the medieval-decor Robin Hood restaurants. By the decade's end, there were 287 in-store restaurants, 14 Corky's and two Robin Hoods.

A third generation of Walgreens ascended to the company presidency in 1969. C.R. (Cork) Walgreen III was named president, succeeding Alvin Borg, who had become president when Charles Walgreen, Jr., became chairman of the board during a 1963 corporate reorganization. This made Walgreen Co. one of the few companies headed by second- and third-generation descendants of the founder, though the Walgreen family no longer owned a controlling share of company stock. Also in 1963, the company elected its first outside directors to the board.

Several changes occurred in the mid-1970s. In 1974 the company opened its first Wag's restaurant; Wag's were free-standing family restaurants, many open 24 hours a day. That year it also acquired the Liggett chain of 29 Florida drugstores. In 1975 Walgreen Co. moved into a new corporate headquarters in Deerfield, a suburb of Chicago. The previous facility had become inadequate in size and outmoded. Also in 1975, the company completed the first phase of a new drug and cosmetics laboratory in Kalamazoo, Michigan; expanded its distribution center in Berkeley, Illinois; and, in Chicago, replaced its plastic container plant and photo processing studio with new ones. The company surpassed the $1 billion mark in sales in 1975.

In 1976 Charles R. Walgreen III succeeded his father as chairman of the board, and Robert L. Schmitt, who had been with the company since 1948, became president. Schmitt oversaw the liquidation of the Globe chain, which had been showing significant losses. He also was charged with forming a partnership with Schnuck's, a St. Louis grocery store operator, to establish combined supermarkets and drugstores, and with opening optical centers in Walgreen stores. Schmitt's tenure ended, however, when he died suddenly in October 1978. Fred F. Canning, a 32-year company veteran, succeeded him. In 1979 Walgreen Co. acquired 16 Stein drugstores in the Milwaukee area. It closed the 1970s with 688 drugstores, sales of $1.34 billion, and earnings of $30.2 million.

Refocused on Drugstores in 1980s

The company began the 1980s by refocusing on drugstores and eliminating certain businesses. In 1980 it ended the agency program, begun in 1929, which accounted for only 2 percent of sales. This step did not sit well with some former agency stores; a group of store operators in Wisconsin sued Walgreen Co., eventually winning a $431,000 judgment. The following year, Walgreen closed its 27 optical centers and ended the partnership with Schnuck's. The company also eliminated many in-store restaurants, concentrating on Wag's instead; in-store restaurants decreased in number from 231 in 1979 to 119 in 1984.

Expanding the drugstore business, Walgreen Co. brought the Rennehbohm chain, based in Madison, Wisconsin, in 1980. Rennehbohm had 17 drugstores, two clinic pharmacies, two health- and beauty-aid stores, a card shop, and six cafeterias. In 1981 Walgreen bought 21 Kroger SuperX drugstores in Houston. In 1982 the company added additional services to its drugstores: it made next-day photofinishing available chainwide and put grocery departments in some stores located in urban areas.

In 1983 Walgreen completed chainwide installation of its Intercom computerized pharmacy system. By the end of the decade Intercom connected each store in the chain via satellite to a mainframe computer in Des Plaines, Illinois. This system enabled customers to have their prescriptions filled at any Walgreens in the country.

Walgreen opened its 1,000th store, on the near north side of Chicago, in 1984. The company continued expanding in the drugstore area, while divesting itself of other businesses; also in 1984 it sold its interest in Sanborns, by then 46.9 percent, to Sanborns's other principals for about $30 million, a move spurred by Mexico's high inflation rate.

In 1986 Walgreen bought the 66 Medi Mart stores, located primarily in New England, in the company's largest single acquisition ever. That year, the company also bought 25 stores from the Indiana chain, Ribordy, and opened 102 new stores, making 1986 Walgreen's biggest year for expansion yet.

In 1988, continuing to trim non-drugstore businesses, Walgreen sold its 87 freestanding Wag's restaurants to Marriott Corporation. In 1988 the Haft family sought regulatory clearance to acquire a block of Walgreen stock—a move that company officials feared would lead to an unfriendly takeover bid, as the Hafts had tried to acquire other retailers. Walgreen responded with a move that was seen as an antitakeover device—the establishment of "golden parachutes," payments to be made to executives if they left the firm after a takeover. No bid came through, however.

In 1989 the company opened four mini-drugstores called Walgreens RxPress, which offered a full-service pharmacy and popular non-prescription items in areas where full-sized store locations were difficult to find. By the mid-1990s, these 2,000-square-foot units, some of which offered one-hour photofinishing services, also featured convenient drive-through pharmacies. There were 25 RxPress locations by 1996.

Accelerated Expansion in the 1990s

For Walgreen, the 1990s were dominated by an unprecedented rate of expansion. Walgreen ended the 1980s with 1,484 units. By mid-1997 the company had more than 2,200 units (an increase of almost 50 percent) and was aiming for the 3,000 mark by the new century. Although most of this growth was accomplished organically, the 1990s began with an acquisition, the 1990 purchase of Lee Drug, a nine-unit drugstore chain in New Hampshire and Massachusetts. That same year Fred Canning retired as president. L. Daniel Jorndt, who had been senior vice-president and treasurer, succeeded him.

For the pharmacy industry as a whole, the 1990s were a decade of profound change. Demographically, there were more and more people over the age of 50; as a result, more prescriptions were being filled each year, making pharmacies a hot commodity. Consequently, competition became fiercer as aggressive chains such as Wal-Mart Stores, Inc. challenged Walgreen's leading position in prescription drugs. Additionally, managed care health plans grew increasingly important as the decade progressed, putting pressure on drugstores to lower prices on prescriptions, thereby squeezing margins. Walgreen responded to these challenges by investing heavily in technology and by launching new initiatives aimed directly at taking advantage of the trend toward managed care.

On the technology side, the company improved its inventory management capabilities when it rolled out point-of-sale scanning equipment chainwide in late 1991, followed by the chainwide completion in 1994 of SIMS (Strategic Inventory Management System), which united all elements of the purchasing-distribution-sales cycle. By 1997 Walgreen was rolling out a second-generation Intercom Plus system, which performed more than 200 functions and enabled customers to order prescription refills using the keys on a push-button phone. The system also cut in half the time customers had to wait to receive their prescriptions.

In response to the managed care boom, one byproduct of which was the growth in cost-effective mail-order pharmacies, Walgreen formed a subsidiary—Healthcare Plus—in 1991 to offer managed care providers a pharmacy mail service of its own. Launched with an Orlando, Florida, mail service facility capable of handling 5,000 prescriptions a day, Healthcare Plus added a second facility in late 1994 in Tempe, Arizona, with a capacity of 7,500 prescriptions per day. Mail service sales were expected to hit $500 million by 1998. In the fall of 1995 Walgreen expanded Healthcare Plus into WHP Health Initiatives, Inc.—a pharmacy benefits manager—in order to offer additional products and services to managed care providers, including long-term care pharmacies, durable medical equipment, and home infusion services. WHP was aimed at small and medium-sized employers and HMOs in Walgreens' top 28 retail markets.

Meanwhile, the expansion of the Walgreens chain continued apace, supported by the opening of two more distribution centers—in Lehigh Valley, Pennsylvania, in June 1991, and in Woodland, California, in July 1995—bringing to eight the number of such centers. The Woodland center was particularly important as it supported an aggressive expansion in California, as well as the opening of the first Walgreens in Portland, Oregon. Walgreens also expanded into several other new markets in the mid-1990s, including Dallas/Fort Worth, Detroit, Kansas City, Las Vegas, and Philadelphia. Throughout the 1990s expansion, the chain concentrated on opening freestanding stores, which were considered more convenient than mall stores. The first freestanding store opened in 1992; by 1996 more than half of all Walgreens were freestanding. Drive-through prescription service at more than 700 Walgreens further enhanced the chain's image of convenience. In addition to all the store openings—210 in 1996 alone—the chain also remodeled or closed some of its older units; consequently, the average age of a Walgreens stood at 7.4 years in 1996, about half what it was ten years earlier. Walgreen posted 1996 net sales of $11.78 billion, more than double that of 1989.

In May 1997 Walgreen entered foreign territory for the first time since the failed Sanborns venture. That month the company formed a joint venture—RX Network Inc. (RXN)—with Itochu Corp. and five other Japanese companies to set up a drugstore chain in Japan. RXN aimed to create a 500-unit chain by 2002. In January 1998 Charles R. Walgreen III retired as CEO, with Jorndt succeeding him. Walgreen III remained chairman until 1999, when Jorndt took over that position as well.

A Steady Performer, Late 1990s and Early 2000s

In the late 1990s and into the early years of the 21st century, Walgreen achieved a remarkable record of steady growth and profitability. As revenues more than doubled from $15.31 billion in 1998 to $32.51 billion in 2003, profits increased at a similar pace, jumping from $511 million to $1.18 billion. Throughout this entire period, the net profit margin stayed within a narrow band, between 3.3 percent and 3.7 percent. Moreover, the results for 2003 marked the company's 29th consecutive year of record sales and earnings. Walgreen added about 350 stores per year in this period, opening its 3,000th store in Chicago in March 2000 and its 4,000th store in Van Nuys, California, in March 2003.

This growth was achieved almost entirely organically as Walgreen eschewed the acquisition route to growth of its competitors, who were participating in a huge consolidation wave that was sweeping the drugstore industry. Walgreen preferred to carefully select its own sites for new stores rather than taking on the hodgepodge of stores with some undesirable locations and/or store formats that the typical large acquisition involves. This strategy also supported a more rapid transition of the store base to Walgreen's preferred format—freestanding stores with drive-through pharmacies, usually located on high-traffic corners. By the end of 2003, of the 4,227 company drugstores, 3,363 were freestanding units and 3,280 had drive-through pharmacies; more than half of the stores were less than five years old. To provide further convenience for customers, 1,112 Walgreens outlets were open 24 hours a day (creating combination convenience/drugstores), and nearly all of them offered one-hour photofinishing services.

There were a number of other important developments during this period. In 1999 Walgreen launched a comprehensive online pharmacy that enabled customers to order prescriptions for instore pickup or mail delivery and also offered access to the health and wellness content of Mayo Clinic Health Information. The following year the web site was expanded to include front-of-the-store merchandise, such as nail polish and shampoo. After the company celebrated its 100th anniversary in 2001, another change in leadership occurred. In January 2002 David Bernauer, a former pharmacist and lifelong Walgreen employee who most recently served as president and chief operating officer, was named CEO, succeeding Jorndt. Bernauer inherited Jorndt's position of chairman as well one year later. In support of its rapid expansion, Walgreen opened major new distribution centers in Jupiter, Florida, and Dallas (both in 2002); in Perrysburg, Ohio (2003); and in Moreno Valley, California (2004)—bringing the total number of such facilities to 11. Late in 2003 Walgreen ended 17 years on the acquisition sideline when it purchased 11 stores and the pharmacy files of five others from Hi-School Pharmacy. The stores were located in the Portland, Oregon, and Vancouver, Washington, metropolitan areas.

Although Walgreen's competition seemed to grow increasingly fierce both at the retail level and in the form of the nascent mail-order pharmacy industry, no clear evidence had arisen suggesting that the company's steady growth was likely to come to an end. The aging U.S. population, coupled with the introduction of innovative new drugs, was fueling prescription growth, and the portion of revenues that Walgreen derived from prescriptions continued to increase, surging from less than 50 percent in 1996 to 62 percent by 2003. The company was seeking to add a net 365 stores during 2004—supported by capital expenditures of $1 billion—toward a longer term goal of 7,000 stores by 2010. Among the markets targeted for major expansion was New York City, where Walgreen had only a small presence.

Principal Subsidiaries

Walgreen Arizona Drug Co.; Bond Drug Company of Illinois; Walgreens Home Care, Inc.; Walgreens Healthcare Plus, Inc.;

Walgreens.com, Inc.; WHP Health Initiatives, Inc.; Walgreen Louisiana Co., Inc.; Walgreen Hastings Co.; Walgreen Eastern Co., Inc.; Walgreen of Puerto Rico, Inc.; Walgreen of San Patricio, Inc.

Principal Competitors

CVS Corporation; Rite Aid Corporation; Wal-Mart Stores, Inc.; The Jean Coutu Group (PJC) Inc.

Further Reading

Bacon, John U., *America's Corner Store: Walgreens' Prescription for Success,* Hoboken, N.J.: Wiley, 2004, 255 p.

Baeb, Eddie, ''Headaches Awaiting Walgreen's New CEO: Grow Store Base, Guard Margins,'' *Crain's Chicago Business,* July 23, 2001, p. 3.

Block, Toddi Gutner, ''We Need You, You Need Us: Drug Benefit Managers Have Grabbed Power in the Retail Pharmacy Industry. Walgreen Co. Is Grabbing It Back,'' *Forbes,* May 8, 1995, pp. 66–67, 70.

Brookman, Faye, ''Innovative Chain Ranks No. 1,'' *Stores,* April 1993, pp. 21–23.

Byrne, Harlan S., ''Good Prescription: Walgreen's Long Skein of Profit Gains Continues,'' *Barron's,* October 12, 1998, p. 15.

——, ''Prescription for Profits,'' *Barron's,* January 12, 2004, p. 23.

——, ''Rx for Growth,'' *Barron's,* January 7, 2002, p. 14.

——, ''A Winning Prescription,'' *Barron's,* March 7, 1994, p. 21.

''A Century of Growth Comes Full Circle,'' *Chain Store Age,* December 2000, pp. 250, 252.

Clepper, Irene, ''Walgreens: One of the Oldest and Still Growing,'' *Drug Topics,* April 8, 1996, pp. 116, 118.

Dubashi, Jagannath, ''Walgreen: Just What the Doctor Ordered,'' *Financial World,* May 1, 1990, p. 20.

''Flourishing Walgreen: It Has Found the Right Prescription for a Retail Drug Chain,'' *Barron's,* April 14, 1958, p. 9.

Garbato, Debby, ''A Model of Efficiency,'' *Retail Merchandiser,* June 2004, pp. 16, 18, 20.

Heller, Laura, ''Steering Chain Along a Profitable Course,'' *Drug Store News,* March 25, 2002, pp. 20, 22.

Henkoff, Ronald, ''A High-Tech Rx for Profits,'' *Fortune,* March 23, 1992, pp. 106–07.

Jones, Sandra, ''Walgreen Doctoring Stores,'' *Crain's Chicago Business,* September 8, 2003, p. 3.

Kogan, Herman, and Rick Kogan, *Pharmacist to the Nation: A History of Walgreen Co., America's Leading Drug Store Chain,* Deerfield, Ill.: Walgreen Co., 1989.

Kramer, Louise, ''Walgreen to Take on New York City,'' *Crain's New York Business,* July 5, 2004, p. 3.

Kruger, Renée Marisa, ''Walgreens: America's Corner Drugstore,'' *Retail Merchandiser,* December 2000, pp. 25–27.

Lambert, Emily, ''In the Pill Box,'' *Forbes,* April 26, 2004, pp. 54–56.

Simon, Ruth, ''Pills and Profits,'' *Forbes,* June 30, 1986, p. 33.

Spurgeon, Devon, ''Walgreen Takes Aim at Discount Chains, Supermarkets,'' *Wall Street Journal,* June 29, 2000, p. B4.

''Walgreen Company: The Accomplishments and Prospects of the Second Largest American Drug-Store Chain,'' *Barron's,* October 15, 1934, p. 16.

''The Walgreen Formula: Digging in for New Growth in Drug Retailing,'' *Business Week,* March 1, 1982, pp. 84+.

''Walgreen Likely to Score Its Best Showing Ever,'' *Barron's,* July 25, 1966, p. 24.

—Trudy Ring
—update: David E. Salamie

WebMD Corporation

669 River Drive, Center 2
Elmwood Park, New Jersey 07407-1361
U.S.A.
Telephone: (201) 703-3400
Fax: (201) 703-3401
Web site: http://www.webmd.com

Public Company
Incorporated: 1995 as Healtheon Corporation
Employees: 5,635
Sales: $964.0 million (2003)
Stock Exchanges: NASDAQ
Ticker Symbol: HLTH
NAIC: 518210 Data Processing, Hosting, and Related
    Services

WebMD Corporation, based in Elmwood Park, New Jersey, is best known for its consumer-focused healthcare information web site, but the company also offers a range of transaction and technology solutions for physicians, providers, and health plans. The company's WebMD Health unit operates the health information web site, which attracts more than 20 million visitors each month. WebMD also distributes its content and services to other Internet portals such as AOL and MSN, and media distribution partner News Corporation. Medscape from WebMD offers online education tools and medical information to more than 575,000 physicians and 1.6 million other healthcare professionals. WebMD Envoy provides electronic data interchange for the healthcare industry to determine eligibility and coverage, bill patients, process claims, and make reimbursements. WebMD Practice Services, through The Medical Manager, provides integrated practice management systems to help physicians automate appointment scheduling, maintain medical histories and charts, and streamline billing. The unit's professional Internet portal also offers members medical research, news, professional journals, and Web-based continuing medical education. WebMD is a public company trading on the NASDAQ.

Forming the Corporation in 1995

The legal history of WebMD Corporation began in December 1995 with the formation of Healtheon Corporation, but the company did not take its present shape until the 1999 merger with WebMD, Inc. In a sense, the men who launched these two enterprises cofounded today's hybrid WebMD. Healtheon's founder, James H. Clark, was already a famous entrepreneur before he turned his attention to the healthcare field. He was born in Plainview, Texas, in 1944 and endured a troubled childhood. His father earned money from doing odd jobs but suffered from a drinking problem, while his mother worked in a doctor's office to help support the family. After his parents divorced when he was 14, even though Clark was highly intelligent, especially in math, and enjoyed working on ham radios, he was bored in school and all too often found trouble. He let loose a skunk at a dance and set off a smoke bomb on the band bus, but did not get suspended until he told a teacher to go to hell. In his junior year in high school Clark simply dropped out. He enlisted in the Navy in 1961 and it was there that he resumed his education and launched his first business: a loan sharking operation that charged sailors 40 percent interest on money lent until payday. He earned his high school equivalency diploma in the Navy, and when he scored at the top on a math test he was promoted to algebra instructor. It was also in the Navy that he first became acquainted with computers and began taking college classes at Tulane University in New Orleans.

Discharged from the service, Clark married and worked as a full-time computer programmer while continuing his college education. He earned a B.S. and master's degree in physics from Louisiana State University, then in 1974 earned his Ph.D. in computer science from the University of Utah, where he began working on computer graphics. His doctoral thesis dealt with building special purpose hardware for 3-D graphics applications. With the intent of becoming a professor, Clark took a teaching position at the University of Santa Cruz, followed by stints at the New York Institute of Technology and University of California at Berkeley, before accepting a position as an associate professor at Stanford University in 1979. Along with six graduate students, Clark worked on three-dimensional graphics, developing what he called a Geometry Engine. He tried to sell the technology to such

357

---

companies as IBM and DEC but found no takers. Instead, Clark quit Stanford in 1981 and founded Silicon Graphics, Inc. (SGI) with his students. SGI quickly became a leader in workstation three-dimensional computer applications, which would find a multitude of uses, such as movie special effects. By 1995 SGI would be generating more than $2 billion in annual revenues, but Clark would have moved on by then.

Clark resigned as chairman of the SGI board in February 1994, frustrated by the board's resistance to his idea to apply the company's technology to interactive television and digital game players. Clark's plan after leaving SGI was to pursue interactive television, but he quickly dropped that idea after becoming convinced that the Internet was the next wave to catch. The Internet had been around for a number of years but required knowledge of arcane and unforgiving programming commands. Then the University of Illinois created Mosaic, the first graphical user interface for the World Wide Web, which would revolutionize the Internet. Clark contacted the lead programmer on the Mosaic project, 23-year-old Marc Andreessen, and they agreed to launch their own company to create an improved and more commercial Mosaic browser. The result was Netscape Communications, launched in April 1994. It was an immediate success.

Presenting the Idea for the Company to the Netscape Board in 1995

Even as Netscape was preparing to go public in August 1995, completing an offering that would make him the first Internet billionaire, Clark was developing his next big idea: finding a way to transform industries by way of Web communications. Having experienced the frustration of filling out medical forms and waiting in doctors' offices, and given the size of the healthcare industry, Clark decided to create an Internet-based system that would create a central depository for patients' medical and billing records and cut through all of the red tape that restricted the efficiency of the healthcare field. He presented the idea to the Netscape board in 1995. The company's CEO, Jim Barksdale, had the first right of refusal, and declined the opportunity. But board member John Doerr, who was a partner with the venture capital firm Klein Perkins Caufield & Byers was interested. He brought Clark together with a partner in his firm, David Schnell, who was also a Harvard-trained doctor and already interested in involving the Internet with healthcare. Together Clark and Schnell devoted four months to customer research, agreed on a mission for the company, and then Clark recruited an SGI engineer, Pavan Nigam, to head a technical team that included other SGI alumni. The company's original name was Healthscape, but that was scrapped because of another product using it and a desire to differentiate the venture from Netscape. In December 1995 the business was incorporated as Healtheon Corp.

With Clark putting up $16 million of his own money, and venture capital from Kleiner Perkins and New Enterprise Associates, Healtheon set up shop for four months in Kleiner Perkins's "incubation suite" of offices reserved for start-ups. Schnell served as the company's initial chief executive officer. The initial focus was on developing software that allowed employees to manage health benefits by way of the Internet, an outsourcing service that connected employers to HMOs and insurance companies. Unfortunately, the idea received a less than enthusiastic response from potential customers. According to a 2001 *Fortune* profile of the company, Clark's original vision was flawed, not taking into account a number of obstacles: "For one thing, most doctors don't like computers; local hospitals are filled with old mainframe and minicomputers that don't talk to one another, let alone to physicians' offices a mile away. Putting patients' medical records online also stirs panic over privacy and confidentiality issues. . . . And the health-care industry is one of the stingiest spenders on IT. What's more, says Clark, the system's wastefulness is entrenched." After a year, Healtheon was adrift, Schnell quit, and Doerr stepped up efforts to woo the man he wanted to take over as CEO: Michael Long, the head of Continuum, an Austin, Texas, IT consulting company.

Long took over as Healtheon's CEO in July 1997 and soon convinced Clark to lead the company in a new direction. Rather than trying to automate insurers, Long wanted to focus on automating physicians, developing software that would allow them to accomplish such online tasks as checking a patient's coverage or making a referral to a specialist. In October, Long signed his first significant contract, a $25 million project to bring Internet processing services to Brown & Toland, a collection of 1,250 San Francisco-area physicians. In February 1998 he completed a major acquisition, the $150 million purchase of ActaMed, a medical records clearinghouse for doctors and insurers. The addition of ActaMed brought with it actual customers and cash flow, important because Healtheon was preparing to make an initial public offering (IPO) of stock.

Healtheon's 1999 IPO

Healthon filed to go public in July 1998 but canceled the October offering. Press reports claimed the company's road show was a disaster. According to the *Wall Street Journal,* one source "said executives fumbled basic questions concerning their proposed business model." Delays in the Brown & Toland project were also leading to unwanted notoriety. Moreover, market conditions for IPOs suddenly turned volatile. Healtheon's executives regrouped for four months, refined their business plan, finalized marketing partnerships with heavy hitters IBM and AT&T, and then successfully completed the offering in February 1999. Investors now began to embrace the stock, bidding it up by 700 percent in a matter of ten weeks. Much of that excitement was due to an announcement that Healtheon planned to acquire Atlanta-based WebMD, a healthcare informational web site. Now Healtheon would become multidimensional, able to serve both consumers and the professional community. In the words of an analyst quoted by the *Wall Street Journal,* "WebMD is the front end and Healtheon is the back end of an integrated company."

WebMD's wonder kid founder, Jeffrey T. Arnold, shared some of the same traits as Healtheon's Clark. He was an indifferent student at the University of Georgia, where he studied communications before dropping out in 1993, only a few credits shy of graduation. While visiting his fiancée at a hospital where she worked he developed a concept for a business: a remote system that would allow cardiac patients to record any problems on a monitoring device, which could then create an electrocardiogram that could be transmitted to a computer and faxed to a doctor. Borrowing $25,000 from her father, the two launched Quality Diagnostic, grew it into a successful company and after two years sold it for $25 million. Arnold was just 26 years old. He used some of that money to launch his next business, a web site to offer free healthcare information to consumers and subscription services to doctors. He was less interested in developing technology than he was in signing up companies to provide medical information or services on his site, in this way securing content ahead of the competition. Another important decision was to employ the memorable WebMD name, paying $10,000 to a Web development company for the rights to it. After just a year, Arnold had lined up $720 million in long-term commitments from such companies as DuPont and CNN. During an Easter weekend vacation in 1999 Arnold and board member Boland Jones decided to cold call Microsoft and suggest a partnership. Within a matter of days, Microsoft was poised to invest $100 million in WebMD. Getting wind of the deal, Long cold called Arnold and set up a meeting to discuss a possible merger. Given how Microsoft had crushed Netscape in the Web browser field, Clark and Long wanted to avoid taking on Microsoft. Arnold was obligated to present the merger proposal to Microsoft and soon received their blessing on the deal.

When the Healtheon and WebMD $7 billion merger was consummated in November 1999 it included two smaller companies: Mede America and Greenberg News Networks. The resulting company became Healtheon/WebMD (the name would be shortened to WebMD Corporation less than a year later). Arnold became CEO and Long became COO and chairman of the board. The addition of Mede America, which operated an electronic processing system that handled some 350 million medical transactions a year, and Greenberg News, a daily news and information service for doctors, was just the first in a series of acquisitions and alliances that WebMD completed over the next several months in an effort to fill out the business. It acquired Medical Manager Corp., an established provider of management systems to physicians, and its subsidiary, Carelnsite, Inc., a provider of technology that allowed confidential information to be shared between patients, physicians, health plans, and other parties. WebMD paid $2.5 billion to

acquire Envoy, which added significantly to its electronic data interchange capabilities and customer base. WebMD also established a partnership with the CVS drugstore chain to sell products on the Web as well as connect its pharmacists to insurers, and a four-year $100 million partnership with Medtronic Inc. to provide healthcare information on the Internet and other media to consumers and physicians. In addition, WebMD forged alliances with Medibuy.com, an online medical equipment supplier; Humana, a managed care network that processed claims between doctors and insurers; pharmaceutical Eli Lilly to promote Prozac and other drugs; IDX Systems Corp., a healthcare information systems company; and media mogul Rupert Murdoch's News Corporation to take WebMD overseas.

WebMD was certainly getting larger, but it remained uncertain that scale provided the kind of benefit that the company's business model assumed. Regional companies chipped away while WebMD struggled to get a handle on its business and achieve profitability. In mid-2000 the company began to reorganize and cost-cutting measures were implemented. As part of this housecleaning effort Arnold was forced to share power with Martin Wygod, a veteran healthcare executive who came to WebMD as part of the Medical Manager deal. More serious changes in the top ranks of management would soon follow. Nigram retired as chief technology officer, expressing a desire to go into semi-retirement and spend more time with his family. A few days later Arnold resigned as co-CEO and relinquished his position as a board member. Clark also resigned from the board. Both would soon be caught up in new ventures.

WebMD wrote down the value of many of its acquisitions leading to massive losses. After trading at higher than $100 the company's stock plunged to $3 in late 2001. Revenues grew steadily, however, improving from $102.1 million in 1999 to $964 million in 2003. After losing more than $3 billion in 2000 and another $6.7 billion in 2001, WebMD finally became marginally profitable in 2003, with expectations of posting at least $150 million in profits in 2004. Long gone, however, was Clark's dream of creating an overarching web-based system or his original idea to use the Internet to make healthcare transactions more efficient. Instead, WebMD evolved into a company with related product lines and some successful, albeit not interconnected, Internet portals. On the positive side, the company had achieved some diversity and was positioned not only to take advantage of the government requirement that all records be digitized but of other trends in the healthcare field as well. Of some concern to investors was that WebMD's two largest business areas, claims transaction services and physicians, were not experiencing the kind of internal growth for which investors had hoped. According to one analyst quoted by *Business Week Online,* the company's management team was ''good at cutting costs and doing deals—but not at executing on an operating basis. . . . All the pieces are there. They just need capable people to put it together and make it work.'' Many investors believed that given time WebMD could live up to its potential, but in the words of *Business Week Online,* ''many of them won't jump into the stock until WebMD shows it's made good on its promises.''

Principal Subsidiaries

Envoy Corporation; Healtheon/WebMD Internet Corporation; WebMD, Inc.; WebMD Practice Services, Inc.

Principal Competitors

International Business Machines Corporation; McKesson Corporation; NDCHealth Corporation.

Further Reading

Anders, George, ''Resistant Strain: Healtheon Struggles in Efforts to Remedy Doctors' Paper Plague,'' *Wall Street Journal,* October 2, 1998, p. A1.

Carrns, Ann, ''Young Atlantan Makes Billions with MedMD,'' *Wall Street Journal,* May 21, 1999, p. B1.

Creswell, Julie, ''What the Heck Is Healtheon?,'' *Fortune,* February 21, 2000, p. 175.

Foust, Dean, ''Man in a Hurry,'' *Business Week,* July 24, 2000, p. EB64.

Hamm, Steve, ''Jim Clark Is Off and Running Again,'' *Business Week,* October 12, 1998, p. 64.

McHugh, Josh, ''Digital Medicine Men,'' *Forbes,* June 1, 1998, p. 146.

Prial, Dunstan, ''Healtheon Formula Equals Quick Success,'' *Wall Street Journal,* June 14, 1999, p. C18.

Ransdell, Eric, ''Silicon Valley's King Midas: Can the Founder of Netscape and Silicon Graphics Do It Again?,'' *U.S. News & World Report,* December 9, 1996, p. 69.

Setton, Dolly, ''Sick Days,'' *Forbes,* July 17, 2000, p. 56.

Tsao, Amy, ''WebMD's Achilles' Heel,'' *Business Week Online,* April 8, 2004.

—Ed Dinger

Williams Scotsman, Inc.

8211 Town Center Dr.
Baltimore, Maryland 21236
U.S.A.
Telephone: (410) 931-6000
Toll Free: (800) 782-1500
Fax: (410) 931-6047
Web site: http://www.willscot.com

Private Company
Incorporated: 1990
Employees: 1,150
Sales: $437.8 million (2003)
NAIC: 532420 Office Machinery and Equipment Rental and Leasing

Williams Scotsman, Inc. is one of the leading providers of mobile and modular office space, serving more than 24,000 customers through over 90 offices in the United States, Canada, and Mexico. The company leases a fleet of more than 94,000 units of mobile offices, portable classrooms, and storage products. Offices and classrooms are available in single-wide, double-wide, and custom sizes. The unique Redi-Space Solutions product line offers flexibility in both size and floor plan. Amenities to mobile structures include heating, air conditioning, plumbing, and high technology infrastructure. Williams Scotsman constructs, delivers, and installs modular buildings in single-story or multi-story configurations, an alternative to site-built structures when rapid construction is required. The company's storage products, including vans, trailers, and containers, are intended for onsite use, such as for retail overflow inventory during the Christmas shopping season. Specialty products include pole trailers and reel trailers, for hauling equipment, and enclosed fiber optic trailers, for situations where high technology equipment is used.

With more than 50 years in business, Williams Scotsman is known for providing quality products and excellent customer service. The company finds its customers in more than 400 industries, including hospitals, schools and universities, construction companies, government agencies, and small and large corporations.

Merger of Regional Companies, Intentions for National Expansion: 1990

Williams Scotsman formed in 1990, through the merger of Williams Mobile Offices/Modular Structures and Scotsman Manufacturing Co. From Baltimore, Maryland, and Gardena, California, respectively, the two companies combined their geographically disparate operations for the purpose of developing a national company. The two companies brought more than 40 years to their combined business.

Williams Mobile Offices, founded in 1944, originally sold construction trailers small enough to be towed by a car. Later, the company began to sell and lease mobile double-wide office structures. During the 1960s, the company expanded outside the Baltimore area for the first time with branch locations in Atlanta and Chicago. Leasing its signature, two-tone green mobile structures, Williams developed business operations along the East Coast and into the Midwest. During the 1980s Williams began to manufacture and install modular office structures. Though not less expensive than site-built offices, modular construction offered a rapid construction process, significantly reducing required construction time. Contrary to the stereotype, modular structures could be designed with aesthetic considerations in mind, such as the architecture in the surrounding community, with masonry, stucco, wood, and brick exteriors possible. Williams offered modular office structures in one-story design or multiple stories with complex architectural dimensions and such interior options as fine cherry wood paneling. Williams built a new company headquarters in Baltimore from modular structures in 1986.

Scotsman Manufacturing, founded in 1945, manufactured recreational vehicles for rental companies. The company began to lease mobile office structures in 1965, as manufacturers started offering larger structures with amenities, such as toilets and showers. Scotsman leased these structures to movie studios for dressing rooms. Eventually, the company entered the market for modular office structures.

At the time of the merger between Williams and Scotsman Manufacturing, Williams was the second largest supplier of mobile offices in the United States, with 15,000 rental units

361

leased through 17 offices in 13 Eastern states. Scotsman operated 11 offices in four Western states with a fleet of 7,500 rental units. The merger was recorded as an acquisition of Williams Mobile Offices from the Williams Family Trust by the Trijka Family Trust, which owned Scotsman Manufacturing. The new company, Williams Scotsman, continued to be family operated.

Williams Scotsman intended to develop a national network of mobile structure lessors. The new company inherited manufacturing facilities from its two predecessors, but decided to close them in order to concentrate on its leasing operations. The company grew slowly, with a focus on internal growth through fleet expansion; only three branch offices opened over the next few years. By 1993 Williams Scotsman owned a fleet of 25,000 mobile office and storage units leased through 31 offices in 18 states.

New Owners Providing Impetus for Rapid 1990s Expansion

Odyssey Partners, a private investment group, acquired Williams Scotsman for $234 million in 1993. The new owners, having the financial capability to develop Williams Scotsman rapidly on a national level, acquired 19 mobile office leasing companies between 1994 and 1997, adding 23,000 units to the fleet. In 1996 Williams Scotsman entered the market for storage products for onsite use, including vans, trailers, and ground level containers. Some customers used the containers for temporary storage during a building or renovation project; Wal-Mart and Kmart used the storage units to hold extra merchandise inventory during the Christmas season. By the end of 1997 Williams Scotsman generated $235 million in revenues through 73 branch offices in 38 states, leasing a fleet of 48,000 mobile offices; the company served more than 12,500 customers in 450 different industries.

Recapitalization of Williams Scotsman in 1997 weakened the company's financial position, however. That year the Cypress Group and Keystone, Inc., two private investment firms, acquired a 90 percent ownership in Williams Scotsman for $675 million. Senior managers acquired a minority stake, and Odyssey Partners also retained a minority stake. The Cypress Group and Keystone funded the acquisition with $400 million in senior notes and a $300 million revolving credit facility. This left Williams Scotsman with $112 million negative equity as of December 31, 1997, and encumbered the company with a high level of interest expense.

Opportunities for growth as a national company prompted Williams Scotsman to continue its acquisition strategy. In July 1998 the company announced an agreement to acquire SpaceMaster International, Inc, of Atlanta, for $273 million, including assumption of debt. SpaceMaster complemented Williams Scotsman's geographic base, with 26 branch offices in 13 states concentrated in the southeastern United States, operating a fleet of more than 12,800 lease units. The acquisition potentially added $325 million in revenues. Williams Scotsman funded the acquisition with bank debt and equity investment from the company's owners; the company refinanced the assumed debt.

A significant portion of SpaceMaster's fleet included portable classrooms, an important area of growth for Williams Scotsman, as the market for portable classrooms experienced significant growth during the 1990s. While schools had used portable classrooms since the early 1980s, their popularity as a low-cost alternative facilitated growth, whether used instead of permanent buildings or as temporary structures while permanent facilities were constructed. Schools felt pressured to build quickly as enrollment increased and then President Clinton's education initiative reduced classroom size. The move into portable classrooms was a natural fit for Williams Scotsman, and by 1999 the company owned a fleet of 12,000 rental units.

Internal growth and new acquisitions expanded Williams Scotsman's presence with facilities in new and existing markets. The company expanded outside the United States for the first time in late 1998, opening its first office in Canada, in Toronto, Ontario. In February 1999 the company acquired Evergreen Mobile Company of Seattle, the largest mobile office dealer in Washington, for $36.2 million. Evergreen owned a fleet of 2,000 portable classrooms and modular structures. The August 2000 acquisition of Truck and Trailer Sales (TNT) strengthened Williams Scotsman's regional operations in Missouri and southern Illinois. In addition to expanding its fleet of mobile offices and storage products, TNT added fiber optic trailers, pole trailers, and Wells Cargo reel trailers. Williams Scotsman combined its St. Louis office with the nearby TNT office. In February 2001 Williams Scotsman acquired McKinney Mobile Modular for $26 million, obtaining a fleet of 1,600 mobile units. Based in California, the sales and leasing company was notable for its strength in the modular classrooms market in the Pacific Northwest. Williams Scotsman expanded its storage product and mobile structures fleet through new factory purchases.

By the end of 2001 Williams Scotsman owned a fleet of 93,900 units, including mobile offices, portable classrooms, and storage products. The company operated 88 branch offices in the United States and Canada. The company generated revenue of $492.2 million and net income of $22.7 million. Approximately half of revenues originated with the company's leasing operations, at $238.2 million. Sales of new and used equipment accounted for $113.3 million, delivery and installation for $97.3 million, and parts, supplies, and other sources at $43.4 million. Educational institutions accounted for 21 percent of overall revenue. Williams Scotsman's equity position improved slightly.

2002–04: New Products and Services and International Development

Williams Scotsman began to offer value-added services to its customers. In response to customer inquiries, Williams

Scotsman offered customers a cellular technology security system for temporary or permanent structures through an exclusive agreement with Tattletale Portable Alarm Systems. The security system was of particular interest for construction companies seeking to protect machinery from theft. For its modular building customers, Williams Scotsman offered real-time viewing of project construction through a web-camera service. Inet OnSite allowed customers to inspect the construction process without having to travel to the site, saving time and money, especially if out-of-town. The service doubled as security surveillance.

With its national base of operations in a strong position, Williams Scotsman expanded its operations in Canada. In August 2002 the company acquired the storage products and mobile office fleet from Northgate Industries, Ltd., which served industrial markets in Edmonton, Alberta. Williams Scotsman paid $7 million for its fleet of 500 units. In June 2003 the company acquired the leasing operations of AFA Locations, Inc., of Montreal, for $3.2 million, involving 300 units.

Williams Scotsman introduced new products to enhance the company's ability to serve the education market in 2002. These included Type IV Classrooms which provided mobility with minimum impact at the location of use. Type VI Classrooms offered a low-cost option in refurbished units recommended for short-term lease, such as when renovation of a permanent structure required a temporary alternative. With Dell Computer Corporation, Williams Scotsman introduced CyberSpaces, modular classrooms customized with computer equipment. Customers chose from desktop or laptop computers, hardwired or wireless; hardware systems options included network servers and peripherals. Optional classroom amenities included appropriate furniture, a printer/scanner, a mobile wireless cart, and a SmartBoard, an electronic whiteboard that substituted for a conventional chalkboard. The new classroom structures were introduced at Williams Scotsman's Orlando branch office, as the State of Florida had passed a constitutional amendment that limited class-size. Along with new state funding for pre-kindergarten classes for four-year olds, Williams Scotsman expected significant immediate demand for portable classrooms in Florida.

Already the largest provider of mobile classrooms in California, Williams Scotsman acquired the California "Division of State Architects" (DSA) classroom units from GE Modular Space in March 2004. The acquisition involved 3,800 single and double-wide units, with 95 percent already under lease by K-12 public schools throughout the state. Williams Scotsman paid $43 million for the fleet and expected to earn $10 million in annual revenue with an average lease rate of $235 per month, slightly lower than the company's average of $249 per month at the time of the acquisition.

In 2004 the company launched its innovative new product line, Redi-Space Solutions, described as "the fastest, most flexible and durable family of relocatable buildings available." The three components of the product included the Redi-Plex Building, a columnless module that could be used singly or placed in a group to create a larger structure. Vinyl-covered Redi-Wall Systems provided quick adjustment to whatever floor plan a customer required. The third component, Redi-Access Systems, added ramps and steps. Williams Scotsman designed the system for situations when a building is needed in a hurry, but promoted it to all of its customer markets. The company projected that the product would change its industry's approach to mobile and modular space design.

Williams Scotsman announced international expansion with new operations in Europe and Mexico in August 2004. The company formed Williams Scotsman Europe, S.L. to acquire a minor interest in privately held Wiron Prefabricados Modulares, S.A., in Parla, Spain, near Madrid. Wiron owned several thousand modular units that the company leased through offices in all major cities in Spain. Williams Scotsman gained a seat on the board of directors, to begin learning about the company and operations in Spain, and obtained the right of first refusal for the sale of any additional shares of Wiron stock. In Mexico Williams Scotsman opened its main office in Mexico City and located a branch office in Monterey. The company accessed national distribution opportunities through an agreement with SaniRest, a major waste disposal company with 27 offices in Mexico.

Principal Subsidiaries

Evergreen Mobile Company; Space Master International, Inc.; Truck and Trailer Sales, Inc.; Williams Scotsman Europe, S.L.; Williams Scotsman of Canada, Inc.; Willscot Equipment, LLC.

Principal Competitors

GE Capital Modular Space; McGrath RentCorp; Mobile Mini, Inc.; Modtech Holdings Inc.; Transport International Pool, Inc.

Further Reading

"Baltimore-Based Williams Scotsman Inc. Provides Every Kind of Mobile Office Space," *Daily Record (Baltimore, MD)*, February 22, 2002.

"California Company Acquires Williams Mobile Offices," *Washington Post*, January 8, 1990, p. F11.

"Dell and Williams Scotsman Outfit Mobile Classrooms," *Electronic Education Report*, August 2, 2002.

Henry, Tamara, "With Portable Pride, Pupils Celebrate Separation," *USA Today*, June 2, 1999, p. 5D.

Janecke, Ron, "Permanent Market, Temporary Walls," *St. Louis Business Journal*, September 14, 2001, p. 15.

''Odyssey Partners to Acquire Scotsman Group,'' *New York Times,* December 2, 1993, p. D5.

''Williams Scotsman Acquires GE Modular Space's Fleet of Single-Wide and Double-Wide California DSA Classrooms,'' *Canada News Wire,* March 26, 2004.

''Williams Scotsman Buys Northgate Industries,'' *Daily Record (Baltimore, MD),* August 2, 2002.

''Williams Scotsman Sale Set for $675 Million,'' *New York Times,* April 15, 1997, p. D4.

—Mary Tradii

Wisconsin Alumni Research Foundation

Wisconsin Alumni Research Foundation

614 Walnut Street, 13th Floor
Madison, Wisconsin 53726
U.S.A.
Telephone: (608) 263-2500
Fax: (608) 263-1064
Web site: http://www.warf.ws

Nonprofit Company
Incorporated: 1925
Employees: 50
Sales: $38.7 million (2003)
NAIC: 541710 Research and Development in the
Physical, Engineering and Life Sciences; 541720
Research and Development in the Social Sciences and
Humanities; 541690 Other Scientific and Technical
Consulting Services

Wisconsin Alumni Research Foundation, known as WARF, is a nonprofit foundation that patents discoveries made by researchers at the University of Wisconsin. WARF was the first such intellectual property organization in the United States, and it became a model for foundations at other leading research universities. WARF is a separate legal entity from the University of Wisconsin, though it stands on the university campus. It files patents for university researchers, licenses its patented products and processes, and then uses these funds to make grants to the university and to invest in start-up companies. WARF was founded with a small endowment from university alumni, and based its early fortunes principally on its first patent, for the production of vitamin D. By the early 2000s, WARF's endowment had grown to some $1.3 billion. It returned about $40 million annually to the University of Wisconsin.

A New Way to Fund Research in the 1920s

The Wisconsin Alumni Research Foundation began with a discovery made by biochemist Harry Steenbock in 1923. Dr. Steenbock was working on the enormous public health problem of the bone-softening disease rickets. Rickets affected a huge proportion of children—up to 50 percent—in the United States, causing skeletal malformations. Vitamin D had recently been discovered by one of Steenbock's colleagues, and this substance was known to prevent rickets. Sunlight also was known to prevent rickets, but scientists did not yet understand how this worked. Steenbock discovered that exposing rat food to sunlight or ultraviolet light synthesized vitamin D in the grain. Rats fed this irradiated food did not develop rickets.

Steenbock was sure he had discovered something vastly important, and he worried about the best way to get his idea from the laboratory to the public. He did not want to patent the vitamin D process himself, both because of the initial expense and because he believed that the University of Wisconsin should have the rights to what its faculty invented. Yet the university had already turned down an earlier offer from Dr. Steenbock to handle his patent on the isolation of vitamin A. Although the University of Wisconsin was at that time the leading American university in the number of doctorates in the sciences it awarded, the school was having trouble resolving how its researchers could be funded. In 1925, the University of Wisconsin accepted a private donation of $12,500 that came from John D. Rockefeller and the Republican Party. This gift ignited a long-brewing fight about private gifts to the school, and in August of that year, the university's governing board of regents resolved that it would no longer accept gifts from corporations or similar bodies. The intent was to free researchers from any taint that they could be bought by corporate or political interests. Yet the resolution also kept the university's regents from considering lucrative propositions in their own back yard, so to speak. Steenbock's vitamin D process was clearly valuable. He was unable to interest his own university in taking out a patent on it, yet the Quaker Oats Company was ready to pay him $900,000 for exclusive rights to it.

Finally Dr. Steenbock met with Charles Schlichter, dean of the university's graduate school. Schlichter was appalled that no one at the university had shown any interest in Steenbock's patent. Schlichter immediately went to New York and Chicago to contact some university alumni. He raised $10,000 from Wisconsin alumni, with the goal of setting up a private foundation. The foundation was to be entirely distinct from the University of Wisconsin. It would take out the vitamin D patent on Dr. Steenbock's behalf, and use royalties from the patent to fund further research. Schlichter next met with eight prominent men, including a leading Chicago patent attorney, a local judge, and the head of the University of Wisconsin alumni association. It turned out that Schlichter had not raised quite enough money to handle Steenbock's patent, and he asked the men gathered at his fishing shack to each contribute $100. With the money Schlichter had already raised and this additional $900, the group chartered the Wisconsin Alumni Research Foundation in November 1925.

Steenbock signed over his rights to the vitamin D process for a nominal fee of $10. WARF then licensed the process to the Quaker Oats Company, which had been trying for years to get the rights. Several pharmaceutical companies also bought rights to the process from WARF, and they made vitamin D concentrate available to consumers for the first time. Then WARF licensed the process to dairy producers. Milk was an ideal carrier for vitamin D, which is soluble in fat. Over the next decade, milk enriched with vitamin D became widely available, and rickets began to disappear. By 1945, when Steenbock's patent expired, it had brought WARF some $8 million in net royalties.

Managing the Foundation Through the Depression and World War II

WARF was initially run by a group of trustees. In 1929, the organization had grown to the point where it needed a full-time manager. The dean of the university's school of natural sciences, H.L. Russell, resigned that position in 1929 to take over WARF. He oversaw the foundation until his retirement in 1939. At first, WARF ran out of a small office in the basement of a university building. In 1930, WARF also established a testing laboratory, where it conducted quality control tests, principally on irradiated foods.

The U.S. economy had boomed through the 1920s, and hit a wall with the stock market crash of October 1929. The University of Wisconsin, supported primarily through state funds, was hit hard by the Great Depression. In 1932, the state legislature cut the university's research budget in half. The university was faced with the prospect of laying off even senior faculty, and junior faculty and graduate students had little hope of seeing fellowship money. Then WARF, still flush with money from

licensing Steenbock's patent, stepped in. WARF had given the university some money annually, beginning in 1928. In 1931, WARF donated some $18,000, as grants for ten different projects. In 1933, with the university desperate for funds, WARF donated more than $147,000. The money went to research fellowships for students and faculty. Although most of the WARF funds went to faculty in the sciences, it also began funding scholars in the humanities and social sciences. With generous backing from WARF, the University of Wisconsin remained one of the leading U.S. universities in the sciences throughout the years of the Depression.

World War II also put a strain on the university. WARF increased the amount of money it donated to the university year by year through the 1930s and 1940s. It also put special funds to use in researching war materials. With gasoline and rubber rationed because of the war, WARF invested in research on artificial gasoline and artificial rubber. WARF also funded researchers at the university who developed high-yielding strains of penicillin. Immediately after the war, the university burgeoned, as former soldiers returned to school. In 1951, WARF made a special grant of $2.8 million to the university, which went to build badly needed new housing.

WARF brought in millions from Dr. Steenbock's work on vitamin D. It took out many other patents on behalf of other faculty. WARF's initial arrangement was to split the net royalties of a patent with its inventor 85–15, with the inventor getting the smaller cut. WARF took out about 60 patents a year, though only a very few of these yielded marketable products. Aside from Steenbock's vitamin D patents, WARF had claim to one other set of extraordinarily valuable patents. These were for the work in the 1930s and 1940s of Dr. Karl Paul Link, who invented the blood anticoagulants dicumarol and warfarin. Link investigated the strange phenomenon of dairy cows that hemorrhaged to death after eating spoiled clover hay. Link isolated the factor that made the cows ill, publishing his first paper on the subject in 1941. Link discovered that the factor in the spoiled hay, which he named dicumarol, could be used to keep blood from clotting, and this became a widely used drug. Later in the 1940s, Link thought of developing a variant of dicumarol that could be used to poison rats and mice. WARF provided the funds for his research, and Link named his new poison for the foundation: warfarin. Warfarin was widely used around the world as a rodenticide as well as to treat some medical conditions in humans. Warfarin was patented in 1950 and was a large source of royalties for WARF.

Quieter Times: 1970s–80s

Although Steenbock's initial patents expired in 1945, WARF continued to bring in royalties for other work related to vitamin D. WARF supported Steenbock's student Hector DeLuca in the 1960s and 1970s. The work of DeLuca and others meant that WARF still derived 70 percent of its patent income from vitamin D-related work as late as the 2000s. In 1969, WARF began building itself a huge new building on the University of Wisconsin campus. WARF took only the top two floors of the distinctive triangular high-rise for itself, and leased the rest to the university as office and laboratory space. WARF funded more than a thousand projects at the University of Wisconsin (including both the Madison and Milwaukee campuses)

Key Dates:

1925: Wisconsin Alumni Research Foundation (WARF) is formed.
1929: The first full-time director is hired.
1933: WARF quadruples its grant to the University of Wisconsin.
1951: WARF makes a major grant to the university to build new housing.
1972: The IRS challenges WARF's nonprofit status.
1983: WARF alters the formula for splitting royalties with inventors.
1993: An equity stake in the company is taken for the first time in lieu of a licensing fee.
2000: Wisys and Wicell subsidiaries are formed.

in 1969, and its total grants to the university topped $3 million. The foundation paid for named professorships for top faculty, for grants to promising junior faculty, for laboratories, and for other special projects. According to an article in the *Wisconsin (Madison) State Journal* (November 9, 1971), many university faculty thought that WARF's money was absolutely essential to maintaining Wisconsin's eminence in the sciences: "The income from these funds, they say, makes the difference between greatness and mediocrity."

WARF began to run into some difficulties in the early 1970s, however. Most of WARF's grants had gone to the main Madison campus of the university, with about 20 percent earmarked for the Milwaukee campus since the late 1960s. But the University of Wisconsin unified into a larger state college system in 1971, sparking fears that WARF's money might have to be spread among the smaller, far-flung campuses as well. Then in 1972, the Internal Revenue Service (IRS) challenged WARF's nonprofit status. The IRS claimed that WARF should not be exempt from taxes because it was in fact a for-profit organization. WARF contested this, and won back its tax-exempt standing, but only after it sold off its development laboratories. According to *Forbes* magazine (May 24, 2004), the brouhaha with the IRS changed WARF from an entrepreneurial institution to a much more cautious one. According to *Forbes,* "For the next 20 years, WARF was run like a stuffy investment portfolio." The foundation revealed in 1976 that it had assets of more than $1 million. By that year, WARF had 42 patents that had become profitable. Of these, three had earned more than $1 million, and 23 had earned from $10,000 to $1 million, leaving almost half its patents earning less than $10,000. WARF's goal in the mid-1970s was said to be satisfying intellectual curiosity, rather than looking for short-term gain in marketable ideas.

WARF continued to give large grants to the University of Wisconsin annually. By the mid-1980s, it was giving out about $8 million. In 1983, WARF changed the formula that it used to divide royalties with inventors. WARF added an initial payment of $1,000 for a patentable idea, and set aside 20 percent of gross income from the invention for the inventor. WARF also allotted 15 percent of gross income for a patent for the inventor's graduate school. But the foundation was making money off only a small percentage of its patents. By 1983, WARF claimed only

76 patents that had made any money at all, and it derived 90 percent of its income from just ten patents. Total income from patents was about $30 million in the mid-1980s.

WARF was one of the largest patent-driven foundations in the country in the early 1990s, in fourth place behind the University of California, Stanford University, and Columbia University. Nevertheless, patent income had fallen sharply, from some $30 million in 1986 to $15.8 million in 1993. That year WARF recruited a new director, a former pharmaceutical company executive, Richard Leazer.

Entrepreneurial Spirit in the 1990s and 2000s

Leazer began to move WARF into a more aggressive stance. The foundation, still maintaining its nonprofit status, began taking an equity stake in young companies working to commercialize WARF patents. WARF also upped the pace at which it issued licenses for patents. When Leazer became managing director in 1993, WARF issued only 21 licenses. Over the 1996–97 academic year, that number increased to 61, and two years later WARF issued 92 licenses.

WARF had asked for large fees from companies wishing to license its patented technology. In 1993, WARF came to what was then a unique agreement with a genetic testing company cofounded by a University of Wisconsin chemistry professor. The company's principals told WARF they could not afford the licensing fee, but they were nevertheless sure they could make money on their genetic diagnostics. According to the *Milwaukee Journal* (June 14, 2003), they told WARF, "We want you to trust us." WARF took an equity stake in the company, Third Wave Technologies, which ten years later had gone public on NASDAQ and expected sales of around $39 million.

Leazer retired in 1999, and was succeeded by WARF's former director of patents and licensing, Carl Gulbrandsen. Gulbrandsen continued in the direction Leazer had mapped out. Three years into his tenure as managing director, WARF had equity stakes in almost 30 start-up companies, which were developing everything from cancer treatment devices to pharmaceuticals to plant-based sweeteners to nanotechnology. WARF also formed two new subsidiaries in the early 2000s. WARF had worked almost exclusively with researchers from the University of Wisconsin's main Madison campus. In 2000, WARF formed a subsidiary called WiSys Technology Foundation, which sought out patents and provided patent licensing for inventions discovered at other University of Wisconsin campuses. The next year, the WiSys subsidiary entered an agreement with a consortium of Milwaukee-area colleges to promote technological development in the broader southeastern Wisconsin region. Then in 2002, WARF opened its first satellite office. The foundation hoped to take advantage of the concentration of new technology companies on the West Coast by opening an office in San Diego, California. This was in line with WARF's push in the 2000s to commercialize its patents more quickly. WARF had an enormous number of patents, owning rights to some 1,700 inventions by 2003.

WARF opened another subsidiary in the 2000s, the Wicell Research Institute. This was a private, nonprofit institute that researched embryonic stem cells. University of Wisconsin professor James Thomson was at the forefront of this research, working with cells derived from human embryos that could then transform into various kinds of tissue. Thomson was the first to isolate these so-called master cells in 1998. Stem cell research held out hope for sufferers of various diseases, including Parkinson's disease and diabetes, but it was also controversial. Federal regulations restricted research on cells derived from human embryos or fetuses. WARF set up Thomson's lab as a private foundation in 2000, and it began licensing one of its stem cell lines to other laboratories. Thomson became a noted figure in the national debate over embryonic vs. adult stem cell research. WARF controlled his patents, not only to the cell lines he had derived, but also for the methods used in the laboratory to grow the cells. In 2001, President George W. Bush declared that federal money could be used to support embryonic stem cell research, as long as it was restricted to certain already existing cell lines. Five of these existing lines were WARF's. WARF hoped to distribute the technology widely, to encourage the quickest and best applications of stem cell technology to medical problems. It sued Geron Corp., a California company that also had funded Thomson and claimed rights to some of his inventions, in 2001. The suit was settled in 2002, with Geron taking exclusive rights to half of Thomson's cell lines. On settling the suit, WARF hoped to lay the legal issues to rest so that it could proceed with licensing this new medical research, though the ethical issues would still remain.

By the mid-2000s, WARF ranked as one of the top earners from university-based patents. It signed more than 150 patent licensing agreements in 2002, and estimated that during 2003, more than $1 billion worth of products based on its patents were sold around the world. It still derived a large proportion of its income from vitamin D research, as several new drugs were under development based on patents held by WARF for Dr. Steenbock's student Hector DeLuca. But WARF had also moved in many new directions in the past ten years, taking stakes in a cadre of small young companies. Since its inception, WARF had contributed some $650 million to the University of Wisconsin, and it continued to help the university uphold its reputation as a leader in the sciences. In the mid-2000s WARF earmarked $80 million for a building grant to the university, contributing to the construction of four new biochemistry buildings. WARF's en-

dowment had grown to $1.3 billion by 2004, and its research grant to the university reached about $40 million annually.

Principal Subsidiaries

Wicell Research Institute; Wisys Technology Foundation.

Principal Competitors

Columbia University; University of California; Stanford University.

Further Reading

Behnke, Clifford C., "Merger Stirs Fears Over Split of UW's WARF, Trust Funds," *Wisconsin State Journal,* November 9, 1971, pp. 1–2.

Fred, E.B., *The Role of the Wisconsin Alumni Research Foundation in the Support of Research at the University of Wisconsin,* Madison: Wisconsin Alumni Research Foundation, 1973.

Gertzen, Jason, "The Mother of Inventions," *Milwaukee Journal,* June 14, 2003.

"Group Benefits Researchers," *Wisconsin State Journal,* February 28, 1986, p. 6.

Johnson, Paul, "Patents, Licensing Lucrative for WARF," *Wisconsin State Journal,* January 26, 1995, p. 1F.

Jordan, William R., ed., *WARF: Fifty Years,* Madison: Wisconsin Alumni Research Foundation, 1976.

Matheson, Helen, "WARF and the UW: 50 Years of Support," *Wisconsin State Journal,* January 18, 1976, pp. 1, 5.

McDade, Phil, "A Key Patent Expires and WARF Loses Millions in Income," *Wisconsin State Journal,* January 27, 1996, p. 1B.

Tatge, Mark, "Miracle in the Midwest," *Forbes,* May 24, 2004, pp. 120–28.

Trewyn, Phill, "TechStar Enters Partnership with UW's Tech Licensing Arm," *Business Journal-Milwaukee,* November 30, 2001, p. 4.

Vogel, Gretchen, "Wisconsin to Distribute Embryonic Cell Lines," *Science,* February 11, 2000, p. 948.

"WARF and Geron Settle Suit," *Technology Access Report,* January 2002, p. 1.

"WARF's Role Grows Stronger," *Wisconsin State Journal,* May 30, 2000, p. 9A.

—A. Woodward

Workflow Management, Inc.

240 Royal Palm Way
Palm Beach, Florida 33480
U.S.A.
Telephone: (561) 659-6551
Fax: (561) 659-7793
Web site: http://www.workflowmanagement.com

Private Company
Incorporated: 1998
Employees: 2,800
Sales: $622.72 million (2003)
NAIC: 323119 Other Commercial Printing

Workflow Management, Inc. tries to simplify its clients' business operations by taking care of all of their print and office supply needs. The company's goal is to help clients cut costs by reducing storage and distribution inefficiencies, rather than by just offering the lowest bid for a print job. Workflow can produce printed materials such as envelopes, invoices, annual reports, and direct mail pieces at one of its dozen manufacturing facilities, or it can act as a print distributor and send out jobs through its network. Once the materials are printed, they can be stored at one of Workflow's warehousing facilities in order to cut down on the client's storage requirements. Workflow's online ordering system, iGetSmart, allows clients to view reports on past deliveries and product consumption and uses a prearranged profile to help them order the right products and stay within budget. While online, clients can also order general office supplies or process an urgent print job using the print-on-demand feature. Workflow rounds out its range of services by offering workflow consulting and document design. The company's clients range from small businesses to corporate giants such as Wells Fargo, Kraft Foods, and Chase Manhattan Bank. Workflow was incorporated in 1998, but it has its roots in a small Virginia printer that merged with a New York firm in 1988 and grew rapidly throughout the 1990s by acquiring dozens of smaller print distributors.

Standard Forms, A Small Print Distributor: 1927–88

Workflow's history can be traced back to a regional print distributor known as Standard Forms. For about six decades,

Standard Forms operated as a small but successful print distributor in Norfolk, Virginia. The company was originally established as Standard Salesbook Company in downtown Norfolk in 1927. The founder, S.S. Bohannan, already owned a printing plant in nearby Newport News as well as a plant in Sturgis, Michigan, both operating under the name Sturgis Newport Business Forms. Bohannan founded Standard Salesbook to act as a sales division for the manufacturing facilities. But Standard Salesbook did more than just direct business to Bohannan's plants; it operated as a general print distributor, brokering out print jobs to outside facilities. Salesbooks sold well, but eventually Standard Salesbook changed its name to Standard Forms to indicate that it could also produce other types of business forms. For the next few decades, Standard Forms operated successfully as a sales intermediary for print jobs.

In the 1970s Standard Forms bought its own printing equipment and set up a manufacturing facility at a new headquarters in east Norfolk. Sales and executive offices moved to this site as well. For the first time, Standard Forms could process jobs internally. Nevertheless, the company continued to send some jobs to outside printers since its own print capacity was limited. At the time the new headquarters was built, Standard Forms had about 30 sales representatives and had opened a few branch offices on the East Coast. By the mid-1980s the company had opened branches in New York City, Boston, Philadelphia, Milwaukee, Portsmouth (Virginia), Richmond (Virginia), and in New Jersey. All of the offices operated under the name "Standard Forms" except for the Milwaukee office, which was known as "Accurate Business Forms."

Merger and Rapid Growth: 1988–95

In 1988 a merger with a New York firm set Standard Forms on the course that would transform it into an industry leader. The merger came about when Tom Cunningham, the president of Standard Forms in the 1980s, became acquainted with Thomas D'Agostino, who owned a paper and office supply distributor in New York City known as Forms and Peripherals. In 1986 D'Agostino had gone through a difficult year: his friend and business partner Robert Clemente died and he lost his largest account. In a casual meeting with Cunningham, D'Agostino expressed interest in taking a closer look at Standard Forms. The business appeared sound, so in 1988 he acquired majority control of the company and merged Forms and Peripherals into Standard Forms Inc., or SFI. At the time, Standard Forms had annual sales of about $17 million; the merger brought that figure to $23 million. The employee owners of Standard Forms approved the transaction unanimously, anticipating that it would give them a better presence in New York.

From the beginning, D'Agostino and Cunningham planned to develop the firm with an aggressive acquisition strategy. They chose this approach over internal growth because they found it difficult to hire new sales representatives—many of them had signed noncompete contracts with previous employers. A better strategy was to purchase an entire small office. Accordingly, SFI put out the word through trade journals and word-of-mouth that it was looking to buy, and by 1994 the company had acquired 14 separate firms. Most of them were small businesses along the East Coast with sales of $2 million to $3 million. Generally, SFI would provide a small down payment upfront and then pay off the remaining purchase price over the years with a dedicated percentage of revenue. The firm would be fully integrated as a branch office of SFI, with the former owner of the business often continuing to manage the branch. One particularly notable acquisition was the purchase of the print manufacturer Hano Business Forms in early 1993. Hano was a major manufacturer with plants in Springfield, Massachusetts; St. Louis, Missouri; and Conyers, Georgia. This purchase turned SFI into a true manufacturer and allowed it to fulfill a larger number of its contracts internally.

While the economy as a whole was suffering in the early 1990s, SFI was expanding and enhancing its services. In addition to the acquisition activity, SFI began implementing a technological development program early that decade. The company spent $3.5 million over two years for new hardware equipment and a custom-designed software package that was more in-depth than off-the-shelf products. The result was a computer system that allowed customers to order online and track inventory electronically. Clients could call up reports showing purchasing activity over the past several years, making it possible to tailor orders to annual fluctuations in usage of office supplies and printed goods. This system was operating by the end of 1993 after an early programming mistake that delayed the launch of the new system and cost SFI $500,000. Other service enhancements that were introduced during this time included "just-in-time" printing that saved clients from having to store large inventories and a pricing program that wrote a baseline price into the contract and gave the client a quarterly overview of any errors, late deliveries, and changes in purchase amounts. SFI also added new product lines such as general office supplies, janitorial supplies, and promo-

tional products so that the client could receive a single invoice for most consumable office items. The service enhancements of the early 1990s were part of an industrywide evolution from basic print distribution to the more service-oriented "forms management."

In 1995 SFI acquired three Atlanta-area firms: the printer Indelible Inc. and the forms management companies Creative Business Systems and Data Formation/Prime Source Group. This purchase gave SFI a total of 17 branch offices along the East Coast and a half dozen distribution centers. Sales had grown from $45 million in 1993 with 120 employees to $309.4 million in 1995 with 275 employees. The firm decided it was time to pursue a public listing. A registration statement was drawn up and underwriters were selected—but at the last minute, U.S. Office Products Co., a fast-growing Washington-based company, approached SFI about a possible acquisition. The initial public offering (IPO) was postponed and in January 1997 U.S. Office Products bought SFI for about $65 million in stock.

Creation and Expansion of Workflow Management: 1998–2002

Only a year later, however, U.S. Office Products carried out a restructuring to divest itself of peripheral operations. The Print Management Division—formerly SFI—was spun off in June 1998 into Workflow Management, Inc., a new corporation based in Palm Springs, Florida. The company began trading on NASDAQ under the symbol WORK. Thomas D'Agostino was chairman and CEO of Workflow and his son Thomas, Jr., was president of the SFI subsidiary. They planned to continue expanding on the same pattern as SFI, buying small printing companies and integrating them as branch offices. Later that same year Workflow bought Penn-Grover Envelope Corporation, a Long Island-based printer of envelopes and direct-mail products. The company was expected to contribute annual revenues of around $15 million. In November Workflow also purchased the New York company Direct Pro LLC for $7 million.

Workflow started 1999 with another string of acquisitions. In February, March, and April the company spent more than $50 million for six firms collectively expected to generate annual revenues of about $90 million. The companies were Pacific Admail of California, a producer of direct mail materials; Freedom Graphics Services, a New Jersey print distributor; Premier Graphics of Columbia, South Carolina, a maker of high-end labeling material; the commercial printer Sundog Printing Limited of Alberta, Canada; Universal Folding Box Co., Inc. of New Jersey, a maker of printed packaging; and the New York City-based Superior Graphics, Inc. These companies brought in clients including Caterpillar, Coca-Cola, and Microsoft. A few months later Workflow made its largest single acquisition yet, paying $14 million for Graphic Management Corp. of Green Bay, Wisconsin, a print distributor with sales of around $30 million. This company's clients included Kraft Foods and Kay-Bee Toys (which would cause trouble for Workflow a few years later). In October Workflow paid $8.9 million for two Anaheim, California-based printers, Sundance Litho, Inc. and Irvine Commercial Printers. The company also made a few other small acquisitions that year and sold its print manufacturer Hano because of declining sales. By the end of the year, Workflow was the largest print distributor on the East Coast.

Key Dates:

1927: Standard Salesbook is founded in Norfolk as a print distributor.

1970s: Now known as Standard Forms, the company buys its own printing equipment and builds a new headquarters.

1988: Standard Forms merges with Forms and Peripherals of New York and begins seeking acquisitions.

1995: Standard Forms has acquired 17 small print distributors and is considering an IPO.

1997: U.S. Office Products buys Standard Forms.

1998: U.S. Office Products spins off Standard Forms into Workflow Management, Inc.

2002: After making well over a dozen new acquisitions, Workflow switches its focus to internal integration.

2004: Workflow goes private in a deal arranged by two private equity firms.

In mid-1999 Workflow created iGetSmart.com as a separate business unit for its online ordering system iGetSmart. The company was planning a public offering for this unit, and anticipation of the IPO pushed Workflow's share price to three times its usual trading level in late 1999. But the subsequent bear market for technology stocks led Workflow to cancel the offering and create iGetSmart.com, Inc. as an independent subsidiary in 2000. Tom D'Agostino, Jr., became CEO of iGetSmart.com and Roger Kimps, former president of Graphic Management Corp., replaced D'Agostino as CEO of SFI. The new subsidiary was preparing to make Workflow's internal e-commerce system available to other print distributors through licensing agreements. For example, in late 1999 the large international printer Quebecor Printing of Montreal signed an agreement to use iGetSmart for its own customers, and in early 2000 American Identity, a Missouri-based distributor of promotional products with more than 20,000 corporate accounts, bought a license for iGetSmart.

Acquisitions also continued through 2000 and into 2001. In early 2000 Workflow bought ALF Graphics, Inc., a print distributor in New York City with $8 million in annual sales. In March Workflow made its largest acquisition ever when it bought Office Electronics, Inc. of Chicago, a $55 million company. Workflow sold the company's print manufacturing facilities and retained the sales force only, thereby nearly recovering the total cost of the acquisition. Office Electronics greatly expanded Workflow's presence in the Midwest, with sales offices in Des Moines, Minneapolis, Cincinnati, and Milwaukee. The company also had offices in Houston, Dallas, and Nashville, which were new locations for Workflow, as well as offices in several other major cities. In late 2000 Workflow purchased two companies that outsourced promotional products and advertising specialties: For Magic Results, Inc. (dba A-lad-in Advertising Company), located in Great Neck, New York, and Inform Graphics of Beaverton, Oregon. The acquisitions of the last few years brought Workflow's annual sales to $547.1 million in 2000 with a net income of $23.15 million.

Workflow's purchases in 2001 included Webtrend Direct, Inc. and Webtrend Graphics, Inc., two direct-mail and commercial printers based in southern California. In July the subsidiary iGetSmart.com bought Document Options.company of Nashville. This company offered workflow consulting and print outsourcing and like iGetSmart.com was focused on reducing hidden costs for customers. In April Robert "Rick" Wesley became president of the SFI subsidiary, replacing Roger Kimps who was returning to his home state of Wisconsin. Wesley had joined SFI as a mergers and acquisitions consultant in 1992 and subsequently played a large role in promoting iGetSmart.com.

Focusing on Integration: 2002–04

In 2002 Workflow's acquisition spree came to an end as the company shifted its focus to integration of its many branches. Annual sales that year were $619 million, but net profit was only $9.2 million. After a difficult year, longtime CEO Thomas D'Agostino, Sr., stepped down in early 2003; he was eventually replaced by Gary Ampulski, former president of the document and forms companies TAB Products Company and Moore North America. Board member Gerald F. Mahoney replaced D'Agostino as chairman, and Thomas D'Agostino, Jr., was terminated as a division president. The new management faced a growing debt problem. Loans totaling $50 million were due in 2003.

Meanwhile, the SFI subsidiary adopted a new image in 2003, changing its name to "Workflow" with the motto "consult create connect." The company launched a "Business Revolution" marketing campaign emphasizing its ability to improve business processes, cut costs, and connect companies with products from a variety of manufacturers.

A net loss of $39.9 million for fiscal 2003 exacerbated Workflow's financial problems. Contributing to the company's difficulties was the fact that its client KB Toys Inc., which owed Workflow $5 million, was going through bankruptcy proceedings. Leadership at Workflow was divided over whether to seek refinancing or accept an offer to go private. In the course of the conflict, CEO Gary Ampulski was terminated after less than a year at Workflow. He claimed that the board was neglecting shareholder interests by rushing into a private buyout proposed by the private equity firms Perseus LLC and Renaissance Group. One of Workflow's major shareholders, Pacific Coast Investment Partners, also opposed the merger and proposed several alternate recapitalization plans. Nevertheless, in April 2004 Workflow succeeded in gaining 70 percent shareholder approval for a merger into WF Holdings Inc., a private company created by Perseus and Renaissance for the purpose of the deal. The equity firms had boosted their per-share payment twice in order to gain approval. The new CEO of Workflow was Greg Mosher of Renaissance Group. Mosher said he looked forward to guiding the company into a new era based on its existing customer base and services.

Principal Subsidiaries

DirectPro LLC; Freedom Graphic Services, Inc.; iGetSmart.com, Inc.; Premier Graphics Inc.; SFI of Delaware, LLC; United Envelope, LLC; Workflow Direct, Inc.; Workflow Management Acquisition II Corp.; Data Business Forms Limited (Canada).

Principal Divisions

Fulfillment Division; Integrated Business Service Division; iGetSmart.com Division.

Principal Competitors

Moore Wallace Inc.; Standard Register Co.; Relizon Company; Mail-Well, Inc.; MeadWestvaco Corporation; Atlantic Envelope Co.; Xerox Corporation; Consolidated Graphics, Inc.

Further Reading

Clifton, Alexandra Navarro, "Workflow Holders OK Sales," *Palm Beach Post,* April 10, 2004, p. 10C.

DeWitt, Maggie, "Workflow Gears Up for a Business Revolution," *Business Forms, Labels & Systems,* January 2004.

"Ex Mail-Well Exec to Head Workflow Management," *Printing Impressions,* March 2003, p. 5.

Fakler, John T., "Workflow Beats Earnings Expectations, Signs NYC Contract," *South Florida Business Journal,* January 5, 2001, p. 16.

Londner, Robin, "Workflow, Ex-CEO in War of Words over Dismissal," *South Florida Business Journal,* March 12, 2004, p. 17.

Mangalindan, Mylene, "Norfolk Firm Keeping Track of Changes in Technology," *Ledger-Star* (Norfolk, Va.), March 21, 1995, p. D1.

Mayfield, Dave, "Norfolk-Based Forms Company Sold," *Virginian-Pilot,* February 5, 1997, p. 1.

"No Recession Here: Standard Forms Has Constant Sales Growth," *Long Island Business News,* July 26, 1993, p. 25.

"Setting Standards for the Future," *Long Island Business News,* May 16, 1994, p. 24.

Shean, Tom, "Spinoff Transforms Norfolk Business," *Virginian-Pilot,* June 13, 1998, p. D1.

—Sarah Ruth Lorenz

World Publications, LLC

460 Orlando Avenue, Suite 200
Winter Park, Florida 32789
U.S.A.
Telephone: (407) 628-4802
Fax: (407) 628-7061
Web site: http://www.worldpub.net

Private Company
Incorporated: 1978
Employees: 275
Sales: $60 million (2003 est.)
NAIC: 511120 Periodical Publishers; 711320 Promoters
   of Performing Arts, Sports, and Similar Events
   Without Facilities

World Publications, LLC is a leading publisher of water sports and leisure-oriented magazines, and also operates web sites, promotes sporting events, and produces television programs. The company's 18 magazine titles include *WaterSki, Boating Life, Sport Diver, Spa, Garden Design,* and *Saveur,* and the firm also runs the Pro Water Skiing Tour and several similar events, and produces their telecasts as well as other video programming related to its publications. Founder/CEO Terry Snow owns controlling interest in the company.

Beginnings

World Publications' origins date to 1978, when a 24-year-old Miami, Florida waterskiing champion named Terry Snow decided to put together a magazine on the sport, which he called *WaterSkiing.* Snow, who had graduated from the University of Florida with a finance degree in 1976, sold the first copies to fellow enthusiasts out of his Dodge van, and the response was strong enough that he made plans to produce more issues. In 1979 he changed the magazine's name to *World WaterSkiing,* and expanded it to a bimonthly in 1980. That same year Snow started publishing a second title, *WindRider,* which covered the sport of windsurfing.

Over the next several years *World WaterSkiing* grew into one of the top two titles in its subject area, and in 1984 Snow

bought its main competitor, *Spray,* and merged them to form *WaterSki.* By this time his company had taken the name World Publications, Inc. In 1986 he started another new magazine, *Sport Fishing,* and late the next year bought *Women's Sport and Fitness,* which boasted circulation of 350,000. It was the company's first mass-market title, competing on newsstands with the likes of *Self* and *Shape.*

In 1988 World Publications took over the Professional Water Ski Tour and formed a sports marketing division to run it. The new unit also began producing a telecast of the tour for cable outlet ESPN, and later began to create other television programming based on the company's magazine properties. The year 1988 also saw both *WindRider* and *Sport Fishing* boost their publishing frequency to eight issues per year. The growing company was now running out of room, and it moved to larger quarters in its home base of Winter Park, Florida.

World Publications' primary audience consisted of individuals on the upper end of the income scale, and the topics its publications covered were typically somewhat expensive to pursue and often required considerable leisure time. This demographic group was a desirable one for advertisers, especially those that produced goods used in the different sports involved, and the firm could often sell ads for several of its publications to the same companies. The affluent clientele also rendered the company's offerings relatively recession-proof, and the magazines, with circulation of roughly 50,000 to 100,000 copies per issue, provided a steady profit from their respective niche markets.

Despite, or perhaps because of, its growing expertise with special-interest sports magazines, the company was having little success with its lone mass-market title, and in 1989 *Women's Sports and Fitness* was leased to Rocky Mountain Sports & Fitness, which would later buy it outright. The next year saw World Publications buy *WindRider*'s sole competitor, *Windsurf,* after which the two were merged into the renamed *WindSurfing.*

Continuing Growth in the Early 1990s

In 1992 the company purchased an upscale fishing magazine called *Marlin,* which was distributed internationally. The following year the popularity of new water sports ski-boarding and knee-boarding inspired the creation of *Wake Boarding* maga-

---

Company Perspectives:

Our Mission: World Publications aspires to be, and be recognized as, the leading force in selected lifestyle and recreational markets by:

Providing participants with information, entertainment, knowledge and inspiration through appropriate interactive media. Building relationships with marketing partners by offering them opportunities, our expertise and access to participants and each other. Contributing to the betterment of the natural environment and the activities in which we function. Nurturing, supporting and inspiring our fellow team members and by creating tangible gain for all.

---

zine, which would start with circulation of 25,000 copies. The quarterly publication had a cover price of $2.95. During 1993 the firm also introduced diving-themed *Sport Diver.*

In 1995 World Publications formed a new division named World Entertainment to provide professional waterskiers for theme parks and other live event situations. It won contracts from SeaWorld parks in Texas, California, Ohio, and Florida over the next several years, as well as Jazzland in New Orleans. Other clients included corporations and the G-7 international economic summit. The unit later also organized a multimedia event called Viva for SeaWorld of Texas that involved synchronized swimmers and divers performing alongside whales and dolphins.

In 1996 the company brought out a 138-page watercraft buyers' guide called *SportBoats. WaterSki,* which now had circulation of 125,000, also had begun publishing a trade magazine called *WaterSki Business* by this time. Total circulation for all of the firm's publications now topped 500,000.

In late 1996 the company acquired *Caribbean Life & Travel,* publishers of a bimonthly, ten-year-old magazine of the same name; *Caribbean Life Made Easy,* an annual; and an in-flight magazine called *American Eagle Latitudes.* The publications, which employed 20, were based in Silver Spring, Maryland. World Publications would integrate some content from the new titles into its existing ones, as well as bundling them into the package deals it offered advertisers. The sale boosted the company's total circulation to 800,000.

In February 1997 another new magazine, *Boating Life,* was introduced. The bimonthly publication targeted owners of 16- to 25-foot boats as well as novices to the field. A total of 155,000 copies would be printed, with 80,000 sold on newsstands and the rest given to attendees of boat shows. Single copies retailed for $3.50.

In 1998 and 1999 the company acquired *Dive Travel* and *Aqua* magazines, which were merged into *Sport Diver. Aqua* was the official magazine of the PADI Diving Society, and *Sport Diver* took on this role. The year 1999 also saw the purchase of *Fly Fishing in Salt Waters* and the launch of a new "extreme sports" title, *Kite Boarding.* By now World Publications was operating web sites for its publications, with a total of eight different ones online by mid-1999. They offered informational databases, archived articles, Web-exclusive content, and links to advertisers.

Purchase of Garden Design *and* Saveur *in 2000*

In January 2000 World Publications acquired three magazines from the struggling New York-based Meigher Communications, which had been founded by an ex-Time, Inc. executive. The reported $7 million "fire sale" deal brought the company upscale landscaping magazine *Garden Design,* gourmet food and travel monthly *Saveur,* and a smaller title called *Friends.* The purchase of *Saveur,* which had circulation of 375,000, and *Garden Design,* with 430,000, had reportedly been the inspiration of Terry Snow's wife Donna, a fan of the magazines.

Following the purchase, additional advertising and marketing employees were hired to boost the new magazines' revenues, and web sites were launched for each. Their editorial functions would continue to be run out of New York, though some business operations were relocated to Florida. The company now had a total of 200 employees.

The former Meigher publications had been struggling for some time, and over the first 18 months of Snow's ownership a number of staffers and some advertisers jumped ship. In the summer of 2001 World Publications moved the offices of *Garden Design* to Florida, which caused its employees to resign en masse, forcing the company to build a new staff from scratch. The firm soon hired publishing industry veteran Richard Amann to manage the Meigher titles, and he quickly took steps to improve staff morale and boost advertising sales.

Seeking an infusion of capital, in January 2002 Snow sold a 49 percent stake in the firm to Boston Ventures Management, Inc., a private equity firm with media and entertainment industry holdings. That June, however, Amann quit over strategic differences with Snow. Although *Saveur*'s circulation had remained steady at 375,000, *Garden Design*'s had fallen from 425,000 to 300,000 since the sale.

Adding Sailing World *and* Cruising World *in 2002*

Shortly after Amann's departure, World Publications bought *Sailing World* and *Cruising World* from Miller Publishing Group for an estimated $10 million. The two new magazines were based in Newport, Rhode Island, where their editorial operations would remain. The monthly *Cruising World* focused on sailing waterways, and had circulation of 155,000, while *Sailing World,* which covered the field of competitive sailing, published ten issues per year and had circulation of 55,000. Annual revenue from the two titles was approximately $10 million. The deal also included several sporting events that the magazines sponsored, the largest of which was the National Offshore One Design Regattas, the largest sailing-regatta series in the United States.

In November 2003 World Publications assisted with the launch of a new music magazine, *Tracks,* which was produced by Sub Rosa Communications, and run by former *Spin, Vibe,* and *Rolling Stone* staffers Alan Light and John Rollins. World Publications took a small equity stake in exchange for the use of some of its New York office space and the support of its business and circulation departments. The magazine was dedicated to covering "music built to last" for the baby boomer generation, with artists including Sting and R.E.M. spotlighted in the debut issue. A total of 100,000 copies would be circulated. Although it had little in common thematically with

---

Key Dates:

1978: Terry Snow creates *WaterSkiing* magazine.
1980: *WindRider* is introduced; six issues of the renamed *World WaterSkiing* are printed.
1986: *Sport Fishing* is launched.
1988: A sports marketing division is formed to run the Pro Water Ski Tour and to produce TV shows.
1992: *Marlin* magazine is acquired.
1993: *Water Boarding* and *Sport Diver* are launched.
1995: The World Entertainment unit is created to manage professional waterskiers.
1997: *Boating Life* debuts; *Caribbean Travel & Life* is acquired.
1999: Web sites are launched; *Fly Fishing in Salt Waters* is bought; *Kite Boarding* bows.
2000: *Saveur, Garden Design,* and *Friends* magazines are purchased.
2002: Boston Ventures Management, Inc. buys a 49 percent stake in the firm; *Cruising World* and *Sailing World* magazines are acquired.
2004: *Spa, Islands,* and *Resorts & Great Hotels* are bought; *Power Cruising* is launched.

Snow's other publications, the target audience was similarly well-to-do.

February 2004 saw the company introduce a new aquatic title, *Power Cruising,* which was aimed at the owners of yachts and other large boats. A total of 35,000 copies would be printed initially, with two issues scheduled for 2004 and expansion to a bimonthly expected in 2005.

In April 2004 World Publications bought three titles from Island Media for a reported $17.5 million. The bimonthly *Spa,* which covered beauty, healthy living, and spa vacations, had circulation of 85,000, and the exotic travel title *Islands,* with eight issues per year, had circulation of 200,000 and also offered a 200,000-circulation offshoot called *Island Weddings & Honeymoons.* The third title, an annual called *Resorts & Great Hotels,* focused on luxury destinations and circulated 340,000 copies. They were published in Santa Barbara, California, where their editorial headquarters would remain. As with past acquisitions, the so-called back-office business functions were relocated to Winter Park. The year also saw the purchase of UsedBoats.com, a company that ran several web sites for

boat sales. It was the firm's first Internet venture not directly related to one of its print offerings.

By now, total circulation for all of World Publications' titles was significantly more than two million, and it had successfully launched a string of related web sites. The company's sports and marketing division continued to produce the Pro Water Ski Tour and its accompanying television broadcast, as well as the Pro Wakeboard Tour and the Vans Triple Crown of Wakeboarding events and their respective telecasts. The company also was having success with its World Entertainment subsidiary, which provided professional waterskiers and other programming for theme parks, and another unit that published custom titles for special events.

After more than a quarter-century, World Publications, LLC had grown into a leading publisher of water sports, travel, and lifestyle magazines for an upscale audience. The company also had branched out into promoting sporting events, producing television programs, and operating web sites based on its publications. Its dominance of a number of niche markets with loyal audiences put it in a strong position for continued success.

Principal Subsidiaries

World Sports & Marketing; World Entertainment Services; Syndication and Custom Publishing; New World Travel.

Principal Competitors

Primedia, Inc.; Hachette Filipacchi Medias; Time, Inc.; Condé Nast Publications; The Hearst Corporation.

Further Reading

Adams, Mark, "New World Order (Terry Snow and World Publications)," *Brandweek,* March 5, 2001.

Boyd, Christopher, "Key Deals Open Up World of Publishing Possibilities in Winter Park, Fla.," *Orlando Sentinel,* December 1, 2003.

"Caribbean Travel and Life Sold to World Publications," *Media Daily,* December 11, 1996.

Kelly, Keith J., "Execs Score in Meigher Sale; Investors Left with Nothing," *New York Post,* December 30, 1999, p. 31.

Maurer, Rolf, "Get a Boating Life," *Folio,* February 1, 1997, p. 25.

Morgan, Richard, "World Publications Gets Three More," *TheDeal.com,* April 28, 2004.

"Terry Snow to Take 'Garden Design' Circ-Backward/Quality-Forward," *MIN Media Industry Newsletter,* April 30, 2001.

White, Carolyn, "Sports Magazines Changes at Top," *USA Today,* December 3, 1987, p. 2C.

—Frank Uhle

INDEX TO COMPANIES

Index to Companies

Listings in this index are arranged in alphabetical order under the company name. Company names beginning with a letter or proper name such as Eli Lilly & Co. will be found under the first letter of the company name. Definite articles (The, Le, La) are ignored for alphabetical purposes as are forms of incorporation that precede the company name (AB, NV). Company names printed in bold type have full, historical essays on the page numbers appearing in bold. Updates to entries that appeared in earlier volumes are signified by the notation **(upd.)**. Company names in light type are references within an essay to that company, not full historical essays. This index is cumulative with volume numbers printed in bold type.

379

INDEX TO INDUSTRIES

Index to Industries

AUTOMOTIVE

Takara Holdings Inc., 62
The Terlato Wine Group, 48
Todhunter International, Inc., 27
Triarc Companies, Inc., 34 (upd.)
Tsingtao Brewery Group, 49
Tully's Coffee Corporation, 51
Van Houtte Inc., 39
Vermont Pure Holdings, Ltd., 51
Vin & Spirit AB, 31
Viña Concha y Toro S.A., 45
Vincor International Inc., 50
Whitbread and Company PLC, I
William Grant & Sons Ltd., 60
The Wine Group, Inc., 39
The Wolverhampton & Dudley Breweries, PLC, 57
Young & Co.'s Brewery, P.L.C., 38

BIOTECHNOLOGY

Amersham PLC, 50
Amgen, Inc., 10; 30 (upd.)
Biogen Inc., 14; 36 (upd.)
Cambrex Corporation, 44 (upd.)
Centocor Inc., 14
Charles River Laboratories International, Inc., 42
Chiron Corporation, 10; 36 (upd.)
Covance Inc., 30
CryoLife, Inc., 46
Delta and Pine Land Company, 33
Dionex Corporation, 46
Enzo Biochem, Inc., 41
Genentech, Inc., 32 (upd.)
Genzyme Corporation, 38 (upd.)
Gilead Sciences, Inc., 54
Howard Hughes Medical Institute, 39
Huntingdon Life Sciences Group plc, 42
IDEXX Laboratories, Inc., 23
ImClone Systems Inc., 58
Immunex Corporation, 14; 50 (upd.)
IMPATH Inc., 45
Incyte Genomics, Inc., 52
Inverness Medical Innovations, Inc., 63
Invitrogen Corporation, 52
The Judge Group, Inc., 51
Life Technologies, Inc., 17
Martek Biosciences Corporation, 65
Medtronic, Inc., 30 (upd.)
Millipore Corporation, 25
Minntech Corporation, 22
Mycogen Corporation, 21
New Brunswick Scientific Co., Inc., 45
Qiagen N.V., 39
Quintiles Transnational Corporation, 21
Seminis, Inc., 29
Serologicals Corporation, 63
Sigma-Aldrich Corporation, 36 (upd.)
Starkey Laboratories, Inc., 52
STERIS Corporation, 29
TECHNE Corporation, 52
Waters Corporation, 43
Whatman plc, 46
Wisconsin Alumni Research Foundation, 65
Wyeth, 50 (upd.)

CHEMICALS

A. Schulman, Inc., 8
Aceto Corp., 38
Air Products and Chemicals, Inc., I; 10 (upd.)
Airgas, Inc., 54
Akzo Nobel N.V., 13
Albemarle Corporation, 59
AlliedSignal Inc., 22 (upd.)
American Cyanamid, I; 8 (upd.)
American Vanguard Corporation, 47

ARCO Chemical Company, 10
Asahi Denka Kogyo KK, 64
Atanor S.A., 62
Atochem S.A., I
Avecia Group PLC, 63
Baker Hughes Incorporated, 22 (upd.); 57 (upd.)
Balchem Corporation, 42
BASF Aktiengesellschaft, I; 18 (upd.); 50 (upd.)
Bayer A.G., I; 13 (upd.); 41 (upd.)
Betz Laboratories, Inc., I; 10 (upd.)
The BFGoodrich Company, 19 (upd.)
BOC Group plc, I; 25 (upd.)
Brenntag AG, 8; 23 (upd.)
Burmah Castrol PLC, 30 (upd.)
Cabot Corporation, 8; 29 (upd.)
Cambrex Corporation, 16
Catalytica Energy Systems, Inc., 44
Celanese Corporation, I
Celanese Mexicana, S.A. de C.V., 54
Chemcentral Corporation, 8
Chemi-Trol Chemical Co., 16
Church & Dwight Co., Inc., 29
Ciba-Geigy Ltd., I; 8 (upd.)
The Clorox Company, 22 (upd.)
Croda International Plc, 45
Crompton & Knowles, 9
Crompton Corporation, 36 (upd.)
Cytec Industries Inc., 27
Degussa-Hüls AG, 32 (upd.)
DeKalb Genetics Corporation, 17
The Dexter Corporation, I; 12 (upd.)
Dionex Corporation, 46
The Dow Chemical Company, I; 8 (upd.); 50 (upd.)
DSM N.V., I; 56 (upd.)
E.I. du Pont de Nemours & Company, I; 8 (upd.); 26 (upd.)
Eastman Chemical Company, 14; 38 (upd.)
Ecolab Inc., I; 13 (upd.); 34 (upd.)
Elementis plc, 40 (upd.)
English China Clays Ltd., 15 (upd.); 40 (upd.)
ERLY Industries Inc., 17
Ethyl Corporation, I; 10 (upd.)
Ferro Corporation, 8; 56 (upd.)
Firmenich International S.A., 60
First Mississippi Corporation, 8
Formosa Plastics Corporation, 14; 58 (upd.)
Fort James Corporation, 22 (upd.)
G.A.F., I
The General Chemical Group Inc., 37
Georgia Gulf Corporation, 9; 61 (upd.)
Givaudan SA, 43
Great Lakes Chemical Corporation, I; 14 (upd.)
Guerbet Group, 46
H.B. Fuller Company, 32 (upd.)
Hauser, Inc., 46
Hawkins Chemical, Inc., 16
Henkel KGaA, 34 (upd.)
Hercules Inc., I; 22 (upd.)
Hoechst A.G., I; 18 (upd.)
Hoechst Celanese Corporation, 13
Huls A.G., I
Huntsman Chemical Corporation, 8
IMC Fertilizer Group, Inc., 8
Imperial Chemical Industries PLC, I; 50 (upd.)
International Flavors & Fragrances Inc., 9; 38 (upd.)
Israel Chemicals Ltd., 55
Koppers Industries, Inc., I; 26 (upd.)
L'Air Liquide SA, I; 47 (upd.)
Lawter International Inc., 14

LeaRonal, Inc., 23
Loctite Corporation, 30 (upd.)
Lubrizol Corporation, I; 30 (upd.)
Lyondell Chemical Company, 45 (upd.)
M.A. Hanna Company, 8
MacDermid Incorporated, 32
Mallinckrodt Group Inc., 19
MBC Holding Company, 40
Melamine Chemicals, Inc., 27
Methanex Corporation, 40
Minerals Technologies Inc., 52 (upd.)
Mississippi Chemical Corporation, 39
Mitsubishi Chemical Corporation, I; 56 (upd.)
Mitsui Petrochemical Industries, Ltd., 9
Monsanto Company, I; 9 (upd.); 29 (upd.)
Montedison SpA, I
Morton International Inc., 9 (upd.)
Morton Thiokol, Inc., I
Nagase & Company, Ltd., 8
Nalco Chemical Corporation, I; 12 (upd.)
National Distillers and Chemical Corporation, I
National Sanitary Supply Co., 16
National Starch and Chemical Company, 49
NCH Corporation, 8
NL Industries, Inc., 10
Nobel Industries AB, 9
Norsk Hydro ASA, 35 (upd.)
Novacor Chemicals Ltd., 12
NutraSweet Company, 8
Olin Corporation, I; 13 (upd.)
OM Group, Inc., 17
OMNOVA Solutions Inc., 59
Penford Corporation, 55
Pennwalt Corporation, I
Perstorp AB, I; 51 (upd.)
Petrolite Corporation, 15
Pioneer Hi-Bred International, Inc., 41 (upd.)
Praxair, Inc., 11
Quantum Chemical Corporation, 8
Reichhold Chemicals, Inc., 10
Rhodia SA, 38
Rhône-Poulenc S.A., I; 10 (upd.)
Robertet SA, 39
Rohm and Haas Company, I; 26 (upd.)
Roussel Uclaf, I; 8 (upd.)
RPM, Inc., 36 (upd.)
RWE AG, 50 (upd.)
The Scotts Company, 22
SCP Pool Corporation, 39
Sequa Corp., 13
Shanghai Petrochemical Co., Ltd., 18
Sigma-Aldrich Corporation, 36 (upd.)
Solutia Inc., 52
Solvay S.A., I; 21 (upd.); 61 (upd.)
Stepan Company, 30
Sterling Chemicals, Inc., 16
Sumitomo Chemical Company Ltd., I
Takeda Chemical Industries, Ltd., 46 (upd.)
Terra Industries, Inc., 13
Teva Pharmaceutical Industries Ltd., 22
Total Fina Elf S.A., 24 (upd.); 50 (upd.)
Ube Industries, Ltd., 38 (upd.)
Union Carbide Corporation, I; 9 (upd.)
Univar Corporation, 9
The Valspar Corporation, 32 (upd.)
Vista Chemical Company, I
Witco Corporation, I; 16 (upd.)
Yule Catto & Company plc, 54
Zeneca Group PLC, 21

CONGLOMERATES

A.P. Møller - Maersk A/S, 57
Accor SA, 10; 27 (upd.)

ENGINEERING & MANAGEMENT SERVICES

ENTERTAINMENT & LEISURE

INSURANCE

PAPER & FORESTRY

PERSONAL SERVICES

WASTE SERVICES

GEOGRAPHIC INDEX

Geographic Index

Italy (continued)

Montedison SpA, I; 24 (upd.)
Officine Alfieri Maserati S.p.A., 13
Olivetti S.p.A., 34 (upd.)
Parmalat Finanziaria SpA, 50
Piaggio & C. S.p.A., 20
Pirelli S.p.A., V; 15 (upd.)
Reno de Medici S.p.A., 41
Riunione Adriatica di Sicurtè SpA, III
Safilo SpA, 54
Salvatore Ferragamo Italia S.p.A., 62
Sanpaolo IMI S.p.A., 50
Seat Pagine Gialle S.p.A., 47
Società Finanziaria Telefonica per Azioni, V
Società Sportiva Lazio SpA, 44
Stefanel SpA, 63
Telecom Italia Mobile S.p.A., 63
Telecom Italia S.p.A., 43
Tiscali SpA, 48

Jamaica

Air Jamaica Limited, 54

Japan

Aisin Seiki Co., Ltd., III; 48 (upd.)
Aiwa Co., Ltd., 30
Ajinomoto Co., Inc., II; 28 (upd.)
All Nippon Airways Co., Ltd., 6; 38 (upd.)
Alpine Electronics, Inc., 13
Alps Electric Co., Ltd., II; 44 (upd.)
Asahi Breweries, Ltd., I; 20 (upd.); 52 (upd.)
Asahi Denka Kogyo KK, 64
Asahi Glass Company, Ltd., III; 48 (upd.)
Asahi National Broadcasting Company, Ltd., 9
ASICS Corporation, 57
Bandai Co., Ltd., 55
Bank of Tokyo-Mitsubishi Ltd., II; 15 (upd.)
Bridgestone Corporation, V; 21 (upd.); 59 (upd.)
Brother Industries, Ltd., 14
C. Itoh & Company Ltd., I
Canon Inc., III; 18 (upd.)
CASIO Computer Co., Ltd., III; 16 (upd.); 40 (upd.)
Central Japan Railway Company, 43
Chubu Electric Power Company, Inc., V; 46 (upd.)
Chugai Pharmaceutical Co., Ltd., 50
Chugoku Electric Power Company Inc., V; 53 (upd.)
Citizen Watch Co., Ltd., III; 21 (upd.)
Clarion Company Ltd., 64
Cosmo Oil Co., Ltd., IV; 53 (upd.)
Dai Nippon Printing Co., Ltd., IV; 57 (upd.)
Dai-Ichi Kangyo Bank Ltd., The, II
Daido Steel Co., Ltd., IV
Daiei, Inc., The, V; 17 (upd.); 41 (upd.)
Daihatsu Motor Company, Ltd., 7; 21 (upd.)
Daikin Industries, Ltd., III
Daimaru, Inc., The, V; 42 (upd.)
Daio Paper Corporation, IV
Daishowa Paper Manufacturing Co., Ltd., IV; 57 (upd.)
Daiwa Bank, Ltd., The, II; 39 (upd.)
Daiwa Securities Group Inc., II; 55 (upd.)
DDI Corporation, 7
DENSO Corporation, 46 (upd.)
Dentsu Inc., I; 16 (upd.); 40 (upd.)
East Japan Railway Company, V
Fanuc Ltd., III; 17 (upd.)

Fuji Bank, Ltd., The, II
Fuji Electric Co., Ltd., II; 48 (upd.)
Fuji Photo Film Co., Ltd., III; 18 (upd.)
Fujisawa Pharmaceutical Company, Ltd., I; 58 (upd.)
Fujitsu Limited, III; 16 (upd.); 42 (upd.)
Funai Electric Company Ltd., 62
Furukawa Electric Co., Ltd., The, III
General Sekiyu K.K., IV
Hakuhodo, Inc., 6; 42 (upd.)
Hankyu Department Stores, Inc., V; 23 (upd.); 62 (upd.)
Hino Motors, Ltd., 7; 21 (upd.)
Hitachi, Ltd., I; 12 (upd.); 40 (upd.)
Hitachi Metals, Ltd., IV
Hitachi Zosen Corporation, III; 53 (upd.)
Hokkaido Electric Power Company Inc. (HEPCO), V; 58 (upd.)
Hokuriku Electric Power Company, V
Honda Motor Company Limited, I; 10 (upd.); 29 (upd.)
Honshu Paper Co., Ltd., IV
Hoshino Gakki Co. Ltd., 55
Idemitsu Kosan Co., Ltd., IV; 49 (upd.)
Industrial Bank of Japan, Ltd., The, II
Isetan Company Limited, V; 36 (upd.)
Ishikawajima-Harima Heavy Industries Co., Ltd., III
Isuzu Motors, Ltd., 9; 23 (upd.); 57 (upd.)
Ito-Yokado Co., Ltd., V; 42 (upd.)
ITOCHU Corporation, 32 (upd.)
Itoham Foods Inc., II; 61 (upd.)
Japan Airlines Company, Ltd., I; 32 (upd.)
Japan Broadcasting Corporation, 7
Japan Leasing Corporation, 8
Japan Pulp and Paper Company Limited, IV
Japan Tobacco Inc., V; 46 (upd.)
Jujo Paper Co., Ltd., IV
JUSCO Co., Ltd., V
Kajima Corporation, I; 51 (upd.)
Kanebo, Ltd., 53
Kanematsu Corporation, IV; 24 (upd.)
Kansai Electric Power Company, Inc., The, V; 62 (upd.)
Kao Corporation, III; 20 (upd.)
Kawasaki Heavy Industries, Ltd., III; 63 (upd.)
Kawasaki Kisen Kaisha, Ltd., V; 56 (upd.)
Kawasaki Steel Corporation, IV
Keio Teito Electric Railway Company, V
Kenwood Corporation, 31
Kewpie Kabushiki Kaisha, 57
Kikkoman Corporation, 14; 47 (upd.)
Kinki Nippon Railway Company Ltd., V
Kirin Brewery Company, Limited, I; 21 (upd.); 63 (upd.)
Kobe Steel, Ltd., IV; 19 (upd.)
Kodansha Ltd., IV; 38 (upd.)
Komatsu Ltd., III; 16 (upd.); 52 (upd.)
Konica Corporation, III; 30 (upd.)
Kotobukiya Co., Ltd., V; 56 (upd.)
Kubota Corporation, III; 26 (upd.)
Kumagai Gumi Company, Ltd., I
Kyocera Corporation, II; 21 (upd.)
Kyowa Hakko Kogyo Co., Ltd., III; 48 (upd.)
Kyushu Electric Power Company Inc., V
Lion Corporation, III; 51 (upd.)
Long-Term Credit Bank of Japan, Ltd., II
Makita Corporation, 22; 59 (upd.)
Marubeni Corporation, I; 24 (upd.)
Marui Company Ltd., V; 62 (upd.)
Maruzen Co., Limited, 18
Matsushita Electric Industrial Co., Ltd., II; 64 (upd.)

Matsushita Electric Works, Ltd., III; 7 (upd.)
Matsuzakaya Company Ltd., V; 64 (upd.)
Mazda Motor Corporation, 9; 23 (upd.); 63 (upd.)
Meiji Milk Products Company, Limited, II
Meiji Mutual Life Insurance Company, The, III
Meiji Seika Kaisha Ltd., II; 64 (upd.)
Millea Holdings Inc., 64 (upd.)
Minolta Co., Ltd., III; 18 (upd.); 43 (upd.)
Mitsubishi Bank, Ltd., The, II
Mitsubishi Chemical Corporation, I; 56 (upd.)
Mitsubishi Corporation, I; 12 (upd.)
Mitsubishi Electric Corporation, II; 44 (upd.)
Mitsubishi Estate Company, Limited, IV; 61 (upd.)
Mitsubishi Heavy Industries, Ltd., III; 7 (upd.); 40 (upd.)
Mitsubishi Materials Corporation, III
Mitsubishi Motors Corporation, 9; 23 (upd.); 57 (upd.)
Mitsubishi Oil Co., Ltd., IV
Mitsubishi Rayon Co., Ltd., V
Mitsubishi Trust & Banking Corporation, The, II
Mitsui & Co., Ltd., 28 (upd.)
Mitsui Bank, Ltd., The, II
Mitsui Bussan K.K., I
Mitsui Marine and Fire Insurance Company, Limited, III
Mitsui Mining & Smelting Co., Ltd., IV
Mitsui Mining Company, Limited, IV
Mitsui Mutual Life Insurance Company, III; 39 (upd.)
Mitsui O.S.K. Lines, Ltd., V
Mitsui Petrochemical Industries, Ltd., 9
Mitsui Real Estate Development Co., Ltd., IV
Mitsui Trust & Banking Company, Ltd., The, II
Mitsukoshi Ltd., V; 56 (upd.)
Mizuho Financial Group Inc., 58 (upd.)
Mizuno Corporation, 25
Morinaga & Co. Ltd., 61
Nagasakiya Co., Ltd., V
Nagase & Co., Ltd., 8; 61 (upd.)
NEC Corporation, II; 21 (upd.); 57 (upd.)
NHK Spring Co., Ltd., III
Nichii Co., Ltd., V
Nichimen Corporation, IV; 24 (upd.)
Nidec Corporation, 59
Nihon Keizai Shimbun, Inc., IV
Nikko Securities Company Limited, The, II; 9 (upd.)
Nikon Corporation, III; 48 (upd.)
Nintendo Co., Ltd., III; 7 (upd.); 28 (upd.)
Nippon Credit Bank, II
Nippon Express Company, Ltd., V; 64 (upd.)
Nippon Life Insurance Company, III; 60 (upd.)
Nippon Light Metal Company, Ltd., IV
Nippon Meat Packers, Inc., II
Nippon Oil Corporation, IV; 63 (upd.)
Nippon Seiko K.K., III
Nippon Sheet Glass Company, Limited, III
Nippon Shinpan Co., Ltd., II; 61 (upd.)
Nippon Steel Corporation, 17 (upd.)
Nippon Suisan Kaisha, Limited, IV
Nippon Telegraph and Telephone Corporation, V; 51 (upd.)
Nippon Yusen Kabushiki Kaisha, V
Nippondenso Co., Ltd., III

NOTES ON CONTRIBUTORS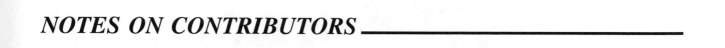

Notes on Contributors

BAXTER, Melissa Rigney. Researcher and writer.

COHEN, M. L. Novelist and researcher living in Paris.

COVELL, Jeffrey L. Seattle-based writer.

CULLIGAN, Susan B. Minnesota-based writer.

DINGER, Ed. Writer and editor based in Bronx, New York.

FUJINAKA, Mariko. Writer and editor living in California.

INGRAM, Frederick C. Utah-based business writer who has contributed to *GSA Business, Appalachian Trailway News,* the *Encyclopedia of Business,* the *Encyclopedia of Global Industries,* the *Encyclopedia of Consumer Brands,* and other regional and trade publications.

LORENZ, Sarah Ruth. Minnesota-based writer.

PEIPPO, Kathleen. Minneapolis-based writer.

RHODES, Nelson. Editor, writer, and consultant in the Chicago area.

ROTHBURD, Carrie. Writer and editor specializing in corporate profiles, academic texts, and academic journal articles.

SALAMIE, David E. Part-owner of InfoWorks Development Group, a reference publication development and editorial services company.

TRADII, Mary. Writer based in Denver, Colorado.

UHLE, Frank. Ann-Arbor-based writer, movie projectionist, disk jockey, and staff member of *Psychotronic Video* magazine.

WOODWARD, A. Wisconsin-based writer.